Leisure Matters:
The State and Future of Leisure Studies

Leisure Matters:
The State and Future of Leisure Studies

Edited by
Gordon J. Walker, David Scott, and Monika Stodolska

Venture Publishing, Inc.
State College, Pennsylvania

Venture Publishing, Inc.
1999 Cato Avenue
State College, PA 16801
Phone (814) 234-4561
Fax (814) 234-1651

Cover Design by StepUp Communications, Inc.

Library of Congress Catalogue Card Number: 2015950388

ISBN-10: 1-939476-06-2
ISBN-13: 978-1-939476-06-7

Dedication

This book is dedicated to our spouses, Janet, Susan, and Matthew.

Table of Contents

SECTION 1: EXPLORING LEISURE

1.1 Disciplinary Perspectives

1.2 Cognate Area Perspectives

1.3 International Perspectives

SECTION 2: EXPERIENCING LEISURE

2.1 Antecedents and Styles

2.2 Diverse Populations

2.3 Time and Technology

2.4 Place and Community

SECTION 3: DELIVERING LEISURE

List of Tables and Figures

Foreword
Assessing Leisure Studies

Thomas L. (Tim) Burton (Professor Emeritus, University of Alberta)

While there is no standard model by which to chart the advancement of leisure studies in Canada[1], there are markers that permit the historian (and the merely curious) to examine how the field has unfolded. They fall into two categories which, though interconnected, may be reviewed separately: instruction and research.

Important markers in the *instruction* category include: the introduction of baccalaureate degree programs in the 1960s[2]; the development of Master's degree programs in the latter half of the 1970s; and the introduction of Doctoral programs in the mid-1990s.

Notable markers on the *research* side include: stand-alone research initiatives published in journals from other fields; formal gatherings of leisure researchers[3]; and the establishment of leisure research journals[4]. But perhaps one of the most significant markers is the periodic examination of the state-of-the-art in the field. This has been done in two forms: in theme editions of journals, and in edited texts that have surveyed the field. The remainder of my remarks here will focus on three edited texts.

In 1989, Ed Jackson and I edited a book entitled *Understanding Leisure and Recreation: Mapping the Past, Charting the Future*. Since knowledge is enhanced not only by original research but also by consolidation and critical assessment of what has already been learned, we set out to assess the then state of leisure studies by reference to both what had been achieved and the judgments of scholars about its condition. We found a "widespread belief... that the quality of research has not kept pace with its quantity" (Jackson & Burton, 1989, p. 2).

A decade later we edited a second text, *Leisure Studies: Prospects for the Twenty-First Century* (1999) that examined how the field had developed and changed in the decade since the first publication. We concluded that while there was cause for concern and self-criticism about particular activities, topics and methods, there was "a strong foundation on which to build as we in leisure studies enter the third millennium" (Jackson & Burton, 1999, p. 521).

And so I come to the current volume. Sixteen years after the publication of our second text, the time is ripe for another look at the state-of-the-art in leisure studies. The purpose of the editors is twofold: "to provide an overview of the state of leisure studies . . . in terms of our understanding of approximately 40 different leisure concepts, topics and areas" and "to be daring and speculate imaginatively about the future of leisure studies" (Walker, Stodolska, & Scott, 2015). I look forward eagerly to seeing where scholars believe we currently stand in a field that is now a half-century old.

[1] I am unfamiliar with details in the U.S., so have restricted myself primarily to events in Canada.

[2] The earliest Bachelor's degree programs went by various names: recreation administration, parks and recreation resources, recreation and leisure studies, and more. I have used the generic term *leisure studies*.

[3] The first *Canadian Congress on Leisure Research* was convened in 1975. It has since continued as a triennial gathering and successfully held its 14th edition in 2014.

[4] The *Journal of Leisure Research* was founded in 1969, followed by *Leisure Sciences* in 1977.

REFERENCES

Jackson, E. L., & Burton, T. L. (Eds.). (1989). *Understanding leisure and recreation: Mapping the past, charting the future*. State College, PA: Venture Publishing, Inc.

Jackson, E. L., & Burton, T. L. (Eds.). (1999). *Leisure studies: Prospects for the twenty-first century*. State College, PA: Venture Publishing, Inc.

Walker, G. J., Stodolska, M., & Scott, D. (2015). Introduction. *Leisure matters: The state and future of leisure studies* (pp. xix–xx). State College, PA: Venture Publishing, Inc.

Foreword
Leisure Studies: Celebrating the Past, Looking to the Future

Edgar L. Jackson (Professor Emeritus, University of Alberta)

You may be surprised to learn that the story of *Leisure Matters* began on a beautifully warm and sunny day on the patio of the Faculty Club at the University of Alberta in the summer of 1984. I was teaching a class in geography that summer, and I had a lunch date with my friend and colleague from the Department of Recreation and Leisure Studies, Tim Burton.

What Tim and I had most in common was the notion that everything had to be placed in context—one always has to keep in mind the "big picture," even when researching relatively small and focused issues. We also subsequently discovered that we were highly compatible as writers, so much so that the pieces we wrote together became seamless; to this day I can still read our own chapters in our first book (Jackson & Burton, 1989), and not be able to tell who wrote which part.

Although my undergraduate and graduate research had been in entirely different areas, I was asked in 1977 to teach a graduate course called "Outdoor Recreation Geography." I quickly became intrigued with what at that time I thought of as *Recreation Research* and then came to realize was part of the broader, vibrant, yet still relatively young field of *Leisure Studies*. I knew I'd found my niche and, while I kept up peripheral interests in the research areas from my student years, I began what was to become the rest of my career in leisure studies.

I soon came to realize three things. First, my ignorance about leisure studies was expanding exponentially faster than my knowledge. Second, although much literature about recreation and leisure was already available, few attempts had been made to integrate leisure studies into a cohesive whole—the "big picture" was missing. Third, there were frequently if not immediately obvious connections between seemingly disparate concepts and issues. For example, after spending a few years on the idea of the negotiation of leisure constraints, I suddenly realized that the perfect conceptual framework for the next step lay in a single table published in an influential 1960s paper on human adjustment to flood hazard (White, 1961).

All of this sets the scene for what Tim and I set out to do, so perhaps it is now appropriate to say something about how we tackled the first of the two predecessors to this book (Jackson & Burton, 1989). That first day we set up a three-column handwritten spreadsheet. In column one we listed topics we thought ought to be covered—the economics of recreation and leisure, the philosophical foundations of the concepts of leisure and of leisure research, and the idea of satisfaction, to name but a few. Then, in column two, we listed authors who we believed would best be able to write about those issues. Last, we made a list of people who we thought should be represented in the book because they had established reputations in important areas of recreation and leisure research and whose contributions would lend weight to what we hoped might become a milestone in the integration of what was then known about leisure. And there we had it: an embryo outline of what eventually became *Understanding Leisure*.

Despite our initial enthusiasm, it wasn't until 1986 that we became serious, revisited the lists, and made changes. Then we sent invitation letters to everyone on our combined list. I recall that, somewhat to our surprise, every single one accepted. Next, we held a short meeting of those authors who were present at the 1987 Canadian Congress on Leisure Research, partly to introduce ourselves, partly to give them more detail about what we had in mind, and partly to convince Geof Godbey that Venture Publishing, Inc. would be the best publisher for the book.

After that the chapters began to arrive and both Tim and I meticulously reviewed each one and put together a package of suggested revisions in much the same way a journal article is handled. Then, in August 1988, we convened a three-day meeting at the University of Alberta to which we invited some 20 of the authors from Canada, the USA, and the United Kingdom. Each had an assigned responsibility to present his or her chapter, as well as act as lead critic on another chapter. After each chapter was presented and criticized the floor was thrown open to a lively discussion which contributed substantially to the quality of the chapters. The editing process was completed within a year and we submitted the manuscript to Venture.

Several years after that, beginning in 1997, we repeated the process, deleting some of the previous chapters, asking for updates in other cases, and commissioning entirely new chapters on emerging topics from new contributors. This resulted in the publication of *Leisure Studies: Prospects for the Twenty-First Century* (Jackson & Burton, 1999).

Neither Tim nor I had any overt plans for a 2009 follow-up, and indeed we both retired before the time would have arrived to begin a repeat of the whole process. Thus, I was particularly pleased when Gordon Walker told me that he, Monika Stodolska, and David Scott were planning a new version of the book. I knew immediately that the project was in good hands.

This book was destined to be good from the outset, and I've been struck by the vision of the editors and the scope of the issues that they have included. Topics are covered that Tim and I never even imagined 29 and 17 years ago, and new scholars have emerged to help outline what is known and to set the scene for the future. One key element that was missing from the earlier books was coverage of leisure issues in various cultures, and I think it's been a fine strategy to commission chapters on leisure in most regions of the world and to broaden the geographic locations of the contributors[1]. The one thing that has struck me about the chapters I've read—apart from their outstanding quality—is how each manages to explore a topic in depth but still succinctly and with reference to key literature from both within *and* outside the conventional leisure research publications, while at the same time providing an important sense of context.

So here we are, full circle, emphasizing depth of knowledge, linkages, integration, context, debate, and vision. Leisure *does* matter, and from where I sit, the future of leisure studies looks good. *Leisure Matters* is testimony to that.

[1] This provides a much-needed cross-cultural view of leisure studies and counters a criticism rightly leveled at the Jackson & Burton books: their North American/Western-centrism.

REFERENCES

Jackson, E. L., & Burton, T. L. (Eds.). (1989). *Understanding leisure and recreation: Mapping the past, charting the future*. State College, PA: Venture Publishing, Inc.

Jackson, E. L., & Burton, T. L. (Eds.). (1999). *Leisure studies: Prospects for the twenty-first century*. State College, PA: Venture Publishing, Inc.

White, G. F. (1961). The choice of use in resources management. *Natural Resources Journal*, 1, 23–40.

Introduction

Gordon J. Walker (University of Alberta), Monika Stodolska (University of Illinois at Urbana-Champaign), and David Scott (Texas A&M University)

Given *Leisure Matters: The State and Future of Leisure Studies* is a successor to (and, we can only hope, will be as successful as) *Mapping the Past, Charting the Future* (1989) and *Leisure Studies: Prospects for the Twenty-First Century* (1999), it is not surprising that we asked Thomas L. Burton and Edgar L. Jackson to write our Forewords[1]. But readers may not be aware that our ties date back nearly two decades; with David having co-authored with Ed (e.g., Jackson & Scott, 1999), Monika having been Ed's doctoral student, and Gordon having been hired by Ed and Tim as an Assistant Professor. Thus, in some ways it was almost inevitable that the three of us would initiate and edit this updated and expanded volume.

As we informed potential authors, the purpose of *Leisure Matters: The State and Future of Leisure Studies* was twofold; with:

- approximately 80% of each chapter being focused on providing an overview of the state of leisure studies, specifically in terms of our current understanding of approximately 40 different leisure concepts, topics, and areas.
- approximately 20% of each chapter being daring and speculating imaginatively (Crawford & Jackson, 2005, p. 165) about the future of leisure studies, specifically in terms of these same concepts, topics, and areas.

We further stipulated that each chapter not only be accessible to senior undergraduate and new graduate students but that it also be limited to approximately 6,000 words, including references. The latter proviso brings to mind French philosopher Blaise Pascal's (1656) oft-cited apology that "I have only made this letter longer because I have not had the time to make it shorter"—a constraint more than a few of our authors also apparently faced but that, when pressed, were able to negotiate.

The three editions of this book—from 1989's *Mapping the Past, Charting the Future*, through 1999's *Leisure Studies: Prospects for the Twenty-First Century*, to 2016's *Leisure Matters: The State and Future of Leisure Studies*—have undergone certain changes in terms of their structure, the chapters included, and the authors who were asked to contribute their expertise. These changes were driven by the new developments in the discipline, by the new and upcoming experts in the specific areas and the retirement of others, and by the pragmatic aspects of the publishing process.

In particular, the current edition features new sections on *Disciplinary Perspectives* (including chapters on anthropology, history, philosophy, psychology, sociology, biology, and economics of leisure), *Cognate Area Perspectives* (including chapters on leisure, health, and physical activity; leisure and religion/spirituality; sport as leisure; and tourism), and *International Perspectives*. Inclusion of these new sections reflects increased attention to issues of health and physical activity in our discipline, and our desire to highlight linkages between the allied fields of sport and tourism. Moreover, it is a testimony to the growing popularity of leisure research in other areas of the world including Africa, Asia, Australia/New Zealand, and Latin America.

Inclusion of these new sections necessitated leaving out some chapters that were included in previous versions, such as those on the benefits of leisure, leisure and conflict, crowding and carrying capacity in outdoor recreation, and recreation and conservation. This is not an indication that research in these areas has diminished or lost importance, but rather that the editors had to make some hard choices to keep the book within a manageable length.

[1] It should be noted here that, in our initial correspondence, we misspelled "foreword" as "forward"—an error Ed was quick to point out. We prefer to think this slip-up was because we wanted our authors be "forward-thinking", rather than an indication of our editorial ability.

At the same time, we also decided to retain some major sections of Jackson and Burton's (1999) book, including Experiencing Leisure, Delivering Leisure, and Debating Leisure. A number of other chapters have been retained, but moved to new sections of the book. For example, new sections on Place and Community, Time and Technology, and Diverse Populations have been created.

In conclusion, we believe *Leisure Matters: The State and Future of Leisure Studies* maintains the spirit and rigor of Tim and Ed's earlier books while also reflecting the growth and maturity that has subsequently occurred in our field. We also hope that the gap between *Leisure Matters* and the next book in this "series" is much shorter than the gap between our work and that of the volume that preceded it.

REFERENCES

Crawford, D., & Jackson, E. (2005). Leisure constraints theory: Dimensions, directions, and dilemmas. In E. Jackson (Ed.), *Constraints to leisure*, (pp. 153–167). State College, PA: Venture Publishing, Inc.

Jackson, E. L., & Burton, T. L. (Eds.). (1989). *Understanding leisure and recreation: Mapping the past, charting the future*. State College, PA: Venture Publishing, Inc.

Jackson, E. L., & Burton, T. L. (Eds.). (1999). *Leisure studies: Prospects for the twenty-first century*. State College, PA: Venture Publishing, Inc.

Jackson, E. L., & Scott, D. (1999). Constraints to leisure. *Leisure studies: Prospects for the twenty-first century* (pp. 299–321). State College, PA: Venture Publishing, Inc.

Pascal, B. (1656). *Provincial letters: Letter XVI.*

Editors and Contributors

Tony Blackshaw is Reader in the Academy of Sport and Physical Activity at Sheffield Hallam University in the United Kingdom. He gained his Ph.D. at Leeds Metropolitan University, the thesis of which was subsequently published as *Leisure Life* (2003). His latest books include the edited collection *Routledge Handbook of Leisure Studies* (2013) and *Leisure* (2010) in Routledge's Key Ideas series. Tony's current interests are in the connections between modernity, leisure, and the lived life. Outside the academy, he is a keen runner and likes to kid himself that he can profit from gambling.

Jason N. Bocarro received his Ph.D. from the Department of Recreation, Park & Tourism Sciences at Texas A&M University. He is currently an Associate Professor in the Department of Parks, Recreation & Tourism Management at North Carolina State University. Dr. Bocarro's research focuses on examining how parks, recreation, and youth sport programs can increase the physical activity level and overall health of children and adolescents. In his leisure time Jason enjoys running, playing and watching soccer, hiking, traveling, and chasing after his two young children, Mia and Liam.

Kelly S. Bricker is a Professor and Chair in the Department of Parks, Recreation, and Tourism at the University of Utah. She earned a Ph.D. from The Pennsylvania State University, specializing in sustainable tourism and natural resources. Kelly has presented and published research on ecotourism, sense of place, natural resources, heritage tourism, social justice, ecotourism certification and policy, and community quality of life stemming from sustainable tourism. With her husband Nathan, Kelly developed an ecotourism enterprise, Rivers Fiji, in the South Pacific. Kelly serves as Chair of The International Ecotourism Society and Vice Chair and Treasurer of the Global Sustainable Tourism Council and enjoys sea kayaking, scuba diving, and running and hiking with her dog TuiWai.

Thomas L. (Tim) Burton holds B.Sc. and Ph.D. degrees (Economics, Land Economics) from the University of London (England). He spent the final 21 years of his academic career at the University of Alberta, taking early retirement for personal reasons in 1997. He was Founding President of the Canadian Association for Leisure Studies (1981–1984). He has volunteered with the Alberta Recreation and Parks Association for the past 14 years, serving consecutive two-year terms as Vice-President, President, and Past-President. In 2005, he was awarded the *Alberta Centennial Medal* for outstanding contributions to the people and Province of Alberta during its first century.

Linda L. Caldwell is Distinguished Professor of Recreation, Park, and Tourism Management and Human Development and Family Studies at The Pennsylvania State University. She received her B.S. from The Pennsylvania State University, her M.S. from North Carolina State University, and her Ph.D. from the University of Maryland in 1986. Her research focuses primarily on interventions that develop youth competencies, promote healthy lifestyles, and reduce risky behavior in and through leisure. She loves Muay Thai kickboxing, traveling, photography, gardening, cooking, being in nature (especially scuba diving, hiking and camping), and spending time with her husband and cats.

Laurence Chalip is the Brightbill/Sapora Professor at the University of Illinois, where he serves as Head of the Department of Recreation, Sport and Tourism. He earned his Ph.D. in Policy Studies from the University of Chicago. He has authored over 100 articles and chapters, as well as several books and monographs. He serves on the editorial boards of nine scholarly journals, and consults widely to the recreation, sport, and tourism industry. For his contributions to sport policy, he has received the Earle F. Zeigler Award from the North American Society for Sport Management and the Distinguished Service Award from the Sport Management Association of Australia and New Zealand.

Garry Chick received a B.S. in psychology from Purdue University and a Ph.D. in anthropology from the University of Pittsburgh. His primary research interests include leisure and health and adult play and games. He has conducted field research in Mexico, the northeastern United States, mainland China, and Taiwan. He joined the faculty at The Pennsylvania State University in 1999 after 18 years in the Department of Leisure Studies at the University of Illinois at Urbana-Champaign. He is past editor of *Leisure Sciences* and a past president of The Association for the Anthropological Study of Play and of the Society for Cross-Cultural Research.

John Dattilo is a Professor in the Department of Recreation, Park and Tourism Management in the College of Health and Human Development at The Pennsylvania State University where he teaches about inclusive leisure services from an applied, philosophical, and ethical perspective. The overarching purpose of his research is to examine effects of services designed to empower individuals who are experiencing constraints to their leisure so that their lives become more meaningful and enjoyable. John relishes his relationships with his family and friends and feels that his wife Amy and his sons, David and Steven, are his most precious gifts.

Lee Davidson is a Senior Lecturer in the School of Art History, Classics and Religious Studies at Victoria University, Wellington, New Zealand. She holds a Ph.D. from Monash University, Australia, a B.A. (Hons) History, from Otago University, and a M.A. (Applied) Recreation and Leisure Studies, Victoria University, New Zealand. Lee teaches in the Museum and Heritage Studies programme and previously in Recreation and Leisure Studies. Her research interests include nature-based leisure and the links between heritage, travel and interculturality. She enjoys alpine recreation and cultural tourism.

Rodney B. Dieser is a Professor of Leisure, Youth, and Human Services at the University of Northern Iowa. Rod holds a Ph.D. in Physical Education and Recreation from the University of Alberta. His research and teaching interests include: (a) cross-cultural therapeutic recreation/inclusive recreation and leisure service delivery, (b) leisure education intervention, (c) leisure and mental health, (d) historical and philosophical foundations of leisure, youth, and nonprofit human services, including Hull-House, 1889–1953, and (e) the philanthropic labor and leisure endeavors of Bruce Springsteen. His leisure consists of mountain biking, judo, playing the harmonica to Bruce Springsteen songs, and most importantly, being with his wife/sons and the family pets (2 dogs, 2 guinea pigs, 2 hedgehogs, and one cat).

Daniel L. Dustin is a Professor in the Department of Parks, Recreation, and Tourism at the University of Utah. He earned a Ph.D. in Education with an emphasis in recreation and park administration from the University of Minnesota. Dan is interested in national park policy, wilderness policy, and environmental ethics. He likes to hike, bike, fish, read, and attend the theater.

Michael B. Edwards is an Associate Professor in the Department of Parks, Recreation & Tourism Management at North Carolina State University where he also received his Ph.D. Dr. Edwards' research interests center on health disparities, particularly related to accessibility to health-promoting resources provided by sport and recreation. He is also interested in the role of leisure and recreation in rural community health development. Dr. Edwards' teaching interests focus on organizational management and research methods. In his leisure time, Mike enjoys running, playing and watching soccer, and engaging in numerous outdoor recreational activities with his family.

Gary Ellis is Head of the Department of Recreation, Park and Tourism Sciences in the Texas A&M University System, a position he has held since 2008. He previously served as Professor and Chair of the Department of Parks, Recreation, and Tourism at the University of Utah (1985–2008; 1994–2006 as Chair). He was a member of the Western Kentucky University faculty from 1983–1985. He holds a Ph.D. in Higher Education Administration from the University of North Texas (1983) and Master's and Baccalaureate degrees in Recreation and Park Administration from the University of Kentucky (1979) and Eastern Kentucky University (1978). Gary has served a variety of leadership positions in professional organizations. His research interests include measurement and facilitation of guest experiences and park, recreation, and tourism management.

Myron F. Floyd earned his Ph.D. in Recreation and Resources Development from Texas A&M University. He is Professor and Department Head in the Department of Parks, Recreation and Tourism Management at North Carolina State University. He has a longstanding interest in how race and ethnicity influence participation in outdoor recreation. His current research examines the capacity of public parks and green space to promote public health, particularly among low-income and racial and ethnic minority populations. His research appears in a wide variety of scientific journals and book chapters. He is a Fellow of the Academy of Leisure Sciences and is the 2008 recipient of the Theodore and Franklin Roosevelt Award for Excellence in Recreation and Park Research. When not working, Myron enjoys reading Civil War history and listening to and singing gospel music.

Karen M. Fox is a Professor of leisure studies at the Faculty of Physical Education and Recreation at the University of Alberta. Her research has examined leisure honoring insights from people or groups not typically appearing in leisure research, such as urban Aboriginal hip-hop cultures, Kanaka Maoli, Navajo peoples, and self-supported long-distance bicycle tourers. She is particularly interested in ways to decentre dominant conceptions and understandings of leisure that intersect with ethics, environmental and sustainability concerns, and rethink our understanding of self, community, and the cosmos. Her publications reflect a deep commitment to collaborative and participatory research/authorship with other scholars, students, and community members.

Simone Fullagar has recently moved to the University of Bath, United Kingdom, to take up a Professorship in Sport and Physical Cultural Studies. She holds a Ph.D. in sociology from the University of New South Wales and a B.A. (Hons) in Leisure Studies from the University of Technology, Sydney. Simone is an interdisciplinary sociologist who has published widely across the areas of health/well-being, leisure, sport and tourism, using poststructuralist and feminist perspectives. She is the past president of the Australian and New Zealand Association for Leisure Studies. Simone has a diverse leisure repertoire that includes cycle touring, running, slow food, and enjoying the arts.

Heather Gibson is a Professor in the Department of Tourism, Recreation and Sport Management at the University of Florida and an Associate Director of the Eric Friedheim Tourism Institute. People often ask "Does Heather specialize in tourism, sport, or leisure?" The answer is all three. She graduated from Brighton Polytechnic in the United Kingdom with a Bachelor's in physical education and a specialization in sport sociology. This focus on the sociology of sport and leisure led her to the University of Connecticut where she earned her Master's and Ph.D. and was introduced to tourism as a field of study. Currently, Professor Gibson teaches classes in leisure theory, tourism, and research methods. She also leads study abroad programs to Australia, New Zealand and Fiji. Her research interests include sport tourism with a particular focus on sport-related travel in later life and small-scale events; leisure and tourism in later life; women travelers; and perceived risk in travel. Professor Gibson's research appears in such journals as the *Annals of Tourism Research*, *Tourism Management*, *Leisure Sciences*, and the *Journal of Sport Management*. She also edited the book *Sport Tourism: Concepts and Theories* and co-edited with Jerome Singleton *Leisure and Aging: Theory and Practice*.

Troy D. Glover received his Ph.D. from the Department of Recreation and Leisure Studies at the University of Waterloo where he now works as a Professor. His research explores the role(s) of leisure in advancing or deterring the realization of healthy communities, often through the development of social capital. When not engaged in academic-related pursuits, Dr. Glover enjoys hanging out with his family, tweeting, and listening to CBC Radio One. He's unstoppable one-on-one on his driveway hoop and loves to keep fit.

Geoffrey Godbey received his Ph.D. from The Pennsylvania State University in Recreation and Parks. He is currently Professor Emeritus in that department. His interests include leisure constraints, futures research, leisure and health, and tourism. He has been involved with Chinese leisure scholars for 20 years.

Daniel Guttentag is currently pursuing a Ph.D. in the Recreation and Leisure Studies Department at the University of Waterloo in Ontario, Canada. He previously received a Master's degree in Tourism Policy and Planning from the same university. He is interested in a range of research topics, including the psychology of leisure, gambling behavior, innovations in tourism accommodation, and volunteer tourism. Daniel's favorite leisure activities include playing with his newborn daughter, (occasionally) beating his wife at board games, participating in all sorts of water sports, reading long-form journalism, and watching the Carolina Panthers football team.

Mark Havitz is Professor and Chair in the University of Waterloo's Department of Recreation and Leisure Studies. He earned B.Sc. and M.Sc. degrees from Michigan State University and a Ph.D. from Texas A&M University. His teaching interests include understanding recreation marketing, finance, and management. His academic research has focused on public and not-for-profit leisure marketing and understanding ego involvements, commitments and loyalties in sport, tourism and recreation contexts. He is a Fellow in the Academy of Leisure Sciences and the World Leisure Academy. His leisure interests include four decades of distance running, 25 years of volunteering with Habitat for Humanity, and a lifetime researching family and university history and walking through parks with his wife Sue and their dogs.

Paul Heintzman is an Associate Professor of Leisure Studies at the University of Ottawa in Ottawa, Canada. He received his Ph.D. in Recreation and Leisure Studies from the University of Waterloo with a thesis titled *Leisure and Spiritual Well-Being: A Social Scientific Exploration*. His research interests include leisure and spirituality, parks, outdoor recreation and education, and the philosophy and ethics of leisure. He is author of the book *Leisure and Spirituality: Biblical, Historical and Contemporary Perspectives*. Teaching areas include recreation and the environment and the concepts of leisure. He enjoys competitive running, cross-country skiing as well as a variety of outdoor activities with his family.

John L. Hemingway was educated at Grinnell College (B.A., political science, 1971) and after military service at the University of Iowa (Ph.D., political science, 1979; M.A., recreation education, 1983), Hemingway has taught in the recreation and leisure services field for 30 years; the last decade at Western Illinois University. His research interests are the expression of freedom in leisure and the connections between leisure and civic engagement. He has published a number of essays on these themes. A strong believer in practicing what we preach, he is serving his third term as a member of the local park district's board of commissioners, of which he is president.

Karla A. Henderson is Professor Emeritus in the Department of Parks, Recreation, and Tourism management at North Carolina State University. She has been a faculty member at the University of Minnesota, University of Wisconsin-Madison, Texas Woman's University, and the University of North Carolina-Chapel Hill. Henderson is a Fellow in the Academy of Leisure Sciences and the American Academy of Park and Recreation Administrators. She has received many awards including the National Recreation and Park Associations Roosevelt Award for Research Excellence, both the World Leisure George Torkildsen Literary Award and National Recreation and Park Association Literary Award in 2010, and the Lifetime Achievement Award from North Carolina State University. She received her Ph.D. from the University of Minnesota and holds a Sc.D. (honoris causa) from the University of Waterloo.

Yoshitaka Iwasaki is a Professor in the Faculty of Extension at the University of Alberta, as well as Associate Dean, Research. He holds a doctorate in recreation and leisure studies from the University of Waterloo. His expertise includes culture/diversity, leisure, and health; meaning-making, coping/healing, and life quality; and community-based research with marginalized populations such as Indigenous peoples, cultural minorities with disabilities, and high-risk youth. Dr. Iwasaki has over 70 refereed journal articles and over $5 million in research funding. In 2008, he was inducted into the Academy of Leisure Sciences, and was a recipient of the Distinguished Alumni Award, Department of Recreation and Leisure Studies, University of Waterloo.

Edgar L. Jackson earned degrees in Geography from the London School of Economics and the Universities of Calgary and Toronto, before joining the University of Alberta in 1975. In the last 20 years of his career he concentrated on constraints to leisure, an area in which he published many journal articles, book chapters, and contract reports for the Alberta government. In 2005 Dr. Jackson completed editing *Constraints to Leisure*. He initiated and maintained the websites for the Academy of Leisure Sciences and the Canadian Association for Leisure Studies. Dr. Jackson retired in 2007 and now spends his time on personal projects and hobbies, enjoying free time rather than—as an academic—studying it.

Corey W. Johnson is a Professor in the Department of Recreation and Leisure Studies at The University of Waterloo. He teaches courses on social justice, gender and sexuality, qualitative data collection, ethnography, and philosophy of science. His scholarship focuses on the power relations between dominant and non-dominant populations in the cultural contexts of leisure. This examination provides important insight into both the privileging and discriminatory practices that occur in contemporary settings. In 2012 he received the University of Georgia President's Martin Luther King Jr. Achieving the Dream award for his efforts to make society more just.

Debra J. Jordan earned her degrees from Indiana University (Re.D.), Western Illinois University (M.S.), and Slippery Rock University of Pennsylvania (B.S.); all in parks and recreation. She is currently a Professor in the Recreation and Leisure Studies Department at East Carolina University. where she teaches in areas such as leadership; leisure behavior in parks; social psychology of leisure; and diversity as it relates to parks, recreation, and leisure studies. Jordan is a fellow in the Academy of Leisure Sciences and in the American Academy of Parks and Recreation Administration.

Fiona Jordan is Associate Dean (External Engagement) in the Faculty of Business and Law at the University of the West of England in the United Kingdom. She has worked in higher education for more than 20 years. Fiona has been the Leisure Subject Editor on the Editorial Board of the *Journal of Hospitality, Leisure, Sport and Tourism Education*, Secretary of the UK Leisure Studies Association, a member of the World Leisure International Scholarship Committee, and an invited member of the International Society of Eastern Sports and Physical Education and the Pan-Asian Society of Sports and Physical Education. Fiona's research centres on the representation and gendered consumption of leisure and tourism spaces and places. Her recent publications focus on the experiences of women traveling alone, examination of the links between tourism and body image, and exploration of the representation of leisure and tourism in popular cultural forms such as women's and men's lifestyle magazines.

Douglas A. Kleiber is Professor of Counseling and Human Development Services and adjunct faculty in Psychology and Gerontology at the University of Georgia. He received an A.B in Psychology from Cornell University in 1969 and a Ph.D. in Educational Psychology from the University of Texas at Austin in 1972. His research on the psychology of leisure has resulted in over 80 articles in refereed journals, as well as 20 chapters and four books, including *Leisure Experience and Human Development* (Basic Books). He is a charter member of the Association of Psychological Science and a past president of the Academy of Leisure Sciences.

Shintaro Kono received his M.S. in Recreation, Sport, and Tourism from the University of Illinois at Urbana-Champaign. He is currently a Ph.D. candidate in the Faculty of Physical Education and Recreation at the University of Alberta. His research interests encompass subjective well-being and leisure, leisure in cross-cultural settings, Japanese culture and leisure, and disasters and leisure. He loves to have relaxing moments, taking a hot bath and watching TV shows and movies. He also enjoys various recreational activities, including basketball, squash, golf, badminton, and swimming, as well as creative activities such as cooking, singing, and drawing. Above all, socialization with his colleagues has always kept motivating him to do research.

Gerard Kyle is a Professor within the Department of Recreation, Park and Tourism Sciences at Texas A&M University. He is also the director of the Human Dimensions of Natural Resources Laboratory (HDNR). Staff within the HDNR Lab draw from several social science disciplines and methods of enquiry to explore human dimensions-related issues impacting natural resource conservation across the globe. His own work is informed by psychological theory of human-environment relationships. These theories drive the development of models aimed at documenting psychological processes that shape behavior in relation to the environment.

Geoff Lacher is an economist with the research and consulting firm, Tourism Economics. He holds a Ph.D. from Clemson University's Parks, Tourism and Recreation Management Department. His research is focused on the economics of tourism and recreation with an emphasis on sustainable tourism and tourism in the developing world. He has previous research experience in Thailand, the Dominican Republic, and Tanzania, as well as the United States.

Jin-Hyung Lee received his Ph.D. in Recreation, Park and Tourism Sciences from Texas A&M University. Currently, he is an Associate Professor in the Department of Tourism Management at Mokpo National University, South Korea. His general research interests include socio-cultural aspects of leisure and tourism, community-based tourism development, and ecotourism and resource interpretation. He teaches courses in introduction of leisure studies, ecotourism, and community-based tourism development. He is regularly involved in table tennis, trail hiking, and walking at community parks.

KangJae Jerry Lee is an Assistant Teaching Professor at the Department of Parks, Recreation and Tourism in the University of Missouri. He received a Ph.D. in Recreation, Park and Tourism Sciences from the Texas A&M University (2013). He is a recipient of the 2013 U.S. Senator Phil Gramm Doctoral Fellowship from Texas A&M and 2012 Diversity Scholarship from National Recreation and Park Association. His research interests include sociology of leisure, leisure behavior of race/ethnic minorities, serious leisure and recreation specialization, and racism and intergroup contact in leisure context. His dissertation research utilized Pierre Bourdieu's sociological theory to examine African Americans' under-representation at parks and the great outdoors.

Monica Z. Li is currently an Assistant Professor at the School of Tourism Management at Beijing International Studies University. She was a University of Illinois graduate, where she earned her Master's degree in Tourism Management in 2003 and her doctoral degree in Leisure Behavior in 2007. Her primary research interests lie in leisure and travel experiences of minority populations in China and overseas. Other areas of her research include social and cultural aspects of tourism and its implications for tourism sustainability. In her spare time, she loves traveling to meet different people and learn different cultures.

Huimei Liu is a Professor, Director of International Communications at the Asian Pacific Centre for the Education and Study of Leisure, Deputy Director of Institute of Cross-Cultural and Regional Studies, Zhejiang University, China. She was a Fulbright Scholar at the Department of Parks, Recreation and Tourism, Pennsylvania State University (2007–2008) and a Visiting Professor at the Faculty of Physical Education and Recreation, University of Alberta (2012–2014). Her research explores the effects of culture and ethnicity on leisure, and she has also worked on several projects on heritage and tourism (leisure) sponsored by the Chinese government. She has a strong passion to promote leisure studies in China.

Roger C. Mannell received his Ph.D. in psychology at the University of Windsor and is a Professor of leisure and health sciences in the Department of Recreation and Leisure Studies, and School of Public Health and Health Systems at the University of Waterloo. He studies and writes about the determinants of lifestyle choices and health, and the role of leisure in coping with time pressure and stress, negative life events such as bereavement, and the challenges of care giving. His leisure passions include outdoor recreation and building and renovating.

Alcyane Marinho is a lecturer at Santa Catarina State University (College of Health and Sport Science, CEFID) in Brazil and leader of the Leisure and Physical Activity Research Laboratory in this institution. She completed her Bachelor's degree in physical education at São Paulo State University (Unesp) in 1995, her Master's degree in 2001 and her Ph.D. in 2006 at Campinas State University (Unicamp). She is also a lecturer in the physical education postgraduate program at the Federal University of Santa Catarina, focusing on "Pedagogical Theory and Practice in Physical Education."

Bryan McCormick holds degrees from The Pennsylvania State University and Clemson University. He is a Professor in the Department of Recreation, Park & Tourism Studies at Indiana University, where he has been on faculty since 1995. He is a past president of the American Therapeutic Recreation Association and is a Fellow in the Academy of Leisure Sciences and the National Academy of Recreational Therapists. He is the author or co-author of over 60 peer-reviewed publications and 11 book chapters. His research has focused on social and community functioning of adults with severe mental illnesses.

Steven E. Mock received his Ph.D. in developmental psychology at Cornell University and completed a postdoc at Yale. He is an Associate Professor in the Department of Recreation and Leisure Studies at the University of Waterloo and the Director of the RBC Retirement Research Centre. His research interests are in the area of lifespan developmental psychology with a focus on coping with stigmatization, sexual minority adult development, leisure as a coping resource, and retirement planning. His leisure pursuits include travel, cooking, watching movies and plays, and a life-long devotion to horses and riding, in particular, dressage.

Andrew J. Mowen is an Associate Professor in the Department of Recreation, Park and Tourism Management at The Pennsylvania State University. His research focuses on the health contributions of public parks and how to better position park and recreation services among local decision makers. In his leisure time, Dr. Mowen enjoys bicycling, paddleboarding, waterfowl and upland game hunting, and fishing.

Maliga Naidoo is a part-time Leisure Science Lecturer in the School of Health Sciences at the University of KwaZulu Natal, Durban. She has been involved in generating vocational leisure qualifications since 2001, which are registered with the South African Qualifications Authority. Her review of the curriculum at the University resulted in the introduction of the Leisure Science stream to provide further education and training at tertiary level in this sector. She is particularly interested in developing curriculum and continuing education of leisure professionals to meet the growing demand for these skills in the public service. Maliga is the founding member of the Leisure and Recreation Association of South Africa (LARASA). Her leisure time is spent traveling, listening to music, and enjoying the outdoors.

Galit Nimrod is an Associate Professor at the Department of Communication Studies and a Research Fellow at the Center for Multidisciplinary Research in Aging at Ben-Gurion University of the Negev, Israel. She holds a Ph.D. in Communication and Journalism from the Hebrew University of Jerusalem, and she was a Fulbright post-doctoral scholar at the University of Georgia. Dr. Nimrod studies psychological and sociological aspects of leisure and media use among populations with special needs such as older adults and people with disabilities. Her leisure interests include traveling, exercising, dancing, cooking, reading, and enjoying the wonderful beaches of Tel Aviv.

Chi-Ok Oh is an Associate Professor in the Graduate School of Culture at Chonnam National University, South Korea. His research interests are in tourism and recreation economics and human dimensions of natural resources, with a particular interest in estimating social and economic benefits of tourism and recreation activities and related natural resources. His research delves into environmental, economic and sociopolitical sustainability by asking how people view, value, and use natural resources, particularly in the areas of parks and protected areas.

Tetsuya Onda is a Professor at Tokai University, Japan, in the School of Physical Education, Sports & Leisure Management Program. He completed his Ph.D. from the University of Sheffield, UK, in the Department of Medical Physics Clinical Engineering of Sports Science. Dr. Onda's research and scholarly expertise includes health, fitness, and life-long sport; sport and leisure education; and sport and leisure management.

Diana C. Parry is an Associate Professor in the Faculty of Applied Health Sciences and the Special Advisor to the President on Women's and Gender Issues at the University of Waterloo, Waterloo Ontario, Canada. Utilizing a feminist lens, Diana's research explores the personal and political links between women's leisure and women's health, broadly defined. Diana's research privileges women's standpoints and aims to enact social justice by challenging the medical model of scholarship.

Arianne C. Reis is a Research Fellow with the School of Business and Tourism (Tourism and Hospitality Management) at Southern Cross University, Australia. Dr. Reis is originally from Brazil, where she completed her undergraduate and Master's studies in physical education and sports sciences. Before doing her Ph.D. at the University of Otago, New Zealand, she worked for several years for public and private institutions in Brazil in the fields of nature-based recreation and sports management. Her research interests developed from these professional experiences, focusing on outdoor recreation and the sustainability issues of sport events.

Robert Richardson is an applied economist and Associate Professor in the Department of Community Sustainability at Michigan State University. He holds a Ph.D. in agricultural and resource economics, and his research focuses mainly on sustainable development, and the role of ecosystem services in supporting the welfare and livelihoods of households and communities.

Diane M. Samdahl is a Professor Emerita at the University of Georgia. She received an M.A. in sociology from the University of Washington and a Ph.D. in leisure studies from the University of Illinois. Her early training in survey research gave way to qualitative methods as her interests moved towards feminist theory and the study of marginalized populations. Her work has explored the ways leisure mirrors and maintains social inequities as well the ways leisure can reshape cultural norms and discourse. She retired in 2014.

Thitikan Satchabut is an associate dean in the University of the Thai Chamber of Commerce (UTCC), Thailand. With the sponsorship from the UTCC, she received her doctorate in Recreation, Park and Tourism Sciences from Texas A&M University (2013). She was granted the HM Queen Sirikit's scholarship, which sponsored by the Royal Thai Government to pursue her Master's degree in Natural Resources Management at the Asian Institute of Technology, Thailand (2007–2009). Fully funded by the University of Arkansas at Pine Bluff, she graduated her Bachelor's degree in Environmental Biology with First-Class Honor (2007). Thitikan's current research interests include environmental concern, recreation participation, and ecotourism. Her deepest passion is to conduct all research by using experimental design.

Ingrid E. Schneider is a Professor in the Department of Forest Resources at the University of Minnesota where she teaches in the park and protected area concentration and concurrently serves as Director of the University's Tourism Center. She received her Bachelor's and Master's degrees from the University of Minnesota and her Ph.D. from Clemson University. Ingrid's research focuses on visitor behavior with an emphasis on leisure constraints, response to recreation conflict, and nature-based tourism. Beyond academia, she has experience in the service industry and as an outdoor recreation planner. Ingrid seeks life balance through yoga, tennis, hiking, reading, attending movies, and cooking.

Keri A. Schwab is an Assistant Professor in the Recreation, Parks, and Tourism Administration Department at California Polytechnic State University, San Luis Obispo. She earned a Ph.D. from the University of Utah. Her academic interests center on youth development, family leisure, community recreation, social justice, and scholarly teaching. Keri enjoys running, hiking, camping, practicing yoga, and spending time with family and friends.

David Scott is a Professor in the Department of Recreation, Park and Tourism Sciences at Texas A&M University. Between 1991 and 1994, he served as Manager of Research and Program Evaluation for Cleveland Metroparks in Cleveland, Ohio. David's undergraduate work was completed at Purdue University, where he majored in sociology and wrestled heavyweight for the Boilermakers. He holds advanced degrees from The Pennsylvania State University. His research focuses on recreation specialization, serious leisure, and leisure constraints. David has published over 75 articles in scholarly journals and served as the Editor of the *Journal of Leisure Research* from 2002 to 2007. He was elected as a Fellow to the Academy of Leisure Sciences in 2007 and was the 2011 recipient of the Theodore and Franklin Roosevelt Award for Excellence in Recreation and Park Research presented annually by National Recreation and Park Association. His leisure interests include birdwatching, reading (history), watching old movies, bicycling, cooking, and playing games with family and friends.

Monika Stodolska is a Professor in the Department of Recreation, Sport and Tourism at the University of Illinois at Urbana-Champaign. She received her Ph.D. in Earth and Atmospheric Sciences from the University of Alberta, Canada. Her research focuses on issues of cultural change and quality of life and their relationship to leisure behavior among ethnic and racial minorities. She explores subjects such as the adaptation processes among minority groups, the effects of leisure on identity development among immigrants, and transnationalism. Other subjects that are prominent in her research include ethnic and racial discrimination in leisure settings, recreation behavior of minority populations in natural environments, physical activity among minority groups, and constraints on leisure. In 2013, Monika was elected to the Academy of Leisure Sciences and in 2014 she co-edited *Race, Ethnicity, and Leisure* with Gordon Walker, Kim Shinew, and Myron Floyd. Monika's leisure activities include hiking in the mountains of Montana, skiing, and adventure travel.

Charles Sylvester received his doctorate from the University of Oregon. He is a Professor in the Department of Physical Education, Health, and Recreation at Western Washington University in Bellingham, Washington. Besides history and philosophy of leisure, his research includes philosophy of therapeutic recreation. He teaches a humanities course on work and leisure. From the age of 7 to 60, he played baseball. Now he rides his bike wherever it takes him.

Dawn E. Trussell is an Assistant Professor in the Department of Recreation and Leisure Studies at Brock University in Ontario, Canada. She serves as a program committee member for Brock University's Centre for Women's and Gender Studies. Her research has focused on diverse social contexts and issues of power and social inclusion, particularly related to constructs of family, gender, sexuality, age, and rurality. Her current projects include family leisure, the transition to motherhood, and organized youth sport—all with an emphasis to the connection to gender and parenting ideologies. Dawn's leisure interests include playing volleyball, yoga as well as enjoying hiking, camping, and canoeing with her family.

A. J. (Tony) Veal was awarded a Bachelor's degree in economics by the University of Bristol in 1966. He is currently Adjunct Professor in the Business School at the University of Technology, Sydney. His research interests lie in the areas of leisure policy, planning and participation patterns, and lifestyle. He is past president of the Australian and New Zealand Association for Leisure Studies and of the UK Leisure Studies Association. His leisure activities include a little gardening, followed by admiring his handiwork over an occasional glass of wine from the nearby Hunter Valley, New South Wales.

Gordon J. Walker is a Professor in the Faculty of Physical Education and Recreation at the University of Alberta. He received his Bachelor's degree from the University of Regina; his Master's degree from Arizona State University; and his Ph.D. from Virginia Tech. Gordon's research program focuses on how culture and ethnicity affect leisure behavior (e.g., motivations for, constraints to, experiences during, and outcomes of, leisure). In 2009, he was elected to the Academy of Leisure Sciences; in 2011, he co-authored the second edition of *A Social Psychology of Leisure* with Doug Kleiber and Roger Mannell; and in 2014, he co-edited *Race, Ethnicity, and Leisure* with Monika Stodolska, Kim Shinew, and Myron Floyd. Gordon's leisure activities include canoeing, reading books (mostly histories and mysteries), listening to music (from Beethoven to Bruce Springsteen to Bruno Mars), and traveling with his wife, Janet (including trips to Mongolia, Mozambique, and Moose Jaw).

D J WILLIAMS received a Ph.D. from the University of Alberta. He is currently the Director of Social Work and an Associate Professor of Sociology, Social Work, and Criminal Justice at Idaho State University. He is also the Director of Research for the Center for Positive Sexuality in Los Angeles. D J's scholarly interests include consensual sadomasochism, self-identified vampires, and leisure as it relates to both criminogenesis and offender rehabilitation. His leisure interests include hiking the rugged mountains of Idaho and playing creatively in active deviant spaces in Los Angeles.

1

Anthropology and Leisure

Garry Chick (The Pennsylvania State University)

Anthropology has traditionally consisted of four separate, but related, subfields. These include *cultural anthropology*, which addresses issues such as how people make their livings, raise their families, and create meaning in their lives; *archeology*, which examines similar issues in historic and prehistoric societies through the analysis of their artifacts and material remnants; *biological anthropology*, which addresses the evolution of humans and our close biological relatives as well as modern human variation; and *anthropological linguistics*, which is devoted to the historical development, structure, and comparison of human languages. All of these, with the exception of biological anthropology, deal with culture in one form or another although it could be argued that biological anthropology addresses the mental capacity for culture. Each has its own relevance to the study of leisure and recreation.

Biological anthropologists might ask, for example, "Do nonhuman primates, such as apes or monkeys, or other animals experience leisure?" While this may first appear to be a peculiar question, we know that animals, mammals in particular, engage in play, especially as juveniles. And play is commonly a part of human leisure experiences. What does animal play and the fact that many animals have plenty of what we could call "free time" mean for the definition of leisure, for example? Archeologists sometimes address the reconstruction of leisure and recreational behavior of past societies, particularly common folk as opposed to just the elites and ruling classes. Linguistic anthropologists might examine whether the English word "leisure" has equivalents in other languages and whether having or not having an equivalent influences thinking and behavior with regard to leisure. Most anthropological research on leisure, however, is based in cultural anthropology.

In keeping with their name, cultural anthropologists study "culture." But, like many concepts in both the social and natural sciences, anthropologists have failed to reach an agreed-upon definition of the term. This, in turn, renders its measurement even more problematic. While there are tens, if not hundreds, of definitions of culture, they do seem to converge on whether or not they are completely cognitive in nature; that is, they involve things like knowledge, beliefs, and values—things in the heads of members of particular cultural groups—or whether they also include characteristic behaviors and/or artifacts (Chick, 1997).

Culturally specific behaviors include taboos, or proscriptions on doing certain things, such as eating red meat on Fridays among Catholics or wearing revealing clothing among traditional Muslim women. They also include prescriptive behaviors, such as holding festivals in honor of particular saints in traditional Latin American communities. Artifacts associated with particular cultures might include the igloo among the Inuit and the boomerang among Australian Aborigines. A problem with definitions that include behavior and/or artifacts, however, is that culture cannot then be used to explain the existence of particular behaviors or artifacts since those behaviors and artifacts are part of the definition of culture (D'Andrade, 1995).

To solve this problem, many anthropologists have adopted a cognitive view of culture wherein culture is considered to be knowledge, beliefs, values, or, more generally, information, that is learned and shared and that influences behavior, including the manufacture of artifacts. For example, in 1957, the anthropologist Ward Goodenough defined culture as what a person needs to know in order to function adequately in a particular social group. This knowledge is learned and shared among members of those social groups and is encoded in the form of cultural models. So, if you go to a restaurant, you have a cultural model of how to order dinner, pay for it, and otherwise behave appropriately. If your cultural model is different from the one that is standard in the local culture, you might leave a tip when none is expected or, possibly worse, not leave one when it is expected.

Four topical areas, each commonly studied by anthropologists in other contexts, provide a basis for the anthropological study of leisure. These are: (a) the ethnography, or intensive description in the local cultural context, of leisure; (b) an examination of whether leisure is a useful adaptive response to the physical and social environment; (c) how leisure, in the context of culture, evolves over time; and (d) whether leisure is a valid concept across different languages and cultures (Chick, 1998). Each of these has been addressed, to greater or lesser extents, in recent years, and will be discussed below.

THE ETHNOGRAPHY OF LEISURE

Anthropology, as a formal discipline, dates to the second half of the nineteenth century with ethnography as its hallmark. Ethnography has traditionally involved holistic description—that is, the description of a total cultural setting. Conventionally, an ethnography requires a long stay in the setting of interest, typically at least a year, in order to experience the entire annual cycle. In recent years, "microethnography," or the description of smaller parts or systems within total cultures, has become popular. These have focused on things such as the organization of a classroom (Smith, 2006), the workings of a business (Hay, 1990), the social dynamics in a gay bar (Johnson & Samdahl, 2005), or the analysis of problem behavior in a campground (Clark, Hendee, & Campbell, 2009) and may require a much shorter time period and less than total immersion in the local culture (Bernard, 2011).

Ethnographic approaches to leisure or leisure activities in non-Western settings have been undertaken only sporadically throughout the history of the discipline but include studies such as Blanchard's (1981) detailed description of leisure among the Mississippi Choctaws, or Chick's (1991) examination of how religious festivals in traditional communities in highland Mexico provide community-wide recreational opportunities. More frequently, ethnographers or compilers of ethnographies have addressed particular instances of leisure, such as Geertz's (1973) classic study of the social organization of cockfighting in Bali, or kinds of leisure, such as games (e.g., Culin's [1907] *Games of the North American Indians* and Stern's [1948] *The Rubber Ball Games of the Americas*), music (e.g., Kaemmer's [1993] *Music in Human Life*), or dance (e.g., Royce's [1977] *The Anthropology of Dance*).

Ethnographic research on leisure itself, or with leisure as one variable among others, has accelerated somewhat in recent years, however. Dressler and his colleagues used free listing, where individuals are asked to list as many items in a particular category as they can think of, to create inventories of leisure activities in a Brazilian city and in a small, largely African American community in the southern United States (Dressler et al., 1998; Dressler & Bindon, 2000). They used these lists in later research and found that informants held some leisure activities to be more important than others for having a good lifestyle. Dressler and his colleagues referred to the ability of individuals to participate in activities that were agreed upon as more important than others as "cultural consonance." Individuals who exhibited high cultural consonance—that is, who had the means to engage in activities culturally agreed upon as important—also had more positive measures of physical (e.g., blood pressure, body mass index) and mental (e.g., stress, depression) health (Dressler et al., 2012). Similar research, relating the importance of leisure constraints and cultural consonance in the importance of leisure activities to self-rated health among informants from six cities in China, has equivalent findings (Chick, Dong, & Iarmolenko, 2014).

Dong and Chick (2012) examined correlates of 37 leisure constraints—that is, things such as lack of time, lack of money, or need to care for elders that either impede or prevent leisure participation—in five Chinese cities (Beijing, Shanghai, Hangzhou, Qingdao, and Chengdu). To obtain the list, samples of approximately 30 individuals in each city were asked to name as many leisure constraints as they could think of in about two minutes. Thus, the lists of leisure constraints were based on local informant knowledge, not predetermined and imposed on them by the researchers. Lack of time and lack of money were the most common factors that constrained leisure among informants across the cities studied. Ethnographic field research, including methods such as free listing, allows researchers to develop locally relevant inventories of leisure activities or leisure constraints in specific cultural settings as part of an overall ethnography of leisure in a given cultural setting.

Ethnographic research relevant to the study of leisure in technologically simple societies often involves the examination of how people allocate their time. Sometimes such studies involve only one cultural group but comparisons between two or more are also possible. For example, Johnson (1978) found that, among the Machiguenga, a small-scale horticultural, food collecting, and hunting society of the upper Amazon basin of Southeastern Peru, men averaged 14.8 hours of free time per day (which included nocturnal sleep) while their counterparts in France averaged only 9.6. Machiguenga females had 14.7 hours of free time per day, on average, while French women averaged 9.4, if married, and 9.8, if unmarried (again including nocturnal sleep). In a more recent study, Gurven and Kaplan (2006) used time allocation to show that adult married men among the Machiguenga and the Piro, also of the upper Amazon basin, had more time for leisure, which they operationalized as idleness, socializing, playing games, and other non-productive activities, than in productive work (388.8 and 408.6 minutes per day, respectively versus 203.5 and 347.9 minutes per day). While adult married Machiguenga women spent more time in leisure than in work (347.4 versus 244.8 minutes per day), adult married Piro women spent more time working (442.9 minutes per day) than in leisure (386.0 minutes per day). These studies suggest that the availability of free time varies substantially cross-culturally, particularly when societies at different levels of cultural complexity are compared, and that time constraints on leisure may be considerably more important in some societies than others.

Secondary ethnographic data is also useful for the examination of leisure. Cross-cultural comparative researchers have used data from sources such as the Human Relations Area Files (HRAF), in order to examine the relationship of leisure to other aspects of culture. The HRAF is a large database of ethnographic materials on approximately 400 societies, both historical and present and ranging from the technologically simple to the complex, from around the world. It is now available in electronic format for a randomly chosen sample of 280 societies (the eHRAF). Unfortunately, only a handful of HRAF-based studies have addressed leisure. Broude and Greene (1983), for example, found that in cultures where husbands and wives spend leisure together, they also do other activities, such as eating and sleeping, together. But, where they do not engage in leisure together, they also remain separate for most other common activities. Chick (1995) hypothesized that the amount of time devoted to leisure cross-culturally would follow an inverted parabola (a U shape) when compared to measures of cultural complexity. In other words, members of technologically simple and technologically complex cultures should have more leisure available to them than members of simple agricultural societies. This hypothesis was not supported, based on data from sample of 43 societies selected from the HRAF. This may be because people attempt to devote approximately the same amount of time to work and to leisure cross-culturally but then adjust other things, such as their activity levels in leisure, to compensate for variation in caloric intake. Indeed, that is exactly what Rubin, Flowers, and Gross (1986), discussed below, found. Chick (1995) did determine that children in societies of midrange complexity began productive work at a younger age than those in either simple or complex societies, probably because simple agricultural and food preparation tasks are more easily learned than the complex knowledge needed for hunting and food collection among technologically simple groups and the extensive education required in modern, complex societies. He also found that the number of children born to women in societies of midrange cultural complexity was higher than for either simple or complex societies. Again, this may be due to the fact that children can contribute productive labor in societies of moderate complexity, thus freeing adults for about the same amount of leisure experienced by adults in simpler or more complex societies. A later study (Chick & Shen, 2011), using time allocation data from 12 small-scale societies, supported Chick's (1995) earlier finding that the amount of leisure time available to adults is highly variable among cultures but does not differ systematically across the range of complexity.

The Internet has become both a rich source of ethnographic material on leisure as well as a tool for conducting ethnographic research on leisure. Snodgrass and his colleagues (2011a, 2011b, 2012), for example, examined the experiences of online gamers, specifically *World of Warcraft* (*WoW*) players. They were particularly interested in situations wherein players confound identification of their everyday lives with their in-game selves. They found that such experiences, for some individuals, lead to improved mental well-being while others may suffer harmful outcomes, including addiction to the games. According to Snodgrass et al. (2011a), "Failure to balance *WoW* and actual-world participation has reached urban legend status. Colorful stories include those of desiccated bodies found in front of computers, leading many games to suggest changing *WoW*'s name to World of War*crack*" (p. 50). In a related study, Snodgrass et al. (2011b) found that *WoW* gamers who played with real-life friends are better able to manage their real-world lives and maintain distance from the game, thus avoiding addictive-like behaviors.

Using the Internet to do ethnographic research is also becoming more common. "Netnography" can be described as a method for doing ethnographic research of online leisure-based cultures (Kozinets, 2010). Stebbins (2010) describes it as a useful means for Internet data collection of qualitative data on leisure but it can also be very easily used for other ethnographic techniques such as free listing, interviews, surveys, blogs, newsgroups, chatrooms, or document analysis (Stebbins 2010). Kozinets (1997), for example, conducted a netnography of X-Philes, a group dedicated to the TV series, *The X-Files*. He determined that *The X-Files* fans are united by the themes of "The truth is out there," "I want to believe," and "Trust no one" (Kozinets, 1997, p. 472). Mkono (2012) used netnography to examine tourist experiences that would otherwise be inaccessible to traditional methods such as interviews and surveys. Williams (2007) examined online identities, created via avatars, in order to determine how participants represent themselves using visual stimuli compared to online text-based discourse. He found, for example, that "physical appearance within Cyberworlds is regarded with more importance than within text-only environments" (Williams, 2007, p. 13). This may be because the visual status of avatars permits observers to make judgments about others more rapidly than is possible with textual communication.

Anthropological research on leisure use of the Internet typically involves traditional anthropological methods such as participant-observation, interviews, surveys, and quasi-experiments (Chick, 2013) but, unfortunately, these carry traditional drawbacks. Studies tend to be based on samples that are small, nonrandom, often self-selected and localized, and generally in North America. As the studies are neither experimental nor longitudinal, the determination of causality is not possible. On the other hand, like traditional ethnographic and cross-cultural research, netnographies can foster the development of research themes and questions for future exploration. Areas such as online gaming and social media are examples of the evolution of leisure as a part of culture. As such, they provide new opportunities for anthropologically oriented researchers with interests in leisure and recreation.

LEISURE AS ADAPTATION

Adaptation refers to the process by which organisms come to function well in their environments, primarily in terms of survival and reproduction (Barash, 1979). Probably the best anthropological study of the adaptive value of leisure was conducted in the Amazon rainforest and published by Rubin, Flowers, and Gross in 1986. They examined patterns of time allocation among individuals in four culturally similar groups living in the Amazon basin. Residents of Kanela, Bororo, Xavante, and Mekranoti communities lived by slash-and-burn agriculture augmented by hunting, fishing, and selling handicrafts. The habitats of all four groups were similar but those of the Kanela and Bororo had poorer soil and lower forest biomass. The Mekranoti and Xavante had the most favorable diets but, despite these differences, adults in all four groups devoted about the same amount of time to productive activities. The Kanela and Bororo spent significantly less of their leisure time in high-energy activities (25.3% and 33.4% respectively), however, when compared to the Xavante and Mekranoti (47.4% and 48.6% respectively). The differences among children under age 15 were even more striking. Kanela children spent twice as much time sleeping or resting during daylight hours than they did in active play while Bororo children spent more time in inactive than active play. In contrast, Xavante and Mekranoti children spent the majority of their free time in active play. Rubin et al. (1986) interpreted these findings as indicating that individuals in these communities adjusted their free time energy use based on the amount of energy required to obtain adequate nutrition. That is, they managed their leisure to help them adapt to their habitat.

In more recent research, Reyes-García and her colleagues (2009) investigated how social versus solitary leisure affected happiness and well-being among the Tsimane' of the Bolivian Amazon. Over a year, the researchers observed and interviewed Tsimane' informants to measure their happiness while they gauged the amount of time they spent in both solitary and social leisure. They found that "social, not solitary, leisure has a positive and statistically significant association with subjective well-being" (Reyes-García et al., 2009, p. 432). In another study, Godoy et al. (2009, p. 564) found that "sharing leisure time with kin and friends" was one of the top ten reasons for being happy among the Tsimane'." The studies described above show that leisure can be a critical factor in adaptation to both the physical and the social environments of individuals and groups in certain circumstances. Leisure could also be thought of as an adaptive response to stress and stress-related lifestyle diseases such as high blood pressure, heart disease, obesity, and depression (Ho, 1996; Iwasaki & Bartlett, 2006; Iwasaki, Mactavish, & MacKay, 2005; Iwasaki, Zuzanek, & Mannell, 2001). However, too little research has been conducted to date where leisure has been conceptualized as an adaptive response to individual, social, or environmental conditions to permit any firm conclusions or generalizations.

LEISURE AND CULTURE CHANGE

Bronislaw Malinowski, a Polish anthropologist famous for his studies in the Trobriand Islands, located off the eastern coast of New Guinea, referred to leisure and recreation as creative elements in culture and suggested that "the vanguard of progress is often found in works of leisure" (Malinowski, 1931, p. 643). Alfred L. Kroeber (1948), one of the most famous American anthropologists of the twentieth century, claimed that inventions such as the bicycle, the bow and arrow, and the automobile were developed in recreational contexts with their utilitarian values recognized later. Finally, Felix Keesing, an Australian anthropologist, recognized the need for a systemic analysis of leisure and recreation as an element in culture change and evolution. He focused his interest on relaxation, leisure, play, and entertainment because he felt that evidence in the ethnographic record suggested that these areas are "notably open to innovation and cross-cultural transfer (Keesing, 1960, p. 130). Unfortunately, these observations and recommendations went largely unheeded as anthropologists have shown little interest in, and devoted little attention to, the place of leisure and recreation in culture change until very recently.

Human culture history is characterized by several technological revolutions. The first of these is termed either the Neolithic Revolution or the Agricultural Revolution and denotes the change from subsistence based on food collection to one based on food production. This began about 12,000 years ago in several areas around the world but the *fertile crescent*, which includes the upper Nile River basin and ancient Mesopotamia, the region between and surrounding the Tigris and Euphrates Rivers, mostly in modern day Iraq, is generally thought to be the most important (Diamond, 1997). The Agricultural Revolution was accompanied by urbanization as humans began to live in settled communities in close proximity to their crops rather than moving through relatively large territories in search of edible plants and animals. The Industrial Revolution, beginning primarily in England around 1760, brought fundamental changes to transportation, agriculture, and manufacturing, largely by the augmentation, and eventual replacement, of human and animal power by mechanical power, such as the steam engine. Many historians, economists, and other social scientists feel that we are now in the middle of a third major culture change, variously called the Information, Computer, or Digital Revolution. The Digital Revolution is characterized by the transition from analog to digital technology and its beginning could be pinpointed by the invention of the transistor in 1947. The transistor led to the development of the ubiquitous electronic devices that have transformed many, perhaps nearly all, aspects of human life in modern and modernizing areas of the world, including recreation and leisure. Hilbert (2012) claims the digital age started in 2002, the year that humans first stored more information in digital than analog form.

Digital technology has had major impacts on leisure and recreation. Mannell, Zuzanek, and Aronson (2005) showed, based on data from time use surveys, that a sample of Canadian adolescents ($n = 219$) between the ages of 12 and 19 years spent 28.6% of their free time, which made up about 40% of their overall waking time, watching TV or videos, 6.2% playing video games, 5.2% surfing the Internet, 5.5% reading, 21.3% in social activities, and 15.6% in physically active leisure. The authors' conclusion was that TV, computer/video games, and Internet use was displacing other forms of leisure, particularly physically active recreation.

Computers, tablets, cell phones and similar devices are becoming ever more important for leisure via social media, such as Facebook, chatrooms, online games (including gambling), online shopping, participation in virtual communities, newsgroups, pornography, and other uses. Arora (2011), in a comparison of the development of parks to online social networking sites, claimed that early parks served as locations for meeting people and socializing but that the Internet has now become the medium of choice for such activities. While the use of tablet computers, smartphones, and portable media players is often associated primarily with younger people, Nimrod (2011) studied the postings of jokes, stories, and social games to online communities by senior citizens over the course of a year. She found that seniors with a basic understanding of computers and the Internet can develop online networks as their offline social circles shrink. Online games may also help seniors maintain cognitive health.

Culture change resulting from the Digital Revolution is accelerating with no end in sight. In 2010, Google CEO Eric Schmidt claimed, "Between the birth of the world and 2003, there were five exabytes of information created. We [now] create five exabytes every two days" (quoted in Wu, 2011, p. 531) (five exabytes is 10^{18} bytes). As of 2012, we were producing information at least twice as fast as in 2010 (Hilbert, 2012). While there is little hope for individuals to keep abreast of even a tiny percentage of this information, much of which is relevant to leisure and recreation (see Nimrod, Chapter 30), methods such as netnography are more promising than traditional ethnographic approaches.

LEISURE AND LANGUAGE

Few languages have terms that translate more or less directly into English as "leisure" (Chick, 1998). In Mandarin Chinese, for example, *xiu xian* (pronounced in English, phonetically, something like "shee-oo shee-an") has a meaning very similar to the English word *leisure*. However, it is composed of not one but two characters (休閒 in traditional Chinese) and may be a relatively recent addition to the lexicon even though the concepts involved are ancient (Liu et al., 2008; see also Chapter 14). Moreover, the historical roots of *xiu xian* are very different from those of leisure. Circumlocutions, such as "free time" (e.g., *Freizeit* in German, *tempo libero* in Italian) are used in many languages while some appear to lack even the concept of leisure completely (Chick, 1998). However, other than the study by Liu et al., (2008), and a recent Canadian-Japanese comparative study (Ito & Walker, 2014), anthropologists, linguists, and others have not examined how leisure is either conceptualized or communicated in non-European languages. Hence, this remains a fertile area for research.

NEW APPROACHES IN ANTHROPOLOGY

Dressler and his colleagues (1998, 2000, 2012) have shown that individuals' ability to participate in agreed-upon models of preferred lifestyles relates to important markers of both mental and physical health. This is a major step forward in medical anthropology and, because the models of preferred lifestyles include leisure activities, the research represents a new frontier in relating cultural aspects of leisure to individual health. Similarly, Iwasaki and Bartlett (2006) have shown that culturally appropriate forms of leisure, including native arts and crafts, dance, music, and spiritual activities, are important stress-coping mechanisms for urban Aboriginal Canadians suffering from diabetes. Yeh et al. (2010) found that greater perceived importance of leisure constraints accompanies lower levels of leisure satisfaction and self-rated health. Additional work in this area is ongoing (e.g., Chick et al., 2014). These studies reflect a biocultural approach, a relatively new perspective in anthropology wherein humans are regarded as the product of both biological and cultural evolution and live in, and interact with, particular social and physical environments (Dressler et al., 2012).

A related perspective is that of sustainability, the idea that human and natural well-being, both present and future, depend on our wise use and preservation of Earth's resources. Anthropologists have been active in promoting environmentally conscious tourism as a means to simultaneously meet human needs and desires while protecting the natural environment (Stronza, 2007; Mbaiwa & Stronza, 2010). Stronza and Gordillo (2008) found that while ecotourism provides an incentive for the residents of areas visited to conserve the environment, in three Amazonian communities in this case, the economic development that results can have both positive and negative outcomes. Positive changes included better quality of life for residents through improved employment opportunities, increased self-esteem, and greater community organization but negative consequences, such as new time restrictions, reductions in reciprocity, and increased social conflict also emerged. Therefore, the degree of, and manner in which, tourism influences sustainability is uncertain and points out the need for both additional research and attention to management practices.

CONCLUSION

Understanding of phenomena always begins with description and, according to some (e.g., Achen, 1982), analysis in social science may be little more than thorough description. Unfortunately, ethnographic description has not been common in leisure and recreation research while the study of leisure and recreation has held relatively little interest for ethnographers (Chick, 1999). This may be changing with the recent research by Dressler and his colleagues on lifestyles and their relationship to health. Similarly, the research by Snodgrass and his colleagues on video game play and its effects on gamers represents a change from anthropology's traditional emphasis on the study of technologically simple cultures to aspects of those of the very highest complexity. Importantly, the work by Snodgrass and his colleagues emphasizes an important recreational pursuit for millions of people around the world.

Biocultural approaches and concern with sustainability offer new opportunities for anthropologists to use their toolkit of concepts, particularly the concept of culture, and methods, such as participant-observation, to address leisure and recreation, including tourism. Moreover, because these approaches include how such activities relate to human health, well-being, and happiness as well as the preservation of the natural environment, they are more problem-oriented than was the case with past anthropological research directed largely at dispassionate ethnographic description. This is important as anthropology, along with other social sciences such as sociology (see Blackshaw, Chapter 7), has been in an era of reformulation in recent years, one version of which is elimination. For anthropology to remain relevant, new perspectives, such as the biocultural approach and those afforded by the concept of sustainability, seem to be needed along with new subject matter, such as the Internet and video game cultures and leisure and recreation, more generally.

REFERENCES

Achen, C. H. (1982). *Interpreting and using regression.* Sage University Paper Series on Quantitative Applications in the Social Sciences no. 07-029. Beverly Hills and London: Sage Publications.

Arora, P. (2011). Online social sites as virtual parks: An investigation into leisure online and offline. *The Information Society: An International Journal, 27,*113–120.

Barash, D. (1979). *The whisperings within.* New York: Penguin Books.

Bernard, H. R. (2011). *Research methods in anthropology* (5th Ed.). Langham, MD: Altamira Press.

Blanchard, K. (1981). *The Mississippi Choctaws at play: The serious side of leisure.* Urbana: University of Illinois Press.

Broude, G., & Greene, S. J. (1983). Husband-wife relationships. *Ethnology, 22,* 263–280.

Chick, G. (1991). Acculturation and community recreation in rural Mexico. *Play & Culture, 4,* 185–193.

Chick, G. (1995). The adaptive qualities of leisure: A cross-cultural survey. In C. Simpson & B. Gidlow (Eds.), *Proceedings of the ANZALS Conference, 1995* (pp. 158–163). Canterbury, New Zealand: Australian and New Zealand Association for Leisure Studies.

Chick, G. (1997). Cultural complexity: The concept and its measurement. *Cross-Cultural Research, 31,* 275–307.

Chick, G. (1998). Leisure and culture: Issues for an anthropology of leisure. *Leisure Sciences, 20,* 111–133.

Chick, G. (1999). Leisure's anthropology and the anthropology of leisure: An examination of the coverage of leisure in anthropology texts and anthropology in leisure texts. *Schole, 14,* 19–35.

Chick, G. (2013). Leisure in culture. In T. Blackshaw (Ed.), *The Routledge international handbook of leisure studies* (pp. 202–215). London: Routledge.

Chick, G., Dong, E., & Iarmolenko, S. (2014). Cultural consonance in leisure activities and self-rated health in six cities in China. *World Leisure Journal, 56,* 110–119.

Chick, G., & Shen, S. X. (2011). Leisure and cultural complexity. *Cross-Cultural Research, 45,* 59–81.

Clark, R. N., Hendee, J. C., & Campbell, F. L. (2009). Values, behavior, and conflict in modern camping culture. *Journal of Leisure Research, 41,* 377–393.

Culin, S. (1907). *Games of the North American Indians.* 24th Annual Report, Bureau of American Ethnology, Washington, DC: U.S. Government Printing Office.

D'Andrade, R. G. (1995). *The development of cognitive anthropology.* Cambridge: Cambridge University Press.

Diamond, J. (1997). *Guns, germs, and steel: The fates of human societies.* New York: W. W. Norton & Company.

Dong, E., & Chick, G. (2012). Leisure constraints in six Chinese cities. *Leisure Sciences, 34,* 417–435.

Dressler, W. W., Balieiro, M. C., & Dos Santos, J. E. (1998). Culture, socioeconomic status and physical and mental health in Brazil. *Medical Anthropology Quarterly, 12,* 424–446.

Dressler, W. W., & Bindon, J. R. (2000). The health consequences of cultural consensus: Cultural dimensions of lifestyle, social support, and blood pressure in an African American community. *American Anthropologist, 102,* 244–260.

Dressler, W. W., Oths, K. S., Balieiro, M. C., Ribeiro, R. P., & Santos, J. E. D. (2012). How culture shapes the body: Cultural consonance and body mass in urban Brazil. *American Journal of Human Biology, 24,* 325–331.

Geertz, C. (1973). Deep play: Notes on the Balinese cockfight. In C. Geertz (Ed.), *The interpretation of cultures* (pp. 412–453). New York: Basic Books.

Godoy, R., Reyes-García, V., Gravlee, C. C., Huanca, T., Leonard, W. R., McDade, T. W., Tanner, S., and the TAPS Bolivia Study Team. (2009). Moving beyond a snapshot to understand changes in the well-being of native Amazonians. *Current Anthropology, 50,* 563–573.

Goodenough, W. H. (1957). Cultural anthropology and linguistics. In P. L. Garvin (Ed.), *Report of the 7th annual round table meeting on linguistics and language study, monograph series on languages and linguistics, no.* 9 (pp. 167–173). Washington, DC: Georgetown University Press.

Gurven, M., & Kaplan, H. (2006). Determinants of time allocation across the lifespan. *Human Nature, 17,* 1–49.

Hay, F. J. (1990). Microethnography of a Haitian boutique. *Social and Economic Studies, 39,* 153–166.

Hilbert, M. (2012). How much information is there in the "information society?" *Significance, 9,* 4, 8–12.

Ho, J. T. S. (1996). Stress, health and leisure satisfaction: The case of teachers. *The International Journal of Educational Management, 10,* 41–50.

Ito, E., & Walker, G. J. (2014). Similarities and differences in leisure conceptualizations between Japan and Canada and between two Japanese leisure-like terms. *Leisure/Loisir, 38,* 1–19.

Iwasaki, Y., & Bartlett, J. G. (2006). Culturally meaningful leisure as a way of coping with stress among aboriginal individuals with diabetes. *Journal of Leisure Research, 38,* 321–338.

Iwasaki, Y., Mactavish, J. M., & MacKay, K. (2005). Building on strengths and resilience: Leisure as a stress survival strategy. *British Journal of Guidance and Counseling, 33,* 81–100.

Iwasaki, Y., Zuzanek, J., & Mannell, R. C. (2001). The effects of physically active leisure on stress-health relationships. *Canadian Journal of Public Health, 92,* 214–218.

Johnson, A. (1978). In search of the affluent society. *Human Nature, 1,* 50–59.

Johnson, C. W., & Samdahl, D. M. (2005). "The night they took over": Misogyny in a country-western gay bar. *Leisure Sciences, 27,* 331–348.

Kaemmer, J. E. (1993). *Music in human life.* Austin, TX: University of Texas Press.

Keesing, F. (1960). Recreative behavior and culture change. In A. F. C. Wallace (Ed.), *Men and cultures* (pp. 130–133). Philadelphia: University of Pennsylvania Press.

Kozinets, R. V. (1997). "I want to believe": A netnography of the X-Philes subculture of consumption. *Advances in Consumer Research, 24,* 470–475.

Kozinets, R. V. (2010). *Netnography: Doing ethnographic research online.* Thousand Oaks, CA: Sage.

Kroeber, A. L. (1948). *Anthropology.* New York: Harcourt Brace.

Liu, H., Yeh, C. K., Chick, G., & Zinn, H. (2008). An Exploration of the meanings of leisure: A Chinese perspective. *Leisure Sciences, 30,* 482–488.

Malinowski, B. (1931). Culture. In E. R. A. Seligman (Ed.), *Encyclopedia of the social sciences* (Vol. 4, pp. 621–646). New York: Macmillan.

Mannell, R. C., Zuzanek, J., & Aronson, R. (2005). *Internet/computer use and adolescent leisure behavior, flow experiences and psychological well-being: The displacement hypothesis.* Eleventh Canadian Congress on Leisure Research, Nanaimo, B.C., May 17th–20th.

Mbaiwa, J. E., & Stronza, A. L. (2010). The effects of tourism development on rural livelihoods in the Okavango Delta, Botswana. *Journal of Sustainable Tourism, 18,* 635–656.

Mkono, M. (2012). Netnographic tourist research: The Internet as a virtual fieldwork site. *Tourism Analysis, 17,* 553–555.

Nimrod, G. (2011). The fun culture in seniors' online communities. *The Gerontologist, 51,* 226–237.

Reyes-García, V., Godoy, R. A., Vadez, V., Ruíz-Mallén, I., Huanca, T., Leonard, W. R., McDade, T. W., Tanner, S., & the TAPS Bolivian Study Team. (2009). The pay-offs to sociability: Do solitary and social leisure relate to happiness? *Human Nature, 20,* 431–446.

Royce, A. P. (1977). *The anthropology of dance.* Bloomington, IN: Indiana University Press.

Rubin, J., Flowers, N. M., & Gross, D. R. (1986). The adaptive dimensions of leisure. *American Ethnologist, 13,* 524–536.

Smith, L. M. (2006). The micro-ethnography of the classroom. *Psychology in the Schools, 4,* 216–221.

Snodgrass, J. G., Dengah, H. J. F., II, Lacy, M. G., Fagan, J., & Most, D. (2011a). Magical flight and monstrous stress: Technologies of absorption and mental wellness in Azeroth. *Culture, Medicine, and Psychiatry, 35,* 26–62.

Snodgrass, J. G., Dengah, H. J. F., II, Lacy, M. G., Fagan, J., Most, D., Blank, M., Howard, L., Kershner, C. R., Krambeer, G., Leavitt-Reynolds, A., Reynolds, A. Vyvial-Larson, J., Whaley, J. & Wintersteen, B. (2012). Restorative magical adventure or Warcrack? Motivated MMO play and the pleasures and perils of online experience. *Games and Culture, 7,* 3–28.

Snodgrass, J. G., Lacy, M. G., Dengah, H. J. F., II, & Fagan, J. (2011b). Enhancing one life rather than living two: Playing MMOs with offline friends. *Computers in Human Behavior, 27,* 1211–1222.

Stebbins, R. (2010). The Internet as a scientific tool for studying leisure activities: Exploratory internet data collection. *Leisure Studies, 29,* 469–47.

Stern, T. (1948). *The rubber ball games of the Americas.* Seattle: University of Washington Press.

Stronza, A. (2007). The economic promise of ecotourism for conservation. *Journal of Ecotourism, 6,* 210–230.

Stronza, A., & Gordillo, J. (2008). Community views of ecotourism. *Annals of Tourism Research, 35,* 448–428.

Williams, M. (2007). Avatar watching: Participant observation in graphical online environments. *Qualitative Research, 7,* 5–24.

Wu, M. M. (2011). Building a collaborative digital collection: A necessary evolution in libraries. *Law Library Journal, 103,* 527–551.

Yeh, C. K., Hsu, Y. C., Chick, G., & Dong, E. (2010). *Leisure, leisure satisfaction, and perceived health in urban Mainland China and Taiwan.* 11th World Leisure Congress, Chuncheon, South Korea, September 1.

2

Leisure at the Biological Level

Bryan McCormick (Indiana University)

Although recreation and leisure have long been studied from sociological, psychological, and economic perspectives, there are growing opportunities to consider a biological perspective to understand recreation, leisure, and play. While Smith (1991) first proposed a biological basis for recreation via the experience of pleasure, considerable development in understanding the human organism has occurred in the ensuing decades. For example, improved knowledge of endocrine and neurotransmitter systems has the capacity to increase our understanding of both antecedents and results of recreation and leisure behavior. There is also reason to consider a broader view of the biological basis for recreation and leisure beyond just pleasure. True, pleasure seems to be one of the hallmark traits of recreation and leisure across most definitional approaches. At the same time, while some leisure behaviors are solitary in nature, there is a strong social element in leisure as well (Kleiber, Walker, & Mannell, 2011). From a psychological view, the need for relatedness is asserted as a basic human need (Deci & Ryan, 1985); however, few social organisms demonstrate the complexity of social behaviors in humans. Yet we still may consider what aspects of social behavior humans share with other social animals. This chapter explores these two foundational elements of recreation and leisure at the biological level.

AFFILIATION AND SOCIAL BEHAVIOR AS BIOLOGICAL PHENOMENA

Given the highly social nature of play, recreation, and leisure there is reason to explore how bonding and affiliation are expressed and encoded in the brain. The neuropeptide ocytocin (OT) and arginine vasopressin (AVP) have been identified in both mother-infant bonding as well as pair-bonding in a number of nonhuman animals (Insel, 2010). Neuropeptides are molecules made up of short chains of amino acids that are produced and released by neurons (Burbach, 2011). Largely produced in hypothalamus portion of the brain, OT and AVP are signaling neuropeptides that facilitate communication from one nerve cell to another. Both have been widely studied in animals and humans as biological factors that are intimately involved in a variety of social processes. Both are synthesized throughout the central and peripheral structures of the human nervous system including the brain, heart, gastrointestinal tract, and reproductive organs (Gordon, Martin, Feldman, & Leckman, 2011). Their receptor systems are also widely distributed throughout the central and peripheral nervous system. The principal linkages of OT and AVP to social behavior are in their associations with fundamental elements of social behavior. Considered as broad areas of function we can consider social perception, social understanding and empathy, and social interaction as fundamental aspects of social behavior.

Social Perception

One of the first requirements for social interaction is social perception (Bos, Panksepp, Bluthe, & van Honk, 2012). In other words, in order to engage in social relationships we have to perceive and recognize others. Experimental studies in humans have found that the administration of OT via nasal spray improves memory of social stimuli such as faces and human movement over memory of non-social stimuli (Keri & Benedek, 2009; Rimmele, Hediger, Heinrichs, & Klaver, 2009). In addition, AVP also appears to be particularly related to social recognition and emotional expression. For example, Guastella and colleagues (2010) found that among adult males, nasal administration of AVP was significantly associated with enhanced memory of happy and angry faces. Additionally, AVP has been found to enhance angry facial responses toward neutral same-sex faces in males; whereas in females AVP reduced angry facial expressions toward happy and angry faces (Thompson, George, Walton, Orr, & Benson, 2006).

Social Understanding and Empathy

Another factor in social behavior is the ability to understand others. This form of perception is known as social cognition and is fundamental to functioning in complex social situations (Gallese, Keysers, & Rizzolatti, 2004). Through social cognition we are able to make inferences about the mental experience of others and thus coordinate social behavior. Deficits in social cognition are frequently identified as fundamental contributors to social dysfunction in such disorders as autism and schizophrenia. Domes and colleagues (2007) found that nasal administration of OT improved the ability of subjects to infer the mental states of others from subtle facial cues. Similarly, emotion perception and empathy also appears to be enhanced through the administration of OT such that people increase their sensitivity and speed of emotional perception (Leknes et al., 2013; Marsh, Yu, Pine, & Blair, 2010). OT particularly may increase emotional empathy in men. Hurlemann and colleagues (2010) found that administration of OT in male volunteers increased the valence of emotional evaluation of emotional pictures. That is, the emotional content of the picture was unaffected by the administration of OT, while the strength of emotional experience was increased. Finally, while most of the previous research has examined increases in empathy resulting from OT administration, one study examined the effect of emotional experience on OT production, empathy, and generosity. In this case, Barraza and Zak (2009) found that viewing an emotional video increased blood level OT as compared to viewing an emotionally neutral video. In addition, they found that greater empathy was positively associated with OT level and generosity.

Social Interaction

Finally, a number of elements of social interaction have been examined as a function of both OT and AVP. One of the primary elements of social interaction is arguably interpersonal trust. Administration of OT has been demonstrated to increase interpersonal trust related to sharing of such goods as money (Kosfeld, Heinrichs, Zak, Fischbacher, & Fehr, 2005), confidential information (Mikolajczak, Pinon, Lane, de Timary, & Luminet, 2010), and emotional experiences (Lane et al., 2013). Along similar lines, AVP has been found to be associated with increased cooperative behavior among men in response to a cooperative gesture (Rilling et al., 2012). More broadly, there is also evidence that OT acts to reduce attention to negative social stimuli and social anxiety (Heinrichs, von Dawans, & Domes, 2009) as well as increasing attention to positive social stimuli (Guastella, Mitchell, & Mathews, 2008). Kemp and Guastella (2011) asserted that OT's principal role in social behavior is to enhance social approach behaviors as well as inhibiting social withdrawal behaviors. Somewhat in a complementary sense, there is also general agreement that AVP works to heighten neural and physiological response to social challenge; however, the nature of the response appears to be sex-linked (Bos et al., 2012). That is, while males are more likely to respond via "fight or flight," females may turn to a "tend and befriend" response (Taylor, 2006). Overall, there is general indication that AVP's role in social behavior is to heighten attention and attentiveness to emotional expression in others.

Affiliative Behavior and Leisure Behavior

Although there are few direct examinations of AVP or OT in leisure and recreation behavior, there are some implications. In two studies of fathers and their play behavior with their children, Naber and colleagues (2010; 2013) found that intranasal administration of OT was found to increase sensitive play, more optimal stimulation of their child, and less hostility for fathers of both typically developing toddlers as well as toddlers with autism. Nasal OT administration has also been found to increase prosocial helping behavior toward an excluded player in a ball tossing game; however this only applied to participants from supportive families (Riem, Bakermans-Kranenburg, Huffmeijer, & van Ijzendoorn, 2013). In addition, Pepping and Timmermans (2012), identified that all of the identified social emotions and social perceptions implicated in OT response are related to successful performance in sport activities. They noted that empathy, trust, generosity and cooperation were implicated, particularly in team sports in which participants relied on one another. Finally, while much of the research on OT and AVP has focused on the influence of these neuropeptides on social behavior, there are some indications that social behavior may influence their production. Taylor proposed that OT increases in response to relationship distress or social isolation, thus providing an impetus for social contact (Taylor, 2006). To the extent that such affiliative needs are met, stress is reduced; however if unmet, stress levels appear to heighten.

THE NEUROANATOMY OF PLEASURE

Pleasure can be thought of as fundamental to leisure and recreation. Regardless of whether the definition takes a sociological (e.g., Dumazedier, 1974), psychological (e.g., Neulinger, 1981) or social psychological (e.g., Kleiber et al., 2011) orientation, there is a general agreement that leisure contains elements of pleasure that can exist in anticipation, experience, and recollection of experience. Smith (1991) asserted that a discussion of leisure that failed to consider the phenomenon of pleasure to be a "serious flaw." He contended that understanding pleasure was critical to understanding leisure, particularly due to its implications in motivation for leisure behavior. There are many reasons that understanding pleasure is important for understanding leisure behavior. Principal among these is the association of leisure activity with intrinsic motive that springs from the desire to engage in behavior as its own form of reward. Another reason to consider pleasure in leisure behavior has to do with the linkages of pleasure with happiness (Kringelbach & Berridge, 2009). From a philosophical point of view, happiness has been conceptualized as comprised of both hedonic (pleasurable) and eudaimonic (a life well-lived) components, yet pleasure alone was seen as inadequate to a life of virtue (Kesebir & Diener, 2008). In addition, while humans experience a number of basic pleasures such as food, sex, and social contact as do other animals (Kringelbach, 2010), we also have the capacity to derive pleasure from a multitude of other, non-basic activities.

What is Pleasure?

Any examination of pleasure then begs the question, what is pleasure? At its most basic, pleasure denotes a positive evaluation of an event, object, experience, or act (Frijda, 2010). In this way pleasure has been characterized as a "niceness gloss" or "hedonic gloss" attached to a stimulus. This notion adds to the understanding of pleasure in that pleasure always exists in relation to something else; that is, feelings of pleasure are always about something. Another characteristic of pleasure noted early in its examination was its evanescent character (Titchener, 1908). A focus on pleasure itself, as opposed to the stimulus to which it is attached, will cause pleasure to evaporate. Further, although perhaps implied in the preceding discussion is the assumption that pleasure must be a conscious experience, there are compelling arguments that certain aspects of pleasure exist at the subconscious level (Berridge & Kringelbach, 2008, 2013). Thus the linkage of the experience of pleasure to reward, reward to motivation, and motivation to behavior connect the biological experience of pleasure to leisure behavior.

From the view of affective neuroscience, reward is considered as a biological mechanism that mediates behavior stimulated by events, and pleasure is implicated in the experience of reward (Esch & Stefano, 2004). From a behavioral psychology point of view, this approach is highly consistent with concepts of reinforcement as seen by some of its earliest proponents. For example, Plaud and Gaither (1996) noted that Thorndike's law of effect stated that a pleasant event subsequent to an organism's response strengthens that response in the future. The relationship of pleasure and reinforcement theory is seen most clearly in the reward component of learning as noted below. In addition, reward can be seen as a multi-component phenomenon comprised of liking, wanting and learning; each of which appears to be mediated by different brain structures within the limbic system and cortex (Berridge & Kringelbach, 2013). In this model, liking is the pleasure or hedonic component of reward, wanting represents the motivational component of reward, and learning connects past reward to anticipated future reward.

Liking

The hedonic element of liking can be further specified along the lines of subjective liking, in which there is a conscious recognition of pleasure, and a core "liking" that is not necessarily conscious (Kringelbach & Berridge, 2010). In searching for the biological basis of such subconscious "liking" the neurotransmitter dopamine was first proposed as this key to translating sensory inputs "into the hedonic messages we experience as pleasure, euphoria, or 'yumminess'" (Wise, 1980, p. 94). The ensuing 30 years of neuroscientific research has failed to support this initial hypotheses. Although dopamine remains implicated in a more complex role in motivation and reward reinforcement, its role in the experience of pleasure has been largely discounted (Berridge, 2007; Salamone & Correa, 2012). Instead, naturally generated opiates and GABA (gamma-aminobutyric acid) appear to be implicated in the euphorigenic component of "liking" (Burgdorf & Panksepp, 2006). It should also be noted that this euphoric experience is also seen in similar psychostimulant substances of abuse (e.g., amphetamines, barbiturates, nicotine, and opiates).

The prototypical reward stimuli of reward "liking," include food, sex, and to some degree social contact, which have been studied extensively. Arguments for such sensory reward stimuli as basic to human and other animal experience is typically couched in evolutionary terms related to survival and procreation advantages (Kringelbach, 2010). Others, however, have suggested that pleasure can be considered well beyond sensory experience. Frijda (2007) suggested that pleasure can be further distinguished as (a) nonsensory likings (e.g., preference for people, objects, possessions), (b) pleasures of gain and relief (e.g., changes from previous states), (c) achievement pleasures (e.g., mastering a skill or achieving a goal), (d) social pleasures (e.g., chatting, participating in a group), (e) activity pleasures (e.g., activities providing intrinsic reward), and (f) esthetic pleasures (e.g., appreciation or contemplation of objects, people, ideas). Within this broader view, recreation and leisure behaviors would appear to fit easily.

Wanting

The hedonic pleasure of liking is translated into a motivational process in the reward component of wanting (Kringelbach & Berridge, 2009). Although Smith (1991) initially cited classical work by Olds (1956) on the brain's "pleasure centers," this work has more recently been reinterpreted according to the different reward functions (Berridge, 2003). Re-examination of this work more accurately indicates that although stimulation of such brain structures increases the wanting for a reward, it does not appear to increase the hedonic experience of objective "liking" of the reward. As noted previously, dopamine has largely been discounted as a neurotransmitter associated with the hedonic aspect of reward, but instead is implicated through incentive salience that makes stimuli attractive and thus wanted (Berridge, 2007). Simply, incentive salience is established through dopamine release in the presence of reward-related conditioned or unconditioned stimuli. The salience value is recreated each time the reward stimulus is experienced. With repeated exposure, "the incentive salience value draws on both pre-existing reward-related associations and current neurobiological states" (Berridge, p. 409). Thus, it is possible that a condition of strong irrational desire can develop in which one wants something that she or he neither likes nor expects to like. Such a condition has been demonstrated in an number of drugs of abuse as well as in certain forms of Parkinson's disease (Berridge, 2007). Not surprisingly, much of the research in this area has focused on understanding addictive behavior. While substance addictions have been the principal focus of addiction research, there have also been studies of leisure behaviors (e.g., gambling and video gaming) that have also been examined. For example, among a sample of adults with video game addiction, it was found that the presentation of gaming images activated brain regions consistent with that of substance dependence for cue-induced craving (Ko et al., 2009). Another study found that video gaming was associated with an increase in dopamine release in the brain during game play (Koepp et al., 1998) consistent with the incentive salience hypothesis.

Learning

Finally, from the neuroscience point of view, learning is a part of the reward system through which connections of past experience impinge upon the associations and predictions of future reward (Berridge & Kringelbach, 2008). Similar to the liking component, learning can be seen as both explicit cognitive predictions as well as implicit associative conditioning. In combination with the liking and wanting processes of reward, it is through basic Pavlovian learning processes that stimuli or cues are associated with pleasure. As noted above, this learning is a combination of previous and current neurobiological states indicating that previously learned stimuli can be reversed based on current state (Robinson & Berridge, 2013). Simply put, those stimuli that elicit strong liking and wanting responses are learned such that they are subsequently sought out.

CONCEPTUALIZING PLEASURE IN LEISURE

The role of pleasure in liking, wanting, and learning has been extensively studied in primary rewards such as food and sexual activity. At the same time, if complex behaviors such as those in leisure are pleasurable, how do they compare to more primary pleasures? Although there is limited scientific research examining such higher order pleasures, one conceptualization asserts that higher order pleasures are "higher-dimensional combinations of the basic pleasures and as such may reuse some of the same brain mechanisms" (Kringelbach, 2010, p. 203). For example, McLean et al. (2009) found that viewing soccer goals by soccer supporters demonstrated activation in brain regions indicative of pleasure processing. In contrast, Sescousse et al. (2013) found that while primary rewards (e.g., food and sexual stimulation) and secondary reward (e.g., money) activated common brain networks, the secondary reward also activated cortical regions of the brain. Thus, while a similar brain network was activated, secondary reward also activated a more recently evolved portion of the human brain as compared to primary reward. Others have sought to identify how aesthetic experience such as art and music can be experienced as pleasurable. These studies have also indicated that while such aesthetic activities engage similar brain regions as those of primary rewards, they also demonstrate more cortical region activity (Skov, 2010; Vuust & Kringelbach, 2010). Part of the challenge with understanding more complex behaviors and reward is that such behaviors typically require the involvement of other brain functions (e.g., perception, cognition) that are interrelated with reward processing.

Another approach to exploring how complex behaviors may elicit pleasure akin to basic rewards may be through examination of more general behaviors implicated in leisure. For example, although not extensively examined within leisure research, curiosity would seem implicated in leisure behavior through such elements as personality traits of autotelic (Baumann, 2012) and sensation seeking types (Carnelley & Ruscher, 2000). Litman (2005) offered a model of curiosity that explicitly connected curiosity to reward through its wanting and liking components. Drawing on animal studies, Litman noted that both dopaminergic (wanting) and opioid (liking) activation is present in approach and inspection behavior among nonhuman animals when presented with novel stimuli. While the wanting element of reward is relatively well-established in seeking behavior and curiosity (Alcaro, Huber, & Panksepp, 2007), liking of complex sensory stimuli may be a function of the degree to which they are cognitively and perceptually "interpretable" (Litman). From such a perspective one may "acquire a taste" for stimuli through repeated exposure leading to more easily interpreted, and therefore better liked, stimuli.

A final area to consider is how pleasure as a hallmark of leisure may contribute to a broader human benefit such as happiness. One avenue for this connection may be through the creation of positive emotional states that can contribute to improved cognitive and emotional resources over time (Fredrickson, 2001). Furthermore, Kringlebach, and Berridge (2009) argued that while positive emotion and affect may be built upon a hedonic "liking" reaction, conscious experiences of pleasure and affective states through cognitive processes is required "to form a higher level of hedonic awareness" (p. 480). Although previously considered from a philosophical point of view, neuroscience also supports that hedonic experience alone is an insufficient cause for happiness. The translation of pleasure into happiness requires the involvement of cognitive appraisals of meaning and life satisfaction. Thus, while leisure behaviors may be pleasurable in their experience, their contribution to happiness may lie as much in the degree to which these behaviors are involved in cognitive appraisals of a meaningful and satisfying life (see also Hemingway, Chapter 4, and Mock, Mannell, & Guttentag, Chapter 6).

CONCLUSION

The study of leisure and recreation behavior has had a long tradition of study in the social sciences and humanities. A great deal has been learned about leisure as a psychological, economic, social, and cultural phenomenon. At the same time we know very little about leisure, recreation, and play at the biological level from direct analysis. Perhaps part of the limitation has been that studying such complex human behavior has presented significant methodological challenges in measuring such things as neurotransmission and brain circuitry. Although brain imaging technology continues to develop rapidly, it remains quite difficult to see the brain in action in the complexity of the natural environment.

Another challenge to knowing leisure as a biological phenomenon is that there are almost no investigators with the biological training to carry out such work. It would appear that the development of a bio-psycho-social understanding of leisure and recreation will be more likely to result through the creation of interdisciplinary collaborations in which leisure researchers work with biological and neuropsychological investigators to understand such phenomena. While leisure behavior has psychological, social, and cultural implications, it is experienced by living organisms whose neurobiological systems process such experiences and render them meaningful. If leisure is to matter we must also know it as a biological phenomenon as well.

What might we learn from exploring leisure at the biological level? One interesting area of exploration would be the social nature of leisure. From one point of view, social leisure may be determined by neuropeptides that drive us toward affiliative behavior. From another point of view, social contact is a primary reward associated with pleasure and thus reinforces social affiliation. Another area could be to explore the biological nature of curiosity as a component of leisure behavior. The pursuit of novel stimuli would appear to be a hallmark of curiosity and leisure. Yet curiosity presents a paradox such that once novel stimuli become "known," curiosity and the associated pleasure are reduced. How do leisure behaviors remain "permanently interesting" and maintain their pleasurable components while at the same time being highly familiar to their participants? Finally, leisure research may also be important in understanding addictive behavior. From social drinking to recreational drug use to shopping to gaming, virtually all addictions begin first as leisure and recreation behaviors. What are the biological phenomena that translate pleasurable liking into addictive wanting?

REFERENCES

Alcaro, A., Huber, R., & Panksepp, J. (2007). Behavioral functions of the mesolimbic dopaminergic system: An affective neuroethological perspective. *Brain Research Reviews, 56*, 283–321. doi: 10.1016/j.brainresrev.2007.07.014

Barraza, J. A., & Zak, P. J. (2009). Empathy toward strangers triggers oxytocin release and subsequent generosity. In S. Atran, A. Navarro, K. Ochsner, A. Tobena, & O. Vilarroya (Eds.), *Values, empathy, and fairness across social barriers* (Vol. 1167, pp. 182–189).

Baumann, N. (2012). Autotelic Personality. In S. Engeser (Ed.), *Advances in flow research* (pp. 165–186). New York: Springer.

Berridge, K. C. (2003). Pleasures of the brain. *Brain and Cognition, 52*, 106–128. doi: 10.1016/s0278-2626(03)00014-9

Berridge, K. C. (2007). The debate over dopamine's role in reward: the case for incentive salience. *Psychopharmacology, 191*, 391–431. doi: 10.1007/s00213-006-0578-x

Berridge, K. C., & Kringelbach, M. L. (2008). Affective neuroscience of pleasure: reward in humans and animals. *Psychopharmacology, 199*, 457–480. doi: 10.1007/s00213-008-1099-6

Berridge, K. C., & Kringelbach, M. L. (2013). Neuroscience of affect: brain mechanisms of pleasure and displeasure.

Current Opinion in Neurobiology, 23, 294–303. doi: 10.1016/j.conb.2013.01.017

Bos, P. A., Panksepp, J., Bluthe, R., & van Honk, J. (2012). Acute effects of steroid hormones and neuropeptides on human social-emotional behavior: A review of single administration studies. *Frontiers in Neuroendocrinology, 33*, 17–35. doi: 10.1016/j.yfrne.2011.01.002

Burbach, J. P. H. (2011). What Are neuropeptides? In A. Merighi (Ed.), *Neuropeptides* (Vol. 789, pp. 1–36): Humana Press.

Burgdorf, J., & Panksepp, J. (2006). The neurobiology of positive emotions. *Neuroscience and Biobehavioral Reviews, 30*, 173–187. doi: 10.1016/j.neubiorev.2005.06.001

Carnelley, K. B., & Ruscher, J. B. (2000). Adult attachment and exploratory behavior in leisure. *Journal of Social Behavior and Personality, 15*, 153–165.

Deci, E. L., & Ryan, R. M. (1985). *Intrinsic motivation and self-determination in human behavior*. New York: Plenum Press.

Domes, G., Heinrichs, M., Michel, A., Berger, C., & Herpertz, S. C. (2007). Oxytocin improves "mind-reading" in humans. [Article]. *Biological Psychiatry, 61*, 731–733. doi: 10.1016/j.biopsych.2006.07.015

Dumazedier, J. (1974). *Sociology of leisure*. Amsterdam: Elsevier.

Esch, T., & Stefano, G. B. (2004). The neurobiology of pleasure, reward processes, addiction and their health implications. *Neuroendocrinology Letters, 25*(4), 235–251.

Fredrickson, B. L. (2001). The role of positive emotions in positive psychology. The broaden-and-build theory of positive emotions. [Research Support, Non-U.S. Gov't
Research Support, U.S. Gov't, P.H.S.]. *Am Psychol, 56*(3), 218-226.

Frijda, N. H. (2007). *The laws of emotion*. Mawah, NJ: Lawrence Earlbaum.

Frijda, N. H. (2010). On the nature and function of pleasure. In M. L. Kringelbach & K. C. Berridge (Eds.), *Pleasures of the brain* (pp. 99–112). New York: Oxford.

Gallese, V., Keysers, C., & Rizzolatti, G. (2004). A unifying view of the basis of social cognition. Trends in Cognitive Sciences, 8, 396–403. doi: http://dx.doi.org/10.1016/j.tics.2004.07.002

Gordon, I., Martin, C., Feldman, R., & Leckman, J. F. (2011). Oxytocin and social motivation. [Review]. *Developmental Cognitive Neuroscience, 1*, 471–493. doi: 10.1016/j.dcn.2011.07.007

Guastella, A. J., Kenyon, A. R., Alvares, G. A., Carson, D. S., & Hickie, I. B. (2010). Intranasal Arginine Vasopressin Enhances the Encoding of Happy and Angry Faces in Humans. *Biological Psychiatry, 67*, 1220–1222. doi: 10.1016/j.biopsych.2010.03.014

Guastella, A. J., Mitchell, P. B., & Mathews, F. (2008). Oxytocin enhances the encoding of positive social memories in humans. *Biological Psychiatry, 64*, 256–258. doi: 10.1016/j.biopsych.2008.02.008

Heinrichs, M., von Dawans, B., & Domes, G. (2009). Oxytocin, vasopressin, and human social behavior. *Frontiers in Neuroendocrinology, 30*, 548–557. doi: 10.1016/j.yfrne.2009.05.005

Hurlemann, R., Patin, A., Onur, O. A., Cohen, M. X., Baumgartner, T., Metzler, S., . . . Kendrick, K. M. (2010). Oxytocin enhances amygdala-dependent, socially reinforced learning and emotional empathy in humans. *Journal of Neuroscience, 30*, 4999–5007. doi: 10.1523/jneurosci.5538-09.2010

Insel, T. R. (2010). The challenge of translation in social neuroscience: A review of oxytocin, vasopressin, and affiliative behavior. *Neuron, 65*, 768–779. doi: 10.1016/j.neuron.2010.03.005

Kemp, A. H., & Guastella, A. J. (2011). The role of oxytocin in human affect: A novel hypothesis. *Current Directions in Psychological Science, 20*, 222–231. doi: 10.1177/0963721411417547

Keri, S., & Benedek, G. (2009). Oxytocin enhances the perception of biological motion in humans. *Cognitive Affective & Behavioral Neuroscience, 9*, 237–241. doi: 10.3758/cabn.9.3.237

Kesebir, P., & Diener, E. D. (2008). In pursuit of happiness: Empirical answers to philosophical questions. *Perspectives on Psychological Science, 3*, 117–125. doi: 10.1111/j.1745-6916.2008.00069.x

Kleiber, D. A., Walker, G. J., & Mannell, R. C. (2011). *A social psychology of leisure* (2nd ed.). State College, PA: Venture Publishing, Inc.

Ko, C. H., Liu, G. C., Hsiao, S. M., Yen, J. Y., Yang, M. J., Lin, W. C., . . . Chen, C. S. (2009). Brain activities associated with gaming urge of online gaming addiction. *Journal of Psychiatric Research, 43*, 739–747. doi: 10.1016/j.jpsychires.2008.09.012

Koepp, M. J., Gunn, R. N., Lawrence, A. D., Cunningham, V. J., Dagher, A., Jones, T., . . . Grasby, P. M. (1998). Evidence for striatal dopamine release during a video game. *Nature, 393*, 266–268.

Kosfeld, M., Heinrichs, M., Zak, P. J., Fischbacher, U., & Fehr, E. (2005). Oxytocin increases trust in humans. *Nature, 435*, 673–676. doi: 10.1038/nature03701

Kringelbach, M. L. (2010). The hedonic brain: A functional neuroanatomy of human pleasure. In M. L. Kringelbach & K. C. Berridge (Eds.), *Pleasures of the brain* (pp. 202–221). New York: Oxford.

Kringelbach, M. L., & Berridge, K. C. (2009). Towards a functional neuroanatomy of pleasure and happiness. *Trends in Cognitive Sciences, 13*, 479–487. doi: 10.1016/j.tics.2009.08.006

Kringelbach, M. L., & Berridge, K. C. (2010). *Pleasures of the brain*. New York: Oxford University Press.

Lane, A., Luminet, O., Rime, B., Gross, J. J., de Timary, P., & Mikolajczak, M. (2013). Oxytocin increases willingness to socially share one's emotions. *International Journal of Psychology, 48*, 676–681. doi: 10.1080/00207594.2012.677540

Leknes, S., Wessberg, J., Ellingsen, D. M., Chelnokova, O., Olausson, H., & Laeng, B. (2013). Oxytocin enhances pupil dilation and sensitivity to "hidden" emotional expressions. [Article]. *Social Cognitive and Affective Neuroscience, 8*, 741–749. doi: 10.1093/scan/nss062

Litman, J. A. (2005). Curiosity and the pleasures of learning: Wanting and liking new information. *Cognition & Emotion, 19*, 793–814. doi: 10.1080/02699930541000101

Marsh, A. A., Yu, H. H., Pine, D. S., & Blair, R. J. R. (2010). Oxytocin improves specific recognition of positive facial expressions. *Psychopharmacology, 209*, 225–232. doi: 10.1007/s00213-010-1780-4

McLean, J., Brennan, D., Wyper, D., Condon, B., Hadley, D., & Cavanagh, J. (2009). Localisation of regions of intense pleasure response evoked by soccer goals. *Psychiatry Research-Neuroimaging, 171*, 33–43. doi: 10.1016/j.pscychresns.2008.02.005

Mikolajczak, M., Pinon, N., Lane, A., de Timary, P., & Luminet, O. (2010). Oxytocin not only increases trust when money is at stake, but also when confidential information is in the balance. [Article]. *Biological Psychology, 85*, 182–184. doi: 10.1016/j.biopsycho.2010.05.010

Naber, F., van Ijzendoorn, M. H., Deschamps, P., van Engeland, H., & Bakermans-Kranenburg, M. J. (2010). Intranasal oxytocin increases fathers' observed responsiveness during play with their children: A double-blind within-subject experiment. *Psychoneuroendocrinology, 35*, 1583–1586. doi: 10.1016/j.psyneuen.2010.04.007

Naber, F. B. A., Poslawsky, I. E., van Ijzendoorn, M. H., Van Engeland, H., & Bakermans-Kranenburg, M. J. (2013). Brief Report: Oxytocin enhances paternal sensitivity to a child with autism: A double-blind within-subject experiment with intranasally administered oxytocin. *Journal of Autism and Developmental Disorders, 43*, 224–229. doi: 10.1007/s10803-012-1536-6

Neulinger, J. (1981). *The psychology of leisure* (2nd. ed). Springfield, IL: C.C. Thomas.

Olds, J. (1956). Pleasure centers in the brain. *Scientific American, 195*, 105–116.

Pepping, G.-J., & Timmermans, E. J. (2012). Oxytocin and the biopsychology of performance in team sports. *Scientific World Journal*. doi: 10.1100/2012/567363

Plaud, J. J., & Gaither, G. A. (1996). Behavioral momentum—Implications and development from reinforcement theories. *Behavior Modification, 20*, 183–201. doi: 10.1177/01454455960202003

Riem, M. M. E., Bakermans-Kranenburg, M. J., Huffmeijer, R., & van Ijzendoorn, M. H. (2013). Does intranasal oxytocin promote prosocial behavior to an excluded fellow player? A randomized-controlled trial with Cyberball. *Psychoneuroendocrinology, 38*, 1418–1425. doi: 10.1016/j.psyneuen.2012.12.023

Rilling, J. K., DeMarco, A. C., Hackett, P. D., Thompson, R., Ditzen, B., Patel, R., & Pagnoni, G. (2012). Effects of intranasal oxytocin and vasopressin on cooperative behavior and associated brain activity in men. *Psychoneuroendocrinology, 37*, 447–461. doi: 10.1016/j.psyneuen.2011.07.013

Rimmele, U., Hediger, K., Heinrichs, M., & Klaver, P. (2009). Oxytocin makes a face in memory familiar. *Journal of Neuroscience, 29*, 38–42. doi: 10.1523/jneurosci.4260-08.2009

Robinson, M. J. F., & Berridge, K. C. (2013). Instant transformation of learned repulsion into motivational "wanting." *Current Biology, 23*, 282–289. doi: 10.1016/j.cub.2013.01.016

Salamone, J. D., & Correa, M. (2012). The mysterious motivational functions of mesolimbic dopamine. *Neuron, 76*, 470–485. doi: 10.1016/j.neuron.2012.10.021

Sescousse, G., Caldu, X., Segura, B., & Dreher, J.-C. (2013). Processing of primary and secondary rewards: A quantitative meta-analysis and review of human functional neuroimaging studies. *Neuroscience and Biobehavioral Reviews, 37*, 681–696. doi: 10.1016/j.neubiorev.2013.02.002

Skov, M. (2010). The pleasure of art. In M. L. Kringelbach & K. C. Berridge (Eds.), *Pleasures of the brain* (pp. 270–283). New York: Oxford.

Smith, S. L. J. (1991). On the biological basis for pleasure: Some implications for leisure policy. In T. A. Goodale & P. A. Witt (Eds.), *Recreation and leisure: Issues in an era of change* (3rd ed., pp. 73–84).

Taylor, S. E. (2006). Tend and befriend: Biobehavioral bases of affiliation under stress. *Current Directions in Psychological Science, 15*, 273–277. doi: 10.1111/j.1467-8721.2006.00451.x

Thompson, R. R., George, K., Walton, J. C., Orr, S. P., & Benson, J. (2006). Sex-specific influences of vasopressin on human social communication. *Proceedings of the National Academy of Sciences of the United States of America, 103*, 7889–7894. doi: 10.1073/pnas.06 0040 6103

Titchener, E. B. (1908). *Lectures on the Elementary Psychology of Feeling and Attention*. New York: McMillan.

Vuust, P., & Kringelbach, M. L. (2010). The pleasure of music. In M. L. Kringelbach & K. C. Berridge (Eds.), *Pleasures of the brain* (pp. 225–269). New York: Oxford.

Wise, R. (1980). The dopamine synapse and the notion of pleasure centers in the brain. *Trends in Neurosciences, 3*(4), 91–95. doi: 10.1016/0166-2236(80)90035-1

3

Economic Decision Making in Leisure and Recreation

Chi-Ok Oh (Chonnam National University), Robert B. Richardson (Michigan State University), and Geoff Lacher (Tourism Economics)

The study of economics is ultimately concerned with understanding tradeoffs in decision making, assuming that choices are based on calculations of the relative benefits and costs of various alternatives. Leisure and recreation (hereafter referred to simply as leisure) is frequently conceptualized in terms of participation in particular *activities*, and in that sense, economists treat leisure activities in the context of the production and consumption of goods and services. Leisure experiences often require the use of equipment, materials, and facilities that are produced in economic markets, and these products are sold to consumers and retailers. Some leisure experiences are not tangible, but are rather consumed as services, such as travel or entertainment. Examples of leisure goods and services would include outdoor recreation, ecotourism, concert tickets, museum visits, and spa therapy. Leisure intersects with numerous economic sectors, including real estate, transportation, food, communication, and fashion, and the leisure economy includes all kinds of organizations from major international corporations to small, local service businesses. In this sense, leisure is much more than merely the opposite of work. It is a major segment of the global economy, and represents dozens of industries, millions of jobs, and hundreds of billions of dollars in consumer spending (Clawson & Knetsch, 1966; Freysinger & Kelly, 2004; Loomis & Walsh, 1997).

This chapter will begin by describing the overall relationship between leisure and economics, including the role of leisure in the global economy and the market for leisure goods and services, then discuss the demand for leisure experiences, including the determinants of demand and its measurement, the estimation of the economic benefits of leisure and applications of benefit-cost analysis in leisure decision making, and conclude with a discussion of future directions of economics of leisure.

THE RELATIONSHIP BETWEEN LEISURE AND ECONOMICS

Economics has a significant influence on leisure decisions and choices, and on the provision of leisure activities. Economics plays a role in how leisure time is spent, such as whether to play tennis, go to a baseball game, or just stay home. Understanding how individuals perceive leisure experiences involves understanding how they make choices in light of their preferences, free time, and resources at their disposal. The frequency of leisure participation, perceptions of quality, impacts of price increases, and the benefits of leisure are all of concern to economists.

Economists assume that individuals seek to maximize their utility, benefits or satisfaction, subject to budget constraints, and that utility increases with consumption, meaning that increasing consumption of goods and services leads to higher levels of satisfaction. In this way, leisure activities are treated like consumer goods that are intended to produce benefits or satisfaction. It is further assumed that, given a set of choices and costs, individuals will choose the alternative that provides the greatest level of benefits. Therefore, among a set of alternative leisure pursuits, individuals will consider their own preferences and budget, and choose the activity that generates the greatest benefits to them.

Measuring the economic value of specific leisure activities requires three kinds of data. First, it is necessary to estimate the *quantity* of leisure activities consumed in some discrete unit of measurement, such as numbers of kayaking trips taken or movie tickets purchased. The second kind of data relates to the concept of *price*—that is, the economic value of some leisure activity would depend on the direct cost of participating in that activity. The third piece of information relates to the sensitivity or *elasticity* of demand to changes in price. When leisure activities are consumed in the market economy, estimation of the economic value of those activities is generally simple and can be readily quantified.

In many cases, however, leisure activities are not consumed in the market economy and, thus, economic valuation methods are employed to approximate the quantity demanded and the price. For example, walks on the beach or visits to a state park are not priced in any market, but they certainly have value with diverse benefits to individuals. Individual consumers incur expenses including travel costs and opportunity costs related to their travel time. Such indirect costs may not appear as monetary expenditures, but they represent real tradeoffs and foregone opportunities. Therefore, a reasonable estimate of the total price of a leisure activity would be the sum of direct monetary and non-monetary costs incurred in the consumption of the activity. Nevertheless, the estimation of economic value is not straightforward and data collection can be challenging. Leisure experiences such as outdoor recreation activities are frequently dependent upon high levels of environmental quality, such as hiking to a scenic view or fishing in a pristine alpine lake, and their value would be diminished in a degraded environment. Also, given the importance of style and status in the marketing of leisure, experiences are rarely homogenous and are therefore not easily substitutable. Most visitors to the Grand Canyon would probably agree that their visit was a unique experience, and that there is no other place quite like it.

Furthermore, while markets function reasonably well for rationing consumer goods and services for a price, they fail to capture the economic value of so-called public goods, because such goods are not consumed in the same manner as private or market goods. This is important because many leisure experiences such as outdoor recreation activities occur in places that possess characteristics of public goods, such as rivers, lakes, national parks, and public beaches. Therefore, the economic value of such leisure experiences requires the use of non-market valuation techniques that attempt to replicate the decision-making environment of economic markets in circumstances where markets do not operate, in order to understand the demand for those activities. For example, numerous studies have used non-market valuation techniques to estimate the benefits derived from recreational wildlife viewing, wetland conservation, and improvements in environmental quality (e.g., Boyer & Polasky, 2004; Navrud & Mungatanga, 1994; Pate & Loomis, 1997). Nevertheless, the role of markets in the provision of leisure experiences has expanded significantly, as leisure and recreation continue to develop new products and services with which to appeal to our discretionary income. The development of new technologies that integrate leisure in our everyday experiences—such as the development of electronic games and applications for personal computers and mobile telephones—blurs the lines between work and leisure.

LEISURE AND RECREATION DEMAND

Utility and Demand

Economists often measure leisure benefits in terms of the amount of utility provided (Clawson & Knetsch, 1966). Utility refers to the amount of benefits, enjoyment, or satisfaction gained from a product or experience. Utility itself is difficult to quantify and measure, so researchers instead look to measure what individuals spend (in terms of money and time) to gain utility as an indirect measure of utility itself. It is generally assumed that rational individuals will work to maximize the amount of utility they gain from time and money spent on leisure. Hence, an assumption can be made that individuals spend more money on products and services that provide them more utility. In this manner, utility is often quantified as an individual's willingness-to-pay (WTP) for a product or service.

Demand for products is created out of a desire for utility. Individuals will have a higher demand for services that they believe will provide them with more utility. Demand in economic terms equates to something close to desire, and it is important to note that total demand for a service is unaffected by the price of the product; what is influenced by price is the quantity of that product demanded, called actual or realized demand. An individual's demand (or desire) to see a movie is the same no matter if the movie is $2 or $20. What does change with price (and a number of other key attributes) is quantity demanded; so that at a price of $20, going to a movie might be a very rare treat, but at $2 it is a frequent occurrence. Similarly, an individual may have a higher demand for a jet ski than a fishing rod, but given the high price of jet skis, the individual may actually purchase more fishing rods. Quantity demanded of a service can change in the short term for a variety of reasons, but it should be noted that there is a long-term trend (over the past century or more) of increases in the quantity of recreation and leisure services demanded. A number of factors may be influencing this increase, including rising income, decreasing costs of recreation products and services, greater provision of public recreation services (recent trends notwithstanding), an increase in the variety of recreation activities, and an increase in the availability of these activities.

Cultural, Demographic, and Personal Effects on Demand

Demand for leisure goods and services can vary greatly from individual to individual. Demographic, cultural, and psychological factors influence demand for leisure services in several ways. In general, individuals will have a higher demand for activities that mesh with their individual tastes, and these tastes can be molded by cultural and demographic factors, as well as previous experiences and perceptions of quality.

Across the world, various leisure activities can be associated with certain cultures and countries; for example, we can assume that Brazilians will have higher demand for soccer balls than hockey pucks. Even within individual countries certain demographic groups may be more prone to certain forms of leisure activities. For instance, a majority of visitors to national parks in the USA are middle-to-upper-class, non-Hispanic Whites. This may be partly a cultural phenomenon in which individuals who visited national parks as youths continue to visit parks into their adulthood and eventually take their children to parks, thus continuing the demographic pattern. It may also speak to disinterest or lack of financial resources in other demographic groups. The U.S. National Park Service has a long-running concern over its relative unpopularity with certain demographic groups and has worked to examine the underlying reasons behind the relative unpopularity with certain demographics and worked to find new attractions and services that these demographics might be interested in, but fighting this demographic inclination is difficult and actual changes caused by these programs appear minor (see Stodolska & Floyd, Chapter 28).

On a personal level, tastes may change as an individual ages. Young people typically express demand for less organized play and leisure experiences. Individuals in early adulthood are more likely to become interested in more demanding recreation activities and often form the majority of participants in outdoor recreation activities such as mountain biking or whitewater kayaking (see Caldwell, Chapter 21). Older adults typically prefer more organized and social recreation activities, with less emphasis on physically demanding activities (see Kleiber, Chapter 23).

Consumers will have higher demand for services and experiences that they deem to be of higher quality. This perception could be a result of actual quality, positive past experiences, or effective advertising. Branding can also play a key role in indicating quality and shaping demand. National and even international recognition of natural features and cultural heritage sites from agencies such as the U.S. National Park Service and the United Nations Environmental, Scientific, and Cultural Organization (UNESCO) is highly sought after and can lead to a sudden spike in attendance figures for recently recognized attractions. Consumers recognize brands such as these as seals of approval from esteemed organizations, and markers of high-quality experiences. Consumers may also become loyal to certain brands or locations and display a higher than expected demand for them. Many companies work hard to ensure customer satisfaction as repeat users/visitors frequently make up a large proportion of their client base, and the cost of attracting new customers is often much higher than working to keep the existing customer base satisfied.

Elasticities of Demand

Culture, demographics, personal tastes, and perceptions can yield insights into the baseline of demand for a service, and understanding various elasticities of demand may help us understand how and why the quantity demanded of a service may change over time. Elasticity refers to how the quantity of a good (or service) demanded may shift in response to changes in another variable such as the good's own price, household income, or the price of related goods (other types of elasticity exist, but are less frequently encountered).

The most commonly analyzed type of elasticity is own-price elasticity of demand, which measures how a change in a good's price will affect the quantity demanded of that good. The formula for measuring own-price elasticity is fairly simple:

$$\text{OWN-PRICE ELASTICITY} = \frac{\text{\% CHANGE IN QUANTITY OF GOOD/SERVICE DEMANDED}}{\text{\% CHANGE IN PRICE}}$$

Typically the absolute value of this will be taken to make the result positive.

A good with an own-price elasticity between 0 and 1 is said to have inelastic demand, meaning that a change in price has a relatively low effect on quantity demanded. Meanwhile, a good with an own-price elasticity greater than 1 is said to have elastic demand, meaning that a change in price has a relatively high effect on quantity demanded. A good with an own-price elasticity equal to 1 is consider unit elastic, and a percent change in its price will be result to an equal change in the quantity demand of that product.

A variety of factors may affect the own-price elasticity of a good including the availability of acceptable substitutes, the necessity of the good, and length of time considered (in the long term, prices tend to be more elastic as individuals have more time to consider substitutes and change their expenditure habits). The more specifically a leisure good or service is defined, the more likely it is to be elastic. For instance, the own-price elasticity of a particular brand of fishing rod is likely elastic, however, the own-price elasticity for fishing rods in general is likely inelastic. For example, if fishing rod manufacturer *Shakespeare*® were to suddenly increase its price, fishermen would likely switch to similar, cheaper brands and greatly reduce sales of *Shakespeare*® rods. However, if all fishing rods increased in price, the decrease in demand would likely to match the increase in price given that rods are an integral part of the fishing experience and that fishing rods may represent only a fraction of the fisherman's overall fishing budget (which might include bait, tackle, a boat, marina fees, travel, and a license). While it is a rare phenomenon, it is worth mentioning Veblen goods. This is a good or service in which quantity demanded actually increases as its price increases, and thus would have a negative own-price elasticity. Their existence may not be common but it is hypothesized that individuals occasionally desire the prestige that comes with purchasing expensive items.

The relationship between income and leisure expenditures is complex and nuanced. While overall expenditure on recreation increases with overall income, what is often under more scrutiny is the income elasticity of demand for leisure. This concept examines the percentage change in demand for goods and services relative to the percentage change in average household income, and the formula is as follows:

$$\text{INCOME ELASTICITY} = \frac{\text{\% CHANGE IN QUANTITY OF GOOD/SERVICE DEMANDED}}{\text{\% CHANGE IN INCOME}}$$

If an individual's income increases and the percentage of expenditure on a good decreases, it is considered a normal good. While if expenditure on a good increases with an increase in income it is considered a luxury good. While leisure would generally be thought of as a luxury good (and therefore would receive a higher percentage of expenditure as income increases) empirical results are mixed. Whether or not leisure is considered a luxury or normal good seems largely dependent on the population measured and what types of expenditure are considered leisure (see Pawlowski & Breuer, 2012). Despite this issue, empirical evidence does support the assumption that overall expenditure on leisure increases with income.

A final type of elasticity worth noting is the cross-price elasticity of a good. This concept refers to how a change in price of one good or service affects the demand for another related good or service. This is expressed as:

$$\text{CROSS-PRICE ELASTICITY} = \frac{\text{\% CHANGE IN QUANTITY OF GOOD ``A'' DEMANDED}}{\text{\% CHANGE IN PRICE OF GOOD ``B''}}$$

While often the price of one good will have no effect on demand for another good, some closely related goods may affect demand for one another. Related goods fall into two categories: substitutes and complements. Substitutes are goods that are closely related and may compete over the same expenditure. A positive cross-price elasticity indicates that two goods are substitutes and thus an increase in the price of a good's substitute will affect the increase the demand for the other good in question. For example, an increase in the price of tickets to an amusement park may lead to an increase in the demand for movies at the cinema. Complementary goods, as their name suggests, are those whose use are directly related to one another, such as fishing rods and tackle boxes. Complementary goods have negative cross-price elasticities and thus an increase in price of a good's complement will reduce the demand for the good in question. For example, the demand for recreational boats might be affected by the prices of motorcycles, all-terrain vehicles, or recreational vehicles, which could be considered substitutes. Changes in the prices of these other vehicles might inversely affect the demand for boats. At the same time, marina fees may be considered a complementary good to the boats; the changes in price of the marina fees will inversely affect demand for boats.

PROVISIONING PUBLIC SERVICES AND COST-BENEFIT ANALYSIS

Understanding and quantifying consumer demand and willingness-to-pay for leisure activities can be an essential part of a cost-benefit analysis which may determine when and where these leisure services need to be provided. Leisure activities are considered goods and services that produce diverse private and social benefits. Because a good fraction of leisure services are provided by the public sector, leisure services often show public good or common property characteristics including non-excludability, non-rivalry, and externalities (Cooke, 1994). Excludability indicates that with the well-defined owner's rights, individuals can effectively prevent others from the use of their goods and services. Rivalry means that an individual's consumption reduces availability to others. For example, an individual's purchase of an ice cream cone implies that others be excluded from its consumption (i.e., excludability) unless that person is willing to share it, and that individual's consumption of ice cream means it is no longer available to others (i.e., rivalry) even if (s)he is willing to share it.

Some leisure activities such as visits to a local park and catching fish in a public lake, however, suffer from the absence of the clearly defined owner's rights and the characteristics of non-excludability and non-rivalry are more relevant. The provision of public goods and services often raises a concern about a free-rider problem, indicating individuals who do not pay for a service have a strong incentive to free-ride (i.e., free access to the service) (Tietenberg, 2000). Thus, without the existence of some mechanism that effectively enforces all consumers pay their dues, a free-rider problem usually results in under-supply of public goods and services or over-consumption of common property resources (Cooke, 1994). Also, leisure activities usually exhibit the characteristic of externalities, indicating an unintended effect of an individual's consumption or production on the benefits or costs of an uninvolved third party such as environmental degradation and noise pollution from motorized recreation. While externalities can be either positive or negative, there can be three different types: unpaid costs and benefits; underpaid costs and benefits; and positive and negative side effects (Vanhove, 2013). Among them, underpaid costs and benefits draw special attention in that underpaid costs are related to the concept of opportunity costs (of foregone opportunities) and underpaid benefits are connected with the concept of consumer surplus (or net benefits). Further, unpaid costs and benefits as well as positive and negative side effects requires economists to take into account social benefits and costs beyond the scope of those of an individual, that provides an important theoretical foundation of cost-benefit analysis.

Cost-benefit analysis (CBA) is perhaps the most popularly used economic framework for making public decisions, such as choices about the management of public recreation areas. CBA, often called social or public cost-benefit analysis, intends to consider all relevant benefits and costs to society as a whole and helps decision makers choose public projects that generate the largest increases in social well-being or welfare (Freeman, 2003; Vanhove, 2013). As a result, CBA is an important project or policy evaluation approach to making optimal decisions regarding proposed public projects. The basic principle of CBA is to support any projects if the present value of benefits are greater the costs, and to choose the one with greatest positive net benefits among competing projects (Loomis & Walsh, 1997). When a camping site in a national forest area considers the provision of additional camping access and facilities, CBA is a useful tool in helping to evaluate proposed project scenarios and make effective decisions regarding the optimal alternative for site and facility development. For example, managers of the Francis Marion National Forest in South Carolina proposed seven different competing scenarios with development of facilities, CBA helped assess the net benefits of each scenario and choose one with the greatest present value of net benefits that included additional recreational vehicle sites and expanded camping bath houses and day use parking areas (Hallo, Oh, Draper, & Bixler, 2008).

Prior to discussion of the measurement of economic benefits and costs, it is important to recognize several assumptions of CBA. First, CBA aims to achieve the condition of Pareto efficiency, meaning that if the benefit gainers could sufficiently compensate the losers, there exist alternative resource allocations and this process continues until net benefits are maximized by an efficient allocation (Freeman, 2003; Tietenberg, 2000). Nevertheless, Pareto efficiency is a theoretical concept and in reality, the gainers do not compensate the losers. Consequently, CBA is often criticized in that equity and fairness such as income redistribution are ignored in pursuit of economic efficiency. Second, social costs should take into account opportunity costs. If the resources had not been used for the most beneficial production of the service, for instance, they would have been used for the next most beneficial production. In this case, social costs also need to reflect the opportunity costs as the potential benefits foregone if the resources had been used for an alternative service. Third, CBA often fails to account for intangibles (i.e., intangible costs and benefits which cannot be easily quantifiable in monetary values). Valuing social benefits or well-being is inherently based on an anthropocentric view of the resources. Consequently, intangibles such as intrinsic value are excluded from CBA results regardless of their importance in the policy decision-making process (Holland, Sanchirico, Johnston, & Joglekar, 2010). Nevertheless, it is increasingly required by policymakers that the significance of intangibles be highlighted and explained in CBA results.

Valuation of Social Benefits (and Costs)

When people think of economic benefits, they often picture economic impact such as the impact of new tourism programs on employment, income, and tax revenues. However, in economic analysis, there are two different types of economic benefits: economic value and economic impact using the concept of primary and secondary benefits. According to Loomis and Walsh (1997), individuals receive primary benefits, called net willingness-to-pay or consumer surplus, through participation in leisure activities and the summation of all of individuals' primary benefits is equal to social benefits, which provide the foundation for CBA. Similarly, there are the secondary benefits (called economic impact) to the local or regional economy as these programs are provided to individuals in the area. The former is called economic value and the latter is economic impact. Although CBA only accounts for primary benefits to individuals for comparing benefits to costs, public decision-makers are also eager to acquire the information of economic impact analysis to assess the contribution of public programs to economic prosperity in the area of concern. As a result, economic impact analysis is commonly included in CBA as supplemental information.

As indicated above, economic values indicate the exchange value individuals place on use or recognition of leisure and recreational services and resources such as beaches, historic sites, and parks. Economic valuation is usually complex since many leisure services and resources are not generally traded in the marketplace. Thus, exchange value is often different from its price consumers pay for. For example, park visitors pay only their entrance fee while enjoying the park but the value of their experiences is not fully reflected in their spending. Net willingness-to-pay or consumer surplus is defined as the value of the total experiences minus total trip expenditures, indicating recreationists' primary benefits from consuming non-tradable leisure and recreation services.

Total economic values are composed of multiple components: use value, option value and existence value (Krutilla, 1967; Freeman, 2003). Use value measures the benefits from direct use of the services or resources such as participation in recreation activities; option value reflects the deferred benefits from future use (e.g., an option of being able to visit a wilderness area in the future); and existence value derives from non-use motivations such as bequest or intrinsic rights of the resources (e.g., the value that individuals receive from simply knowing that the Antarctica is preserved).

The choice of valuation methods usually depends on the types of economic values that researchers intend to measure. Two different valuation methods are commonly used for valuing leisure and recreation services: (a) revealed preference methods, and (b) stated preference methods. Revealed preference approaches rely on market decisions to infer benefits for the services not exchanged in the marketplace (Ward & Beal, 2000). As indicated above, the number of trips taken to a particular location also tends to be inversely related to travel cost. Travel cost method, as a revealed preference method, makes use of these two variables as principal surrogates of quantity and price for trip decisions in order to derive a demand curve for estimating economic benefits. Given that recreational anglers recurrently visit a certain fishing site, for example, Oh, Ditton, Anderson, Scott, and Stoll (2005) used travel cost method and reported that an average angler gained $334 in use value from their fishing trips to the site, Sam Rayburn reservoir in Texas. Travel cost method takes advantage of actual behavioral data and thus reduces the possibility of strategic behaviors or biases that may influence hypothetical valuation outcomes. Despite this advantage, however, a drawback of this method is that it can measure only use value.

On the other hand, stated preference approaches including contingent valuation method and choice modeling uses some form of contingent circumstances to elicit a response based upon the assumption of the contingency becoming reality (Freeman, 2003). Thus, questions often include "What would you do if ...?" or "Would you be willing to pay if...?" and in this sense, they are hypothetical in nature. This has been a source of criticism but well-designed studies have become widely accepted to provide reliable and valid estimates for use in CBA. Stated preference methods are particularly beneficial to estimate service and resource values if new programs or policies have not been adopted yet but are of interest for future changes.

The contingent valuation method usually asks respondents to consider a single set of program or policy changes. This single-item nature can result in failure to identify the relative and interacting importance of one program (or policy) option to another (i.e., tradeoffs). As a result, decision-makers risk having very little insight into individuals' actual tradeoff-oriented preferences when developing practical program or policy measures. Choice modeling, instead, makes use of hypothetical scenarios to elicit respondents' responses regarding their overall preferences (e.g., preferred attributes of experiences, products, or outcomes). Based on the assumption that respondents' decisions involve several factors being considered simultaneously, choice modeling allows for an understanding of the relationship of multiple factors (i.e., tradeoff relationships) as they contribute to preferences or choice behavior (Louviere, Hensher, & Swait, 2000). As choice modeling enables researchers to identify the relative importance of program or policy attributes, it is seen as a major improvement for understanding recreationists' preferences. For example, Schroeder and Louviere (1999) employed choice modeling to examine the impact of an increase in user fees at public recreation sites. Their study results indicated that individuals were well aware of tradeoff relationships between different park characteristics and were willing to accept higher user fees to enjoy improved quality of various site amenity features. Richardson and Loomis (2004) used choice modeling approaches to estimate the impact of climate change on national park visitation.

Economic Impact

Recreationists to a particular region bring in money from outside the region for local spending on goods and services. Their expenditures support jobs and income for local residents. They also increase local and state tax revenues. The economic impact analysis begins with the estimation of visitors' expenditures or direct economic impacts. This new money that remains in the economy generates secondary effects (i.e., indirect and induced impacts) on local and state economies. Indirect impacts imply that beneficiaries from direct expenditures spend part of the receipts on the purchase of trip-related products and services from local suppliers. Induced impacts are generated from the circulation of wages and salaries paid by the employers of directly and indirectly related industries. The additional ripples of indirect and induced impacts are created in a cycle and contribute to total economic impact. The total economic impact is the sum of direct, indirect, and induced effects. Although economic impact analysis is not directly included in CBA, this information is useful in future decision-making processes related to economic development. In particular, economic impact analysis can be used as an evaluation tool for local and state and governments to assess financial benefits generated from leisure and recreation programs and resources. The importance of leisure is widely reported using economic impact analysis. For example, a 2012 report by the Outdoor Industry Association estimated that the outdoor recreation economy includes private consumer expenditures of $646 billion on outdoor recreation per year in the USA, and that spending supports 6.1 million direct jobs and $80 billion in federal, state, and local tax revenues (Outdoor Industry Association, 2012).

CONCLUSION

Economics often takes a less prominent role in leisure research due to its relatively heavy reliance on mathematical models compared to other social sciences such as psychology, geography, and anthropology. Nevertheless, along with other social sciences, economics is concerned with observing and explaining human behavior. In that sense, leisure scholars in economics are interested in understanding leisure choices and decisions such as how individuals allocate time between leisure and work and how individuals choose between alternative leisure activities, and how consumption of leisure experiences and activities differs across demographic variables such as age, sex, ethnicity, and education level (see Chapters 21 to 28). Seen this way, economic perspectives on leisure are useful in understanding the demand for leisure and the scope of the leisure economy and assisting the society in making more effective policy and project decisions.

In brief, some future directions related to economics of leisure are worth noting here. First, interdisciplinary approaches that incorporate some other disciplinary perspectives into economics will be beneficial. Understanding leisure phenomena will be enhanced with an interdisciplinary research approach but the lack of cross-fertilization is often criticized in the field. In particular, researchers may want to apply concepts and methods derived from other disciplines such as psychology, sociology, and geography in economic analysis to promote more holistic understandings of leisure behavior. An example may include that because individuals are not a homogeneous group and show variations in leisure behavior and preferences within a population, concepts such as serious leisure and recreation specialization can be used to take into account group differences in recreationists' economic benefits of and preferences for leisure management and policy development (see Scott, Chapter 19).

Second, the evaluation of the economic impact of recreation venues and events continues to be reconsidered and is an evolving topic. Critics have asserted that economic impact reports tend to be biased and use improper methodologies to inflate results. More reliable estimates of the economic benefits of venues and events can lead to better policy and management decisions. This is especially important as mega-events and large stadiums increasingly rely on public dollars for support; while they often appear to create enormous influxes of new money, research is beginning to assert that they are often not worth the investment for the local governments. A better understanding of the economic impacts may lead to better use of public funds in the future.

Third, to assess economic values of non-market goods and services, different valuation tools have been adopted based on the ideal assumption that individuals fully process information with unlimited information processing capabilities. However, they are not perfect and behavioral economics verifies that individuals are limited in their abilities to manage information processing tasks due to imperfect knowledge, lack of time and limited cognitive capacities. Thus, recent study findings show that such psychological insights during the information process need to be incorporated into modeling efforts to explain many behavioral deviations. Increasing the accuracy of information is an ultimate goal of economic valuation studies, and therefore recent developments in decision sciences should be incorporated. Future research is required to better understand individuals' decision-making behavior by detecting observed regularities and the investigation of these issues will be an important line of future research.

Finally, benefit transfer is an emerging area of leisure economics research. To account for all of the segments or sites in a single study is not practicable and thus benefit transfer is a useful means to help researchers test whether benefits of certain segments or sites included in a study are transferrable to those of others not included. Nevertheless, transfer of benefits inevitably generates transfer error, which is defined as the difference between original benefit estimates at a study site and predicted benefit information at a policy site. The goal of benefit transfer, as a cost-effective method, is to minimize the magnitude of transfer error for more effective management decision making and still requires various studies to enhance the reliability and validity of these methods. For instance, to increase the explanatory power of the transfer models, incorporating more sophisticated independent variables such as recreationists' attitudes, beliefs, and perceptions may be promising. Oh (2013) indicates that in leisure and recreation management, theory-driven latent variables such as place attachment, experience use history, and recreation substitution might have been used as "well-behaved" variables that can help increase an explanatory power of the model specification and help decrease transfer error.

Concepts, methods, and applications of economics in leisure contexts continue to evolve and it is important to understand how economics can be used to promote leisure opportunities. In particular, given recent trends of making various public leisure services such as parks and protected areas more independent of public subsidies (i.e., self-sufficiency), the importance of economics of leisure may be increasingly brought to the forefront as organizations are eager to know about the supply and demand of leisure services and their benefits and costs for effective decision making. Additionally, economic analysis including CBA can provide crucial guidance in support of protecting parks and wildlands or providing municipal recreation services. While leisure practitioners know that there are numerous psychological and health benefits provided by leisure, information derived from economics is often needed to convince diverse stakeholders and policymakers of the importance of leisure programs and resources in communities. The power and widespread appeal of economic information ensure that economics continues to play a key role in leisure and recreation for years to come.

REFERENCES

Boyer, T., & Polasky, S. (2004). Valuing urban wetlands: A review of non-market valuation studies. *Wetlands, 24*, 744–755.

Clawson, M., & Knetsch, J. L. (1966). *Economics of outdoor recreation*. Baltimore, MD: The Johns Hopkins Press.

Cooke, A. (1994). *The economics of leisure and sport*. London, UK: Routledge.

Freeman III, A. M. (2003). Economic valuation: What and why. In P. A. Champ, K. J. Boyle, & T. C. Brown (Eds.), *A primer on non-market valuation* (pp. 1–26). Boston, MA: Kluwer Academic Publishers.

Freysinger, V. J., & Kelly, J. R. (2004). *21st Century Leisure: Current Issues* (2nd ed.). State College, PA: Venture Publishing, Inc.

Hallo, J. C., Oh, C., Draper, J., & Bixler, R. (2008). *Needs and feasibility assessment for the development of additional campground facilities at Buck Hall recreation area*. Clemson, SC: Department of Parks, Recreation and Tourism Management, Clemson University.

Holland, D., Sanchirico, J., Johnston, R., & Joglekar, D. (2010). *Economic analysis for ecosystem-applications to marine and coastal environments*. Washington DC: Resources for the Future.

Krutilla, J. (1967). Conservation Reconsidered. *American Economic Review, 57*, 777–786.

Loomis, J. B., & Walsh, R. G. (1997). *Recreation economic decision: Comparing benefits and costs*. State College, PA: Venture Publishing, Inc.

Louviere, J. J., Hensher, D., & Swait, J. (2000). *Stated choice methods: Analysis and application*. Cambridge, UK: Cambridge University Press.

Navrud, S., & Mungatanga, E. D. (1994). Environmental valuation in developing countries: The recreational value of wildlife viewing. *Ecological Economics, 11*, 135–151.

Oh, C. (2013). Incorporating simplified decision rules into tourist decision making processes: A case of fishing trips. *Ocean & Coastal Management, 71*, 79–87.

Oh, C., Ditton, R. B., Anderson, D. K., Scott, D., & Stoll, J. R. (2005). Understanding differences in nonmarket valuation by angler specialization level. *Leisure Sciences, 27*, 263–277.

Outdoor Industry Association. (2012). *The outdoor recreation economy*. Boulder, CO: Outdoor Industry Association.

Pate, J., & Loomis, J. (1997). The effect of distance on willingness to pay values: a case study of wetlands and salmon in California. *Ecological Economics, 20*, 199–207.

Pawlowski, T., & Breuer, C. (2012). Expenditure elasticities of the demand for leisure services. *Applied Economics, 44*, 3461–3477.

Richardson, R. B., & Loomis, J. B. (2004). Adaptive recreation planning and climate change: A contingent visitation approach. *Ecological Economics, 50*, 83–99.

Schroeder, H. W., & Louviere, J. (1999). Stated choice models for predicting the impact of user fees at public recreation sites. *Journal of Leisure Research, 31*, 300–324.

Tietenberg, T. (2000). *Environmental and natural resource economics*. New York: Addison-Wesley.

Vanhove, N. (2013). Tourism projects and cost-benefit analysis. In C. Tisdell (Ed.), *Handbook of tourism economics* (pp. 393–415). Hackensack, NJ: World Scientific Publishing Company.

Ward, F. A., & Beal, D. (2000). *Valuing nature with travel cost models*. Northampton, MA: Edward Elgar Publishing.

4
History of Leisure

John L. Hemingway (Western Illinois University)

To understand the history of leisure requires us to ask some fundamental questions.[1] What is history? Does leisure have a single continuous history, or multiple often intersecting histories? Is a final, definitive history of leisure possible, or does leisure's history continue evolving though the events it deals with may be long past? Difficult questions indeed, but we need answer them here only in sufficient detail to appreciate why leisure's history matters to us as members of contemporary society and as leisure services professionals.

LEISURE AND HISTORICAL STUDY

When you began studying leisure, it probably did not take long to realize that leisure has been defined in many ways. Sometimes this definitional multiplicity is frustrating, but rather than throw up our hands, we should take it as a sign that leisure is a very complex phenomenon closely interwoven with other fundamental elements of our individual and social beings. This does not mean we are free to choose whichever definition of leisure seems convenient and go from there. Definitions must be consistent with what we are studying, with why and how we are doing so. We must expect from our subject only what it can give. Just as our questions must match what we study, so must our methods and the precision expected in our answers. These considerations should guide us in defining leisure for historical study.

We cannot go back in time to conduct surveys about leisure motivations or experiences. We can, however, examine the historical record to learn what people regarded as leisure, when they had leisure and how much, who participated in what forms of leisure and the meanings attached to them, and the importance leisure had to what kinds of people. The nature of many historical sources means we must often be content with narrative description rather than correlational or causal analysis. But this is a problem only if we expect more of the historical record than it can actually give.

What we look for in the historical record are patterns of activity regarded as leisure by the people who engaged in them and the meanings they attached to it. Rather than imposing our preconceived definitions and meanings, the people we study historically must be allowed to reveal *their* definitions and meanings to us through the historical record. It is our task to explore and interpret that record. In doing so, however, we must avoid "presentism," the error of expecting to find people attaching the same meanings and values as we do to words like leisure, labor, work, free time, recreation, play, idleness, or fun. We must not, that is, regard contemporary leisure as a standard for evaluating historical leisure.

We must instead take the historical record and the people who made it as much as possible on their own terms. Encountering activities or beliefs contrary to our own, the proper response is to ask why reasonably intelligent people came to engage in those activities or hold those beliefs. Why did they attract and make sense to those people? How did they help organize experience and help people understand their world?

What we search for in the historical record, then, is evidence about the *social practices* that constituted leisure. Social practices are coherent sets of activities that make sense to their participants, structuring and giving meaning to their social worlds. Social practices make sense because they are governed by largely informal rules and expectations about how to conduct ourselves and deal with other people. Our shared, usually tacit understanding of these rules and expectations creates the sociocultural contexts within which most of daily life occurs. We are seldom moved to question these

[1] This chapter was completed during a semester leave funded by the Office of the Provost and Vice-President of Academic Affairs at Western Illinois University. I take this opportunity to express my thanks for this support.

rules and expectations, which are as natural to us as water is to fish. Indeed, one value of historical study is that exploring past social practices may prompt us to examine our own. Our leisure practices are constructed from the same building blocks as historical leisure practices: sociocultural expectations about the activities constituting leisure and the accepted uses of time and space for leisure.

WHAT HISTORY IS

In defining leisure for historical study, we have also arrived at a preliminary definition of history: the study of past leisure practices, how they were constructed, and what they meant to the people who participated in them. To understand why leisure's history matters, we now need to expand this definition a little further.

Let us start with the phrase "past leisure practices," which should not mislead us into thinking that leisure's history involves only the distant past. Leisure's history begins now, at the present moment. One reason for studying leisure historically is that current leisure practices, however new or different they seem, are built on those of the past. Today's technologically sophisticated role-playing games have roots in earlier games like "Dungeons and Dragons" along with fantasy and science fiction literature and films. Strategy games have a history reaching back to the invention of chess, about 600 in India. Many other examples, particularly from sports and games, could be cited, of course, and there is a long tradition of chronicling them in the study of leisure (Dulles, 1965, is the most distinguished contribution here).

For leisure's history to matter, however, historical study must go beyond chronicling earlier activities and their possible connections to later ones. Chronicling tends toward "presentism" in two ways. First, it emphasizes apparent similarities of past leisure practices to later or present ones, not the importance of past leisure practices to the people who engaged in them. Second, it tends to assume a direct line of descent from past to later or present leisure practices, treating more recent practices as an assumed standard. Yet when people in the past engaged in leisure, they thought of themselves as doing just that, and not as blazing a trail to our present leisure.

Chronicling is also limited by its emphasis on description over analysis. The past tends to be presented as fixed, as being what it had to be. *Human agency,* the ability of people to act deliberately and consequentially, is thus downplayed. Human agency is one of those "big questions" in historical study. Happily, we do not need to resolve it here, but we do need to know what it involves. Human action is deeply nuanced. Its scope is shaped and at times outright limited by many different *bounding factors,* but there is almost always some range, wider or narrower, of alternative actions from which people may choose. What people understood these alternatives to be and why they chose from among them as they did are questions lying at the core of historical inquiry. Rather than pursue this difficult question further, however, for our purposes it is enough to say that human beings make their own history, though not always as they want or intend to, in ways they recognize at the time, or with the consequences they expect.

Historians of leisure explore the leisure practices people constructed within the limits imposed by various bounding factors. Among these factors are the shared cultural capacities—what Bourdieu (1989, pp. 14, 18–19) calls "schemes of perception, thought, and action"—that create the immediate social world within which so much of our activity occurs, leisure very much included. Especially since the 1980s, historians have come more and more to study how these cultural capacities shape leisure practices. As a result, the scope of what is considered relevant to leisure's history has expanded considerably. No longer is leisure's history restricted to formally structured activities, institutions and organizations, and a few professional leaders and great events. Historians now find it necessary to examine patterns of consumption, property ownership, housing and domestic furnishings, diet, employment patterns, salaries and wages, the domestic economy, slave owning, civic participation, fraternal and social groups, education and literacy, music, reading tastes, religion, and much more.

Perhaps the most important consequence of this widened scope for historical analysis has been a clear recognition that there can be no single, unified history of leisure, that leisure has multiple histories, maybe even as multiple as the factors shaping people's leisure choices and activities. With this has come more open acknowledgement that histories, including histories of leisure, inevitably reflect the perspectives from which they are written, the questions they address, and the data used to answer them. This is *not* to say that relativism is acceptable or that we can make history be whatever we want it to be. It *is* to say that history reflects the angle from which we look at it, the questions we bring to it, the landmarks that catch (or do not catch) our attention. What appear to be the same events are experienced and understood differently by people who are differently situated, who see them from different angles of vision. This applies equally to historians and to participants in events.

History is about events, their causes and consequences, how people experienced them, and the meanings people attached to them. All this is open to multiple understandings depending on the angles from which we approach it. It is no surprise, then, that as our historical understanding expands, we are likely to find history itself changing as what once seemed certain turns out not to be so after all. However discomfiting, our best response is to remember that what changes most as our historical understanding matures is not so much history but us, and for the better.

WHY LEISURE'S HISTORIES MATTER

Any number of reasons may be given why the histories of leisure matter, but at the risk of considerable simplification they will be divided here into two broad classes: enriched professional education and practical application.

Enriched Professional Education

All professions expect their members to have a basic knowledge of the profession's history if for no other reason than to establish professional identity and continuity. To be a leisure services professional in the U.S. therefore means knowing something about, for examples, the playground movement, the urban reform movement and creation of urban parks, the emergence of organized camping, the genesis of the national parks, and the evolution of professional leisure services organizations.

Such basic understanding, usually acquired during early professional training, is a good beginning. Leisure is such a remarkably multifaceted phenomenon, however, that a basic understanding may leave us unaware of the full richness of leisure's histories and thus unable to draw on it either in understanding contemporary leisure or in arguing for its significance. Enriched professional education goes beyond the basics to explore the factors that shaped leisure's histories and the influence of historical leisure on the structure and content of contemporary leisure. Not only do we become more effective advocates for leisure, an obligation that comes with being a member of the leisure services profession, but we also become more sensitive to important developments in leisure's wider field. Given how easily our focus can be narrowed down to our immediate professional issues and settings, we need regular reminders that much if not most leisure occurs outside those settings while still influencing the attitudes and expectations brought into them. An enriched understanding of leisure's histories is both a good preventive and effective cure for such narrowness.

Practical Application

The most obvious examples here are historically-oriented programs and facilities (e.g., living history, reenactments, special events, historic sites, and museums). Such programs and facilities are worthwhile in themselves but are also often vital components in creating a viable tourism industry, especially in areas otherwise lacking in attractions. Considerable preliminary research and preparation are necessary to develop historically-oriented programs and facilities. A surprising amount of what has been aptly labeled "fakelore" (Nabokov & Loendorf, 2004, pp. 21–28) is embedded in everything from local legends, tour guidebooks, and interpretive materials to scholarly books. It is imperative to identify and address such misinformation to maintain the credibility of historically-oriented programs and facilities. Visitors to historically-oriented attractions are quite often very well-informed. They will be quick to spot inaccuracies and are not likely to be shy about pointing them out. Thus not only must features of an historically-oriented attraction like structures, implements, and costumes be highly accurate, but staff and volunteers must be as knowledgeable as possible about the attraction itself and its wider historical context. This very much includes the history of leisure, which often holds particular fascination for visitors.

Another practical application for historical methods is the creation and preservation of organizational memory. Every organization maintains administrative files, but the extent and value of these files can vary considerably. By creating an archive, however, an organization can preserve a far richer historical record of its culture, mission, activities, and relationships with service populations. Materials of all sorts can then be made available as needed, such as during employee orientations or on symbolic occasions to reinforce organizational identity and loyalty.

THE HISTORICAL RECORD: SOURCES

The phrase "historical record" has appeared here more than once. It is time to give it a concrete meaning. Stated briefly, the historical record consists of all the sources available to us for historical inquiry. The record will be more complete in some cases than in others, but there will almost always be gaps. Nor will the sources be impartial. They will always have a point of view, and there will always be other points of view. When going to the historical record, then, keep in mind that history is subject to multiple understandings, reflecting the perspectives from which it is viewed.

Four basic types of sources are available to historians: physical, written, visual, and aural. *Physical sources* include actual sites (e.g., parks, playing fields), structures (e.g., buildings, stadia), and artifacts (e.g., toys, equipment, apparatus, implements). Some research purposes require first-hand inspection of physical sources; nothing else will do. *Written sources* are probably the most familiar; they include text documents of all types and all media. *Visual sources* consist of glyphs (e.g., pictographs), paintings and drawings, and other art objects. For much of history, these were the primary means to record both the appearance of things and events. More recently, of course, photography and videography have replaced them. Finally, *aural sources* are sound recordings (including voice, music, and environmental). Despite some overlap among these types of sources, there are reasonably clear expectations about appropriate methods for analyzing each of them and about their appropriate uses in historical research. Historians tend to emphasize written sources, but the others may be equally useful and in some cases essential.

There is a hierarchy of sources, based on their presumed accuracy, reliability, and usefulness. *Primary sources* stand at the top of this hierarchy. Of particular interest to historians are accounts by participants in or observers of events, notably those accounts dating from the time of the events or soon afterwards. The immediacy of such accounts presumably increases their accuracy. Human memory is both fragile and malleable. Accounts recorded long after events may be inaccurate or perhaps adjusted based on subsequent developments. Diaries, letters, and memoirs written by participants or observers closer to events are therefore privileged over later accounts.

Government documents at all levels are also important primary sources. Some are more familiar in leisure services (e.g., reports from the Bureau of the Census and Bureau of Labor Statistics) than others (e.g., committee reports and hearings transcripts). Recreation and social service program brochures are classified as government documents. If necessary, federal and state freedom of information (FOIA) acts can assist researchers in obtaining records not immediately available.

Other useful primary sources are community directories and almanacs that list businesses and other organizations (sometimes with their missions and activities). These are useful to track voluntary, nonprofit, fraternal, or social groups. Remember that such groups may issue annual or other reports. Corporate and business reports are also helpful if they are available, as are sales catalogs and advertisements in newspapers and magazines which provide an idea of the availability of leisure goods and services (see Cross's, 1997, innovative study of children's toys). Finally, written materials, movies, TV and radio shows, and artwork can also be primary sources. Examined carefully, with due attention to point of view and intended audience, these may offer rich clues about the structure and contents of leisure at specific times and places.

Libraries, academic and public, are good starting points for locating primary sources. Many serve as depositories for government documents and other records. Ask a reference librarian for assistance. Do not overlook historical or professional associations, which may have useful although narrow holdings. So, too, do government agencies, usually required by law to preserve public records and make them available. In any case, the more precisely you identify what you are looking for, the better your chances of finding it.

Readers are likely already familiar with *secondary sources*. This is, after all, what most textbooks are. Secondary sources may be scholarly or popular, prepared after the events discussed by people who did not participate in or observe them. Most secondary sources are books or journal articles, though documentary films are also possible. A good secondary source is clearly based on independent research using primary sources, clearly identified and referenced, and makes extensive use of relevant secondary sources. When relying on secondary sources, good practice requires providing two or more sources in support of important points and to avoid using any source repetitively.

Tertiary sources are derivative reports at third-hand for which an author has done little or no independent research. They make little direct use of primary sources and summarize the existing secondary literature without adding anything new to it. What use there is of primary sources is indirect, signaled by references including the phrase "as quoted by" indicating the author has not checked the primary source but is relying on another author. Unavoidable at times, it is far more often a sign that the author's research lacks thoroughness and rigor. Avoid tertiary sources as a general rule.

No historical source is infallible. The best-intentioned historian, the most scrupulous report writer, the most observant eyewitness: All can and do make errors of fact and interpretation. Historical analysis thus requires using as many different sources as possible while adopting a critical, analytical stance that challenges each one: What do you know? How do you know it? Why do you want me to know it, too?

GENRES OF HISTORY

To close this chapter, it is appropriate to look at several genres of leisure history to get a brief notion of what they involve. And *brief* is all that is possible. Having once recognized the full complexity of leisure, historians responded with a steady expansion of their inquiries far beyond traditional disciplinary boundaries. The result is a growing literature whose richness can scarcely be suggested here.

First, though, a *genre of history* is simply a body of research with an identifiable literature linked by shared themes, questions, research methods, and assumptions about the factors shaping human activity. Genres are not necessarily a formal category, though often enough they form the basis of academic curricula and have professional societies, journals, and conferences devoted to them. Some genres are highly specialized, others are more diffuse. Finally, most genres come in several different flavors, between which non-specialists can have trouble distinguishing, a difficulty that appears to be growing, not diminishing.

Social History

Of all genres of history, social history has seen the greatest expansion over the past 50 years, partly because so much can be included in it and partly in reaction against traditional history. Social history addresses the activities and experiences of the ordinary people so often hidden from view by traditional history's emphasis on political, diplomatic, military, and economic events and leaders. In contrast, social history examines such themes as gender, race, ethnicity, the family, domesticity, and work. There is significant crossover among social history's sub-genres as well as between it and other disciplines. Peiss's (1986) study of young working women from immigrant families in New York between roughly the 1880s and 1920s is an excellent example of social history that pulls together a number of themes (e.g., ethnicity, gender, class, technology) to demonstrate how these women used leisure to create identities independent of the patriarchal family structures in which they lived.

Peiss' (1986) study highlights opportunities created by new modes of entertainment and transportation. Movies created new spaces in which mixed audiences could mingle away from parental supervision. Expanded urban streetcar service allowed escape from one's neighborhood at least temporarily and enabled access to commercial leisure centers that attracted people of many different classes. Among the most well known of these was Coney Island, to which Peiss devotes a chapter and Kasson (1978) a short but highly informative book. Rabinovitz (1998, 2012) also explores the role of movies and amusement parks for women and American culture generally. Cross (1990) touches on these and related themes.

Commercial leisure and leisure-based consumption draw considerable attention from social historians, largely because in a market-based society like the U.S., being able to consume and knowing what to consume are important factors in establishing both personal identity and social standing. Some historians (e.g., Hurley, 2001; Nasaw, 1993) have studied commercial recreation's creation of sites for social interaction, including how the changing nature of these sites affects the interactions occurring there. Though the significance of consumption is already evident in the eighteenth and early nineteenth centuries (e.g., Breen, 2004; Bushman, 1992), its growing importance in the late nineteenth and twentieth centuries has been particularly studied (e.g., Cohen, 2003; Cross, 2000; Leach, 1993). The dependence of consumption-based leisure on one's work-based earnings is an irony some critics have pointed out (e.g., Butsch, 1990; Cook, 2001). A further criticism has been that some consumption-based leisure activities reinforce workplace roles and attitudes (e.g., Gelber's, 1999, study of hobbies).

The study of the routine activities and settings of daily life is worth mentioning here as a final sub-genre of social history. By setting leisure in context, whether in the early settlements (e.g., Hawke, 1988) or more recently (e.g., Kyvig, 2002), the analysis of daily life provides vital clues for understanding the structure and content of leisure, and the meanings attached to it.

Labor History and Shorter Hours

Although sometimes treated as a sub-genre of social history, labor history—the study of work, wages, working conditions, unions, and work hours—has enough substance to stand on its own. The influence of work on free time and earnings makes it difficult to imagine an adequate historical understanding of leisure without some sustained attention to labor history as well.

In two widely influential works, English historian E. P. Thompson (1963, 1967) identifies the early development of factory-based timed labor as the vital element in the emergence of an identifiable working class. In contrast, some U. S. labor historians (e.g., Montgomery, 1968, 1979, 1993) argue that working-class interests emerged before American industrialization, specifically among wage-earning artisans in the urban workshops. As soon as they had the means, these artisans hoped to open their own workshops or to relocate and take up farming. A great many actually did just this, establishing an idealized pattern that became embedded in American culture (e.g., Foner, 1995).

This ideal became increasingly difficult to achieve in the second half of the nineteenth century. Particularly in the North and parts of the Midwest, the Civil War encouraged industrialization, larger businesses, and concentration around railroad networks. The capital required to open an independent business increased accordingly. Good agricultural land became increasingly scarce, making it necessary to relocate considerable distances if one wanted to farm. Urban populations grew in cities old and new (e.g., Cronon, 1996). Skilled artisanal work was more difficult to find, wages for unskilled work remained low. A permanent class of wage earners emerged, followed by workers' associations and unions. Among their first concerns was the length of the working day.

Artisans' complaints about long working days involved their negative effects on family life, church involvement, self-improvement activities, and civic engagement (e.g., Roediger & Foner, 1989, Chapters 1–2). These complaints were understandable from men (which almost all artisans were) having realistic hopes of advancing beyond wage earning. For later wage earners, without the artisans' hopes, a shorter work day was a simple matter of survival. These workers made shorter work days a primary goal, as they organized, repeating the artisans' earlier concerns while increasingly emphasizing worker health and safety. Labor historian B. K. Hunnicutt (1984, 1988) traced the growth of the shorter hours movement among workers, social activists, clergy, and educators. He finds a steady decline in work hours from the late nineteenth century until the Great Depression, when legislation was introduced in Congress to establish a six-hour work day as a means of spreading available employment more widely, thereby alleviating some effects of the Depression. Known as the Black and Connery Bills, this legislation actually passed the Senate, but business opposition and a shift by President Roosevelt prevented further action. Subsequent policy decisions by the Roosevelt administration favored job creation through government economic stimulus over job sharing as an answer to unemployment. A number of firms nonetheless adopted the six-hour work day voluntarily, among them the Kellogg's Corporation. Kellogg's continued to have workers on the six-hour day until 1984, though in steadily declining numbers. Hunnicutt (1996) tells this story with fascinating insights into the conflicting meanings the additional free time had for Kellogg's workers.

Park History

This genre, considerably narrower than other more widely recognized genres, has clear relevance to leisure history and the leisure services profession. The creation of urban, state, and especially national parks is often pointed to as among the proudest achievements of the U.S., for which there is surely considerable justification. As historians have explored the history of American parks, however, it has become increasingly clear that their creation reflected existing patterns of political, economic, and social power far more than is acknowledged in the official histories or in more traditional celebratory accounts (e.g., Tilden, 1968, on national parks).

Cranz's (1982) now classic history illustrates this for urban parks, where expectations about park users and the perceived need for social control often dominated park planning and design. Parks were often enough located to the advantage of privileged groups and the disadvantage of others, including using the creation of parks to eliminate unwanted shanty towns and even more substantial housing. Rosenzweig's (1987) study of Worcester, Massachusetts, revealed that far from maintaining parks in immigrant neighborhoods, some were actually used as dumps. Worries that immigrants might penetrate middle- and upper-class neighborhoods were reflected in conflicts over the use of public space, with most parks designed along Olmstedian principles that discouraged free play, sports, and spontaneous socializing. Only after sustained political conflict was it finally agreed that immigrant parks would be improved and maintained.

National parks exhibit a somewhat similar pattern. Though wilderness, the frontier, and the West were all originally regarded as threats to civilization (e.g., Marx, 1964; Nash, 2001; Smith, 1978), they eventually became symbols of American strength and virtue. This did not prevent steady encroachment on any land with economic value, however, prompting growing concern that what was most unique about the U.S. would be swallowed up. Not until Yellowstone was a large block of land designated as (supposedly) protected from development. The Yellowstone effort was successful, as Runte (1997) points out, because at the time no one saw any economic value in the land set aside, except perhaps some local and railroad visionaries who recognized its potential tourism value. The Yellowstone effort was also successful because Native Americans, particularly the feared Blackfeet, had finally been destroyed. Only then were systematic exploring and surveying of the Yellowstone territory deemed sufficiently safe (e.g., Black, 2012).

THE FUTURE OF LEISURE'S PAST

There's a touch of irony in speculating about the future of leisure's history, but the issue is real and so should be concern at the prospects. Put simply, the future of leisure history lies in hands other than those of the leisure services profession, practitioner, or academic. Leisure services is an applied field. It does not prepare its own historians, and with limited exceptions there is no recognized professional specialty in history. Few trained historians are recruited to or attracted by the field. Almost all historical study of leisure is therefore carried on outside leisure services, with the consequence that it is disconnected from the field's historical needs and concerns. Given this, what paths is historical study of leisure likely to follow in the next decade?

Social history will continue growing, though more slowly. Historians will continue giving critical attention to gender, race, and ethnicity, exploring these in a widening range of times and places. We will learn more about patterns of daily life, domestic relations, and the structure of local communities. The effects of demographic changes—the aging boomers, later marriages and fewer children, population shifts, individual mobility—will attract interest as post-boomer generations become more dominant (see Chapters 21 to 28).

The lines between *labor history and social history* will blur further, reflecting the changing nature of work in the twentieth century. Attention will shift from work hours to the broader question of free time in quality of life (e.g., Hunnicutt, 2013). Stagnant income growth and persistently imbalanced distributions of wealth may stir interest in class as a research focus, especially regarding leisure-based consumption.

The *effects of technology change on leisure* will see dramatically increased attention. Accelerating through the twentieth century and then fairly exploding with the digital revolution, innovations in transportation, recreational equipment, and electronic devices have reshaped leisure. Historians of leisure and leisure services practitioners both will need to respond to these dramatic changes (see Nimrod, Chapter 30).

Historically-oriented programming and facilities are likely to remain popular. Historic preservation has received increased emphasis from government and citizen groups, reflecting widespread interest in establishing contact with human and natural heritages. The economic value of historical tourism is a further reason to anticipate further, if possibly slower growth in this area.

CONCLUSION

Underlying this chapter is this basic assumption: there is great value in studying leisure's history and indeed any history in order to understand the past out of which the present has emerged and from this to further understand the role of human action in creating our present world. We all too often take the world as given, as fixed. We resign ourselves to making do with what is or finding small ways around it. History shows us that human action has limits, yes, but it also shows us that human action has possibilities. The work of historians may show us that the past was not what we thought it was, but the more we understand the past, the more we can free ourselves from it by challenging the existing in the name of the possible.

REFERENCES

Black, G. (2012). *Empire of shadows: The epic story of Yellowstone.* New York: St. Martin's Griffin.

Bourdieu, P. (1989). Social space and symbolic power (L. J. D. Wacquant, Trans.). *Sociological Theory, 7,* 14–25.

Breen, T. H. (2004). *The marketplace of the Revolution: How consumer politics shaped American independence.* New York: Oxford University Press.

Bushman, R. L. (1992). *The refinement of America: Persons, houses, cities.* New York: Vintage Books.

Butsch, R. (Ed.). (1990). *For fun and profit: The transformation of leisure into consumption.* Philadelphia: Temple University Press.

Cohen, L. (2003). *A consumer's republic: The politics of mass consumption in postwar America.* New York: Alfred A. Knopf.

Cook, D. T. (2001). The elephant in the living room. *Leisure Sciences, 23,* 67–70.

Cranz, G. (1982). *The politics of park design: A history of urban parks in America.* Cambridge, MA: MIT Press.

Cronon, W. (Ed.). (1996). *Uncommon ground: Rethinking the human place in nature.* New York: W. W. Norton.

Cross, G. (1990). *A social history of leisure since 1600.* State College, PA: Venture Publishing.

Cross, G. (1997). *Kids' stuff: Toys and the changing world of American childhood.* Cambridge, MA: Harvard University Press.

Cross, G. (2000). *An all-consuming century: Why commercialism won in modern America.* New York: Columbia University Press.

Dulles, F. R. (1965). *A history of recreation: America learns to play* (2nd ed.). New York: Appleton, Century, Crofts.

Foner, E. (1995). *Free soil, free labor, free men: The ideology of the Republican Party before the Civil War.* New York: Oxford University Press. [Originally published 1970]

Gelber, S. M. (1999). *Hobbies: Leisure and the culture of work in America.* New York: Columbia University Press.

Hawke, D. F. (1988). *Everyday life in early America.* New York: Harper & Row.

Hunnicutt, B. K. (1984). The end of shorter hours. *Labor History, 25,* 373–405.

Hunnicutt, B. K. (1988). *Work without end: Abandoning shorter hours for the right to work.* Philadelphia: Temple University Press.

Hunnicutt, B. K. (1996). *Kellogg's six-hour day.* Philadelphia: Temple University Press.

Hunnicutt, B. K. (2013). *Free time: The forgotten American dream.* Philadelphia, PA: Temple University Press.

Hurley, A. (2001). *Diners, bowling alleys, and trailer parks: Chasing the American dream in postwar consumer culture.* New York: Basic Books.

Kasson, J. (1978). *Amusing the million: Coney Island at the turn of the century.* New York: Hill & Wang.

Kyvig, D. E. (2002). *Daily life in the United States, 1920–1940: How Americans lived through the "Roaring Twenties" and the Great Depression.* Chicago: Ivan R. Dee.

Leach, W. (1993). *Land of desire: Merchants, power, and the rise of a new American culture.* New York: Vintage Books.

Marx, L. (1964). *The machine in the garden: Technology and the pastoral ideal in America.* New York: Oxford University Press.

Montgomery, D. (1968). The working classes of the preindustrial American city. *Labor History, 9,* 3–22.

Montgomery, D. (1979). *Workers control in America: Studies in the history of work, technology, and labor struggles.* Cambridge, MA: Cambridge University Press.

Montgomery, D. (1993). *Citizen worker: The experience of workers in the United States with democracy and the free market during the nineteenth century.* New York: Cambridge University Press.

Nabokov, P., & Loendorf, L. (2004). *Restoring a presence: American Indians and Yellowstone National Park.* Norman, OK: University of Oklahoma Press.

Nasaw, D. (1993). *Going out: The rise and fall of public amusements.* New York: Basic Books.

Nash, R. (2001). *Wilderness and the American mind* (4th ed.). New Haven, CN: Yale University Press.

Peiss, K. (1986). *Cheap amusements: Working women and leisure in turn of the century New York.* Philadelphia, PA: Temple University Press.

Rabinovitz, L. (1998). *For the love of pleasure: Women, movies, and culture in turn-of-the-century Chicago.* New Brunswick, NJ: Rutgers University Press.

Rabinovitz, L. (2012). *Electric dreamland: Amusement parks, movies, and American modernity.* New York: Columbia University Press.

Roediger, D., & Foner, P. (1989). *Our own time: A history of American labor and the working day.* Westport, CT: Greenwood Press.

Rosenzweig, R. (1987). Middle-class parks and working-class play: The struggle over recreational space in Worcester, Massachusetts, 1870–1910. In H. G. Gutman & D. H. Bell (Eds.), *The New England working class and the new labor history* (pp. 214–230). Urbana, IL: University of Illinois Press.

Runte, A. (1997). *National parks: The American experience* (3rd ed.). Lincoln, NE: University of Nebraska Press.

Smith, H. N. (1978). *Virgin land: The American West as symbol and myth.* Cambridge, MA: Harvard University Press.

Thompson, E. P. (1963). *The making of the English working class.* New York: Random House.

Thompson, E. P. (1967). Time, work-discipline, and industrial capitalism. *Past and Present, 38,* 56–97.

Tilden, F. (1968). *The national parks* (Rev. & enlarged ed.). New York: Alfred A. Knopf.

5

Philosophy and Leisure Studies

Charles Sylvester (Western Washington University)

Recognizing that the majority of readers may have limited background in philosophy, I intend to provide a bit of guidance in the course of this survey while sparing as much technical terminology as possible. Further, philosophy is the broadest of subjects in this book. By seeking to go everywhere philosophy appears in leisure studies, however, we risk getting nowhere. So rather than attempt the impossible of covering all of the pertinent literature in an overview limited by space, I have selectively searched for contributions that are particularly useful for discerning the presence of philosophy in leisure studies. Also, I concentrate more on the discipline of leisure studies, rather than on specializations associated with it (e.g., sport and tourism), except where they help to explain better some aspect of philosophy. After a few remarks on the meaning and purpose of philosophy, I will survey leisure studies using four of the major departments of philosophy: ontology, epistemology, ethics, and social philosophy. It will be followed by a cursory account of postmodernism and, finally, comments on the future of philosophy and leisure.

A Very Brief Introduction to Philosophy

From the Greek, φιλοσοφία (*philosophia*), philosophy literally means "love of wisdom." Without some background on the origins of philosophy, it unfortunately does not explain much, particularly about modern philosophy. Further, philosophy is not as easy to nail down as other disciplines, having what seems like "as many meanings as philosophers engaging in it" (Angeles, 1981, p. 211). Nonetheless, the practice of subjecting *everything* to questioning is a good place to start for grasping what makes philosophy distinctive. For example, theories of leisure make certain assumptions, such as free will, autonomy, and self-determination. Taking nothing for granted, philosophy critically examines theoretical assumptions and conceptual foundations of leisure. In the course of questioning, philosophy aims to achieve logically justified explanations that are clear, critical, coherent, and rigorous. Based on the results of philosophical inquiry, the dialectical (question and answer) process continues, leading to further questions and rational arguments. For instance, ancient philosophers asked, "What is justice?" Repeatedly argued across the centuries, justice is a question that occupies leisure studies today (e.g., Paisley & Dustin, 2011; Rojek, 2005). On the important questions of life (e.g., truth, goodness, beauty, justice, love, death, freedom, society, peace, happiness) the final word has not been written. Philosophy, then, is radically the continuous practice of asking and answering fundamental questions in all areas of life using the tools of conceptual analysis.

Before moving on to discuss the main intersections between philosophy and leisure studies, I want to share a final thought on the purpose of philosophy, which happens to be my favorite. In the introduction to *The Human Condition*, Hannah Arendt (1998) wrote, "What I propose, therefore, is very simple: *it is nothing more than to think what we are doing*" (emphasis added) (p. 5). In that spirit, this chapter explores some of the philosophical thinking in contemporary leisure studies that asks the plain, but challenging question—"What *are* we doing?"

Ontology

Ontology involves questions about existence or reality. When we say leisure *is* something, whether a period of time, an activity, or a state of mind, we are engaging in ontology by asserting ways in which we believe leisure exists. Socrates often began his philosophical conversations with an ontological question. For instance, in Plato's *Meno*, the question is raised whether virtue (moral excellence) can be taught. Socrates insists that virtue first be defined, arguing that before it can be determined if something can be taught or not, we need to know what it is. Similarly, how we study, teach, manage, and participate in leisure depend on what we believe it *is*. As such, ontology is no mere exercise in semantics. For example, embedded in an ontological hierarchy based on degrees of natural freedom (Stocks, 1939), Aristotle concluded that slaves and women were unfit by nature for leisure, effectively excluding them from social and political participation (Sylvester, 1999). The ontological task of defining leisure, then, matters greatly, producing social, ethical, and political implications that have real consequences.

Two important ontological inquiries that actually predate leisure studies are worth mentioning for their historical significance and engaging narratives, making them excellent introductions to the philosophy of leisure. *Leisure, the Basis of Culture*, by Josef Pieper (1952), argues that the essence of leisure is not time remaining after work, but is rather a spiritual condition embodied in an open, wondrous attitude toward life, making inner freedom the existentially defining quality of leisure. Sebastian de Grazia's (1962) *Of Time, Work, and Leisure* also questions the ontological assumption that leisure *is* free time. Drawing mainly from Aristotle, de Grazia asserts that leisure is a condition of being free from the need to labor, offering opportunities to enjoy activity worthy for its own sake, citing music, friendship, and, above all, contemplation. As such, leisure exists as an objective condition of social, economic, and political freedom (see Sylvester, 2013).

Only a few studies in leisure studies have made the ontology of leisure their direct target. Otherwise, studies either substantially address ontology as one part of a systematic theory of leisure (e.g., Aitchison, 2003; Blackshaw, 2010; Rojek, 1995) or refer to it, but lack philosophical analysis. Unable to cover the array of ontological perspectives, I will present examples, followed by prevalent positions.

Coincidentally oriented to authenticity, the following three studies are an instructive gateway to ontology. Asking directly, "What kind of thing is leisure?" (p. 54), Cooper (1989) presented an "expressivist conception of leisure, emphasizing its role in leading an authentic life" (p. 59). What makes leisure a value-laden concept in the first place, according to Cooper, is that by its very nature leisure is an authentic "kind of thing" or way of being. Borrowing Martin Heidegger's conception of authenticity, Aho (2007) explored the ancient idea of leisure as a way of recovering authenticity today. Like Cooper, Aho's inquiry stands out for showing that questions important to previous cultures—authenticity and leisure in this case—remain relevant today. Finally, if authenticity is the extent of being one's "true self," Blackshaw's (2010) theory of *liquid leisure* is also ontologically rooted in authenticity. Like many leisure theorists, Blackshaw situates leisure in individual freedom. The practical advantage of liquid leisure rests in it being "the principal driving force for meaning and our thirst for giving our lives purpose" (p. 120). While identity will continue to be influenced by such factors as class, gender, and ethnicity, individual identity will always be a "work in progress" open to "infinite interpretability" (p. 144; see also Blackshaw, Chapter 7).

As an aside, Blackshaw's (2010) ontology is also notable for its ethical implications. Resembling Nietzsche's "will to power," liquid leisure is a "devotional practice" whereby individuals freely commit themselves to whatever they find personally meaningful, boundlessly "stretching from extreme sport to extreme cuisine to extreme pornography" (p. 144). Regarding "anything goes" so long as it springs from the free will as characteristic of the modern crisis, Alastair MacIntyre (1984), in his acclaimed study, *After Virtue*, turned to the authority of traditional practices as an alternative to the anti-authority of theories like liquid leisure.

Ontology can be approached from many perspectives. Spracklen (2009) described three main ontological views appearing in leisure studies that correspond to historically significant sociopolitical frameworks:

- Free choice in a structured world (liberal perspective), whereby people are free to make their own leisure choices that express their self-determining values.
- Structurally constrained choice (structuralist perspective), whereby people's choices are determined more by social and cultural factors than by autonomously self-determined choices.
- Complete free choice in a structurally disintegrating world (postmodern perspective), whereby social and cultural norms are arbitrary, leaving it to individuals to continuously create their own values in the absence of any universal or pre-existing principles around which to center their lives. (pp. 13–17)

Ontology has more generally taken one of several basic forms in leisure studies. *Materialism* holds that reality, including human beings and everything surrounding them, consists of objectively natural properties that can be independently studied. Chick's (1998) defense of a cultural anthropology of leisure, for example, is situated in the materialist camp (see Loy, 1998, for his philosophical analysis of Chick's ontology; cf. Chick, Chapter 1). *Idealism* contends that reality is principally organized or structured as mental states. Psychological theories of leisure that take the subjective definition of leisure as a starting point are often idealist in varying degrees. For instance, Neulinger (1981), theorized leisure as a state of mind consisting of two conditions—perceived freedom and intrinsic motivation. Of the two, perceived freedom is most fundamental, for "leisure has one and only one essential criterion, and that is the condition of perceived freedom" (Neulinger, p. 15), meaning that "no activity is inherently not a leisure activity" (p. 35) as long as the individual perceives it as such. In other words, the reality of leisure occurs through a structuring mental process involving perceptions of freedom and intrinsic motivation. Indicative of differences within disciplines, other psychological theories are more complex in their ontological approaches, such as social psychology (e.g., Kleiber, Walker, & Mannell, 2011).

The *linguistic perspective* rejects the existence of leisure as a "thing" at all, whether as a physical object (e.g., free time behavior) or as a psychological construct (e.g., perceived leisure). Language is not a mirror that reflects reality. Language actually creates reality. In the simplest of terms, language does not have a direct, one-to-one correspondence to things that allows words like tree, dog, man, woman, democracy, work, and leisure to be matched with their counterparts in the real world. Words are thus cultural tools that enable people to organize their lives for a variety of purposes, such as survival, relationships, and self-expression. As such, one word does *not* fit all, meaning that language and the reality it describes are dependent on time and place. Definitions do not provide true, eternal, and universal descriptions of what exists. They instead consist of symbols that are useful for satisfying our needs and desires through acts of communication. Blackshaw (2010) suggested that rather than attempt to discover what leisure *really* is or what the purposes of leisure *really* are, we should explore how leisure is *used* in association with other words (e.g., work, class, gender, freedom, authenticity, credibility, creativity, happiness) in different contexts and the effects it has on people's lives. For instance, dissatisfied with modern linguistic frameworks of leisure built around freedom and self-determination, Rojek's (2009) "labour of leisure" creatively reinvents leisure with words more typically associated with work—competence, relevance, and credibility—offering a fresh vantage on leisure and its possibilities. The ontological challenge is to "make the application of any of our conceptual schema clear by thinking it through" (Blackshaw, p. xi), including how it matters in our lives. Studies of leisure, then, should be ontologically explicit, because, as Socrates suggested, figuring out where to go and how to get there are improbable without first some sense of where one is coming from.

EPISTEMOLOGY

Closely related to ontology is epistemology, which is concerned with the question of knowledge and methods of acquiring it. With variations in between, epistemology of leisure can be roughly divided between *positivism* and *interpretivism*. Positivism holds that genuine knowledge is attained through the scientific process of empirical observation, hypothesis testing, and theory building. A pioneer in the social psychology of leisure, Iso-Ahola's (1980) claim that research (the search for genuine knowledge) "is *only* possible in the stages of social empiricism and social analysis" (p. 48) (emphasis added) exemplifies the positivist view. According to interpretivism, people interactively create knowledge through language, leaving what we know open to diverse explanations depending on when and where they culturally occur. Hemingway (1995) delivered a critique of positivism and defense of interpretivism, arguing that questions about meaning and value, which positivism rejects in favor of generalizable explanations, are only answerable through interpretive inquiry.

The "positivist-interpretivist" epistemological debate has benefited from assessments tracing its development along the complex contours of leisure studies. Characterizing leisure studies as being in a period of "epistemological challenge" (p. 119), Samdahl (1999) contended that epistemology "may be the most important issue facing leisure studies today" (p. 130). In terms of camps, the consensus is that the positivist tradition is, with exceptions, mostly characteristic of North American research (Coalter, 1999; Rojek, 2009). Conversely, interpretivist approaches, such as cultural studies, are more prevalent in Great Britain, other parts of Europe, and Australasia. Seeing the debate as an unproductive standoff, Henderson (2011) recommended getting past dichotomies to "post-positivism," where methods from both perspectives could be pragmatically suited to the particular problem or issue, rather than driven by ideology (Kelly, 1994) or technique (Hemingway, 1995).

While others might disagree, the steady stream of dialogue on epistemology suggests progress and perhaps even modest appreciation for diverse approaches to understanding the complexity of leisure. Among other possibilities, the next phase of the philosophical dialogue might be linking epistemology more systematically to ontology, ethics, and politics, similar to Rojek's (2005) "action theory" and Aitchison's (2003) social-cultural analysis of gender.

ETHICS

Ontology and epistemology ask, "Where am I?" and "How do I know?" Ethics asks, "What should I do and what kind of person should I be?" Socrates shifted the path of philosophy from the first two questions to the question of ethics or how to live, to which he answered a life of virtue. Since then ethics has taken a number of well-traveled routes in philosophy. Although less clearly marked, the path of ethics in leisure studies contains enough traffic to form impressions.

In a paper presented at the 1996 Leisure Studies Association Conference, McNamee and Brackenridge (2006) offered an assessment of ethics in leisure studies that remains mostly unchanged. They concluded, "dependent upon how the term 'ethics' was interpreted almost everything and almost nothing might be included in leisure research" (p. 45). By "everything," they meant that the field of leisure studies abounds with descriptions of ethical problems and dilemmas related to people, policies, and practices, such as abuse, cheating, and inequity. The ubiquity of ethics in leisure studies is indeed as evident today as it was for McNamee and Brackenridge roughly two decades ago.

On the other hand, McNamee and Brackenridge (2006) noted that ethics as *moral philosophy*, meaning "the systematic conceptual enquiry of questions regarding how we ought to live our lives" (p. 45) had little to offer leisure studies. Philosopher Sarah Broadie (2006) confirmed the shortage, observing, "there has been practically no modern ethical discussion of leisure" (p. 357). Yet, while the portion of moral philosophy on the plate of leisure studies has been meager, it is not altogether bare.

Ethics manifests in two ways in leisure studies: theoretical and applied. Theoretical ethics deals with more abstract questions (e.g., principles of right conduct, elements of good character), while applied ethics addresses particular, concrete matters, such as professional behavior and the actions of people while at leisure. Although virtually all moral philosophy in leisure studies is applied to a degree, some studies are more substantively theoretical. For example, Mason (1999) compared five moral theories, both traditional (utilitarianism, rights theory, and virtue ethics) and modern (narrative ethics and feminist ethics), for their efficacy in assessing the moral effects of the body-shape industries on women. Another excellent example of moral analysis, McNamee, Sheridan, and Buswell (2001) examined the potential of utilitarianism as a professional ethic for guiding policy planning and implementation in public leisure services. First, they historically situated utilitarianism, explaining its roots, development, and varieties. Second, they modeled dialectical reasoning by asking clear questions, followed by rigorous analysis, leading to sound premises that reach a logically valid conclusion. Finally, they recognized that the period and place in which utilitarianism originally developed—late eighteenth century England—are different than our own, requiring adjustments to interpretation and application more suitable for contemporary times.

The majority of the literature on applied ethics addresses principles of right conduct and ethical decision making in a variety of fields, such as outdoor recreation (e.g., Hunt Jr., 1994), sport (e.g., Morgan, 2007), tourism (e.g., Fennell, 2006), and recreation and leisure services (e.g., McLean & Yoder, 2005). Virtue ethics, which concerns the moral character of individuals, has also attracted some interest. Pearce, Filep, and Ross (2011) associated such virtues as wisdom, volunteering (altruism), resilience, and creativity with greater justice and well-being in tourism. Virtue ethics has also been discussed in the literature of therapeutic recreation (Sylvester, 2009).

In sum, leisure studies is paradoxically awash in moral matters and wanting in moral philosophy. Perhaps the tradition of liberalism is one of the reasons behind the contradiction. Classical liberalism espouses maximizing individual freedom in society while leaving how freedom is expressed to each individual so long as the freedom of others is not infringed upon. Fearing state control and "tyranny of the majority," there has been resistance in liberal democracies to installing, much less legislating, particular values and ways of living, leaving it to individual conscience and choice. Of course, values constantly intersect and often collide. And not all ways of living are equally desirable or worthwhile. Moreover, the world, including leisure studies, is replete with "moralizing," which is different than moral philosophy. Whatever the reasons, moral philosophy of leisure needs to catch up with ethics in leisure.

One area where moral philosophy of leisure has an opportunity to gain ground is the burgeoning study of happiness. The field of positive psychology draws heavily from philosophy in theorizing happiness or flourishing (e.g., Seligman, 2002). Emulating positive psychology, happiness and leisure are being addressed (e.g., Nawijn & Veenhoven, 2013) by the incipient field of "positive leisure science" (Freire, 2013; Mock, Mannell, & Guttentag, Chapter 6). Furthermore, two recent works, *How Much is Enough: Money and the Good Life* (Skidelsky & Skidelsky, 2012) and *Happiness and the Good Life* (Martin, 2012), are excellent examples of the application of moral philosophy to leisure.

SOCIAL PHILOSOPHY

Social philosophy broadly includes law, ethics, political philosophy, and the philosophy of social science. Political philosophy, for its part, examines the nature, role, and authority of institutions in all areas of people's lives (Audi, 1999). Because of the vast number of issues, (e.g., power, authority, conflict, rights, culture, economics, and law), social philosophy can seem unfathomable. So I will again limit discussion to some of the major developments in leisure studies.

Karl Marx (1845/1998) famously remarked that "philosophers have only *interpreted* the world, in various ways; the point is to change it" (p. 571). In that spirit, the duo of critique and change has been a major theme in leisure studies, with Marxism serving as one of the main portals of inquiry. Chastising leisure studies for complacency, Clarke and Critcher's (1985) groundbreaking study, *The Devil Makes Work*, embodied Marxist elements, emphasizing the effects of class, consumption, and capitalism on leisure. Feminist theorists have also used Marxism to explore the subordination of women in leisure (e.g., Aitchison, 2003; Deem, 1986).

Indicative of Marxism's widening lens, Bramham (2013) assessed cultural studies from the context of postmodernity, tracing key intersections between Marx and leisure studies in the process. And nearly three decades after his first encounter with Marxism (Rojek, 1985), Rojek (2013) reaffirmed its relevance as "a pivotal resource for the study of leisure" (p. 31).

Marxism has spawned other neo-Marxist forms of critique, the main one being critical theory. As a philosophical movement, critical theory began with a group of intellectuals who formed the Institute for Social Research in 1923, later known as the "Frankfurt School." Fundamentally, critical theory consists of descriptive and normative social inquiry that seeks to lessen domination and enhance freedom (Bohman, 2013). Therefore, critical theory attempts to combine philosophy and social science (Bohman), valuing the contributions of both for increasing what it describes as "emancipation." Philosophers of critical theory have attracted attention in leisure, including Walter Benjamin (Rojek, 1997), Theodor Adorno (Mussell, 2013), and Michel Foucault (Miller, 2013). The work of Jürgen Habermas, the most recent of the major critical theorists, has also been studied. One of most salient aspects of Habermas' prolific social theory is the concept of rationality or ways of reasoning. Two types of rationality, instrumental and communicative, are characteristic of modern society. Typical of technology, administration, and capitalism, instrumental rationality is deliberation on the most efficient means to achieve predetermined ends. Conversely, communicative rationality is the free and open sharing of ideas that takes place in human interaction. Hemingway (1997) and Spracklen (2009, 2013) incisively assessed how instrumental rationality constrains people in their leisure while emancipatory leisure offers opportunities for communicative rationality and genuine freedom.

As an "ideology and social political movement" (Henderson, 2013, p. 26) that aims to critique and change society, feminism is one of the most viable currents of social philosophy in leisure studies (e.g., Aitchison, 2003; Deem, 1987; Parry, Chapter 24). It has been approached from multiple views, including liberal, socialist, radical, and more recently, poststructuralist perspectives (Henderson). Although feminism typically springs from social philosophy due to its roots in the oppression of women, it has also made significant contributions to other areas of philosophy, including ontology and epistemology (e.g., Aitchison, 2003) and ethics (e.g., Henderson, 1997).

While issues of justice pervade leisure studies (Allison, 2000), such as race (e.g., Arai & Kivel, 2009), gender (e.g., Freysinger, Shaw, Henderson, & Bialeschki, 2013), and disability (e.g., Sylvester, 2011), there is surprisingly scant political philosophy to match. The otherwise outstanding collection of essays on social and environmental justice, *Speaking Up and Speaking Out* (Paisley & Dustin, 2011), contains only scatterings of philosophical analysis. There are noteworthy exceptions. Analyses by Veal (1998) on social democracy, Hemingway (1988, 1999) on civility, social capital, and democracy, and Arai and Pedlar (2003) on communitarianism stand out as social philosophy. Nonetheless, similar to the situation described earlier regarding ethics and moral philosophy, leisure studies is laden with descriptive and normative accounts of justice, but offers only a modicum of political philosophy.

POSTMODERNISM

Blackshaw's (2009) pithy description uncovers the nub of postmodernism: "At the heart of postmodernism is the idea that the moral universe is no longer stable, that the areas of agreement about values and ethics have disappeared. There is no such thing as objective truth" (p. 166). Since the days of Socrates, Plato, and Aristotle, philosophy has sought a unitary theory of truth, goodness, and beauty, a coherent, timeless, all-encompassing account of reality. According to postmodernism, the quest has been nothing but a mirage, a fiction. The search for *the* truth about nature, ethics, politics, society, and everything associated with them (e.g., rights, sexuality, freedom, democracy, leisure) is thwarted by methods and foundations that are not objective, independent, and value-free, but instead products of particular cultures. Rather than the record of grand theories making steady progress in the competition to discover the truth in all spheres of life, history is simply a collection of stories about the beliefs of different cultures and societies, none ultimately truer than others. In short, truth is inescapably relative to time and place. As such, there is no essential theory of leisure—no definitive ontology, epistemology, ethics, or social philosophy—"no longer any reliable signposts" (Coalter, 1999, p. 511). Leisure is just a piece of language used in infinite ways and for countless purposes. In Shakespearean terms, "All the world's a stage," a play, in other words, and leisure is one of the players on the world stage. Instead of "truthfulness," postmodern leisure is predicated on "playfulness." The goal of leisure studies, as such, is not to *end* the modern quest by searching deeply enough to one day discover the true meaning and purpose of leisure, but to keep the "game" going by freeing the study of leisure to *endless* possibilities.

A number of theorists have looked at leisure through the kaleidoscope of postmodernism (e.g., Aitchison, 2003; Blackshaw, 2010; Bramham, 2013; Rojek, 1995). Arguably the most profound, prolific, and provocative theorist of leisure, Rojek deserves credit for substantively articulating postmodernism. *Decentring Leisure* (Rojek) was groundbreaking, not only for introducing postmodernism, but also for breaking the ground beneath the concept of leisure, where he endeavored to expose all attempts to discover the "real" leisure as false. Blackshaw's study of modern leisure was another postmodern blow that seemed to stagger the rationality of modern philosophy and the search for—if not foundations—footing in beliefs and values that are more than just aesthetic performances. Undoubtedly, then, postmodernism's impact has been significant. Whether it has actually made the philosophy of leisure irrelevant will be touched upon next in the conclusion.

A TALE OF TWO PHILOSOPHIES

Like any survey, this one is superficial relative to the actual depth, variety, and complexity of philosophy in leisure studies. Nonetheless, even a tour along the surface is sufficient for the sake of gleaning a few impressions.

Most impressively, philosophy is inherent and ubiquitous in leisure studies. Understanding why is not a mystery—values are unavoidable, theories are value-laden (the goal of value-free research is itself a value), assumptions and methods are not self-justifying, everything social involves power and is thus political, and all things can, and should, be questioned. If leisure is anything, therefore, it is radically philosophical—an open, unfinished, ongoing practice. I can confidently state, then, that there is philosophy *in* leisure studies, much of which has occurred in Great Britain and Australasia through social, cultural, and historical studies that are philosophically informed.

On the other hand, countervailing that impression is how little philosophy *of* leisure is evident. While teeming with philosophical issues related to ontology, epistemology, ethics, and social philosophy, leisure studies suffers from a shortage of analyses that employ philosophical method. While I have steered readers to some notable exceptions for both evidentiary and pedagogical purposes, they make the dearth of genuine philosophy all the more obvious.

Interestingly, a burst of books on philosophy of leisure studies appeared in the period between of 1987 and 1991. *The Concept of Leisure in Western Thought* (Dare, Welton, & Coe, 1987) was a history of the influence by major philosophers and schools of philosophy on the idea of leisure. *The Evolution of Leisure* (Goodale & Godbey, 1988) traced the concept of leisure from antiquity to the present. The *Philosophy of Leisure* (Winifred & Cyril, 1989) and *Leisure and Ethics* (Fain, 1991) featured collected essays. Nothing to my knowledge appeared since that period until Karl Spracklen's (2011) *Constructing Leisure: Historical and Philosophical Debates* and a short chapter on the philosophy of leisure by Alex Sager (2013). Philosophy's star that shot across the sky of leisure studies in the late 1980s and early 1990s waned quickly.

Being a part of the scene in the United States during philosophy's brief surge in the 1980s and 1990s, I remember the excitement in the humanities sessions at the Leisure Research Symposium. Philosophy and the rest of the humanities started to languish, however, around the time the Symposium switched from organizing sessions by disciplines to thematic tracks. While a structural change may have dampened philosophy, however, it did not cause its decline. In all likelihood, multiple factors explain the debilitated state of the philosophy of leisure. Positivism is likely one reason for its decline, especially where it marginalizes ethics and social philosophy. But philosophy of leisure thrived for a short period when positivism was absolute lord in leisure studies. So there must be more behind the story. I suspect one of the main reasons has been the rise of careerism and specializations in the recreation and leisure industry, such as tourism, sport management, recreational therapy, and administration in general. For instance, *The Council on Accreditation of Parks, Recreation, Tourism, and Related Professions* (2013) refers to philosophy only as it relates to *professional* foundations. Moreover, the word *leisure* appears nowhere in the document. Since most students come seeking careers in the manifold leisure industry, it not surprising that leisure studies in general and philosophy in particular are, if not sidelined, mostly sideshows.

Furthermore, since postmodernism concludes that the search for "reliable signposts" (Coalter, 1999, p. 511) is futile, one might wonder why bother with philosophy at all, resorting instead to "free play." When "free play," however, lacks rules, principles, values—"signposts"—it risks becoming a "free for all" where anything goes. Although postmodernism is criticized as self-refuting by asserting as fundamentally true that there is no fundamental truth, it has far too much important to say to disregard. Nonetheless, while appreciating the insights and lessons of postmodernism, I do not regard it as representing the end of philosophy, but rather another way of philosophizing or asking questions. Indeed, leisure studies' most prominent postmodern pair, Blackshaw (2010) and Rojek (2009) use *schole*, as foundational a concept as there is in leisure studies, in their recent work. Moreover, Rojek's (2005) action approach to leisure, while borrowing aspects of postmodernism, contains an unmistakable air of Enlightenment philosophy. Perhaps, then, what we should strive for is a bit of balance, something in between absolute signposts and none whatsoever (Harvey, 1990), thus redeeming philosophy.

For the time being, I am optimistic that as long as leisure studies continues, either on its own or as a part of other disciplines, such as cultural studies, philosophy *in* leisure studies will endure. Seeing few philosophers on the scene and even fewer on the horizon, however, I am concerned for the future of the philosophy *of* leisure in leisure studies. As cliché as it may sound, the chances of recovery mostly rest in the hands of students. According to Plato, Socrates remarked, "The unexamined life"—meaning a life without philosophy—"is not worth living." We may not wish to go that far. Yet if a worthy life that is just, free, wise, and flourishing depends on asking intelligent questions and searching for thoughtful answers, then philosophy is paramount. Daring to embrace the questions, "What *are* we doing?" and "Where *are* we going?" philosophy has much to offer leisure studies. And while there is definitely something worth receiving from philosophy *in* leisure studies, there is even more that needs to be given by way of philosophy *to* leisure studies. I urge readers, especially students, both to receive *and* to give.

REFERENCES

Aho, K. (2007). Recovering play: On the relationship between leisure and authenticity. *Janus Head, 10*(1), 217–238.

Aitchison, C. M. (2003). *Gender and leisure: Social and cultural perspectives.*

Allison, M. T. (2000). Leisure, diversity, and social justice. *Journal of Leisure Research, 32*(1), 2–6.

Angeles, P. A. (1981). *Dictionary of philosophy*. New York: Barnes & Noble Books.

Arai, S., & Pedlar, A. (2003). Moving beyond individualism in leisure theory: A critical analysis of concepts of community and social engagement. *Leisure Studies, 22*, 185–222.

Arai, S., & Kivel, B. (2009). Critical race theory and social justice perspectives on whiteness, difference(s) and (anti)racism: A fourth wave of race research in leisure studies. *Journal of Leisure Research, 41*(4). Retrieved from http://js.sagamorepub.com/jlr/article/view/391

Arendt, H. (1998). *The human condition*. Chicago: University of Chicago Press.

Audi, R. (1999). *The Cambridge dictionary of philosophy*. New York: Cambridge University.

Blackshaw, T. (2009). Postmodernism. In T. Blackshaw, & G. Crawford (Eds.), *The Sage dictionary of leisure studies* (p. 166). London: Sage.

Blackshaw, T. (2010). *Leisure*. New York: Routledge.

Bohman, J., "Critical Theory", *The Stanford Encyclopedia of Philosophy* (Spring 2013 Edition), Edward N. Zalta (ed.), Retrieved from http://plato.stanford.edu/archives/spr2013/entries/critical-theory/

Bramham, P. (2013). Theorizing social class, culture and leisure. In T. Blackshaw (Ed.), *The Routledge handbook of leisure studies*, (pp. 103–201). New York: Routledge.

Broadie, S. (2006). Aristotle and contemporary ethics. In R. Kraut (Ed.), *The Blackwell guide to Aristotle's Nicomachean Ethics*, (pp. 342–361). Malden, MA: Blackwell.

Chick, G. (1998). Leisure and culture: Issues for an anthropology of leisure. *Leisure Sciences, 20*(2), 111–133.

Clarke, J., & Critcher, C. (1985). *The devil makes work*. London: Macmillan.

Coalter, F. (1999). Leisure sciences and leisure studies: The challenge of meaning. In E. L. Jackson and T. L. Burton (Eds.), *Leisure studies: Prospects for the twenty-first century* (pp. 507–522). State College, PA: Venture Publishing, Inc.

Cooper, W. E. (1989). What kind of thing is leisure? *Philosophy in Context, 19*, 59–73.

Council on Accreditation of Parks, Recreation, Tourism, and Related Professions. (2013). Retrieved from http://www.nrpa.org/uploadedFiles/nrpa.org/Professional_Development/Accreditation/COAPRT/2013%20COAPRT%20Standards_04-30-13.pdf

Dare, B., Welton, G., & Coe, W. (1987). *Concepts of leisure in western thought: A critical and historical analysis.* Dubuque, IA: Kendall Hunt.

de Grazia, S. (1962). *Of time, work, and leisure*. New York: Twentieth Century Fund.

Deem, R. (1987). *All work and no play: The sociology of women and leisure*. Berkshire, UK: Open University Press.

Fain, G. S. (1991). *Leisure and ethics: Reflections on the philosophy of recreation and leisure*. Reston, VA: American Alliance of Health, Physical Education, Recreation, and Dance.

Fennell, D. (2006). *Tourism ethics*. Clevedon, England: Channel View.

Freire, T. (2013). *Positive leisure science*. Netherlands: Springer.

Freysinger, V. J., Shaw, S. M., Henderson, K. A., & Bialeschki, M. D. (2013). *Leisure, women, and gender*. State College, PA: Venture Publishing, Inc.

Goodale, T., & Godbey, G. (1988). *The evolution of leisure: Historical and philosophical perspectives*. State College, PA: Venture Publishing, Inc.

Harvey, D. (1990). *The condition of postmodernity*. Madden, MA: Blackwell.

Henderson, K. A. (1997). Just recreation: Ethics, gender, and equity. *Journal of Park and Recreation Administration, 15*(2), 16–31.

Henderson, K. A. (2011). Post-positivism and the pragmatics of leisure research. *Leisure Sciences, 33*(4), 341–346.

Henderson, K. A. (2013). Feminist leisure studies: Origins, accomplishments and prospects. In T. Blackshaw (Ed.), *The Routledge handbook of leisure studies*, (pp. 26–39). New York: Routledge.

Hemingway, J. L. (1988). Leisure and civility: Reflections on a Greek ideal. *Leisure Sciences, 22*, 185–202.

Hemingway, J. L. (1995). Leisure studies and interpretive social inquiry. *Leisure Studies, 14*, 32–47.

Hemingway, J. L. (1997). Emancipating leisure: The recovery of freedom in leisure. *Journal of Leisure Research, 28*(1), 27–43.

Hemingway, J. L. (1999). Leisure, social capital, and democratic citizenship. *Journal of Leisure Research, 31*, 150–165.

Hunt Jr., J. (2002). *Ethical issues in experiential education*. Dubuque, IA: Kendall Hunt.

Iso-Ahola, S. (1980). *The social psychology of leisure and recreation*. Dubuque, IW: William C. Brown.

Kelly, J. R. (1994). The symbolic interaction metaphor and leisure. *Leisure Studies, 12*, 81–96.

Kleiber, D. A., Walker, G. J., & Mannell, R. C. (2011). *A social psychology of leisure* (2nd ed.). State College, PA: Venture Publishing, Inc.

Loy, J. W. (1998). An explication of the philosophical premises underlying "leisure and culture: Issues for an anthropology of leisure." *Leisure Sciences, 20*(2), 135–141.

MacIntyre, A. (1984). *After virtue* (2nd ed.). South Bend, IN: University of Notre Dame.

Mason, S. (1999). Beyond flow: The need for a feminist ethics of leisure. *Leisure Studies, 18*(3), 233–248.

Martin, M. W. (2012). *Happiness and the good life*. New York: Oxford.

McLean, D., & Yoder, D. (2005). *Issues in recreation and leisure: Ethical decision making*. Champaign, IL: Human Kinetics.

McNamee, M. J., & Brackenridge, C. (2006). Ethics in leisure: An agenda for research. In E. Kennedy & H. Pussard (Eds.), *Defining the field: 30 years of the Leisure Studies Association*, (pp. 43–56). Eastbourne, UK: Leisure Studies Association.

McNamee, M. J., Sheridan, H., & Buswell, J. (2001). The limits of utilitarianism as a professional ethic in public sector leisure policy and provision *Leisure Studies, 20*(3), 173–197.

Miller, T. (2013). Michel Foucault and leisure. In T. Blackshaw, (Ed.), *The Routledge handbook of leisure studies*. (pp. 99–109). New York: Routledge.

Morgan, W. J. (2007). *Sports ethics* (2nd ed.). Champaign, IL: Human Kinetics.

Mussell, S. (2013). Theodor W. Adorno, the culture industry and leisure. In T. Blackshaw (Ed.), *The Routledge handbook of leisure studies*, (pp. 133–140). New York: Routledge.

Nawijn, J., & Veenhoven, R. (2013). Happiness through leisure. In T. Freire (Ed.), *Positive leisure science* (pp. 193–202). Netherlands: Springer.

Neulinger, J. (1981). *To leisure*. Boston, MA: Allyn & Bacon.

Paisley, K., & Dustin, D. (2011). *Speaking up and speaking out: Working for social and environmental justice through parks, recreation, and leisure*. Champaign, IL: Sagamore.

Pearce, P., Filep, S., & Ross, G. (2011). *Tourists, tourism and the good life*. New York: Routledge.

Pieper, J. (1952). *Leisure, the basis of culture* (Tr. Alexander Dru). New York: Mentor Books.

Rojek, C. (1985). *Capitalism and leisure theory*. London: Tavistock.

Rojek, C. (1995). *Decentring leisure: Rethinking leisure theory*. London: Sage.

Rojek, C. (1997). 'Leisure' in the writings of Walter Benjamin. *Leisure Studies, 16*, 155–171.

Rojek, C. (2005). An outline of the action approach to leisure studies. *Leisure Studies, 24*, 13–25.

Rojek, C. (2009). *The labour of leisure: The culture of free time*. London: Sage.

Rojek, C. (2013). Is Marx still relevant to the study of leisure? *Leisure Studies, 32*(1), 19–33.

Sager, A. (2013). Philosophy of leisure. In T. Blackshaw (Ed.), *Routledge handbook of leisure studies* (pp. 5–14). New York: Routledge.

Samdahl, D. M. (1999). Epistemological and methodological issues in leisure research. In E. L. Jackson & T. L. Burton (Eds.), *Leisure studies* (p. 119–132). State College, PA: Venture Publishing, Inc.

Seligman, M. E. P. (2002). *Authentic happiness: Using the new positive psychology to realize your potential for lasting fulfillment*. New York: Free Press.

Skidelsky, R., & Skidelsky, E. (2012). *How much is enough? Money and the good life*. New York: Other Press.

Spracklen, K. (2009). *The meaning and purpose of leisure: Habermas and leisure at the end of modernity*. Basingstoke, UK: Palgrave Macmillan.

Spracklen, K. (2011). *Constructing leisure: Historical and philosophical debates*. Basingstoke, UK: Palgrave Macmillan.

Spracklen, K. (2013). Leisure at the end of modernity: Jürgen Habermas on the purpose of leisure. In T. Blackwell (Ed.), *The Routledge Handbook of leisure studies* (pp. 141–149). New York: Routledge.

Stocks, J. L. (1939). Leisure. In D. M. Emmet (Ed.), *Reason and intuition, and other essays* (pp. 152–171). London: Oxford University Press.

Sylvester, C. (1999). The classical idea of leisure: Cultural ideal or class prejudice? *Leisure Sciences, 21*(1), 3–16.

Sylvester, C. (2009). A virtue-based approach to therapeutic recreation practice. *Therapeutic Recreation Journal, 43*(3), 9–25.

Sylvester, C. (2011). Therapeutic recreation, the International Classification of Functioning, Disability, and Health, and the Capability Approach. *Therapeutic Recreation Journal, 45*(2) 85–104.

Sylvester, C. (2013). [Review of the book *Of time, work, and leisure*.] *Journal of Leisure Research, 45*(2), 253–258.

Veal, T. (1998). Leisure studies, pluralism and social democracy, *Leisure Studies, 17*, 249–267.

Winnifrith, T., & Barrett, C. (1989). *Philosophy of leisure*. Basingstoke, England: Palgrave Macmillan.

6

Psychology of Leisure, Positive Psychology, and "Psychologizing" Leisure Theory

Steven E. Mock (University of Waterloo), Roger C. Mannell (Professor Emeritus, University of Waterloo), and Daniel Guttentag (University of Waterloo)

Some scholars have lamented what they see as a struggle to demonstrate the relevance of leisure studies (Shaw, 2007), arguing that the inability to do so has led to insularity with leisure researchers speaking only to themselves (Dustin, Schwab, & Bricker, Chapter 40; Samdahl, 1999). These concerns are also applicable to the psychology of leisure in spite of the fact that the leisure domain is increasingly seen as relevant to understanding behavior in other domains of life (e.g., work, family) and that emerging forms of leisure (e.g., gambling, online gaming) are being studied outside of leisure studies by psychologically-oriented researchers. The challenges of relevancy and insularity can also result from the failure to cite work from outside of leisure studies, which in turn decreases the likelihood that leisure research will be cited by other disciplines (Mannell & Kleiber, 2013; Shaw, 2007). There are however excellent opportunities for cross-fertilization.

One such area that not only can contribute to the psychological study of leisure, but also to which the psychology of leisure can contribute, is the *positive psychology movement* (Seligman & Csikzentmihalyi, 2000). Emerging in areas of psychology concerned with human development and mental health, this movement reflects a shift in focus from pathology to the well-being and flourishing of individuals and communities (Kahneman & Krueger, 2006). Importantly, leisure is a domain of human behavior shown to be a critical context for enhancing well-being and development (Iwasaki, 2007; Mannell, 2007). However, explicit interest in this movement in leisure studies, and specifically the psychology of leisure, has only been recent (e.g., Freire, 2013; Kleiber, Walker, & Mannell, 2011; Stebbins, 2006). This chapter will provide an overview of positive psychology, describe fundamental links between positive psychology and the psychology of leisure, examine the extent to which the psychology of leisure can or should be positive psychology, and propose ways leisure studies theories and models can be further developed by applying psychological thinking. It will be argued that psychological approaches including positive psychology can be used to "psychologize" established leisure theories that are in part based on implicit and rather vague emotional, motivational, and cognitive processes that need exposition and systematic study if progress is to be made.

POSITIVE PSYCHOLOGY

Positive psychology is "the study of optimal human functioning" (Linley, Joseph, Harrington & Wood, 2006, p. 8) and focused on understanding well-being, happiness, satisfaction, contentment, flourishing, and thriving (Gable & Haidt, 2005). Often referred to as a "movement" (e.g., Diener, 2009; Gable & Haidt, 2005; Lazarus, 2003; Linley et al., 2006), it began with Martin Seligman's 1998 American Psychological Association presidential address (see Seligman, 1999) and a special issue of *American Psychologist* (Seligman & Csikszentmihalyi, 2000). Positive psychology has since become firmly established in the field of psychology (Diener, 2009; Seligman & Csikszentmihalyi, 2000). The *Journals of Happiness Studies* and *Positive Psychology* have since been established, numerous books have been published (e.g., Carr, 2004; Peterson, 2006; Snyder & Lopez, 2009), and regular conferences held (Gable & Haidt, 2005). Research continues to grow and falls into three broad areas originally suggested by Seligman (1998) and Seligman and Csikszentmihalyi (2000) that include subjective positive experience, positive individual traits, and positive groups and institutions.

Subjective positive experience or well-being refers to a person's present happiness, contentment with the past, and optimism regarding the future (Diener & Ryan, 2009; Seligman & Csikszentmihalyi, 2000). Researchers have investigated differences in well-being, happiness, and life satisfaction based on sociodemographic characteristics and culture (e.g., Biswas-Diener, Vittersø, & Diener, 2005; Morrison, Tay, & Diener, 2011), and the benefits of subjective well-being for physical health, social relationships, and workplace experience

(Diener & Ryan, 2009). Theoretical frameworks have been proposed to conceptualize subjective well-being, including: (a) telic theories (i.e., happiness is achieved when goals are met), (b) top-down theories (i.e., the innate tendency towards happiness influences experience), (c) bottom-up theories (i.e., positive and negative experiences sum to total happiness), (d) cognitive theories (i.e., interpretive processes influence how life is experienced), and (e) evolutionary theories (i.e., feelings of well-being evolved to assist species survival) (Diener & Ryan, 2009). Interest has also been shown in positive traits that foster subjective well-being (Peterson & Park, 2009) as well as the ability of social institutions such as the family and schools to promote and sustain them (e.g., Diener & Diener, 2009). With respect to the former, traits such as wisdom, courage, humanity, justice, temperance, and transcendence have been proposed (Seligman, Steen, Park, & Peterson, 2005) and measures developed (Peterson & Seligman, 2004) to investigate their presence in various populations (e.g., Gillham et al., 2011; Linley et al., 2007).

Before moving on to discuss the relevance of positive psychology to the psychological study of leisure, it should be noted that critics have argued that the contributions of humanistic psychology, which emerged in the middle of the last century, have not been adequately recognized (e.g., Robbins, 2008). In fact, interest in the positive aspects of life and how to foster them can be found in the work of psychologists such as William James, Carl Rogers, and Abraham Maslow, all advocates of humanistic psychology, who were interested in positive development including "the fully functioning person" and self-actualization (Gable & Haidt, 2005; Linley et al., 2006). Also, dividing human experience into the "positive" and "negative," of which positive psychology has been accused, is seen as problematic. As Lazarus (2003) remarked, "this polarity represents two sides of the same coin of life... you can't separate them and make good sense" (p. 94). Many emotions or traits are not completely good or bad; for example, anger may be positive when people are standing up for themselves against injustice, and high self-esteem may encourage risky or harmful behaviors (Baumeister, Smart, & Boden, 1996).

LEISURE STUDIES, PSYCHOLOGY OF LEISURE, AND POSITIVE PSYCHOLOGY

Although interest in the potential contributions of positive psychology to leisure studies is recent, social, personality, and developmental psychologies have long been influential in leisure studies (Mannell & Kleiber, 2013). The psychology of leisure is concerned with how people choose to fill and structure their free or leisure time with behavior and experience and why they make these choices. It is also concerned with the relationship between what people do in their leisure and what they do in the other domains of their lives, such as work, family, and community. Finally, the psychology of leisure is concerned with the impact of these leisure choices on well-being (Kleiber et al., 2011). In fact, a recent and extensive meta-analysis supports the claim that leisure participation and satisfaction with leisure play an important role in enhancing subjective well-being (Kuykendall, Tay, & Ng, 2015). It is this latter area of theory and research that has a clear link to the positive psychology movement.

In the leisure studies field, much speculation and many unsubstantiated claims have been made for the beneficial psychological effects of leisure. However, starting in the early 1970s, North American and British researchers began promoting and contributing to the psychological study of leisure. Since the early 1990s, interest in the benefits of leisure (Driver & Bruns, 1999), including well-being (Mannell, 2007), as well as health promotion (Godbey, Caldwell, Floyd, & Payne, 2005) and leisure constraints (Jackson, 2005), have strongly influenced psychologically-oriented research in leisure studies. Additionally, the influence of leisure on family and interpersonal relationships, unemployment, work, work-life balance, and sense of community has been studied (see Kleiber et al., 2011). Finally, there has been growth in research on leisure and gender (see Henderson, Hodges, & Kivel, 2002), sexual orientation (e.g., Mock & Hummel, 2012), potentially negative life events such as caregiving (e.g., Dupuis, 2000), disability (e.g., Hutchinson, Loy, Kleiber, & Dattilo, 2003), and cross-cultural similarities and differences (e.g., Walker, Deng, & Dieser, 2005).

Mainstream social psychological theories have been used and, in some cases, these theories have influenced the development of leisure-specific social psychological theories in leisure studies. For example, the theory of intrinsic motivation and self-determination (Ryan & Deci, 2000) has been used extensively and leisure-specific social psychological theories built on ideas of intrinsic motivation include models of leisure experience (Neulinger, 1974) and tests of them (see Iso-Ahola, 1979). Psychological reactance theory has been used to explain and design tests of the influence of perceived freedom on flow experiences (Csikszentmihalyi, 1990) in leisure activities (Mannell & Bradley, 1986) and as the basis for a theory of the substitutability of leisure behavior (Iso-Ahola, 1986). The theory of transactional stress coping (Folkman & Lazarus, 1988) has been used in developing new theory about the role of leisure in coping with stress (Iwasaki, 2003). Also, self-efficacy theory has been used (e.g., Loucks-Atkinson & Mannell, 2007) to extend leisure constraint theory by describing the social cognitive processes underlying the perception and operation of constraints.

Personality psychology also has been used and stable psychological dispositions have been examined as causes of leisure behavior and experience (e.g., Knopf, 1983). Conversely, leisure has been studied as an influence on personality—on identity formation in particular (e.g., Collinson & Hickey, 2007). Leisure researchers have proposed and developed measures of leisure-specific personality traits (Mannell, 1984). For example, playfulness is a personality construct that has been measured reliably in children (Barnett & Kleiber, 1984), adolescents (Staempfli, 2007), and young adults (Barnett, 2007), and in later life playfulness appears to be related to leisure choices characterized by unconventionality and fun (Yarnal, Chick, & Kerstetter, 2008). A related personality trait has been measured with the intrinsic leisure motivation scale (Weissinger & Bandalos, 1995) and people with high scores have been found to be less likely to experience boredom during leisure. Currently, personality approaches are being used to provide insights into new and emerging forms of leisure such as Internet use and online gaming (e.g., Orchard & Fullwood, 2010).

The influence of developmental psychology also is evident in the psychological study of leisure. Age has been shown to be a significant context influencing leisure interests, activities, and experience over the lifespan. Interest in leisure socialization and the influence of lifespan changes on leisure have continued to grow. Greater attention is being given to the role of leisure in childhood and adolescent development (Hutchinson, Baldwin, & Caldwell, 2003) as well as the ways in which leisure activity and experience contribute to adjusting to life events, both predictable (e.g., parenthood, retirement) and unpredictable (e.g., unemployment, widowhood) (Kleiber, 1999).

Clearly, psychologically-oriented researchers have demonstrated that leisure behavior and experience can, under the right conditions, contribute to well-being and personal growth and development. These benefits can be classified according to a number of themes consistent with the idea that leisure can be a positive force in people's lives. Leisure is seen to potentially contribute to well-being by "keeping idle hands and minds busy"; providing pleasure, relaxation, and fun; fostering personal growth; encouraging identity formation and affirmation; and functioning as a coping resource (see Kleiber et al., 2011; Mannell, 2007). However, although much of this theory and research is consistent with the aim of positive psychology to identify factors that foster well-being and personal growth and development, leisure researchers have only recently explicitly suggested that positive psychology can contribute to the study of leisure (e.g., Freire, 2013; Kleiber et al., 2011; Stebbins, 2006). In particular, a recent edited book (Freire, 2013) identifies a number of areas where leisure researchers could incorporate thinking and findings from positive psychology. The editor and contributors discuss the potential role that leisure can play in well-being and quality of life, positive living across the lifespan, and human growth and development. Stebbins (2006, 2013) has also been an advocate of the important role leisure studies can play in promoting the positive psychology agenda. He argues that leisure is uniquely linked with well-being and happiness because leisure activities are more likely to be engaged in due to their desired outcomes of enjoyment, satisfaction, or fulfillment (Stebbins, 2006). Stebbins goes so far as to suggest that "leisure studies is the only, essentially, *happy science*" (p. 20, italics in original), and posits "no other sphere of human activity can be so exclusively characterized as 'upbeat'" (p. 21).

Although this characterization by Stebbins is provocative, it is perhaps a bit extreme. Freire and Caldwell (2013, p. 218–219) note in their assessment of the development of "positive leisure science" that participation in leisure activities can also produce negative outcomes and consequences. Such consequences may be far more significant than the relatively small frustrations that Stebbins (2006) acknowledges. For example, passive forms of leisure (e.g., video games) have been found to be negatively associated with well-being (Leung & Lee, 2005; Holder, Coleman, & Sehn, 2009), and leisure activities like gambling can be detrimental when engaged in at high levels (Korn & Shaffer, 1999). Moreover, even seemingly beneficial forms of leisure, like physical exercise (Paradis, Cooke, Martin, & Hall, 2013), when engaged in at high levels, may have serious detrimental consequences for the work and family domains of life. In fact, there has long been a debate in leisure studies that the assumption that leisure is "good" can create conceptual blinkers that limit researchers' ability to not only identify all the consequences—both positive and negative—of leisure behavior, but also our understanding of the factors and processes that contribute to these various outcomes (e.g., Freire & Caldwell, 2013; Mannell & Loucks-Atkinson, 2005).

However, just as it is valuable to view and study leisure from social, personality, and developmental psychological perspectives, there are a number of interesting and potentially useful ideas in the positive psychology movement that are relevant to the development of leisure theory. We now turn our attention to some examples of leisure theory and the potential insights that positive psychology can contribute.

POTENTIAL CONTRIBUTIONS OF POSITIVE PSYCHOLOGY TO "PSYCHOLOGIZING" LEISURE THEORIES

As suggested above, psychological theory and research can contribute to leisure studies by providing a better understanding of psychological outcomes, potential mechanisms, and explanatory factors that describe motivations for leisure participation and its effects on peoples' lives (Kleiber et al., 2011; Mannell & Kleiber, 2013). Theory and research in positive psychology can extend these contributions, and in the remainder of the chapter, some examples are provided using several major conceptual models developed in leisure studies.

A number of facets of well-being and flourishing have been mentioned thus far, including happiness, life satisfaction, growth, and self-efficacy. Within positive psychology, these diverse components of well-being are often classified as *hedonic* well-being and *eudaimonic* well-being. Hedonic well-being refers to happiness, pleasure, and positive affect (Ryan & Deci, 2001). In contrast, eudaimonic well-being taps into aspects more closely related to meaning and purpose in life, areas such as mastery, positive social relations, and personal growth (Ryan & Deci, 2001; Ryff & Keyes, 1995). Although these two components of well-being may be related to each other, hedonic enjoyment does not necessarily co-occur with pursuit of meaning and purpose in life. For example, the pleasure derived from eating a delicious piece of cheesecake does not necessarily induce a sense of meaning and purpose in life, and the sense of mastery derived from learning how to bake a cheesecake may not always be accompanied by feelings of happiness (e.g., because of frustration procuring the right ingredients, anxiety about cracks forming during baking). Importantly, this typology provides numerous ways of conceptualizing leisure outcomes. Commonly used measures of happiness include the Positive and Negative Affect Schedule (PANAS; Watson, Clark, & Tellegen, 1988) that contrasts positive feelings (e.g., excited, enthusiastic) with negative feelings (e.g., distressed, irritable), and the Satisfaction with Life Scale (Diener, Emmons, Larsen, & Griffin, 1985). Ryff and colleagues have developed measures of eudaimonic well-being that tap into self-acceptance, environmental mastery, positive relations, purpose in life, personal growth, and autonomy (Ryff & Keyes, 1995). Thus, the use of measures developed from principles of positive psychology to assess outcomes in leisure research would help to bridge these two fields.

Although these components and measures help describe and clarify the diverse forms and meanings of well-being, it is important to develop an understanding of the potential role of these psychological factors as mechanisms in explaining the motivation for engaging in leisure and resultant outcomes. For example, Fredrickson's (2001) *broaden-and-build* theory helps explain the potential consequences of positive emotions for cognitive processes, coping, and longer-term well-being. This theory draws on evidence that positive feelings induce breadth of attention and cognitive flexibility (Ashby & Isen, 1999). These cognitive consequences serve as resources for creative problem solving and coping that enhance the likelihood of future positive experiences (Tugade, Fredrickson, & Feldman Barrett, 2004). The implications of Fredrickson's theory are that leisure experiences that create pleasure and positive feelings have consequences extending beyond their immediate rewards. Although Fredrickson's model has been discussed in the leisure literature (e.g., Mitas, Yarnal, Adams, & Ram, 2012), leisure studies researchers have seldom assessed or utilized the full extent of the broaden-and-build model.

Finally, a motivational theory related to a eudaimonic well-being outcome, namely growth, helps explain how people persist in the face of challenge. Although personal growth can be seen as an outcome of learning from setbacks and challenges, growth can also be thought of as a motivational orientation. Dykman (1998) developed a goal orientation inventory that contrasts growth motivation with validation motivation. To be specific, growth-oriented individuals tend to see challenges in life as opportunities for learning, but those with a validation orientation are more likely to view life challenges as a test of self-worth. Dykman developed a growth versus validation goal orientation measure and found that those with a growth orientation had higher levels of task persistence, greater self-actualization, and fewer depressive symptoms over time compared to those with a validation orientation. Thus, goals related to eudaimonic well-being concepts like personal growth also serve as motivational factors with beneficial consequences for well-being and persistence in the face of challenge.

The psychological outcomes, explanatory factors, and motivations discussed above will now be applied to two models developed in leisure studies beginning with the concepts of serious and casual leisure followed by leisure constraints. The serious leisure model describes high investment and personally fulfilling forms of leisure that typically involve long-term learning and socialization processes (Scott, Chapter 19; Stebbins, 1982, 2013). In particular, high investment refers to leisure activities that require perseverance despite obstacles, the notion of a leisure career with stages of achievement, and significant effort to acquire special knowledge, skills, and abilities. The personally fulfilling characteristics of serious leisure include the notion of *durable outcomes* such as social integration and self-actualization through investment in leisure, *unique ethos* of ideals and values shared by fellow participants, and a sense of individual and collective *identity* through leisure participation. The aspects of serious leisure most clearly linked with positive psychology include not only the *durable outcomes* of eudaimonic well-being (e.g., mastery, social integration; Ryff & Keyes, 1995), but the commitment required to persist at serious leisure is likely supported by a growth orientation (Dykman, 1998). Although some research has been conducted connecting serious leisure with positive psychology concepts (e.g., Voigt, Howat, & Brown, 2010), so far, these links are underdeveloped.

Casual leisure activities provide diversionary, pleasurable experiences with play-like qualities and typically relaxing effects (Stebbins, 1997). According to Stebbins' model, types of casual leisure include passive entertainment (i.e., diversion delivered directly to the participant), active entertainment that requires simple involvement (e.g., cards, puzzles), sociable conversation, and sensory stimulation. Although sometimes seen as a less substantial counterpart to serious leisure (e.g., Stebbins, 1997), the health and restorative effects of casual leisure have been recognized. For example, casual leisure participation can enhance mood and, subsequently, health by providing a buffer against stressful events, enhancing coping efforts and helping to maintain or re-establish social ties (Hutchinson & Kleiber, 2005). Thus, the clearest links between casual leisure and positive psychology are in the domain of hedonic well-being as a psychological outcome. To extend Hutchinson and Kleiber's ideas of the health and well-being benefits of casual leisure, Fredrickson's (2001) broaden-and-build model suggests a potential mechanism for explaining these effects. Although such conceptual links have been suggested in the leisure studies literature (e.g., Chun, Lee, Kim, & Heo, 2012; Stenseng, Rise, & Kraft, 2011), little empirical work has been done to test the effect of casual leisure participation on positive mood induction and, subsequently, breadth of attention and cognitive flexibility.

Ideas from positive psychology also have relevance for the leisure constraints model that posits intrapersonal (e.g., personality, attitudes, perceptions), interpersonal (e.g., social facilitation or sanctions), and structural (e.g., time pressure, competing commitments) factors frustrate or hinder leisure participation (Godbey, Crawford, & Shen, 2010; Schneider, Chapter 18). An important extension of this model is the notion of a *constraints negotiation* process; namely, that people respond and manage potential constraints by coping and adapting (Jackson, Crawford, & Godbey, 1993). For example, Hubbard and Mannell (2001) found in a study of employees' use of workplace fitness facilities that greater motivation to participate as well as perceived constraints appeared to initiate a constraints negotiation process that was positively associated with greater participation. As suggested with the serious leisure model, an application of the positive psychology goal orientation approach (i.e., growth versus validation orientation) would be well-suited to research on leisure constraints and negotiation, suggesting that those with a growth orientation may be more likely to engage in leisure constraints negotiation than those with a validation orientation. Consequently, the effort expended in constraints negotiation and potential learning experiences through that process may lead to eudaimonic well-being outcomes such as environmental mastery, personal growth, and positive relations with others.

CONCLUSION

In many respects, the study of leisure, particularly the psychological perspective, has been the study of positive psychology in that this research is focused on uncovering the ways leisure participation contributes to well-being, happiness, meaning and purpose in life, and human flourishing. Thus, the positive psychology movement offers leisure studies researchers a prime opportunity to connect with theory and research in other fields, namely, psychology and other disciplines with an interest in well-being (e.g., sociology, economics, human geography). In this chapter, we have outlined some potential points of intersection between leisure studies, the psychology of leisure and positive psychology by highlighting the potential contributions of research and theory on positive psychology outcomes, explanatory factors, and motivations to the further development of leisure studies models. Leisure scholars are beginning to draw on these theories and measures, and psychological researchers are also recognizing the potential contributions of leisure to a better understanding of positive psychology (e.g., Newman, Tay, & Diener, 2013). However, much work remains to be done to strengthen these interdisciplinary links and thus counter perceptions that leisure research is not relevant (Shaw, 2007) and leisure researchers are speaking only to themselves (Samdahl, 1999).

REFERENCES

Ashby, F. G., & Isen, A. M. (1999). A neuropsychological theory of positive affect and its influence on cognition. *Psychological Review, 106*, 529–550.

Barnett, L. A. (2007). The nature of playfulness in young adults. *Personality and Individual Differences, 43*, 949–958.

Barnett, L. A., & Kleiber, D. A. (1984). Playfulness and the early play environment. *The Journal of Genetic Psychology, 144*, 153–164.

Baumeister, R. F., Smart, L., & Boden, J. M. (1996). Relation of threatened egotism to violence and aggression: The dark side of high self-esteem. *Psychological Review, 103*, 5–33.

Biswas-Diener, R., Vittersø, J., & Diener, E. (2005). Most people are pretty happy, but there is cultural variation: The Inughuit, the Amish, and the Maasai. *Journal of Happiness Studies, 6*, 205–226.

Carr, A. (2004). *Positive Psychology: The science of happiness and human strengths*. New York: Brunner-Routledge.

Chun, S., Lee, Y., Kim, B., & Heo, J. (2012). The contribution of leisure participation and leisure satisfaction to stress-related growth. *Leisure Sciences, 34*, 436–449.

Collinson, J. A., & Hickey, J. (2007). "Working out" identity: Distance runners and the management of disrupted identity. *Leisure Studies, 26*, 381–398.

Csikszentmihalyi, M. (1990). *Flow: The psychology of optimal experience*. New York, NY: Harper Perennial.

Diener, E. (2009). Positive psychology: Past, present, and future. In C. R. Snyder & S. J. Lopez (Eds.), *Oxford handbook of positive psychology* (2nd ed) (pp. 7–11). Toronto: Oxford University Press.

Diener, E., & Diener, C. (2009). Forward. In R. Gilman, E. S. Huebner, & M. J. Furlong (Eds.), *Handbook of positive psychology in schools* (pp. xi–xii). New York: Routledge.

Diener, E. D., Emmons, R. A., Larsen, R. J., & Griffin, S. (1985). The satisfaction with life scale. *Journal of Personality Assessment, 49*, 71–75.

Diener, E., & Ryan, K. (2009). Subjective well-being: A general overview. *South African Journal of Psychology, 39*, 391–406.

Driver, B. L., & Bruns, D. H. (1999). Concepts and uses of the benefits approach to leisure. In E. L. Jackson and T. L. Burton (Eds.), *Leisure studies: Prospects for the twenty-first century* (pp. 349–369). State College, PA: Venture Publishing, Inc.

Dupuis, S. L. (2000). Institution-based caregiving as a container for leisure. *Leisure Sciences, 22*, 259–280.

Dykman, B. M. (1998). Integrating cognitive and motivational factors in depression: Initial tests of a goal-orientation approach. *Journal of Personality and Social Psychology, 74*, 139.

Folkman, S., & Lazarus, R. S. (1988). Coping as a mediator of emotion. *Journal of Personality and Social Psychology, 54*, 466–475.

Fredrickson, B. L. (2001). The role of positive emotions in positive psychology: The broaden-and-build theory of positive emotions. *American Psychologist, 56*, 218–226.

Freire, T. (Ed.). (2013). *Positive leisure science: From subjective experience to social contexts*. New York: Springer.

Freire, T., & Caldwell, L. (2013). Afterthoughts on leisure and future research directions. In T. Freire (Ed.), *Positive leisure science: From subjective experience to social contexts* (pp. 213–223). New York: Springer.

Gable, S. L., & Haidt, J. (2005). What (and why) is positive psychology? *Review of General Psychology, 9*, 103.

Gillham, J., Adams-Deutsch, Z., Werner, J., Reivich, K., Coulter-Heindl, V., Linkins, M., Winder, B., Peterson, C., Park, N., Abenavoli, R., Contero, A., & Seligman, M. E. P. (2011). Character strengths predict subjective well-being during adolescence. *The Journal of Positive Psychology, 6*, 31–44.

Godbey, G. C., Caldwell, L. L., Floyd, M., & Payne, L. L. (2005). Contributions of leisure studies and recreation and park management research to the active living agenda. *American Journal of Preventive Medicine, 28*, 150–158.

Godbey, G. C., Crawford, D. W., & Shen, X. Y. S. (2010). Assessing hierarchical leisure constraints theory after two decades. *Journal of Leisure Research, 42*, 111–134.

Henderson, K. A., Hodges, S., & Kivel, B. D. (2002). Context and dialogue in research on women and leisure. *Journal of Leisure Research, 34*, 253–271.

Holder, M. D., Coleman, B., & Sehn, Z. L. (2009). The contribution of active and passive leisure to children's well-being. *Journal of Health Psychology, 14*, 378–386.

Hubbard, J., & Mannell, R. C. (2001). Testing competing models of the leisure constraint negotiation process in a corporate employee recreation setting. *Leisure Sciences, 23*, 145–163.

Hutchinson, S. L., Baldwin, C. K., & Caldwell, L. L. (2003). Differentiating parent practices related to adolescent behavior in the free time context. *Journal of Leisure Research, 35*, 396–422.

Hutchinson, S. L., Loy, D. P., Kleiber, D. A., & Dattilo, J. (2003). Leisure as a coping resource: Variations in coping with traumatic injury and illness. *Leisure Sciences, 25*, 143–161.

Hutchinson, S. L., & Kleiber, D. A. (2005). Gifts of the ordinary: Casual leisure's contributions to health and well-being. *World Leisure Journal, 47*(3), 2–16.

Iso-Ahola, S. E. (1979). Some social psychological determinants of perceptions of leisure: Preliminary evidence. *Leisure Sciences, 2*, 305–314.

Iso-Ahola, S. E. (1986). A theory of substitutability of leisure behavior. *Leisure Sciences, 8*, 367–389.

Iwasaki, Y. (2003). The impact of leisure coping beliefs and strategies on adaptive outcomes. *Leisure Studies, 22*, 93–108.

Iwasaki, Y. (2007). Leisure and quality of life in an international and multicultural context: What are major pathways linking leisure to quality of life? *Social Indicators Research, 82*, 233–264.

Jackson, E. L. (2005). Leisure constraints research: Overview of a developing theme in leisure studies. In E. L. Jackson (Ed.), *Constraints to leisure* (pp. 3–19). State College, PA: Venture Publishing, Inc.

Jackson, E. L., Crawford, D. W., & Godbey, G. (1993). Negotiation of leisure constraints. *Leisure Sciences, 15*, 1–11.

Kahneman, D., & Krueger, A. B. (2006). Developments in the measurement of subjective well-being. *The Journal of Economic Perspectives, 20*, 3–24.

Kleiber, D. A. (1999). *Leisure experience and human development: A dialectical interpretation*. New York: Basic Books.

Kleiber, D. A., Walker, G. J., & Mannell, R. C. (2011). *A social psychology of leisure* (2nd ed). State College, PA: Venture Publishing, Inc.

Knopf, R. C. (1983). Recreational needs and behavior in natural settings. In I. Altman & J. F. Wohlwill (Eds.), *Behavior and the natural environment* (pp. 205–240). New York: Plenum.

Korn, D. A., & Shaffer, H. J. (1999). Gambling and the health of the public: Adopting a public health perspective. *Journal of Gambling Studies, 15*, 289–365.

Kuykendall, L., Tay, L., & Ng, V. (2015). Leisure engagement and subjective well-being: A meta-analysis. *Psychological Bulletin, 141*, 364–403.

Lazarus, R. S. (2003). Does the positive psychology movement have legs? *Psychological Inquiry, 14*, 93–109.

Leung, L., & Lee, P. S. (2005). Multiple determinants of life quality: The roles of Internet activities, use of new media, social support, and leisure activities. *Telematics and Informatics, 22*, 161–180.

Linley, P. A., Joseph, S., Harrington, S., & Wood, A. M. (2006). Positive psychology: Past, present, and (possible) future. *The Journal of Positive Psychology, 1*, 3–16.

Linley, P. A., Maltby, J., Wood, A. M., Joseph, S., Harrington, S., Peterson, C., Park, N., & Seligman, M. E. P. (2007). Character strengths in the United Kingdom: The VIA inventory of strengths. *Personality and Individual Differences, 43*, 341–351.

Loucks-Atkinson, A., & Mannell, R. C. (2007). Role of self-efficacy in the constraints negotiation process: The case of individuals with fibromyalgia syndrome. *Leisure Sciences, 29*, 19–36.

Mannell, R. C. (1984). Personality in leisure theory: The self-as-entertainment construct. *Loisir et Société/Society and Leisure, 7*, 229–242.

Mannell, R. C. (2007). Leisure, health and well-being. *World Leisure Journal, 49*, 114–128.

Mannell, R. C., & Bradley, W. (1986). Does greater freedom always lead to greater leisure? Testing a person x environment model of freedom and leisure. *Journal of Leisure Research, 18*, 215–230.

Mannell, R. C., & Kleiber, D. A. (2013). Psychology of leisure. In T. Blackshaw (Ed.), *The Routledge International handbook of leisure studies* (pp. 40–51). London, UK: Taylor and Francis.

Mannell, R. C., & Loucks-Atkinson, A. (2005). Why don't people do what's "good" for them? Cross-fertilization among the psychologies of nonparticipation in leisure, health, and exercise behaviors. In E. L. Jackson (Ed.), *Constraints to leisure* (pp. 221–232). State College, PA: Venture Publishing, Inc.

Mitas, O., Yarnal, C., Adams, R., & Ram, N. (2012). Taking a "peak" at leisure travelers' positive emotions. *Leisure Sciences, 34*(2), 115–135.

Mock, S. E., & Hummel, E. M. (2012). Sexual minority adults at a seasonal home campground: An examination of common, unique, and diverse leisure motivations. *Leisure Sciences, 34*, 155–171.

Morrison, M., Tay, L., & Diener, E. (2011). Subjective well-being and national satisfaction findings from a worldwide survey. *Psychological Science, 22*, 166–171.

Neulinger, J. (1974). *The psychology of leisure*. Springfield, IL: Charles C Thomas.

Newman, D. B., Tay, L., & Diener, E. (2014). Leisure and subjective well-being: A model of psychological mechanisms as mediating factors. *Journal of Happiness Studies, 15*, 555–578.

Orchard, L. J., & Fullwood, C. (2010). Current perspectives on personality and Internet use. *Social Science Computer Review, 28*, 155–169.

Paradis, K. F., Cooke, L. M., Martin, L. J., & Hall, C. R. (2013). Too much of a good thing? Examining the relationship between passion for exercise and exercise dependence. *Psychology of Sport and Exercise, 14*, 493–500.

Peterson, C. (2006). *A primer in positive psychology*. Toronto: Oxford University Press.

Peterson, C., & Park, N. (2009). Classifying and measuring strengths of character. In C. R. Snyder & S. J. Lopez (Eds.), *Oxford handbook of positive psychology* (2nd ed) (pp. 25–33). Toronto: Oxford University Press.

Peterson, C., & Seligman, M. E. P. (2004). *Character strengths and virtues: A handbook and classification*. Washington, DC: American Psychological Association.

Robbins, B. D. (2008). What is the good life? Positive psychology and the renaissance of humanistic psychology. *The Humanistic Psychologist, 36*, 96–112.

Ryan, R., & Deci, E. (2000). Self-determination theory and the facilitation of intrinsic motivation, social development, and well-being. *American Psychologist, 55*, 68–78.

Ryan, R. M., & Deci, E. L. (2001). On happiness and human potentials: A review of research on hedonic and eudaimonic well-being. *Annual Review of Psychology, 52*, 141–166.

Ryff, C. D., & Keyes, C. L. M. (1995). The structure of psychological well-being revisited. *Journal of Personality and Social Psychology, 69*, 719.

Samdahl, D. M. (1999). Speaking only to ourselves? Citation analysis of Journal of Leisure Research and Leisure Sciences. *Journal of Leisure Research, 31*, 171–180.

Seligman, M. E. P. (1998). *Positive psychology network concept paper*. Retrieved from http://www.ppc.sas.upenn.edu/ppgrant.htm.

Seligman, M. E. P. (1999). The president's address. *American Psychologist, 54*, 559–562.

Seligman, M. E. P., & Csikszentmihalyi, M. (2000). Positive psychology: An introduction. *American Psychologist, 55*, 5–14.

Seligman, M. E. P., Steen, T. A., Park, N., & Peterson, C. (2005). Positive psychology progress: Empirical validation of interventions. *American Psychologist, 60*, 410.

Shaw, S. M. (2007). Re-framing questions: Assessing the significance of leisure. *World Leisure, 49*, 59–68.

Snyder, C. R., & Lopez, S. J. (Eds.). (2009). *Oxford handbook of positive psychology* (2nd ed.). Toronto: Oxford University Press.

Staempfli, M. B. (2007). Adolescent playfulness, stress perception, coping and well being. *Journal of Leisure Research, 39*, 393–412.

Stebbins, R. A. (1982). Serious leisure: A conceptual statement. *Pacific Sociological Review, 25*, 251–272.

Stebbins, R. A. (1997). Casual leisure: A conceptual statement. *Leisure Studies, 16*, 17–25.

Stebbins, R. A. (2006). Leisure studies: The happy science. *Leisure Studies Association Newsletter, 75*, 20–22.

Stebbins, R. A. (2013). Research and theory on positiveness in the social sciences: The central role of leisure. In T. Freire (Ed.), *Positive leisure science: From subjective experience to social contexts* (pp. 3–19). New York: Springer.

Stenseng, F., Rise, J., & Kraft, P. (2011). The dark side of leisure: Obsessive passion and its covariates and outcomes. *Leisure Studies, 30*, 49–62.

Tugade, M. M., Fredrickson, B. L., & Feldman Barrett, L. (2004). Psychological resilience and positive emotional granularity: Examining the benefits of positive emotions on coping and health. *Journal of Personality, 72*, 1161–1190.

Voigt, C., Howat, G., & Brown, G. (2010). Hedonic and eudaimonic experiences among wellness tourists: An exploratory enquiry. *Annals of Leisure Research, 13*, 541–562.

Walker, G. J., Deng, J., & Dieser, R. B. (2005). Culture, self-construal, and leisure theory and practice. *Journal of Leisure Research, 37*, 77–99.

Watson, D., Clark, L. A., & Tellegen, A. (1988). Development and validation of brief measures of positive and negative affect: The PANAS scales. *Journal of Personality and Social Psychology, 54*, 1063–1070.

Weissinger, E., & Bandalos, D. L. (1995). Development, reliability and validity of a scale to measure intrinsic motivation in leisure. *Journal of Leisure Research, 27*(4), 379–400.

Wiegand, D. M., & Geller, E. S. (2005). Connecting positive psychology and organizational behavior management: Achievement motivation and the power of positive reinforcement. *Journal of Organizational Behavior Management, 24*, 3–25.

Yarnal, C. M., Chick, G., & Kerstetter, D. L. (2008). "I did not have time to play growing up… so this is my play time. It's the best thing I have ever done for myself": What is play to older women? *Leisure Sciences, 30*, 235–252.

7

Rethinking Sociological Leisure Studies for the Twenty-First Century

Tony Blackshaw (Sheffield Hallam University)

It seems to me unlikely that any important sociological theories of leisure will ever be written again. Leisure "Theory" is dead. Theory, that is to say, within the sense of theory as the "founding fathers" of sociology understood it. In the future, I can imagine journal articles and even the odd book still devoted to sociological leisure "Theory." But these will invariably represent flights into the past, package tours to much-loved Arcadias where sociology used to have some especially firm footholds: functionalism, Marxism, symbolic interactionism, feminism, and so on. As is usually the case at properly consoling funerals, those writing these articles or books will not dream of dwelling on the deceased's bad points, because they will no doubt be so carried away by the eulogies that got them thinking about the resurrection in the first place—a bit of nostalgia; those were the days. But nobody should be fooled by what people will be saying at these wakes. Make no mistake about it, leisure "Theory" is dead.

Personally, I see no reason to lament the passing of leisure "Theory"—the talent wasted on theorizing contemporary sociological understandings of leisure should be used for the more urgent task of theorizing *contemporary* leisure. It is, however, worthwhile enquiring why leisure "Theory" has become redundant; it may help us to both understand more closely the sociology of leisure's historical situation and begin to map out for it an alternative future. It is to these two tasks that this chapter is in the main devoted.

The first part of the chapter argues that the beginning of the end of orthodox sociological "Theory" coincided, roughly speaking, with the rise of Chris Rojek's star in leisure studies. I subsequently argue that there is a crisis in leisure theory that has its roots in the central tenets of sociology. Taking its cue from Jacques Rancière's (2004) classic study *The Philosopher and His Poor* the chapter develops the argument that if social inequality was once upon a time the fundamental issue in the discursive formation known as the sociology of leisure, today it urgently needs an alternative cognitive framework for thinking outside this paradigm. In order to substantiate this critique, the discussion considers two leading theoretical perspectives in leisure studies: the sociology of Pierre Bourdieu and feminist sociology, and in particular the emphasis currently placed on the idea of intersectionality. It is argued thereafter that sociologists of leisure, and others who carry out research in leisure studies, generally have a particular activity in view: methodological uniformity of both the employment of research methods and the philosophical study of how, in practice, researchers go about their business. But there are some different "rules of method" when we engage in thinking sociologically after "Theory." As is demonstrated in the final part of the chapter, analysis of this second kind of activity does not rely on the epistemological frameworks and ontological assumptions generally used to make sense of leisure. Instead it develops its own new "rules of method" which turn out to be radical, because they are not "rules of method" at all.

The End of Sociological Leisure "Theory"

If I were asked to mark the moment when the decline of "Theory" became inevitable in leisure studies, by identifying the work of one sociologist, I would choose Chris Rojek. Of the key sociologists in leisure studies, Rojek is an important standard bearer. In books such as *Decentring Leisure* (1995) and *The Labour of Leisure* (2009), we are presented with a sociology that registers no allegiances to "isms" or any other signature gestures. His work offers us not a "Theorist's" world of leisure but one in whose sociological evidence we can believe. As both of these books demonstrate, increasingly from the last three decades of the twentieth century, in pursuing their leisure interests, fewer and fewer individuals have been able to believe in the value of the social roles assigned to them at birth. If, in Rojek's mid-nineties mind, the postmodern imagination emerged as a new way to think and understand how we engage with leisure in modernity, by the end of the 2000s he was just as persuasively arguing that what we call "leisure" today is actually a form of social and cultural life in which "work" and "leisure" often intersect and mutually inform one another. What Rojek's work demonstrates more than anybody else's is that theory continues to prosper when it challenges the intellectual attitude that once defined "Theory." This is one good answer to our original question about the decline of "Theory" in leisure studies.

This answer implies, however, that sociological leisure studies are in rude health. But they are not. To understand why, we must consider a second answer. The discursive formation known as sociological leisure studies is actually in a quiet but deep state of crisis. But what do I mean by crisis? To squeeze together two definitions, the crisis of sociological leisure studies can be understood as a result of a 'legitimation crisis' (Habermas, 1975), reflected in the erosion of the explanatory basis of previously important theoretical perspectives in sociology, which has led to an 'organic crisis' of authority that 'consists precisely in the fact that the old is dying and the new cannot be born; in this interregnum a great variety of morbid symptoms appear' (Gramsci, 1971, p. 276). What sort of crisis is this? My argument is that the situation in sociological leisure studies is part of an intellectual crisis that is mirrored in all areas of leisure studies, which has in no uncertain terms precipitated the decline in the study of leisure in universities across the globe. But what makes this crisis even more serious is that it has been presaged by a 'business as usual' attitude and the deepening of present trends. This crisis presents challenges that deliver some heavy blows to this discursive formation, which despite being relatively new feels more like an aging boxer staggering with exhaustion in the final round of a championship fight, who still thinks he has the right punches and combinations to win, but cannot see that this is more illusion than hit. These challenges bring into question the tacit, invariant assumption of sociology that in order to understand people's leisure choices we need to put their social inequality at the forefront of our analyses. In other words, sociology, in leisure studies, as elsewhere, is the very thought of social inequality (Rancière, 2004). This is the paradox that pervades the discursive formation, for it is in the idea of social inequality that sociology assumes the "truth" about our leisure is located. It is also a paradox of this crisis that its roots are to be found in the circumstances that originally gave rise to sociological leisure studies.

As is well known, in the 1970s the study of leisure was led away from its uncritical comfort zone by bright young academics from disciplines as diverse as urban studies, geography, history, social work, and especially sociology, attracted to a new field of study whose subject burned brightly in their own free time, and who in due course not only produced a new academic discipline, but also a paradigm shift by bringing attention to social inequality as the fundamental issue in the study of leisure. The emergence of this critical sociology of leisure coincided with the collapse of the "positive" values that had hitherto dominated sociology more generally and the concomitant rise in the concern with the study of social class, gender, and "racial" inequalities in cultural studies. In leisure studies, Clarke and Critcher's (1985) seminal book *The Devil Makes Work* is the classic example that captures this moment. The circumstance that social inequality entered sociological debates in leisure studies, at a time of some radical confrontations with these arrangements of social stratification, was to have consequences for the study of leisure for a long time to come.

Yet, at the beginning of the twenty-first century, the crisis in the sociology of leisure has its roots in the aftermath of this paradigm shift. Although the necessity of bringing to attention social inequality in constraining the freedom and reducing the ability of some people to take up "leisure" on their own terms was important 30 or 40 years ago, it has by now run its course and is in need of an alternative vision. Why? By continuing to pose social inequality—particularly though not exclusively of class, of gender, and of "race"—as the primary "fact" that needs to be explained with regard to people's leisure, sociology has ended up explaining its *necessity* (Rancière, 2004). In other words, we have a situation in which the social inequality of certain social groups is presumed and this means that there is a fundamental gap in our understanding of their leisure lives.

This might appear a somewhat scandalous proposition; it is meant to be. As such, it demands a critical discussion of some of the dominant standpoints in the sociology of leisure. Let us consider two. On one hand there is the massive legacy of Bourdieu, the social theorist of *Distinction* (Bourdieu, 1984), whose theories and concepts are some of the most regularly and uncritically applied in leisure studies; on the other is feminist sociology, and in particular its foregrounding of intersectionality in the current theoretical landscape in leisure studies (Henderson, 2013; Watson & Scraton, 2013).

THE SOCIOLOGISTS OF LEISURE AND THEIR "POOR"[1]

Let us begin with Bourdieu. There is a paradox at the heart of his sociology: although it is extremely critical of social inequality, its subjects have no social role in it other than to perform this social inequality as they endure it as their life. As Rancière explains, this leads to "a theory of the *necessary* misrecognition of social relations as the very mechanism of their reproduction" (Swenson, 2006, p. 642). This tautology is important for our purposes since it clearly identifies the limits of Bourdieu's sociology for understanding leisure. Not only is social inequality built into the deep structure of Bourdieu's sociology, but it also performs the brilliant feat of making the "poor" feel ennobled while confirming their extirpation from the world of leisure choices. It is not so much that Bourdieu's sociology places too much emphasis on social structure at the expense of social agency, rather that it does something more fundamental: it denies social actors the leisure to think for themselves and patronizes them by speaking on their behalf. It is not that Bourdieu's respect for the "poor" is not genuine (see for example Bourdieu's magnus opus *The Weight of the World;* Bourdieu et al., 1999), it is simply the case that his insights are not convincingly constituted of the different situations in which social inequality occurs. In a nutshell, the great sociologist of reflexivity thinks that the "poor" do not have any time for leisure and presumes that those who do of being incapable of having any—well, any that does not incite the kind of disapproving, puritanical look made corporate by the Frankfurt School, whose ghost lives on in Bourdieu's sociology—grimly looking down and shaking its mocking head at those among the "poor" "aspiring to reranking [*reclassement*] through [their] feats in the great simile industry of the new petty bourgeoisie: the manufacture of junk jewelry or sale of symbolic services; the commerce of youth leaders, marriage counsellors, sex therapists, advertising executives, or dieticians determined to create within people the symbolic need necessary for the enlargement of their market, hence for the reconquest of their inheritance" (Rancière, 2004, pp. 192–193).

Another version of this theme is replayed in the theoretical perspective and methodology known as "intersectionality" some feminists have adopted in leisure studies, which works on the basis that social inequality in leisure is relational and has multiple dimensions. The clear, rational logic of this argument suggests that by taking into account the concept of "class" multiplied by "gender" multiplied by "race" and so on, what is revealed is something even more unequal. A good example of this approach is Watson and Ratna's (2011) research in the UK. Their article claims that intersectionality offers us a way to move beyond static interpretations of compound social inequality by taking into representations of shifting, multilayered social inequalities which are constructed across racialized, classed, and gendered social relations in particular leisure spaces. Yet it offers very little that is concrete or geared to representing the social conditions under scrutiny.

A further shortcoming of this type of sociology, is that it never stops to consider, that in practice, an odd kind of polarizing effect might just take place in these contexts. Rather than amplifying each other, social inequalities multiplied might just cancel each other out. As is well known, Victor Turner (1969) has skillfully explored the relation between liminality and religious pilgrimages in overturning extant conditions of social inequality. Following Turner, leisure scholars have theorized the impact of liminality in leisure contexts where racial, class, and gender differences are temporarily suspended. Here liminality is not just a leveling process but often a time and space when the features that structure everyday life are turned upside down. A better example, however, of this alternative rationalization is my own life history research in northern England (Blackshaw, 2013), which in contrast to "thinking intersectionally" provides a rather different view of the role of leisure in the lives of those individuals and groups who find themselves in conditions of deprivation. It is only possible to present the ideas emerging from this research in the barest outline here. But the crux of the thesis developed in this book is that multiple social factors can be used to explain how in the period after the Second World War a quiet revolution of sorts occurred within English society. This revolution led to a redefinition of politics as consisting precisely in leisure situations when extant unequal social relations were reconfigured on a permanent basis. Following Rancière, this research suggests that politics, where and when they occur in leisure contexts, are fundamentally democratic and dissensual.

This leads us to a further troubling aspect of "thinking intersectionally." This is the argument that despite its adherents' claims to the contrary, "thinking intersectionally" does a double disservice to the "poor" by not only being resolutely determined to "give voice" to the authenticity of the multiplicity of their subjugation through concepts such as "raceclassgender" (Watson & Scraton, 2013, p. 37), but also by judging "them" as oppressed creatures.

---

[1] My use of the term "poor" here is Rancière's which works with the assumption that the history of Western thought is one in which freedom and the right to think are premised on situating and excluding those whose social role is perceived other than to think. In applying the term in this way I am also using it as a shorthand to include all those social groups who are in one way or another subjugated and/or excluded.

Indeed, in thinking about social inequality and its relationship with leisure through "intersectionality," the world of the research subjects under scrutiny always remains a foreign territory, and if it is one that is successful giving voice, the only voices really heard are those of the sociologists. One of the upshots of this is that "thinking intersectionally" has to nurture with its thought the lives of its "subjects." But what it fails to grasp is that what it is actually doing when bolting together these objectified versions of human existence is forming intersections that never quite cohere with one another. This kind of interpretation is so full of its own virtuousness that it has the reverse effect of the one intended. The result is that the arch structuring the sociology—with its inability to grasp the existential contingency of the individual lives at stake in the commentary—is critically inert. As that most discerning critic of this social scientific fixation with turning subjectivity into objectivity and converting people from subjects into objects of investigation, Jacques Derrida once put it, "One cannot say 'Here are our monsters' without immediately turning the monsters into pets" (1990, p. 80).

What is perhaps most problematic with "thinking intersectionally," then, is that it ends up overstating the significance of the relationship between difference and subjugation. Basically in fixing individuals or social groups in impoverished identities it denies their capacity for agency. As a result, it also fails to register that the satisfaction we find in our leisure is often the satisfaction of finding another aspect of ourselves, which permits us to be somebody else and this has nothing to do with the desire of external powers to recognize us only through our poverty. This constitutes the limit of a particular sort of sociology for which true freedom is only that of the sociologist, which is conceivable and functions as the exact opposite of the ostensible powerlessness of those who are subjugated. As Rancière would say, here sociology once again ends up as the very thought of inequality because by posing social inequality as the primary fact that needs to be explained it ends up explaining its necessity.

What "thinking intersectionally" also does in this regard is deny the interpretive role of the researcher since its conception of reflexivity, in common with Bourdieu's, foregrounds social inequality at the expense of understanding leisure through the self-understandings of social agents. Indeed, the awareness of what is lost, overlooked, and distorted in the process of transforming people's everyday worlds into sociology cannot help but be missing from "thinking intersectionally." And what it shares in common with Bourdieu's sociology is the inability to escape the tendency to impose its own narrative order on all kinds of untidiness—worst of all, the necessities of sociological "Theory" above the identification with and compassion for those whose worlds it claims to be explaining—while failing miserably to reflect on the process by which that order has been achieved.

What the argument developed so far suggests is that in sociological "Theory" the "poor" have to stay in their place: on the one hand, they have no time to go anywhere else because work will not wait for them, which is an empirical fact; and on the other, their immovability rests on the belief that "God mixed iron in their makeup while he mixed gold in the makeup of those who destined to deal with the common good" (Rancière, 2009, p. 276). This second reason is not an empirical fact, but it provides the alchemical myth that underpins the "natural" order of things and which sustains the idea that the "poor" have to remain in their assigned places. In other words, in order for sociology to function it has to rest on the idea that the social divisions and the inequalities emanating from these are performed by those who endure them "as their life, as what they feel, and what they are aware of" (*ibid*). To use one of Rancière's analogies, the identity of someone from the "poor" must fit like a handmade pair of shoes, but the type of shoe is never in question.

Obviously, Rancière does not think that the "poor" actually believe that God mixed iron in their souls and gold in the souls of those higher in the social class system, but it is enough that they *sense* it and as a result feel obliged, responsible, and actively committed to this idea *as if* it were true. In other words, for Rancière, social divisions are not only a reflection of actually existing conditions of existence, but also the extent to which sociologists believe that they are natural and inevitable. In Rancière's scheme of things, myth and reality and activity and passivity are not opposed; just as a reality always goes along with myth, so activity always goes along with passivity. In other words, for Rancière, sociologists give their *own* meaning to different worlds of leisure through the patterns of hierarchy and order which appear in their "Theories" and which they help to create and sustain.

INTERIM SUMMARY

Among all the issues that emanate from the cognitive dissonance discussed in the preceding section of this chapter, the following stand out. First and foremost, too many sociologists equip the "poor" and other subjugated groups with an excess of the most unattractive but also most necessary features of "people like them"—features that while purporting to "give them voice" actually turn them into monsters, or even worse, pets. These are the same social groups whose leisure interests incite the kind of disapproving, puritanical look made universal by the Frankfurt School, which hangs over some sociologies of leisure like a bad dream.

What is also clear from this discussion is that the discursive formation known as the sociology of leisure has been too insular, too parochial, and too complacent in framing the idea of its subject and while many of the once bright young academics from the 1970s are still around, the waves that they make nowadays seem much more modest. Beyond the odd blue-moon gem from Rojek, the sociology of leisure seems to have reduced its ambitions to the shrinking comfort zone of coterie approval that is its key associations, conferences, and journals. Moreover, what is hardly debated in leisure studies is that the subject field has lost its lustre. The study of leisure has by and large dropped off the curriculum at most universities and most bright young postgraduates nowadays seem more attracted to subjects like sport, criminology, and cultural studies (see also Henderson, Chapter 39). The fundamental issue at stake here can be found in the failure to incorporate into the sociology of leisure what has happened in social, cultural, political, and economic life over the last 30 or so years.

It is important to qualify something at this point. I am not suggesting for a moment that social inequality is by now unimportant to leisure studies. That is not my argument. My argument is that there is now an unacceptable gap between sociological accounts and quotidian leisure. This gap has arisen as a result of the discursive formation's anxious reluctance to let go of the "zombie categories" associated with orthodox sociology, which no longer have a compelling grip on reality. What I am talking about in this regard are the zombie concepts associated with social inequality that have a strange ghostlike presence in the sociology of leisure, which still uses them as if they represent something, including power; and to some extent they do still represent power. But the social networks and patronage, the paddings of privilege and the stereotypes left over from the time before modern life changed the nature of individual identity do not carry the same power that they once did—even if sociologists carry on "business as usual." Breaking this spell is a game that sociologists of leisure need to play if the discursive formation is to emerge from the current crisis.

So how to refresh the sociology of leisure in a way that thinks outside social inequality? The first answer to this question must be that the explanations I have given for the decline of sociological "Theory" have implications which reach much further than theory. Indeed, the whole function of sociology is in question if we can no longer accept that the identity of an individual (no matter how underprivileged) and his or her leisure can be adequately established by imposing on these a certain kind of fixity. What this suggests is that the sociology of leisure needs some new "rules of method." To understand why, we must consider yet another answer.

TOWARDS AN ALTERNATIVE SOCIOLOGY OF LEISURE

Today we find ourselves living in a sociality at once strange and yet strangely familiar. It is still far from being an equal one, which means that a democratic deficit continues to bedevil the leisure opportunities of many. However, with the emergence of what Bauman (2000) calls "liquid modernity" there has been a shift from a structured and structuring society in which our identities were largely predetermined by our social class, gender and "race" to an unstructured and de-structuring one in which *individualization* dominates more than anything else, and where our identities always remain a work in progress. Social class, gender, and ethnicity may still exert *some* degree of influence on our leisure lives, but they certainly do not dictate them. There are many reasons why this is so, but it is still difficult to define this change briefly. But what individualization involves, fundamentally, is the change, as Raymond Williams once observed, from *unaware* alignment to *active* commitment, or in other words, the moving of social relationships to human consciousness. Unaware alignment refers to the kind of life you are born into and stuck with, while active commitment refers to the kind of life we make for ourselves because we *feel* it our duty to do so. And this is because all of us—modern men and modern women both rich and poor—are existential agents who are very much aware of our social contingency.

The implications of these observations for sociology are profound. In the rest of the chapter I shall develop a thumbnail sketch of an alternative sociology of leisure with certain epistemological, ontological, and ethical implications. In so doing, my approach differs noticeably from orthodox sociology of leisure, by which I am referring to the knowledge it thinks with, but not about. The views that I shall develop below have their point of origin in another kind of sociological thinking which begins with the assumption that truth is better revealed through essential action rather than "Theory." These views are intimately shaped by the work of social philosophers such as Zygmunt Bauman, Jacques Rancière, Richard Rorty, and Peter Sloterdijk, who each stress the ambivalence and social contingency of modern life, and which culminates in a way of thinking that reverses a number of assumptions underpinning orthodox sociology's rational theorization of the modern world.

The first merit of this way of thinking is that it abandons the binary oppositions orthodox sociology inherited from the Enlightenment tradition. Its second strength, and a considerable one, is that it inscribes social theory within modernity by taking it out of the academy and placing it politically into everyday life (Badiou, 2005). Its third virtue is to foreground the question of what it means to be human in the modern world. In so doing it frames human life as an existential problem. However, contra Heidegger, it stresses "becoming" over "being" and the recognition that modern life is irreducibly mutable and heterogeneous. In addition to this, it argues that rather than finding ourselves merely "being-thrown-in-the-world," we are knowledgeable actors who recognize the conditions of own social contingency. The fourth virtue of this way of thinking is that it replaces the idea of a singular world as an ontological given with the idea that we in fact inhabit pluralized worlds—contingent, shape-shifting, fractured, underdesigned and undesignable, fuzzily-hierarchical, imperceptible worlds—in which life is lived *noch nicht* surrounded by possibilities that have not yet been realized, and where freedom is considered as our duty. Its fifth distinguishing feature, and perhaps its most contentious, is that it brings the idea to sociology that what we understand about the pluralized worlds in which we find ourselves is only knowable through some kind of story.

Let us look at this fifth feature in some more detail. My way of thinking sociologically attempts to fasten the delight we find in the pluralized worlds of liquid modernity onto new kinds of narrative informed by the kind of penetrating exuberance only found in the best works of literature and poetry. In other words, in deconstructing binary oppositions—between "subject" and "object," "concept" and "existence," "knowledge" and "action," and so on—and in the absence of ontological certainty, it is my contention that "rules of method" have to be assigned on what are essentially aesthetic grounds—on the basis of whose narrative has the more attractive language, or the more engaging style.

A good example of this is Wittgenstein's emphasis on *seeing* things differently and the associated notions of pictorial thinking through "family resemblances." As I have argued elsewhere (Blackshaw, 2010), what underpins this approach is the idea that we might not be able to define leisure so accurately as to uncover its "real" meaning, but we might try to understand it in terms of its "family resemblances" and their own internal practices and rules, even if we believe that the very request to define the idea in a definitive way is a mistake. In other words, we should not be asking after the *meaning* and the *purposes* of leisure, but should instead be asking after its *uses*. In other words, our task should be to clarify its contingencies and the ways in which the idea is used by people in different leisure situations rather than trying to it pin down to some absolute meaning.

I have argued that sociology should aspire to the best works of literature and poetry. This is because the strength of the best works of literature and poetry lies in their ability to perceive the lives of men and women within a particular milieu. What this suggests is that trying to understand different worlds with different rules demands a special kind of sociological inquiry. This is the kind of inquiry that takes into account the objective features of the world in question while contemplating its subjective features—research respondents' outer and inner worlds—by accounting for their personal priorities and relationships with others. There are two important building blocks to this kind of inquiry. First it begins with the assumption that the human "becoming-in-the-world" is knit together with its own sense of security and comfort—with *feeling* just right—and second that every world has its own sense of morality—its inhabitants *living* life in a way that they deem right.

As Giddens (1974) has convincingly argued, the relation between sociology and its subject matter—the two-way process by which everyday experience is turned into sociology and sociology is turned into everyday experience—has to be understood in terms of a "double hermeneutic." In volunteering themselves as cultural intermediaries who tell stories about their research respondents' leisure, what sociologists do is demonstrate that virtue is better revealed in action rather than "Theory." In so doing they say "This is my interpretation of the world of my respondents and I'm going to try like hell to make you believe that it's true; all I ask is that you suspend your own ontological assumptions for a little while until I have told you their story."

In other words, sociologists as cultural intermediaries challenge their readers to engage in what Rorty (2007) calls "cultural politics": the beginning of a conversation about what words to use to create a better vision of the society we want to live in. What this tells us is that rather than trust sociological "Theory"; we should trust sociologists' stories instead. This is because sociology conducted under the auspices of cultural politics can only be good or bad in its own categorization. Cultural intermediaries know what they are presenting us with is both a superior and an inferior world than the one we usually live with, but what they demand is that we keep looking steadily at them both (Frye, 1963). Here, no idea of reality is final and no interpretation of leisure, however good, is going to pronounce some final absolute truth. Every new interpretation, every new formulation emerging from this or that interpretation has the potential to change our understanding.

In anticipation of my critics, I am acutely aware that, as the eminent philosopher R. G. Collingwood (1994) famously pointed out, the work of the scholar is constrained by two important issues that need not concern the novelist or the poet. First, its narrative must be localized in a time and space that has actually existed; and second, it must be allied to evidence which the scholar has gathered from reliable sources. In other words, as sociologists, we do not have the freedom of the novelist; we are constrained by the evidence.

Walter Benjamin, a scholar who occupied the opposite pole on the continuum on which the rather conservative Collingwood's views could be plotted, offered a more radical solution. To scholars who wish capture the lives and times of any era, Benjamin (1974) suggested, they should develop a "procedure of empathy" by turning to the period in question in order to redeem its sufferings. Benjamin's invocation gives a crucial role to developing solidarity with the worlds of those whose leisure lives we seek to understand.

CONCLUSION

What these last observations attest is not only that all those awakened to rethinking sociologically anew must be aware that ethical questions are today more difficult (Sloterdijk, 2013, p. 90), but also that sociological theory means something different. As it rises from its death it develops some "new rules of method" which abandon theorizing altogether. In other words, after "Theory," narrative—another expression for storytelling, as says Sloterdijk (p. 11), bent on the "musical-rhapsodic transmission of knowledge rather than the "prosaic-communicative procurement of knowledge"—is now resurrected as a viable alternative to "Theory," and not just as intelligent but better made to the measure of the contemporary world. This "new" method not only entails taking "Theory" out of the academy and placing it politically into everyday life, but relies on interpretations drawn from compelling stories, rather than depending on facts or being fixated with establishing grand "Theory" (see also Walker, Kono, & Dieser, Chapter 36).

Those who use pictorial thinking through "language games" argue two things: firstly, that it is a different way of thinking that recognizes that as the world alters, we need a new vocabulary with which to interpret it; and secondly, that sociologically there are many different stories that we can tell and retell. What these stories do not do is try to *conceptualize* the world through the rules of logic. What they do, instead, is *literalize* metaphor. This is what makes pictorial thinking valuable. It alerts us to what abstract conceptual thinking cannot: those stubbornly universal human dilemmas—questions to which sociologists have found few compelling answers—which have never vanished from life. The hallmark of this "rule of method," then, is that it recurs perennially as our understandings are revised and revivified as society and culture shift and change.

As we have also seen, the practice of pointing out the questionable epistemological grounds which form the basis of orthodox sociological "Theory," while simultaneously asking ones readers to temporarily suspend their own ontological assumptions, is another one of the most distinctive features of this reflexive approach. Some readers will no doubt find the combination of outspoken epistemological criticism and deferred ontological judgment troubling. Others will be equally unhappy about accepting such a frankly novelizing methodological approach, especially when it is applied to certain aspects of deviant leisure (Rojek, 1999), for example. However, the disorderly continuity of modern life is infinitely less predictable and more strangely ambiguous than any sociological "Theory" would suggest. Sociologists must face up to the fact that each and every one of them is standing in a moral quagmire as they try to illuminate the lived (leisure) life through their different stories. As such, to paraphrase Sloterdijk, it is essential to recognize that as sociologists we must be prepared to be challenged where our own tacit assumptions are interrogated. When there is no solid ground under the sociological enterprise, no basis for moral certainty, the truth is that the only other way the authority of any work can be enhanced is through the acknowledgement of its predispositions.

The effects of social inequality, we can agree, continue, and always will be important for understanding leisure. As we have learned from Giddens, the two-way process by which everyday experience is turned into sociology and sociology is turned into everyday experience should always be promoted by sociologists as a democratic activity. Any sociologist intent on revealing the effects of social inequality on leisure must try to ensure that she is showing us *both* of these things. There is no one theory or "rule of method" in this regard; the genuinely reflexive sociologist will write these the way that she must write them. In the most compelling stories the writing will be clear and the ideas will be based on things *seen* by her and *spoken about* by her research respondents rather than on what she thinks as a professional sociologist and is excited to think she now understands it all.

This brings me to the sixth, and final, feature of my "new rules of method." This is the admonition to all sociologists that they must complicate their stories by questioning what it is possible for them as researchers, or anyone else for that matter, to finally "know" about other people. It is all too easy to feel and to theorize people less fortunate than yourself as part of a mass—or any other kind of social grouping vulnerable to political manipulation. It is also all too easy to disprove of what that mass do in *their* leisure. But that kind of feeling and theorizing is as foolish as the disproving is reprehensible. To put some additional gloss on James' (2009, p. 9) perceptive observations, the mass are *us*: a multitude of individuals. They just happen to be leading less fortunate lives. Any sociologist who speaks about social justice from her privileged position will not be able to do so in any compelling ways unless she can dispel the disapproving, puritanical attitude that often pervades sociology. In order to do this, she will not only have to replace this attitude with compassion, but just as importantly recognize that her own fortune begins with her freedom (see also Parry, Chapter 24).

What I have argued in this chapter is that, to paraphrase Bauman (1989), if sociology is going to claim the right to speak with authority about leisure in the twenty-first century, it is going to have to update its theoretical understandings of leisure. Currently it presents us with only a two-dimensional understanding of leisure inherited from the dichotomous thinking that underpins the Enlightenment tradition. We need a third dimension. What I have offered in the second part of the foregoing discussion is an alternative way of thinking sociology that gives us this dimension. This is the path forward for the sociology of leisure. Bauman, Rancière, Rorty and Sloterdijk have led the way. Given the resources of their scholarship, there is no reason not to follow.

REFERENCES

Badiou, A. (2005, September/October) The adventure of French philosophy. *New Left Review, 35*, 67–76.

Bauman, Z. (1989). Hermeneutics and modern social theory. In D. Held & J. B. Thompson (Eds.), *Social theory of modern societies: Anthony Giddens & his critics*. Cambridge: Cambridge University Press.

Bauman, Z. (2000). *Liquid modernity*. Cambridge: Polity Press.

Benjamin, W. (1974). On the concept of history. *Gesammelten Schriften I:2*. Translated by Dennis Redmond 8/4/01. Frankfurt am Main:Suhrkamp, Verlag.

Blackshaw, T. (2010). *Leisure*. London and New York: Routledge.

Blackshaw, T. (2013). *Working-class life in northern England, 1945–2010: The pre-history and after-life of the Inbetweener Generation*. Basingstoke, UK: Palgrave Macmillan.

Bourdieu, P. (1984). *Distinction: A social critique of the judgment of taste*. London: Routledge.

Bourdieu, P. et al. (1999). *The weight of the world: Social suffering in contemporary society*. Cambridge: Polity Press.

Burn, G. (2009). 'Have I broken your heart?' *Guardian Review*, 7th March.

Clarke, J. and Critcher, C. (1985). *The devil makes work*. London: Macmillan.

Collingwood, R. G. (1994). *The idea of history. Revised edition with lectures 1926–1928*. (edited by Jan van Der Dussen) Oxford: Clarendon Press [1946].

Derrida, J. (1990). *Some statements etc*. Stanford: Stanford University Press.

Frye, N. (1963). *The educated imagination*. Toronto: Canadian Broadcasting Corporation.

Giddens, A. (1974) *New rules of sociological method*. London: Hutchinson.

Gramsci, A. (1971). *Selections from the prison notebooks*. Translated and edited by Quintin Hoare and Geoffrey Nowell Smith. New York: International Publishers.

Habermas, J. (1975). *Legitimation crisis*. Translated and with an introduction by Thomas McCarthy. Boston, Beacon Press.

Henderson, K. A. (2013). Feminist leisure studies: Origins, accomplishments and prospects. In T. Blackshaw (Ed.), *The Routledge handbook of leisure studies*. London and New York: Routledge.

James, C. (2009) *The revolt of the pendulum: Essays 2005–2008*. London: Picador.

Rancière, J (2004). *The philosopher and his poor*. Translated by John Drury, Corinne Oster and Andrew Parker. Durham and London: Duke University Press.

Rancière, J (2005). *The politics of aesthetics: The distribution of the sensible*. Translated by Gabriel Rockhill. London: Continuum.

Rancière, J. 2009. Afterword/The method of equality: An answer to some questions. In G. Rockhill & P. Watts (Eds.), *Jacques Rancière: History, politics, aesthetics* (273–288). Durham, NC: Duke University Press.

Rojek, C. (1999). Deviant leisure: The dark side of free-time activity. In E. L. Jackson & T. L. Burton (Eds.), *Leisure studies: Prospects for the twenty-first century*. State College, PA: Venture Publishing, Inc.

Rojek, C. (1995). *Decentring leisure: Rethinking leisure theory*. London: Sage.

Rojek, C. (2010). *The labour of leisure: The culture of free time*. London: Sage.

Rorty, R. (2007). *Philosophy as cultural politics: Philosophical papers volume 4*. Cambridge: Cambridge University Press.

Sloterdijk, P. (2013). *Philosophical temperaments: From Plato to Foucault*. Translated by Thomas Dunlap/ Foreword by Creston Davis. New York: Columbia University Press.

Swenson, J. (2006). Jacques Rancière. In L. D. Kritzman (Ed.), *The Columbia history of twentieth-century French thought*. New York: Columbia University Press.

Turner, V. (1969). *The ritual process: Structure and anti-structure*. Chicago, IL: Aldine.

Watson, B. & Scraton, S. J. (2013). Leisure studies and intersectionality. *Leisure Studies, 32*(1), 35–47.

Watson, B. and Ratna, A. (2011). Bollywood in the park: Thinking intersectionally about public leisure space. *Leisure/Loisir, 35*(1), 71–86.

8

Leisure, Health, and Physical Activity

Jason N. Bocarro (North Carolina State University) and Michael B. Edwards (North Carolina State University)

The parks and recreation field has a long history of managing programs and resources that promote physical activity and health. In fact, the recreation movement in the nineteenth century was largely based on improving urban health conditions, preserving nature and providing opportunities for healthy recreation opportunities such as sports, supervised play, exercise, dance, and outdoor recreation (Godbey, Caldwell, Floyd, & Payne, 2005). Although physical activity and health have been a component of leisure research, it was rarely a prominent form of inquiry (Henderson & Bialeschki, 2005).

However, repositioning leisure programs and services as viable mechanisms to promote physical activity and health has intensified in recent years. This approach has been supported globally through advocacy by the United Nations, World Health Organization (WHO), and many national governments as well as partnerships in the United States between the National Recreation and Park Administration, the Centers for Disease Control and Prevention, and the National Cancer Institute (Godbey et al., 2005). Furthermore, 89% of city managers reported the primary governmental agency responsible for helping to address the U.S. obesity problem is parks and recreation (International City/County Management Association, 2005). This has culminated in other disciplines recognizing that those working within the leisure, parks, and recreation field have an essential role in addressing health outcomes, resulting in more interdisciplinary collaborations (Godbey & Mowen, 2010; Henderson & Bialeschki, 2005).

Defining health can be problematic. For the purpose of this chapter, our discussion is framed around the WHO's (1946) definition that describes health as "a complete state of physical, mental and social well-being, and not merely the absence of disease or infirmity." Dimensions of health include physical, social, emotional, and psychological aspects. The WHO recognizes that governments have a responsibility for the health of their people that can be fulfilled by the provision of adequate health and social measures.

As part of their role in promoting optimal population health, the U.S. government establishes the country's overarching health agenda every 10 years through the Healthy People program (Payne & Orsega-Smith, 2010). The most recent report (Healthy People 2020) outlined four overarching goals:

- To attain high-quality, longer lives free of preventable disease, disability, injury, and premature death
- To achieve health equity, eliminate disparities, and improve the health of all groups
- To create social and physical environments that promote good health for all
- To promote quality of life, healthy development, and healthy behaviors across all life stages.

In 2010, a series of research syntheses summarized some of the contributions from the park and recreation field to this national health agenda. Mowen's (2010) synthesis, commissioned by the Robert Wood Johnson Foundation, summarized some of the major contributions of parks and playgrounds in providing low- or no-cost opportunities for people of all ages to be physically active. Godbey and Mowen's (2010) monograph highlighted the growing recognition among the health community of the value of public parks and recreation in addressing negative health outcomes. Kuo (2010) provided an intriguing summary of new evidence showing that engaging in leisure activities within a natural environment has both important physical and psychological health benefits. Thus, although the goals listed in Healthy People 2020 are beyond the scope of one discipline, our contention is that leisure scholars can bring their expertise and disciplinary perspective in helping to address each of these goals.

With that in mind, this chapter provides an overview of the research on leisure and health, describing the unique perspectives and contributions that leisure scholars and practitioners provide. It also outlines some of the major theoretical frameworks used to understand leisure, health, and physical activity. We also provide a critique of the leisure and health scholarship, recognizing that leisure can have some negative individual and social health outcomes despite the inherently positive discourse. Finally, we describe some strategic gains that have been made as well as critical issues and questions that both leisure practitioners and scholars should consider in the future.

RESEARCHING LEISURE AND HEALTH

Increasingly, leisure researchers have worked with public health scholars to better understand and promote the positive relationship between recreational activities and health (Librett, Henderson, Godbey, & Morrow, 2007; Payne, Ainsworth, & Godbey, 2010). The ultimate goal of this research is to inform benefits-based practices, emphasizing designing and implementing programs and services that promote positive individual and community health outcomes (Driver, Brown, & Peterson, 1991). Central to this relationship is the ability of the recreation profession to promote leisure-time physical activity. This focus is important as increased physical activity has been linked with a host of positive health outcomes, including decreased rates of obesity, lower cardiovascular mortality, reduced risks of some cancers, and improved mental health (Edwards & Casper, 2012).

Leisure researchers often assume leisure services provide space for people who are intrinsically motivated to be physically active while also creating fun and enjoyable environments and programs that include healthy components and attract wider participation from people who may not be motivated solely by exercise (Henderson & Ainsworth, 2003). While most of the research examining the benefits from participating in these recreational activities have focused on increased physical activity, other health benefits of recreation and leisure have been identified (e.g., reduced stress or increased socialization) (Iwasaki & Mannell, 2000). Indeed, some scholars have argued that the primary value of leisure and recreation is its capacity to promote more holistic health outcomes (Dustin, Bricker, & Schwab, 2009).

FRAMEWORKS FOR UNDERSTANDING LEISURE AND HEALTH

Similar to public health, leisure studies apply theoretical frameworks from several disciplines (e.g., psychology, planning, sociology, anthropology, and kinesiology) to help understand and explain human behavior. This approach follows the prevention model of public health. That is, research is designed to ultimately inform practices that lead to the prevention of negative health outcomes (Caldwell, 2005). However, many researchers are also interested in understanding how leisure and recreation help individuals cope with or improve poor health through recreational activities (Caldwell, 2005). When researching the role of recreation and leisure to prevent negative health outcomes, scholars often want to know why people do or do not engage in healthy leisure activities, how social groups support or discourage participation in healthy leisure activities, how physical environments (e.g., parks and recreation programs) contribute to community health promotion, and how public policy influences opportunities for health-promoting recreation and leisure. While there have been multiple theories and disciplinary approaches examining this relationship between environments and health outcomes, the social-ecological framework (McLeroy, Bibeau, Steckler, & Glanz, 1988) has been the predominant model for understanding leisure and recreation's contribution to health promotion.

Health promotion through leisure and recreation is a multifaceted phenomenon. The social-ecological framework recognizes that different systems within the environment (i.e., progressing from the individual to societal level) have the potential to shape human behavior. Social-ecological health proponents argue that health behavior is influenced by multiple interactions with physical and social environments that can either facilitate or constrain individual health (Kaczynski & Henderson, 2007; McLeroy et al., 1988).

Leisure research has made significant contributions to our understanding of the role of leisure and recreation in promoting physical activity and health. While much of this research has been published in scholarly journals traditionally focused on leisure and recreation (e.g., *Journal of Leisure Research, Leisure Sciences,* and *Journal of Park and Recreation Administration*), many leisure scholars have found public health journals receptive to publishing research in this area. This research has focused on all levels of the social-ecological framework within six analytical perspectives: (a) intrapersonal, (b) interpersonal, (c) lifespan, (d) constraints, (e) environments, and (f) management and policy.

Intrapersonal Perspectives

Intrapersonal perspectives are represented by the work of earliest leisure theorists (e.g., Csikszentmihalyi, 1990; Iso-Ahola, 1980; Neulinger, 1981), who developed highly-individualized theories of leisure motivation. The most prevalent research that emerged from this tradition has focused on individual motivations. This perspective assumes that, although external environments influence decisions, people are internally motivated to intentionally act based upon cognitive or emotional responses (Newton, Watson, Kim, & Beacham, 2006). Psychologically-based intrinsic motivation is the primary guiding influence to participation in healthy leisure activities. This perspective provides the foundation for self-determination theory (Deci & Ryan, 1985; Iso-Ahola, 1980). Using self-determination theory, researchers suggested activities must support an individual's intrinsic need for autonomy, competence, and relatedness to sufficiently motivate participation in the activity (Lloyd & Little, 2010; Walker, Chapter 17).

Because self-determination theory often fails to adequately account for social factors that lead to motivation or condition participation, some researchers have adopted approaches that use Ajzen's (1991) theory of planned behavior. A measure of intention, the theory of planned behavior incorporates constructs of attitudes and subjective norms, along with perceived behavioral control, a derivative of the social cognitive ideas of self-efficacy and locus of control (Ajzen, 2002). From this perspective, research suggests that perceived behavioral control has an important effect on motivation to participate in physically active recreation, even when individuals perceive barriers to participation (Tsai & Coleman, 2009).

Interpersonal Perspectives

Interpersonal perspectives are also interested in examining motivations to participate in healthy leisure activities, but are more intentional about understanding how social relations influence motivation. Using frameworks such as social cognitive theory (Bandura, 1986) and social support theory, researchers account for the importance of significant others, particularly friends and family, to shape beliefs and attitudes about participation (Orsega-Smith, Payne, Mowen, Ching-Hua, & Godbey, 2007). Interpersonal perspectives have found social support to be a key predictor of motivation to participate in healthy leisure activities (Cardenas, Henderson, & Wilson, 2009). Drawing from social learning theory, a few researchers have examined the socialization process, rather than individual motivation, to understand how individuals become involved in healthy leisure (Mannell & Kleiber, 1997). For example, Kenyon and McPherson (1973) proposed three interrelated components (i.e., personal attributes, significant others, and the socialization situation) contributed to role learning in children and provided a foundation for future participation in physically active leisure.

Lifespan Perspectives

Another way in which leisure researchers have approached recreation and health is to examine factors that encourage participation across parts of the lifespan. This research often focuses on why some individuals maintain leisure activities from childhood into and through adulthood, while others withdraw from these activities at transitional points during their life. This perspective has been informed by a number of theoretical frameworks, including: continuity theory (Atchley, 1989), social learning theory (Csikszentmihalyi, 1997), life course theory (Zick, Smith, Brown, Fan, & Kowaleski-Jones, 2007), leisure repertoire model (Bocarro, Kanters, Casper, & Forrester, 2008; Iso-Ahola, 1980; Iso-Ahola, Jackson, & Dunn, 1994), and model of successful aging (Payne, Mowen, & Montoro-Rodriguez, 2006). This approach suggests that major socializing agents (e.g., schools, communities, parents, peers, and teachers) shape lifetime attitudes towards participation. Additionally, adults often gain self-efficacy to participate in healthy leisure based upon opportunities available during childhood and adolescence. As individuals age, they will seek to maintain continuity in activities with which they are familiar and will be less likely to take up new activities (Atchley, 1989). People may also be more determined to continue healthy activities in which they participated at earlier life stages even when external barriers exist (Pagano, Barkhoff, Heiby, & Schlicht, 2006). This research suggests that individuals should be provided with multiple opportunities to learn and participate in healthy leisure activities in childhood so their participation can be maintained in adulthood (Caldwell, Chapter 21; Iso-Ahola, 1980).

Constraints Perspectives

One often-used approach to examine the role of leisure and recreation in promoting health is leisure constraints (Jackson, 2000; Schneider, Chapter 18). Similar to previous perspectives, constraints approaches are often interested in understanding what prevents or facilitates an individual's participation in healthy leisure activities. However, this research often bridges the traditional ontological divide between agency and structure, thus providing a link between personal-level and environmental approaches. Overall, many people report a perceived lack of time (Kimm et al., 2006), dependence on screen-based entertainment (Godbey, 1997), and not having other people to participate with (Thompson, Rehman, & Humbert, 2005; Wilhelm Stanis, Schneider, & Anderson, 2009) as important constraints to participating in healthy leisure behavior. Demographic and stratification frameworks have also been used to understand how groups of people experience constraints differently. Significant evidence supports the idea that woman, racial/ethnic minorities, economically disadvantaged, and people living in specific areas (e.g., inner cities, rural areas, or developing nations) have poorer health outcomes than more advantaged groups. Based on the constraints perspective, the literature suggests that these disadvantaged groups perceive higher constraints to their participation in healthy leisure activities, particularly structural constraints (e.g., institutional discrimination, racism, cost, lack of transportation, and governmental restrictions) (Edwards & Cunningham, 2013; Harrolle, Floyd, Casper, Kelley, & Bruton, 2013).

Environmental Perspectives

The use of environmental perspectives has intensified in recent years, particularly as public health research has focused nearly exclusively on the role of physical environments to promote physical activity. However, some of the theoretical origins of this approach may be based in Hendee's (1969) opportunity theory that argues recreation participation is dependent on the availability of proximate low- or no-cost resources. Thus, environmental perspectives have primarily examined the correlation between parks and recreation spaces and levels of physical activity. Much of the early research in this area has suggested proximity to parks and other spaces (e.g., walking trails and greenways) is associated with higher use and increased physical activity (Kaczynski & Havitz, 2009; Kaczynski & Henderson, 2007).

As research in this area has evolved, scholars have become interested in understanding what features of parks and recreational areas encourage physical activity (Giles-Corti et al., 2005). This research suggests that larger parks and the presence of trails, playgrounds, sports facilities, and other amenities are associated with higher use and levels of physical activity (Floyd et al., 2011; Kaczynski & Havitz, 2009). People also are more likely to visit and be physically active in parks that are aesthetically appealing and free of disorder (Ridgers, Stratton, Fairclough, & Twisk, 2007). Another important environmental factor that encourages participation in physical activity seems to be the presence of other people (Floyd et al., 2011). Additional research has suggested that the availability of structured programs (Wolch et al., 2011) and media promotion (Leahy, Shugrue, Daigle, & Daniel, 2009) within parks are critical to facilitating physical activity among park users.

Similar to the constraints perspective, the environmental perspective has been useful in understanding neighborhood and community disparities. This research has often been based within the framework of deprivation amplification that argues that individuals with the highest need have the lowest access to health-promoting environments (Edwards, Bocarro, & Kanters, 2013; Macintyre, Ellaway, & Cummins, 2002). Most of this research has suggested that individuals living within more socio-economically disadvantaged neighborhoods have access to fewer parks and recreational resources, and perceive parks as unsafe and being inferior in quality in comparison to more advantaged neighborhoods (Slater, Fitzgibbon, & Floyd, 2013; Stodolska & Floyd, Chapter 28; Stodolska, Shinew, Acevedo, & Roman, 2012).

Management and Policy Perspectives

Although less studied than other perspectives, research has focused on broader policy and management issues related to leisure, recreation, and health. Limited research has examined macro-level policies in the United States. Most notably, county-level analyses in West Virginia, Oregon, and North Carolina suggested increased allocation of recreational resources was associated with positive health outcomes (Edwards, Jilcott, Floyd, & Moore, 2011). Additionally, a state survey of parks and recreation directors in North Carolina suggested that health and physical activity, especially for children, were organizational priorities (Bocarro, Casper et al., 2009). Research has also argued for the potential of recreation and leisure to develop community-level capacity to address local physical and social health issues (Edwards, Miller, & Blackburn, 2011; Glover & Bates, 2006). Specifically, this research has stressed the importance of leveraging inter-organizational partnerships (Bruton et al., 2011) and joint use agreements (Spengler, Young, & Linton, 2007) to maximize community resources and increase accessibility (Glover, Chapter 32).

Less research has been conducted that informs our understanding of how people use leisure time to advocate or raise awareness for improved population and community health. We know that people use their leisure time to participate in health support groups, community organizing, community coalitions, and direct political action designed to improve the health and well-being of themselves and their communities (Labonte, 1994). Wheaton (2007) examined the role of surfers in the UK to advocate for cleaner beaches. There have also been examinations of the efficacy and politics of groups such as volunteers for breast cancer awareness (King, 2006) and reducing incidents of drunk driving (DeJong, 1996). However, little is known about the role of these voluntary leisure activities in promoting community health.

CRITIQUES OF RESEARCH ON LEISURE AND HEALTH

The leisure and health research has been criticized for its almost evangelical discourse seeking to document leisure's benefits, functionalist perspective, and domination of physical health outcomes (Stewart, Parry, & Glover, 2008). Critics of benefits-based leisure and health research argue this research often assumes health is universally and uncritically defined, when health is often a concept that is culturally and politically constructed (Fullagar, 2002). It has been suggested that more critical debate is necessary to prevent leisure from being used as a mechanism to reinforce social order and reproduce health inequality (Rojek, 2000). In this sense, we have to ensure research on leisure and health does not lead to blaming individuals or specific social groups for their own poor health outcomes.

Additionally, more holistic and multidimensional conceptualizations of health are needed to develop a fuller understanding of leisure's role in promoting health.

Rojek (1999) criticized leisure scholars for assuming leisure is inherently positive, particularly within Western society (Williams, Chapter 20). Thus, although researchers, practitioners, and advocates of leisure and recreation espouse its health benefits, negative health aspects of leisure should be recognized. For example, it is possible that even leisure-time physical activity can produce significant negative effects, such as detrimental cravings for leisure-time physical activity, excessive exercise focused on cosmetic fitness and body image issues, and injuries (Hausenblas & Symons Downs, 2002).

As leisure has become more "professionalized," the associated costs have resulted in less accessibility, particularly among already disadvantaged groups (Edwards & Casper, 2012). One area that has seen this occur is in youth sports. John Engh, the CEO of National Alliance for Youth Sports, pointed out that in an era of reduced municipal budgets and the push to include children in organized sports at a younger age, the traditional parks and recreation sports leagues have virtually disappeared (Tanier, 2012). Furthermore, towns across America have focused resources in new sport venues designed exclusively to accommodate elite-level sport tournaments making recreation settings designed to provide leisure-time physical activity inaccessible to many local residents (Hyman, 2012).

Research on the benefits of leisure settings has shown that simply being close to parks and other recreation amenities has positive physical and mental health benefits (Kaczynski & Henderson, 2007; Kuo, 2010). However, the recognition of these benefits has resulted in an increase in property values (e.g., Crompton, 2010). Thus, there may be unintended consequences of developing recreational spaces in ways that promote physical activity. Specifically, some areas have seen the gentrification of communities where lower income citizens, the ones disproportionately impacted by negative health, may be displaced by largely White, middle-class populations seeking better access to recreational amenities (Fraser, 2004; García, 2013). Because gentrification is symptomatic of larger issues surrounding economic disparity, solutions to address it are difficult. The exclusion of certain groups from participation in sports and the loss of access to parks and natural spaces may lead to less leisure-time physical activity and more health risks. However, García (2013) suggested that by better translating their research findings, leisure scholars can help to address various health inequities.

CRITICAL QUESTIONS AND ISSUES FOR THE FUTURE

In 2005, Godbey et al. and Henderson and Bialeschki outlined a number of suggestions in order for leisure research to play a more prominent role in transdisciplinary efforts to promote health and physical activity. Since then, the role of leisure researchers has become more prominent, addressing many of those suggestions (Bocarro & Wells, 2009). These have included special issues of journals focused on this topic (e.g., *Leisure Sciences*, 2005; *Journal of Physical Activity & Health*, 2007; *Journal of Park and Recreation Administration*, 2009), conferences focused on the contribution of leisure, parks, and recreation to physical activity and health (Cooper Institute, Active Living Research, 2006), and more leisure scholars publishing in journals outside of the leisure discipline (Godbey & Mowen, 2010). Furthermore, leisure scholars have developed validated measurement tools that are being widely adopted by practitioners and researchers from other disciplines (e.g., Bocarro, Floyd et al., 2009; Kaczynski, Wilhelm Stanis, & Besenyi, 2012).

While there has been tremendous growth and recognition in leisure research and practice in regards to physical activity and health, we feel there are five issues future research should consider.

- Although Godbey and Mowen (2010) recognized the success in leisure scholars publishing in journals outside of our field, this could be problematic. Without a strong and vibrant body of knowledge within our own journals, some may question leisure scholars' contribution and unique perspective to research on physical activity and health. Although we agree that leisure researchers should publish some of their work in journals outside of their discipline, we argue that the next step is to encourage researchers from other disciplines to read our literature and journals to better understand leisure's contribution to this issue.
- Over the past decade, leisure researchers and practitioners have engaged in partnerships to address many of the health issues. These partners have predominately come from disciplines such as urban planning, landscape design, public health, sociology, geography, exercise science, and others from within the medical community. However, we suggest that practitioners and leisure researchers consider partners from other disciplines to help address different research questions. These could include partners more engaged in policy work, political science, economics, computer science, and neuroscience.

- Leisure researchers should consider what the best opportunities are to affect environmental and policy change. As we point out earlier in this chapter, there has been less work focused on management and policy implications related to leisure, health, and physical activity. Bocarro and Stodolska (2013), in challenging leisure researchers to be more relevant, suggested aligning research to policy change and engaging communities where the research is taking place; particularly when examining issues of social and environmental injustice or health inequities (see also Veal, Chapter 33).
- It will be critically important to consider how information regarding leisure research is disseminated. For example, the concept of translational research is becoming more valued within academia; however, leisure and recreation academic departments still struggle to incentivize this type of scholarship (Bocarro & Stodolska, 2013). Furthermore, leisure researchers should consider other means of disseminating the value of their research and focus questions examining the effectiveness of the translational process.
- Finally, as new technologies develop, it will be important to consider their use in our research to answer relevant questions using new tools. For example, Aspinall, Mavros, Coyne, & Roe (2013) investigated the use of mobile electroencephalography (EEG) as a method to record and analyze the emotional experience of a group of walkers in three types of urban environments. Other researchers (e.g., Hipp, Adlakha, Chang, Eyler,, & Pless, 2013) have experimented with new technology to help them capture big data from multiple locations using webcams and crowdsourcing. Furthermore, as technology has progressed, the analysis of large amounts of data has gained significant attention from the scientific community (Halevi & Moed, 2012). Having access to the skills required to work with big data will be critical to understanding broader geographical and societal trends.

CONCLUSION

The World Health Organization points out that the adoption of "Western" lifestyles throughout the world and non-communicable diseases will become an increasing threat to global health. As this chapter illustrates, leisure has the potential to mitigate some of these negative health outcomes. With that in mind, we propose some research topics and questions for future researchers to consider. First, as this chapter described, more research is needed on the impact of public policy on the organization and management of leisure programs for health. Furthermore, along with increased calls for translational health research that directly influences policy decisions, research questions evaluating the process of how research affects policy change will be critical. Second, although people use their leisure time to participate in activities designed to improve their own health and well-being, limited research exists showing how people use leisure time to advocate or raise awareness for improved population and community health. Third, we often assume that leisure is inherently beneficial for our health. Therefore, there is a need to increase our understanding related to the potentially negative health aspects of leisure. Fourth, the continued fragmentation of society will require that leisure researchers understand more about the health of specific communities with different needs, specifically veterans, people with physical and mental disabilities (Dattilo, Chapter 26), and different immigrant and ethnic populations (Stodolska & Floyd, Chapter 28). For example, a 2013 NIH RFP called for a greater understanding regarding the health of LBGTQ populations (Johnson, Chapter 25). Finally, increasing our understanding of other health benefits (e.g., cognitive/mental health, social, spiritual) related to leisure programs and the places they occur will be imperative.

REFERENCES

Ajzen, I. (1991). The theory of planned behavior. *Organizational Behavior and Human Decision Processes, 50*, 179–211.

Ajzen, I. (2002). Perceived behavioral control, self-efficacy, locus of control, and the theory of planned behavior. *Journal of Applied Social Psychology, 32*(4), 665–683.

Aspinall, P., Mavros, P., Coyne, R., & Roe, J. (2013). The urban brain: Analysing outdoor physical activity with mobile EEG. *British Journal of Sports Medicine*. doi: 10.1136/bjsports-2012-091877

Atchley, R. (1989). The continuity theory of normal aging. *The Gerontologist, 29*, 183–190.

Bandura, A. (1986). *Social foundations of thought and action: A social cognitive theory*. Englewood Cliffs, NJ: Prentice Hall.

Bocarro, J. N., Casper, J., Henderson, K. A., Floyd, M. F., Moore, R., Kanters, M. A., . . . Edwards, M. B. (2009). Physical activity promotion in North Carolina: Perceptions of public park and recreation directors. *Journal of Park & Recreation Administration, 27*(1), 1–16.

Bocarro, J. N., Floyd, M. F., Moore, R., Baran, P., Danninger, T., Smith, W., & Cosco, N. (2009). Developing a reliable measure of physical activity among children in different age groups using the System for Observing Physical

Activity and Recreation in Communities (SOPARC). *Journal of Physical Activity and Health, 6*(6), 699–707.

Bocarro, J. N., Kanters, M. A., Casper, J., & Forrester, S. (2008). School physical education, extracurricular sports, and lifelong active living. *Journal of Teaching in Physical Education, 27*, 155–166.

Bocarro, J. N., & Stodolska, M. (2013). Researcher and advocate: Using research to promote social justice change. *Journal of Leisure Research, 45*(1), 2–6.

Bocarro, J. N., & Wells, M. S. (2009). Making a difference through parks and recreation: Reflections on physical activity, health and wellness research. *Journal of Park and Recreation Administration, 27*(3), 1–7.

Bruton, C. M., Floyd, M. F., Bocarro, J. N., Henderson, K. A., Casper, J. M., & Kanters, M. A. (2011). Physical activity and health partnerships among park and recreation departments in North Carolina. *Journal of Park & Recreation Administration, 29*(2), 55–68.

Caldwell, L. (2005). Leisure and health: Why is leisure therapeutic? *British Journal of Guidance & Counselling, 33*(1), 7–26.

Cardenas, D., Henderson, K. A., & Wilson, B. E. (2009). Experiences of participation in senior games among older adults. *Journal of Leisure Research, 41*(1), 41–56.

Crompton, J. L. (2010). *Measuring the economic impact of park and recreation services.* National Recreation and Parks Association. Retrieved 3rd August, 2013, from http://www.nrpa.org/uploadedFiles/nrpa.org/Publications_and_Research/Research/Papers/Crompton-Research-Paper.pdf

Csikszentmihalyi, M. (1990). *Flow: The psychology of optimal experience.* New York: Harper & Row.

Csikszentmihalyi, M. (1997). Activity, experience, and personal growth. In J. Curtis & S. Russell (Eds.), *Physical activity in human experiences: Interdisciplinary perspectives.* Champaign, IL: Human Kinetics.

Deci, E. L., & Ryan, R. M. (1985). *Intrinsic motivation and self-determination in human behavior.* New York: Plenum Press.

DeJong, W. (1996). MADD Massachusetts versus Senator Burke: A media advocacy case study. *Health Education & Behavior, 23*(3), 318–329.

Driver, B. L., Brown, P. J., & Peterson, G. L. (1991). *Benefits of leisure.* State College, PA: Venture Publishing, Inc.

Dustin, D. L., Bricker, K. S., & Schwab, K. A. (2009). People and nature: Toward an ecological model of health promotion. *Leisure Sciences, 32*(1), 3–14.

Edwards, M. B., Bocarro, J. N., & Kanters, M. A. (2013). Place disparities in access to supportive environments for extracurricular physical activity in North Carolina middle schools. *Youth & Society, 45*(2), 265–285.

Edwards, M. B., & Casper, J. M. (2012). Sport and Health. In G. B. Cunningham & J. D. Singer (Eds.), *Sociology of sport and physical activity* (2nd ed., pp. 69–98). College Station, TX: Center for Sport Management Research and Education.

Edwards, M. B., & Cunningham, G. B. (2013). Examining the associations of perceived community racism with self-reported physical activity levels and health among older racial minority adults. *Journal of Physical Activity and Health, 10*, 932–939.

Edwards, M. B., Jilcott, S. B., Floyd, M. F., & Moore, J. B. (2011). County-level disparities in access to recreational resources and associations with adult obesity. *Journal of Park & Recreation Administration, 29*(2), 39–54.

Edwards, M. B., Miller, J. L., & Blackburn, L. (2011). After-school programs for health promotion in rural communities: Ashe County Middle School 4-H After-School Program. *Journal of Public Health Management & Practice, 17*(3), 283–287.

Floyd, M. F., Bocarro, J. N., Smith, W. R., Baran, P. K., Moore, R. C., Cosco, N. G., . . . Fang, K. (2011). Park-based physical activity among children and adolescents. *American Journal of Preventive Medicine, 41*(3), 258–265.

Fraser, J. (2004). Beyond gentrification: Mobilizing communities and claiming space. *Urban Geography, 25*(5), 437–457.

Fullagar, S. (2002). Governing the healthy body: Discourses of leisure and lifestyle within Australian health policy. *Health, 6*(1), 69–84.

García, R. (2013). The George Butler Lecture—Social justice and leisure: The usefulness and uselessness of research. *Journal of Leisure Research, 45*(1), 7–22.

Giles-Corti, B., Broomhall, M. H., Knuiman, M., Collins, C., Douglas, K., Ng, K., . . . Donovan, R. J. (2005). Increasing walking: How important is distance to, attractiveness, and size of public open space? *American Journal of Preventive Medicine, 28*(2, Supplement 2), 169–176.

Glover, T. D., & Bates, N. R. (2006). Recapturing a sense of neighbourhood since lost: Nostalgia and the formation of First String, a Community Team Inc. *Leisure Studies, 25*(3), 329–351.

Godbey, G. C. (1997). *Leisure and leisure services in the 21st century.* State College, PA: Venture Publishing, Inc.

Godbey, G. C., Caldwell, L. L., Floyd, M., & Payne, L. L. (2005). Contributions of leisure studies and recreation and park management research to the active living agenda. *American Journal of Preventive Medicine, 28*, 150–158.

Godbey, G. C., & Mowen, A. (2010). *The benefits of physical activity provided by Park and Recreation services: The scientific evidence*. National Recreation and Parks Association. Retrieved from http://www.nrpa.org/uploadedFiles/nrpa.org/Publications_and_Research/Research/Papers/Godbey-Mowen-Research-Paper.pdf

Halevi, G., & Moed, H. (2012). The evolution of big data as a research and scientific topic. *Research Trends, 30*, 3–6. Retrieved from http://www.researchtrends.com/wpcontent/uploads/2012/09/Research_Trends_Issue30.pdf

Harrolle, M. G., Floyd, M. F., Casper, J. M., Kelley, K. E., & Bruton, C. M. (2013). Physical activity constraints among Latinos. *Journal of Leisure Research, 45*(1), 74–90.

Hausenblas, H. A., & Symons Downs, D. (2002). Exercise dependence: A systematic review. *Psychology of Sport and Exercise, 3*(2), 89–123.

Healthy People 2020. Retrieved from http://www.healthypeople.gov/2020/topicsobjectives2020/pdfs/HP2020objectives.pdf

Hendee, J. C. (1969). Rural-urban differences reflected in outdoor recreation participation. *Journal of Leisure Research, 1*, 333–341.

Henderson, K. A., & Ainsworth, B. E. (2003). Enjoyment: A link to physical activity, leisure and health. *Journal of Park & Recreation Administration, 21*(1), 130–146.

Henderson, K. A., & Bialeschki, M. D. (2005). Leisure and active lifestyles: Research reflections. *Leisure Sciences, 27*(5), 355–365.

Hipp, J. A., Adlakha, D., Chang, B., Eyler, A. A., & Pless, R. B. (2013). Emerging technologies: Webcams and crowdsourcing to identify active transportation. *American Journal of Preventive Medicine, 44*(1), 96–97.

Hyman, M. (2012). *The most expensive game in town: The rising cost of youth sports and the toll on today's family*. Boston, MA: Beacon Press.

International City/County Management Association. (2005). *Active Living Approaches by Local Governments, 2004*. Retrieved from http://www2.icma.org/main/ld.asp?from=search&ldid=18012&hsid=1

Iso-Ahola, S. E. (1980). *The social psychology of leisure and recreation*. Dubuque, IA: W. C. Brown Co. Publishers.

Iso-Ahola, S. E., Jackson, E. L., & Dunn, E. (1994). Starting, ceasing, and replacing leisure activities over the life-span. *Journal of Leisure Research, 26*(3), 227–249.

Iwasaki, Y., & Mannell, R. (2000). Hierarchical dimensions of leisure stress coping. *Leisure Sciences, 22*(2), 163–181.

Jackson, E. L. (2000). Will research on leisure constraints still be relevant in the twenty-first century? *Journal of Leisure Research, 32*, 62–68.

Kaczynski, A. T., & Havitz, M. E. (2009). Examining the relationship between proximal park features and residents' physical activity in neighborhood parks. *Journal of Park & Recreation Administration, 27*(3), 42–58.

Kaczynski, A. T., & Henderson, K. A. (2007). Environmental correlates of physical activity: A review of evidence about parks and recreation. *Leisure Sciences, 29*(4), 315–354.

Kaczynski, A. T., Wilhelm Stanis, S. A., & Besenyi, G. M. (2012). Development and testing of a community stakeholder park audit tool. *American Journal of Preventive Medicine, 42*(3), 242–249.

Kenyon, G. S., & McPherson, B. D. (1973). Becoming involved in physical activity and sport: A process of socialization. In G. L. Rarick (Ed.), *Physical activity: Human Growth and development* (pp. 303–322). New York: Academic Press.

Kimm, S. Y. S., Glynn, N. W., McMahon, R. P., Vorhees, C. C., Striegel-Moore, R. H., & Daniels, S. R. (2006). Self-perceived barriers to activity participation among sedentary adolescent girls. *Medicine & Science in Sports & Exercise, 38*(3), 534–540.

King, S. (2006). *Pink Ribbon, Inc.: Breast cancer and the politics of philanthropy*. Minneapolis, MN: University of Minnesota.

Kuo, F. (2010). *Parks and other green environments: Essential components of a healthy human habitat*. National Recreation and Parks Association. Retrieved from http://www.nrpa.org/uploadedFiles/nrpa.org/Publications_and_Research/Research/Papers/MingKuo-Research-Paper.pdf

Labonte, R. (1994). Health promotion and empowerment: Reflections on professional practice. *Health Education & Behavior, 21*(2), 253–268.

Leahy, J., Shugrue, M., Daigle, J., & Daniel, H. (2009). Local and visitor physical activity through media messages: A specialized benefits-based management application at Acadia National Park. *Journal of Park & Recreation Administration, 27*(3), 59–77.

Librett, J. J., Henderson, K. A., Godbey, G. C., & Morrow, J. R. (2007). An introduction to parks, recreation, and public health: Collaborative frameworks for promoting physical activity. *Journal of Physical Activity and Health, 4*(1), S1–S13.

Lloyd, K., & Little, D. E. (2010). Self-determination theory as a framework for understanding women's psychological well-being outcomes from leisure-time physical activity. *Leisure Sciences, 32*(4), 369–385.

Macintyre, S., Ellaway, A., & Cummins, S. (2002). Place effects on health: How can we conceptualise, operationalise and measure them? *Social Science & Medicine, 55*(1), 125–139.

Mannell, R. C., & Kleiber, D. A. (1997). *A social psychology of leisure*. State College, PA: Venture Publishing.

McLeroy, K. R., Bibeau, D., Steckler, A., & Glanz, K. (1988). An ecological perspective on health promotion programs. *Health Education Quarterly, 15*, 351–377.

Mowen, A. (2010). *Parks, Playgrounds and Active Living. Robert Wood Johnson Foundation*. Retrieved from http://activelivingresearch.org/files/Synthesis_Mowen_Feb2010_0.pdf

Neulinger, J. (1981). *The psychology of leisure* (2nd ed.). Springfield, IL: C.C. Thomas.

Newton, M., Watson, D. L., Kim, M. S., & Beacham, A. O. (2006). Understanding motivation of underserved youth in physical activity settings. *Youth & Society, 37*(3), 348–371.

Orsega-Smith, E. M., Payne, L. L., Mowen, A. J., Ching-Hua, H., & Godbey, G. C. (2007). The role of social support and self-efficacy in shaping the leisure time physical activity of older adults. *Journal of Leisure Research, 39*(4), 705–727.

Pagano, I. S., Barkhoff, H., Heiby, E. M., & Schlicht, W. (2006). Dynamical modeling of the relations between leisure activities and health indicators. *Journal of Leisure Research, 38*(1), 61–77.

Payne, L. L., Ainsworth, B. E., & Godbey, G. (2010). *Leisure and health: Making the connection*. State College, PA: Venture Publishing, Inc.

Payne, L. L., Mowen, A. J., & Montoro-Rodriguez, J. (2006). The role of leisure style in maintaining the health of older adults with arthritis. *Journal of Leisure Research, 38*(1), 20–45.

Payne, L. L., & Orsega-Smith, E. (2010). Relations between leisure, health and wellness. In L.L. Payne, B. Ainsworth, & G. Godbey (Eds.), *Leisure, health, and wellness: Making the connections*. State College, PA: Venture Publishing, Inc.

Ridgers, N. D., Stratton, G., Fairclough, S. J., & Twisk, J. W. R. (2007). Long-term effects of a playground markings and physical structures on children's recess physical activity levels. *Preventive Medicine, 44*(5), 393–397.

Rojek, C. (1999). Deviant leisure: The dark side of free-time activity. In E. L. Jackson & T. L. Burton (Eds.), *Leisure studies: Prospects for the twenty-first century* (pp. 81–95). State College, PA: Venture Publishing, Inc.

Rojek, C. (2000). *Leisure and culture*. New York: St. Martin's Press.

Slater, S., Fitzgibbon, M., & Floyd, M. F. (2013). Urban adolescents' perceptions of their neighborhood physical activity environments. *Leisure Sciences, 35*(2), 167–183.

Spengler, J. O., Young, S. J., & Linton, L. S. (2007). Schools as a community resource for physical activity: Legal considerations for decision makers. *American Journal of Health Promotion, 21*(4s), 390–396.

Stewart, W. P., Parry, D. C., & Glover, T. D. (2008). Writing leisure: Values and ideologies of research. *Journal of Leisure Research, 40*(3), 360–384.

Stodolska, M., Shinew, K. J., Acevedo, J. C., & Roman, C. G. (2012). "I was born in the hood": Fear of crime, outdoor recreation and physical activity among Mexican-American urban adolescents. *Leisure Sciences, 35*(1), 1–15.

Tanier, M. (April 12, 2012). *Big Price Tags Attached to Even the Littlest Leagues*. New York Times. http://www.nytimes.com/2012/04/24/sports/big-price-tags-attached-to-even-the-littlest-leagues.html?pagewanted=all&_r=2&

Thompson, A., Rehman, L., & Humbert, M. (2005). Factors influencing the physically active leisure of children and youth: A qualitative study. *Leisure Sciences, 27*, 421–438.

Tsai, E. H.-L., & Coleman, D. J. (2009). The influence of constraints and self-efficacies on participation in regular active recreation. *Leisure Sciences, 31*(4), 364–383.

Wheaton, B. (2007). Identity, politics, and the beach: Environmental activism in Surfers Against Sewage. *Leisure Studies, 26*(3), 279–302.

Wilhelm Stanis, S. A., Schneider, I. E., & Anderson, D. H. (2009). State park visitors' leisure time physical activity, constraints, and negotiation strategies. *Journal of Park & Recreation Administration, 27*(3), 21–41.

Wolch, J., Jerrett, M., Reynolds, K., McConnell, R., Chang, R., Dahmann, N., . . . Berhane, K. (2011). Childhood obesity and proximity to urban parks and recreational resources: A longitudinal cohort study. *Health & Place, 17*(1), 207–214. doi: http://dx.doi.org/10.1016/j.healthplace.2010.10.001

World Health Organization. (1946). *Preamble to the Constitution of the World Health Organization*. Paper presented at the International Health Conference, New York.

Zick, C. D., Smith, K. R., Brown, B. B., Fan, J. X., & Kowaleski-Jones, L. (2007). Physical activity during the transition from adolescence to adulthood. *Journal of Physical Activity and Health, 4*, 125–137.

9

Leisure and Religion/Spirituality

Paul Heintzman (University of Ottawa)

Religion is important in the daily lives of approximately 68% of the world's population or 4.6 billion people (Diener, Tay, & Myers, 2011). A recent survey of Canadians found that 73% considered themselves either religious and/or spiritual while 27% considered themselves neither religious or spiritual (Angus Reid Institute, 2015). The English word "spirituality" comes from the Latin, *spiritus,* meaning "breath of life" and can be traced to the Greek word *pneuma* used in the New Testament to describe a person's spirit guided by God's Spirit. Today, spirituality may be defined as "the feelings, thoughts, experiences, and behaviors that arise from a search for the sacred" (i.e., divine being, Ultimate Reality or Ultimate Truth) (Larson, Swyers, & McCullough, 1998, p. 21). The English word "religion" is related to the Latin word *legare,* which means to connect. The main goal of religion is the facilitation of spirituality as defined above, and it may also include: (a) a search for non-sacred goals such as identity and belongingness and (b) "the means and methods . . . of the search that receive validation and support from within an identifiable group of people" (Larson et al., 1998, p. 21).

During recent decades there has been increasing discussion of spirituality within leisure studies and services. Perusal of a community's recreation programs often reveals activities that have spiritual elements. However, the relationship between leisure and spirituality is not a recent development. In Judaism, the practice of Sabbath rest is "paradigmatic for leisure in general and . . . may serve as a model for an ethic of leisure" (Lamm, n.d.). Jewish scriptures instruct Jews to refrain from work on the Sabbath, however, a corollary of abstaining from work is rest, which was created on the seventh day and is the culmination of creation. Thus Sabbath is a time of celebration: "not a date but an atmosphere" (Heschel, 1951, p. 21) that permeates all of life.

In Christianity, Augustine (345–430CE), Aquinas (1225–1274CE) and medieval monastics saw the contemplative life or the life of leisure *(otium)* as important and essential to spirituality. This spiritual understanding of leisure was summarized by Pieper (1963): "Leisure . . . is in the first place, an attitude of mind, a condition of the soul . . . a contemplative attitude . . ." (pp. 40–41). Contemporary Christian views of leisure include: classical, especially among Roman Catholics (e.g., Doohan, 1990; Pieper), activity (e.g., Ryken, 1995), time (e.g., Neville, 2004) and holistic (e.g., Heintzman, 2015; Joblin, 2009) concepts.

The activity view of leisure is prominent in Islam (Martin & Mason, 2004). The prophet Mohammed (570–633CE) stated, "Recreate your hearts hour after hour, for the tired hearts go blind" and "Teach your children swimming, shooting, and horseback riding" (Ibrahim, 1991, p. 206). In Islam, leisure activities fulfill three desires: amusement, relaxation, and laughter; rhythmic tunes and the experience of objects through the senses; and the desire to wonder, learn, and gain knowledge.

While the classical definition of leisure as a state of being has had spiritual overtones for centuries, other conceptualizations of leisure are also associated with spirituality. When leisure is defined as free time, the free time can be used for spiritual growth. When leisure is defined as activity, spiritual activities can be included. Peak experience, optimal experience, and flow, which are associated with the state of mind view of leisure, have also been used to describe spiritual experiences. Holistic leisure overlaps with spirituality as a way of being.

SYNTHESIS OF EMPIRICAL RESEARCH

The remainder of the chapter will synthesize empirical findings on leisure (excluding tourism and outdoor/adventure education) and spirituality using a framework

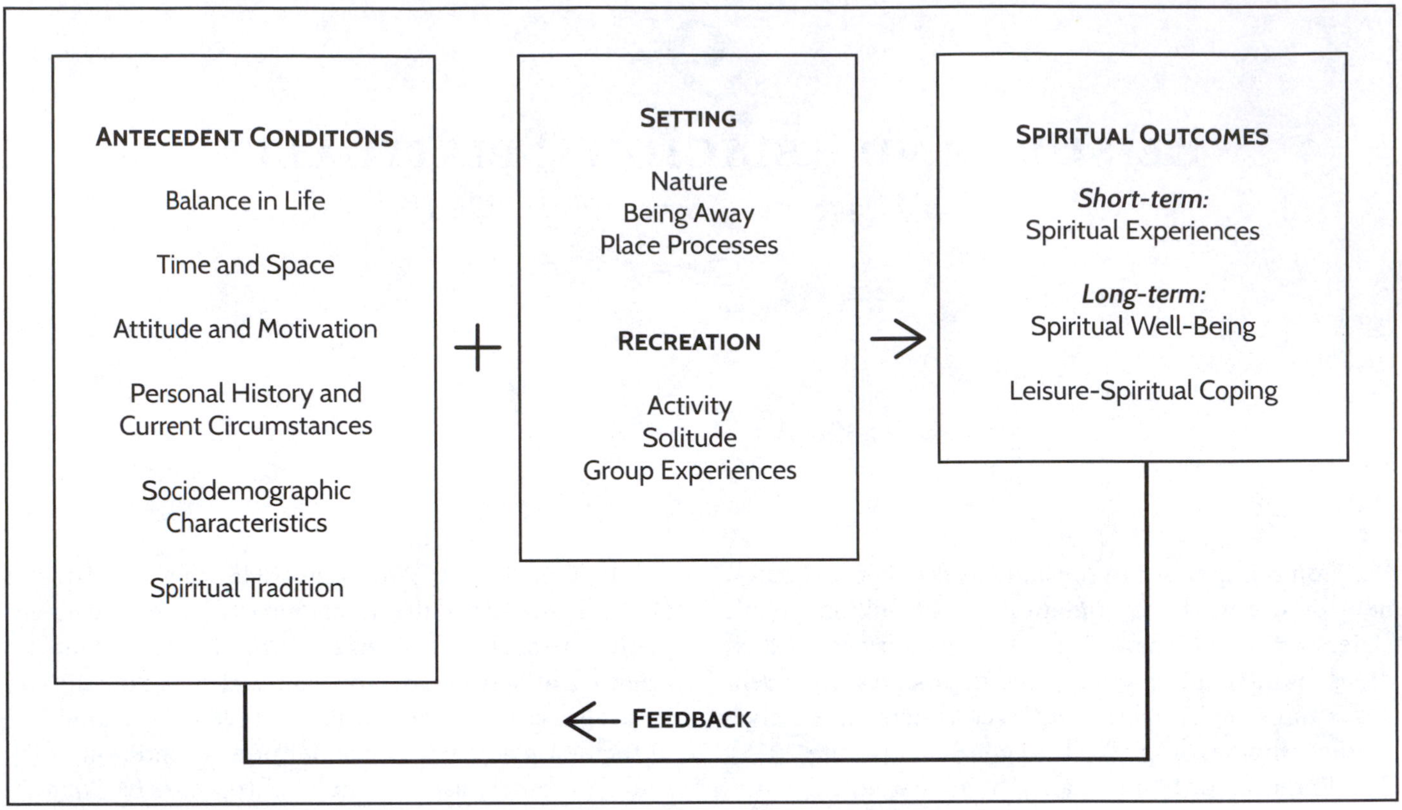

Figure 9.1. Leisure and Spirituality

that includes antecedent conditions, setting and recreation factors, and spiritual outcomes (see Figure 9.1). The framework identifies factors that influence spiritual outcomes. Not all of the factors are necessary or sufficient for spiritual outcomes. The specific factors and combination of factors may vary.

Spiritual Outcomes

The most common outcome studied is *spiritual experience* which often includes affective dimensions (feelings such as peace, awe, love), cognitive processes (e.g., contemplation), transcendence of one's self and environment, and a high level of emotional intensity (Stringer & McAvoy, 1992). Schmidt and Little's (2007) phenomenological study of leisure as a spiritual experience found it to be characterized by expressions of sensation and emotion as the spiritual dimensions of leisure were experienced affectively. Spiritual experience in nature settings has been characterized by emotions of awe and wonderment, feelings of connectedness, heightened senses, inner calm, joy, inner peace, inner happiness, and elatedness (Fox, 1997); intense and often positive emotions (Stringer & McAvoy, 1992); peacefulness, including peace with oneself and the world (Heintzman, 2007); and religious-like or self-transcending feelings of peace and humility (Fredrickson & Anderson, 1999). Positive feelings experienced at camp about oneself and camp, such as happiness, love, and peace, enhanced youth campers' spirituality (Sweatman & Heintzman, 2004). Feelings of unity with oneself and with nature were mentioned by urban park visitors as a spiritual component of the park experience (Chiesura, 2004).

Haluza-Delay (2000) criticized these types of studies as focusing exclusively on pleasant emotional states and urged investigation on whether or not the experiences lead to life transformation which has been considered in some recent research. McDonald, Wearing, and Ponting (2009) discovered that participants' peak experiences in wilderness facilitated the sacredness of life, meaning and purpose, and transcendent dimensions of spirituality. An indirect, but not direct relationship has been found between the spiritual experiences of surfers and scuba divers and environmentalism (Moore, 2011). Forest recreationists who were spirituality seekers in terms of place meanings held preservationist values based on spiritual beliefs related to revering and preserving the landscape (Hutson & Montgomery, 2010).

An outcome that reflects life transformation is *spiritual well-being,* which Hawks (1994) defined as:

> A high level of faith, hope, and commitment in relation to a well-defined worldview or belief system that provides a sense of meaning and purpose to existence in general, and that offers an ethical path to personal fulfilment which includes connectedness with self, others, and a higher power or larger reality. (p. 6)

A quantitative study ($N = 361$) found significant positive correlations between spiritual well-being scores and leisure participation, motivation, attitude, and satisfaction scores, but not with constraints on participation (Ragheb, 1989). In a subsequent study ($N = 219$), frequency of leisure participation and level of leisure satisfaction were positively associated with spiritual wellness (Ragheb, 1993). Higher levels of satisfaction with the relaxational and aesthetic-environmental components of leisure were dominant in their contributions to spiritual wellness. A limitation of these studies was the measurement of spiritual well-being with just one or two questionnaire items, making it difficult to capture the complexity of spiritual well-being and assess the reliability of its measurement. Using six items to measure perceived spiritual wellness Tsai and Wu (2005) discovered correlations between leisure participation and perceived spiritual wellness among adults aged 55–75 in Taiwan.

A more specific study ($N = 268$) of leisure and spiritual well-being that investigated the relationship between four dimensions of leisure style (activity, motivation, setting, time) and spiritual well-being as measured by two scales (Heintzman, 1999). In regards to *leisure settings*, those who pursued leisure in quiet urban recreation areas and their own homes reported higher levels of spiritual well-being. Participation in personal development activities was the best predictor of spiritual well-being, followed by stimulus-avoidance motivations and frequency of engaging in leisure in one's own home.

The concept of spiritual well-being has also been used in studies of park visitors (Lemieux et al., 2012), wilderness canoeists (Heintzman, 2007, 2008b), yoga (Pham, 2013), and college students' leisure preferences (Doi, 2004). Few studies have examined whether leisure negatively impacts spirituality; however, studies suggest leisure can both enhance and detract from spiritual well-being (see Figure 9.2) (Heintzman, 1999, 2000).

Another outcome is *leisure-spiritual coping* which refers to the ways people receive help, in the context of their leisure, from spiritual resources (e.g., higher power, spiritual practices, faith community) during periods of life stress (Heintzman, 2008a). Studies illustrate the importance of spirituality in the leisure coping process:

- Women who had experienced a major life change (e.g., deterioration of personal health, major career change, death of a loved one) found that a wilderness trip afforded the opportunity to leave everyday life stresses and experience spiritual rejuvenation (Fredrickson & Anderson, 1999).
- Spiritual functions of leisure such as sacralisation (leisure sensitizes one to the spiritual) and place processes (nature, sense of place, being away) ameliorated the negative influence of time pressure on spiritual well-being (Heintzman & Mannell, 2003).
- Spiritual engagement during the leisure of unpaid caregivers served as a means of coping with challenging and stressful life experiences (Rehman, Reading, & Unruh, 2009).
- Leisure has been used to spiritually cope with cancer through dragon boat racing (Parry, 2009; Unruh & Elvin, 2004), gardening (Unruh, Smith, & Scammell, 2000), and a recreation therapy and exercise program (Groff, Battaglini, Sipes, O'Keefe, & Peppercorn, 2009).
- In studies on marginal groups (e.g., Aboriginal people) Iwasaki, MacKay, Mactavish, Ristock, and

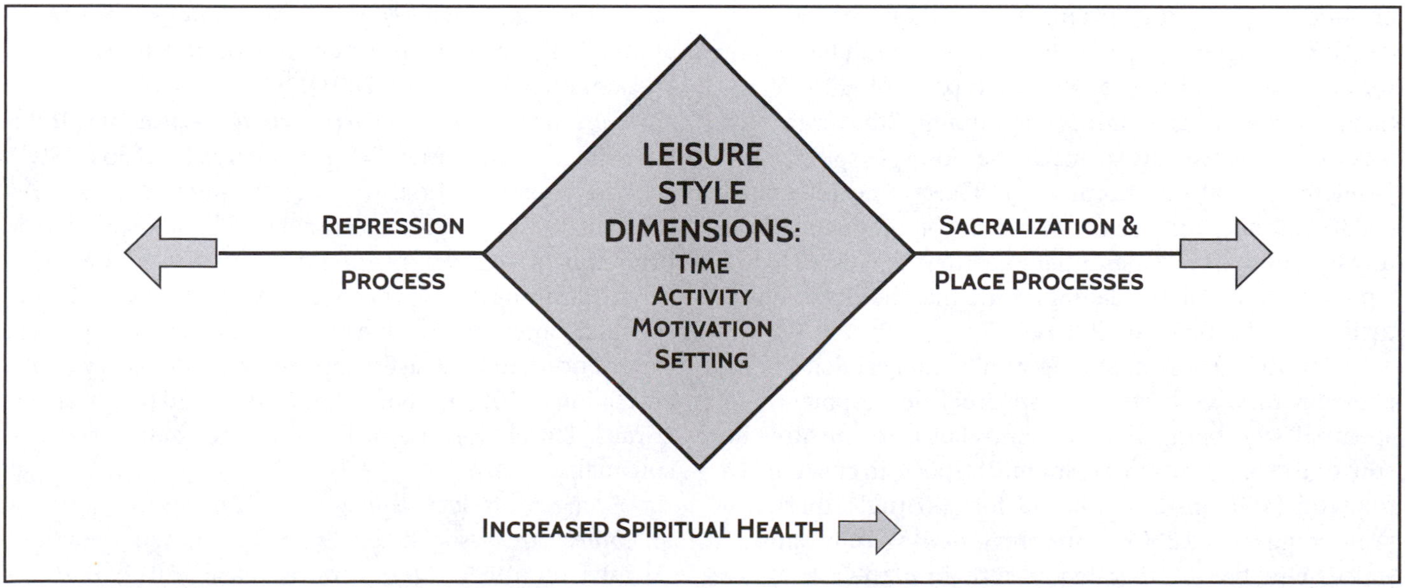

Figure 9.2. Model of Leisure and Spiritual Health

Bartlett (2006) found that using active leisure to cope with stress included both spiritual activities (e.g., spiritual reading) pursued in leisure to cope with stress and the opportunity to obtain spiritual meanings.

- Leisure experience facilitated spirituality as a key coping mechanism for parents of children with cancer (Schneider & Mannell, 2006).

An illustration of meaning-making through leisure-spiritual coping is provided by a study of the leisure experiences of older women living with HIV/AIDS (Gosselink & Myllykangas, 2007). These women were disenfranchised and encountered economic, social, and structural constraints. Following HIV/AIDS diagnosis, the meaning of leisure was transformed for all of the women in the study. As their disease progressed the women experienced spiritual transcendence and developed a spiritual view of leisure, which became a metaphor for meaning in life. Leisure advanced the women's well-being through therapeutic benefits, such as resilience in transcending systemic barriers they faced as a result of being female, over 50, and HIV/AIDS infected. As the disease progressed, the women's transcendence matured and their resolve to overcome obstacles increased. The newfound spirituality of all the women "continued to grow and provide meaning such that they viewed nature, animals, friends, family, and advocacy as leisure vehicles through which they could express their spirituality" (p. 16).

Antecedent Conditions

Antecedent conditions refer to people's characteristics prior to their leisure experience. For example, *balance in life*, in contrast to busyness, has been identified as conducive to spiritual well-being (Heintzman, 2000). Leisure provided opportunities for mental health professionals to develop a balanced life which overlapped with the search for an integrated life (i.e., physical, psychological, emotional, and spiritual) and it was through "the search for integration, that leisure seemed to be closest to spirituality" (Anderegg et al., 2002, p. 194). Those who integrated leisure into their life, as compared to compartmentalizing it, were more open to spiritual experiences; leisure led to a more balanced and meaningful life that facilitated spirituality (Grafanaki et al., 2005).

Findings from qualitative studies suggest that leisure provides *time and space*: for spiritual development and spiritual well-being (Heintzman, 2000); to nurture the spiritual dimension of life (Schmidt, 2006); to create space for God (Williams, 2010); and for spiritual experience (Anderegg et al., 2002). Anderegg et al.'s study showed those who have integrated leisure into their lives, in comparison to those trying to set aside a special time for leisure, were more receptive to spiritual experiences that occurred during the course of everyday life. Some marginalized persons may deliberately create a spiritual leisure space or an oasis where they can renew themselves (Iwasaki et al., 2005).

Leisure created "time and space" does not necessarily guarantee spiritual well-being, rather a key factor is the *attitude* brought to an activity, one characterized by "keeping awareness open," "seeing with new eyes," "intentionality," "discernment," and "being open to seeing" (Heintzman, 2000). Leisure characterized by a sense of gratitude, a celebration of life and creation, and being in the moment was associated with spirituality, "changing the most ordinary of experiences into something extraordinary, miraculous, and spiritual" (Anderegg et al., 2002, p. 174). For belly dancers, dancing becomes spiritual when they let go, are introspective and "get into a zone" (Kraus, 2009, p. 612). Being "in the zone" is also a factor for snowboarders (Elliot, 2010).

Closely related to attitude is *motivation*. Higher levels of *leisure motivation* have been correlated with spiritual well-being (Heintzman, 1999; Ragheb, 1989), as has leisure engaged in for intellectual (e.g., discover new things, be creative) and stimulus-avoidance (e.g., slow down, rest) motives (Heintzman, 1999). A positive correlation has been found between spiritual motivations for surfing and Spiritual Experience Assessment scores that reflect the occurrence and magnitude of spiritual experience post-activity (Moore, 2011). While some qualitative studies suggest that some wilderness recreationists did not experience spiritual outcomes because they were not seeking them (Heintzman, 2007; Stringer & McAvoy, 1992), quantitative studies suggest many (46% to 82%) but not all wilderness/park visitors are motivated by spiritual outcomes (e.g., Brayley & Fox, 1998; Lemieux et al., 2012), although these outcomes may not be the most valued (Behan, Richards, & Lee, 2001).

Personal history and current circumstances may influence spiritual outcomes. Baggage such as fear (Fox, 1999), spiritual mentorship from another person or a book (Foster, 2012), previous awareness of one's spirituality, prior spiritual experiences, and needing to address personal questions (Stringer & McAvoy, 1992) may influence spiritual outcomes during wilderness recreation. More experienced, in contrast to less experienced, snowboarders (Elliot, 2010), climbers (Pond, 2013) and belly dancers (Kraus, 2009) were more likely to see their activity as spiritual.

In regards to *sociodemographic characteristics*, spiritual outcomes: are associated more with women than men (Heintzman, 1999, 2012; Lemieux et al., 2012; Lusby & Anderson, 2010), are described more completely by women

(Unruh & Hutchison, 2011), increase with age (Heintzman, 2012); increase with education (Heintzman, 2012; Moore, 2011; Winter, 2007); and decrease with income (Heintzman, 2012; Lemieux et al., 2012).

Spiritual tradition was identified as the most dominant factor in spiritual experience during one's surfing or scuba diving (Moore, 2011). Spiritual outcomes may vary based on one's spiritual tradition. There is a difference in the leisure activities of New Christians and New Spirituals (Berkers, 2012). Wilderness visitors with Christian understandings of spirituality viewed nature as God's creation, which is entwined with their spirituality (Foster, 2012, Heintzman, 2008b). Gardeners with religious views viewed their garden "as an extension of their spirituality and a confirmation of their beliefs" while those with secular views tended to "embed their spirituality in their relationship with nature as manifested in their garden" (Unruh & Hutchinson, 2011, p. 572). Those from a religious spiritual tradition articulated a metaphysical framework in which their spiritual experiences in nature were viewed as purposeful and intelligible while those with nonreligious spiritual perspectives struggled to come up with, or resisted interpretations of their spiritual experiences that gave any substantial meaning other than being pleasant or extraordinary psychological states (Snell & Simmonds, 2012). One's spiritual tradition influenced if and how the activities of climbing (Pond, 2013), belly dancing (Kraus, 2009) and snowboarding (Elliot, 2010) were perceived as spiritual. The pagan and Satanist spirituality of fringes of the Goth Scene influences, and is interwoven with, their use of dark leisure (Spracklen & Spracklen, 2013).

Setting Factors

Factors related to leisure settings, such as being in nature, being away to a different environment and place processes, may influence spiritual outcomes. Qualitative studies on leisure in all settings have determined *nature* to be conducive to spiritual outcomes for a variety of reasons as nature: elicits a sense of wonder, awe, and amazement (Anderegg et al., 2002; Ellard et al., 2009; Fox, 1997; Heintzman, 2000) that may lead to spiritual meditation and reflection (Anderegg et al., 2002); provides opportunity to connect with God or a higher power (Ellard et al., 2009; Heintzman, 2000, 2007, 2008b; Hoover, 2012; Livengood, 2009); gives a sense of peacefulness, freedom, calm, stillness, or tranquility (Fox, 1997; Heintzman, 2007; Sweatman & Heintzman, 2004); offers therapeutic (Fox, 1997), life-giving (Heintzman, 2000), and healing benefits (Lusby & Anderson, 2010); stimulates peak experiences that facilitate spiritual expression (McDonald et al., 2009); and nurtures the spirit (Lafrance, 2011). Schmidt and Little (2007) observed that nature triggered respondents' spiritual experience through inspiration, connection, escape, sense of place, peace, and wholeness. The biophysical characteristics of *bona fide* wilderness and direct contact with nature (Fredrickson & Anderson, 1999) and the natural backcountry setting (Marsh, 2008) have been associated with spirituality.

Being away to a different environment is conducive to spiritual outcomes. Stringer and McAvoy (1992) observed the greater opportunities and enhancement of spiritual experiences in the wilderness were usually ascribed to the lack of constraints and responsibilities characteristic of everyday life. Being away has been identified as facilitating spiritual outcomes in studies of: youth residential campers who were away from technology, pollution, and busy cities (Sweatman & Heintzman, 2004); canoeists away from everyday routine (Heintzman, 2007, 2008b) and information technology (Foster, 2012); Montana' vacationers who became spiritually grounded, re-centred, and refocused (Ellard et al., 2009); and monastery visitors (Ouellette, Kaplan, & Kaplan, 2005).

Various *place* concepts and processes during leisure have been associated with spirituality. Leisure settings that have a sense of personal history (e.g., childhood places) (Heintzman, 2000) or human history (e.g., old buildings) (Fox, 1999; Heintzman, 2000) have been found to be conducive to spiritual outcomes. The leisure-spiritual process of *sense of place* has been positively correlated with spiritual well-being (Heintzman, 1999), and the relationship between leisure activity participation and spiritual well-being has been mediated by the "place" spiritual function of leisure (Heintzman & Mannell, 2003). Introspection (e.g., "think about my personal and/or spiritual values") by wildlife related recreationists was positively associated with *place identity* (Anderson & Fulton, 2008) while spiritually inspirational characteristics of wilderness recreation have been linked to "*place attachment*" and "*sacred space*" (Fredrickson & Anderson, 1999; Kyle, Chapter 31). Finally, spiritual *place meanings* have been associated with: sacred sites by Apostle Islands' visitors (Salk, Schneider & McAvoy, 2010), natural environments by outdoor recreation professionals (Hutson, Montgomery, & Caneday, 2010), and personally significant Niagara Escarpment places by forest recreationists (Hutson & Montgomery, 2010).

Recreation Factors

Participants in qualitative studies have identified numerous and diverse leisure *activities* that they associate with spiritual outcomes (Berkers, 2012; Heintzman, 2000; Schmidt & Little, 2007; Stringer & McAvoy, 1992). Spiritual outcomes have also been documented in studies of belly dancing (Kraus, 2009, 2010, 2012; Moe, 2012), climbing

(Pond, 2013), dragon boat racing (Parry, 2009; Unruh & Elvin, 2004) gardening (Unruh & Hutchison, 2011; Unruh et al., 2000) four-wheel driving (Narayanan & Macbeth, 2009), snowboarding (Elliot, 2010), surfing and scuba diving (Moore, 2011), yacht cruising (Lusby & Anderson, 2010) and yoga (Odenheimer, 2012; Pham, 2013). While activities which facilitate spirituality vary from person to person, research suggests leisure activities that help people get in touch with themselves, express their personality, and are compatible with who they are, are the ones that promote spiritual well-being (Heintzman, 2000).

Significant positive relationships have been found between spiritual well-being and overall leisure activity participation, as well as engagement in the leisure activity categories of personal development activities, cultural activities, outdoor activities, and hobbies (Heintzman, 1999). There were negative correlations between spiritual well-being and watching television and videos, social dancing, and adventure trekking. Strong correlations have been found between reading and spiritual wellness (Heintzman, 1999; Ragheb, 1993). The use of leisure-spiritual processes to achieve spiritual well-being was significantly higher for college students who preferred outdoor activities compared to students who preferred playing sports (Doi, 2004). In regards to overall *leisure style*, that considers motivation as well as activity, a "mass media" leisure style (low leisure activity participation except for high participation in mass media activities and low leisure motivation) has been clearly associated with low spiritual well-being (Heintzman, 1999). Both those who might be characterized as having what might be termed a "personal development" leisure style (i.e., high level of participation in personal development activities) and those with an "overall active" leisure style (i.e., high level of participation in all leisure activity categories) were associated with higher levels of spiritual well-being.

Ontario Parks' visitors who spent most of their time at a park in more nature-oriented activities (e.g., viewing/photographing nature, guided hikes/walks) rated higher on the degree to which introspection/spirituality added to their satisfaction than did campers who spent most of their time in activities such as biking and motor boating (Heintzman, 1999, 2012). Similarly, Behan et al. (2001) found that spiritual benefits were valued more by foot travelers than by mountain bikers as it was easier for non-mechanized travelers to focus on nature. Nevertheless, four-wheel drive travel in the Australian desert has been found to have a spiritual dimension (Narayanan & Macbeth, 2009).

Challenging activities is a common theme in facilitating leisure as spiritual experience (Schmidt & Little, 2007). The physical challenge of canoeing and hiking (Fredrickson & Anderson, 1999) adventure, and mental and physical exercise (Marsh, 2008), have all been associated with spirituality. The type of spiritual outcome may also be influenced by the type of activity engaged in. Canoeists have been found to have had spiritual experiences focused on interconnections with people while mountain hikers described spiritual experiences involving appreciation of wilderness beauty (Stringer & McAvoy, 1992).

A qualitative study found that leisure activities characterized by *solitude* and quiet were conducive to spiritual well-being (Heintzman, 2000), while a quantitative study found a positive relationship between solitary leisure activity participation and spiritual well-being (Heintzman, 1999). The importance of solitude for spirituality has also been reported by canoeists who participated in a solo experience (Heintzman, 2007) or solo expedition (Swatton & Potter, 1998), solo hikers (Coble, Selin, & Erickson, 2003), backcountry adventurers (Marsh, 2008), and youth residential campers (Sweatman & Heintzman, 2004). In quantitative studies, Ontario Parks' campers who visited a park alone rated introspection/spirituality higher than those who were with others (Heintzman, 2012) while outdoor recreation professionals who held spiritual place meanings towards natural environments needed solitary contemplation in outdoor places (Hutson et al., 2010). Solitude in wilderness settings has led to peace, tranquility, a chance for an inner journey, time for self-reflection (Fox, 1997), and renewal resulting from contemplation of life's deepest questions, which can be difficult during everyday life (Fredrickson & Anderson, 1999).

While solitude is important to spiritual well-being, this theme is not the same as isolation; rather, solitude is balanced with community and *connections with others* (Heintzman, 2000). Connections with others during leisure (Berkers, 2012; Schmidt & Little, 2007), formal and informal social experiences of youth campers with camp staff and other camp participants (Sweatman & Heintzman, 2004), and care for others, community, and relatedness in mental health professionals lives (Anderegg et al., 2002) all contributed to spirituality. Bonds among climbers have spiritual implications (Pond, 2013) while connections with others is a factor in belly dance being considered spiritual (Kraus, 2009). Within the context of nature-based recreation, spirituality is linked to group experiences, including the sharing of experiences, ideas and friendship (Fredrickson & Anderson, 1999; Heintzman, 2007; Stringer & McAvoy, 1992); and teamwork (Fox, 1997). Conversations and discussions on one wilderness trip facilitated ongoing spiritual friendships (Heintzman, 2008b). Being part of a male-only or female-only group has also played an important role in spiritual outcomes (Fox, 1997; Fredrickson & Anderson, 1999; Heintzman, 2008b).

CONCLUSION

Recently Bouwer (2013) concluded,"existent evidence for supporting the statement that leisure is a moderator for spiritual well-being is (conceptually) too weak to make a valid case for it" (p. 292). For the most part Brouwer's conclusion is true. Despite dramatic increase in the social scientific study of the relationship between leisure and spirituality in the last 15 years, few of these studies are quantitative, and even fewer use the concept of spiritual well-being or spiritual well-being scales used frequently in other disciplines. Most studies to date are qualitative, with small sample sizes that allow for participants to self-define spirituality so there is little conceptual clarity regarding the spiritual outcomes that are mentioned in these studies. Nevertheless, the increasing numbers of studies suggest we can speculate on a number of factors, as outlined in this chapter, that connect leisure with spiritual outcomes of one form or another. Furthermore many factors conducive to spirituality, as identified by recent empirical research, are not necessarily new. These factors, such as time and space, balance, an attitude of receptivity and being in nature, being away, solitude, and connections with others have been advocated within Christian spirituality—and other traditional spiritual traditions—and passed down through the centuries through experiential knowledge and wisdom (Heintzman, 2015).

The theoretical framework presented in this paper (see Figure 9.1, p. 68), based on extant empirical research in contrast to earlier speculative frameworks (Deschênes, 2002; Heintzman, 2002; Karlis, Grafanaki, & Abbas, 2002), can serve as a guide in conducting future research on this topic, just as an earlier version focused on nature-based recreation (Heintzman, 2010) was used for research on surfing and scuba diving (Moore, 2011). The framework provides a way to explore the processes that link leisure and spirituality and help explain the complexity of the relationships between these two phenomena. Research needs to be continued and developed in nine ways. First, there has been a disproportionate emphasis upon nature-based recreation; more research is needed on leisure in other settings. Second, as suggested by Haluza-Delay (2000), research on spiritual behaviors and the long-term consequences rather than just the immediate feelings of leisure-based spiritual experiences is needed. Third, research has focused on the personal spiritual benefits with little attention to social relationships and the social and environmental justice dimensions of spirituality. Fourth, the concept of spiritual well-being and the use of spiritual well-being scales, prevalent in other social science disciplines, need to be expanded. Fifth, most research on this topic has been qualitative and more quantitative research is needed to determine whether qualitative findings can be generalized to larger populations. Sixth, it is important not to confuse spiritual outcomes and well-being with psychological outcomes and well-being (Bouwer, 2013). Seventh, although recent studies (Kraus, 2010, 2012; Pond, 2013) have explored specific serious leisure activities, more research is needed to understand spirituality within serious leisure contexts. Eighth, research is needed on how leisure represses as well as facilitates spiritual benefits. Ninth, as the experience of spirituality is different for diverse population groups, it is important to expand the study of these groups.

REFERENCES

Anderegg, M., Cini, F., Godula, M., MacKenzie, S. N., Nason, S., Pearson, D., & Grafanaki. S. (2002). *"When Heaven and Earth meet": A qualitative study on the experience of leisure and spirituality among mental health professionals* (Unpublished master's research project). Ottawa, ON: St. Paul University.

Anderson, D. H., & Fulton, D. C. (2008). Experience preference as mediators of the wildlife related recreation participation: Place attachment relationship. *Human Dimensions of Wildlife, 13,* 73–88.

Angus Reid Institute. (2015, March 26). Religion and faith in Canada today: Strong belief, ambivalence and rejection define our views. Retrieved from: http://angusreid.org/faith-in-canada/

Behan, J. R., Richards, M. T., & Lee, M. E. (2001). Effects of tour jeeps in a wildland setting on non-motorized recreationist benefits. *Journal of Park and Recreation Administration, 19*(2), 1–19.

Berkers, V. (2012). *Religion, spirituality and leisure: A relational approach. The experience of religion and spirituality of Dutch New Christians and New Spirituals during leisure activities* (Unpublished master's thesis). Utrecht University. Utrecht, Netherlands.

Bouwer, J. (2013). Leisure as moderator for spiritual well-being? In H. Westerink (Ed.), *Constructs of meaning and religious transformation: Current issues in the psychology of religion* (Vol. 4), (pp. 275–274). Göttingen, Germany: V& R Unipress.

Brayley, R. E., & Fox, K. M. (1998). Introspection and spirituality in the backcountry recreation experience. In M. D. Bialeshki & W. P. Stewart (Eds.), *Abstracts from the 1998 Symposium on Leisure Research* (p. 24). Ashburn, VA: National Recreation and Parks Association.

Chiesura, A. (2004). The role of urban parks for the sustainable city. *Landscape and Urban Planning, 68,* 129–138.

Coble, T. G., Selin, S. W., & Erickson, B. B. (2003). Hiking alone: Understanding fear, negotiation strategies and leisure experience. *Journal of Leisure Research, 35,* 1–22.

Dechênes, G. (2002). Pour une spiritualité du loisir. *Society and Leisure, 25*, 173–202.

Diener, E., Tay, L., & Myers, D. G. (2011). The religion paradox: If religion makes people happy, why are so many dropping out? *Journal of Personality and Social Psychology, 101*(6), 1278–1290.

Doi, A. S. (2004). *Spiritual well-being and leisure preferences in college students* (Unpublished master's thesis). Springfield College, Springfield, MA.

Doohan, L. (1990). *Leisure: A spiritual need.* Notre Dame, IN: Ave Maria Press.

Ellard, A., Nickerson, N., & Dvorak, R. (2009). The spiritual dimension of the Montana vacation experience. *Leisure/Loisir, 33*, 269–289.

Elliot, N. M. R. (2010). *'Soulriding' and the spirituality of snowboarding* (Unpublished doctoral dissertation). Kingston University. London, England.

Foster, I. M. (2012). *Wilderness, a spiritual antidote to the everyday: A phenomenology of spiritual experiences in the Boundary Waters Canoe Area Wilderness* (Unpublished master's thesis). University of Montana. Missoula, MT.

Fox, R. J. (1997). Women, nature and spirituality: A qualitative study exploring women's wilderness experience. In D. Rowe & P. Brown (Eds.), *Proceedings, ANZALS conference 1997* (pp. 59–64). Newcastle, NSW: Australian and New Zealand Association for Leisure Studies, and the Department of Leisure and Tourism Studies, The University of Newcastle.

Fox, R. (1999). Enhancing spiritual experience in adventure programs. In J. C. Miles & S. Priest (Eds.), *Adventure programming* (pp. 455–461). State College, PA: Venture Publishing, Inc.

Fredrickson, L. M., & Anderson, D. H. (1999). A qualitative exploration of the wilderness experience as a source of spiritual inspiration. *Journal of Environmental Psychology, 19*, 21–39.

Gosselink, C. A., & Myllykangas, S. A. (2007). The leisure experiences of older U.S. women living with HIV/AIDS. *Health Care for Women International, 28*, 3–20.

Grafanaki, S., Pearson, D., Cini, F., Godula, B., McKenzie, B., Nason, S., & Anderegg, M. (2005). Sources of renewal: A qualitative study of the experience and role of leisure in the life of counselors and psychologists. *Counselling Psychology Quarterly, 18*, 31–40.

Groff, D., Battaglini, C., Sipes, C., O'Keefe, C., & Peppercorn, J. (2009). Lessons from breast cancer survivors: The role of recreation therapy in facilitating spirituality and well-being. *Leisure/Loisir, 33*, 341–365.

Haluza-Delay, R. (2000). Green fire and religious spirit. *The Journal of Experiential Education, 23*, 143–149.

Hawks, S. (1994). Spiritual health: Definition and theory. *Wellness Perspectives, 10*, 3–13.

Heintzman, P. (1999). *Leisure and spiritual well-being: A social scientific exploration* (Unpublished doctoral dissertation). University of Waterloo, Waterloo, ON.

Heintzman, P. (2000). Leisure and spiritual well-being relationships: A qualitative study. *Society and Leisure, 23*, 41–69.

Heintzman, P. (2002). A conceptual model of leisure and spiritual well-being. *Journal of Park and Recreation Administration, 20*(4), 147–169.

Heintzman, P. (2007). Men's wilderness experience and spirituality: A qualitative study. In R. Burns & K. Robinson (Comps.), *Proceedings of the 2006 Northeastern Recreation Research Symposium* (pp. 216–225) (Gen. Tech. Rep. NRS-P-14). Newton Square, PA: U.S. Department of Agriculture, Forest Services, Northern Research Station.

Heintzman, P. (2008a). Leisure-spiritual coping: A model for therapeutic recreation and leisure services. *Therapeutic Recreation Journal, 42*, 56–73.

Heintzman, P. (2008b). Men's wilderness experience and spirituality: Further explorations. In C. LeBlanc & C. Vogt (Eds.), *Proceedings of the 2007 Northeastern Recreation Research Symposium* (pp. 55–59) (Gen. Tech. Rep. NRS-P-23). Newton Square, PA: U.S. Department of Agriculture, Forest Services, Northern Research Station.

Heintzman, P. (2010). Nature-based recreation and spirituality: A complex relationship. *Leisure Sciences, 32*, 72–89.

Heintzman, P. (2012). The spiritual dimension of campers' park experience: Management implications. *Managing Leisure, 17*, 370–385.

Heintzman, P. (2015). *Leisure and spirituality: Biblical, historical and contemporary perspectives.* Grand Rapids, MI: Baker Academic.

Heintzman, P., & Mannell, R. (2003). Spiritual functions of leisure and spiritual well-being: Coping with time pressure. *Leisure Sciences, 25*, 207–230.

Heschel, A. J. (1951). *The Sabbath.* New York: Farrar, Straus, & Giroux.

Hoover, M. (2012). Understanding National Park visitor experiences through backcountry register content analysis. In J. Bocarro & M. Stodolska (Eds.), *Abstracts from the 2012 Leisure Research Symposium.* Ashburn, VA: National Recreation and Park Association.

Hutson, G., & Montgomery, D. (2010). Stakeholder views of place meanings along the Niagara Escarpment: An exploratory Q methodological inquiry. *Leisure/Loisir, 34*, 421–442.

Hutson, G., Montgomery, D., & Caneday, L. (2010). Perceptions of outdoor recreation professionals toward place meanings in natural environments: A Q-method inquiry. *Journal of Leisure Research, 42*, 417–442.

Ibrahim, H. (1991). Leisure and Islam. In G. S. Fain (Ed.), *Leisure and ethics: Reflections on the philosophy of leisure* (pp. 203–220). Reston, VA: American Association for the study of Leisure and Recreation.

Iwasaki, Y., MacKay, K. J., Mactavish, J. B., Ristock, J., & Bartlett, J. (2006). Voices from the margins: Stress, active living, and leisure as a contributor to coping with stress. *Leisure Sciences, 28,* 163–180.

Iwasaki, Y., Mactavish, J., & MacKay, K. (2005). Building on strengths and resilience: Leisure as a stress survival strategy. *British Journal of Guidance and Counselling, 33*, 81–100.

Joblin, D. (2009). Leisure and spirituality: An engaged and responsible pursuit of freedom in work, play, and worship. *Leisure/Loisir, 33*, 95–120.

Karlis, G., Grafanaki, S., & Abbas, J. (2002). Leisure and spirituality: A theoretical model. *Society and Leisure, 25*, 205–214.

Kraus, R. (2009). Straddling the sacred and secular: Creating a spiritual experience through belly dance. *Sociological Spectrum, 29,* 598–625.

Kraus, R. (2010). They danced in the bible: Identity integration among Christian women who belly dance. *Sociology of Religion, 71*, 457–482.

Kraus, R. (2012). Spiritual origins and belly dance: How and when artistic leisure becomes spiritual. *Journal of Dance and Somatic Practices, 4*, 59–77.

Lafrance, M. N. (2011). Reproducing, resisting and transcending discourses of femininity: A discourse analysis of women's accounts of leisure. *Qualitative Research in Sport, Exercise and Health, 3*, 80–98.

Lamm, N. (n.d.). *A Jewish ethic of leisure*. Retrieved from: http://www.innernet.org.il/article.php?aid=356

Larson, D. B., Swyers, J. P., & McCullough, M. E. (1998). *Scientific research on spirituality and health: A consensus report*. Rockville, MD: National Institute for Health Care Research.

Lemieux, C. J., Eagles, P. F. J., Slocombe, D. S., Doherty, S. T., Elliot, S. J., & Mock, S. E. (2012). Human health and well-being motivations and benefits associated with protected area experiences: An opportunity for transforming policy and management in Canada. *Parks: The International Journal of Protected Areas and Conservation, 18*(1), 71–85.

Livengood, J. (2009). The role of leisure in the spirituality of New Paradigm Christians. *Leisure/Loisir, 33*, 389–417.

Lusby, C., & Anderson, S. (2010). Ocean cruising—a lifestyle process. *Leisure/Loisir, 34*, 85–105.

Marsh, P. E. (2008). Backcountry adventure as spiritual experience: A means-end study. *Journal of Experiential Education, 30*, 290–293.

Martin, W. M., & Mason, S. (2004). Leisure in an Islamic context. *World Leisure Journal, 46*(1), 4–13.

McDonald, M. G., Wearing, S., & Ponting, J. (2009). The nature of peak experiences in wilderness. *Humanistic Psychology, 37*, 370–385.

Moe, A. M. (2012). Beyond the belly: An appraisal of Middle Eastern dance (aka belly dance) as leisure. *Journal of Leisure Research, 44*, 201–233.

Moore, C. (2011). *Spiritual experiences and environmentalism of recreational users in the marine environment: New Zealand surfers and scuba divers* (Unpublished master's thesis). Lincoln, New Zealand: Lincoln University.

Narayanan, Y., & Macbeth, J. (2009). Deep in the desert: Merging the desert and the spiritual through 4WD tourism. *Tourism Geographies, 11*, 369–389.

Neville, G. (2004). *Free time: Toward a theology of leisure*. Birmingham, UK: University of Birmingham Press.

Odenheimer, E. F. (2012). *Adaptations of yoga: Christian interpretations* (Unpublished doctoral dissertation). University of Tennessee, Knoxville, TN.

Ouellette, P., Kaplan, R., & Kaplan, S. (2005). The monastery as a restorative environment. *Journal of Environmental Psychology, 25*, 178–188.

Parry, D. C. (2009). Dragon boat racing for breast cancer survivors: Leisure as a context for spiritual outcomes. *Leisure/Loisir, 33,* 317–340.

Pham, K. H. (2013). *Outcomes of a recreation therapy yoga meditation intervention on prison inmates' spiritual well-being* (Unpublished master's thesis). San Jose State University, California.

Pieper, J. (1963). *Leisure: The basis of culture*. New York: The New American Library.

Pond, M. F. (2013). *Investigating climbing as a spiritual experience* (Unpublished master's thesis). Ohio University, Athens, OH.

Ragheb, M. G. (1989). Step-wise regression analysis of leisure domains and the reported contribution of leisure activities to individuals' well-being: An exploratory study. *Society and Leisure, 12*, 399–412.

Ragheb, M. G. (1993). Leisure and perceived wellness: A field investigation. *Leisure Sciences, 15*, 13–24.

Rehman, L., Reading, C., & Unruh, A. (2009). "You grow from it…you get more spiritual": An exploration of spirituality, health, and leisure for unpaid caregivers. *Leisure/Loisir, 33*, 367–388.

Ryken, L. (1995). *Redeeming the time: A Christian approach to work and leisure*. Grand Rapids, MI: Baker Books.

Salk, R., Schneider, I. E., & McAvoy, L. H. (2010). Perspectives of sacred sites on Lake Superior: The case of the Apostle Islands. *Tourism in Marine Environments, 6*, 89–99.

Schmidt, C. (2006). The lived experience of the spiritual potential of leisure. *Annals of Leisure Research, 9*, 173–193.

Schmidt, C., & Little, D. E. (2007). Qualitative insights into leisure as a spiritual experience. *Journal of Leisure Research, 39*, 222–247.

Schneider, M. A., & Mannell, R. C. (2006). Beacon in the storm: An exploration of the spirituality and faith of parents whose children have cancer. *Issues in Comprehensive Pediatric Nursing, 29*, 3–24.

Snell, T. L., & Simmonds, J. G. (2012) "Being in that environment can be very therapeutic": Spiritual experiences in nature. *Ecopsychology, 4*, 326–335.

Spracklen, K., & Spacklen, B. (2013). Pagans and Satan and Goth, oh my: Dark leisure as communicative agency and communal identity on the fringes of the modern Goth scene. *World Leisure Journal, 54*, 350–362.

Stringer, L. A., & McAvoy, L. H. (1992). The need for something different: Spirituality and the wilderness adventure. *The Journal of Experiential Education, 15*, 13–21.

Swatton, A. G., & Potter, T. G. (1998). The personal growth of outstanding canoeists resulting from extended solo canoe expeditions. *Pathways: The Ontario Journal of Outdoor Education, 9*(6), 13–16.

Sweatman, M., & Heintzman, P. (2004). The perceived impact of outdoor residential camp experience on the spirituality of youth. *World Leisure Journal, 46*, 23–31.

Tsai, C-Y., & Wu, M-T. (2005). Relationship between leisure participation and perceived wellness among older persons in Taiwan. *Journal of ICHPER, 41*(3), 44–50.

Unruh, A. M., & Elvin, N. (2004). In the eye of the dragon: Women's experience of breast cancer, and the occupation of dragon boat racing. *Canadian Journal of Occupational Therapy, 71*, 138–149.

Unruh, A. M., & Hutchinson, S. (2011). Embedded spirituality: Gardening in daily life and stressful experiences. *Scandinavian Journal of Caring Sciences, 25*, 567–574.

Unruh, A. M., Smith, N., & Scammell, C. (2000). The occupation of gardening in life-threatening illness: A qualitative pilot study. *Canadian Journal of Occupational Therapy, 67*, 70–77.

Williams, R. R. (2010). Space for God: Lived religion at work, home and play. *Sociology of Religion, 71*, 257–279.

Winter, C. (2007). The intrinsic, instrumental and spiritual value of natural area visitors and the general public: A comparative study. *Journal of Sustainable Tourism, 15*, 599–614.

10

Sport as a Leisure Behavior

Laurence Chalip (University of Illinois)

Sport is one of the most ubiquitous leisure behaviors. Given the size of the sports market, the National Sporting Goods Association (NSGA) has tracked participation in 88 sports and recreational activities annually since 1993 among Americans age 7 and above (NSGA data are available via SBRnet). Not all sports have been tracked each year, and participation numbers vary somewhat each year in each sport. Nevertheless, the numbers present a picture of sport participation that demonstrates not merely that sport participation is widespread, but also that the patterns of participation do not track with the cultural saliency of particular sports. In 2012, for example, 57.7 million Americans exercised with equipment, 48.6 million swam, 40 million ran or jogged, and 35.5 million went bowling. Participation in culturally salient sports was also high, but somewhat lower, as 25.6 million played basketball, 21.1 million played golf (other than miniature golf), 13.7 million played soccer, 13.7 million played tennis, 12.1 million played baseball, and 7.9 million played (American) football.

It might be argued that many participants did these activities recreationally, rather than as competitive sports, or as training for competitive sport. There have been many efforts to define sport, and to differentiate it from recreation, typically requiring sports to include social comparison and physical activity. The problem is that some activities that meet those criteria (e.g., competitive ballroom dancing, piano competitions) are not popularly treated as sports, while some Olympic sports (e.g., archery, shooting) require negligible physicality. Although defining sport may give the appearance of academic rigor, allowing definitional taxonomies to shape or direct research is counterproductive, as strict distinctions between sport and recreation impose false rigor. Participants rarely care if their running, surfing, dancing, bowling, archery, or golf are recreations or sports. The activities in which people engage may (or may not) be physically demanding, and people may sometimes engage in social comparisons, but neither fact is routinely paramount to those who participate. Socializing, mastery of a skill, or a sense of well-being can be more important to participants (Ashford, Biddle, & Goudas, 1993; McCarthy & Jones, 2007). Further, motives are situational, subject to individual interpretation, and can change across the life course (Beltman & Volet, 2007; Lamprecht & Starnm, 1996). In other words, participation is so complexly determined that strict demarcation of sport from recreation risks blurring, truncating, or shrouding research insights because the primary (and important) scholarly concerns with causes and consequences of human activity, as well as the ramifications of variations in human activity, are thereby abridged.

More Americans watch sport than play sport. (SBRnet conducts an annual survey of Americans 13 years of age and older to determine how many Americans watch or attend a professional sport event each year.) Over half the American population was estimated to have watched (on television or over the Internet) or attended a professional sport event in 2012. Football, baseball, and basketball were the most popular sports to watch, with 152.7 million Americans having watched at least one NFL game, 120.3 million having watched at least one Major League Baseball game, and 85.6 million having watched at least one NBA game. The NHL (ice hockey), NASCAR, Mixed Martial Arts, IndyCar, and professional lacrosse also posted numbers that exceed or are equivalent to participation rates in America's most popular participation sports. Thus, sport as a passive entertainment is an even more ubiquitous leisure behavior than is sport as an active pursuit.

The study of sport behaviors has burgeoned in recent decades, and there has been substantial proliferation of research topics and theories. Although a wide array of questions are now addressed, eight big questions undergird sport studies:

1. Why do people watch (or not watch) sport?
2. Why do people do (or not do) sport?

3. What facilitates and what inhibits watching sport?
4. What facilitates and what inhibits doing sport?
5. What are the social and psychological effects, if any, of sport fanship?
6. What are the social and psychological effects, if any, of doing sport?
7. What is the relationship between watching sport and doing sport?
8. How can answers to the first seven questions be used to manage and market sport most effectively and efficiently?

Answers to these questions are clearly culturally dependent. Even though a sport may look the same in different cultures, it is unlikely to *mean* the same in different cultures (Markus, Uchida, Omoregie, Townsend, & Kitayama, 2006; Stewart & Lacassagne, 2005). It is a common mistake for researchers and practitioners to treat sport as if it were a universal language. Despite the ubiquity of claims about sport's universal character, despite the global presence of sport competitions, and despite the increasing use of sport as a tool for development, sport is not interpreted, valued, or organized in a singular manner across the globe (see Chapters 12 to 16). In fact, the nature of variations in cultural constructions of sport, as well as the causes and consequences of those variations, are themselves noteworthy topics for research.

Two interrelated claims are commonly used to undergird assertions regarding sport's universal value. The first asserts that competitiveness is intrinsic to human nature. The second asserts that the competitive experiences that sport provides render social and psychological benefits. Both claims are false. Research by anthropologists and cross-cultural psychologists finds that cultures (and, consequently, people living in those cultures) vary greatly in the degree to which they value competition, if at all (Hayward & Kemmelmeier, 2007; Mead, 1961). There are also substantial differences in the value placed upon competition among ethnic groups residing in the same country or community (Madsen, 1971; Sommerlad & Bellingham, 1972). These differences are important because they affect preferred styles of play (Allison, 1980; Light, 2000), requisite designs for coaching (Greenman, 2005), and even whether a particular set of rules or game behaviors is acceptable to a target population (Ager, 1977; Vander Velden, 1986). Similarly, research finds that competition is rarely, if ever, preferable to cooperation as a condition for personal or social development (Kohn, 1992).

It is instructive to consider that universalist claims about sport and competition have retained their traction despite decades of evidence falsifying those claims. In order for sport research to contribute fully to our understandings of the causes and consequences of sport behaviors, it is first necessary to shed false presuppositions. Sport has certainly become a salient conduit for international exchange; but effective management, marketing, and use of sport require cultural sensitivity and an analytic perspective on competition. Since the overwhelming majority of research addressing the eight big questions has been undertaken in developed Western (and typically urban) cultural settings, the following review pertains particularly to those settings. More work is needed to explore the big eight questions beyond Western (and urban) settings.

Sport behaviors often differ as a function of age, gender, ethnicity, and social class (Coakley, 2009). Some research incorporates one or more of these variables, but it is rare for all four to be included simultaneously. Each is best understood as a proxy for particular social, cultural, or psychological conditions. For example, age effects are generally attributed to life course differences in life tasks or scripts (Ostrow, Jones, & Spiker, 1981; Tischer, Hartmann-Tews, & Combrink, 2011); gender differences are commonly attributed to male and female socialization into culturally prescribed gender roles (Koivula, 1999; Lamprecht & Starnm, 1996; Matteo, 1986); effects of ethnicity and social class are typically ascribed to class and culture differences in values and/or beliefs (Ager, 1977; Light, 2000; Watson, 1977a). More work is needed to elaborate and explain age, gender, ethnicity, and social class effects in sport jointly and in reference to the big eight questions.

The following section considers what is known about watching sport, including implications of current knowledge (Questions 1, 3, 5, and 8). The subsequent section considers what is known about doing sport (Questions 2, 4, 6, and 8). A short section then considers the relationship between watching and doing sport (Question 7). A brief integrative conclusion is then provided.

WATCHING SPORT

Watching sport takes place in different contexts. Watching sport *in situ* (i.e., live at the competition) and watching sport on television or over the Internet are different, but both are typically social. The crowd is commonly understood to be a key attraction for watching sport events *in situ*. Melnick (1993) argued that attendance at sport events is, in fact, a search for social interaction. Menzies and Nguyen (2012) found that attendees at a motor sport event sought to escape everyday life by socializing with family or other attendees in the context of the event. Lee, Lee, Seo, and Green (2012) found that the crowd at sport events enhances the physical sense of social interaction because it elevates the sensory stimulation that spectators obtain. Holt (1995) spent two years observing baseball spectators, finding that being present at a game enables socializing, and that interpersonal interactions among spectators play vital roles in the ways that spectators interpret events on the field. Holt also found that spectators often engage in imaginary interactions with players, managers, and umpires, and sometimes develop a sense of relationship with them even though they have not met. The social character of sport events is fundamental to the spectator's game experience.

Watching sport on television or the Internet also has a social aspect despite the lack of a crowd. Of course, fans who use media, even exclusively, do develop a sense of relationship with favored teams, as demonstrated by the ways that they bask in the reflected glory (BIRG) when a favorite team wins (Dalakas, Madrigal, & Anderson, 2004). Fans also invite one another to watch sport at each others' homes. This is especially true for events with high social salience, such as the Super Bowl or an Olympic Games. Rothenbuhler (1988) found, for example, that Olympic viewers treat the event as a social holiday during which they invited family and friends to watch, typically sharing food, drink, and conversation. Fans also seek out bars and restaurants as venues to watch sport because those venues enable some of the sociability that is otherwise obtained by watching an event *in situ* (Eastman & Land, 1997). It has been estimated that the vast majority of those who watch sport on television or the Internet simultaneously use social media, especially Twitter and Facebook, to foster and amplify the social experience they obtain while watching (Wang, 2013).

Social connection and interaction, whether real or imagined, are consequently key to the value that spectators obtain from the experience of watching sport—a fact that has commercial relevance. Melnik (1993) recommended that sport teams and event organizers should find ways to foster sociability among spectators. Hognestad (2012) demonstrated that European soccer fans often maintain an interest in multiple clubs because following the performances of multiple clubs enhances their social networking. Fairley and Tyler (2012) found that providing sites (e.g., movie theaters) where fans who are not attending a sport event can gather to watch a sport event enables a social environment that fans value. Indeed, some fans preferred the theater venue to the stadium because they felt a stronger sense of community among spectators at the theater. Large events, such as the Olympic Games and the World Cup capitalize on this insight by incorporating "live sites" or "celebration sites" where spectators can gather in a public place to watch events on a large screen, usually accompanied by other musical or theatrical performances. These sites are expected to enhance the quality of social life in the communities where they are situated because they promote social interaction which, in turn, enables a shared sense of celebration (Chalip, 2006).

Social interaction while watching sport is dominated by conversation, which takes varied forms (Holt, 1995). The conversation includes speculations about what will happen, analysis of what has happened, and judgments about both. The conversation can occur before, during, or after the event as speculations and interpretations become the central feature of discussion. Consequently, the opportunities engendered for social interaction (even after the event is over) are a core reason that people watch sport events even when their favorite team is not playing (Fink & Parker, 2009). Indeed, when fanship of a particular sport, team, or event is ubiquitous, sport becomes such a substantial element of conversation that even non-fans feel compelled to follow the sport, team, or event sufficiently to be able to converse about it (Lever, 1983). Thus, sport becomes a social lubricant that facilitates social discourse, even across ethnic, social class, and gender lines. The actual facts of the contest are less important for this purpose than are the speculations, judgments, and interpretations that become grist for social discourse.

There have been several scales developed to measure fan motives (e.g., Trail & James, 2001; Wann & Branscombe, 1993). Although the dimensions of each scale vary somewhat, they all find a social motive for watching sport. Other important dimensions include drama and aesthetics. Although the scales typically measure the motive to socialize as if it were separate from and parallel to aesthetics and drama, it is more likely that drama and aesthetics enable the social interactions necessary for the social motive to be fulfilled. In other words, drama and aesthetics foster the social discourse that is a central feature of watching sport; they serve socialization, and are not merely motives that are parallel to it.

Evidence for that claim comes from experimental studies of people watching sport contests. Spectators find sport contests more appealing and more enjoyable when there are risky but effective plays, and when they are aware of personal stakes for the athletes and/or teams (Zillman, Bryant, & Sapolsky, 1989). The *in situ* study of sport spectators finds that significant and/or unusual plays, as well as the importance of those plays for the players or game outcomes, provide the specific instances for speculations, judgments, and interpretations that form the basis of spectator conversations (Holt, 1995). Further, even if fans watch alone, they typically seek to share their reactions and interpretations via social media (Wang, 2013).

In the process of interpreting plays and stakes, spectators make meaning from sport. There is nothing intrinsically significant about being able to kick an inflated white sphere into a net (soccer), hit a small round ball with a cylindrical piece of wood (baseball), carry a piece of pigskin across a line (American football), toss a large rubber sphere into a hoop (basketball), run around an oval (track), or swim from wall to wall (competitive swimming). These are invented activities with arbitrary rules, which are frequently rewritten. The activities become meaningful via the interpretations we make about them. Although interpretations may incorporate detailed analysis of the stakes of the game, specific plays, and particular outcomes, the deeper question to be asked about sport discourse is why any of that matters at all. The meanings that sport contests have for people are not intrinsic to the sport itself, but are socially constructed. They are stories we tell ourselves about ourselves.

In his analysis of sport story forms, Gusfield (1987) concluded that sports "are described in the dramatic language of conflict and . . . use commonplace metaphors and myths" (p. 209). In other words, because sports are contests, they enable stories. Further, those stories gain their power because they draw on classic mythic forms (e.g., David and Goliath) or because they become metaphors for contemporary concerns (e.g., when national rivals square off). Chalip (1997) studied the ways that athletes attain heroic status, and found that the narratives about those athletes described them in a manner that demonstrates the potential for transformation of self and society, the capacity to overcome adversity, the qualities requisite for achievement, and transcendence of the mundane. In other words, athletes who rise to heroic status are described by narratives that resonate with classic heroic templates. These findings demonstrate that the social consumption of sport is anchored in the story narratives that make sport meaningful to audiences. Much of sport's power is consequently at a non-conscious level; it is felt rather than analyzed. People may not be aware of the deeper meanings that make sport an attractive social engagement, and the non-conscious nature of those deeper meanings may enhance their attractiveness (Chartrand & Bargh, 2002). Further, by embedding non-sport genres (e.g., rituals, spectacle, and festival) and by layering symbols (e.g., mascots, awards, logos), the felt sense of meaning can be boosted (Chalip, 1992).

Audiences are attracted and built through the narratives and meanings that social interaction enables. Failures to create or sustain audience interest are grounded in failures to foster narratives that engender meanings and animate social interaction. Given the practical value that sport narratives have, one would expect there to have been a great deal of research into the construction and use of sport narratives in order to activate and capitalize upon the non-conscious motives of target audiences. There has been scant study of sport narratives, except to map particular thematic content. There has been no systematic study of the ways that audiences interpret different narratives, how audiences reinterpret and change narratives as they share and retell stories over time, or why particular narratives become significant while others are readily forgotten. We need a better understanding of the ways that episodic narratives (stories about a contest or an athlete) become meaningful to audiences, how episodic narratives can be strung together over time to create an appealing story arc, and the uses of backstory to add depth and added meaning to sport narratives. We need to know more about the interplay of genres and symbols with the ways that audiences interpret sport events. What we know about each of these matters is at best intuitive, as the necessary research has not yet been forthcoming.

DOING SPORT

When adults or children are asked why they do sport, the most common answer is that it is "fun" (Weiss & Chaumeton, 1992), and when people quit sport or choose not to do sport, the most common reason they give is that doing sport would not be "fun" (Carpenter & Scanlon, 1998). Of course, fun is not itself an explanation. It is a summary description of an hedonic sense of enjoyment. The key question is: what makes sport "fun?"

Several studies have sought to unpack what makes sport fun, especially for children and adolescents. Involvement in the action (Harris, 1984), a sense of adequate skill combined with quality feedback (Mandigo & Couture, 1996), and positive support from family, coaches, and teammates (Scanlan, Carpenter, Lobel, & Simons, 1993) are each associated with a sense of fun. Interestingly, although winning can enhance the sense of fun, it is not essential. Fun depends more on the sense of having performed well against the challenges that were faced (Wankel & Sefton, 1989). Coaches play a pivotal role in the ways that athletes make that determination (Cummming, Smoll, Smith, & Grossbard, 2007).

Although these factors are clearly important, they do not adequately predict or explain sport participation. The relative popularity of particular sports changes as people age (National Sporting Goods Association, reported in SBRnet), suggesting that age-related factors and a sport's organization play a significant role in the degree to which a sport is attractive to participants. This is important because it demonstrates that people take up different sports at different ages, either for the first time or as a substitute for sports that they have discontinued. There has been a great deal of concern about sport participation levels because physical activity is vital for health, and aggregate national declines in physical play are thought to contribute to increased rates of cardiovascular disease, diabetes, and other infirmities associated with a sedentary lifestyle (MacCallum, Howson, & Gopu, 2012). Although it is clear that the total volume of sport participation, especially among children, has been declining in recent years, the data also suggest that sport participation can be fostered among adolescents, young adults, and even among middle-aged adults if the nature of the sport and the ways it is organized are appropriate. It would be helpful to learn what makes golfing attractive to middle-aged Americans, why baseball participation peaks in childhood but rises again slightly in early adulthood, why basketball and volleyball are particularly popular sports for adolescents, why participation in gymnastics and soccer plummets after childhood, and why bowling is among the nation's most popular sports for participation at nearly every age and for both men and women (see also Bocarro & Edwards, Chapter 8; Caldwell, Chapter 21; and Kleiber, Chapter 23).

There is evidence that the ways sport is organized affects enjoyment, which should ultimately affect participation and retention. Adolescents experience informal sport settings as most enjoyable, formal sport training and competitions as least enjoyable, and sport during physical education as midway between informal and formal sport (Chalip, Csikszentmihalyi, Kleiber, & Larson, 1984). These findings suggest that the greater the degree of adult supervision and control, the less adolescents enjoy sport settings. This would be consistent with the developmental challenge of separation from adult control that is focal during adolescence (Smetana, 2005). Interestingly, coaches generally seek greater control over athletes during the adolescent years than they do with younger athletes. The increase in coach assertion of control during adolescence has been attributed to coaches' views that fun and mastery of sport skills are incompatible (Bengoechea, Strean, & Williams, 2004). One source of this view is the model of sport represented by professional teams, leagues, and events—a model that stresses work over play, specialization over variety, and rules designed for players who are mature, dedicated, and elite. Professional sports create a cultural pull to systems of sport that can be less-than-ideal for attracting, retaining, and developing athletes who are not (or not yet) elite (Chalip & Green, 1998). More work is needed to identify and test age- and skill-appropriate design and coaching of sport programs. Given the cultural pull to professionalized models of sport, even when such models are inappropriate, work is also required to formulate means to establish and maintain programs that differ from professional sport models by being more age- and skill-appropriate.

As with watching sport, participating in sport is fundamentally social, even if the sport is an individual sport. Sport participation is typically organized around clubs or teams, especially in the Western world, so the social climate of clubs and teams makes a difference. Youth sport that takes place outside of school in the United States is typically organized around parent-run clubs and leagues. The degree that those clubs and leagues are attractive to families depends on the sense of community that they engender among members (Chalip, Lin, Green, & Dixon, 2013). Although coaching and competition are important, those are ultimately judged in the context of the community feeling that is rendered by the experience of training and competing through the club and league.

Much the same is true in school and university sport, although variations in the ways that a sport is organized affect the ways that sense of community is enabled or hindered (Warner, Dixon, & Chalip, 2012). When the sport is managed by athletes themselves, as in the case of intramural or university club sport, the necessity that athletes take on the roles necessary to run their sport creates shared administrative activities that cultivate a sense of community. That does not occur when athletes play little or no role in running their sport, as in the case of American varsity sports. Yet sense of community can occur there nonetheless, because varsity athletes share a focus on quality sport competition. In other words, sport settings can enable a sense of community when there is a shared purpose, but differences in the ways that settings are structured will affect the intensity and quality of community that athletes experience.

Obtaining a sense of community in sport is complicated by the mere fact that sport is competitive. Competition can render social forces that lead to rancor (Watson, 1977b), dropout (Roberts & Chick, 1984), and consequent dysfunction or dissolution of sport programs and leagues (Chalip & Scott, 2005; Sharpe, 2003). This occurs for child, adolescent, and adult sport. If sport programs are to be managed effectively, then the disruptive social climate that sport competition can encourage also needs to be managed. The necessary means are not yet well understood, and are therefore in need of further study.

Despite the centrifugal social forces that sport can fuel, sport experiences are popularly believed to provide a means to socialize people, particularly children and adolescents, into preferred values and beliefs (Watson, 1977a). It is as if the team and competition experiences intrinsic to sport were sufficient to impart socially desired values and beliefs. In fact, however, whether sport provides positive, negative, or any benefits for socialization depends entirely on the nature and quality of experiences that the sport program provides and enables, especially the social dealings that athletes consequently obtain with family, coaches, and peers (Fraser-Thomas & Côté, 2009; Kremer-Sadlik & Kim, 2007). Just as the choice to participate in sport depends on the ways that sport programs are organized and experienced, so do the effects that sport has.

THE RELATIONSHIP BETWEEN WATCHING SPORT AND DOING SPORT

Intuitively, one would expect that having played a sport would make one more likely to watch sport, and that watching sport should inspire people to do sport. That expectation was central to the social mission that became the modern Olympic Movement (MacAloon, 1981), and there is evidence that knowledge about a sport can buttress watching the sport (Zhang, Smith, Pease, & Mahar, 1996). Yet the few empirical studies to date examining the relationship between watching sport and having done sport find little or no connection. The lack of a relationship has been demonstrated using different measures and methods among American adults (Burnett, Menon, & Smart, 1993), French adults (Irlinger, 1994), and Estonian children (Saar & Jürimäe, 2007).

It is not clear whether the lack of any demonstrable relationship between watching sport and doing sport is a consequence of differing motives for doing sport than for watching sport, or is a consequence of deficient marketing imagination among sport marketers. The lack of a relationship might indicate that watching sport and doing sport are fundamentally incongruous, or it might be a consequence of marketers' failure to create (and capitalize upon) potential symbioses between the two. Some American professional teams (e.g., Chicago Blackhawks, San Antonio Spurs) have incorporated support of participation-based programs into their community relations undertakings. The effectiveness of such support for either participating or watching remains unevaluated. More work is needed to determine whether watching and doing sport can be made symbiotic and, if so, how.

CONCLUSION

Watching sport and doing sport are among the most ubiquitous of leisure behaviors, as over half the American population watches sport each year, at least occasionally, and a third or more of the American population participates in sport annually, at least as an occasional recreation. Effective management and marketing of sport intended to attract audiences requires that narratives be cultivated to enable and encourage conversations that interpret sport expectations and outcomes. Effective management and marketing of sport as a participative activity requires that sport clubs, teams, and leagues foster a sense of community among participants and their families, including design and delivery of programs for which the design may differ significantly from professional sport models. There is a great deal more to be learned about the development of effective narratives, the design and marketing of age-appropriate and skill-appropriate sport programs, and the cross-leverage of sport spectating and sport participation.

REFERENCES

Ager, L. P. (1977). The reflection of cultural values in Eskimo children's games. In D. F. Lancy & B. A. Tindall (Eds.), *The study of play: Problems and prospects* (pp. 92–98). West Point, NY: Leisure Press.

Allison, M. T. (1980). Competition and cooperation: A sociocultural perspective. *International Review for the Sociology of Sport, 15*(3–4), 93–104.

Ashford, B., Biddle, S., & Goudas, M. (1993). Participation in community sports centres: Motives and predictors of enjoyment. *Journal of Sports Sciences, 11*, 249–256.

Beltman, S., & Volet, S. (2007). Exploring the complex and dynamic nature of sustained motivation. *European Psychologist, 12*, 314–323.

Bengoechea, E. G., Strean, W. B., & Williams, D. J. (2004). Understanding and promoting fun in youth sport: Coaches' perspectives. *Physical Education and Sport Pedagogy, 9*, 197–214.

Burnett, J., Menon, A., & Smart, D.T. (1993). Sports marketing: A new ball game with new rules. *Journal of Advertising Research, 33*, 21–35.

Carpenter, P. J., & Scanlan, T. K. (1998). Changes over time in the determinants of sport commitment. *Pediatric Exercise Science, 10*, 307–321.

Chalip, L. (1992). The construction and use of polysemic structures: Olympic lessons for sport marketing. *Journal of Sport Management, 6*, 87–98.

Chalip, L. (1997). Celebrity or hero? Toward a conceptual framework for athlete promotion. In D. Shilbury & L. Chalip (Eds.), *Advancing management of Australian and New Zealand sport* (42–56). Burwood, Victoria: SMAANZ.

Chalip, L. (2006). Towards social leverage of sport events. *Journal of Sport & Tourism, 11*, 109–127.

Chalip, L., Csikszentmihalyi, M., Kleiber, D., & Larson, R. (1984). Variations of experience in formal and informal sport. *Research Quarterly for Exercise and Sport, 55*, 109–116.

Chalip, L., & Green, B. C. (1998). Establishing and maintaining a modified youth sport program: Lessons from Hotelling's location game. *Sociology of Sport Journal, 15*, 326–342.

Chalip, L., Lin, Y. C., Green, B. C., & Dixon, M. A. (2013). The essential role of community in consumption of a shared experience: Lessons from youth sport. In J. Sundbo & F. Sørensen (Eds.), *Handbook on the experience economy* (pp. 325–338). Cheltenham, UK: Edward Elgar Publishing.

Chalip, L., & Scott, E. P. (2005). Centrifugal social forces in a youth sport league. *Sport Management Review, 8*, 43–67.

Chartrand, T. L., & Bargh, J. A. (2002). Nonconscious motivations: Their activation, operation, and consequences. In A. Tesser, D. A. Stapel, & J. V. Wood (Eds.), *Self and motivation: Emerging psychological perspectives* (pp. 13–42). Washington, DC: American Psychological Association.

Coakley, J. (2009). *Sports in society: Issues and controversies* (10th ed.). Boston: McGraw-Hill.

Cumming, S. P., Smoll, F. L., Smith, R. E., & Grossbard, J. R. (2007). Is winning everything? The relative contributions of motivational climate and won-lost percentage in youth sports. *Journal of Applied Sport Psychology, 19*, 322–336.

Dalakas, V., Madrigal, R., & Anderson, K. L. (2004). "We are number one!" The phenomenon of Basking-in-Reflected-Glory and its implications for sports marketing. In L. R. Kahle & C. Riley (Eds.), *Sports marketing and the psychology of marketing communication* (pp. 67–79). Mahwah, NJ: Erlbaum.

Eastman, S. T., & Land, A. M. (1997). The best of both worlds: Sport fans find good seats at the bar. *Journal of Sport & Social Issues, 21*, 156–178.

Fairley, S., & Tyler, B. D. (2012). Bringing baseball to the big screen: Building sense of community outside of the ballpark. *Journal of Sport Management, 26*, 258–270.

Fink, J. S., & Parker, H. M. (2009). Spectator motives: Why do we watch when our favorite team is not playing? *Sport Marketing Quarterly, 18*, 210–217.

Fraser-Thomas, J., & Côté, J. (2009). Understanding adolescents' positive and negative developmental experiences in sport. *Sport Psychologist, 23*, 3–23.

Greenman, N. (2005). Anthropology applied to education. In K. Satish & J. van Willigen (Eds.), *Domains of application* (pp. 263–306). Westport, RI: Praeger.

Gusfield, J. (1987). Sports as story: Content and form in agonistic games. In S-P. Kang, J. MacAloon, & R. DaMatta (Eds.), *The Olympics and cultural exchange* (pp. 207–234). Seoul: Hanyang Institute for Ethnological Studies.

Harris, J. C. (1984). Interpreting youth baseball players' understandings of fun, and excitement, danger and boredom. *Research Quarterly for Exercise and Sport, 4*, 379–382.

Hayward, R. D., & Kemmelmeier, M. (2007). How competition is viewed across cultures: A test of four theories. *Cross-Cultural Research, 41*, 364–395.

Hognestad, H. K. (2012). Split loyalties: Football is a community business. *Soccer & Society, 13*, 377–391.

Holt, D. B. (1995). How consumers consume: A typology of consumption practices. *Journal of Consumer Research, 22*, 1–16.

Irlinger, P, (1994). The contribution of televised sports to the spread of sports activities. *International Review for the Sociology of Sport, 29*, 201–210.

Kohn, A. (1992). *No contest: The case against competition* (Rev. ed.). Boston: Houghton Mifflin.

Koivula, N. (1999). Sport participation differences in motivation and actual participation due to gender typing. *Journal of Sport Behavior, 22*, 360–380.

Kremer-Sadlik, L, & Kim, J. L. (2007). Lessons from sports: Children's socialization to values through family interaction during sports activities. *Discourse & Society, 18*, 35–52.

Lamprecht, M., & Starnm, H. (1996). Age and gender patterns of sport involvement among the Swiss labor force. *Sociology of Sport Journal, 13*, 274–287.

Lee, S., Lee, H. J., Seo, W. J., & Green, C. (2012). A new approach to stadium experience: The dynamics of the sensoryscape, social interaction, and sense of home. *Journal of Sport Management, 26*, 490–505.

Lever, J. (1983). *Soccer madness*. Chicago: University of Chicago Press.

Light, R. (2000). Culture at play: A comparative study of masculinity and game style in Japanese and Australian school rugby. *International Sports Studies, 22*(2), 26–41.

MacAloon, J. J. (1981). *This great symbol: Pierre de Coubertin and the origins of the modern Olympic Games*. Chicago: University of Chicago Press.

MacCallum, L., Howson, N., & Gopu, N. (2012). *Designed to move: A physical activity action agenda*. Beaverton, OR: Nike.

Madsen, M. C. (1971). Developmental and cross-cultural differences in the cooperative and competitive behavior of young children. *Journal of Cross-Cultural Psychology, 2*, 365–371.

Mandigo, J. L., & Couture, R. T. (1996). An overview of the components of fun in physical education, sport and physical activity programs. *Avante, 2*(3), 56–72.

Marcus, H. R., Uchida, Y., Omoregie, H., Townsend, S. S. M., & Kitayama, S. (2006). Going for the gold: Models of agency in Japanese and American contexts. *Psychological Science, 17*, 103–112.

Matteo, S. (1986). The effect of sex and gender-schematic processing on sport participation. *Sex Roles, 15*, 517–432.

McCarthy, P. J., & Jones, M. V. (2007). A qualitative study of sport enjoyment in the sampling years. *Sport Psychologist, 21*, 400–416.

Mead, M. (Ed.). (1961). *Cooperation and competition among primitive peoples* (Rev. ed.). Boston: Beacon Press.

Melnick, M. J. (1993). Searching for sociability in the stands: A theory of sports spectating. *Journal of Sport Management, 7*, 44–60.

Menzies, J. L., & Nguyen, S. N. (2012). An exploration of the motivation to attend for spectators of the Lexmark Indy 300 Champ Car event, Gold Coast. *Journal of Sport & Tourism, 17*, 183–200.

Ostrow, A. C., Jones, D. C., & Spiker, D. D. (1981). Age role expectations and sex role expectations for selected sport activities. *Research Quarterly for Exercise & Sport, 52*, 216–227.

Roberts, J. M., & Chick, G. E. (1984). Quitting the game: Covert disengagement from Butler County Eight Ball. *American Anthropologist, 86*, 549–567.

Rothenbuhler, E. W. (1988). The living room celebration of the Olympic Games. *Journal of Communication, 38*, 61–81.

Saar, M., & Jürimäe, T. (2007). Sports participation outside school in total physical activity of children. *Perceptual & Motor Skills, 105*, 559–562.

SBRnet (nd). Available for purchase at www.SBRnet.com

Scanlan, T. K., Carpenter, P. J., Lobel, M., & Simons, J. (1993). Sources of enjoyment for youth sport athletes. *Pediatric Exercise Science, 5*, 275–285.

Sharpe, E. K. (2003). "It's not fun anymore": A case study of organizing a contemporary grasssroots recreation association. *Loisir et Société/Society and Leisure, 26*, 431–452.

Smetana, J. (Ed.) (2005). *Changing boundaries of parental authority during adolescence.* San Francisco: Jossey-Bass.

Sommerlad, E. A., & Bellingham, W. P. (1972). Cooperation-competition: A comparison of Australian European and Aboriginal school children. *Journal of Cross-Cultural Psychology, 3*, 149–157.

Stewart, I., & Lacassagne, M-F. (2005). Social representations as a diagnostic tool for identifying cultural and other group differences. *Psychology & Marketing, 22*, 721–738.

Tischer, U., Hartmann-Tews, I., & Combrink, C. (2011). Sport participation of the elderly: The role of gender, age, and social class. *European Reviews of Aging & Physical Activity, 8*(2), 83–91.

Trail, G. T., & James, J. D. (2001). The motivation scale for sport consumption: Assessment of the scale's psychometric properties. *Journal of Sport Behavior, 24*, 108–127.

Vander Velden, L. (1986). Heroes and bad winners: Cultural differences. In L. Vander Velden & J. H. Humphrey (Eds.), *Psychology and sociology of sport: Current selected research* (Vol. 1, pp. 205–220). New York: AMS Press.

Wang, X. (2013). Applying the integrative model of behavioral prediction and attitude functions in the context of social media use while viewing mediated sports. *Computers in Human Behavior, 29*, 1538–1545.

Wankel, L. M., & Sefton, J. M. (1989). A season-long investigation of fun in youth sports. *Journal of Sport and Exercise Psychology, 11*, 355–366.

Wann, D. L., & Branscombe, N. R. (1993). Sport fans: Measuring degree of identification with their team. *International Journal of Sport Psychology, 24*, 1–17.

Warner, S., Dixon, M. A., & Chalip, L. (2012). The impact of formal versus informal sport: Mapping the differences in sense of community. *Journal of Community Psychology, 40*, 983–1003.

Watson, G. G. (1977a). Games, socialization and parental values: Social class differences in parental evaluation of Little League baseball. *International Review for the Sociology of Sport, 12*(1), 17–48.

Watson, G. G. (1977b). Social conflict and parental involvement in Little League baseball. *Quest, 27*, 71–86.

Weiss, M. R., & Chaumeton, N. (1992). Motivational orientations in sport. In T. S. Horn (Ed.), *Advances in sport psychology* (pp. 61–100). Champaign, IL: Human Kinetics.

Zhang, J. J., Smith, D. W., Pease, D. G., & Mahar, M. T. (1996). Spectator knowledge of hockey as a significant predictor of game attendance. *Sport Marketing Quarterly, 5*(3), 41–48.

Zillman, D., Bryant, J., & Sapolsky, B. S. (1989). Enjoyment from spectator sports. In J. H. Goldstein (Ed.), *Sports, games, and play: Social and psychological viewpoints* (2nd ed., pp. 241–278). Hillsdale, NJ: Lawrence Erlbaum.

11
Tourism

Heather J. Gibson (University of Florida)

Travel and tourism is one of the largest industries in the world, and for many countries it may be the biggest contributor to their Gross Domestic Product (GDP) (World Travel and Tourism Council; WTTC, 2013). In 2012, travel and tourism comprised 9.3% of global GDP and employed over 261 million people (WTTC, 2013). While the economic impact of travel and tourism is a good place to start, the business side of the industry is one perspective. Tourism can also be approached as a social phenomenon (Higgins-Desboilles, 2006), and as such helps in understanding such topics as the contribution of travel to quality of life (Dolnicar, Yanamandram, & Cliff, 2012), or the negative impacts of tourism on host communities (Smith, 1989). Treating tourism as a social phenomenon also facilitates further understanding as to how tourism relates to leisure.

It is generally recognized that travel consists of three major types: (a) pleasure travel, (b) business travel, and (c) visiting friends and relatives (Goeldner & Ritchie, 2011). In 2011 direct spending on leisure-related travel constituted 76% of tourism-related GDP, whereas, business-related travel spending comprised 24% (WTTC, 2013). Thus, travel for leisure is the predominant purpose of trips that many people take. Therefore, in this chapter, Cohen's (1974) classic definition of tourism as a special form of leisure will be used as a conceptual foundation. Cohen identified six dimensions of a tourist. Their trips are: (a) temporary, (b) taken voluntarily, (c) involve a round trip (i.e., come back home), (d) relatively long (here cultural perceptions are influential), (e) non-recurrent (i.e., do not happen on a regular basis), and (f) non-instrumental (i.e., they are for pleasure, not for work). It is evident that some of Cohen's dimensions share key characteristics with definitions of leisure and, as with debates over what constitutes leisure, sometimes different types of travel may be a combination of work and leisure. For example, a business trip where an individual visits a tourist attraction while they are in town is a gray area as the trip cannot be totally described as leisure-travel. However, as with all types of leisure behavior, ambiguity is addressed by focusing on the meanings that a behavior has for the individual and if they perceive the trip to be leisure. Thus, in this chapter we will focus on tourism as a social phenomenon and adopt the perspective that tourism is a special form of leisure.

LEISURE AND TOURISM CONNECTION

Despite the close connection between leisure and tourism, there has been a tendency to treat them as separate dimensions of life and fields of study (Moore, Cushman, & Simmon, 1995; Smith & Godbey, 1991). Over the years, scholars have proposed conceptual models suggesting how leisure and tourism behavior are related. Currie (1997) developed the Liminoidal, Inversionary, and Prosaic (LIP) behavior framework to examine the impact of daily behaviors (including leisure) on tourist behaviors. He argued that the prevailing sentiment in tourism research was that tourist behaviors tended to be conceptualized as being opposite to home-based activities. Instead, Currie suggested that tourist behaviors may be based on everyday activities because even though vacations might encourage individuals to participate in different activities, the underlying motives, needs, and desires behind a trip still reflect home-based lifestyles. Similarly, Carr (2002) suggested that leisure and tourism could be conceptualized along a continuum. He found that individuals retain the same values from their everyday life and some consistency between leisure and tourism exists, even though tourist behaviors might be more hedonic-oriented than leisure behaviors. Carr suggested that this consistency could be explained by subjective norms, values, attitudes, personality, and deep-rooted habits. In recent years, there has been a resurgence of interest in understanding tourism-based choices within the context of wider life styles, including leisure. This type of approach particularly lends itself to understanding some of the niche forms of tourism such as sport-related travel (Chang & Gibson, 2011).

SETTING THE SCENE FOR UNDERSTANDING TODAY'S TOURISM

The study of tourism as a social phenomenon largely began in the 1970s as anthropologists started raising concerns about the growth of tourism and the impacts on what were then referred to as members of host communities, or what are called today, residents of tourist destinations. Valene Smith's (1977/1989) book *Hosts and Guests* is a good example of this type of work. Similarly, sociologists, while concerned about the changes wrought by tourism on communities were beginning to focus on the actual tourists. Cohen (1972) argued that there "is not one type of tourist;" that different types of tourists could be identified and it is important to understand that each type of tourist can have potentially different impacts on host communities largely due to their preferences for familiarity or strangeness (novelty). He proposed a typology of four tourist roles that could be distinguished along a continuum of strangeness and familiarity. *Organized mass tourists* and *independent mass tourists*, Cohen suggested, are familiarity seekers in their preferences for Western-style accommodation and food and tend to visit regular tourist attractions. Potentially, these types of tourists have the most impact initially on host communities as they require the most change in a destination in the form of Westernized hotels and food. Today, the organized and independent mass tourists are still attracted to destinations such as Orlando, Florida and Waikiki, Hawaii; however, even these mass tourists are motivated by a search for novelty, and as new destinations develop to receive them, concerns first raised in the 1970s are still relevant.

On the other end of the continuum, Cohen (1972) identified two types of tourist that can be distinguished by a preference for higher degrees of strangeness or novelty. The *explorer* prefers to visit places that are away from the regular tourist attractions, interact with local people and try the local food, but there is still a degree of familiarity in their trip largely related to choice of accommodations. While they may not want a chain-style hotel, they still prefer accommodations with familiar amenities. Today, much of the youth budget/backpacker travel may be classified as explorers as would some of the newer niche styles of ecotourism, cultural, and heritage tourism.

According to Cohen's (1972) original classification, the tourist role which described a style of travel that attempted to escape the 'regular tourist route' was that of the *drifter*. Cohen (1973) referred to drifters as "children of affluence" and used this classification to describe the extended trips of young adults around the world that he saw occurring in the 1970s, where the goal was to encounter destinations in a largely unchanged state, to interact with the local people, and accept whatever style of accommodations were available. Because drifters tend to adapt to the local way of life, they invoke less change and may have the most economic and social benefits for a community. In fact, the goals of many of the more recent types of low impact tourism would be in line with the original drifter role. However, the proportion of drifters in the traveling population is quite low. My own research has shown through the years the proportion of drifters in a sample of U.S. residents is about 8% and preference for the drifter role is largely confined to young adults (Gibson & Yiannakis, 2002). Today, even with the prevalence of young budget travelers, many of them resemble explorers, and as the backpacker infrastructure becomes more institutionalized (i.e., more developed and mass-tourism-like) some budget travelers may be more akin to independent mass tourists (Larsen, Ogaard, & Brun, 2011), exchanging backpacks for wheeled suitcases, motivated less by altruism and more by hedonism (Lyons, Hanley, Wearing, & Neil, 2012).

So how is work that was first written in the 1970s still relevant to our understanding of tourism today? Cohen's (1972) tourist role typology initially resulted in a succession of work on different types of tourists (tourist roles) (e.g., Mo, Howard, & Havitz, 1993; Pearce, 1985; Yiannakis & Gibson, 1992), and has been applied to understand different tourist contexts such as perceived risk (Lepp & Gibson, 2003), women's tourist experiences (Wickens, 2002) and ecotourism (Havenegaard, 2002). Indeed, Cohen's seminal paper can be regarded as the foundation for much of our work today, especially in relation to understanding the variety of tourist behaviors and activities as tourism continues to specialize into different niches.

GROWING SPECIALIZATION OF TOURISM: NICHE TOURISM

The specialization of tourism into different niches has continued over the past decade. Cohen's (1972) statement that "there is not one type of tourist" was prophetic in that while the traditional beach or sight-seeing vacations are still popular, today it is common to hear about specialized tourism segments and many universities offer classes related to specific niche forms such as ecotourism or sport tourism. Various terms have been used to describe this segmentation of tourism types, including special interest tourism (Hall & Weiler, 1992), niche tourism (Novelli, 2005), even adjectival tourism (Robinette, 2011). Nonetheless, while this segmentation of tourism has not been without criticism as there seems to be a multitude of tourism types (e.g., tea tourism, shark tourism, bookstore tourism) and the utility of such narrow specialties for either academic study or market segmentation is being questioned, a viable body of knowledge and social policy has been built around some of the earlier niches including ecotourism, sport tourism, and dark tourism.

Ecotourism

Some of the first academic studies on ecotourism emerged during the early 1990s and were in response to growing concerns about the negative environmental, social, and even economic effects of many forms of tourism (Diamantis, 1999). As the global economies shifted in the 1980s from a reliance on traditional manufacturing industries into the service sector, tourism was identified as a form of economic development. However, in response to concerns about mass corporate tourism, an alternative model of tourism emerged (Epler Wood, 2010).

Over the years there have been various definitions of ecotourism, largely based on such concepts as nature, environmentally sensitive, low impact, and socially responsible travel. In the 1990s, the popularity of the term had grown to such an extent that ecotourism was largely considered to be a "buzzword" often applied to forms of tourism that did not resemble ecotourism (Diamantis, 1999) and could be at best described as nature-based tourism (tourism taking place outdoors or involving some sort of animal, fish or bird, while disregarding ecotourism principles). Even today where there is a growing consensus as to the basic principles of ecotourism, there are charges of "green washing" whereby tourism agencies use the term as a marketing strategy with little concern for ecotourism principles (Honey, 2003). Indeed, Fennel and Weaver (2005) suggested that the overall credibility of ecotourism is threatened by the failure of many destinations and operators to incorporate the three core principles of ecotourism (ecological and social sustainability; nature-based attraction; and education) into their businesses. Similarly, the International Ecotourism Society (TIES) suggested that the term ecotourism should be reserved for tourism operations that minimize both social and environmental impact; develop environmental and cultural awareness and respect; provide positive experiences for both residents and tourists; yield direct financial benefits for conservation; provide financial benefits and empowerment for the local people; raise sensitivity of the host country's political, environmental and social climate; and support international human rights and labor agreements (Epler Wood, 2010).

In terms of trends, Weaver and Lawton (2007) noted a growing specialization within ecotourism. Specialized sub-types of ecotourism are becoming evident such as ecotourism centered on indigenous people (Zeppel, 2006) or a specific type of species such as whale watching (Curtin, 2003). Much of the early work was also focused on the lesser developed countries such as Costa Rica (Weaver, 1999), whereas over the past decade attention has shifted to more developed countries such as Australia (Buckley, 2004). Weaver and Lawton also noted a shift in the focus of research from ecotourism in publicly protected lands (e.g., national parks) to an understanding of the role of private lands to ecotourism operations.

Today, while ecotourism is still a recognizable niche with a substantive body of academic research (Weaver & Lawton, 2007), the growing movement towards sustainable development, and sustainable tourism in particular (Liu, 2003), may serve to diminish the distinctiveness of ecotourism. Moreover, Weaver and Lawton argued that the development of ecotourism is further challenged by a number of failures including quality control and the unequal enforcement of standards in the industry. They also charged that while there is plenty of ecotourism-related academic work, it largely lacks a conceptual foundation and a sense of coherence as a body of knowledge.

Sport Tourism

Travel for sport is nothing new in and of itself. The Ancient Greeks and Romans were avid sport tourists with journeys to Olympia and the Coliseum in Rome as both athletes and spectators. However, in line with the trend towards economic development through tourism and the need to re-image and regenerate the former industrial cities (Austrian & Rosentraub, 2002) or to project a positive image for the newly emerging global powers such as China (Gibson, Qi, & Zhang, 2008), over the last decade sport tourism has developed into both a government policy (Swart & Bob, 2007) and a field of study.

Through the mid- to late-1990s as increased attention was given to the relationship between sport and tourism, much of the debate was about how to define sport-related travel (Gibson, 1998; Hinch & Higham, 2001; Standevan & DeKnop, 1999; Weed & Bull, 2004). Interestingly, some of the earliest work on sport tourism was presented at leisure studies conferences (e.g., Redmond 1990 at the Leisure Studies Association Conference, UK) or published in leisure journals (De Knop, 1990). Following the lead of these early scholars I suggested that there are three broad types of sport tourism (Gibson, 1998): (a) *active sport tourism*, where individuals travel to take part in sport; (b) *event sport tourism*, whereby individuals travel to watch sport; and (c) *nostalgia sport tourism* which encompasses travel to sport-related attractions such as Cooperstown, New York, and the National Baseball Hall of Fame and Museum, or visits to sporting facilities such as Olympic Park in Montreal, Canada. Since the late 1990s, academic work on sport tourism has grown immensely and has been an area of study that has bridged the gaps between tourism, sport management, recreation and leisure, and increasingly the emerging area of event management.

In the active sport tourism realm, the early work focused on golf (Petric, 2002) or snow sports (Williams & Fidgeon, 2000), but more recently, attention has shifted to event-related contexts such as master's sports (Gillet & Kelly, 2006) or triathlons (Lamont & Kennelly, 2012). There is also a growing line of work which incorporates the relationship between leisure behavior and active sport tourism choices with the premise that people who travel to take part in physical activity are likely to be highly involved in these sports in their everyday leisure (Chang & Gibson, 2012). In the realm of event sport tourism, most of the focus has been on the mega-events such as the Olympic Games (Kaplanidou, 2012) or the FIFA World Cup (Cornelissen, Bob, & Swart, 2011). Although as questions are being raised about the costs of hosting these events and the legacies accruing from them, there has been a movement among smaller communities to emphasize hosting what are often referred to as the small-scale events (Higham, 1999). In many North American communities there is a growing realization that there is economic potential in hosting amateur sports events such as youth soccer, or leveraging the tourism potential from local college and university sports (Gibson, Willming, & Holdnak, 2003). Many of these initiatives involve the parks and recreation departments as they frequently manage the available sports facilities in a community and often have the relevant human capital in the form of sports officials, event managers, and volunteers needed to host these events (see http://www.ci.newberry.fl.us/recreational-sports-info/). The realm of nostalgia sport tourism is probably the least developed in terms of research, although a special issue of the *Journal of Sport & Tourism* in 2005 [vol. 10 (4)] featured articles on this topic. Moreover, research on specific nostalgia related venues such as fantasy camps (Gammon, 2002), stadium tours (Ramshaw, Gammon, & Huang, 2013) and halls of fame (Fyfe, 2008) is becoming more pervasive.

Dark Tourism

Throughout the 2000s there has been growth in a niche of tourism devoted to "travel to sites of death, disaster, or the macabre" (Stone, 2013 http://lgn1331135353.site-fusion.co.uk/)[1]. The term dark tourism is commonly used to describe this type of travel, although other terms such as thanatourism (Seaton, 1998) have been used. Tourist fascination with ghosts (Inglis & Holmes, 2003), Dracula (Light, 2007), concentration camps (Biran, Poria, & Oren, 2011), or prisons (Strange & Kempa, 2003), among others, have provided some interesting insights into what motivates people to visit these sights, which some find distasteful, but others find fascinating. Dark tourism is one of the niches that has received some critique as to whether it is a distinct form of tourism, or just a form of adjectival tourism. Some of the concerns arise as to whether, for example, visits to battlefield sites or former concentrations camps such as Auschwitz are dark tourism that is motivated by fascination with death and the macabre or are instead a form of heritage tourism where interest is centered on an historical quest or a sense of mourning if the site is one that has personal significance to the tourist (Biran et al., 2011). In addition to issues of motivation, there are questions as to whether all of these different types of sights and attractions can be categorized under one umbrella term. For example, is ghost tourism or Dracula tourism the same as disaster tourism, for example, visiting New Orleans after Hurricane Katrina?

More recently, some of the newer forms of tourism such as poverty tourism or what is increasingly termed pro-poor tourism where tourists visit shanty towns (slums, favelas, etc.) have attracted similar concerns (Rolfes, 2010). Rolfes explained that some of the concerns with pro-poor tourism or disaster tourism are voyeurism and the commodification of less fortunate people's circumstances. Although, on the other side, some forms of pro-poor tourism where the tours are run by the local people, are educational, and financial benefits accrue to the community are lauded as valuable forms of economic development (Ashley, Roe, & Goodwin, 2001). Indeed, Nyapane and Poudell (2011) in the context of Nepal, found that small locally run ecotourism operations can help alleviate poverty and encourage an appreciation for the value of biodiversity in a community. The debates over dark tourism are set to continue and it will be interesting to see how it develops in the future. As Rojek (1997, p. 63) commented, since the early pilgrimages humans have visited sites associated with death, or what he calls Black Spots, but perhaps more recently the rising interest in places associated with major disasters might be better classified as 'sensation sights' which tend towards a heightened sense of voyeurism.

LOOKING FORWARD

Since the 1950s, tourism has grown in popularity as taking an annual summer vacation became part of everyday life (Parrinello, 1993) and international travel was opened to the masses with the advent of charter flights and packaged vacations. By the 1990s, many people were taking multiple trips per year as the relative cost of travel had declined and they were enticed by increasingly diverse travel offerings. However, after the record-breaking millennial year 2000,

[1] The University of Central Lancashire in the UK hosts the Institute for Dark Tourism Research, a group of researchers focused on increasing our understanding of dark tourism and forging academic and industry partnerships in this form of tourism around the world.

up until 2011, the travel and tourism industry experienced a turbulent decade with financial crises, terrorist attacks, natural disasters, and the threat of epidemics, among others, and what had been a growth industry for 50 years suddenly saw negative growth and unpredictability in traveler patterns. Since 2012, the UNWTO reported that for two consecutive years (2011 and 2012), international travel receipts have grown by 4% each year (UNWTO, 2013). Thus, after a decade of instability, global tourism may be on the road to recovery. During this period of instability, a number of trends in both the academic field and the industry became apparent and have given rise to a number of new foci.

Not surprisingly, the issue of safety and security and disaster recovery became a topic of interest over the past decade. Through the 1980s and 1990s, scholars had paid some attention to tourism and crime (Pizam, 1999) and terrorism (Sönmez & Graefe, 1998) as there was a growing realization that the stability of the tourism industry was related to safety and security. This growing awareness in the 1980s arose out of a number of incidents; however, with the advent of 9/11, travel and tourism changed forever. As discussed above, over the past 30 years many communities had focused on tourism as their primary economic source and when tourists stop visiting, the financial well-being of those destinations is adversely affected. Thus, literature has emerged around perceived risk and understanding who will travel when perceptions of risk are high (Lepp & Gibson, 2003; Sönmez & Graefe, 1998). Lepp and Gibson found that risk perception level is correlated to Cohen's (1972) tourist role type with Organized Mass Tourists being the most risk averse and drifters being the most likely to travel when risks are higher. On the destination side, a related body of knowledge has developed on disaster recovery and recovery marketing (Faulkner, 2001) to help destinations in the aftermath of both natural and human-derived events (see: http://tcmi.hhp.ufl.edu/).

Another trend that is set to continue is related to a movement that also began in the late 1980s, that of low impact tourism. With growing concerns about global climate change and the long-term viability of tourism destinations (Hall & Higham, 2005), there has been an increasing focus on sustainability and sustainable tourism (Liu, 2003). Sustainability is conceptualized in terms of three components: economic, social, and environmental, and in some tourism circles a fourth dimension has been added, climate responsiveness (UNWTO, 2007). While this holistic approach to sustainability is advocated, so far many of the industry responses have been to focus on a "greening of the industry" with the hospitality sector being early adopters in terms of encouraging guests to reuse sheets and towels and to reduce their electric and water usage, followed by the airline industry where concerns have been related to fuel conservation. Discussions about sustainability are also spreading into the tourism niches with attention on the sustainability of event and sport tourism (O'Brien & Chalip, 2008) and heritage tourism (Chhabra, 2010), and the development of specialist degree programs in sustainable tourism.

Surprisingly, the topic of tourism and well-being has received little attention through the years and is just starting to appear in the literature (Gilbert & Abdullah, 2004). The guiding philosophy of North American leisure studies has always been that leisure is beneficial for individuals (Payne, Ainsworth, & Godbey, 2010) and communities, and concerns are being raised about the lack of leisure as part of a focus on work-life balance (Hillbrecht, Shaw, Johnson, & Andrey, 2008). Whereas, in tourism studies, investigations of related concepts such as quality of life have largely focused on the impact of tourism on the residents of tourist destinations (Purdue, Long, & Allen, 1990) rather than understanding how taking a vacation contributes to quality of life for the tourist. However, studies of such concepts as the contribution of vacations to a sense of well-being (Gilbert & Abdullah, 2004), quality of life (Dolnicar et al., 2012), and specific areas of life such as family functioning (Lehto, Choi, Lin, & MacDermid, 2009) have begun to appear in the literature. Certainly, if we maintain the philosophy that leisure and tourism are integrally related, then there are many opportunities for researchers to collaborate and contribute to the wider body of knowledge on work-life balance and health and well-being through leisure and tourism.

In the U.S., attention to the idea of vacations and health and well-being is starting to occur among various industy associations, but one suspects that it is driven by a spirit of captialism; that is, persuading Americans to take vacations not necessarily for their own good, but for the good of the tourism industry negatively affected by the recent recession (U.S. Travel Association, 2010). Nonetheless, if we adopt a leisure studies philosophy, then advocating for vacation time and time spent with friends and family away from everyday life is definitely an issue and a research area that needs more attention. Another related area that is growing in importance is the role of technology in tourism.

Technology and tourism have been approached from several perspectives. Much of the early work focused on the supply side of the industry, notably change in distribution channels away from the travel agent to online reservation systems (Goeldner & Ritchie, 2011) and also the use of the Internet in destination marketing (Gretzel, Yuan, & Fesenmaier, 2000). A growing area of concern is the use of technology by the tourists themselves. In the not-so-distant past, when individuals took a vacation they were pretty much cut off from home and certainly from work. A pay phone and the odd postcard were the extent of many vacationers' connections with home. With the advent of mobile technology, the impact of being connected with home (i.e., living in two worlds) while traveling has been raised (White & White, 2007) and questions about the intrusion of the everyday, particularly the blurring of the boundaries between work and vacation are of increasing concern as individuals never seem to experience the true sense of escape a vacation is supposed to provide.

CONCLUSION

Thus, it appears there are a number of promising avenues for potential study and practice in the realm of travel and tourism. Certainly, a number of demographic trends are already beginning to impact the tourism industry, such as the increased propensity for travel among the BRIC nations of Brazil, Russia, India, and China (see Liu and Li's section in Chapter 14; and Marinho and Reis, Chapter 16). For several years, the industry has been adapting to the needs of these customers, but as yet academic research in this area is scarce (Reisinger, 2009). Similarly, within North America increasing population diversity has been largely ignored by academics. In 1995, Richter and Butler noted that tourism researchers had tended to ignore gender and race in their work. While gender-related research, particularly women as tourists, has grown over the past 20 years, there still remains a paucity of attention focused on race, ethnicity, and tourism (see Stodolska & Floyd, Chapter 28). Another growth area is the retiring baby boomers who are looking forward to enjoying the increasing number of travel choices available to them. For many people, travel is an important part of their lives and as such should be examined from an interdisciplinary perspective that encompasses social science, environmental, and business to fully understand its role in societies and individual lives.

REFERENCES

Ashley, C., Roe, D., & Goodwin, H. (2001). *Pro-poor tourism strategies: Making tourism work for the poor: A review of experiences.* Nottingham, UK: Russell Press.

Austrian, Z., & Rosentraub, M. (2002). Cities, sports and economic change: A retrospective assessment. *Journal of Urban Affairs, 25*(5), 549–563.

Biran, A., Poria, Y., & Oren, G., (2011). Sought experiences at (dark) heritage sites. *Annals of Tourism Research, 38*(3), 820–841.

Buckley, R. (2004). Partnerships in ecotourism: Australian political frameworks. *International Journal of Tourism Research, 6*(2), 75–83.

Carr, N. (2002). The tourism-leisure behavioral continuum. *Annals of Tourism Research, 29*, 972–986.

Chang, S., & Gibson, H. (2011). Physically active leisure and tourism connection: Leisure involvement and choice of tourism activities among paddlers. *Leisure Sciences, 33,* 162–181.

Chhabra, D. (2010). *Sustainable marketing of cultural and heritage tourism.* Wallingford, Cabi International.

Cohen, E. (1972). Toward a sociology of international tourism. *Social Research, 39*, 164–182.

Cohen, E. (1973). Nomads from affluence: Notes on the phenomenon of drifter tourism. *International Journal of Comparative Sociology, 14*, 89–103.

Cohen, E. (1974). Who is a tourist?: A conceptual clarification. *Sociological Review, 22,* 527–553.

Cornelissen, S., Bob, U., & Swart, K. (2011). Sport mega-events and their legacies: The 2010 FIFA World Cup. *Development Southern Africa, 28*, 305–306.

Currie, R. R. (1997). A pleasure-tourism behaviors framework. *Annals of Tourism Research, 24,* 884–897.

Curtin, S. (2003). Whale watching in Kaikoura: Sustainable destination development? *Journal of Ecotourism, 2*(3), 173–195.

De Knop, P. (1990). Sport for all and active tourism. *World Leisure and Recreation, 32*, 30–36.

Diamantis, D. (1999). The concept of ecotourism: Evolution and trends. *Current Issues in Tourism, 2*(2/3), 93–122.

Dolnicar, S., Yanamandram, V., & Cliff, K. (2012). The contribution of vacations to quality of life. *Annals of Tourism Research, 39*(1), 59–83.

Epler Wood, M. (2010). Ecotourism then & now: Ecotourism key milestones & current developments. Retrieved from http://www.ecotourism.org/ecotourism-then-and-now.

Faulkner, B. (2001). Towards a framework for tourism disaster management. *Tourism Management, 22*, 135–147.

Fennell, D., & Weaver, D. (2005). The ecotourism concept and tourism-conservation symbiosis. *Journal of Sustainable Tourism, 13,* 373–390.

Fyfe, D. (2008). Birthplace of baseball or village of museums? The packaging of heritage tourism in Cooperstown, New York. *Journal of Sport & Tourism, 13*, 135–153.

Gammon, S. (2002). Fantasy, nostalgia and the pursuit of what never. In S. Gammon & J. Kurtzman (Eds.), *Sport tourism: Practices and principles*, (pp. 61–71), Eastbourne, UK: LSA Publications.

Gibson, H. (1998). Sport tourism: A critical analysis of research. *Sport Management Review, 1,* 45–76.

Gibson, H., Qi, C., & Zhang, J. (2008). Destination image and intent to visit China, and the 2008 Beijing Olympic Games. *Journal of Sport Management 22*, 427–450.

Gibson, H., Willming, C., & Holdnak, A. (2003). Small-scale event sport tourism: Fans as tourists. *Tourism Management, 24,* 181–190.

Gibson, H., & Yiannakis, A. (2002). Tourist roles: Needs and the adult life course. *Annals of Tourism Research, 29*(2), 358–383.

Gilbert, D., & Abdullah, J. (2004). Holiday taking and the sense of well-being. *Annals of Tourism Research, 31*, 103–121.

Gillet, P., & Kelly, S. (2006). "Non-local" Masters games participants: An investigation of competitive active sport tourist motives. *Journal of Sport & Tourism, 11* (3/4), 239–258.

Goeldner, C., & Ritchie, J. R. B. (2011). *Tourism: principles, practices, philosophies* (12th ed.). New York: John Wiley & Sons.

Gretzel, U., Yuan, Y., & Fesenmeier, D. (2000). Preparing for the new economy: Advertising strategies and change in destination marketing organizations. *Journal of Travel Research, 39*(2), 146–156.

Hall, C. M., & Higham, J. (Eds.). (2005). *Tourism, recreation and climate change.* Clevedon, UK: Channel View Publications.

Hall, C. M., & Weiler, B. (Eds.). (1992). *Special interest tourism.* London: Belhaven Press.

Havenegaard, G. (2002). Using tourist typologies for ecotourism research. *Journal of Ecotourism, 1*(1), 7–18.

Higgins-Desboilles, F. (2006). More than an "industry:" The forgotten power of tourism as a social force. *Tourism Management, 27*, 1192–1208.

Higham, J. (1999). Commentary-Sport as an avenue of tourism development: An analysis of the positive and negative impacts of sport tourism. *Current Issues in Tourism, 2*, 82–90.

Hillbrecht, M., Shaw, S., Johnson, L., & Andrey, J. (2008). "I'm home for the kids:" Contradictory implications for work-life balance of teleworking mothers. *Gender, Work & Organization, 14*, 454–476.

Hinch, T., & Higham, J. (2001). Sport tourism: A framework for research. *International Journal of Tourism Research, 3*, 45–58.

Honey, M. (2003). Protecting Eden: Setting green standards for the tourism industry. *Environment: Science and Policy for Sustainable Development, 45*(6), 8–20.

Inglis, D., & Holmes, M. (2003). Highland and other haunts: Ghosts in Scottish tourism. *Annals of Tourism Research, 30*(1), 50–63.

Kaplanidou, K. (2012). The importance of legacy outcomes for Olympic Games four summer host cities residents' quality of life: 1996–2008. *European Sport Management Quarterly, 12*, 397–433.

Lamont, M., & Kennelly, M. (2012). A qualitative exploration of participant motives among committed amateur triathletes. *Leisure Sciences, 34*, 236–255.

Larsen, S., Ogaard, T., & Brun, W. (2011). Backpackers and mainstreamers: Realities and Myths. *Annals of Tourism Research, 38*(2), 690–707.

Lehto, X., Choi, S., Lin, Y., & MacDermid, S. (2009). Vacation and family functioning. *Annals of Tourism Research, 36*, 459–479.

Lepp, A., & Gibson, H. (2003). Tourist roles, perceived risk and international tourism. *Annals of Tourism Research, 30*, 606–624.

Light D. (2007). Dracula tourism in Romania: Cultural identity and the state. *Annals of Tourism Research, 34*, 746–765.

Liu, Z. (2003). Sustainable tourism development: A critique. *Journal of Sustainable Tourism, 11*, 459–475.

Lyons, K., Hanley, J., Wearing, S., & Neil, J. (2012). Gap year volunteer tourism: Myths of global citizenship. *Annals of Tourism Research, 39*(1), 361–378.

Mo, C., Howard, D., & Havitz, M. (1993). Testing an international tourist role typology. *Annals of Tourism Research, 20*, 319–335.

Moore, K., Cushman, G., & Simmons, D. (1995). Behavioral conceptualization of tourism and leisure. *Annals of Tourism Research, 22*, 67–85.

Novelli, M. (2005). *Niche tourism: Contemporary issues, trends and cases.* London, UK: Elsevier Ltd.

Nyaupane, G., & Poudel, S. (2011). Linkages among biodiversity, livelihood and tourism. *Annals of Tourism Research, 38*, 1344–1366.

O'Brien, D., & Chalip, L. (2008). Sport events and strategic leveraging: Pushing towards the triple bottom line. In A. Woodside & D. Martin, (Eds.), *Tourism management: Analysis, behaviour and strategy*, (pp. 318–338). Wallingford, UK: CAB International.

Parrinello, G. (1993). Motivation and anticipation in post-industrial tourism. *Annals of Tourism Research, 20*, 233–249.

Payne, L., Ainsworth, B., & Godbey, G. (2010). *Leisure, health and wellness: Making the connections.* State College, PA: Venture Publishing, Inc.

Pearce, P. (1985). A systematic comparison of travel-related roles. *Human Relations, 38*, 1001–1011.

Petric, J. (2002). An examination of golf vacationer's novelty. *Annals of Tourism Research, 29*, 384–400.

Pizam, A. (1999). A comprehensive approach to classifying acts of crime and violence at tourism destinations. *Journal of Travel Research, 38*(1), 5–12.

Purdue, R., Long, P., & Allen, L. (1990). Resident support for tourism development. *Annals of Tourism Research, 17*, 586–599.

Ramshaw, G., Gammon, S., & Huang, W. (2013). Acquired pasts and the commodification of borrowed heritage: The case of the Bank of America Stadium tour. *Journal of Sport & Tourism, 18*(1), 17–31.

Redmond, G. (1990). Points of increasing contact: Sport and tourism in the modern world. In A. Tomlinson,

(Ed.), *Proceedings of the Leisure Studies Association Second International Conference, Leisure, Labour, and Lifestyles: International Comparisons* (pp. 158–169), Conference Papers no. 43. Eastbourne, UK: LSA Publications.

Reisinger, Y. (2009). *International tourism: Cultures and behavior.* Oxford, UK: Butterworth-Heinemann.

Richter, L., & Butler, R. (1995). Gender and race: neglected variables in tourism research. In R. Butler and D. Pearce (Eds.), *Change in tourism: People places, processes* (pp. 71–91). London, UK: Routledge.

Robinette, R. (2011). What are adjectival, specialty niche tourisms? Retrieved from http://cultural-heritage-tourism.com/what-are-adjectival-specialty-niche-tourisms.

Rojek, C. (1997). Indexing, dragging and the social construction of tourist sights. In C. Rojek and J. Urry (Eds.), *Touring cultures: Transformations of travel and theory* (pp. 52–74). London: Routledge.

Rolfes, M. (2010). Poverty tourism: Theoretical reflections and empirical findings regarding an extraordinary form of tourism. *GeoJournal, 75*, 421–442.

Seaton, A. (1998). War and thanatourism: Waterloo 1815–1914. *Annals of Tourism Research, 26,* 130–158.

Smith, S., & Godbey. G. (1991). Leisure, recreation and tourism. *Annals of Tourism Research, 18*, 85–100.

Smith, V. L. (1989). *Hosts and guests: The anthropology of tourism*. Philadelphia, PA: University of Pennsylvania Press.

Sönmez, S., & Graefe, A. (1998). Influence of terrorism risk on foreign tourism decisions. *Annals of Tourism Research, 25,* 112–44.

Standevan, J. & De Knop, P. (1999). *Sport tourism*. Champaign, IL: Human Kinetics.

Strange, C., & Kempa, M. (2003). Shades of dark tourism: Alcatraz and Robben Island. *Annals of Tourism Research, 30*(2), 386–405.

Stone, P. (2013). Institute for Dark Tourism Research Retrieved from http://lgn1331135353.site-fusion.co.uk/) at the University of Central Lancashire, UK July 3rd, 2013.

Swart, K., & Bob, U. (2007). The eluding link: Toward developing a national sport tourism strategy in South Africa beyond 2010. *Politkon, 34*(3), 373–391.

U.S. Travel Association. (2010). *The benefits are everywhere: The personal benefits of travel and taking a vacation.* Retrieved from http://www.travelmontana.mt.gov/tourism_week/benefits_of_travel.pdf.

UNWTO. (2007). *From Davos to Bali: A tourism contribution to the challenge of climate change.* Retrieved from www.unwto.org

UNWTO. (2013). *International tourism receipts grew by 4% in 2012.* Retrieved from http://media.unwto.org/en/press-release/2013-05-15/international-tourism-receipts-grew-4-2012.

Weaver, D. (1999). Magnitude of ecotourism in Costa Rica and Kenya. *Annals of Tourism Research, 26*, 792–816.

Weaver, D., & Lawton, L. (2007). Twenty years on: The state of contemporary ecotourism research. *Tourism Management, 28*, 1168–1179.

Weed, M., & Bull, C. (2004). *Sports tourism: Participants, policy and providers.* London: Butterworth-Heinemann.

White, N., & White, P. (2007). Home and away: Tourists in a connected world. *Annals of Tourism Research, 34*(1), 88–104.

Wickens, E. (2002). The sacred and the profane: A tourist typology. *Annals of Tourism Research, 29*(3), 834–851.

Williams, P., & Fidgeon, P. (2000). Addressing participation constraint: A case study of potential skiers. *Tourism Management, 21*, 379–393.

World Travel and Tourism Council. (2013). *Travel and tourism economic impact 2013: World.* Retrieved from http://www.wttc.org/research/economic-impact-research/

Yiannakis, A., & Gibson, H. (1992). Roles tourists play. *Annals of Tourism Research, 19*(2), 287–303.

Zeppel, H. (2006). *Indigenous ecotourism: Sustainable development and management.* Wallingford, UK: CAB International.

12

Leisure in Africa

Maliga Naidoo (University of KwaZulu Natal, South Africa)

Africa is the second largest continent and the second most populous in the world, comprising 61 countries including the Indian Ocean islands, each with its own ruling government, culture, and traditions. With a population of 1.2 billion and with varying degrees of wealth and poverty, it is rich in its diversity of vibrant cultures, languages, and traditions. Leisure in Africa is shaped by its history. To appreciate leisure on this continent, it is necessary to understand the influences of the colonial past and how it affected sport and leisure practices in the African communities.

The momentous hosting of the 2010 Fédération Internationale de Football Association (FIFA) World Cup in South Africa was a significant mega event in the sporting history and in the lives of all Africans. According to Akyeampong and Ambler (2002), soccer reflects a passion and a pleasure among many African men while the women either have no time for leisure or their activities revolve around the social pastimes of visiting family and friends or other pleasurable activities (Martin, 2002). This passion for soccer is echoed in the celebrations which followed the victory of Senegal against the defending French champions during the 2002 FIFA World Cup. To the Senegalese players the win was not a technical or conventional one. The victors triumphantly expressed, "Today's victory is a victory for all of Africa. . . . Between Senegal and France, there is a lot of history" (Akyeampong & Ambler, 2002, p. 1). The sentiments of the Senegalese players after 42 years of independence from the French government may be viewed as a retribution for the time they served as subjects during the colonial years.

This chapter examines the concept of leisure in Africa during the precolonial times and attempts to address to what extent colonialism enhanced or suppressed leisure in African society. Generally, very little is known about leisure in Africa and this chapter will attempt to provide the reader with a historic overview of colonialism and its effect on the participation in sport and leisure among the colonized in Ghana, Nigeria, Zanzibar, Kenya, and South Africa. In conclusion, we will consider the challenges experienced by African communities in the twenty-first century, and assess if these can be ameliorated through the provision of scholarly research and implementation of sustainable leisure services.

THE CONCEPT OF LEISURE IN AFRICA

Akyeampong and Ambler (2002) described leisure in African society post-colonialism as an important domain of activity and a time for reflection, when socially valuable constructs were established: time spent with family and friends, community activities, an opportunity to develop a social identity, participation for fun or pleasure, and a time to rest and rejuvenate from the demands of work. These cultural activities were enjoyed as part of the daily routine interspersed with work activities (Regi, 2012).

In the days preceding colonization, people participated in recreation activities involving traditional culture after or during the day's work. Activities engaged in for enjoyment and rejuvenation incorporated physical exercises during dance, acrobatic and gymnastic displays, and cultural festivals (Asagba, 2007). Children were encouraged to participate in play activities such as jumping, climbing a tree, hiking up a mountain, riding a horse or donkey, dancing, singing, and acrobatic acts (Omoruan, 1996).

It was believed that through playing games and sports and attending traditional religious festivals the African child would develop physical, emotional, aesthetic, and social skills which prepared him or her for a well-adjusted adult life. Such traditions were practiced extensively in Nigeria and included activities such as festivals, moonlight stories, meetings at the village square, hunting, dancing, wrestling, fishing, swimming, and playing various types of games during free time (Ipinmoroti, 2004).

In his paper on leisure and culture, Chick (1998) questioned to what extent leisure as a concept is valid in other cultures. While Western scholars defined leisure as free time, activity away from personal obligations, an experience or a state of mind, Chick pondered whether any or all of these definitions could be applied to the behavior or experiences of people living in non-Western cultures. It can be argued that in the precolonial times, leisure practices in Africa were driven more by the desire to preserve a tradition rather than based on conceptual theories as described in the West. This dichotomous understanding of leisure later on may have precipitated the antagonism between the local people and their European employers. Cross-cultural problems in defining leisure, for example, were observed in the 1920s during events organized by the Europeans for the local population. What was perceived to be appropriate leisure activities organized for the benefit of workers, resulted in clashes between colonial officials and employees (Akyeampong & Ambler, 2002). The attempt to provide worker relief by introducing European soccer to the employees at the Northern Rhodesian Copperbelt was met with very little enthusiasm and support (Akyeampong & Ambler, 2002).

Leisure practice within defined boundaries contributed to tensions between different cultural groups, since African workers attempted to preserve their independence and struggled against the imposition of leisure activities and loss of control over their free time (Ambler, 2003). The concept of leisure is bound by social and cultural constructs with different cultures interpreting the meaning of leisure based on race, ethnicity, gender, class, and age. Such a misunderstanding between the managers and mine workers exposed the problems related to the understanding of leisure practice in Africa. The position of the manager at the mine was occupied by a male middle-class Englishman who may not have had a thorough understanding of the nature of African leisure traditions (Ambler, 2003).

The language barrier and the absence of the word "leisure" within the African cultures may have further compounded the breakdown in communication, which resulted in increased resistance of the African people towards the British (Chick, 1998). From an anthropological perspective, informal research by Chick (1998) suggested not all languages have words that could be translated into the English word "leisure." Chick explained only 7 of the 11 languages spoken by students in his study had the same words to mean leisure, while the French language was the only language which correctly translated and back translated the word "leisure." "Leisure" in other languages was back translated to mean "free time" or a close equivalent of this term. In some African languages, the word "leisure" could not be translated and then translated back into English.

Another consideration in understanding African leisure is how, and by whom, activities come to be defined as leisure. Leisure is an intangible concept with a variety of definitions and understandings dependent on the context. Workers who settled in urban centers in the early 1930s brought with them their own philosophies or ideas of leisure activity, which did not include soccer and drill teams, as it was imposed by the European managers (Akyeampong & Ambler, 2002).

Colonizers who observed the leisure activities of African people described them as either "wasting time" or "celebrating life." Dances at funerals were an expression of celebrating the life of the deceased while "wasting time" made reference to "Africa time." Africans generally did not subscribe or pay serious attention to punctuality (Ekpo, 1990). This wastage of time, as interpreted by Westerners, was closely associated with idleness and irresponsible behavior. For Africans, however, it was a time when socializing, and fun activities such as singing and dancing, took place before the function or event commenced. It was an important time during which people connected and shared a sense of community. The issue of time and its uses, which has always been of concern to man, must be re-examined with respect to changing societal trends in Africa. It is relevant to accord leisure and recreation their rightful place in the political, educational, social, and economic planning, especially in developing nations (Ekpo 1990).

THE INFLUENCE OF COLONIZATION ON AFRICA

The colonization of Africa by the major European powers of Britain, France, Belgium, Italy, Spain, and Portugal took place between 1870 and 1900 (Iweriebor, 2011). These European settlements imposed political and economic control over Africa resulting in the division of the local people and the creation of a multitude of diverse cultures and ethnicities (Howard, 1999). Many factors and events shaped the attitudes of the African people towards the colonizers, which helped them prepare to fight for the right to govern themselves. Life under colonial rule was very difficult for the people of Africa because colonizers maintained colonies for their own benefit. Colonization worked to the advantage of the mother countries who sought areas rich in natural resources, cheap labor, and for commercial purposes.

The partition of Africa and struggle for power to own the rich natural resources of the continent lasted between 60 and 80 years, enslaving most of the people in African countries (Toyin, 2004). Colonizers imposed control to maintain order and to demonstrate superiority by overlooking and isolating the local population's culture and way of life. The changes emanating from the partitioning of the continent left deep scars, affecting the social, economic, and political characteristics of the colonized people and countries, their culture and the way the local people think and act today. Conquests, colonization, the slave trade, the influence of different religions and cultural elements, and recently the spread of commercialization have all transformed Africa over the years. The exploitation that prevailed during this period also changed the way the whole world viewed Africa; as a source of slave trade and as a continent whose economic development trailed behind the rest of the world (Toyin, 2004).

Colonizers created divisions among their subordinate societies by appointing and training a few subjects to work within the administration of the colonies while at the same time expecting passive compliance from the majority of the population. The establishment of municipalities and bureaucracies managed by local people resulted in competition, power struggles, and conflict between ethnic and social groups. This prompted distrust and anger, resulting in nationalist tensions that progressively grew into a state of dissatisfaction against the rule of the European superiors. Rising nationalist sentiments throughout Africa brought about a new paradigm shift against the oppressors (Hutchison, 2009). Nationalist sentiments continued to rise since 1930 encouraged by educated leaders in the fight for independence and self-governance.

THE RISE OF AFRICAN NATIONALISM THROUGH SPORT AND LEISURE

During the colonial era the relationship that existed between the colonizers and the African people was a painful one. Between 1940 and 1950 the elite class of Africans who attended Western schools became exposed to a different lifestyle of self-determination and independence. Knowledge gained by studying historical wars for freedom and class battles empowered the elite leaders to take action within Africa. This was a turning point in the history of Africa, when scholars and soldiers returned armed with knowledge and a thirst for freedom which gave rise to a stronger resistance movement and determination for self-governance (Howard, 1999).

While sport activities in the British colonies were planned to control the local population, they worked radically against them after World War I. Sport served to unite the local people in a climate of social and political unrest. Although the British developed and administered the rules of play, the selection and organization of teams fell outside of their influence. Teams were planned and organized by the African people, which helped to unify them across social, cultural, and economic divisions to resist the colonizers. On the playing field during the matches, the players were cheered and motivated by the mesmerizing rituals and sounds of song and dance, which helped to strengthen the African spirit against the oppressor (Hutchison, 2009).

The most popular sports played across the African diaspora were soccer, cricket, boxing, and field hockey. Boxing in Ghana and soccer in Senegal evolved from an ethnic precolonial tradition of participation in athletic activities such as spear throwing, warrior training, wrestling, and other combat actions that had their foundations in leisure. During sport matches, people casually engaged in debates over drinks, as crowds would gather around televisions or in stadiums to watch their teams play. Sport events played a pivotal role in bringing together people from across a diverse community, strengthening their resolve against the colonial rulers (Hutchison, 2009).

In the period when colonial power in Africa began to decline, the International Olympic Committee (IOC) showed an interest in developing sport in Africa. Influenced by the philosophy of the Olympics, the founder of the Olympic Committee, Pierre de Coubertin, proposed a program initiating the African Games to encourage "athletic activity among indigenous youth" (Chatziefstathiou, Henry, & Theodoraki, 2004, p. 111). This initiative was rejected by the colonial governments for fear of being defeated by the African players or encouraging the growth of nationalism at sporting events (Chatziefstathiou et al., 2004).

As the interest and passion for sport developed in Africa, the British rulers had little influence on the transformation of leisure and recreational pursuits of the colonized. In her writings, Fair (1997) described sport played in colonial Zanzibar as having political undertones and, at the same time, providing an opportunity for social experiences for both the players and the spectators. As players and spectators battled and mingled on and off the field, new urban networks were formed, friendships developed, and new jobs sought. Soccer prowess enabled players to boost their reputations and become recognized as important team, neighborhood, and nationalist leaders (Fair, 1997). Soccer events played a central role in developing community identity. After the matches, the clubhouse served as a meeting place to foster unity among men, women, and children (Fair, 1997).

While the newfound freedom in participating in soccer was developing, another form of recreational activity was becoming popular in colonial Zanzibar. Competitions between dance and singing groups took place daily, organized by people from diverse African ethnic communities (Fair, 1997). These pastimes served as an important avenue to reflect and reinforce the diversity of the communities based on class, ethnicity, socioeconomic status, and neighborhoods. Leisure-time activities integrated players and dancers from poor and socially marginalized backgrounds. While a match took place, spectators used the opportunity to engage in leisure-time activities which served as a stimulus to strengthen mass action (Fair, 1997).

Leisure and sport seemed to play an equally important role in colonial South Africa during the years of the struggle for freedom. The black freedom movement in South Africa, which united those Africans living under the discriminatory laws, allowed them to resist not only the elite ruling class black Africans, but also their White colonizers. Soccer helped the freedom fighters to shape relationships into common bonds and provided relief from social and political anxieties (Alegi, 2002).

Sport and leisure as a form of resistance was widely publicized in South Africa. The non-racial sport movement which began in South Africa in the 1950s was formed primarily to end racism in sport and to end apartheid in society. Apartheid was a system of segregation enacted by law to classify people based on color which was strongly opposed by the non-racial sporting movement. The South African Non-Racial Olympic Committee (SANROC) based in London, commenced a series of attempts to isolate South Africa from the international community as well as the international sporting arena, which was achieved when the IOC expelled South Africa in 1970 (Nongongo, 2012). Overall, during the time of struggle for independence, sport and leisure events provided opportunities for the people of Africa to stand united in bringing about change through sociopolitical and cultural agendas.

URBANIZATION AND LEISURE

Between 1951 and 1993 all African countries gained their independence from colonial rule. Since independence, African countries have adopted a commitment to urbanization and modernity with the emphasis on becoming self-sufficient, promoting nation building, and improving standards of living of the local population. Efforts were directed towards achieving national growth by developing a set of new values for a free and just society and nation building. The rapid urbanization that followed redefined how the Africans viewed work and free time and led to concerns related to the impact of urban life on the traditional values (Okolo, 2011). Work, and the availability of leisure time as a reward for work, affected relationships and traditional values of the Africans in the post-colonial period. Leisure in Africa was starting to closely resemble that in the West. The values assigned to leisure and strong work orientation in the Western countries have been attributed to the Protestant work ethic and shaped by the Industrial Revolution of the nineteenth century (Brightbill, 1960). Similarly, urbanization in Africa and the drive to material progress achieved through work, created a new value system which went against the traditional norms as practiced by the rural population.

During the precolonial era work was necessary for survival, to support tribal customs and family obligations of accumulating enough wealth to pay a dowry for a bride, or improve one's social status. As the level of education and employment opportunities increased, the urban African was set to progress and earn more financial rewards. The traditional value of concern and respect for the elders, which played a significant role in the lives of the younger generations, was slowly eroded. Urbanization and employment meant long hours at the office or on the farms and this new lifestyle, governed by work-related schedule affected how African people engaged in their old traditional leisure activities (Okolo, 2011).

The migration to the cities also had an impact on family life when working-class mothers enjoyed less time for family and leisure. During the precolonial era, women stayed at home and worked on the land around the living area. They played a central role in organizing family activities which changed noticeably during the period of urbanization. Much of the struggles were also related to the quality of life in the cities. Many people were forced to relocate to urban areas because of poverty, drought or unrest. Cities grew exponentially without concomitant expansion in infrastructure and safe housing with proper public services for healthy living. The rapid and unorganized development of cities may have contributed to the some of the challenges outlined below.

LEISURE IN CONTEMPORARY AFRICA

There is very little documented evidence explaining leisure practices in contemporary Africa. Since the time of the Pharoahs, board games were a popular pastime played on the ground or on exquisitely carved wood or ivory platforms. The continent is known for one of the oldest board games, called Senet, which was played in Egypt around 3,500 B,C. Another popular board game in Africa, that also has its origin in ancient times, is Mancala/Mankala which is played and enjoyed by all. African children play a large variety of games, with or without equipment, such as "hide and seek" and "leap frog." Toys for children are usually handmade from everyday materials such as hoops made from the rims of tires, skipping ropes made from grass, or homemade wooden dolls (SOS Children's Villages, 2014).

The most popular sport played in Africa is soccer. It is not unusual to see youngsters in most cities and rural areas of Africa kicking a football. To fulfill the sporting prowess of athletes, Africa has its own Olympic Games, the All

Africa Games which are hosted every four years by a different country. Cricket and golf are played mostly in South Africa and Zimbabwe. Among younger generations, capoeira—a martial art with elements of dance, acrobatics, and music—is hugely popular in countries such as Mozambique and Angola. It is played in a circle on the ground and requires nothing more than a few meters of flat space for the participants to have fun. With its energetic combination of kicks and acrobatics, capoeira is all about directing energy and aggression through physical challenge (SOS Children's Villages, 2014).

CHALLENGES IN AFRICA

African countries across the continent face numerous challenges in their quest to provide adequate services to improve quality of life of the local population. According to the ranking of countries based on the human development index (HDI) for Africa, most countries fall within the medium to low development levels. However, between 2005 and 2013 countries such as Ghana, South Africa, Libya, Tunisia, and other North African countries reported improved indicators for well-being and quality of life. Notwithstanding this improvement in some countries, the majority of African people face the challenges of inadequate access to education, high youth unemployment, increased burden of disease, gender inequity, and poverty (World Helath Organization, 2009), which places the provision of recreation and leisure services low on the priority list for service delivery in Africa.

The health challenges confronting Africa may be a manifestation of low literacy rates and high levels of insanitary living conditions. According to the Global Health Risk report burden of disease statistics (World Health Organization, 2009), Africa has the highest rate of HIV and sexually transmitted diseases, number of deaths under 60 years of age due to elevated blood pressure, and deaths under 60 years of age caused by obesity. For instance, according to a study by Caldwell et al. (2004), 54% of the population of South Africa is below 25 years of age and has the highest incidence of HIV in the world. The high incidence of HIV, increased substance abuse and early sexual activity necessitated the need for an intervention directed at reducing the health risk profile among adolescents. The Health Wise program based on the successful USA Time Wise project was integrated into the Life Skills curriculum at schools in the Cape Flats district, Cape Town, where teachers helped students to identify their leisure interests, find local resources, motivate them to pursue their interests, and anticipate ways to overcome obstacles (Caldwell & Baldwin, 2004). Positive changes in behavior and time management helped the youth develop new strategies for healthy living. Another growing global public health concern is the high incidence of obesity as a risk factor for non-communicable diseases. Developing nations of South Africa, Zimbabwe, Kenya, and Ghana are particularly affected and have an increased rate of obesity across all economic levels and age groups (World Health Organization, 2009).

Many of these problems are related to people's lifestyles, which can be addressed by increasing leisure-time physical activity (Poirier & Despres, 2001). In particular, physical activity reduces the risk of cardiovascular disease, some cancers and type 2 diabetes. Participation in leisure-time physical activity allows an individual to socialize within a positive environment and to gain access to various resources. Physically active participants also enjoy a higher life satisfaction and quality of life compared to those who are physically inactive (Ramírez-Marrero, Smith, Meléndez-Brau, & Santana-Bagur, 2004). Physical activity can be easily incorporated into daily activities including work, transportation, domestic chores, and leisure (World Health Organization, 2009).

Rates of work- and transportation-related physical activity in Africa were found to be high, while physical activity during leisure time was not common (Guthold et al., 2011). In a study of 22 African countries, physical activity levels varied greatly across areas and population subgroups with leisure-time physical activity being consistently low (Guthold et al., 2011). Low levels of participation in leisure-time physical activity across Africa are influenced by cultural and religious attitudes and behavior. A combination of poor environmental conditions with lack of facilities and high crime rates, and the absence of a national policy to promote leisure services, seem to contribute to low levels of physical activity among South Africans (South African Medical Research Council, 2010).

Mental disorders account for a large proportion of the disease burden among young people in all societies, especially among youth between 12 to 24 years of age (Patel, Flisher, Hetrick, & McGorry, 2007). Poor mental health is strongly related to other health and development concerns in young people, notably lower educational achievements, substance abuse, violence, and poor reproductive and sexual health. Health-system responses to mental health problems among youth in Africa have been inadequate in developing countries, which has obvious implications for public health if these disorders persist into adulthood (Patel et al., 2007). Leisure and leisure education play an important role in maintaining good mental health levels. For instance, studies have shown that participating in physical activity—either walking or cycling to work or school—has a beneficial effect (Ohta, Mizoue, Mishima, & Ikeda, 2007; Wiles et al., 2008). Leisure education, well-informed teachers and public service officials can effectively transfer the message of the benefits of leisure through the implementation of programs and services.

Sivan (1997) explained that leisure and education are interconnected. She suggested that leisure education plays an important role in nurturing and stimulating the interest of cultures and societies in the pursuit of pleasure-seeking activities that are socially acceptable and individually satisfying. The context within which leisure education is created and implemented is crucial to the acquisition of leisure-related skills, knowledge, attitudes, and perceptions (Yankholmes & Lin, 2012). The acquisition of skills and the pursuit of socially acceptable activities may assume a much more important role in transforming youth by enhancing an individual's quality of life and identity (Yankholmes & Lin, 2012).

Leisure education provides a systematic approach to influencing services and motivating people to participate in leisure-time activities. During adolescence, children are allowed greater freedom of choice to engage in self-managed leisure-time activities and to demonstrate their level of responsibility by engaging in healthy behavior and attitudes. Teachers, parents and public service officials play an important role in educating the youth to make good choices (Caldwell & Baldwin, 2004).

The availability of leisure education and activities within the public service is dependent on the quality of skills and knowledge of young African people to make an essential contribution to today's societies and future generations. They will be better educated and more aware of global opportunities than previous generations, giving them high expectations of a better life and future. Faced with limited opportunities to improve social well-being and enhance their human development, young people in Africa have become victims of social and economic problems that originated in the preceding decades (Janneh, 2011). Future success of the youth in transforming their lives and their cities would therefore depend on university administrators, educators, and campus recreation professionals to provide positive leisure and recreation programs for college students on campus (Yang & Guo, 2011).

Central to the empowerment of youth, it is essential to consider the role and status of mothers and women in Africa. Women spend most of their leisure in and around the home with family and in activities that are congruent with the primary domestic dual roles of wife and mother. Most women in Africa engage in convenient leisure activities that coincide with the needs of the family, that are easily accessible, low cost, and easy to perform (Muiruri, 1994). In Africa, roles within the family remain mutually exclusive and unequal; they are allocated not on the basis of ability or choice but on the basis of gender. Even successful career women have to perform their stereotypical gender roles at home (Muiruri, 1994). The burden placed on women to balance work and life issues is influenced by years of traditional upbringing where women had to fulfill the roles of mother and wife.

The roles of women are learned and transmitted from one generation to the next. Individuals may make changes by adapting to the changing times to keep pace with the social developments or challenges taking place in the wider society, and design services that contribute to social good. Recreation in the family should be encouraged because of its positive values and influence on human development (Trussell, Chapter 22; Wiles et al., 2008). Helping women to learn to use their discretionary time effectively in the most enjoyable and rewarding ways can boost self-esteem and address the issues of gender inequality (Muiruri, 1994). It is during leisure-time engagements that women explore and review themselves as encompassing many roles and multiple identities. Green (1998) suggested that an opportunity to spend leisure tome with other women may help them assess and shape their lives. Satisfying interactions and a sense of belonging can sustain the identities of women (Green, 1998; Parry, Chapter 24).

CONCLUSION

The discussion presented in this chapter has focused on the long journey of Africans from the oppressive days of colonialism to the twenty-first century where the aim and focus of countries is to achieve a better quality of life for the people. This is reflected in the adoption of the strategies for sustained economic growth, poverty reduction and attainment of the Millennium Development Goals (MDGs). However, the challenge confronting most African countries is the ability to pursue development initiatives in a manner that preserves the environment for economic growth and poverty reduction.

In the last 40 years, the field of leisure has made great strides in scientifically demonstrating the benefits of leisure services (Driver, Brown, & Peterson, 2009). Some of the measurable outcomes of leisure participation include improving the human condition, boosting youth resiliency, and poverty alleviation. Thus, sustainable and quality leisure services in communities are also likely to contribute to improving the human development index in Africa. The challenge today is to reposition leisure services within the sociopolitical landscape to alleviate some of the burdens facing the continent.

The low level of research and documented evidence in this field may be attributed to the small number of tertiary institutions offering leisure education to fully train professionals in this field. An Internet search for universities offering Bachelor degree programs in leisure sciences in Africa revealed only seven countries out of 55 and approximately 10 institutions on the continent offering this training. It is imperative that more professionals are trained in the sector of parks and recreation to address some of the challenges and at the same time improve the quality of life of all. An evaluation of the existing academic programs is necessary to understand skills development and the availability of professionals in this sector.

While large investments have been made to promote tourism and attract leisure travelers to Africa, further research and investment is needed in infrastructure, leisure education, and understanding the leisure perception and needs of the people. Research evidence based on leisure-related issues within the African context will assist policymakers to make informed decisions for change.

More scholarly research on leisure in Africa is deemed necessary to understand the full extent of leisure practices and attitudes. An exploration of government policy and strategies in different countries will provide essential information on the mandate for leisure service delivery. Based on my review of the literature, low levels of participation in leisure-time physical activity, the growing burden of disease, risky behavior of youth, and environmental concerns across Africa provide numerous opportunities for research. Further research on cultural and traditional practices, leisure among women, and the availability of resources, and infrastructure for leisure participation could provide the basis to justify the implementation of sustainable leisure services.

Another focus for scholarly investigation is the availability of youth services and leisure programs to boost resiliency and contribute to alleviating some of the challenges such as unemployment and risky leisure behavior patterns among youth (Caldwell, Chapter 21).

Finally, the solutions to Africa's challenges and the drive towards self-realization, empowerment, and identity are dependent on internal knowledge production and the African renaissance.

REFERENCES

Akyeampong, E., & Ambler, C. (2002). Leisure in African history: An introduction. *The International Journal of African Historical Studies, 35*(1), 1–16.

Alegi, P. C. (2002). Playing to the gallery? Sport, cultural performance, and social identity in South Africa, 1920s–1945. *International Journal of African Historical Studies, 35*(1), 17–38.

Ambler, C. (2003). Writing African leisure history. In T. Zeleza & C. R. Veney (Eds.), *Leisure in Urban Africa* (pp. 3–18). Trenton, NJ: Africa World Press.

Asagba, B. O. (2007). Perceived impact Of leisure activities To societal development of the Indigenous People Of Kwara Central Zone Kwara State Nigeria. *International Journal of African and American Studies, VI*(2).

Brightbill, C. (1960). *The challenge of leisure*. Englewood Cliffs, NJ: Prentice Hall.

Caldwell, L. L., & Baldwin, C. (2004). Preliminary effects of leisure education program to promote healthyuse of free time among middle school adolescence. *Journal of Leisure Research, 36*(3), 310–335.

Caldwell, L. L., Smith, E. A., L, F., Wegner, L., Vergnani, T., Mathews, C., & Mpofu, E. (2004). Healthwise South Africa: Development of a life skills curriculum for young adults. *World Leisure Journal, 3,* 4–17.

Chatziefstathiou, D., Henry, I., & Theodoraki, D. (2004). *Coubertin, colonialism and control of the spread of Olympic sport in Africa*. Retrieved from http://easm.net/download/2004/06213503c2a0e7a076746794609fe9ef.pdf

Chick, C. (1998). Leisure and culture: Issues for an anthropology of leisure. *Leisure Sciences, 20*(2), 111–133. doi: 10.1080/01490409809512269

Driver, B. L., Brown, P. J., & Peterson, G. L. (2009). *The benefits of leisure.* State College, PA: Venture Publishing, Inc.

Ekpo, K. (1990). Re-education for the management of enforced leisure through leisure hours *World Leisure & Recreation, 32(4)*, 27–31. doi: 10.1080/102611 33.1990.10559128

Fair, F. (1997). Kickin' it: leisure, politics and football in colonial Zanzibar, 1900s–1950s *Journal of the International African Institute, 67*(02), 224–251. doi: 10.2307/1161443

Green, E. (1998). "Women Doing Friendship": An analysis of women's leisure as a site of identity construction, empowerment and resistance. *Leisure Studies, 17*, 171–185.

Guthold, R., Louazani, S. A., Riley, L. M., Cowan, M. J., Bovet, P., Damasceno, A., . . . Armstrong, T. P. (2011). Physical activity in 22 African countries: Results from the World Health Organization STEPwise approach to chronic disease risk factor surveillance. *American Journal of Preventitive Medicine, 41*(1), 52–60. doi: 10.1016/j.amepre.2011.03.008

Howard, A. (1999). When the people decide: A study of the independence movement in Ghana. http://digitalcollections.sit.edu/african_diaspora_isp/41

Hutchison, P. M. (2009). Breaking boundaries: Football and colonialism in the British Empire. *International Student Journal, 1*(11).

Ipinmoroti, O. A. (2004). Provision of recreational facilities. An imperative for the Nigerian school system. *Education Today, 1*(1), 4–9.

Iweriebor, E. E. G. (2011). The colonisation of Africa. Retrieved from http://exhibitions.nypl.org/africanaage/essay-colonization-of-africa.html

Janneh, A. (2011). African Youth Report 2011. Addis Ababa: United Nations.

Martin, P. (2002). Leisure and society in colonial Brazzaville. Cambridge University Press.

Muiruri, P. W. (1994). Leisure for urban working women : A case study of Nairobi, Kenya. http://publications.ossrea.net/index.php?option=com_sobi2&sobi2Task=sobi2Details&sobi2Id=464&Itemid=0

Nongongo, P. (2012). *Sports around the world*. J. Nauright & C. Parrish (Eds.). United States of America: ABC-CLIO.

Ohta, M., Mizoue, T., Mishima, N., & Ikeda, M. (2007). Effect of the physical activities in leisure time and commuting to work on mental health. *Journal of Occupational Health, 49*(1), 46–52.

Okolo, C. B. (2011). *Urbanization and African traditional values*. Washington, DC: Council for Research in Values and Philosophy.

Omoruan, J. C. (1996). *A handbook on physical education, sport and recreation*. Zamaru, Zaria: Akesome and Company.

Patel, V., Flisher, A. J., Hetrick, S., & McGorry, P. (2007). Mental health of young people: A global public-health challenge. *Lancet, 369*, 1302–1313.

Poirier, P., & Despres, J. P. (2001). Exercise in weight management of obesity. *Cardiology Clinics, 19*(3), 459–470.

Ramírez-Marrero, F. A., Smith, B. A., Meléndez-Brau, N., & Santana-Bagur, J. L. (2004). Physical and leisure activity, body composition, and life satisfaction in HIV-positive Hispanics in Puerto Rico. *The Journal of the Association of Nurses in AIDS Care : JANAC, 15*(4), 68–77.

Regi, T. (2012). Tourism, leisure and work in an east African pastoral society. *Anthropology Today, 28*(5), 3–7.

Sivan, A. (1997). Recent developments in leisure education research and implementation. *World Leisure & Recreation, 39*(2), 41–44.

South African Medical Research Council. (2010). *The second South African national youth risk behavior survey 2008*. Cape Town: South African Medical Research Council.

SOS Children's Villages. (2014). Our Africa - Games and Sport. Retrieved from http://www.our-africa.org/games-and-sports

Toyin, F. (2004). *The dark webs: Perspectives on colonialism in Africa*. Durham, NC: Carolina Academic Press.

World Health Organization. (2009). *Global health risks: Mortality and burden of disease attributable to selected major risks*. Geneva: World Health Organization.

Wiles, N. J., Jones, G. T., Haase, A. M., Lawlor, D. A., Macfarlane, G. J., & Lewis, G. (2008). Physical activity and emotional problems amongst adolescents: a longitudinal study. *Social Psychiatry and Psychiatric Epidemiology, 43*(10), 765–772. doi: 10.1007/s00127-008-0362-9

Yang, H., & Guo, L. (2011). Relationship between self-esteem and leisure boredom among college students. *LARNet The Cyber Journal of Applied Leisure and Recreation Research, 14*(1), 1–12.

Yankholmes, A., & Lin, S. (2012). Leisure and education in Ghana: An exploratory study of university students' leisure lifestyles. *World Leisure Journal, 54*(1), 58–68. doi: 10.1080/04419057.2012.668044

13

LEISURE IN AUSTRALIA AND NEW ZEALAND

Simone Fullagar (University of Bath, United Kingdom)
and Lee Davidson (Victoria University, New Zealand)

In this chapter we outline some of the major leisure-related policy and participation trends in Australia and New Zealand as neighboring countries with a number of similarities and yet quite distinct cultures. New Zealand and Australia have enjoyed a close economic and social relationship over a long period of time, yet the friendship is often "tested" in the sport arena with intense rivalry in football, netball, and cricket. In this chapter we examine several tensions that exist between constructions of national identity around the "sporting nation" and leisure participation trends (see also Bennett, Bustamante, & Frow, 2013; Veal, Darcy, & Lynch, 2013). Australia, for example, has promoted active lifestyles for several decades yet low rates of physical activity persist as patterns of sport and recreation change, while high levels of accumulated annual leave and long working hours continue (Australian Bureau of Statistics, 2013a,b; Commonwealth of Australia, 2010; Hajkowicz, Cook, Wilhelmseder, & Boughen, 2013). Unlike the severe economic downturn experienced by many other Organization for Economic Co-operation and Development (OECD) countries across the globe, Australia and New Zealand have enjoyed higher levels of economic prosperity, low unemployment, and at the same time have had to respond to number of major natural disasters (e.g., earthquakes, fires, and floods). In addition, inequalities continue to be evident in relation to patterns of leisure participation within organized sport, recreation, and cultural pursuits. We provide a brief overview of the historical and cultural context that has shaped the meaning and forms of leisure provision and participation in both countries before examining a number of specific issues in greater detail.

HISTORICAL AND CULTURAL CONTEXT

Modern Australia was founded on colonial rule with distinctly British traditions employed to create a new industrial society that was defined against the customs and knowledge of the original Aboriginal custodians who had no equivalent notion of "leisure" and were subject to the oppressive conditions of white rule (Veal et al., 2013). For the many different clans of Aboriginal people there was no oppositional construction of work and leisure practices, rather there existed varied expressions of playful activity and cultural ritual that are deeply tied to notions of kinship and a spiritual relationship to "country" that continue in the post-colonial context today (Tsai, Cushman, Gidlow, & Toohey, 2013). British inflected leisure practices (e.g., gambling, drinking, sport) in post-colonial Australia have also been shaped by several waves of migration from many parts of the world which has led to the emergence of a multicultural society with a distinct cosmopolitan orientation.

The existing "work-leisure" relationship for New Zealand's indigenous Māori was disrupted by the arrival of missionaries in the early nineteenth century and the introduction of European sports and pastimes. The loss of traditional cultural practices was further exacerbated by the alienation of Māori land during the colonial period and increasing urbanization in the twentieth century (Smith, 1998). Leisure in New Zealand's predominantly male "frontier society" was characterized by heavy drinking, gambling, and tough physical sports, reflecting the rugged conditions of a life extracting resources and "taming" the landscape for pastoral production (Watson, 1998). While these tendencies declined as society became more settled, they never entirely disappeared. The discipline of team sports such as rugby was encouraged, as they served the interests of capitalism and imperialism, as well as encouraging egalitarian values (Watson, 1998). While international sporting success on the rugby field has been important for developing a sense of national identity and pride, the culture of the "national game" remains associated, to a certain extent, with alcohol consumption and violence.

However, the contemporary sporting landscape of New Zealand is more diverse, reflecting an increasingly multicultural population and a trend towards individual rather than team sports (Watson, 1998). While rugby remains popular for Māori adults, a renaissance of Māori culture in the last few decades has seen the growing popularity of recreational and sporting interests that retain a connection with cultural traditions and practices. Another important legacy of New Zealand's colonial past is found in the practice of nature-based recreation. It retains strong values of self-sufficiency, resourcefulness, and endurance associated with the pioneering tradition of European settlers, as well as a love of New Zealand's distinctive flora, fauna, marine, and alpine landscapes, which are also significant sources of national identity (Davidson, 2002, 2011). This tradition is reflected in international success in sports such as mountaineering, sailing, and adventure racing, as well as a reputation for adventure tourism. However, there is concern that participation in outdoor recreation is declining, while a number of tragic accidents involving adventure tourism operators, such as the deaths of an English tourist in a river-boarding accident in 2008, have led to stricter safety regulations (Dignan & Cessford, 2009; *Group targets New Zealand adventure tourism*, 2010).

Both countries are also shaped by popular tourist imaginaries that emphasize outdoor lifestyles, inviting natural landscapes, cosmopolitan cultures, Indigenous histories, and friendly people. Yet, each country experiences increasing wealth disparities, an aging population with limited financial resources for a leisurely retirement and sustainability challenges related to urban sprawl and densification (Fullagar, Pavlidis, Reid, & Lloyd, 2013). Our perusal of recent media reports also reveals the continuation of an historical preoccupation with moral questions about acceptable leisure practices and limits of freedom. For example, debates continue over the problematic effects of alcohol in the night time leisure economy, drugs in elite and community sport that compromise the spirit of fair play, public outcry over aggressively promoted online gambling during live sport coverage, and the opening up of national parks to uses deemed incompatible with conservation (e.g., cattle grazing, hunting). The shifting patterns and meanings of leisure in Australia and New Zealand highlight the complex relationship between notions of individual freedom to choose and deeply held cultural beliefs about the "good life" within the context of advanced liberalism, consumerism, and national identity.

CHANGING LEISURE PARTICIPATION

Much has changed in the Australian leisure landscape since the establishment of the first Commonwealth Department for Tourism and Recreation in 1973 by the progressive Whitlam Labor government. With concerns about the implications of a future leisure society, a focus on quality of life, health, and equality, Whitlam famously declared in his 1972 election speech:

> There is no greater social problem facing Australia than the good use of expanding leisure. It is the problem of all modern and wealthy communities. It is, above all, the problem of urban societies and thus, in Australia, the most urbanized nation on earth, a problem more pressing for us than for any other nation on earth. For such a nation as ours, this may very well be the problem of the 1980's; so we must prepare now; prepare the generation of the '80s—the children and youth of the '70s—to be able to enjoy and enrich their growing hours of leisure. (http://whitlamdismissal.com/1972/11/13/whitlam-1972-election-policy-speech.html#sthash.uJhYZlF2.dpuf)

While the leisure society faded into obscurity and working hours increased, the concern with quality of life, health, and participation remained central to contemporary leisure policy in an ever more complex globalized world. In their recent report on the future of Australian sport, Hajkowicz et al. (2013) identified trends related to time use and changing work, home, and leisure relationships and commitments. Drawing upon national time use data they discussed how time for recreation reduced by one hour and 45 minutes per week from 1997 to 2006, while time spent working increased. Hajkowicz et al. (2013, p. 8) stated that:

> people are spending less time playing sport and more time watching screens. The amount of time people spend engaging in 'sport and outdoor activities' has decreased even more, by 30 percent, from 27 minutes per day to only 19 minutes. Time spent on audiovisual entertainment has increased by eight percent from 2:10 to 2:20 per day (Australian Bureau of Statistics, 2011).

In response to these trends there has been a rise in gym membership, personal training and overall growth in the fitness industry. If we look at the top 10 active leisure pursuits with the greatest participation from 2001 to 2010 we see a strong emphasis on individual activities, fitness orientation, and a lesser focus on organized sport. According to Hajkowicz et al. (2013), these activities include: walking, aerobics/fitness, swimming, cycling, running, golf, tennis, bushwalking, outdoor soccer, and netball. Another related trend that was identified with Australian culture is the growing visibility of "lifestyle sports" (e.g., skateboarding, surfing, rock climbing, mountain biking, slack lining, parkour, and roller derby) (Pavlidis & Fullagar, 2013). Hajkowicz et al. (2013) suggested that "These sports are gaining popularity among large segments of Generation Y (born between 1978–1995) who connect to a counter-culture of irreverence, adventure, and freedom of expression" (p. 12). This interest in "new" or adventurous sports has emerged in the form of organized events that range from volunteer-based free five kilometre weekly runs (parkrun: www.parkrun.com.au) to endurance oriented events (triathalons, Iron Man, marathon and half marathon races, The Stampede, and Tough Mudder: www.toughmudder.com.au). Hajkowicz et al. (2013) provided an example that also illustrates the social camaraderie and sense of community that is associated with these physically challenging events:

> In Australia the inaugural Tough Mudder challenge took place in Phillip Island, Victoria on 31 March 2012. Tickets were sold out to 15,000 participants (The Age Newspaper, 2012) with prices ranging from $A90 to $A150 (Tough Mudder, 2012). The Tough Mudder philosophy on the company website is about overcoming challenges and helping teammates, rather than winning. The popularity of these events reveals a significant niche consumer segment and social demographic, seeking physically demanding endurance sports. (p. 14)

Acknowledging some differences in the surveys between countries, New Zealand's 10 most popular sport and recreation activities in terms of annual participation are: walking, gardening, swimming, equipment-based exercise, cycling, jogging/running, fishing (marine/saltwater), golf, dance, and tramping (bushwalking) (Sport and Recreation New Zealand, 2008). A recent report examining trends between 1997 and 2007 found overall participation rates had largely been maintained, however there were worrying declines within certain demographic groups. Although most young New Zealanders (18- to 24-year-olds) are playing sport, levels of participation in this age group have declined. Participation among Pacific Peoples, who make up a growing proportion of the New Zealand population, and adults of Other Ethnicity (i.e., outside the four major ethnic groups of New Zealand Asian, European, Māori, and Pacific) is also declining (Sport New Zealand, 2013). There is additional evidence of the growing popularity of individual-based sports such as running and cycling, while membership of sports clubs and fitness centers is in decline (Sport New Zealand, 2013). Although tramping makes it into the top 10 list and participation appears to remain consistent over the past decade, concerns have been raised about potential future declines. Alongside urbanization and an increasing preference for passive, home-based activities, demographic trends are predicted to affect the prevalence of outdoor recreation as the population ages and becomes more ethnically diverse (Dignan & Cessford, 2009; Lovelock, Farminer, & Reis, 2011).

In a distinct contrast to physically challenging forms of leisure, watching television remains a major leisure-time pursuit in Australian and New Zealand homes and the experience is being augmented by other kinds of screen technology. In 2013 Australians viewed an average of 92 hours and 39 minutes of TV each month (3.3 hours per day), while New Zealanders were spending an average of 2 hours and 8 minutes a day watching television in 2009/10 (up 7 minutes over the previous decade). Indeed, over 80% of all leisure time (4 hours and 36 minutes a day on average) for New Zealanders over the age of 12 was spent on passive mass media (e.g., watching television and video) and social entertainment (e.g., socializing, conversation) activities. In contrast, New Zealanders spent only an average of 19 minutes a day on all primary exercise or sporting activities (Statistics New Zealand, 2011).

As early adopters of new technology, three in five Australians use a smartphone and "27 percent of Australian homes have each of the four screen types: TV, PC, tablet and mobile phone, up from 16 percent a year ago" (Nielsen, 2013, p. 2). People are also increasingly engaging with technology in multiple "time deepening" ways. For instance, in 2012, 74% of Australians aged 16 and over who had online access said that they multitask—up 14% from 2011. From the late 1990s, Internet use in New Zealand has steadily risen, reaching 86% in 2011. There is evidence, however, of a persistent "digital divide," with most of those without Internet access aged over 60 and/or in a low-income household, while younger, wealthier, urban New Zealanders are most likely to view the Internet as an important part of their daily lives (Smith et al., 2011). Smartphone use has increased rapidly, with mobile handset subscriber numbers rising 34% in 2012 over the previous year, to total more than half of the population (Statistics New Zealand, 2012). Significantly, increasing mobility through wireless access is seeing more usage in open, communal spaces. However, television retains its top spot as the primary entertainment medium, with New Zealanders rating the Internet more highly for providing access to information than for entertainment. Nonetheless, social network site membership increased by a third between 2009 and 2011 to almost two-thirds of Internet users. In 2011, more than a quarter of Internet users reported having made new friends online, and half of those went on to meet them in person (Smith et al., 2011).

There has been much moral debate about the health implications of screen-based leisure in light of government imperatives to reduce the costs of non-communicable diseases. For example, the Commonwealth Government of

Australia (2009) highlighted the need to understand parental attitudes towards active living in relation to the range of children's leisure choices within and beyond home. The growth of screen-based leisure (e.g., computer games, TV) has been positioned in opposition to the sport and recreation participation agenda. Yet, there is a complex relationship to be further explored between technology and active/passive forms of leisure. As Hajkowicz et al. (2013) pointed out, the rise of Wii Fit and interactive computer games questions this opposition, while technology and social media have also been identified as crucial to shaping new ways of organizing recreation and sport activity in more spontaneous and less structured formats. The relatively recent growth of canyoning in New Zealand is a case in point. When Dan Clearwater began canyoning in 2005, it was very difficult to find other enthusiasts or information on the sport. As a result he founded the KiwiCanyons.org website which offers practical advice, technical tips, and descriptions of canyons around the country. The website is complemented by a Facebook group where over 200 members share stories, post photos and videos, and invite each other on trips. While in the past networks of clubs were the mainstay of outdoor activities in New Zealand, Clearwater thinks people are moving away from that kind of structure and towards more online organization.

> I don't think [New Zealand], the world even, does clubs much anymore. I think the sort of electronic club system will be the one that will reign for the foreseeable future. People don't meet and sit and talk about canyoning formally, they just go on trips together. Clubs are a thing of the past. (D. Clearwater, personal communication, March 7, 2013)

We also see technology being used globally in democratic ways to collectively 'map' leisure practices and knowledge so that it may be stored and widely shared. For example, the growing interest in cycling and strong sales of bicycles have informed the emergence of crowdsourced website maps of cycling routes that include cafés, scenic information and risk conditions (e.g., on/off road). There are also broad sustainability-oriented 'eco spot' maps that invite citizens to create virtual communities, alternative leisure spaces, and eco practices that counter consumerist imperatives[1].

LEISURE AND CULTURAL PARTICIPATION

Despite the significance of sport and outdoor recreation for New Zealand and Australia's cultural heritage and identity, the arts and culture also play an important role. A 2002 survey reported a high level of engagement with cultural activities among New Zealanders aged 15 and over. Ninety-three percent had participated in at least one cultural activity surveyed, ranging from purchasing books and visiting public libraries (44 and 39%, respectively in the previous four weeks), to visiting museums/art galleries and attending live performances of popular music (48 and 37%, respectively in the previous 12 months). Most New Zealanders (85% in 2011) also either attend or participate in the arts, with half being actively involved in at least one arts event in the past 12 months, and one-quarter (25%) participating at least monthly (Creative New Zealand, 2011). Australians are also enthusiastic participants in arts, entertainment, and culture with greatest involvement in commercial activities (cinema and pop concerts), regular visitation to public facilities such as libraries and varied engagement in other forms (e.g., galleries, dance, theatre) over time (Veal et al., 2013). Generally, participation in most cultural activities tends to be higher among those people with higher education, those in the labor force, earning higher incomes, and living in urban centers (Ministry for Culture and Heritage, 2003).

Arts and culture have also been significant in recent urban regeneration strategies throughout New Zealand, with regional centers branding themselves as heritage tourism attractions (e.g., art deco in Napier and Victorian heritage in Oamaru), while major cities compete with events, festivals, and cultural institutions. A particularly successful example of the re-imaging of a post-industrial urban landscape has been the capital, Wellington, which historically suffered from a negative image as a city populated by politicians and civil servants. Over the past two decades, however, Wellington has achieved significant growth in tourist arrivals as it has overcome its dull image and established itself as an attractive destination with a mix of cultural attractions and events, as well as a general "vibe" created by its cafés, restaurants, and shops (Carey, Davidson, & Sahli, 2012). In 2010, Lonely Planet ranked Wellington fourth among the world's top city destinations, while in a recent Quality of Life survey, 90% of Wellingtonians agreed that their city has a culturally rich and diverse arts scene, compared with an average of 47% across other urban areas nationwide (ACNielsen, 2013).

The building of a new national museum on the city's waterfront has been an integral part of this development. Opened in 1998, the Museum of New Zealand Te Papa Tongarewa (Te Papa) sought to attract a broader audience than its predecessor by reflecting the country's bicultural identity, and offering engaging and interactive displays along with complementary retail and hospitality functions. With an average annual visitation of 1.3 million in its first decade of operation, more than five times that of the previous

[1] See http://www.urban-growth.com/2013/03/my-eco-city-sharing-eco-spots-of.html

museum, Te Papa has largely achieved its democratizing agenda and ranks as the most visited museum or cultural institution in Australasia. Visitation from the local community is high and encompasses a broad range of leisure contexts, while many domestic tourists travel to visit international touring exhibitions that offer experiences of art and culture they have few chances to see due to New Zealand's geographic isolation. Among international visitors (around 40% of total visitation) Te Papa has a strong reputation as a place to learn about the country's unique history and culture (Davidson & Sibley, 2011).

LEISURE PARTICIPATION FOR ALL CITIZENS?

Despite the more recent challenges arising from the global economic downturn in 2008, there have been growing levels of prosperity over the last two decades and the unemployment rate has more than halved in Australia. Yet, these benefits have not eliminated social inequality. In New Zealand, income inequality increased significantly and rapidly following neo-liberal economic reforms in the 1980s, taking New Zealand from well under the OECD average to well above by the mid-1990s (Perry, 2013). Income inequality in New Zealand is similar to that in Australia, Ireland, Canada and Japan, with socioeconomic disadvantage borne largely by Māori and Pacific Peoples, teenage mothers, and sole parent families (Quality of Life Project, 2007).

In 2010, a quarter of Australians aged 15 years plus experienced some degree of social exclusion from marginal to deeper forms that affected their life opportunities. Those most at risk of greater disadvantage include the unemployed, Indigenous Australians, people with a long-term health condition or disability, lone parents, and people with low educational attainment. Australians residing in more disadvantaged areas also experience much higher rates of chronic disease and mental health problems (McLachlan, Gilfillan, & Gordon, 2013). Children from socioeconomically disadvantaged families have a more difficult start to life than their more advantaged peers. Higher incomes are also associated with better average development scores among 4- to 5-year-old Australian children.

These inequalities persist in relation to leisure opportunities for children and adults who experience disadvantage. The Australian Bureau of Statistics suggested that public health campaigns about physical activity may have contributed to a 3% increase in children's sport and recreation participation from 2000 to 2006 (Australian Bureau of Statistics, 2009, p. 8). However, there has been no increase in participation rates for children from more disadvantaged areas, migrant backgrounds, sole parent families, or among girls (Australian Bureau of Statistics, 2012). There are also concerning figures in the most recent Australian Bureau of Statistics (2011, p. 1) data on adult participation in a sport or recreational activity (occurring at least once a year) that identified a decrease from 66% in 2005–2006 to 64% in 2009–2010 that was attributed to a drop in women's participation. Only 30% of the Australian population (aged over 15 years) participated regularly (more than twice a week): 80% of people with higher incomes participated in sport and recreation compared with 45% of those with household incomes in the lowest quintile bands (Australian Bureau of Statistics, 2011, p. 2).

The focus on the promotion of physical activity for health has continued in Australian health policy with the increased recognition of prevention, early intervention, and healthy lifestyles (Commonwealth Government of Australia, 2009). Health issues have also been incorporated more specifically into the rationale of sport and recreation policy along with a renewed focus on community participation (Fullagar & Harrington, 2009). In the last decade, Australian physical activity campaigns have consistently urged citizens to find ways to engage in a minimum of 30 minutes a day for adults, or 60 minutes for children, to gain health benefits. The benefits of physical activity are well-cited in a range of public policy areas that emphasize the potential economic and health outcomes for individuals and the nation (Commonwealth Government of Australia, 2009).

Similarly, a national Physical Activity Taskforce was established in New Zealand in 1998 to address inactivity among the local population. In 1999, the social marketing campaign Push Play was launched to encourage all adults to participate for 30 minutes a day, five times a week, in moderate-intensity physical activity. An evaluation conducted in 2002 found that although the campaign had resulted in increased message recognition and intention to become more active, there were no sustained changes in physical activity (Bauman et al., 2003). The most recent attempts to measure physical activity levels in New Zealand found that 48% (44% among women and 52% among men) of adults achieved the national physical activity guideline (Sport and Recreation New Zealand, 2008). Internationally, New Zealand and Australia rank in the top five countries for the proportion of the population engaging in "high" levels of physical activity (Bauman et al., 2009).

Yet, the individualized emphasis on greater responsibility for healthy lifestyles raises questions about how effectively parents and children in disadvantaged communities are supported by governments and leisure services to enable participation. While sport and recreation are popularly conceived as a domain of free choice, there is a growing body of literature that has identified a range of factors that contribute to nonparticipation and sedentary lifestyles, such as beliefs about risk, family circumstances, cultural norms, school and community opportunities, as well as the broader social, political, and economic context of advanced liberalism (Bauman et al., 2009; Fullagar & Harrington, 2009).

It is perhaps not surprising that Australian active living campaigns have had limited success with increasing participation and the development of physical activity policy has been inconsistent (Bellew, Schöeppe, Bull, & Bauman 2008). Governments at different levels face major challenges in mobilizing adults and children to take up the "active living imperative" to change their lifestyles through greater commuting/transport and recreation/sport activity (Harrington & Fullagar, 2013). In the domain of sport, play, and recreation, state and local governments also have to plan for and manage population demand for infrastructure (e.g., parks, bikeways, pools, sport fields) and targeted services (e.g., youth, family, culturally specific) within the context of a market-based leisure economy that is comprised of public, commercial, and third sector organizations (e.g., youth centers, gyms, sport clubs) (Coalter, 2007).

The Victorian Health Promotion Foundation recommended that further Australian research be conducted to examine the effects of parental perceptions of risk and fear as a significant issue limiting children's independent mobility and opportunities for physical activity (Zubrick et al., 2010). The changing leisure context of Australian families has also been identified in Cleland's et al. (2009) urban study that described a significant decline in time that children spent participating in outdoor activities over a five-year period. This study also raised concerns about the gendered effects of risk discourses on active participation, as older girls were initially identified as spending less time in outdoor activities than older boys, and this difference was exacerbated over time for older girls. This study identified how parental encouragement was significantly greater among older boys than older girls. In this sense, both the active lifestyle decisions of families and the directions of health promotion policies and campaigns are "governed" and shaped by particular meanings about risk and moral conduct (Fullagar & Harrington, 2009). Crawford (2000) described the permutation of health anxiety and desire through individual lives and state concerns as "healthism." From this perspective, leisure practices are not simply a private realm of free choice, consumption and socialization, rather they are increasingly part of a bio-political field that is shaping the form and conduct of health in relation to risk.

Similar to the concept of leisure, the meaning of health and well-being is also culturally specific and produced through different histories, norms, and social organization. Collectivist cultures often construct health and well-being in terms of the social (and spiritual) relationships that people have with nature or place, as well as family and community. For example, many Indigenous Australians do not view health or illness via an individualist biomedical paradigm but rather in terms of changes in relationship to "country," ancestors, and kinship. An Australian report recently examined the relationship between well-being and culturally specific leisure practices such as Indigenous events and festivals (Phipps & Slater, 2010). Indigenous festivals (e.g., music, cultural heritage, arts, sport) were identified as a significant source of positive identity that countered negative stereotypes and racist narratives. In addition, such leisure spaces facilitated social relationships, engagement with services, employment, and skill development that all contribute to community well-being.

The question of how leisure participation is and will continue to be shaped by culturally diverse participants and an aging demographic profile of Australia has been raised in a recent national report The Future of Australian Sport (Hajkowicz et al., 2013). One-quarter of Australians were born overseas and multicultural policies identify sport as a site for social inclusion for new and established immigrants. There are major challenges in terms of adequate provision of programs for diverse participants as the community sport sector is largely supported by volunteers who may, or may not, have cultural awareness. Organized sport will need to change in order to be more responsive to the growing needs of older participants and immigrants who do not bring with them a cultural affiliation with dominant sports. As Hajkowicz et al. (2013, p. 21) pointed out, "Fourteen percent of the Australian population is currently over 65 years of age. This is forecast to reach between 23 and 25 percent by 2056." In addition, Australians with some form of disability make up approximately one-fifth of the total population and yet their participation rates in sport and recreation remain low at around 25% (Hajkowicz et al., 2013). With women living longer than men, on lower incomes and experiencing declining rates of active participation over a lifetime, there is an important gendered dimension to the debate about the provision of services to support active aging. Many older people are living independently and alone, which suggests the importance of socially oriented leisure provision to support civic participation and mental health.

With continued growth projected for Māori, Asian and Pacific populations, growing ethnic diversity and multiculturalism is making its mark on New Zealand's leisure landscape. Sports popular with Asian New Zealanders include pilates/yoga, badminton, and basketball, leading to greater demand in these areas (Sport and Recreation New Zealand, 2008). Participation in Māori arts is increasing, with 14% of New Zealanders being involved annually, and more than two-thirds of young New Zealanders participating in Māori cultural activities such as singing, dancing, kapa haka, carving, and weaving (Creative New Zealand, 2011). A growing sport with great cultural heritage value for Māori and Pacific Peoples is waka ama (outrigger canoeing), with an estimated 15,000 participants nationwide. A week-long National Championships consistently attracts upwards of 2,000 competitors (Nga Kaihoe o Aotearoa New Zealand, 2009).

However, Māori, Pacific Islanders, and other ethnic groups, as well as older adults, people with disabilities, and those on low incomes are underrepresented in general outdoor recreation (Dignan & Cessford, 2009). This poses challenges for park managers to improve access and attract more diverse populations to New Zealand's conservation estate, which accounts for roughly one-third of the country's total surface area. Other challenges include managing conflicts between an increasing diversity of activities (e.g., mountain biking, canyoning, and commercial versus recreational users), as well as mitigating the social and physical impacts of crowding, as international visitors are drawn to popular multiday walking tracks and iconic scenic destinations such as Milford Sound and Tongariro National Park (Davidson, 2011; Lovelock et al., 2011).

CONCLUSION

In this chapter we have provided a broad overview of some of the major social issues and trends that affect leisure participation in New Zealand and Australia. Framing our discussion in a historical context we have identified persistent patterns of inequality relating to class, gender, culture, age, and disability that continue to shape the "individual freedom" to choose leisure within global capitalism. With the rise of healthism we have also seen how sport and active living policies frame participation in terms of instrumental health outcomes and yet they struggle to address questions of inequality. As residents of countries with relatively small populations and significant geographic distances, Australians and New Zealanders have become "early adopters" of technology and this trend is profoundly shaping leisure practices and social relations. As multicultural nations with aging populations, there are a number of key challenges and opportunities ahead for government policy and leisure service provision across the commercial, voluntary, and public sectors. There remain a number of issues that we have not been able to cover in this chapter but we mention several of them here for future consideration. The looming issue of climate change and the impact on leisure provision, opportunities, and inequalities is a key area that is fraught with political, economic, and cultural complexities. As an important domain of quality of life, leisure is paradoxically positioned in ways that contribute to climate change (e.g., hyperconsumption, carbon emissions, energy and waste issues) and can also help reduce negative environmental impacts (e.g., the emergence of sustainable leisure practices, walking and cycling, the protection of natural areas, and alternative cultures of anti-consumption). Policy debates about the need to change our leisure lifestyles to help mitigate the pace and effects of climate change will have to wrestle with fundamental questions about the competing freedoms and rights of individuals, societies, and non-human species. Acknowledging the high levels of individual energy use and consumption in Australia and New Zealand, both governments have been at the forefront of debates to address climate change (Garnaut, 2008). Yet, the political will that is required to implement effective policy has reduced in the face of concerns over short-term national competitiveness in the global market and prevailing neo-liberal notions of individual choice. The interconnected nature of climate change has moved national debate from individual countries to the regional and global level to open up dialogue with neighboring cultures. The Asia Pacific region is undergoing changes along multiple dimensions with rising sea levels, the growth of people seeking asylum from persecution, the rise of middle-class tourism, and increased trade flows from China and Indonesia. The future of New Zealand and Australian leisure practices will be shaped by these global movements of populations, the challenges of climate change, and the opportunities arising from greater cultural diversity.

REFERENCES

ACNielsen. (2013). *Quality of life survey 2012 six councils report*. Wellington: Quality of Life Survey Team.

Australian Bureau of Statistics (2009). *Research paper: Children's participation in organised sporting activity*, Cat. No.1351.0.55.028. Canberra: ABS.

Australian Bureau of Statistics (2011). *Australian social trends June 2011, sport and physical recreation*, Cat. No.4102.0, Canberra: ABS.

Australian Bureau of Statistics (2012). *Gender indicators, Australia*, Cat. No. 4125.0, Canberra: ABS.

Australian Bureau of Statistics (2013a). *Australian health survey: Physical activity, 2011–12*, Cat. No.4364.0.55.004. Canberra: ABS.

Australian Bureau of Statistics (2013b). *Profiles of health, Australia, 2011–13*, Cat. No. 4338.0. Canberra: ABS.

Bauman, A., Bull, F., Chey, T., Craig, C., Ainsworth, B., Sallis, J., et al. (2009). The international prevalence study on physical activity: Results from 20 countries. *International Journal of Behavioral Nutrition and Physical Activity, 6*(21). doi: 10.1186/1479-5868-6-21

Bauman, A., McLean, G., Hurdle, D., Walker, S., Boyd, J., van Aalst, I., et al. (2003). Evaluation of the national 'Push Play' campaign in New Zealand—creating population awareness of physical activity. *New Zealand Medical Journal, 116*(1179). Retrieved from http://journal.nzma.org.nz/journal/116-1179/535/

Bellew, B. Schöeppe, S., Bull, F., & Bauman, A. (2008). The rise and fall of Australian physical activity policy 1996–2006: A national review framed in an international context. *Australia and New Zealand Health Policy, 5*(1), 18, 1–10.

Bennett, T., Bustamante, M., & Frow, J. (2013). The Australian space of lifestyles in comparative perspective. *Journal of Sociology, 49*(2–3), 224–255.

Carey, S., Davidson, L., & Sahli, M. (2013). Capital city museums and tourism flows: An empirical study of the Museum of New Zealand Te Papa Tongarewa. *International Journal of Tourism Research, 15*, 554–569.

Cleland, V., Timperio, A., Salmon, J., Hume, C., Baur, L. A., & Crawford, D. (2009). Predictors of time spent outdoors among children: 5-year longitudinal findings, *Journal of Epidemiology & Community Health, 64*, 400–406.

Coalter, F. (2007). *A wider social role for sport: Who's keeping the score?* London: Routledge.

Commonwealth Government of Australia. (2009). *Australia: The healthiest country by 2020, National Preventative Health Strategy*. Canberra: National Preventative Health Taskforce.

Commonwealth of Australia. (2010). *Australian sport: Pathways to success.*

Crawford, R. (2000). The ritual of health promotion. In S. Williams, J. Gabe, & M. Calnan (Eds.), *Health, medicine and society: Key theories, future agendas,* London: Routledge.

Creative New Zealand. (2011). *New Zealanders and the arts: Attitudes, attendance and participation in 2011*. Wellington, New Zealand: Creative New Zealand.

Davidson, L. (2002). The 'spirit of the hills': Mountaineering in northwest Otago, New Zealand 1882–1940. *Tourism Geographies, 4*(1), 44–61.

Davidson, L. (2011). On nature's terms: Preserving the practice of traditional backcountry recreation in New Zealand's national parks. In E. Dorfman (Ed.), *Intangible natural heritage: New perspectives on natural objects* (pp. 105–124). New York: Routledge.

Davidson, L., & Sibley, P. (2011). Audiences at the 'new' museum: Visitor commitment, diversity and leisure at the Museum of New Zealand Te Papa Tongarewa. *Visitor Studies, 14*(2), 176–194.

Dignan, A., & Cessford, G. (2009). *Outdoor recreation participation and incidents in New Zealand: A scoping study relating incidents with participation levels*. Wellington: Mountain Safety Council.

Fullagar, S., Pavlidis, A., Reid, S., & Lloyd, K. (2013). Living it up in the new 'world city': High-rise development and the promise of liveability. *Annals of Leisure Research,* doi: 10.1080/11745398.2013.840946

Fullagar, S., & Harrington, M. (2009). Negotiating the imperative to be healthy: Australian family repertoires of risk, leisure and healthy lifestyles. *Annals of Leisure Research, 12*(2), 195–215.

Garnaut, R. (2008). The Garnaut climate change review. *Global Environmental Change, 13*, 1–5.

Group targets New Zealand adventure tourism. (2010). Retrieved from http://www.stuff.co.nz/national/3219503/Group-targets-New-Zealand-adventure-tourism

Hajkowicz, S. A., Cook, H., Wilhelmseder, L., & Boughen, N. (2013). The future of Australian sport: Megatrends shaping the sports sector over coming decades. A Consultancy Report for the Australian Sports Commission. CSIRO, Australia.

Harrington, M., & Fullagar, S. (2013). Challenges for active living provision in an era of healthism. *Journal of Policy Research in Tourism, Leisure and Events, 31*(1), 1–19.

Lovelock, B., Farminer, A., & Reis, A. C. (2011). *A synthesis and gap analysis of research on visitors to public conservation areas in New Zealand 1995–2010*. Wellington, NZ: Department of Conservation.

McLachlan, R., Gilfillan, G., & Gordon, J. (2013). Deep and persistent disadvantage in Australia. *Productivity Commission Staff Working Paper*, Canberra.

Ministry for Culture and Heritage. (2003). *A measure of culture: Cultural experiences and cultural spending in New Zealand*. Wellington, New Zealand: Ministry for Culture and Heritage.

Nga Kaihoe o Aotearoa New Zealand. (2009). *Three year strategic plan for the sport of waka ama, August 2009 to July 2012*. Retrieved from http://s3.wakaama.co.nz/story/1001890/attachments/Waka_Ama_Strategic_Plan_Final.pdf

Nielsen Australia (2013). Australian multi-screen report: Quarter 1 2013, http://www.nielsen.com/au/en/news-insights/press-room/2013/australian-multi-screen-report-q1-2013.html#sthash.FUC6ukjp.dpuf

Pavlidis, A., & Fullagar, S. (2013). Becoming roller derby grrrls: Exploring the gendered play of affect in mediated sport cultures. *International Review for the Sociology of Sport.* doi: 10.1177/1012690212446451

Perry, B. (2013). *Household incomes in New Zealand: Trends in indicators of inequality and hardship 1982 to 2012*. Wellington, New Zealand: Ministry of Social Development.

Phipps, P., & Slater, L. (2010). *Indigenous cultural festivals: Evaluating impact on community health and wellbeing.* Melbourne: Globalism Research Centre, RMIT University.

Quality of Life Project. (2007). *Quality of life in twelve of New Zealand's cities 2007*. Retrieved from http://www.

qualityoflifeproject.govt.nz/pdfs/2007/Quality_of_Life_2007.pdf

Smith, A. (1998). Māori and leisure: A survey. In H. Perkins and G. Cushman (Eds.), *Time out? Leisure, recreation and tourism in New Zealand and Australia* (pp. 51–63). Auckland, NZ: Longman.

Smith, P., Gibson, A., Crothers, C., Billot, J., & Bell, A. (2011). *The internet in New Zealand 2011*. Auckland, New Zealand: Institute of Culture, Discourse & Communication, AUT University.

Statistics New Zealand. (2012). *Internet service provider survey: 2012*. Wellington: Statistics New Zealand.

Sport and Recreation New Zealand. (2008). *Sport, recreation & physical activity participation among New Zealand adults: Key findings of the 2007/08 Active New Zealand Survey*. Wellington: SPARC.

Sport New Zealand. (2013). *Sport and recreation participation trends 1997–2007*. Wellington: Sport New Zealand.

Statistics New Zealand. (2011). *Time use survey: 2009/10*. Wellington: Statistics New Zealand.

Tsai, E. H., Cushman, G., Gidlow, B., & Toohey, G. (2013). Research in Australia and New Zealand. In M. Stodolska, K. Shinew, M. F. Floyd, & G. J. Walker (Eds.), *Race, ethnicity and leisure: Perspectives on research, theory, and practice* (pp. 247–296). Champaign, IL: Human Kinetics.

Veal, A., Darcy, S., & Lynch, R. (2013). *Australian leisure* (4th ed.). Sydney: Pearson.

Watson, J. (1998). From the frontier to cyberspace: A history of leisure, recreation and tourism in New Zealand. In H. Perkins and G. Cushman (Eds.), *Time out? Leisure, recreation and tourism in New Zealand and Australia* (pp. 16–33). Auckland, NZ: Longman.

Whitlam, G. (1972). *It's time: Whitlam's 1972 election policy speech*, November 13, retrieved from http://whitlamdismissal.com/1972/11/13/whitlam-1972-election-policy-speech.html#sthash.uJhYZlF2.dpuf, 13/7/2013

Zubrick, S., Wood, L., Villanueva, K., Wood, G., Giles-Corti, B., & Christian, H. (2010). *Nothing but fear itself: Parental fear as a determinant of child physical activity and independent mobility*, Melbourne: Victorian Health Promotion Foundation.

14

Leisure in East Asia

Contributing Authors:
Huimei Liu, Monica Z. Li, Yoshitaka Iwasaki, Tetsuya Onda, and Jin-Hyung Lee

INTRODUCTION

Outside the West (i.e., Western Europe, Canada and the United States, and Australia and New Zealand), leisure has been studied for longer and in greater depth in East Asia—and, in particular, in China, Japan, and South Korea—than anywhere else in the world (Ito, Walker, & Liang, 2014). Though there are certainly commonalities in terms of how Chinese, Japanese, and Korean cultures comprehend leisure (because, for example, of the influence of Confucianism on each), there are also important differences in leisure meanings, activity participation patterns, and current and future leisure policy, practice, and research directions. Consequently, rather than have one or two authors attempt to write an all-inclusive chapter on East Asian leisure, the *Leisure Matters* editors asked leading Chinese (Huimei Liu, Zhejiang University; Monica Li, Beijing International Studies University), Japanese (Yoshitaka Iwasaki, University of Alberta; Tetsuya Onda, Tokai University), and Korean (Jin-Hyung Lee, Mokpo National University) scholars to focus on leisure in their own cultures. Their insightful observations and bold speculations follow.

LEISURE IN CHINA

Huimei Liu (Zhejiang University) and Monica Z. Li (Beijing International Studies University)

Despite there not being a Chinese word that can be directly translated into "leisure," this does not mean that Chinese people do not understand the wisdom of leisure. Chinese perceptions of leisure and Chinese ways of spending leisure time are actually deeply rooted in Chinese culture and philosophy. As Gong (2013) argued, "leisure is, in fact, a very important component of traditional Chinese culture, closely related to philosophy, aesthetics, literature and the arts, and practices of health and wellness" (p. 1).

Although cultural traditions have influenced contemporary Chinese citizens' leisure, their leisure experiences cannot be fully understood without reference to the major changes that have more recently taken place in Chinese society. Thus, in this section discussion will center on both the traditional meaning and the contemporary dimensions of Chinese leisure. Additionally, because China consists of 56 ethnic groups, we cannot describe in detail the leisure patterns of each of these groups. Instead, we will focus on the Han people, who represent 90% of China's overall population (National Bureau of Statistics of China, 2010).

The Meaning of Leisure in Chinese Traditions

Xiu Xian (休闲), a combination of two simplified Chinese characters, most closely corresponds with the Western concept of "leisure." The first character, *Xiu* (休), is a compound word consisting of a person (人) and a tree (木), and means a person leaning against a tree. In ancient China, *Xiu* symbolized a break from, or physical relaxation during, labor, such as farm work. The original meaning of this character has since changed to now represent psychological well-being and the finer qualities of people and objects (Liu, Yeh, Chick, & Zinn, 2008). The second character, *Xian* (闲), also consists of two components, a door (门) and a tree used as a log to bar a door (木). *Xian* thus denotes an in-between space that is both protected and undisturbed. When *Xiu* and *Xian* are combined, the positive connotation of being free and unoccupied is reinforced.

Xiu Xian, however, can also have a negative connotation; such as when it is associated with being idle or lazy (Yu, 2005). The reason for this negative attitude toward leisure is based on traditional Chinese philosophical values. Confucianism, for instance, stresses the importance of self-improvement through education

(Schutte & Ciarlante, 1998). Hard work, respect for learning, and the need for an orderly and harmonious society are, therefore, emphasized. Any remaining "spare time" is to be used not in a leisurely manner but rather to further one's education.

Moreover, because Confucianism places great importance on obedience, discipline, devotion, and dutifulness, satisfaction of personal needs is not encouraged in Chinese culture. Confucianism also holds that the rights of the individual are subordinate to those of the group so that social harmony can be achieved and maintained. This emphasis on social needs can be seen in the prominence assigned to family, and the pervasive impact family has on the lives of immediate and extended family members. This phenomenon has been interpreted in terms of Chinese people having an "interdependent self-construal" (Markus & Kitayama, 1991) that, in turn, impacts their emotions, cognitions, and behaviors—including, and perhaps especially, during their leisure (Walker, 2010; Walker, Deng, & Dieser, 2005).

Taoism, another philosophy that has molded Chinese civilization, stresses that people should concentrate on inner spiritual matters and put aside concerns with external rewards such as wealth and fame. Taoism's impact on leisure can be seen "in Chinese people's close connection to the natural world, the concept of holistic wellness and health care, [and] the practice of martial arts, traditional arts such as painting and poetry, enjoyment of cultural activities, celebrations, and tourism" (Wang & Stringer, 2000, p. 33). Taoism holds that improving the body, mind, and spirit can be achieved by pursuing tranquility, peace of mind, and the beauty of nature. Consequently, Chinese people generally prefer quieter and more passive activities during their leisure (Yu & Berryman, 1996). A study by Jackson and Walker (2006) found, for example, that 84% of Mainland Chinese university students reported that their most frequent and/or most enjoyable leisure activities were passive. Tsai, Knutson, and Fung (2006) suggested that such findings were a function of Chinese people generally favoring low-arousal positive affect (e.g., calm) whereas Western people generally preferred high-arousal positive affect (e.g., excited). (See also Walker, Chapter 17.)

In summary, as Confucians, Chinese are work-oriented and often hold less positive attitudes toward leisure. When leisure does occur, it is frequently either family-oriented or focused on learning rather than engaged in for fun or pure pleasure. Taoism, in contrast, considers leisure to be a state of mind or an individual experience that helps cultivate a love of nature and satisfies a person's longing for a peaceful life.

The Meaning of Leisure in Contemporary China

China's economic and political situation dramatically changed in the 1970s with the introduction of economic reforms and the "open door" policy (which allowed foreign businesses to invest China). This transformation granted Chinese people a better life, but at the cost of exceptionally long and hard work. Against this background, Chinese scholars began to recognize the paradox in which Chinese people, on the one hand, became richer in material possessions while, on the other hand, they lacked spiritual and psychological satisfaction. This recognition, coupled with the introduction of leisure concepts and theories from the West, led to *xiu xian* (i.e., leisure) becoming a popular topic of discussion in Chinese universities.

After implementation of the above reforms, Chinese people experienced increasingly more leisure time than ever before. New government policies, such as the five-day workweek, the "golden week" public holidays, and the subsequent eleven-day public holiday, launched in 1994, 1999, and 2008 respectively, allowed Chinese to have more time for leisure. Liu (2004), for instance, found Chinese people's daily leisure time increased from 126 minutes in 1980 to 337 minutes in 1998, while Wang Lei, & Shi (2000) found Beijing residents' leisure time rose from 239 minutes in 1986 to 303 minutes in 1996.

Although studies have identified a variety of popular leisure pursuits in contemporary Chinese society, there are also certain activities that are consistently mentioned. For instance, Yin (2005) found watching television, reading books or newspapers, listening to the radio, playing mah-jong (a tile game involving skill and strategy), and chatting with family members were the most popular leisure activities. Jim and Chen (2009) also discovered watching television, chatting with families or friends, and reading were frequently mentioned activities at home, while walking for leisure and shopping were people's main outdoor activities. Wang, Lei, and Shi (2002) too found television watching was common, with Beijing residents spending on average two hours and 39 minutes, or 46% of their total leisure time, doing so. A recent survey by *Insight Magazine* (2012) suggests that changes may be taking place, however, as their respondents' top choice was surfing the Internet, followed by taking a walk, hiking in the mountains, visiting parks, watching television, and traveling.

Many of these popular leisure activities have a long tradition in China. Both tai chi (a martial art) and mah-jong, for example, date back hundreds of years. But while tai chi is endorsed by the Chinese government as an exercise beneficial for one's health, mah-jong was once banned as a gambling activity and it is still not officially sanctioned by the government—despite Chinese of all ages, occupations, and classes being obsessed with the game (Deng & Liu, 2012). Visiting parks is another popular, and traditional, form of Chinese leisure (Chang & Card, 1992). The royal gardens, built by emperors and imperial families, and private gardens, built by ancient poets, soldiers, scholars, merchants, and government officials, are sites full of cultural relics and historical memories. These places provide families, friends, and relatives peaceful and relaxing leisure experiences. Families, friends, and relatives may also socialize and strengthen interpersonal bonds while eating, which has been called "a national pastime for Chinese people," and food having played "an important role in the history of Chinese leisure" (Chang & Card, 1992, p. 16). Finally, two other, albeit less traditional, leisure activities that are now common in today's China are singing songs in a karaoke room and square dancing. In terms of the latter, dozens to hundreds of people gather together, usually in the early morning or evening, to dance in an urban open space (e.g., a public square). Forty-five percent of the residents of the city of Chongqing, for instance, reported that they square danced on a regular basis (Deng & Liu, 2012).

Conversely, though Chinese people may be eager to enjoy the changes brought about by China's economic and social development, they may simultaneously suffer from the costs and anxieties that accompanying such rapid and radical changes. Two recent nationwide surveys (China Daily, 2012; Echinacities, 2012) found, for example, that because of growing workloads, an immature paid-vacation system, and the pressures of the global market economy, leisure time in China has actually decreased. Other research supports this downward trend, with a 2011 CNN survey indicating that Chinese people enjoyed the fewest number of paid vacation days (10 per year) among 40 nations, while a recent study (Wei & Stodolska, in press) found that Chinese people now had only 130 minutes of free time per day, much less than in the 1990s and much more in line with the early 1980s.

In conclusion, although leisure in China is still pursued in traditional ways, it is now also influenced by globalization and the market economy. As Weber (2002) observed, contemporary Chinese people are facing different challenges and pursuing different opportunities than those of earlier generations. The manifestation of social transformations can be seen in the newly developing leisure culture in China, which entails mixed and complex social realities (Chen, Clark, Gottschang, & Jeffery, 2001; Link, Madsen, & Pickowicz, 2002).

The Future of Leisure in China

China is a country at the crossroads of social, economic, and political transformation, and Chinese people will continue to long for an improved quality of life in which leisure plays an essential role (Deng & Liu, 2012). Consequently, leisure in China must confront certain pressing issues in the future.

First, Chinese leisure scholarship needs to contribute more in terms of leisure research. On the one hand, for the past three decades Chinese leisure studies has benefited from and been nurtured by Western leisure studies. Dozens of Chinese scholars, including those in Taiwan, Hong Kong, and mainland China, have been educated in European, North American, and Australian and New Zealand leisure studies programs. Additionally, a number of classic and current English-language leisure books have been translated into Chinese, which has greatly influenced the development of Chinese leisure research in recent years. On the other hand, how traditional Chinese ideas influence various aspects of leisure, such as meanings (e.g., Liu et al., 2008), motivations (e.g., Walker, 2010), constraints (e.g., Walker, Jackson, & Deng, 2008), and satisfaction and quality of life (e.g., Spiers & Walker, 2009) have become more common in the literature. Efforts of this kind have led to a synthesis of the similarities and differences in Chinese and Western leisure, and the possibility of theory integration (Walker & Liang, 2012). More effort will be needed to continue this type of exploration in the future, but further effort to understand the essence of Chinese leisure—such as peacefulness, tranquility, relaxation, and harmony—could also benefit not only Chinese people but the rest of the world as well.

Second, research and policy attention needs to be directed at "balance" leisure activities, such as tourism, as well as "core" or routine leisure activities, such as daily physical exercise (Godbey, 2013; Kelly, 1999). Currently, China has the world's largest domestic tourism market and Chinese outbound tourists became the world top spenders in 2012. A new trend among Chinese tourists is to increasingly demand customized tourist products of greater choice and quality rather than standardized mass-market packaged holidays. As a favorite leisure activity for more and more Chinese people, tourism will continue to grow in the foreseeable future. On a more daily basis, "core leisure activities will receive more attention in the coming era of Chinese reform" (Godbey, 2013, p. 24). For instance, sport activities among common people, rather than those among sport elites, will become the focus of Chinese leisure in the future.

Third, rapidly increasing leisure needs will give great impetus to demands for leisure services from both the public and private sectors. In terms of the former, rapid urbanization and inefficient planning for public leisure have left shrinking open spaces and limited infrastructure for recreation and leisure in most Chinese cities. For example, Lu and Yu (2005) found that there were no recreational facilities in 37% of residential areas in the capital city of Beijing. Yet the Chinese government cannot simply adopt Western practices to provide leisure opportunities, but instead it must develop its own models. In terms of the latter, the leisure industry is one of the fastest-growing sectors of China's economy. In 2009, domestic leisure consumption reached U.S. $258.4 billion, or 5% of the country's total GDP (Liu, Gao, & Song, 2010). The continued growth of the Chinese leisure economy will create tremendous business opportunities in China and throughout the world.

Last, leisure studies became an acknowledged academic field in China in the middle of 1990s, with intellectuals such as Yu Guangyuan and Ma Huidi initiating early efforts on this topic. Ever since, researchers having different backgrounds have worked together to reinforce the importance of leisure studies among other longer established disciplines. However, leisure as a legitimate subject for research and study is still not fully recognized and appreciated either in Chinese academia or by the Chinese public. Despite these issues, there exist urgent demands for leisure education at various levels as well as well-designed leisure programs that provide personnel with the management and organizational skills that are required to properly deliver leisure services. Thus, continued cooperation between Chinese and Western leisure scholars, in terms of both academic research and practical training, should be pursued in the future.

Conclusion

Traditional philosophies such as Confucianism and Taoism, in conjunction with modern economic, social, and cultural developments, have tremendously impacted Chinese leisure. We believe Chinese people's leisure needs will continue to grow and, therefore, even greater efforts in leisure education, leisure policy, and leisure management (e.g., service delivery) will be required in the future.

LEISURE IN JAPAN

Yoshitaka Iwasaki (University of Alberta) and Tetsuya Onda (Tokai University)

Social, historical, and cultural factors influence leisure in Japan. Based on recent survey data, we describe the types of popular leisure activities and diverse purposes of leisure for Japanese people. We also discuss the need for a more systematic, coordinated approach to more formal, professional leisure/recreation programs and services in Japan. Significantly raising public status and recognition of leisure/recreation professionals is a must, by focusing on public education to enhance Japanese people's awareness about and advocacy for the contribution of life-long leisure and recreation to promoting life quality for all. We begin, however, with a brief overview of the different leisure-related words that are used in Japan.

The Meaning of Leisure in Japanese Culture

Generally, leisure in Japanese means *yoka* (spare time) and is also associated with *goraku* (amusement) and *asobi* (play) (Kubo, 2004). Most Japanese people also understand and use *reja* to imitate the sound of leisure (Iwasaki, Nishino, Onda, & Bowling, 2007). For more on the meaning and usage of these Japanese words, readers are referred to Iwasaki et al. (2007) and Ito and Walker (2014).

Leisure in Contemporary Japan

Social, historical, and cultural factors that influence leisure in Japan.

Japanese traditions continue to influence forms of leisure. Examples include seasonal festivals (e.g., *Ohanami*, or cherry blossom-viewing picnics), martial arts (e.g., judo, kendo), and traditional games (e.g., *Igo* and *Shogi*, Japanese Othello games). These activities provide not only personally satisfying experiences, but they also generate meaningful experiences socially, spiritually, and culturally (e.g., family cohesion, spiritual renewal, cultural identity) (Iwasaki, 2008). On the other hand, Western influences are clearly noticeable in Japanese people's leisure participation. Examples include the popularity of North American and European professional sport broadcasting, Western TV programs, the adoption of Western-style living, and the introduction of Western-based recreation programs.

Japan's landscape allows abundant opportunities to visit parks and enjoy outdoor activities as it is covered by forests and mountains (Ministry of the Environment, Government of Japan, 2007). The Ministry of the Environment (2013) lists 30 national parks comprising approximately 5.5% (i.e., 2.09 million hectares) of the country's total land. Accessibility to a variety of nature-based recreation experiences has been improving, with growing popularity in hiking and nature-oriented activities; although the scale of accommodating a diverse range of visitors seems limited compared to Western parks systems. According to the Ministry of Land, Infrastructure, and Transport (2005), there are more than 89,000 parks throughout the country, including city and sport parks, regional parks, greenbelts, and urban groves.

Technological advances have implications for leisure participation. In particular, the popularity of cell phones (which increased from 0.3% in 1988 to 98% in 2012) and the Internet (approximately 80% penetration in 2011) (Sport Facility Publishing, 2013) seem to have had an impact; especially on technologically oriented younger generations. The nature of these changes and their implications in terms of overall benefits and constraints are still unclear and need to be examined through rigorous research.

Although a gender- and age-based hierarchy still exists, traditional stereotypical roles associated with being a woman or older adult seem no longer prevalent in contemporary Japanese society. Fueled by a stronger advocacy for equality and equity, Japan has increasingly recognized the role of leisure and recreation in enhancing life quality for both women and men and old and young.

This trend toward life-long leisure for all is observable in a recent national survey (Japan Productivity Headquarter, 2012). Participation in various leisure activities increased steadily between 2004 and 2011, particularly among women (e.g., an increase in sport participation and foreign travel). Also, a wider variety of leisure participation patterns (e.g., hobbies/creative activities, games/amusement) has been observed among older adults compared to younger adults, the latter of whom showed higher popularity mostly in pleasure travel and amusement (Japan Productivity Headquarter, 2012).

Diversity and complexity in Japanese people's leisure participation.

Japan is often characterized as a homogenous country due to the large middle-class population and the importance of collective identity. However, leisure in Japan is better appraised in terms of diversity and complexity, illustrated by a combination of consumptive forms of leisure (e.g., travel and tourism, amusement), casual leisure (e.g., relaxing leisure), and serious leisure (e.g., seeking self-actualization; Stebbins, 2006), along with personal, social, spiritual, and cultural dimensions described earlier.

Recent survey data support this. According to a national survey conducted in 2011 (Japan Productivity Headquarter, 2012), the top 10 popular leisure activities in Japan included: (a) domestic travel (54.5 %); (b) dining out (52.4 %); (c) pleasure driving (52.3 %); (d) watching movies (40.6 %); (e) music appreciation (40.1 %); (f) video entertainment (38.8 %); (g) karaoke (38.2 %); (h) lottery (37.5 %); (i) visiting a zoo, aquarium, or museum (36.3 %); and (j) gardening (33.0 %). The same survey also included a "new leisure" category, with the top activities in it including: walking, shopping (at outlet malls), *onsen* (hot spring)/health spa, pets (playing with, taking care of), barbecuing, fashion for pleasure, and volunteering activities. Additionally, according to Sport Life Data (Sasakawa Sports Foundation, 2011), the most popular sport activities in 2010 included walking, exercise, bowling, weight training, golfing, jogging/running, and fishing.

Purposes of leisure for Japanese people.

It is important to understand not only the popularity of different types of leisure activities but also the purposes that underpin leisure engagement. Overall, over 80% of respondents to a 2011 national survey (Japan Productivity Headquarter, 2012) reported that leisure's role in making one's life enjoyable and meaningful was critical. Specifically, Japanese people's reasons for engaging in leisure were quite diverse, and included: (a) peace of mind/tranquility, (b) sense of connection with family and friends, (c) social responsibility/contribution to society, (d) health benefits, and (e) self-identity (Japan Productivity Headquarter, 2012). In terms of the first, *yasuragi* means peace, tranquility, and relaxation. Many Japanese people identify leisure as a restful space or sanctuary wherein they can gain meaning and/or balance in their lives. Examples include feeling a sense of harmony with nature through outdoor activities, a sense of freedom or release via engaging in a preferred leisure activity, and a sense of joy from creating something meaningful (e.g., art). Second, Japanese people value quality social interactions with significant others through leisure to promote positive interpersonal relationships and a sense of connection and belonging. Third, they also value a societal responsibility or altruistic motivation toward improving the life quality of others as well as the overall society, by being a contributive member of the community (e.g., through volunteering). Fourth, a significant role of leisure in promoting and maintaining health (i.e., *kenko*) is well-recognized from a holistic perspective, which encompasses physical, mental, emotional, social, and spiritual health. Finally, Japanese people acknowledge that leisure provides opportunities for both self-discovery/self-identity and learning about the world around them, including other people and various subject areas from a life-long learning perspective. Overall, these five major purposes for Japanese people's leisure represent the multiple roles of leisure in meaning-making or making sense of life (Iwasaki, 2008).

The role of leisure in coping with stress and maintaining a more balanced life.

Of leisure's many universal benefits, being a means of coping with stress may be among its most important (e.g., Coleman & Iso-Ahola, 1993; Iwasaki, 2006; Iwasaki & Mannell, 2000; Iwasaki, MacKay, Mactavish, Ristock, & Bartlett, 2006; Kleiber, Hutchinson, & Williams, 2002). This constructive use of leisure (e.g., exercise, mini-vacation) is popular among many Japanese people (Japan Productivity Headquarter, 2012). Most companies have implemented two-day weekends (approximately 85% in 2011), and vacation time has gradually increased over the years. Quality of life issues have also been emphasized in regard to maintaining a more balanced life, and this has been facilitated by government policies (Japan Productivity Headquarter, 2012). Evidence exists that supports associations between leisure participation and lower depressive symptoms among Japanese people (Wada, Satoh, Tanaka, Tsunoda, & Aizawa, 2007).

Leisure's stress-coping role has implications for a leisure-based intervention as therapeutic recreation (TR) has seen progress in Japan. The number of qualified *fukushi* (welfare) recreation workers has increased significantly (Japan Productivity Headquarter, 2012; Nishino, Chino, Yoshioka, & Gabriella, 2007). Nishino et al. emphasized the importance of a *Japanesed* TR framework that gives attention to traditional Japanese activities—from seasonal activities, such as *Ohanami* (cherry blossom-viewing picnic), the *Bon* Festival (Japanese summer ancestor worship), and *Momijigari* (autumn leaf-viewing picnic) to cultural activities, including *Igo*, *Shogi*, and *Karuta* (a Japanese card game). To develop evidence-based, effective leisure/recreation interventions, research conducted within a Japanese cultural context is essential. This involves examining the applicability and relevance of a Western leisure/recreation framework to Japanese people in a cross-cultural context, and integrating Japanese traditions into the refinement and testing of these frameworks/models.

However, the dark side of leisure cannot be ignored. For example, Japan hosts the world's largest gambling market ($310 billion in 2008) (Manzenreiter, 2013). Pachinko machines alone, which are widespread in Japan, accounted for 59% of the world gaming market in the late 1990s (Dowling, Smith, & Thomas, 2004). Despite the potential benefits of temporal escape and sensation seeking, pathological gambling behavior is problematic: personally, family-wise, and societally (Suissa, 2007). One element of leisure-based intervention includes the provision of healthy, constructive/meaningful recreation pursuits that replace potentially destructive leisure-like behaviors such as pathological gambling and criminal activities.

Leisure Studies in Japan

Because physical education and sport have been more integral to Japanese people's lives than leisure, the concept of leisure appears well-positioned to be integrated into the philosophy and principles of sport and physical education from both educational and research perspectives (Kubo, 2004). This sport-leisure combination is well-reflected in the development of sport/leisure management programs at universities in Japan (Hagi et al., 2010). For example: (a) the very first university-level sport/leisure management course was offered in 1988 at Nippon Sport Science University; (b) a specialization in sport/leisure management was first established in 1993 at Juntendo University; and (c) at a national university level, this type of specialization was first established at the University of Tsukuba in 1997. As of 2010, 64 universities/colleges in Japan offered a sport/leisure management specialization.

Japanese faculties/colleges having a specialization in sport/leisure management can represent: (a) sport and physical education; (b) management economics; (c) education; (d) health; and (e) sociology, human science, and/or tourism (Hagi et al., 2010). Concerning academic philosophy, a higher priority seems given more to sport and leisure business than to conceptualizing sport and leisure as an educational area. However, there is no standardized curriculum of sport/leisure management established in Japan; thus, each university/college has developed its own curriculum (Hagi et al., 2010). Regardless, although there has been steady growth in leisure research in Japan, a disciplinary basis for leisure research has not yet been formally established.

The Future of Leisure in Japan

This rather contradictory reality (i.e., Japanese people increasingly valuing leisure but the study of leisure in Japan not progressing) lends itself to development of a more extensive partnership approach to raising public awareness and advocacy to both better understand leisure phenomena and to improve the provision of leisure education and services in Japan.

A partnership approach to public awareness and advocacy for life-long leisure.

Specifically, a real challenge to advancing Japan's leisure and recreation field is to establish trained professional leadership in communities locally and regionally, with a more systematic and formal regulation by the nation as a whole (Korfhage, Daniel, & Hall, 2007; Nishino et al., 2007). More extensively working with and engaging families, schools, and community agencies/groups to maximize the opportunities for life-long leisure at all levels is important to promote a greater quality of life of all citizens.

It must be noted that since 2003 the Japanese Government has implemented a policy to encourage the use of a partnership approach that involves collaboration between public and private sectors in the delivery of leisure and recreation services (Sport Facility Publishing, 2013). As of April 2012, 61.3% of all facilities have introduced/used this public-private partnership approach, including 87.5% of the recreation and sport facilities across the nation. Approximately 90% of these facilities have used a small-scale partnership approach only at a local level (i.e., cities or towns; Sport Facility Publishing, 2013). This approach typically involves the use of public facilities managed by private agencies for cost-saving, greater employment opportunities, and improved service quality. Stronger partnerships with families, schools, and other community agencies would potentially provide broader population benefits.

A more coordinated approach to formal academic and professional programs.

Rather than relying heavily on volunteers and less formal programs, what is really needed is a more systematic, coordinated approach to formal professional programs and services at federal, regional, and local levels. The establishment and maintenance of a more rigorous professional certification to leisure/recreation managers and professionals is critical to ensure the quality and integrity of leisure/recreation programs and services. In addition, the establishment of an academic accreditation for universities/colleges that offer recreation and leisure studies programs in Japan is needed. This academic and professional rigor-enhancing approach is extremely important to significantly raise public status and recognition of leisure/recreation professionals.

A more comprehensive partnership approach to promoting inclusive life-long leisure.

The major thrust for achieving this goal involves public education to enhance Japanese people's awareness and understanding about the important contribution of life-long leisure and recreation to promoting enjoyment and life quality for all. This life-long leisure/recreation is entitled to everyone, as a global human right endorsed by the United Nations (2013).

The use of a more extensive partnership approach to this public awareness and education process is critical, by working across all stakeholder groups, including all levels of governments, school systems, health-care systems, community services (e.g., social work, sport and recreation agencies, TR programs), business/corporate sectors, and universities/colleges. For example, leisure education that embraces the concept of inclusive life-long leisure for all across the lifespan (regardless of gender, age, race/ethnicity, disabilities/abilities, sexual orientations, etc.) can be formally integrated into Japan's school systems (as an important addition to physical education) at elementary and middle school levels. Researchers should continue to provide tangible evidence about the benefits of leisure and recreation in a Japanese cultural context to offer evidence-based recommendations for developing and administering inclusive leisure/recreation programs and policies. Health-care systems and community service sectors (e.g., social work, sport and recreation agencies, TR programs) can then apply the knowledge about the role of inclusive life-long leisure and recreation in promoting active living, health, and life quality of all citizens to the implementation of health, social, and community programs.

Business/corporate sectors should also recognize the contributions of leisure/recreation to satisfying these sectors' societal responsibilities by having a positive impact on community citizens. For instance, a business sector can administer community grants, in partnership with community agencies, to provide greater opportunities for life-long leisure and recreation for wider population groups (especially for disadvantaged, vulnerable groups such as individuals with disabilities, high-risk youth, and elderly). In addition, commercial benefits of the leisure/recreation and tourism industry to enhance economy are another attractive element for the business/corporate sectors partnering with the local and regional governments for the growth and rejuvenation of local and regional economy. The strategic use of a partnership approach among business and community service sectors and the local government, to establishing recreation facilities and providing greater leisure opportunities, can contribute significantly to both the promotion of life quality among local citizens and the rejuvenation of local economy.

Conclusion

The domain of leisure and recreation is no longer trivial, as all citizens are entitled to enjoyable and meaningful leisure and recreation pursuits. Giving more serious, formalized attention to this domain of life by all stakeholder groups will be a key determinant of healthy, sustainable growth in Japan, by fully realizing the significant role of life-long leisure for all. Raising public status and recognition of leisure/recreation professionals as a legitimate occupation is a must if we strive to ensure a higher quality of life for Japanese people. Critical to achieve this goal is the use of a partnership approach to promoting public awareness and advocacy for social change that supports inclusive life-long leisure for all Japanese citizens. It is a shared responsibility of all who are involved from all sectors (government, community/nonprofit, business, and educational/academic) at local, regional, and national levels.

LEISURE IN KOREA

Jin-Hyung Lee (Mokpo National University)

As in the West, leisure is a significant sphere of life for many contemporary Koreans. It is also an important area of research in Korea for disciplines such as physical education, tourism sciences, and family studies. In this section, leisure and leisure studies in Korea will be briefly introduced and discussed. First, the Korean word *yeoga* ("leisure") and its historical origins will be investigated and the history of leisure in Korea will be discussed. Second, the ways in which contemporary Koreans use their time and participate in leisure activities will be examined. Finally, the principal areas of research on leisure in Korea and their possible directions in the future will be considered.

The Meaning of Leisure in Korean Culture

Yeoga is a Sino-Korean term which is analogous to "leisure" in Western societies. Although the word is widely used in everyday life by contemporary Korean people, it is not clear when it was first used in Korea. Several studies (e.g., Lee, Cho, & Kim, 2006) have suggested that the Chinese characters for *yeoga* (餘暇) were first officially used as a translation of the Western concept of "leisure" in 1924 for labor statistics in Japan. At that time, Korea was under Japanese colonial rule, and these researchers posited that this is how *yeoga* was introduced into Korean society.

However, more recent studies show that the word *yeoga* was already being used in traditional Korean society. Based on a review of the Annals of Chosun dynasty (1392–1910), Shin (2013) found that out of 27 kings' annals, the word *yeoga* was documented 26 times in 25 annals of 12 kings. He also investigated the meaning of *yeoga* in these documents and concluded that the word was used in the context of the lack of free time among the kings and high-ranked government officials of Chosun dynasty. Shin (2013) also insisted that the word *yeoga* had been used for at least 600 years, which supports the idea that the word is more than just a contemporary translation of the Western word "leisure."

Besides *yeoga,* native Korean words that have similar meanings to "leisure" also exist (e.g., *jjam, teum*). From a conceptual point of view, however, these two native Korean words are very much *time-oriented* (i.e., leisure as a brief period of free time) and lack the characteristics of the contemporary Western academic definition of "leisure" (i.e., an activity, state of mind and/or being). Moreover, there was no effort to develop an academic definition of leisure before the 1980s when some Korean social scientists began to research Koreans' participation in leisure (e.g., Lee & Shim, 2009). However, since the 1990s significant academic efforts have been made to define the characteristics of leisure for Koreans and by Korean scholars. Much of these efforts were influenced by Western leisure scholars' (e.g., Nash, De Grazia, Kaplan, Dumazedier, Parker, and Godbey) works, although several studies sought to understand leisure from traditional Asian philosophical and religious perspectives, such as Confucianism, Buddhism, and Taoism (e.g., Hong, 2006).

Before the late nineteenth century, Korea was a feudal society with a closed agricultural economy. People's lives in traditional Korean society were significantly influenced by Asian religions such as Buddhism, Confucianism, and Korean shamanism. In addition, there was also a strict class system in pre-modern Korea. For example, the Chosun dynasty encouraged the entrenchment of Korean Confucian ideals and doctrines in Korean society. There were also four strictly defined social classes: scholars, farmers, artisans, and tradesmen.

Leisure in pre-modern Korea was highly influenced by the socioeconomic, cultural, and political systems present at the time. First of all, 24 annual cyclical holidays, mostly related to agricultural plantings and harvests, were important parts of the traditional leisure lifestyle of Korean people (Yoon, 2000). Among those agricultural holidays, the lunar New Year (*Seollal*) and *Chuseok* (the Korean Thanksgiving day) were the most popular. For example, during the lunar New Year, people played a family board game called yunnori. Men and boys flew rectangular kites called *yeonnalligi,* while women and girls played *neolttwigi*, a game of jumping on a seesaw. For *Chuseok*, Koreans also did *ssireum*, a form of Korean wrestling.

There was also a clear differentiation between the upper classes and lower classes with respect to their leisure participation (Choi & Kim, 2004). For example, lower class people were prohibited from participating in activities like *Kyukkoo* (a Korean version of polo) because it was considered an elegant leisure activity for the nobility, known as the *yangban*. Under the influence of Confucianism and Taoism, *yangban* were only allowed to participate in a leisure activity that was considered to be decent and honorable (Kim, 1997, p. 203). *Pungryu* was the typical leisure activity for the upper classes, which consisted of visiting beautiful mountains and valleys, reciting poems, and playing traditional Korean instruments (Park, 2013).

Leisure in Contemporary South Korea

During the nineteenth century, the Chosun dynasty made every effort to control foreign influence by closing the borders to all nations but China. However, in 1876 Chosun opened Korean ports to foreign countries. Between 1885 and 1909, Western sports such as gymnastics, football, baseball, tennis, and table tennis were introduced to Korea through modern schools and organizations such as YMCA and YWCA, which were founded by Western Christian missionaries (Gwack & Gwack, 2005). It was during the Japanese colonial era (1910–1945) that Western-style commercial leisure was introduced to Korea in the name of modernity (Lee, 2012). For example, department stores and hotels appeared as modern consumption spaces. Cinemas, music cafés, and dance halls became the new commercial leisure spaces, mostly for the elites in colonial

Korea. In addition, tourism was established as a systematic part of colonial policy (Cho, 2012). Based on the railroad systems, sea, and air routes, which were built by the Japanese, the elites of colonial Korea were encouraged to visit Japan to see its advanced economy and to be assimilated into its society. On the other hand, Japanese people were encouraged to visit Korea and Manchuria, which was a part of China, to see their colonial territories and to be proud of being citizens of imperial Japan.

When Korea gained its independence in 1945, it was still an agricultural society with little industrial infrastructure. The Korean War (1950–1953) further devastated the peninsula, pushing the Korean postwar economy into a much worse state than before the war. However, South Korea was transformed into an industrial society during the Park Jung -hee era (Kim & Vogel, 2011). President Park seized power in 1961 through a military coup and led the so-called "Miracle on the Han River" until 1979. The Park Jung-hee era was a period of rapid economic growth in South Korea, even though his authoritarian rule precipitated numerous human rights abuses.

Under President Park's authoritarian leadership, work hours for factory laborers reached 53 hours per week in 1975 (Choi, 2005). Consequently, Koreans had little time to participate in leisure activities during this period. Watching television was the most popular leisure-time activity in the late 1970s among Korean people, followed by watching movies (Choi, 2005). Leisure participation was also limited because a curfew from 11 pm until 4 am was in place.

During this period the Korean central government developed several tourism destinations including Jeju Island and Gyeongju to attract not Korean citizens, but rather foreign tourists, especially those from Japan. At the same time, Koreans themselves were not allowed to travel to other countries except for business and official matters.

Since 1980, Korea has become democratized and more industrialized. Under Chun Do-Hwan's administration from 1980 to 1988, the curfew was abolished, the first professional baseball and soccer leagues in Korea were formed, and two important international mega-events, the Seoul Asian Games (1986) and the Seoul Olympics (1988), were held. Liberalization of overseas travel and tourism destination development including the constructions of condominiums for Korean citizens started during the 1980s. All of these changes meant diversification and commercialization of leisure for Koreans (Choi, 2005).

However, working hours for factory laborers did not decrease at all under President Chun's dictatorship. After the 6/10 June Demography Movement in 1987, the Labor Standard Act was revised, which decreased statuary working hours from 48 to 44 hours per week. The Act also did not allow more than 48 hours of work in a single week (Choi, 2005). Since then, working hours have begun to decrease and leisure has become an important area of life for Koreans. In addition, the five-day workweek started in Korea in 2004, which also had an impact on the Koreans' leisure lifestyle.

Having stated this, only about 40% of Korea people worked 40 hours a week in 2012 (Korea Ministry of Culture, Sport and Tourism , 2012); Korea is second highest out of 32 OCED member countries in its average hours actually worked per year (OECD, 2013). As can been seen Figure 14.1, the average hours actually worked per year in Korea

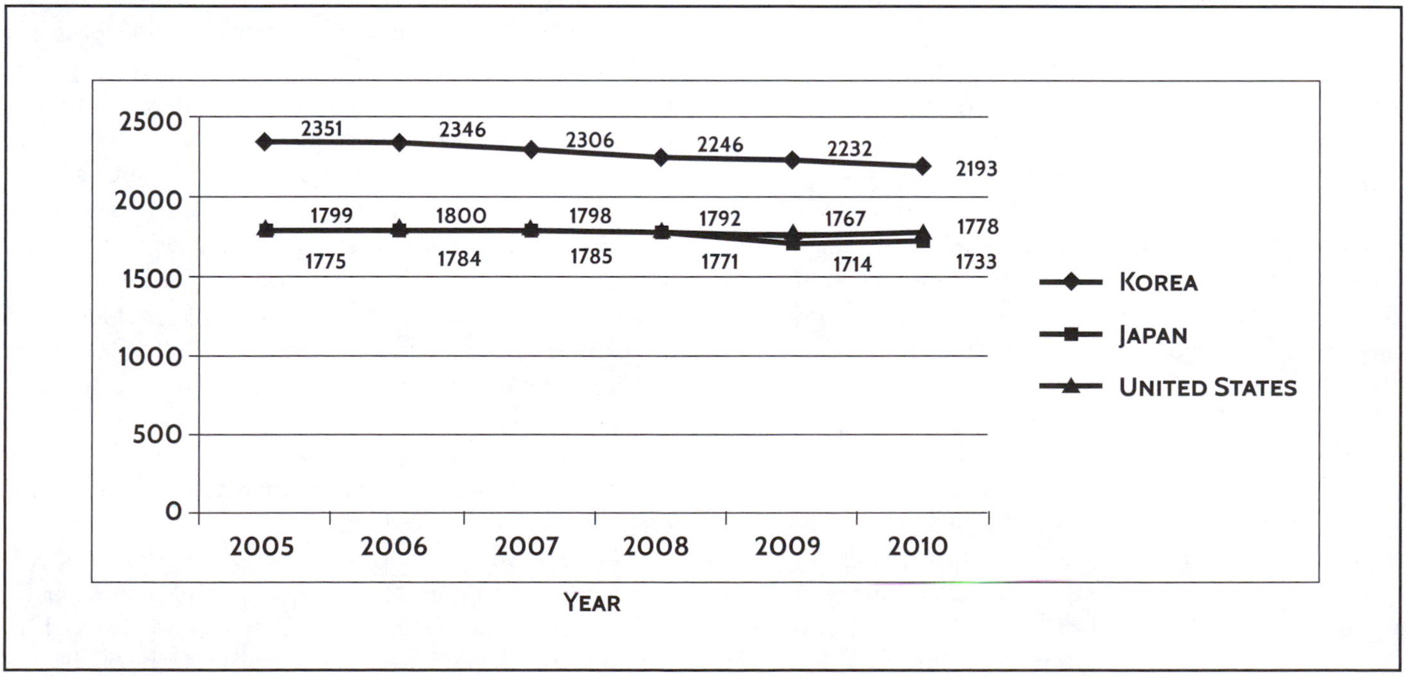

Figure 14.1. Average Hours Worked Per Year: South Korea, Japan, and the United States

was 2,193 (42 hours per week) in 2010, which is about 400 to 500 hours longer than those of the United States and Japan. Indeed, Korea is still an overworked society (Kim, 2013) and some politicians and scholars have even proposed legislating a Leisure Promotion Act to remedy this social problem (Cho, 2010). In fact, according to the official statistics of the Korea Ministry of Culture, Sports and Tourism (2012), Koreans only had 3.5 hours for leisure during weekdays and 5.1 hours during the weekend in 2012, resulting in 27.7 hours of leisure hours per week; far fewer hours than in Japan and the United States.

In terms of leisure activity participation, in 2012 watching television was the most popular leisure activity (77.8%), followed by taking walks (31.2%), taking naps (23.6%), Internet/social networking service (23.5%), hiking (19.4%), watching movies (19.4%), drinking (18.9%), chatting with friends (16.2%), playing games (14.3), and going to fitness centers (6.6%) (Korean Ministry of Culture, Sports and Tourism, 2012). This finding suggests that most of the popular leisure activities in Korea, except for hiking and going to fitness centers, are relaxing activities typically done at home and nearby neighborhood areas (though there are some significant differences between age groups and social classes; Kim, Lee, & Choi, 2012). In addition, Korea has the highest smartphone penetration rate in the world (67.6%), with smartphones being widely used for multiple leisure purposes including: watching television and movies, listening to music, Internet surfing, social network services, and playing games. Finally, as more Koreans have become interested in having a healthier lifestyle, walking has become a very popular leisure activity in Korea—to such a degree, in fact, that it is even described as a "walking fever." One can easily find people walking in neighborhood parks and school playgrounds, especially early in the morning or late at night. Over the last 10 years, numerous walking trails have been developed around the country as tourist attractions.

Sports for all activities are under development in Korea as well, with tennis, table tennis, badminton, and soccer being the most popular. This means that, in addition to causal leisure participants there are also serious and specialized leisure participants (Stebbins, 1992), even though they still make up only about 10% of the Korean population (Korean Ministry of Culture, Sports and Tourism, 2012).

Statistics also show that 13.7 million Korean people (about 27.5% of population) traveled abroad in 2012 (E-daily, 2013 August 5) whereas approximately 85.2% of Korean people participated in domestic tourism during the same year (Korea Ministry of Culture, Sports and Tourism, 2013). The average number of times Koreans over the age of 15 traveled domestically was 4.93 trips per year, and the total number of days per year was, on average, 8.43. The increase in domestic tourism is closely associated with the rise in automobile ownership by Korean households since the late 1990s. Indeed, travel is a popular leisure activity in contemporary Korean society.

The Future of Leisure in South Korea

As mentioned earlier, South Korea was transformed into an industrial society during the 1960s and 1970s, primarily during the Park Jung-hee era. During this time period, the Korean economy developed rapidly but at the expense of higher income and shorter work hours. Given these circumstances, it is not surprising that there were almost no studies on leisure in Korea before the 1980s (with the few exceptions typically being descriptive, policy-driven studies that examined the "good" use of leisure by teenagers, college students, and factory workers; Lee & Shim, 2009). However, in the 1980s, more systemic research on leisure started in some academic fields in Korea, including tourism sciences. Additionally, in 1984 the *Korean Society of Leisure and Recreation* was founded by researchers in physical education.

The number of research articles on leisure has increased significantly since the 1990s. Out of 812 studies on leisure in Korea published between 1990 and 2004 (identified after a search of the Korea National Assembly electronic library database), about 42.2% were in the field of physical education, followed by tourism sciences (15.5%), and then home economics/women's studies (Kim & Kim, 2004). In terms of research themes, leisure behavior (46.8%), including leisure motivations and attitudes, was the most frequent, followed by leisure policy (11.7%), leisure planning and management (5.5%), leisure education (3.6%), tourism (3.7%), leisure and quality of life (3.6%), leisure opportunities for minorities (3.5%), and leisure-related consumer behavior (3.1%) (Kim & Kim, 2004).

Lee and Shim (2009) also examined 75 research articles published in 2 top-tier Korean tourism journals over the last 25 years in terms of their research areas and themes. Of this total, 20 research articles were on leisure behavior and participation, 12 were on the psychology of leisure, 9 were on outdoor recreation management, 8 were on quality of life and another 8 were on leisure management and economics, and 7 were on constraints to leisure. In addition, 5 articles examined Korean leisure from a structural/critical point of view, whereas 4 articles focused on leisure space development.

Lee and Shim (2009) further found that, since 2003, the number of studies on general aspects of leisure participation, leisure management/economics, and the psychology of leisure decreased significantly. Conversely, the number of studies on outdoor recreation management (e.g., recreation specialization, recreational conflict, crowding, carrying capacity), constraints to leisure, and structural/critical approaches to leisure increased significantly. Lastly, in terms of research subjects, Lee and Shim discovered that leisure studies involving social minorities (e.g., women, multicultural families, North Korean defectors, and immigrant workers) had become more common when compared with traditional subjects such as teenagers and college students.

Korean scholars have not yet reached general consensus on the major leisure research topics and themes (Shim, 2004). This suggests that, in South Korea, leisure studies remains a developing academic area and need to do more systemic research studies on diverse subjects. First of all, future leisure research in Korea should focus more on the history of Korean leisure. As mentioned before, leisure studies in Korea tended to be focused on behavioral aspects of leisure and outdoor recreation. Not many studies to date have examined the historical facets of Korean leisure. For example, there has been almost no rigorous study of the social history of modern Korean leisure. Korean academic society needs to systemically investigate how modern leisure was introduced and evolved over time, as Cross (1990) and Nasaw (1993) did in the United States.

More research may also be needed on the Korean leisure industry. As Rojek (1995) pointed out, commercialization or industrialization is one of the key characteristics of modern leisure. In Korea, a white paper on the leisure industry has been published annually since 2007 by a private publishing company, but future research should be more diverse. In particular, the mobile leisure industry (i.e., Internet, television, video, music, and social network site usage) and people's experiences of mobile leisure need to be more thoroughly explored as it has become a very important aspect of Koreans' leisure lifestyle.

Research is also needed on the leisure of older Koreans. Korea became an aging society (7% of population over age 65) in the early 2000s and is expected to become an aged society (14% of population over age 65) in 2019 and post-aged society (20% of population over age 65) in 2026. This suggests that the so-called "silver leisure industry" market, including the silver sport industry, silver tourism industry, silver edutainment industry, and silver leisure facilities, will increase significantly in the near future. This also means that appreciably more research is needed on the relationship between older Koreans' leisure and the silver leisure industry.

Conclusion

As evinced by the above, it is hard to say that Korea has a healthy leisure culture and lifestyle at this point in time. Koreans are overworked and there is a harried leisure class in Korea (Linder, 1970; Schor, 1992). Unlimited materialism and competition are also common in Korean society. Even teenagers do not have enough time to develop leisure skills (e.g., sports, music, and other cultural activities) because of the notorious Korean "private education fever" and "evening self-study session at school." In fact, it is no exaggeration to state that for many Korean adolescents, their mobile phones provide one of their few opportunities for leisure. In conclusion, therefore, Korea's local and central governments should develop diverse measures to remedy these problems by legislating leisure-related laws, creating better work environments, conducting campaigns that encourage more balanced lives, building more public leisure facilities, and enhancing leisure education in schools. To help accomplish these goals, an annual conference should be organized that includes scholars from fields such as sociology, economics, sports sciences, recreation and leisure studies, and tourism sciences, as well as representatives from the Korea Culture and Tourism Institute, Ministry of Culture, Sports and Tourism, and the National Assembly of Korea.

REFERENCES

Chang, Y. S., & Card, J. A. (1992). *The impact of ancient Chinese philosophy on contemporary leisure in China*. (ERIC Document Reproduction Service No. ED 350 295).

Chen, N. N., Clark, C. D., Gottschang, S. Z., & Jeffery, L. (2001). Introduction. In N. N. Chen, C. D. Clark, S. Z., Gottschang, & L. Jeffery (Eds.), *China urban: Ethnographies of contemporary culture* (pp. 1–20). Durham, NC: Duke University Press.

China Daily. (2012). *Lack of leisure time takes toll on workers*. Retrieved from http://english.peopledaily.com.cn/90882/7974087.html

Cho, G-I. (2010). Revisiting the justification for legislation of Leisure Promotion Act. *Journal of Leisure Studies, 2*, 1–31.

Cho, S-W. (2012). *Modern tourism and Japan inspection tours in colonial Korea*. Seoul, Korea: Kyungin Publishing.

Choi, S-H. (2005). *Korean society and Korean leisure: The formation of modern leisure and civilizing process*. Paju, Korea: Korea Studies Information.

Choi, Y-T., & Kim, D-J. (2004). Leisure and recreations during the Chosun dynasty. *Korea Sports Research, 15*, 735–744.

CNN. (2012). *Which country has the most vacation days?* Retrieved from http://www.cnn.com/2011/WORLD/asiapcf/07/29/country.comparisons.vacation/

Coleman, D., & Iso-Ahola, S. E. (1993). Leisure and health: The role of social support and self-determination. *Journal of Leisure Research, 25*, 111–128.

Cross, G. (1990). *A social history of leisure since 1600*. State College, PA: Venture Publishing, Inc.

Deng, J. Y. & Liu, H. M. (2012). Recreation and leisure in China. In *Introduction to recreation and leisure* (2nd ed.) (pp. 399–406). Champaign, IL: Human Kinetics.

Dowling, N., Smith, D., & Thomas, T. (2004). Electronic gaming machines: Are they the 'crack-cocaine' of gambling? *Addiction, 100*, 33–45.

Echinacities. (2012). *Working hard or hardly working? Trends in China's leisure economy*. Retrieved from http://www.echinacities.com/china-media/Working-Hard-or-Hardly-Working-Trends-in-Chinas-Leisure-Economy.

Godbey, G. (2013). Reforming leisure in China. *Proceedings of the 2013 China (Hangzhou) International Leisure Development Forum* (pp. 22–31).

Gong, B. (2013). *Chinese leisure* (In Chinese). Beijing Publishing Group Ltd.

Gwack, A-Y., & Gwack, H-G. (2005). Physical education activities of Christians mission school at the Enlightened Era in Korea. *Korean Journal of History for Physical Education, Sports and Dance*, 16, 27–41.

Hagi, Y., Kurihara, T., Onda, T., Ito, E., Yoshihara, S., & Shimoyamada, S. (2010). *Current Situation Analysis of Sport & Leisure Management Education in Japanese University (College)*. 1–13.

Hong, S. (Ed.). (2006). *Oriental philosophical thoughts and post-modern leisure*. Dague, Korea: Keymung University Press.

Insight Magazine. (2012). *Chinese' leisure time decreased in a row for the past three years and over seventy percent respondents worked overtime* (in Chinese). Retrieved from http://politics.people.com.cn/n/2012/1015/c1001-19261665.html

Ito, E., & Walker, G. J. (2014). Similarities and differences in leisure conceptualizations between Japan and Canada and between two Japanese leisure-like terms. *Leisure/Loisir, 38*, 1–19.

Ito, E., Walker, G. J., & Liang, H. (2014). A systematic review of non-Western and cross-cultural/national leisure research. *Journal of Leisure Research, 46*, 226–239.

Iwasaki, Y. (2006). Counteracting stress through leisure coping: A prospective health study. *Psychology, Health & Medicine, 11*(2), 209–220.

Iwasaki, Y. (2008). Pathways to meaning-making through leisure in global contexts. *Journal of Leisure Research, 40*, 231–249.

Iwasaki, Y., MacKay, K., Mactavish, J., Ristock, J., & Bartlett, J. (2006). Voices from the margins: Stress, active living, and leisure as a contributor to coping with stress. *Leisure Sciences, 28*, 163–180.

Iwasaki, Y., & Mannell, R. C. (2000). Hierarchical dimensions of leisure stress coping. *Leisure Sciences, 22*, 163–181.

Iwasaki, Y., Nishino, H., Onda, T., & Bowling, C. (2007). Leisure research in a global world: Time to reverse the Western domination in leisure research? *Leisure Sciences, 29*, 113–117.

Kleiber, D., Hutchinson, S., & Williams, R. (2002). Leisure as a resource in transcending negative life events: Self-protection, self-restoration, and personal transformation. *Leisure Sciences, 24*, 219–236.

Jackson, E. L., & Walker, G. J. (2006). A cross-cultural comparison of leisure styles and constraints experienced by Chinese and Canadian university students. *Ninth World Leisure Congress Abstracts: Oral and Poster Presentations* (p. 28). Hangzhou, China: World Leisure.

Japan Productivity Headquarter (2012). *Leisure white paper 2012*. Tokyo, Japan: Author.

Jim, C. Y. & Chen, W. Y. (2009). Leisure participation pattern of residents in a new Chinese city. *Annals of the Association of American Geographers, 99*, 657–673.

Kelly, J. R. (1999). Leisure behaviors and styles: Social, economic, and cultural factors. In E. L. Jackson & T. L. Burton (Eds.), *Leisure studies: Prospects for the twenty-first century* (pp. 135–150). State College, PA: Venture Publishing, Inc.

Kim, B-K., & Vogel, E. F. (Eds.). (2011). *The Park Chung Hee era: The transformation of South Korea*. Boston, MA: Harvard University Press.

Kim, G-Y., & Kim, H-I. (2004). An analysis on the leisure research trend in Korea. *The Korean Journal of Physical Education, 43*(5), 689–703.

Kim, S-H. (1997). A cross-cultural comparison of leisure tradition in Korea: The case of play culture. *Korean Journal of Tourism Sciences, 20*(2), 193–207.

Kim, S-J., Lee, M-J., & Choi, S. (2012). Topology of leisure activities in Korea: A focus on the leisure activities types on weekdays and weekend. *Journal of Leisure Studies, 10*(2), 55–85.

Kim, Y-S. (2013). *Overworked society*. Seoul, Korea: Imagine Publishing.

Korea Ministry of Culture, Sports, and Tourism. (2012). *Korea National Leisure Survey*.

Korea Ministry of Culture, Sports, and Tourism. (2013). *Korea National Tourism Survey*.

Korfhage, J., Daniel L., & Hall, B. (2007, May). Parks across the pacific: A trip to Japan reveals a different culture and means of recreating. *Parks & Recreation*, 53–55.

Kubo, M. (2004). The study on the concept of sport and leisure in physical education. *Physical Education and Sport Research*, 1–14.

Lee, I-Y. (2012). The dialectics of modernity and orientalism reflected on the formation of the leisure and tourism pattern: A case study of the Japanese Colonia Era. *Journal of Tourism Sciences, 36*(6), 11–35.

Lee, J-H., Cho, B-S., & Kim, D-J. (2006). The *Yeoga* (Leisure) presented in the Chosun dynasty authentic records. *Journal of Leisure and Recreation Studies, 30*(3), 311–321.

Lee, J-H., & Shim, J-M. (2009). The trend of leisure research appeared in tourism journals in Korea. *Journal of Tourism Sciences, 33*(2), 9–30.

Linder, B. L. (1970). *The harried leisure class*. New York: Columbia University Press.

Link, P., Madsen, R. P., & Pickowicz, P. G. (2002). Introduction. In P. Link, R. P. Madsen, & P. G. Pickowicz (Eds.), *Popular China: Unofficial culture in a globalizing society* (pp. 1–8). Lanham, MA: Rowman & Littlefield Publishers.

Liu, E. (2004). Comparison of time budget and lifestyle between Chinese and American urban residents. *Information Times*, 7.

Liu, D. Q., Gao, S.L., & Song, R. (2010). *China Leisure Greenbook: Report of Chinese leisure development in 2010*. Social Sciences Academic Press (China).

Liu, H. M., Yeh, C. K., Chick, G. E., & Zinn, H. C. (2008). An exploration of meanings of of leisure: A Chinese perspective. *Leisure Sciences, 30*, 482–488.

Lu, Y. Z., & Yu, Y. H. (2005). Investigation on the sports facilities in Beijing residential areas (In Chinese). *Sports Science Research, 26*(5), 20–24.

Markus, H., & Kitayama, S. (1991). Culture and the self: Implications for cognition, emotion, and motivation. *Psychological Review, 98*, 224–253.

Manzenreiter, W. (2013). Playing against all odds: Pachinko and the culture of risk-taking in Japan's crisis economy. *Leisure Studies, 32*, 283–298

Ministry of the Environment, Government of Japan (2007). *The nature of Japan*. Tokyo, Japan: Author.

Ministry of the Environment, Government of Japan. (2013). *National Parks of Japan*. Retrieved from http://www.env.go.jp/en/nature/nps/park/

Ministry of Land, Infrastructure and Transport, Government of Japan. (2005). *Current status of provision of city parks in Japan*. Tokyo, Japan: Author.

Nasaw, D. (1993).*Going out: The rise and fall of public amusement*. Cambridge, MA: Harvard University Press.

National Bureau of Statistics of China. (2010). *The report of the 6th national population census of the People's Republic of China* (in Chinese). Retrieved from http://www.stats.gov.cn/tjfx/jdfx/t20110428_402722253.htm

Nishino, H. J., Chino, H., Yoshioka, N., & Gabriella, J. (2007). Therapeutic recreation in modern Japan: Era of challenge and opportunity. *Therapeutic Recreation Journal, 41*, 119–131.

OECD. (2013). *OECD Factbook 2013*. Retrieved from http://www.oecd-ilibrary.org/content/book/factbook-2013-en

Park, H. (2013). Leisure and culture of entertainment in the view of Pungryu. *Korean Journal of Practice Folkloristics, 21*, 118–219.

Rojek, C. (1995). *Decentring leisure: Rethinking leisure theory*. London: Sage Publications.

Sasakawa Sports Foundation. (2011). *Sport white paper: Sport for everyone*. Tokyo, Japan: Author.

Schutte, H., & Ciarlante, D. (1998). *Consumer behavior in Asia*. Washington Square, NY: New York University Press.

Schor, J. B. (1992). *The overworked American: The unexpected decline of leisure*. New York: Basic Books.

Shim, J. M. (2004). *The evolution of leisure studies in North America and South Korea: A study of cultural consensus*. (Doctoral dissertation, The Pennsylvania State University).

Shin, J-H. (2013). The history of leisure concept in Korea. *Journal of Leisure Studies, 10*, 101–117.

Spiers, A., & Walker, G. J. (2009). The effects of ethnicity and leisure satisfaction on happiness, peacefulness, and quality of life. *Leisure Sciences, 31*, 84–99.

Sport Facility Publishing. (2013). *Sport Facility Monthly*. Tokyo, Japan: Author.

Stebbins, R. A. (1992). *Amateurs, professionals, and serious leisure*. Montreal, PQ & Kingston, ON: McGill-Queen's University Press.

Stebbins, R. A. (2006). Serious leisure. In C. Rojek, S. M. Shaw, & A. J. Veal (Eds.), *A handbook of leisure studies* (pp. 448–456). London: Palgrave Macmillan.

Suissa, A. J. (2007). Gambling addiction as a pathology: Some markers for empowerment. *Journal of Addictions Nursing, 18*(2), 93–101.

Tsai, J. L., Knutson, B., & Fung, H. H. (2006). Cultural variation in affect valuation. *Journal of Personality and Social Psychology*, 90, 288–307.

United Nations. (2013). *United Nations enable development and human rights for all: Article 30—Participation in cultural life, recreation, leisure and sport*. Retrieved from http://www.un.org/disabilities/default.asp?id=290

Wada, K., Satoh, T., Tanaka, K., Tsunoda, M., & Aizawa, Y. (2007). Associations of depressive symptoms with regular leisure activity and family social support among Japanese workers, *Industrial Health, 45*, 181–185.

Wang, J. Y., & Stringer, A. (2000). The impact of Taoism on Chinese leisure. *World Leisure Journal, 42*(3), 33–41

Walker, G. J. (2010). The effects of personal, contextual, and situational factors on the facilitation of intrinsic motivation: The case of Chinese/Canadians. *Journal of Leisure Research, 42*, 43–66.

Walker, G. J., Deng, J., Y. & Dieser, R. B. (2005). Culture, self-construal, and leisure theory and practice. *Journal of Leisure Research, 37*, 77–99.

Walker, G. J., Jackson, E. L., & Deng, J. (2008). The role of self-construal as an intervening variable between culture and leisure constraints: A comparison of Canadian and Mainland Chinese university students. *Journal of Leisure Research, 40*, 90–109.

Walker, G. J., & Liang, H. (2012). An overview of a comprehensive leisure participation framework and its application for cross-cultural leisure research (in Chinese). *Journal of Zhejiang University (Humanities and Social Sciences), 42*, 22–30.

Wang, Q. Y., Lei, T., & Shi, L. (2000). Watching TV the most frequent leisure activity of Beijing residents. *Beijing Statistics, 151*, 19–20.

Weber, I. (2002). Shanghai Baby: Negotiating youth self-identity in urban China. *Social Identities, 8*(2), 347–368.

Wei, X., & Stodolska, M. (2015). Leisure in urban China: General trends based on a nationwide survey. *Journal of Leisure Research, 47*(3), 373–387.

Yin, X. D. (2005). New trends of leisure consumption in China. *Journal of Family and Economic Issues, 26*(1), 175–182.

Yoon, S-M. (2000). Leisure in pre-modern Korean and its modern implications. *The Korean Journal of Physical Education, 39*(4), 1023–1030.

Yu, G. Y. (2005). *On the society of universal leisure*. Beijing, China: Economy Publishing House.

Yu, P., & Berryman, D. L. (1996). The relationship among self-esteem, acculturation, and recreation participation of recently arrived Chinese immigrant adolescents. *Journal of Leisure Research, 28*, 251–273.

15

LOISIR SANS FRONTIERS? LEISURE IN EUROPE

Fiona Jordan (University of the West of England, United Kingdom)

Fully encapsulating within one chapter the changing nature and scope of leisure research in Europe, including its associated disciplines/subject fields such as tourism and sport, and the implications for leisure of the shifting borders of Europe, is a challenging task. Leisure is itself a term covering a broad set of activities and disciplines (the range of topics covered in this edited collection is testament to that) and how to best research this subject across an increasingly legally unified, but still culturally diverse, set of countries is a question subject to debate among leisure scholars and policymakers alike.

According to National Geographic, Europe is the second-smallest continent in terms of area, extending from Iceland in the west to the Ural Mountains of Russia in the east. Europe's northernmost point is the Svalbard archipelago of Norway, and it reaches as far south as the islands of Greece and Malta. The Council of Europe lists 47 countries as members, with 28 of those also forming the European Union (EU) (http://hub.coe.int/web/coe-portal/home). Europe has a population of around 733 million and growing and is the third most populous continent after Africa and Asia. The potential for leisure in Europe and the challenges of providing opportunities for leisure are therefore huge. Within this large landmass there have been seismic shifts in the geo-political landscape over the past 20 years. While this chapter does not discuss in any detail the various political upheavals and conflicts that have characterized the shifts in European geographical, political, and economic boundaries, they provide an essential backdrop to any discussion of leisure in Europe.

In 1997, Mommaas produced a comparative analysis of the history of leisure in six European countries. He concluded that in Europe leisure research had been dominated by sociological perspectives but had moved from an emphasis on issues of collective public concern to a more fragmented consideration of consumption, time, pleasure, and play. He questioned whether leisure studies required a unifying project and if so, what that project would look like. This chapter uses his question to focus on the opportunities and challenges of considering leisure across Europe in the twenty-first century. Rather than a country by country analysis of leisure, this chapter initially considers some of the issues raised in trying to determine the geographical and theoretical borders of leisure research in a changing Europe. The chapter then examines the challenges and opportunities presented by transnational research on leisure in Europe and highlights some of the existing cross-European studies of sport and cultural consumption to illustrate the possibilities for further European leisure research.

LEISURE RESEARCH IN EUROPE: STILL TRYING TO DEFINE THE THEORETICAL AND GEOGRAPHICAL BORDERS

Fox (2006) contends that leisure scholarship has been dominated by Eurocentric practitioners and practice. Roberts (2010), however, has argued that although since the 1960s leisure studies has tended to be Anglophone in its orientation it has also ". . . demonstrated an ability to listen to voices from, and to understand the distinctive properties of leisure in societies outside, the core 'leisure studies' countries" (p. 164). This, he suggests, gives leisure studies a promising base from which to broaden its scope and geographical orientation. This has obvious possibilities for the expansion of leisure studies research across Europe, though to return to the question posed by Mommaas (1997) it is still not clear what the unifying project would look like, or indeed how it would be funded in a time of shrinking research budgets in many countries.

Discussions of the nature, scope, direction, theoretical underpinnings, and future of leisure studies as a field and/or within particular geographical areas such as Europe are not unusual. Some of the most controversial claims and heated academic debates in the field have been catalysed by these so-called "crises" in the subject field. At the turn of the century, for instance, the nature and extent of a crisis in leisure studies was being debated in a series of articles (e.g., Aitchison, 2000; Chick, 1997; Coalter, 1997; Mommaas, 1997). Often the discussions have focused on the relationship between leisure studies and its parent disciplines (see Chapters 1 to 7); the ability of leisure studies to embrace new conceptual challenges (e.g., post-structuralism, cultural studies); the decline of leisure studies as an academic programme of study; concerns about the extent to which leisure studies relates theory to practice (see Walker, Kono, & Dieser, Chapter 36); and the extent to which leisure studies links to or differs from cognate fields/disciplines (or as some authors contend, the subfields) of sport, tourism and most recently events (see Chalip, Chapter 10; and Gibson, Chapter 11). At the time that the predecessor to this volume was written, the turn of the century debate over leisure studies was being played out in key leisure publications. Henderson's Chapter 39 in this volume provides a comprehensive account of these areas of discussion and their influence on the development and direction of leisure as a field of study in North America.

Within the debate at the end of the 1990's, Coalter (1997) put forward the notion that leisure theory was "characterised by different epistemological, methodological, and theoretical perspectives" in the United Kingdom (UK) and North America (cited in Aitchison, 2000, p. 129). He argued that in the UK, leisure theory was oriented towards *leisure studies*, and North America towards *leisure sciences*. Mommaas, however, rejected that claim, arguing instead that "UK and European Leisure Studies have witnessed a shift from American-based scientism and functionalism to Gramscian neo-Marxism, French post-structuralism, semiotics, and psychoanalysis" (cited in Aitchison, 2000, p. 130). At the turn of the century Aitchison was critical of this view, positing that in fact leisure studies had been slow to embrace these rich theoretical perspectives.

Since the turn of the century, it could be argued that France, and in particular French philosophers, have had a profound influence on leisure research generally. Towards the end of the previous millennium and during the first decade of the twenty-first century, poststructuralist perspectives have been adopted by a number of leisure researchers, in particular feminist leisure scholars (e.g., Aitchison, 2001; Fullagar, 2002; Jordan & Aitchison, 2008; Wearing, 1998). The philosophical perspectives of scholars such as Derrida and Foucault have been both adapted and critiqued in analyses of leisure and tourism experience and have informed the debate about the extent to which leisure research should, would, or could, benefit from further exploration of these concepts in seeking to understand power relations and the diversity of leisure behaviors and experiences. Given the political, geographical, social, and cultural diversity of the countries that form Europe, further studies exploring ways in which these factors shape leisure participation and leisure research within local contexts would appear to have merit. However, such a shift could have profound implications for the pursuit of a more unifying view of leisure in Europe.

The challenge of finding a unifying leisure research project for Europe has also become more difficult both with the expansion of the European Union. Since the formation of the European Coal and Steel Community in 1951 with just six members, the EU has expanded to include 28 countries at the time of writing with further expansion imminent. The largest single expansion occurred with the addition of ten new members in 2007 including the Czech Republic, Estonia, Latvia, Lithuania, and Poland. The EU enlargement is inextricably linked to political upheavals and the redrawing of European boundaries, all of which has a profound effect on the everyday lives of citizens, including their leisure time. The redrawing of borders has had a significant influence on migration patterns which culturally shape the nature of leisure activities within different nation states and the extent to which there has been a move towards cultural homogenization. This is an avenue that seems worthy of further exploration within twenty-first century studies of leisure in Europe.

It is clear that the related field of tourism research has taken the opportunity to explore the implications of the changing nature of the EU, with textbooks examining issues such as social tourism in Europe (McCabe, Minnaert, & Diekmann, 2012), the impact of the "new Europe" on small- and medium-sized tourism enterprises (Thomas & Augustyn, 2007), the geography of migrant labor in tourism (Zampoukos & Ioannides, 2011), the challenges and opportunities for tourism of EU enlargement (Hall, Smith & Marciszewska, 2006) and intra-tourism trade in Europe (Petit & Nowak, 2012). Similarly researchers within the subject field of sport have explored the implications of EU for sports policy (see for instance Henry, 2007) and the potential for the flow of ideas on elite sport development from the former Eastern Bloc to Western countries (Green & Oakley, 2001). Researchers such as Coalter (2013) and Palmer (2012) have considered the broader relationship between globalization and sport and other publications make the connection between all three in providing discussion which encompasses European issues (see for instance Veal, 2010). In reviewing the extant literature, it appears that while analyses of related areas such as sport and tourism in the "new" Europe exist it is more difficult to identify studies focusing on the implications of the expansion of the EU specifically for leisure as a topic. The following section examines some of the potential reasons for this.

TRANSNATIONAL LEISURE RESEARCH IN EUROPE: CHALLENGES AND OPPORTUNITIES

Bramham (2006) suggests that leisure research has tended to be focused within nation states, often driven by social policy agendas, rather than undertaking transnational analyses. He argues that this approach needs to change if leisure studies is to survive: "What has become clear is that change can no longer be hermeneutically contained and managed simply within the nation state" (p. 382).

In contrast to the relatively national focus of leisure studies research, the rise of tourism studies in Europe has been fast-paced in the twenty-first century. Could this reflect the fact that as an academic subject field and industry tourism is more inherently international and cross-border? While leisure researchers focus more on leisure within societies, tourism researchers more often explore leisure travel as a phenomenon whereby the interesting aspects of consumer behavior arise primarily from people moving between societies and their impact on the societies they visit. This is not to say that leisure research has completely overlooked these issues, but more that tourism studies has sought to actively embrace them.

One differentiating feature between transnational leisure and tourism research may be a relative lack of coordinated approach to transnational policymaking and funding in leisure. Whereas tourism has organizations such as the United Nations World Tourism Organization (UNWTO) providing an overarching international body to promote: "tourism as a driver of economic growth, inclusive development and environmental sustainability and offers leadership and support to the sector in advancing knowledge and tourism policies worldwide" (http://www2.unwto.org), the same unifying body does not exist for leisure.

Another factor that may contribute to the relative lack of transnational analyses of leisure is the difficulty of obtaining valid data with which to make comparisons. According to van Tuyckom, Bracke, and Scheerder (2011), policy functions and those organizations responsible for funding and publishing research are increasingly interested in comparative cross-country analyses based on data such as that gathered in the Eurobarometer (operated by the European Commission) and the International Social Survey Programme (available at http://www.esds.ac.uk/international/access/I33213.asp). This, they say, has led to an increase in the number of sports-related cross-country studies (e.g., Hovemann, & Wicker, 2009).

While on the surface, greater such availability of cross-national data seems to have potential to contribute to the formation of a unifying European Leisure project, van Tuyckom, Bracke, and Scheerder (2011) raise the question of comparability of such data in respect of cross-cultural sports participation. As they state:

> Cross-national research rests on the assumption of equivalence of meaning, that is, comparisons between countries are only worthwhile when different countries measure things in the same way. Unfortunately, this issue has been seriously underdeveloped in the sports research literature with the consequence that too often researchers find themselves 'reinventing the wheel' or worse, repeating the mistakes of others. (p. 89)

In examining sports participation in the EU, van Bottenburg, Rijnen, and van Sterkenburg (2005) are also critical of the lack of robust comparative data from which to identify trends in sports participation. This lack of meaningful data relates to a variety of factors including dynamic political and social agendas resulting in changing research design making comparisons harder over the longer term and resulting in a lack of longitudinal studies in many European countries. There are also gaps in our understanding of key issues such as motivations for participation and explanation of declining participation.

This is not to say that no such studies exist. A cross-national analysis of gender and leisure-time physical inactivity (LTPI) by van Tuyckom, van de Velde, and Bracke (2013), for instance, used data from the 2005 Eurobarometer and employed two international composite measures of gender-based (in)equality—United Nations Development Programme's Gender Empowerment Measure and the World Economic Forum's Gender Gap Index. Their findings identified gender disparities and cross-national differences in LTPI. They concluded that national social policies had a significant influence over LTPI and that society-level policy interventions addressing gender disparities may be more effective in addressing these issues than European level mass media campaigns.

The lack of sources of comparative European data on general leisure-related activities has led to a number of studies relying either on the Eurobarometer, as one of the few comprehensive datasets available (see later discussion of studies using these data), or on researchers examining specific aspects of leisure through national surveys and then providing a comparative analysis. For example, Garcia, Molina, and Navarro (2007) drew on European Community Household Panel (ECHP) (1994–2001) data from 14 European countries in examining spouse satisfaction with their leisure time. The ECHP is a national sample-based survey designed to be comparable trans-nationally and includes information on individual's work, income, health, and so on. This source was also used by Warren (2010) in her study of European women's temporal and economic well-being. This study, which examined the relationship between women's work and leisure time, concluded that measuring qualitative expressions of satisfaction remains a challenge and this is particularly so when endeavoring to do so across countries. Warren suggests that to fully understand these issues will require researching beyond the chronometric dimensions—a challenge when considering the size of the European population and the diversity of cultures encompassed within the EU.

Mäkinen, Sippola, Borodulin, Rahkonen, Kunst, Klumbiene and Prättälä, (2012) used national health survey data to study the leisure-time physical activities of 30- to 59-year-olds in 12 European countries. They also concluded that physical activity measures varied considerably between countries although they were able to identify some general patterns concerning the relationship between educational level and participation in physical activity. Hovemann and Wicker (2009), having compared data from the Eurobarometer and from 25 individual states, concluded that it was important to take account of "the peculiarities of sports participation" (p. 51) in different countries.

This does raise the question: is it feasible to produce truly comparative cross-country data on leisure participation given the diversity of political, social, and cultural factors shaping each of the countries in Europe and the subjective nature of individual leisure experiences?

MAPPING THE TERRITORY: EXISTING CROSS-EUROPEAN STUDIES OF SPORT AND CULTURAL CONSUMPTION

A number of studies related to specific aspects of leisure such as sport and cultural activities have been undertaken, largely relying on data taken from the Eurobarometer. One such study (Tuyckom & Scheerder, 2010) drew on data from the 2005 Eurobarometer in comparing levels of sporting activity of citizens in different European states. According to the Eurobarometer data 4 out of 10 Europeans are not exposed to sports activity. They related their analyses to EU policy which aims to enhance levels of physical activity of European citizens as a means of tackling growing problems of obesity. van Tuyckom and Scheerder (2010) linked their study to two key white papers: *The White Paper on a Strategy for Europe on Nutrition, Overweight and Obesity-Related Health Issues* (European Commission, 2007a) and the *White Paper on Sport* (European Commission, 2007b). What is notable about these white papers is the pan-European approach taken to tackling health-related issues and to promoting the economic and societal benefits of sport. As the authors point out, this represents an important first step in dealing with sport-related issues in a comprehensive way across Europe. Again, this points to the value and significance of cross-European policy and funding bodies in generating both data and potential funding for cross-Europe research. In addressing the question of what a unifying leisure project in Europe could look like, issues such as consistent European-wide guidelines on health and physical activity have the potential to form a central focus.

Eurobarometer data have also been the basis of limited research in another key leisure-related area, that of cultural consumption and lifestyles. Prior to work by Katz-Gerro (2011), research relying on Eurobarometer data indicated some general themes in cultural consumption in different European states (such as the significance of age, education, and gender) but also showed that the diverse cultures and social structures of different states are highly influential factors where cultural consumption is concerned. van Hek and Kraaykamp (2013) similarly drew on Eurobarometer data in analysing social inequality in cultural consumption. They highlighted the significance of government policy and the economic and social conditions of a country in shaping this aspect of leisure. Gronow and Southerton (2010) used household data and time diary data to study changing socio-geographical patterns of leisure-related activities in Europe. Their conclusion was that while there is some evidence of cultural homogenization, national institutions and characteristics remain fundamental in shaping leisure consumption. This view seems to have resonance for other leisure-related activities too and again relates back to the potential value of a more unified leisure project within and across Europe.

Katz-Gerro (2011) is critical of the lack of cross-national analyses of cultural consumption, highlighting that previously there has been a preponderance of country-specific studies rather than research which is designed as comparative. Despite the challenges of undertaking cross-national comparisons (similar to those outlined above with regards to researching sports participation) Katz-Gerro is strongly in favor of further cross-country research which broadens our understanding of experience in regions such as Eastern Europe. As she says:

> Cross-national projects give researchers a means of confronting findings in an attempt to identify and illuminate similarities and differences, not only in the observed characteristics of particular institutions, systems or practices, but also in the search

for possible explanations in terms of national propensity or disinclination. (p. 360)

A key element of Katz-Gerro's argument is that such comparative research should not only seek to find out what is the same but could also assist in helping us to understand diversity in leisure participation and consumption.

CONCLUSION

So, where does that leave analyses of leisure in Europe and the important question posed by Mommass (1997) about the desirability and feasibility of having a unifying project or approach? In short, there still seem to be more questions than answers. Unlike the United States, Canada, Australia and New Zealand, and the UK there is no one overarching association of leisure studies in Europe. To what extent is there a need for/advantage to be gained by having a more unified approach to leisure research within Europe? Are there key issues common to all of the fields and all of the countries in Europe that could realistically provide a framework around/within which leisure research in Europe could coalesce? There is the potential for relevant subject associations to do this, for instance the UK's Leisure Studies Association and World Leisure, but without there being a driving force, an imperative whether from personal interest, advocacy or necessity it is difficult to see how this would be achieved. The bigger question is to what extent would it be beneficial to do so and beneficial to whom?

In Henderson's (2006) opinion, the future of leisure studies/sciences lies in the ability of Leisure researchers to adopt a "both/and" approach rather than one which is "either/or." Henderson noted, "Thus the strengths of leisure research lie in the notion that leisure is a primary social institution that exists within societies. It can be examined from many perspectives" (p. 393). With the focus of leisure research traditionally grounded more in analyses of nation state, it could be argued that European leisure research has failed to fully grasp the opportunity to examine the major political changes that have occurred with the expansion of the EU and the implications these political upheavals have for provision of and participation in leisure. Expansion and population migration is certainly potentially rich territory for leisure researchers to explore the implications for leisure of changing migration patterns and population shifts.

Favell's (2011) book, *Eurostars and Eurocities: Free Movement and Mobility in an Integrating Europe*, provides some interesting avenues for future work in this area. Focusing on Amsterdam, London, and Brussels, and based on interviews with European migrants, he explores a range of issues such as mobility, sense of identity, integration, and cultural assimilation. Researching the lived experiences of those individuals who move around the new Europe has the potential to provide powerful insights into the extent to which leisure experiences are shaped by being members of migrant communities and the inter-relationship between those who move and the societies that they are moving into. Understanding how the changing geographical map of Europe affects access to, and the nature of, leisure for European citizens is going to be key to any possible pan-European leisure project. The studies of gender and leisure in Europe discussed earlier in this chapter demonstrate clearly that while it is useful to map patterns of leisure participation a more nuanced and in-depth exploration of the societal factors that influence national all aspects of leisure is also important.

There are clearly still many issues to be faced in producing truly comparative cross-national analyses given the social and cultural diversity of the countries that make up Europe and its continually shifting borders. Rather than maybe then seeking just one unifying project for leisure in Europe it may be that the future of research in this area relies upon the ability of scholars and practitioners to identify key cross-cutting themes, such as physical activity and health, that could generate academic interest and funding for projects. Continuation and development of leisure research in Europe may lie in the ability of this subject field to build bridges and learn from related subject areas such as sport, tourism, and cultural consumption where cross-national studies are increasing in number. In line with Katz-Gerro's view, any project examining leisure in Europe should seek to understand not just the similarities but also celebrate the cultural diversity of this unique continent.

REFERENCES

Aitchison, C. (2000). Poststructural feminist theories of representing others: A response to the 'crisis' in leisure studies' discourse. *Leisure Studies, 19*, 127–144.

Aitchison, C. (2001). Theorizing other discourses of tourism, gender and culture: Can the subaltern speak (in tourism)? *Tourist Studies, 1*(2), 133–147.

Bramham, P. (2006). Hard and disappearing work: Making sense of the leisure project. *Leisure Studies, 25*, 379–390.

Chick, G. (1997). Crossroads and crises, or much ado about nothing? A comment on Mommaas and Coalter. *Leisure Sciences, 19*, 285–289.

Clark, G., Oliver, T., Ilbery, B., Chabrel, M., Bousset, J., Skuras, D., Tesitel, J., Marsat, J., Petrou, A., Fiallo-Pantziou, E., Kusová, D., Bartos, M., Cawley, M., Gillmor, D. A., Pantziou, E. F., Dimara, E., Saxena, G., & Kneafsey, M. (2007). Rural tourism in Europe. *Tourism Geographies, 9*, 345–468

Coalter, F (1997). Leisure sciences and leisure studies: Different concept, same crisis? *Leisure Sciences, 19,* 255–268.

Coalter, F. (2013). *Sport for development: What game are we playing?* Oxfordshire, UK: Taylor & Francis Group.

European Commission. (2007a). *White paper on a strategy for Europe on nutrition, overweight and obesity related health issues.* Brussels: Commission of the European Communities.

European Commission. (2007b). *White paper on sport.* Brussels: Commission of the European Communities.

Favell, A. (2011). *Eurostars and Eurocities: Free movement and mobility in an integrating Europe* (Vol. 56). Chichester, UK: John Wiley & Sons.

Fox, K. (2006). Leisure and indigenous peoples. *Leisure Studies, 25,* 403–409.

Fullagar, S. (2002). Narratives of travel: desire and the movement of feminine subjectivity. *Leisure Studies, 21,* 57–74.

García, I., Molina, J. A., & Navarro, M. (2007). How satisfied are spouses with their leisure time? Evidence from Europe. *Journal of Family and Economic Issues, 28,* 546–565.

Green, M. & Oakley, B. (2001). Elite sport development systems and playing to win: uniformity and diversity in international approaches. *Leisure Studies, 20,* 247–267.

Gronow, J., & Southerton, D. (2010). Leisure and consumption in Europe. In S. Immerfall & G. Therborn (Eds.), *Handbook of European societies: Social transformations in the 21st century* (pp. 355–384). New York: Springer.

Hall, D. R., Smith, M. K. & Marciszewska, B. (2006). *Tourism in the new Europe: The challenges and opportunities of EU enlargement.* Wallingford, UK: CABI.

Henderson, K. A. (2006). False dichotomies and leisure research. *Leisure Studies, 25,* 391–395.

Henry, I. (2007). (Ed.). *Transnational and comparative research in sport: Globalisation, governance and sport policy* (Vol. 35). London: Routledge.

Hovemann, G., & Wicker, P. (2009). Determinants of sport participation in the European Union. *European Journal for Sport and Society, 6*(1), 51–59.

Jordan, F. & Aitchison, C. (2008). Tourism and the sexualisation of the gaze: Solo female tourists' experiences of gendered power, surveillance and embodiment, *Leisure Studies, 27,* 329–349.

Katz-Gerro, T. (2011). Cross-national cultural consumption research: Inspirations and disillusions. *Kölner Zeitschrift für Soziologie und Sozialpsychologie, 51,* 339–360.

Mäkinen, T. E., Sippola, R., Borodulin, K., Rahkonen, O., Kunst, A., Klumbiene, J. & Prättälä, R. (2012). Explaining educational differences in leisure-time physical activity in Europe: The contribution of work-related factors. *Scandinavian Journal of Medicine & Science in Sports, 22,* 439–447.

McCabe, S., Minnaert, L. & Diekmann, A. (2012). (Eds.). *Social tourism in Europe: Theory and practice.* Bristol, UK: Channel View.

Mommaas, H. (1997). European leisure studies at the crossroads? A history of leisure research in Europe. *Leisure Sciences, 19,* 241–254.

Palmer, C. (2012). *Global sports policy.* London: Sage.

Petit, S. & Nowak, J. (2012). Intra-tourism trade in Europe. *Tourism Economics, 18,* 1287–1311.

Reisinger, Y. (2013). *Transformational tourism: Tourist perspectives.* Wallingford, UK: CABI.

Roberts, K. (2010). Is leisure studies "ethnocentric"? If so, does this matter? *World Leisure Journal, 52*(3), 164–176.

Thomas, R. & Augustyn, M. (2007). (Eds.). *Tourism in the new Europe: Perspectives on SME policies and practices.* Oxford, UK: Elsevier.

Van Bottenburg, M., Rijnen, B., & Van Sterkenburg, J. (2005). *Sports participation in the European Union: Trends and differences.* Nieuwegein, Netherlands: W. J. H. Mulier Institute and Arko Sports Media.

van Hek, M., & Kraaykamp, G. (2013). Cultural consumption across countries: A multi-level analysis of social inequality in highbrow culture in Europe. *Poetics, 41,* 323–341.

van Tuyckom, C., Bracke, P., & Scheerder, J. (2011). Sports-idrott-esporte-deporte–sportovní-: The problem of equivalence of meaning in comparative sports research. *European Journal for Sport and Society, 8*(1/2), 85–97.

van Tuyckom, C., & Scheerder, J. (2010). Sport for All? Insight into stratification and compensation mechanisms of sporting activity in the 27 European Union member states. *Sport, Education and Society, 15,* 495–512.

van Tuyckom, C., Van de Velde, S., & Bracke, P. (2013). Does country-context matter? A cross-national analysis of gender and leisure time physical inactivity in Europe. *The European Journal of Public Health, 23*(3), 452–457.

Veal, A. (2010). *Leisure, sport and tourism: Politics, policy and planning.* Wallingford, UK: CABI.

Warren, T. (2010). Work time. Leisure time. On women's temporal and economic well-being in Europe. *Community, Work & Family, 13*(4), 365–392.

Wearing, B. (1998). *Leisure and feminist theory.* London: Sage.

Zampoukos, K., & Ioannides, D. (2011). The tourism labour conundrum: Agenda for new research in the geography of hospitality workers. *Hospitality & Society, 1*(1), 25–45.

16
Leisure in Latin America

Alcyane Marinho (Santa Catarina State University, Brazil)
and Arianne C. Reis (Southern Cross University, Australia)

Latin American countries have common characteristics that distinguish them from other continental groups around the world; however, they also possess unique cultural, historical, economic, social, political, ethnic, and environmental issues and features that differentiate them from each other (Galeano, 2009; Gallini, 2009; Gomes, Osorio, Pinto, & Elizalde, 2009). As such, they also have distinctive patterns of leisure practices and traditions that can only be discussed as a group for analytical purposes in order to provide a general overview of how they compare to other major cultures of the world. The purpose of this chapter is to provide such an overview.

Latin America includes the sovereign and non-sovereign states located in South, Central, and North America (Mexico), where the Romanic languages (mostly Spanish, Portuguese, and French) are officially spoken. The term "Latin America" originated in the nineteenth century under the political influence of France and the United States, and has endured as nations achieved independence from their colonizers (Bruit, 2000; Gomes & Elizalde, 2012). Indeed, the term is now well-established and adopted by national and international institutions across the globe, despite its cultural, social, and even geographic inaccuracy.

From Mexico to Argentina the region was mostly colonized by Portugal and Spain during the sixteenth and seventeenth centuries, their influence culminating in the so-called "Latin" culture recognized today. However, what is now perceived as the "Latin American culture" also has important roots, and is still influenced by, the indigenous cultures of the region, the significant presence of African slaves and their post-slavery settlement, and waves of European and Asian migration in the late nineteenth and early twentieth centuries (Bruit, 2000).

In the nineteenth century a process of emancipation took place in the region, with most countries establishing their independence. In the 1990s another significant change occurred, with most countries in the region returning from the dictatorial, military-based regimes that predominated in the twentieth century to more democratic ones. With this, human rights issues became significant points in the region's agenda, and a better integration between Latin American countries and the rest of the world developed (Bruit, 2000; Gomes & Elizalde, 2012). However, as with most formerly colonized regions around the world, Latin American nations continue to face major problems such as struggle for economic independence and social welfare.

It is against this backdrop that we present an overview of leisure matters in Latin America based on a literature review. First, however, it is useful to provide some background related to the theoretical influences on leisure studies in the region.

LEISURE THEORY IN LATIN AMERICA

Dumazedier (1979) has been an influential leisure scholar in countries across this region, and in particular in Brazil. He described a system of constituent characteristics of leisure, composed of a: (a) *discharge character*, meaning that leisure is immune from professional, family, social, spiritual, and political obligations/affiliations, therefore being a result of free choice; (b) *disinterested character*, meaning that leisure is not subjected to a particular end, such as profit or professional development; (c) *hedonistic character*, or the search for a state of satisfaction (pleasure, happiness, enjoyment); and (d) *personal character*, referring to the functions of leisure (e.g., rest, fun, and social and personal development) that meet the needs of individuals arising from obligations imposed by society.

Based on these features, Dumazedier (1979) described leisure as a set of occupations that individuals willingly engage in to relax, have fun, to voluntarily participate in social activities or to develop their creative potential, after being freed from professional, family, and social obligations. Despite the importance of this framework to the development of leisure studies in Latin America, it has been the target of much critique referring mainly to the restriction of the leisure phenomenon to the practice of particular leisure activities, and its opposition to the needs and obligations of everyday life, especially professional work. Gomes (2004) emphasized that work and leisure, despite having distinct features, are part of the same social dynamics and establish dialectical relationships. Thus, one must consider the dynamics of these phenomena, including the interrelationships and contradictions they share. In this way, work and leisure are not polar opposites, considering that there are not always absolute boundaries between these dimensions in everyday life.

Marcellino (1983), another influential leisure scholar in Latin America, defined leisure as culture in its broadest sense, practiced during an "available" time, having the disinterested character as the defining trait of this experience. Redefining leisure as culture, Marcellino presented a possibility to overcome the understanding of leisure as a mere set of occupations. However, his framework is nonetheless influenced by Dumazedier's (1979) work, especially the disinterested character, and the hedonistic and free nature of leisure.

Marcellino (1990) has further advanced his conceptualization of leisure regarding it as a privileged vehicle for education (education *through* leisure), therefore considering its potential to develop individuals socially and personally. He also highlighted the need for learning, encouragement, and initiation into the cultural components of leisure experiences (education *for* leisure). By doing so, such an approach suggests a double aspect for leisure education: one that uses leisure to teach values and content (i.e., education *through* leisure), and another that educates individuals about the interfaces between leisure and culture (i.e., education *for* leisure), making it possible to reach more complex modes of engagement in critical and creative ways.

By highlighting the cultural aspects of leisure, Marcellino (1983) served as a reference for other Latin American authors who also developed their own conceptions of leisure from a cultural framework, such as Melo and Alves Júnior (2003), and Gomes (2004). According to Gomes (2004), leisure can be considered a dimension of culture, constituted by the playful experience of cultural traditions in a time/space acquired by the individual or social group, and establishing dialectical relations with the needs, duties, and obligations of everyday life, particularly with productive work. This understanding of leisure has become particularly strong among Latin American scholars, with the recent work of Gomes et al. (2009) being of special significance.

With this context and the gaps commonly found between theoretical conceptualizations of a phenomenon and the performance of such a phenomenon in academic and daily life in mind, we will now explore some of the most discussed, and arguably the most significant, themes in leisure studies and practice in Latin America. First, however, we provide a brief description of the methodological process used to identify such themes.

METHODOLOGY

The analysis presented in this chapter is based on a thorough review of the literature included in the electronic academic database *Literatura Latino-Americana e do Caribe em Ciências da Saúde* (Latin American and Caribbean Health Sciences Literature or LILACS). A search was performed for full-text articles published between 2008 and 2012 using the title keywords "leisure," "recreation" and "free time" in Portuguese and Spanish (i.e., "lazer," "ócio," "ocio," "recreação," "recreación," "tempo livre" and "tiempo libre"). For each keyword used, an Excel spreadsheet was created containing the title, abstract, language, year of publication, and a reference to the full text. The researchers conducted an analysis of all texts included in the final list and identified five main themes for discussion: Leisure and Health, Public Policy and Leisure, Leisure and Sports, Leisure and the Environment, and Leisure and Physical Education.

It is important to note that the search was conducted in March 2013; therefore, this chapter does not include new publications available in the LILACS database after this period. In addition, the authors and works referenced herein do not represent the totality of works in the leisure studies field in Latin America, but only a portion of the existing academic material on the topic. Identifying the state-of-the-art scientific studies that address leisure in this region would be an endless task and one that is beyond the scope of this chapter. Our aim is solely to raise the main issues regarding leisure and leisure practices in Latin America from the perspective of those who investigate and publish in this field in this region.

RESULTS AND DISCUSSION

In total, 109 articles were selected, with only 14 of them not arising from Brazilian scholars and institutions. This finding emphasizes the growing political and economic strength of Brazil in the region and internationally and, as a consequence, the growth in importance, and therefore funding, of scientific production in Brazil. This is not to say that more academic research is conducted in Brazil than in any other Latin American country, but only that the current economic conditions in Brazil have been conducive for more scientific production and publication in the field of leisure studies.

This finding also means that some bias towards issues of significance to the Brazilian context will be inevitable in the analysis that follows. In order to reduce such a problem, our discussions concentrate on matters that have been raised as being of relevance region-wide in other

Latin American academic fora, such as conferences, seminars, and books to which the authors have either contributed to, or participated in, over the past 10 years.

Table 16.1 presents a summary of the articles included in the analysis by year of publication, theme and keywords used in the search. As can be seen from the data presented in Table 16.1, Leisure and Health was the most prevalent theme found in the review (56 articles), an expected result due to the nature of the database selected—one that focuses mainly on the health sciences. While this limitation is recognized, the selection of the database is justified by its significance in Latin America, its size (i.e., the largest database to focus on Latin American research), and the fact that, albeit focusing mostly on the health sciences, the database also includes publications from the social sciences.

Leisure and Health

The articles under this theme investigated primarily the importance and health benefits of leisure-time physical activity, and approached the topic using a medical lens. In particular, the focus on prevention and treatment of diseases was apparent. In addition, a general concern regarding increasing physical inactivity was highlighted and associated with sociodemographic, economic, and cultural factors (Azevedo, Horta, Gigante, Victora, & Barros, 2008; Martini & Barbisan, 2010; Martins, Assis, Nahas, Gauche, & Moura, 2009; Rocha, Almeida, Araújo, & Virtuoso, 2011). In this sense, it seems that Latin America is not unlike countries of the developed North, where similar patterns of physical inactivity have been reported (cf. Dumith, Hallal, Reis, & Kohl, 2011). What may be different are the cultural and social contingencies that produce such habits and trends. For instance, Abramovay, Castro, Pinheiro, Lima, and Martinelli (2002) discussed how youth in low-income communities across Latin America have limited opportunities for engaging in leisure activities and live in neighborhoods where there is an evident lack of available leisure spaces. Apart from the insufficient number of facilities for social and cultural activities, it was also reported to be a clear disparity in the quality and quantity of what is available between low-income communities and middle-class neighborhoods of most Latin American cities. In this context, soccer is one of the few leisure options available to youth in these poorer communities (Castro, Abramovey, Rua, & Andrade, 2001).

Articles included in this theme also dealt with more topical issues, such as the relationship between aging and quality of life, social participation, motivation, and leisure practice (Cabeza, 2009; Campagna & Schwartz, 2010; Debortoli, 2012; d'Orsi, Xavier, & Ramos, 2011), or addressed health issues related to youth, low-income communities, and idleness, to name but a few (Alberti, Costa, & Moreira, 2011; Andrade & Marcellino, 2011; Lacerda, Gonçalves, Zocoli, Diaz, & Paula, 2011; Marchese, Vilela, & Machado, 2011).

A common finding of studies in the Leisure and Health theme was that men are more engaged in leisure-time physical activity than women, as are those with higher levels of formal education and of higher socioeconomic status (Azevedo et al., 2008, Martins et al., 2009; Rocha et al., 2011). Again, these findings mirror patterns described in the global North (e.g., Canada, Japan, Europe, and the United States; cf. Eyler et al., 2002).

Table 16.1. Number of Articles According to Year of Publication, Theme, and Keywords Used in the Search

Year	Articles	Leisure & Health				Public Policy & Leisure				Leisure & Sports				Leisure & the Environment				Leisure & Physical Education			
Keywords		L	O	R	T	L	O	R	T	L	O	R	T	L	O	R	T	L	O	R	T
2012	25	8	-	-	-	9	-	-	-	4	-	-	-	2	-	-	-	2	-	-	-
2011	37	19	1	-	5	9	-	-	-	1	-	-	-	2	-	-	-	3	-	-	-
2010	16	6	-	-	2	5	-	-	-	-	-	-	2	1	-	-	-	-	-	3	-
2009	16	5	-	-	2	3	-	-	-	2	-	-	-	3	-	-	-	1	-	-	-
2008	6	2	1	-	5	1	-	-	-	-	-	-	-	-	-	-	-	-	-	-	-
TOTAL	109	40	2	0	14	27	0	0	0	7	0	0	2	8	0	0	0	6	0	3	0

L = lazer; O = ócio e ocio; R = recreação e recreación; T = tempo livre e tiempo libre

Studies focusing on the aging population identified walking as the most reported leisure-time physical activity and tended to reflect upon constraints to accessing other forms of active leisure (Krug et al., 2011; Maciel & Veiga, 2012; Santos, Forini, & Chaves, 2009). Sociocultural barriers to accessing leisure have been described as the aspects that may hinder individuals from diversifying their leisure-time activities, such as economic factors, social class, level of education, access to urban spaces, violence, age, gender, and ethnicity (Marcellino, 2012).

In our review, gender was also identified as a key issue, with men reportedly practicing more collective and competitive physical leisure activities, and women engaging in activities that are of an individual and less intense nature (Del Duca, Oliveira, Sousa, Silva, & Nahas, 2011; Sá Silva, Sandre-Pereira, & Salles-Costa, 2011). Studies on children (Lima & Starepravo, 2010; Silva Júnior, 2012) highlighted similar issues: boys tend to be involved in physically active leisure practices; whereas girls are more interested in or encouraged to engage in passive leisure activities, such as listening to music or watching TV. A social explanation raised by the authors for such a phenomenon is that boys in Latin American countries are often encouraged to practice sports from an early age, while girls are encouraged to play indoors, focusing on artistic and manual activities as a way of preparing them for the housework that they will possibly be responsible for in the future. Although similar patterns can be found in developed nations in the global North, it seems that this sociocultural structure is more acute in Latin American countries than in their northern counterparts.

An interesting finding of our analysis of the material included in this theme is that in most studies there is a tendency to consider leisure as simply the time when one can practice (or not) physical activity. Generally, leisure is not directly addressed, but only superficially mentioned, without applying a theoretical framework specific to the area and therefore not allowing for greater depth in the discussions.

The lack of a theoretical framework to study leisure was evident in the different uses and applications of the term when associated with physical activity: "leisure-time physical activity," "physical activity during leisure time," and "physical activity in the context of leisure" (Brasileiro, Machado, Matias, & Santos, 2011; Inácio, Salvador, & Florindo, 2011; Rocha et al., 2011; Salvador, Florindo, Reis, & Costa, 2009). These terms also tended to always be in opposition to the time of productive work. Although, as we discussed previously, this opposition between leisure and work is one of the possibilities of understanding leisure, in most studies this and other theoretical approaches were not mentioned.

Although there may be certain specificities and conceptual-theoretical preferences in the studies described under this theme which do not necessarily encompass the more "accepted" or "utilized" frameworks of leisure theory, it is nonetheless important to note the existence of a reductionist view of the leisure concept, linked mostly to the absence of disease and to experiences that are directly associated with the production and/or promotion of health. According to Carvalho (2005), more profound discussions about leisure are not present in the field of public health (which includes preventive medicine and epidemiology). Here lies an important problem faced by most Latin American countries: leisure is not commonly understood as a social need and right of all citizens. Carvalho (2005) pointed out that the concept of public health incorporates knowledge and perspectives from the humanities, and should therefore include professionals who work in the leisure field. In turn, leisure professionals should understand the pedagogical nature of their intervention, considering cultural, historical, economic, and political factors as significant issues in and of leisure practices. Leisure professionals should also highlight the elements of the physical (bodily) culture as human manifestations and expressions with historicity and meaning in order to serve as a counterpoint to the strict view of a biological body.

In general, however, there is a concern from scholars in this area surrounding the need to highlight the many problems associated with the lack of access to basic health care experienced in Latin American countries. In this vein, some studies under this theme highlighted issues associated with public policies in health care, especially when a positive relationship was found between physical activity and health, or when disturbing data on the prevalence of physical inactivity in different contexts and population groups were evident (Batista, Ribeiro, & Nunes, 2012; Pitanga & Lessa, 2009; Rocha et al., 2011; Zaitune et al., 2010). We now turn our attention to the theme of Public Policy and Leisure.

Public Policy and Leisure

The articles included in this theme critique important issues related to public policy and leisure. They are focused on topics such as the disparities between access to leisure in metropolitan and rural areas, addressing factors such as: urbanization, land speculation, and the growth of metropolitan regions; the absence of effective public policies that take into account different age groups; through to issues involving social policy and class struggles. Some articles also denounced the lack of qualified human resources in the planning and management of public policy, highlighting the need for community participation in decision making, co-management, and sharing responsibility for the use of public spaces and for the different projects and programs (Areias & Borges, 2011; Sawitzki, 2012; Silva & Nunes, 2009; Sousa, Vilela, & Tolocka, 2012).

Along with the demands for quality public policies there was an emphasis on ensuring that it is both safe and viable for individuals from all different socioeconomic classes to engage in leisure activities outside the home, in public spaces, and facilities across the city. The increasing population growth experienced by Latin American cities and the consequences associated with such growth, such as violence and traffic, contribute to leisure practices being more geared to the domestic context (Silva & Nunes, 2009; Sousa et al., 2010).

Another common trend found in the studies within this theme was the discussion surrounding training and professional practice. Frequent mentions of "education for leisure," as developed by Marcellino (1990) and mentioned above, were presented as a potential solution for some existing deadlocks. For these authors, education for leisure should be advocated for and implemented by government organizations through the co-management of public spaces. Melo (2006) called this process "Cultural Animation," composed from the Greek word "anima," meaning soul. According to this perspective, leisure is a fertile opportunity to discuss values and norms, as well as to stimulate critical thinking about the reality. Education should then be directed to understanding the multiple leisure options that people can engage in, developed in the form of a long learning process of persuasion and mediation, in tune with cultural knowledge.

Another important discussion raised in the articles within this theme referred to the need for public policies that contemplate stages of planning, monitoring, and evaluation. In this way, projects or programs promoted by management agencies will be envisioned not only as a means of defining targets and monitoring calendars and cash flow, but also as important tools for improving the decision-making process in management. It is important to verify, as pointed out by Zingoni (2007) and Machado (2012), not only if resources are being used efficiently, but more importantly, if actions and results have contributed to a positive change.

In summary, the articles investigated in this theme demonstrate the importance given to democratic and inclusive public policies to ensure people's right to leisure. Furthermore, the studies reported the problems associated with the absence of sequential planning and delivery of leisure projects and programs, highlighting weaknesses in the implementation of public policies. In this sense, sport, together with leisure, was commonly addressed in the articles studied, with similar issues being raised.

Sport and Leisure

As with the Leisure and Health theme, the approach to leisure in articles within the Sport and Leisure theme referred to a particular "time" for the practice of sports, particularly football (Lages & Silva, 2012; Pizani, Amaral, & Paes, 2012). Apart from some studies challenging this limited view (which prevent other forms of leisure manifesting as an end in themselves), other important issues were identified within this literature.

It is clear that sport plays an important role in human life and there seems to be an agreement among Latin American scholars that it should be understood as a cultural manifestation which is performed in different contexts, such as in clubs, sport organizations, businesses, churches, nursing homes, schools, gyms, and prisons. Sport can be formally or informally organized, and presented in myriad ways in the media. In economic terms, Melo (2004) pointed out that, currently, sport is touted as one of the greatest business products in Latin America, and that the growing professionalization of its management has been able to move dreams, spread ideas, and standardize behaviors and attitudes.

Sport has influenced the history of different nations and the relationships established between them, and such a phenomenon is evident also in Latin America. At the same time, most of the studies analyzed here critically discussed—directly or indirectly—the valorization of sport for its economic potential, as a marketing product, and as a tool of political propaganda. Such valorization has led, according to Ramos and Isayama (2009), to an overemphasis on high-performance sport at the expense of its other forms. In addition, there is a functionalist view of leisure sports which does not value the practice in itself, instead viewing it only as a means to regain the energy to work or to identify and promote high-performance athletes.

Physical Education and Leisure

Among the various knowledge areas that are concerned with leisure practices, physical education has occupied an increasingly significant position among the various research groups based in Latin America (Gomes et al., 2009). Leisure practices and activities are a significant part of interventions in physical education, directly influencing the choices, training, and professional experience of those who work in the physical education field. Considering the sociocultural context of several Latin American countries and their historical and political developments, it is possible to infer that issues related to school- and non-school-based education, scientific production, the labor market, cultural diversity, and health and public policy all work dynamically to build relationships between leisure and physical education. Thus, the material analyzed within this theme pointed to the need to recognize leisure, in the context of physical education, as also being a tool in the building of one's personality and education, and in the development of children, adolescents, adults, and the elderly.

According to Marcellino (2001), physical education, in conjunction with other areas of the curriculum, must demonstrate through its pedagogical practice the importance of leisure in society as a form of human expression. Furthermore, physical education classes should introduce the cultural content of physical activity and sports practices to students in a way that not only creates individuals who actively engage in physical activity and sports but also who enjoy these activities as passive participants. Through such pedagogical practices the student should then be able to realize the inter-relationship that exists between leisure and sports and other cultural expressions of their society. Significantly, in order to achieve such aims, teaching methodologies in physical education should incorporate the ludic as an essential part of the educational process (Marcellino, 2001).

Marinho and Inácio (2007) provided another interesting example of how physical education classes can act to develop more holistic aspects of education. According to these authors, physical education classes in outdoor environments can, apart from developing motor skills and physical abilities, stimulate reflection about environmental issues. The authors argued that outdoor adventure activities, in particular, are excellent ways for developing cognitive, affective, and psychomotor skills while at the same time fostering valuable opportunities for behavior change in regards to care for the environment. In sum, similarly to the previous theme, under this theme the studies identified leisure opportunities within physical education classes as a fertile tool to experiment with situations that can develop curiosity, interest, creativity, and critical thinking.

Environment

The interest in environmental issues among leisure scholars in Latin America was not surprising. Although the relationship between industry and science has contributed to scientific progress and growth in personal mobility, industrial production, and the expansion of human settlements in cities in recent decades, it has also aggravated a number of harmful environmental effects, and led to significant changes in social relations, and in the political, economic, and educational milieus across the region (Dias, 2011).

In this context, a trend against economic rationality was apparent within the work of a number of authors, in what seems to be an attempt to exalt a sociability based on an environmental ethic as an alternative way of surviving in the modern times (Armas & Inácio, 2010; Gomes & Isayama, 2009). There was also a clear consensus about the characteristics governing industrial society and modernity, one which presents a different kind of sensitivity towards nature. Some of these characteristics relate to the unequal and unjust forms of appropriation, excessive consumerism, unequal capital distribution, and also the superficial relationships established between society and nature in modern and postmodern times. These discussions are part of the historical construction of the environmental movement itself that absorbed different ways of thinking about nature and human relations.

Although the focus was not on leisure *per se*, an interesting study by González-Gaudiano and Lorenzetti (2009) highlighted that research in environmental education in Latin America is still an unexplored field. The few initiatives that do exist, mainly originating from Mexico and Brazil, attempt to promote educational research in the area at the institutional level. In other Latin American countries, a few (and institutionally isolated) researchers have led individual and small projects commonly under precarious conditions. Nonetheless, González-Gaudiano and Lorenzetti argued that there is an increasing, albeit slow, growth trend in this field of research in Latin America, and stressed that there is significant potential for environmental education to be included in both formal and non-formal education systems.

THE ROAD AHEAD

From our review of leisure-related topics being investigated by Latin American scholars, two issues seem to cut across different areas and approaches to leisure, and deserve more systematic and integrated research: aging and vocational/professional training.

Population aging has attracted the interest of researchers from public and private agencies particularly due to the significant increase in the number of older adults observed in different countries of Latin America in recent years. In this perspective, attention has been given to the need for new initiatives which meet the requirements and demands of increasingly aging societies, including the possibilities of active participation by the elderly in social life, especially through leisure experiences (cf. Benedetti, Mazo, & Borges, 2012; Oliveira & Queiroz, 2012).

Vocational and professional training came to prominence in Latin America in the 1990s. In this region, it is usually the physical education professional who leads leisure, recreation, and sport activities in the labor market. Recent changes in tertiary education and vocational training for these professionals can be noticed in the evolution of the elements that constitute the concept of "physical education" itself, especially as it concerns target customers/students/markets, the organizations that offer physical education "services," and the learning content associated with physical education. The preparation/education of professionals in this area in Latin America has been characterized by the diversity of training interventions in higher education, suggesting a lack of a general model to qualify the future professionals to perform well and attend the demand for increasingly specialized activities (e.g., outdoor activities, high-performance sports). In this sense, it is increasingly noted in the literature the requirements imposed by the market to "professionalize" all "services" and activities which fit the leisure, recreation, and/or sports realms. The question that remains is how much should education and training be guided by market imperatives.

More broadly, it is noteworthy the absence in the literature, or at least the less prominence, of some acute problems faced by Latin American communities and their interface with leisure. We may have expected the relationships between leisure and social issues such as poverty, conflict, inequality, and exclusion (social, cultural, physical, economic, environmental), to be a priority of researchers who live within this social context (for some exceptions, please see Andrade, & Marcellino, 2011; Peres, Bodstein, Ramos, & Marcondes, 2005; Reis, Sousa-Mast, & Vieira, 2013; Santos, 2010). In this sense, following Gomes and Elizalde (2012), it seems that Latin American scholars, as well as their societies, have too rapidly embraced Euro and North American-centric discourses and approaches to the study of leisure, leaving behind a gamut of leisure practices that do not conform with, or are not available within, colonial ideals. Again, it seems imperative to change this scenario and invest in critical leisure studies; studies which analyze and discuss, for instance, the colonial vestiges of leisure practices and policies in Latin America or the leisure practices and influences of the various ethnic and cultural groups that comprise Latin American communities, particularly those of marginalized status (e.g. Afro-descendants, local Indians, European war immigrants). It is a challenge that we hope will be taken up more broadly and consistently among Latin American scholars in years to come.

CONCLUSION

In an attempt to provide a general overview of the most discussed and relevant themes in leisure studies and practices in Latin America, this chapter reviewed over 100 articles published in the field over five years in this region. The five major themes identified were linked to health issues, public policy, physical education, sport, and the environment. Although contributions emanating from Brazilian scholars were by far the most predominant in the search performed, researchers from Argentina, Chile, Colombia and Peru, in particular, also published a number of studies in the field of leisure practices and experiences in journals indexed by the Latin American and Caribbean Health Sciences Literature database (LILACS). Specifically, Peruvian and Argentinian scholars showed a more pronounced interest in issues related to leisure in physical education classes, while Chile was better represented under the leisure and health theme.

In regard to the general content of these studies, much of the discussions and also, more importantly, the everyday practices described, still seem to reduce leisure to a space in time. They often ignore the importance of leisure as a social right, as a possibility for cultural production, community involvement, and social transformation, and the benefits acknowledged by and sometimes advocated for among Latin American leisure theorists. In this sense we concur with Gomes (2011) that it is necessary to expand our knowledge about the diversity of perspectives and realities of leisure studies and practices in different Latin American countries, considering the relationships between leisure and other dimensions of social life.

More than defining the various terms used in different countries to classify and describe leisure practices, it is necessary to understand the meanings that have historically been built around each of these expressions. This is particularly relevant because they are all commonly, and often interchangeably, used in society and academic literature, but also because, as Debortoli (2012) aptly argued, each term hides and reveals identities and forms of visibility, as well as conditioning concepts and biases, leading to not only an awareness of limitations but also of possibilities.

REFERENCES

Abramovay, M., Castro, M. G., Pinheiro, L.C., Lima, FS., & Martinelli, C.C. (2002). *Juventude, violência e vulnerabilidade social na América Latina: Desafios para políticas públicas*. Brasília: Edições UNESCO BRASIL.

Alberti, S., Costa, A. C., & Moreira, J. de O. (2011). Oficina do ócio: Um convite para o sujeito. *Revista Latinoamericana de Psicopatololia Fundamental, 14*(3), 499–512.

Andrade, C. P. de, & Marcellino, N. C. (2011). O lazer, a periferia da metrópole e os jovens: Algumas relações. *Licere, 14*(2), 1–17.

Areias, K. T. V., & Borges, C. N. F. (2011). As políticas públicas de lazer na mediação entre estado e sociedade: Possibilidades e limitações. *Revista Brasileira de Ciências do Esporte, 33*(3), 573–588.

Armas, C. S., & Inácio, H. L. D. (2010). Seres humanos e natureza: O lazer como mediação. *Licere, 13*(2), 1–29.

Azevedo, M. R., Horta, B. L., Gigante, D. P., Victora, C. G., & Barros, F. C. (2008). Fatores associados ao sedentarismo no lazer de adultos na coorte de nascimentos de 1982, Pelotas, RS. *Revista de Saúde Pública, 42*(supl.2), 70–77.

Batista, J. C., Ribeiro, O. C. F., & Nunes Jr., P. C. (2012). Lazer e saúde: Uma aproximação conveniente. *Licere, 15*(2), 1–16.

Benedetti, T. R. B., Mazo, G. Z., & Borges, J. J. (2012). Condições de saúde e nível de atividade física em idosos participantes e não participantes de grupos de convivência de Florianópolis. *Ciência & Saúde Coletiva, 17*(8), 2087–2093.

Brasileiro, M. D. S., Machado, A. B., Matias, B. A., & Santos, A. da C. (2011). Do diagnóstico à ação: Uma proposta de lazer ativo e envelhecimento. *Revista Brasileira de Atividade Física e Saúde, 16*(3), 271–274.

Bruit, H. H. (2000). *A invenção da América Latina*. In: Anais Eletrônicos do V Encontro da ANPHLAC. Belo Horizonte, 2000. Disponível em: <http://anphlac.org/upload/anais/encontro5/hector_bruit.pdf> Acesso em: 27/7/2013.

Cabeza, M. C. (2009). Más allá del trabajo: el ocio de los jubilados. *Revista Mal-Estar e Subjetividade, 9*(1), 13–42.

Campagna, J., & Schwartz, G. M. (2010). O conteúdo intelectual do lazer no processo do aprender a envelhecer. *Motriz, 16*(2), 414–424.

Carvalho, Y. M. (2005). *Lazer e saúde*. Brasília: SESI/DN.

Castro, M. G., Abramovay, M., Rua, M. G., & Andrade, E. R. (2001). *Cultivando vida, desarmando violências: Experiências em educação, cultura, lazer, esporte e cidadania com jovens em situação de pobreza*. Brasília: UNESCO, Brasil Telecom, Fundação Kellogg, Banco Interamericano de Desenvolvimento.

Debortoli, J. A. O. (2012). Lazer, envelhecimento e participação social. *Licere, 15*(1), 1–29.

Del Duca, G. F., Oliveira, E. S. A. de., Sousa, T. F. de., Silva, K. S. da., & Nahas, M. V. (2011). Inatividade física no lazer em trabalhadores da indústria do Rio Grande do Sul, Brasil. *Motriz, 17*(1), 180–188.

Dias, C. (2011). Perspectivas históricas para o lazer e a educação na natureza. *Licere, 14*(1), 1–15.

d'Orsi, E., Xavier, A. J., & Ramos, L. R. (2011). Trabalho, suporte social e lazer protegem idosos da perda funcional: Estudo epidoso. *Revista de Saúde Pública, 45*(4), 685–692.

Dumazedier, J. (1979). *Sociologia empírica do lazer*. São Paulo, Brazil: SESC.

Dumith, S. C., Hallal, P.C., Reis, R.S., & Kohl III, H.W. (2011). Worldwide prevalence of physical inactivity and its association with human development index in 76 countries. *Preventive Medicine, 53*, 24–28.

Eyler, A. E., Wilcox, S., Matson-Koffman, D., Evenson, K. R., Sanderson, B., Thompson, J. Wilbur, J., & Rohm-Young, D. (2002). Correlates of physical activity among women from diverse racial/ethnic groups. *Journal of Women's Health and Gender-Based Medicine, 11*(3), 239–253.

Galeano, E. (2009). *As veias abertas da América Latina, (49ª ed.)*. São Paulo: Paz e Terra.

Gallini, S. (2009). Historia, ambiente, política: el camino de la historia ambiental en América Latina. *Nómadas (Col), 1*(30), 92–102.

Gomes, C. L. (Ed.). (2004). *Dicionário crítico do lazer*. Belo Horizonte, Brazil: Autêntica.

Gomes, C. L. (2011). *Mapeamento histórico do lazer na América Latina: Em busca de novas abordagens para os estudos sobre o tema*. In H. F. Isayama & S. R. Silva (Orgs.), Estudos do lazer: Um panorama, (pp. 145–164). Belo Horizonte, Brazil: CELAR/UFMG.

Gomes, C. L., & Elizalde, R. (2012). *Horizontes Latino-Americanos do lazer/horizontes Latinoamericanos del ocio*. Belo Horizonte, Brazil: UFMG.

Gomes, C. L., Osorio, E., Pinto, L., & Elizalde, R. (Eds.). (2009). *Lazer na América Latina/ Tiempo libre, ocio y recreación en Latinoamérica*. Belo Horizonte, Brazil: UFMG.

Gomes, O. C., & Isayama, H. F. (2009). Corridas de aventura e lazer: Um percurso analítico para além das trilhas. *Motriz, 15*(1), 69–78.

González-Gaudiano, E., & Lorenzetti, L. (2009). Investigação em educação ambiental na América Latina: Mapeando tendências. *Educação em Revista, 25*(3), 191–211.

Inácio, R. F., Salvador, E. P., & Florindo, A. A. (2011). Análise descritiva da prática de atividade física no lazer de idosos residentes em uma região de baixo nível socioeconômico da zona leste de São Paulo, SP. *Revista Brasileira de Atividade Física e Saúde, 16*(1), 150–155.

Krug, R. R., Marchesan, M., Conceição, J. C. R., Mazo, G. Z., Antunes, G. A., & Romitti, J. C. (2011). Contribuições da caminhada como atividade física de lazer para idosos. *Licere, 14*(4), 1–29.

Lacerda, A. B. M., Gonçalves, C. G. O., Zocoli, A. M. F., Diaz, C., & Paula, K. (2011). Hábitos auditivos e comportamento de adolescentes diante das atividades de lazer ruidosas. *Revista CEFAC, 13*(2), 322–329.

Lages, C. E. D. M., & Silva, S. R. (2012). Futebol e lazer: Diálogos e aproximações. *Licere, 15*(1), 1–13.

Lima, J. C., & Starepravo, F. A. (2010). Lazer e atividade física: Perfil de escolares de 10 a 15 anos e sua relação com as políticas públicas na cidade de Pinhão-PR. *Licere, 13*(4), 1–20.

Machado, G. V. (2012). *Pedagogia do esporte: Organização, sistematização, aplicação e avaliação de conteúdos esportivos na educação não formal. Master's dissertation*. Faculdade de Educação Física - Universidade Estadual de Campinas, Campinas, Brazil.

Maciel, M. G., & Veiga, R. T. (2012). Intenção de mudança de comportamento em adolescentes para a prática de atividades físicas de lazer. *Revista Brasileira de Educação Física e Esporte, 26*(4), 705–716.

Marcellino, N. C. (1983). *Lazer e humanização*. Campinas, Brazil: Papirus.

Marcellino, N. C. (1990). *Lazer e educação, (2nd ed.)*. Campinas, Brazil: Papirus.

Marcellino, N. C. (2001). *O conceito de lazer nas concepções da Educação Física escolar - o dito e o não dito*. In: Anais do XII Congresso Brasileiro de Ciências do Esporte. Campinas-SP: CBCE, p. 1–9.

Marcellino, N. C. (2012). Possíveis relações entre educação física e lazer. *Corpoconsciência, 16*(1), 2–12.

Marchese, D., Vilela Jr., G. B., & Machado, A. A. (2011). O Lazer como possível espaço/tempo para o consumo de drogas. *Licere, 14*(4), 1–22.

Marinho, A., & Inácio, H. L. D. (2007). Educação física, meio ambiente e aventura: Um percurso por vias instigantes. *Revista Brasileira de Ciências do Esporte, 28*, 55–70.

Martini, M. R., & Barbisan, J. N. (2010). Influência da atividade física no tempo livre em pacientes no seguimento de até dois anos após CRM. *Revista Brasileira de Cirurgia Cardiovascular, 25*(3), 359–364.

Martins, T. G., Assis, M. A. A., Nahas, M. V., Gauche, H., & Moura, E. C. (2009). Inatividade física no lazer de adultos e fatores associados. *Revista de Saúde Pública, 43*(5), 814–824.

Melo, V. A. (2004). Los primeros tiempos del deporte en la ciudad de Rio de Janeiro. *Cultura, Ciencia y Deporte, 1*(1), 7–13.

Melo, V. A. (2006). *A animação cultural: Conceitos e propostas*. Campinas, Brazil: Papirus.

Melo, V. A., & Alves Jr., E. D. (2003). *Introdução ao lazer*. Barueri: Manole.

Oliveira, M. Q., & Queiroz, M. B. (2012). O "olhar" da pessoa idosa acerca da participação em grupos de convivência: contribuindo para a melhoria da qualidade de vida? *Revista Portal de Divulgação, 19*, 31–40.

Peres, F. F., Bodstein, R., Ramos, C. L., & Marcondes, W. B. (2005). Lazer, esporte e cultura na agenda local: A experiência de promoção da saúde em Manguinhos. *Ciência & Saúde Coletiva, 10*(3), 757–769.

Pitanga, F. J. G., & Lessa, I. (2009). Associação entre atividade física no tempo livre e proteína C reativa em adultos na cidade de Salvador, Brasil. *Arquivos Brasileiros de Cardiologia, 92*(4), 302–306.

Pizani, R. S., Amaral, S. C. F., & Paes, R. R. (2012). Esporte e lazer: Diálogos possíveis à luz da pedagogia do esporte. *Licere, 15*(3), 1–18.

Ramos, R., & Isayama, H. F. (2009). Lazer e esporte: Olhar dos professores de disciplinas esportivas do curso de educação física. *Revista Brasileira de Educação Física e Esporte, 23*(4), 379–391.

Reis, A. C., Sousa-Mast, F. R., & Vieira, M. C. (2013). Public policies and sports in marginalised communities: The case of Cidade de Deus, Rio de Janeiro, Brazil. *World Leisure Journal, 55*(3), 229–251.

Rocha, S. V., Almeida, M. M. G., Araújo, T. M., & Virtuoso Júnior, J. S. (2011). Fatores associados à atividade física no lazer entre residentes de áreas urbanas de um município do nordeste do Brasil. *Revista Brasileira de Cineantropometria e Desempenho Humano, 13*(4), 257–264.

Sá Silva, S. P., Sandre-Pereira, G., & Salles-Costa, R. (2011). Fatores sociodemográficos e atividade física de lazer entre homens e mulheres de Duque de Caxias/RJ. *Ciência & Saúde Coletiva, 16*(11), 4491–4501.

Salvador, E. P., Florindo, A. A., Reis, R. S., & Costa, E. F. (2009). Percepção do ambiente e prática de atividade física no lazer entre idosos. *Revista de Salud Pública, 43*(6), 972–980.

Santos, E. S. (2010). Experimentando as juventudes num bairro segregado. *Licere, 13*(1), 1–25.

Santos, P. L., Foroni, P. M., & Chaves, M. C. F. (2009). Atividades físicas e de lazer e seu impacto sobre a cognição no envelhecimento. *Medicina, 42*(1), 54–60.

Sawitzki, R. L. (2012). Políticas públicas para esporte e lazer: Para além do calendário de eventos esportivos. *Licere, 15*(1), 1–16.

Silva Jr., V. P. (2012). O lazer de interesse físico/esportivo no cotidiano infantil e sua interface com a saúde. *Licere, 15*(1), 1–20.

Silva Jr., V. P., & Nunes, P. R. M. (2009). Parques públicos de lazer de interesse físico/esportivo, animação sociocultural e população atendida. *Licere, 12*(2), 1–18.

Sousa Jr., J. G., Vilela Jr., G. de B., & Tolocka, R. E. (2010). Mudanças ocorridas na cidade de Uberaba-MG e suas possíveis influências no lazer infantil. *Licere, 13*(3), 1–21.

Zaitune, M. P. A., Barros, M. B. A., César, C. L. G., Carandina, L., Goldbaum, M., & Alves, M. C. G. P. (2010). Fatores associados à prática de atividade física global e de lazer em idosos: inquérito de saúde no estado de São Paulo (ISA-SP), Brazil. *Caderno de Saúde Pública, 26*(8), 1606–1618.

Zingoni, P. (2007). *Marco lógico: Uma metodologia de elaboração, gestão e avaliação de projeto social de lazer*. In L. M. S. M. Pinto, (Org.), Como fazer projetos de lazer: Elaboração, execução e avaliação (pp. 13–81). Campinas, Brazil: Papirus.

17

Leisure, Needs, and Motivations

Gordon J. Walker (University of Alberta)

Leisure needs and motivations, along with leisure constraints and negotiation strategies, leisure experiences, and leisure satisfaction, have been called the "pillars" that underpin the social psychology of leisure (Walker, Halpenny, Spiers, & Deng, 2011). In the first section of this chapter I describe the different types of needs, how leisure may be an especially important life domain for satisfying certain needs, and how need satisfaction during leisure can potentially be fostered by recreation practitioners and facilitate an enhanced quality of life. In the second section, I describe the different types of motivations and how leisure motives may differ from those in other domains. In the final section, I briefly outline the various frameworks that have been developed that link needs and motivations. Throughout the chapter I also identify what research gaps currently exist and suggest where future research should focus.

NEEDS

Needs are commonly divided into two main categories: physiological and psychological (Kleiber, Walker, & Mannell, 2011).

Physiological Needs

Physiological needs are founded on "tissue deficits" or biochemical imbalances (e.g., thirst, hunger, sleep). In terms of leisure, the most relevant need involves the drive to attain one's desired level of stimulation, or optimal arousal. According to Kleiber et al. (2011):

> If a person is under-aroused, or bored, she or he is more likely to seek out leisure activities or settings that are new, challenging, or maybe even risky (e.g., hiking a new trail, playing at a higher level of difficulty in a computer game, going to a casino). If a person is over-aroused, he or she is more likely to seek out leisure activities or settings that are familiar, relaxing, and predictable (e.g., visiting a nearby park, watching a favorite movie). (p. 133)

In the leisure literature, optimal arousal is increasingly paired with research on affect (e.g., Linzmayer, Halpenny, & Walker, 2013; Mercer & Eastwood, 2010). The proposition that affective experiences involve both arousal (ranging from feeling quiet to active) and valence (ranging from feeling pleasant to unpleasant) dates back over a century (Kuppens, Tuerlinckx, Russell, & Feldman Barnett, 2012). Two contemporary examples of this are Russell's (1980) valence-arousal, and Watson and Tellegen's (1985) positive activation-negative activation, models. In the former case, for example, Russell posited that a person's affective state would be situated in one of four quadrants: (a) high-arousal positive (HAP; e.g., enthusiastic); (b) low-arousal positive (LAP; e.g., calm); (c) low-arousal negative (LAN; e.g., dull); or (d) high-arousal negative (HAN; e.g., fearful).

Tsai (2007) held, however, that it was important to examine people's *ideal* affect (i.e., the affective state a person prefers experiencing), as well as how, when, and why it differed from their *actual* affect (i.e., the affective state a person is currently experiencing). According to Tsai there are four types of ideal affective states: (a) ideal high-arousal positive (i.e., I-HAP) and ideal low-arousal positive (i.e., I-LAP), both of which people usually want to experience to a greater degree; and (b) ideal high-arousal negative (i.e., I-HAN) and ideal low-arousal negative (i.e., I-LAN), both of which people usually want to experience less (if at all). Preliminary psychological research demonstrates that, depending on a person's I-HAP or I-LAP preferences, he or she may be more likely to seek out certain leisure activities over others. For instance, in Tsai's study, participants who were I-HAP-oriented engaged in more physically rigorous activities such as exercise, team sports, and running, whereas I-LAP-oriented participants engaged in more passive activities such as reading and computer games. Based on this and related findings, Tsai proposed that if people's actual affect was significantly discrepant from their ideal affect they would engage in certain mood producing or modifying behaviors—such as leisure activities—to minimize this discrepancy.

To date, research on this topic remains rare among leisure scholars. A recent study (Mannell, Walker, & Ito, 2014) of Canadian workers did discover that, during leisure: (a) both males and females realized their desired levels of nervousness and fearfulness (i.e., I-HAN), but (b) only males realized their preferred levels of calmness and relaxation (i.e., I-LAP). Neither males nor females, however, realized the high levels of excitement and enthusiasm (i.e., I-HAP) they preferred, nor the low levels of dullness and sluggishness (i.e., I-LAN) they desired. For comparative purposes, during paid work the same participants did not realize *any* of their ideal affective states. Importantly, the discrepancies between ideal and work HAP and LAP were also significantly higher for females than males. These findings diverged with those of an earlier study (Larson, Richards, & Perry-Jenkins, 1994) wherein females were found to be happier than males at work, but only if the former felt unhurried. Mannell et al. concluded:

> Given the increased frequency of workplace interruptions (e.g., due to email), the increased frequency and intensity of daily hassles in the workplace, and the increased likelihood of poor workplace supervision as a result of high unemployment and low unionization rates, [Larson and associates'] finding induces a certain degree of nostalgia. (p. 32)

In summary, it seems worthwhile to expand leisure research on optimal arousal to include both actual and ideal affect and, further, how the avoidance or lessening of negative affective states and the promotion of positive affective states varies by type of leisure activity and setting as well as across sociodemographic and sociocultural groups.

Psychological Needs

Researchers have paid much greater attention to psychological than physiological needs. In leisure studies, Tinsley, Barrett, and Kass (1977) developed an inventory of 45 needs and then investigated how much each was satisfied by five common leisure activities. They found, for example, that reading and bicycling satiated undergraduate students' need for independence more than watching television, which in turn did so to a greater degree than attending plays or concerts and drinking and socializing. Concurrently, Driver and associates examined how outdoor recreation gratified various psychological needs, albeit while also taking managerial relevance into account (Driver, Tinsley, & Manfredo, 1991). Through the use of literature reviews, focus groups, and scale development and testing, they identified 19 domains—which they came to refer to as recreation experience preferences (REP), likely because some (e.g., "agreeable temperatures") seemed more a matter of personal taste and less a psychological need. A review (Manfredo, Driver, & Tarrant, 1996) of 36 studies that utilized REP scales supported their validity and reliability, which is one reason they are still frequently employed in leisure studies.

Interestingly, mainstream psychology itself has come to focus more on identifying and substantiating "core" or "basic" psychological needs, as well as when and how these are satisfied. Arguably, it was Deci and Ryan's (1985, 2000) designation of autonomy, competence, and interpersonal relatedness as basic needs, along with Baumeister and Leary's (1995) development of criteria by which to validate such needs, that spurred this movement. In terms of the latter, Baumeister and Leary maintained that one such standard was that when a need was not sated, the effects were generally harmful (medically, psychologically, and/or behaviorally). Among their other criteria were that core needs must: (a) operate across a wide variety of settings; (b) impact a broad variety of behaviors, (c) direct cognitive processing, (d) impel toward satisfaction, (e) have affective consequences (e.g., increase happiness); and (f) be universal.

Based on the above benchmarks, Baumeister and Leary (1995) made a convincing case for *belonging* being a basic psychological need. A similar case has been put forth for interpersonal relatedness being a core need. Deci and Ryan (2000) noted that relatedness involves people feeling they are loved by and connected to others; that others understand them; and they are meaningfully involved with the broader social world in which they live. Deci and Ryan (1985; 2000) also proposed that *autonomy* (i.e., which involves freedom to initiate one's behavior, typically through personal choice and control) and *competence* (which involves effective functioning and, in turn, the desire to seek out and conquer ever bigger challenges) were basic human needs.

Basic needs theory (BNT), developed by Deci and Ryan (1985; 2000), should be of interest for both leisure researchers and professionals. BNT maintains that: (a) need satisfaction and facilitation can vary across domains (e.g., work, school, leisure); (b) domain-specific studies "offer a better understanding of the extent to which some general principle 'works' in a specific sphere"; and (c) "domain research is critical because of its applied significance" (Ryan, 1995, p. 412). Unfortunately, in spite of its apparent theoretical and practical relevance, little research has examined BNT in regard to either leisure alone or in combination with other life domains.

Among the few mainstream psychology exceptions is an experience sampling method (ESM) study (Ryan, Bernstein, & Brown, 2010) wherein American adults reported their activities and levels of autonomy, belonging, and competence three times a day for 21 days. Activities were subsequently categorized into work (e.g., at a job, commuting) and non-work (e.g., leisure pursuits, self-maintenance); with findings indicating the former was not only associated with lower satisfaction of the needs for autonomy and belonging but also, unexpectedly, competence. Ryan et al. recognized the inherent diversity within their non-work category, and they added that their findings highlighted the potential importance free time could play in satisfying people's basic psychological needs.

Ryan and associates' (2010) proposition is examined here based on the results of three leisure studies, although some other supportive work does exist (e.g., Lundberg, Groff, & Zabriskie, 2010). First, an ESM study of Chinese-Canadians' basic needs during their self-identified work or leisure or both or neither (Shaw, 1984) found that, when these participants:

> were *alone*, autonomy was satisfied the most during leisure and the least during neither (e.g., doing household chores, driving to work), whereas competence was satisfied the most during work and the least during neither. In contrast, when [they] were *with others*, autonomy and competence were satisfied the most during leisure and the least during work. (Walker & Wang, 2009, cited in Kleiber et al., 2011, p. 139)

Belongingness (which was pertinent only when participants were with others) was also satiated the most during leisure and the least during work.

While the above study suggests that similarities and differences in need satisfaction may exist across domains and social settings, the second study submits that variations might also occur as a consequence of social class. Specifically, Walker and Glover (2013) asked Albertans who worked 20 or more hours per week to rate how well their needs for autonomy, belonging, and competence were satisfied during their leisure and paid work. Based on participants' job titles and descriptions, they were then classified into one of Florida's (2012) four social classes: (a) *super-creative* (e.g., arts, education, and engineering occupations); (b) *creative professional* (e.g., legal, financial, and management occupations); (c) *working* (e.g., extraction, construction, and production occupations); and (d) *service/sales* (e.g., food preparation, personal care, and building cleaning occupations). Analyses indicated that the super-creative class experienced more autonomy during paid work than the service/sales class, and both creative classes experienced more belongingness than the working class in this domain. These results, Walker and Glover maintained, partially supported Florida's contention that the creative class' working conditions are distinct. On the other hand, the working class experienced less belongingness during leisure than the creative professional class but, somewhat surprisingly, more competence than the super-creative class in the same domain.

Follow-up analyses focused on the discrepancies between need satisfaction during paid work and leisure, by social class. Findings contradicted Florida's (2012) claim that work and leisure blur together for the creative class, with autonomy being higher during leisure than work for all four classes. Competence was greater during work than leisure for all four classes—a result consistent with what Ryan et al. (2010) expected but did not actually find. Finally, all but the service/sales class had their need for belongingness satisfied equally during work and leisure, with this difference possibly due to the emotional labor (Hochschild, 1993) demands inherent in these workers' jobs.

Third, the results of a study of Canadian adults (Reid & Mannell, 1993) were largely consistent with the above studies in that social interaction was found to be sated more during leisure whereas achievement was satisfied more during work. However, Reid and Mannell diverged from BNT (Deci & Ryan, 1985, 2000) by also including the needs for self-esteem and escape, with their participants reporting the former was satisfied more during work and the latter was gratified more during leisure. Self-enhancement (which is comparable with self-esteem) is one of four core social needs associated with, but subordinate to, belongingness (Fiske, 2000). Empirical research (Sheldon, Elliott, Kim, & Kasser, 2001) found that U.S. university students ranked self-esteem as their most important need, followed equally by autonomy, belonging, and competence, and then six other needs, such as pleasure-stimulation. Though Sheldon et al. did not include escape in their list of ten potential core needs, Iso-Ahola (1982) developed a model wherein recreationists strove to escape (or, alternately, seek out) personal and interpersonal rewards and environments.

The proposition that leisure activities could not only satisfy basic needs but also provide an escape from the demands of trying to do so has been recognized in mainstream psychology. Baumeister (1991), for instance, deemed that decreased self-esteem could lead to attempts to "escape the self" through various behaviors (e.g., meditation, alcohol use and abuse) or, more commonly, participation in certain types of leisure. Such leisure activities included those that were likely to lead to flow experiences (Csikszentmihalyi, 1990) as well as those that involved either mental focusing (e.g., mountain-climbing, long-distance running) or de-individuation (e.g., attending concerts and sporting events).

Taken together, the above suggests that future research could benefit by: (a) building on BNT (Deci & Ryan, 1985; 2000) while not overlooking other possible core needs, and (b) recognizing that the relationship between leisure and basic needs could be much more complex than simply participation leads to satisfaction. For instance, in terms of the world's most common recreation activity, psychological studies have found that watching television can: (a) fulfill the need for belonging, as well as buffer against the negative effects of a threat to belongingness (Derrick, Gabriel, & Hugenberg, 2009); (b) restore self-control depleted after social interaction (Derrick, 2012), and (c) provide escape when a discrepancy between one's ideal self and actual self is detected (Moskalenko & Heine, 2003). All of these researchers, however, noted that other leisure activities could have similar effects, with Derrick (somewhat disparagingly) stating: "television, movies, and books can be more than *mere* leisure activities; in some cases, they fulfill needs, like restoring self-control, that people are reluctant or unable to fulfill through other means" (italics added; p. 305).

Taking a somewhat different tack, Vallerand (2000) discussed how loss of competence in one domain (e.g., school) could be compensated for in another (e.g., sports). Alas, research on how people respond to "need thwarting" (Ryan & Deci, 2000)—especially in terms of leisure as a surrogate for other need-deficient domains, such as work and school—remains lacking.

Sheldon and associates' (2010) study is important because it discovered that, while self-esteem was the primary need for American students, belongingness was ranked highest among Korean students, followed by self-esteem, and then by autonomy, pleasure-stimulation, and competence equally. Perhaps, therefore, similar to Mannell and colleagues' (2014) comparison of ideal affect and actual affect, future research should consider examining "ideal" core need satisfaction and "actual" core need satisfaction across life domains (e.g., work and leisure) as well as across sociodemographic and sociocultural groups (e.g., men and women, East Asians, and Euro-North-Americans).

It may, however, not only be the case that core needs vary in importance cross-culturally, but also that core needs are interpreted and enacted differently cross-culturally. Fiske and Fiske (2007) described how their five social needs could differ, and provided as an example how an independent American would achieve control by trying to influence the world around them. In contrast, an interdependent Japanese would achieve control by adjusting and compromising to circumstances and relationships. Weisz, Rothbaum, and Blackburn (1984) called the former primary control and the latter secondary control. Morling (2000) used these concepts to differentiate between, respectively, "taking" an aerobics class in the U.S. and "entering" an aerobics class in Japan. An ESM study (Ito & Walker, 2013) of Canadian and Japanese students, however, found that primary control during leisure increased in both cultures. On the other hand, whereas one type of secondary control (i.e., acceptance) decreased in both cultures, another type (i.e., adjustment) increased for Japanese, but decreased for Canadian participants. In summary, these findings suggest that leisure activities may provide opportunities to satisfy certain culturally endorsed needs/need dimensions as well as certain universally shared needs/need dimensions.

Building on existing need satisfaction research could prove beneficial for recreation practice. For example, Veal (Chapter 33) held that while one often-used leisure planning framework did emphasize satisfying people's needs, it was severely limited because it did not define exactly what this concept meant and, consequently, it was often confused with wants, desires, demand, etc. Yet if Baumeister and Leary's (1995) evaluation criteria were employed, a more valid, reliable, and briefer list of core needs could result. For instance, based on BNT's (Deci & Ryan, 1985; 2000) three needs, Gillard, Watts, and Witt (2007) provided a number of youth camp-focused programming recommendations. Adult counselors could, they suggested, support campers' need for autonomy by providing information about options; their need for belongingness by acknowledging campers' feelings; and their need for competence by providing reasons for why the camp had certain rules and structures in place.

Similarly, in an attempt to create a more generic list of practical programming recommendations, I (Walker, 2011) presented the "Eight Simple Need Questions For Front-Line Staff" measure—based on existing SDT need scales (e.g., Van den Broeck, Vansteenkiste, De Witte, Soenens, & Lens, 2010)—at the 2011 Alberta Recreation and Parks Association Conference. Attendees were told that front-line staff should complete this questionnaire before implementing a new or existing program. Specifically, they should indicate how true they thought each of the following statements would be for their program participants using a seven-point scale (1 = not true at all; 4 = somewhat true; 7 = very true). For example, the following item was one of three used to measure participants' need for *autonomy*: "Program participants will be able to freely express their ideas and opinions." *Relatedness* was assessed using two items, one of which was: "There will be lots of opportunities for social interaction." And participants' need for *competence* was measured using three items, including: "Program participants will feel a sense of accomplishment from what they do." Employing these items could aid practitioners attract new participants (assuming they were made aware of how their core needs would be satisfied beforehand), as well as increasing the likelihood current participants would continue (assuming their core needs were indeed satisfactorily met) to engage in the same, or ensuing, programs in the future.

Finally, I began this sub-section by citing Tinsley and colleagues' (1977) nearly 40 year old study of need satisfaction and leisure activities. Their stated rationale for this research was the belief that: "as the available leisure time increases, the life satisfaction of an individual will become increasingly dependent upon the extent to which that person is able to select leisure activities which fulfill his or her needs" (p. 111). Although arguments and counter-arguments can be put forth regarding whether the amount of leisure time has, in fact, increased (Godbey, Chapter 29), there is more certainty that need satisfaction during leisure does positively impact people's subjective well-being (SWB). A summary of 363 research articles led Newman, Tay, and Diener (2014) to identify five psychological mechanisms that leisure potentially triggers to promote leisure-based SWB. These were autonomy, affiliation, and mastery (as per BNT; Deci & Ryan, 1985; 2000); meaning-making (not unlike Baumeister's, 1991, need for purpose), and detachment and recovery from work (not unlike Baumeister's need for escape). Employing this integrative model, with its close ties to core needs, could not only provide scholars with a better understanding of how leisure affects people's SWB (cf. Kuykendall, Tay, & Ng, 2015), but also how leisure studies could begin to move beyond its chronic concern with our field's perceived insularity and irrelevance (Mock, Mannell, and Guttentag, Chapter 6).

MOTIVATIONS

According to Ryan and Deci (2000), "motivation concerns energy, direction, persistence, and [consistent outcomes]—all aspects of activation and intention" (p. 69). Early research (Deci, 1971; Neulinger, 1981) proposed there were two types of motivation—intrinsic (i.e., doing an activity for its own sake) and extrinsic (i.e., doing an activity for a "payoff"). Graef, Csikszentmihalyi, and Gianinno (1983) conducted an ESM study using two questions to measure intrinsic and extrinsic motivation. Overall, 22% of the participants' daily experiences were intrinsic, though percentages varied from 3% during work, to 18% during household chores, to approximately 40% during leisure generally, to nearly 50% when eating meals.

Organismic integration theory (OIT; Deci & Ryan, 1985; Ryan & Deci, 2000) subsequently posited that there were, in fact, multiple kinds of extrinsic motivation. OIT also held that all forms of motivation could be arranged in a systematic manner; ranging from intrinsic (which comprises the greatest degree of "self-determination") to amotivation (which comprises the least degree of "self-determination"), with four types of external motivation in between. *Intrinsic* motivation involves interest, enjoyment, and participation in activities for their own sake. *Integrated* motivation involves evaluation and assimilation into the self, whereas *identified* motivation involves valuing a goal as being personally important. Conversely, *introjected* motivations are performed to enhance pride or avoid guilt, whereas *external* motivations are performed to obtain rewards or avoid punishments. Lastly, *amotivation* entails a person not acting at all, acting but not being cognizant of why he or she is doing so, or acting but only "going through the motions."

In the leisure studies field, Baldwin and Caldwell (2003) developed and tested the free time motivation scale for adolescents (FTMS-A). The FTMS-A measures five of OIT's (Ryan & Deci, 2000) six forms of motivation; with integration being excluded because Baldwin and Caldwell contended that their targeted participants were not yet developmentally capable of experiencing this motive. Caldwell and associates have conducted numerous investigations using the FTMS-A, with a mixed methods study of South African adolescents (Palen, Caldwell, Smith, Gleeson, & Patrick, 2011) comparing and contrasting the resultant quantitative data with qualitative findings from a series of focus groups. Among Palen and associates' results were that intrinsic motivation was the most frequently mentioned form in their focus groups and it had the highest level of agreement in their surveys, followed by identified motivation in both instances. Furthermore, they found that intrinsic motivation, generally, was not limited to any specific kinds of free time activities. Palen et al. recommended longitudinal research be performed in the future to better understand how intrinsic motivation and their other FTMS-A motives might impact positive (e.g., SWB) and negative (e.g., delinquency) outcomes, as well as how to best design recreational programs to promote the former and prevent the latter.

A study (Walker & Wang, 2009) of Chinese and Canadian university students' leisure found that both groups were more intrinsically motivated versus the next highest rated form of motivation (identification in both cases). Other cross-cultural similarities and differences were discovered with, for instance, integration being essentially equal but identification being significantly greater for Canadians. These researchers had hypothesized that the latter would occur as identified motivation involves "conscious valuing of a behavioral goal" (Ryan & Deci, 2000, p. 72), and other empirical work has found that Chinese people typically view leisure less positively than Westerners (e.g., Walker, Deng, & Chapman, 2007). Walker and Wang also hypothesized that intrinsic motivation would *not* vary between their two groups based on Mannell's (2005) contention that "important social psychological and leisure construct, like intrinsic motivation, might operate as a basic psychological process across cultures but affect experiential and behavioral outcomes, including leisure, differently depending on cultural context" (p. 100). As they anticipated, no difference in intrinsic motivation was found.

Finally, an observant reader will have already noticed that the above studies examined either only non-Westerners', or Westerners and non-Westerners', motivations for leisure. This may be one of the few instances in our field where indigenous and comparative cross-national/cultural studies predominate (Ito, Walker, & Liang, 2014). This led a colleague and I (Walker & Deng, 2014) to call for more research on how motives may be similar and different across ethnic and racial groups within, for example, Canada (e.g., British- and Indo-Canadians) and the United States (e.g., White, Hispanic, and African Americans).

THE RELATIONSHIP BETWEEN NEEDS AND MOTIVATIONS

In the previous section, a study (Graef et al., 1983) was described which found that leisure was highly intrinsically motivated whereas work was not. Importantly, Graef et al. also discovered that competence was positively related with intrinsic motivation but negatively related with extrinsic motivation. Other research (Unger & Kernan, 1983) identified a relationship between intrinsic motivation and perceived freedom; with Iso-Ahola (1999) comparing the latter leisure construct with the psychological need for autonomy. If correct, then Neulinger's (1981) paradigm could be considered to be one of the first frameworks linking leisure needs and motivations—or, more accurately, one type of core need (i.e., autonomy) and two broad types of motivation (i.e., intrinsic and extrinsic). Deci and Ryan (2010) advanced this connection when they proposed:

> natural processes such as intrinsic motivation, integration of extrinsic regulations, and movement toward well-being are theorized to operate optimally only to the extent that the nutriments [for experiencing autonomy, belonging, and competence] are immediately present, or, alternatively, to the extent that the individual has sufficient inner resources to find or construct the necessary nourishment. (p. 229)

Based on Deci and Ryan's proposition, Kleiber et al. (2011) adapted the following figure (Figure 17.1, modified slightly here to improve clarity):

Unfortunately, although empirical research in cognate areas, such as physical activity (Wilson, Rodgers, Blanchard, & Gessell, 2003), has successively employed this framework, to date few investigations appears to have done so in leisure studies. Walker (2010) conducted an ESM study with Chinese-Canadians that measured their self-construals (i.e., how they perceived the relationship between self and others; Triandis, 1995) beforehand, and then their motivation for, competence in, and autonomy during, leisure and non-leisure activities. Results indicated that participants who emphasized social cohesion and equality, and who experienced high levels of autonomy, reported *higher* levels of intrinsic motivation. In contrast, those who emphasized social cohesion and either hierarchy or personal and status differences, and who experienced high levels of autonomy, reported *lower*

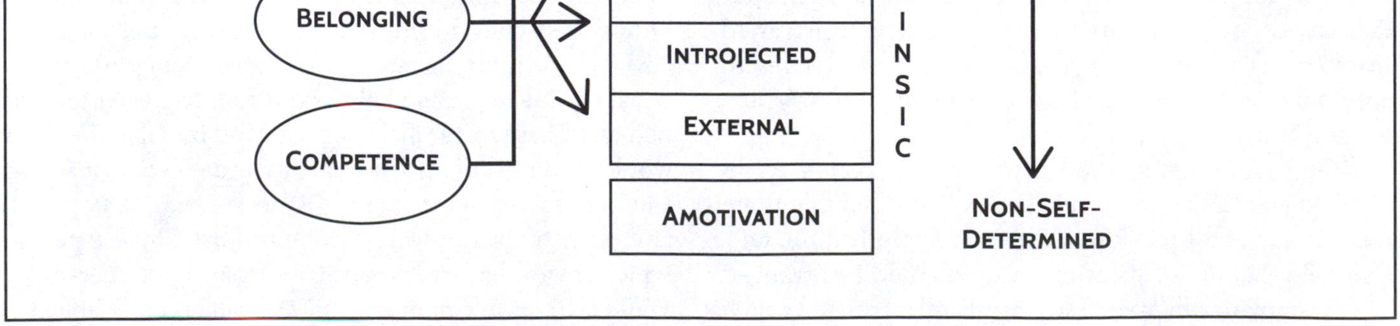

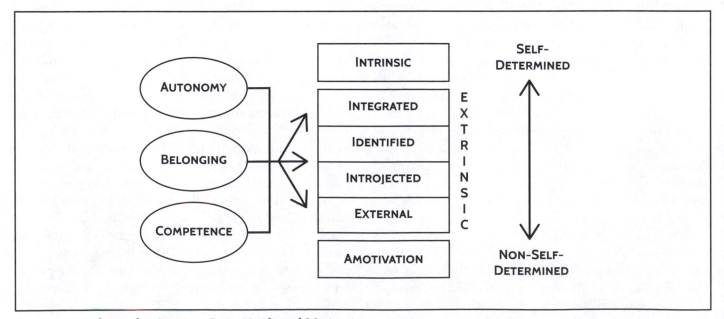

Figure 17.1. Relationship Between Basic Needs and Motivations

levels of intrinsic motivation. In summary, these findings indicate that more leisure research is necessary on the relationship between core needs and motivations; ideally while taking into account the potential effects of race, ethnicity, culture, and self-construal (see also Stodolska, Sharaievska, Tainsky, & Ryan, 2014).

CONCLUSION

As noted in the introduction, leisure needs and motivations have been described as one of the "pillars" that underpins the social psychology of leisure (Walker, et al., 2011). Another such standard—leisure constraints and negotiation strategies—will be described in detail shortly (Schneider, Chapter 18). What will soon become evident is that much greater attention has been paid to the latter pillar by the leisure studies field, in spite of the hierarchical/negotiation constraints model recognizing the key role motivations play in explaining and predicting leisure participation (Jackson, 2005). In conclusion, great gains await leisure researchers who undertake studies on physiological and psychological needs; intrinsic and extrinsic motivations (as well as amotivation); and the relationships that exist among them, especially when done so in conjunction with other important leisure topics, such as constraints and negotiation; race, ethnicity, culture, and self-construal; and subjective well-being (see also Walker, Kono, & Dieser, Chapter 36).

REFERENCES

Baldwin, C. A., & Caldwell, L. L. (2003). Development of the free time motivation scale for adolescents. *Journal of Leisure Research, 35*, 129–151.

Baumeister, R. F. (1991). *Escaping the self: Alcoholism, spirituality, masochism, and other flights from the burden of selfhood*. New York, NY: Basic Books.

Baumeister, R. F., & Leary, M. R. (1995). The need to belong: Desire for interpersonal attachments as a fundamental human motivation. *Psychological Bulletin, 117*, 497–529.

Csikszentmihalyi, M. (1990). *Flow: The psychology of optimal experience*. New York: Harper Perennial.

Deci, E. L. (1971). Effects of externally mediated rewards on intrinsic motivation. *Journal of Personality and Social Psychology, 18*, 105–115.

Deci, E. L., & Ryan, R. M. (1985). *Intrinsic motivation and self-determination in human behavior*. New York, NY: Plenum Press.

Deci, E. L., & Ryan, R. M. (2000). The "What" and "Why" of goal pursuits: Human needs and the self-determination of behavior. *Psychological Inquiry, 11*, 227–268.

Derrick, J. L. (2012). Energized by television: Familiar fictional worlds restore self-control. *Social Psychological and Personality Science, 4*, 299–307.

Derrick, J. L., Gabriel, S., & Hugenberg, K. (2009). Social surrogacy: How favored television programs provide the experience of belonging. *Journal of Experimental Social Psychology, 45*, 352–362.

Driver, B. L., Tinsley, H. E. A., & Manfredo, M. J. (1991). The Paragraphs About Leisure and Recreation Experience Preference scales: Results from two inventories designed to assess the breadth of the perceived psychological benefits of leisure. In B. L. Driver, P. J. Brown, & G. L. Peterson (Eds.), *Benefits of leisure* (pp. 263–286). State College, PA: Venture Publishing, Inc.

Fiske, S. T. (2000). Stereotyping, prejudice, and discrimination at the seam between the centuries: Evolution, culture, mind, and brain. *European Journal of Social Psychology, 30*, 299–322.

Fiske, A. P., & Fiske, S. T. (2007). Social relationships in our species and cultures. In S. Kitayama & D. Cohen (Eds.), *Handbook of cultural psychology* (pp. 283–306). New York: Guilford.

Florida, R. (2012). *The Rise of the Creative Class—Revisited: 10th Anniversary Edition*. New York: Basic Books.

Gillard, A., Watts, C., & Witt, P. (2007). The effect of perceptions of support for autonomy, relatedness, and competence on interest in camp for adolescent girls. In C. LeBlanc & C. Vogt (Compilers), *Proceedings of the 2007 Northeastern Recreation Research Symposium* (pp. 152–159). Newtown Square, PA: USDA Forest Service.

Graef, R., Csikszentmihalyi, M., & Gianinno, S. M. (1983). Measuring intrinsic motivation in everyday life. *Leisure Studies, 2*, 155–168.

Hochschild, A. (1993). *The managed heart: The commercialization of human feeling*. Berkeley, CA: The University of California Press.

Iso-Ahola, S. E. (1982). Toward a social psychological theory of tourism motivation: A rejoinder. *Annals of Tourism Research, 12*, 256–262.

Iso-Ahola, S. E. (1999). Motivational foundations of leisure. In E. L. Jackson & T. L. Burton (Eds.), *Leisure studies: Prospects for the twenty-first century* (pp. 35–51). State College, PA: Venture Publishing, Inc.

Ito, E., & Walker, G. J. (2013). Effects of culture and leisure participation on university students' control. In J. Bocarro & J. Sibthorp (Compilers), *2013 Leisure Research Symposium Book of Abstracts,* p. 73–76. Available at http://academyofleisuresciences.com/sites/default/files/lrs/LRS_2013_BOA.pdf

Ito, E., Walker, G. J., & Liang, H. (2014). A systematic review of non-Western and cross-cultural/national leisure research. *Journal of Leisure Research, 46*, 226–239.

Jackson, E. L. (2005). Leisure constraints research: Overview of a developing theme in leisure studies. In E. L. Jackson

(Ed.), *Constraints to leisure* (pp. 3–19). State College, PA: Venture Publishing, Inc.

Kleiber, D. A., Walker, G. J., & Mannell, R. C. (2011). *A social psychology of leisure* (2nd ed.). State College, PA: Venture Publishing, Inc.

Kuppens, P., Tuerlinckx, F., Russell, J. A., & L. Feldman Barnett. (2012). The relation between valence and arousal in subjective experience. *Psychological Bulletin, 139*, 917–940.

Kuykendall, L., Tay, L., & Ng, V. (2015). Leisure engagement and subjective well-being: A meta-analysis. *Psychological Bulletin, 141*, 364–403.

Larson, R. W., Richards, M. H., & Perry-Jenkins, M. (1994). Divergent worlds: The daily emotional experience of mothers and fathers in the domestic and public spheres. *Journal of Personality and Social Psychology, 67*, 1034–1046.

Linzmayer, C., Halpenny, E., & Walker, G. J. (2013). A multidimensional investigation into children's optimal experiences with nature. *Landscape Research*, 1–21.

Lundberg, N. R., Groff, D. G., & Zabriskie, R. B. (2010). Psychological need satisfaction through sport participation among international athletes with cerebral palsy. *Annals of Leisure Research, 13*(1–2), 102–115.

Manfredo, M. J., Driver, B., & Tarrant, M. (1996). Measuring leisure motivation: A meta-analysis of the Recreation Experience Preference scales. *Journal of Leisure Research, 28*, 188–213.

Mannell, B., Walker, G. J., & Ito, E. (2014). Ideal affect, actual affect, and affect deficiency during leisure and paid work. *Journal of Leisure Research, 46*, 13–37.

Mannell, R. C. (2005). Evolution of cross-cultural analysis in the study of leisure: Commentary on "Culture, self-construal, and leisure theory and practice." *Journal of Leisure Research, 37*, 100–105.

Mercer, K. B., & Eastwood, J. D. (2010). Is boredom associated with problem gambling behaviour? It depends on what you mean by 'boredom.' *International Gambling Studies, 10*, 91–104.

Morling, B. (2000). "Taking" an aerobics class in the U.S. and "entering" an aerobics class in Japan: Primary and secondary control in a fitness context. *Asian Journal of Social Psychology, 3*, 73–85.

Moskalenko, S., & Heine, S. J. (2003). Watching your troubles away: Television viewing as a stimulus for subjective self-awareness. *Personality and Social Psychology Bulletin, 29*, 76–85.

Neulinger, J. (1981). *The psychology of leisure* (2nd ed.). Springfield, IL: Charles C. Thomas.

Newman, D. B., Tay, L., & Diener, E. (2014). Leisure and subjective well-being: A model of psychological mechanisms as mediating factors. *Journal of Happiness Studies, 15*, 555–578.

Palen, L.-A., Caldwell, L. L., Smith, E. A., Gleeson, S. L., & Patrick, M. E. (2011). A mixed-method analysis of free-time involvement and motivation among adolescents in Cape Town, South Africa. *Leisure/Loisir, 35*, 227–252.

Reid, d. G., & Mannell, R. C. (1993). Future possibilities: The changing patterns of work and leisure. In A. J. Veal, P. Jonson, & G. Cushman (Eds.), *Leisure and tourism: Social and environmental change* (pp. 373–378). Sydney, Australia: University of Technology Sydney Press.

Russell, J. A. (1980). A circumplex model of affect. *Journal of Personality and Social Psychology, 39*, 1161–1178.

Ryan, R. (1995). Psychological needs and facilitation of integrative processes. *Journal of Personality, 63*, 397–427.

Ryan, R., Bernstein, J., & Brown, K. (2010). Weekends, work, and well-being: Psychological need satisfactions and day of the week effects on mood, vitality, and physical symptoms. *Journal of Social and Clinical Psychology, 29*, 95–122.

Ryan, R., & Deci, E. (2000). Self-determination theory and the facilitation of intrinsic motivation, social development, and well-being. *American Psychologist, 55*, 68–78.

Shaw, S. (1984). The measurement of leisure: A quality of life issue. *Loisir et Société/Society and Leisure, 7*, 91–107.

Sheldon, K., Elliot, A., Kim, Y., & Kasser, T. (2001). What is satisfying about satisfying events? Testing 10 candidate psychological needs. *Journal of Personality and Social Psychology, 80*, 325–339.

Stodolska, M., Sharaievska, I., Tainsky, S., & Ryan, A. (2014). Minority youth participation in an organized sport program. *Journal of Leisure Research, 46*, 612–634.

Tinsley, H. E. A., Barrett T. C., & Kass, R. A. (1977). Leisure activities and need satisfaction. *Journal of Leisure Research, 9*, 110–120.

Triandis, H. (1995). *Individualism & collectivism*. Boulder, CO: Westview Press.

Tsai, J. L. (2007). Ideal affect: Cultural causes and behavioural consequences. *Perspectives on Psychological Science, 2*, 242–259.

Unger, L. S., & Kernan, J. B. (1983). On the meaning of leisure: An investigation of some determinants of the subjective experience. *Journal of Consumer Research, 9*, 381–392.

Vallerand, R. J. (2000). Deci and Ryan's self-determination theory: A view from the hierarchical model of intrinsic and extrinsic motivation. *Psychological Inquiry, 11*(4), 312–318.

Van den Broeck, A., Vansteenkiste, M., De Witte, H., Soenens, B., & Lens, W. (2010). Capturing autonomy, competence, and relatedness at work: Construction and initial validation of the work-related basic need satisfaction scale. *Journal of Occupational Psychology, 83*, 981–1002.

Walker, G. J. (2010). The effects of personal, contextual, and situational factors on the facilitation of intrinsic motivation: The case of Chinese/Canadians. *Journal of Leisure Research, 42*, 43–66.

Walker, G. J. (2011, October). *Are we really satisfying people's needs?* Paper presented at the Alberta Recreation and Parks Association Conference. Lake Louise, Alberta. Available from the author.

Walker, G. J., & Deng, J. (2014). Leisure among Asian-North Americans. In M. Stodolska, K. Shinew, M. Floyd, & G. J. Walker (Eds.), *Race, ethnicity, and leisure: Perspectives on research, theory, and practice* (pp. 97–109). Champaign, IL: Human Kinetics.

Walker, G. J., Deng, J., & Chapman, R. (2007). Leisure attitudes: A follow-up study comparing Canadians, Chinese in Canada, and Mainland Chinese. *World Leisure Journal, 49*, 207–215.

Walker, G. J., & Glover, T. (2013). Creative class leisure participation and leisure and work need satisfaction. In J. Bocarro & J. Sibthorp (Compilers), *2013 Leisure Research Symposium Book of Abstracts,* p. 241–244. Available at http://academyofleisuresciences.com/sites/default/files/lrs/LRS_2013_BOA.pdf

Walker, G. J., Halpenny, E., Spiers, A., & Deng, J. (2011). A prospective panel study of Chinese-Canadian immigrants' leisure participation and leisure satisfaction. *Leisure Sciences, 33*, 349–365.

Walker, G. J., & Wang, X. (2009). The meaning of leisure for Chinese/Canadians. *Leisure Sciences, 31*, 1–18.

Watson, D., & Tellegen, A. (1985). Toward a consensual structure of mood. *Psychological Bulletin, 98*, 219–235.

Weisz, J., Rothbaum, F., & Blackburn, T. (1984). Standing out and standing in: The psychology of control in America and Japan. *American Psychologist, 39*, 955–969.

Wilson, P. M., Rodgers, W. M., Blanchard, C. M., & Gessell, J. (2003). The relationship between psychological needs, self-determined motivation, exercise attitudes, and physical fitness. *Journal of Applied Social Psychology, 33*, 2373–2392.

18

Leisure Constraints and Negotiation: Highlights from the Journey Past, Present, and Future

Ingrid E. Schneider (University of Minnesota)

In the twenty-first century, the evolution of leisure constraints research finds us at an exciting juncture with evolving models and no shortage of ideas on which roads to take next. In 2000, when asked if leisure constraints research would be relevant in the twenty-first century, often cited constraints author Ed Jackson answered "a guarded yes" (Jackson, 2000). More than a decade into the twenty-first century, I proffer a resounding yes: leisure constraints research is and will remain relevant for the foreseen future.

Constraints are "factors that are assumed by researchers and perceived or experienced by individuals to limit the formation of leisure preferences and to inhibit or prohibit participation and enjoyment in leisure" (Jackson, 1997, p. 461) with additional possibilities to enable leisure (Kleiber, McGuire, & Aybar-Damali, 2004). Why is constraints research relevant and why will it remain so? Researchers Goodale and Witt (1989) suggested "concern about barriers, non-participation in recreation activities, and lack of leisure opportunities has always been an important progenitor of park, recreation, and leisure services" (p. 421). In terms of research on constraints, Jackson (2005) clearly articulated at least three reasons for it: (a) to understand individuals' leisure choices and behavior, (b) to generate new insights into leisure concepts, and (c) to enhance communication among scholars. The manifestation of this constraints research, conceptually and methodologically, is the road before us.

The purpose of this chapter is to assess the state of leisure constraints research and to offer a perspective on its future. To clearly assess the status of leisure constraints, we need to understand the foundation from which it has evolved. Distilling several decades of leisure constraints research into a useful and comprehensive document is a daunting yet necessary task. The prospect is daunting in that Samdahl (2005) suggested, "leisure constraint research represents the largest and most cohesive body of research in the field of leisure studies" (p. 337) and simultaneously Jackson noted that "leisure constraints research is now well-established as a recognizable and distinct subfield within leisure studies" (p. 10). Subsequently, the depth and breadth of leisure constraints research is significant. Previously shared syntheses of leisure constraints research include a book edited by Wade (1985), special issues of *Journal of Leisure Research* and *Leisure Sciences* in 1991, a book chapter by Jackson and Scott (1999), and Jackson's (2005a) edited *Constraints to Leisure* book. The task of synthesizing leisure constraint research is necessary as Jackson (2005b), among others, noted the "... need for and value of synthesis ... to avoid the pitfalls of fragmentation" (p. 11). As such, this chapter offers one assessment of the state of leisure constraints research so readers can identify its foundation and the conceptual and methodological questions at hand. And, while Jackson (2005b) suggested that "periodic efforts ... should stand back from the detail of individual research projects ... to try to detect—or construct—the big picture" (p. 10), some individual research projects are essential to highlight for their role in directing leisure constraints research.

Conceptual Advances and Status

Since the inception of systematic leisure constraints research, conceptual development evolved from (a) initialization to (b) model testing and through (c) model expansion. In this evolution, constraint conceptualization moved from 'barriers' to recreation participation to 'constraints' to leisure preference development and participation through sources of stress and leisure enablers (Crawford & Godbey 1987; Hubbard & Mannell, 2001; Kleiber, McGuire, Aybar-Damali, & Norman, 2008; Schneider & Wilhelm Stanis, 2007; Shogan, 2002).

Initialization

Although part of leisure's fabric, only in the 1960s were 'barriers' called out explicitly as issues to recreation participation (Ferris, 1962) and only a handful of published studies existed prior to 1980 (Jackson, 2005b). Barriers were factors that prevented leisure participation and the initial name for what is termed 'constraints' in the early twenty-first century. In the 1980s, the term barriers fell out of favor when researchers realized constraints could be dealt with and that they influenced more than just participation. Subsequently, constraints became the preferred term. Not until the 1980s were existing leisure constraint studies brought together and highlighted for practitioners and researchers (*Journal of Leisure Research*, 1980; *Leisure Sciences*, 1981; Wade, 1985). Following Wade's book, an even more concentrated effort ensued to understand leisure constraints. Specifically, a line of research by Crawford and colleagues pioneered the path of leisure constraint and negotiation model development (1987, 1991, 1993). Essentially, the authors initially described intrapersonal, interpersonal, and structural barriers to leisure (Crawford & Godbey, 1987) and then arranged them in a hierarchical fashion indicating intrapersonal constraints must first be overcome, then interpersonal and finally structural (Crawford, Jackson, & Godbey, 1991; see Figure 18.1). *Intrapersonal constraints* were identified as personal characteristics and psychological attributes (e.g., fear of violence, fear of heights, self-image) that interact and influence leisure preferences. In contrast, *interpersonal constraints* arise out of interactions with others and coordinating personal resources to engage in recreation and leisure (e.g., unable to coordinate schedules with friends). *Structural constraints* intervened between leisure preference and participation (e.g., time, money, supplies) and have been further differentiated into the natural environment, social environment, territorial, and institutional categories (Walker & Virden, 2003, 2005).

Crawford and colleagues also acknowledged that constraints were frequently negotiated such that leisure participation occurs. Negotiation was defined as the "effort of individuals to use behavioral or cognitive strategies to facilitate leisure participation despite constraints" (Jackson, Crawford, & Godbey, 1993, p. 4). With this definition, Jackson et al. elaborated on how negotiation happens, put forward ideas related to constraints and proposed the outcome of the negotiation process depends on constraints to and motivations for participation.

Negotiation strategies were first conceptualized as strategies to overcome constraints, then as accommodations of existing conditions, and most recently as resistance and coping (Jackson & Rucks, 1995; Kay & Jackson, 1991; Samdahl, Jacobson, & Hutchinson, 1998; Schneider & Wilhelm Stanis, 2007; Scott, 1991; Stalp, 2006). When initially introduced, negotiation strategies included information acquisition, altered scheduling, and skill development (Scott, 1991). In the first study explicitly focused on leisure constraint negotiation, Jackson and Rucks (1995) categorized junior high school student responses to leisure constraints into two basic negotiation strategies: behavioral and cognitive. They then further divided behavioral strategies into time management, skill acquisition, changing interpersonal relationships, improving financial situations, physical therapy, changing leisure aspirations, and a miscellaneous category. Building on this qualitative data, Hubbard and Mannell

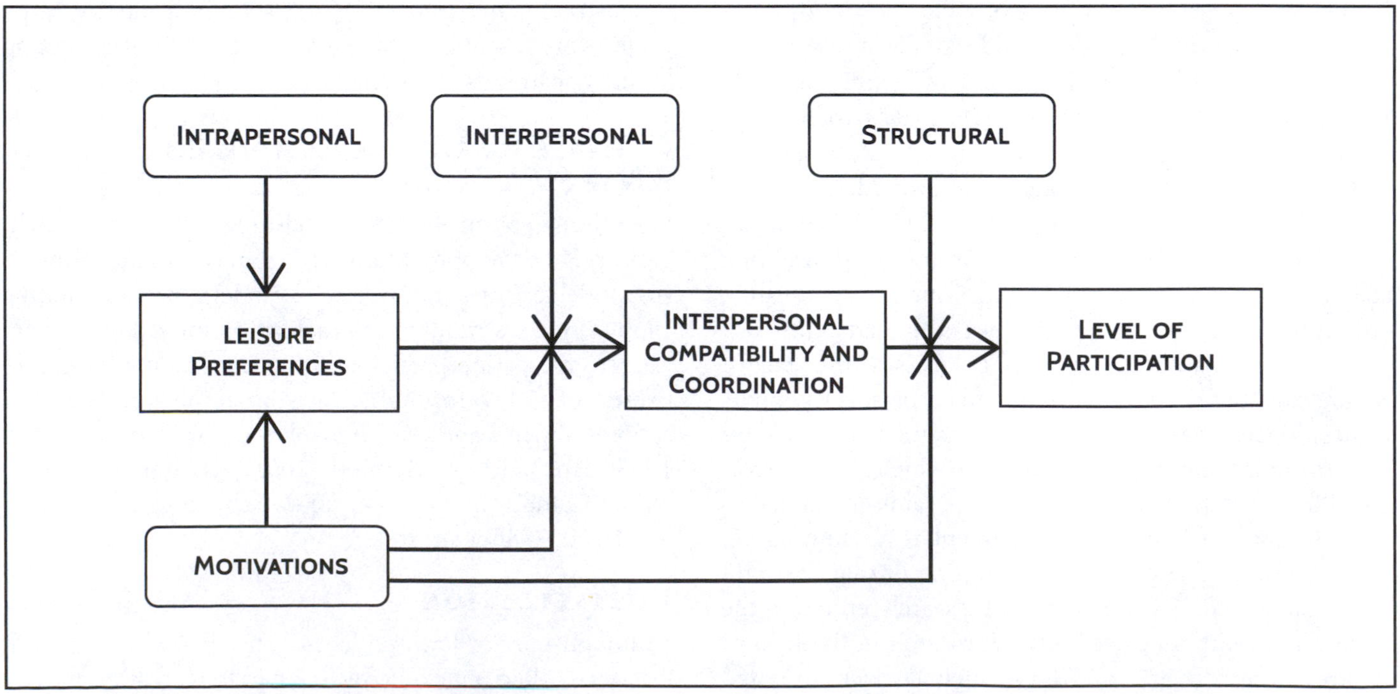

Figure 18.1. Hierarchical Model of Constraints (Crawford, Jackson, & Godbey, 1991)

(2001) developed and tested behavioral negotiation scales: time management, skill acquisition, financial management, and interpersonal coordination. Variations of these scales have been used throughout the twenty-first century. Questions exist if a single list of negotiation measures should be used (Godbey, Crawford, & Shen, 2010) with the arguments including using a single list is useful and appealing to compare study results, but using a single list may exclude strategies researchers have not yet identified.

Model Testing

Empirical examinations of the hierarchical model confirmed constraints and negotiations exist (e.g., Nyaupane, Morais, & Graefe, 2004; Raymore, Godbey, Crawford, & von Eye, 1993). While "a stable and meaningful core of leisure constraints regardless of the specific circumstances of a particular study or the nature of the samples" (Jackson & Scott, 1999, p. 304) may exist, certainly constraint's relative strength and importance vary for different populations and in different circumstances (Godbey et al., 2010; Wade, 1985). Similar to constraints, negotiation or coping strategies have been categorized. Coping strategies are constantly changing cognitive and behavioral efforts to manage a troubled person-environment relationship (Lazarus & Folkman, 1984). They can serve as an alternative to negotiation as they are more encompassing and theoretically based (Schneider & Wilhelm Stanis, 2007). Samdahl and colleagues differentiated negotiation from accommodation. According to them, while negotiation requires someone or something to negotiate, accommodation occurs when individuals accept or adapt to existing conditions that are not challenged or changed (Samdahl et al., 1998; Samdahl, Hutchinson, & Jebokovich, 1999). Research revealed the use of negotiation depends on the person's motivation and self-efficacy (Jun & Kyle, 2011; Son, Mowen, & Kerstetter, 2008; Walker, 2007a; White, 2008), where efficacy refers to "people's confidence in their ability to successfully use negotiation strategies to overcome constraints" (Loucks-Atkinson & Mannell, 2007, p. 20). Within these models, the empirical emphasis has been on structural constraints (Crawford & Jackson, 2005).

Throughout the hierarchical model testing, however, concerns emerged about the existence of the constraint hierarchy (Henderson & Bialeschki, 1993; Shaw, Bonen, & McCabe, 1991). Were the constraints really experienced in a hierarchical fashion or, rather, did they depend on the person and circumstance? Also, concerns focused on a reliance on describing rather than explaining negotiation (Jackson & Scott, 1999; Samdahl & Jekubovich, 1997). The lists of ways to negotiate seemed to be repeated and expanded, rather than significant efforts to explain why negotiation was occurring were made: why were people negotiating? Finally, a focus on participation as the dominant outcome variable seemed limited as surely constraints and negotiation impacted other parts of the experience (Godbey et al., 2010; Jackson & Scott, 1999; McGuire & Norman, 2005; Raymore, 2002; Samdahl, 2005; Samdahl & Jekubovich, 1997).

In response to concerns about the proposition that constraints are experienced hierarchically, Henderson and Bialeschki (1993) conducted interviews about constraints experienced by women and, based on their results, suggested a model where constraints occurred simultaneously and interacted with one another; a model that was supported in subsequent qualitative investigations (McQuarrie & Jackson, 1996; Samdahl & Jekubovich, 1997) and in survey-based studies (Dominguez, 2003; Gilbert & Hudson, 2000; Nadirova & Jackson, 2000). Empirical support for the hierarchical progression exists, though, as tested when initially proposed (Raymore et al., 1993) and in more recent efforts, even cross-culturally (Walker, Jackson, & Deng, 2007; Zhang, Zhang, Cheng, Liu, & Shi, 2012). Godbey et al. (2010) cautioned against strict interpretation of the hierarchy, suggesting the model is circular and does not have to begin with intrapersonal constraints. As such, it seems that depending on approach and focus, the hierarchical model remains relevant but limited in its power.

To understand the role of motivation and constraints in the model, Alexandris and colleagues (1997, 2002 and 2011) initiated a set of studies. First, they explored the relationship between constraints and motivation using a sample of Greek adults living in an urban area. Initial results found a negative relationship between the strength of intrinsic motivation and constraints to participation, meaning those with higher motivation perceived less constraint (Carroll & Alexandris 1997). More recently, Alexandris, Funk, and Pritchard (2011) affirmed the negative relationship between constraints and motivation among a sample of Greek skiers. In 2002, Alexandris, Tsorbatzoudis, and Grouios surveyed an urban Greek population to assess the relationship between constraints and three types of motivations: intrinsic, extrinsic, and amotivation. Results indicated intrinsic motivation intervened between constraints and participation and, in particular, intrapersonal constraints negatively impacted participation. While samples were selective, these research efforts point to the important and different influence of both motivation and constraint types on participation.

In a step toward answering the challenge to "explain negotiation of leisure constraints" (Jackson & Scott, 1999, p. 310), Hubbard and Mannell (2001) tested several leisure constraints and negotiation models and found the strongest statistical model was where constraints decreased participation but also influenced greater use of negotiation, thus counteracting the negative effects of constraints (Figure 18.2). Subsequent modeling efforts found support for this

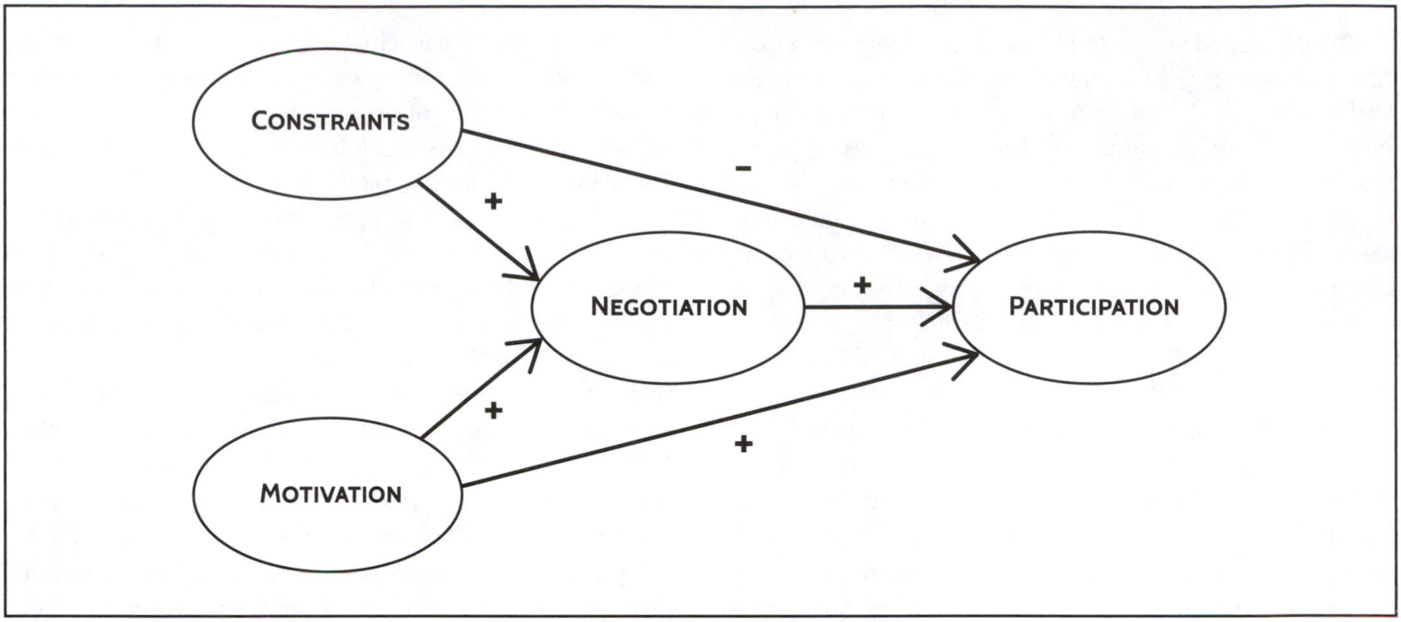

Figure 18.2. Constraints Effects Mitigation Model (Hubbard & Mannell, 2001)

'constraints-effects-mitigation model' (Loucks-Atkinson & Mannell, 2007; Wilhelm Stanis, Schneider, & Russell, 2009). However, Son et al. (2008) found no significant relationship between constraints and negotiation and subsequently renamed their model the 'constraint-negotiation dual channel model' (Figure 18.3). Additional testing will elucidate the type, direction, and strength of these relationships.

Model Expansion

As model testing was occurring, ideas for expansion and theoretical grounding simultaneously emerged. As explained above, some of the expansions were due to criticisms related to the use of participation as the only criterion variable (e.g., McGuire & Norman, 2005; Samdahl & Jekubovich, 1997; Scott & Jackson, 1999), the lack of theoretical grounding (e.g., Henderson, 1997; Jun & Kyle, 2011) or the hierarchical model negating sociocultural influences such as gender expectations or familial support (e.g., Chick & Dong, 2005; Henderson, 1997; Samdahl & Jekubovich, 1997).

Within the social-psychological perspective, several variables were proposed as influential in constraints negotiation. Loucks-Atkinson and Mannell (2007) added negotiation efficacy to the constraints mitigation-effects model, finding it positively related to motivation and negotiation. Their proposition was confirmed by White's (2008) study

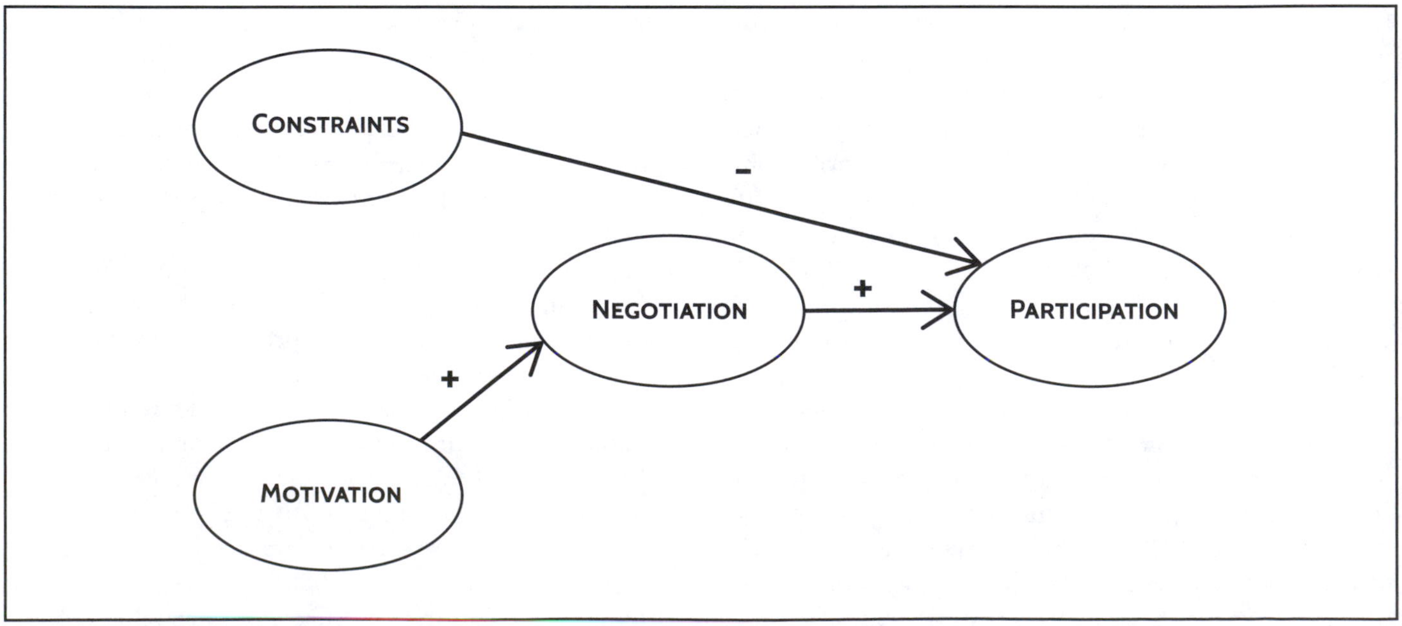

Figure 18.3. Dual Channel Constraints Model (Son et al., 2008)

that found negotiation efficacy positively related to motivation to participate and negotiation. As such, continued attention to the role negotiation efficacy plays is needed for future model development. In a different vein and toward an understanding of how individuals turn constraints into opportunities that may enable leisure (Shogan, 2002), Kleiber and colleagues proposed "the emergence of some limitation or constraint often causes adjustments that brings benefits ...leading to the realization of other desirable opportunities" (Kleiber et al., 2008, p. 345; see also Kleiber et al., 2004; Kleiber Wade, & Loucks-Atkinson, 2005; Kleiber, Chapter 23); which Samdahl (2005) conceptually supported. These beneficial roles of constraints include (a) resilience and deepened commitment; (b) attention to other goals; (c) discovery of previously unattended capacities; (d) changes in attitude toward life and leisure; and (e) goal achievement and well-being (Figure 18.4). For example, when I modify my leisure-time physical activity to participate with family members rather than do it alone, it provides me an opportunity to maintain the activity while achieving multiple goals and promote not only my physical well-being, but also my social bonding and emotional well-being by being with my family and sharing the importance of an active lifestyle. Aybar-Damali and McGuire (2013) indicated "research on how and whether life circumstances limiting actions in some contexts (particularly leisure) provide opportunities that enable human growth is in its infancy" (p. 146) and thus, further research is needed. For example, while Kleiber et al. (2008) focused on older adults, subsequent research can reveal the utility of this constraint benefit idea in other samples and examine additional relationships among negotiation and its outcomes.

Two expanded models, compatible with each other, emerged since the start of the 21st century. Each model expanded existing constraints models in that they recognized negotiation and coping as a process and gave attention to personal and environmental factors (Schneider & Wilhelm Stanis, 2007; Walker & Virden, 2003, 2005). Walker and Virden's model (2003, 2005) included both individual and socially oriented factors such as culture and personality. Further, Walker and Virden (2003, 2005) explicitly called out several stages to the model: the decision to participate, a

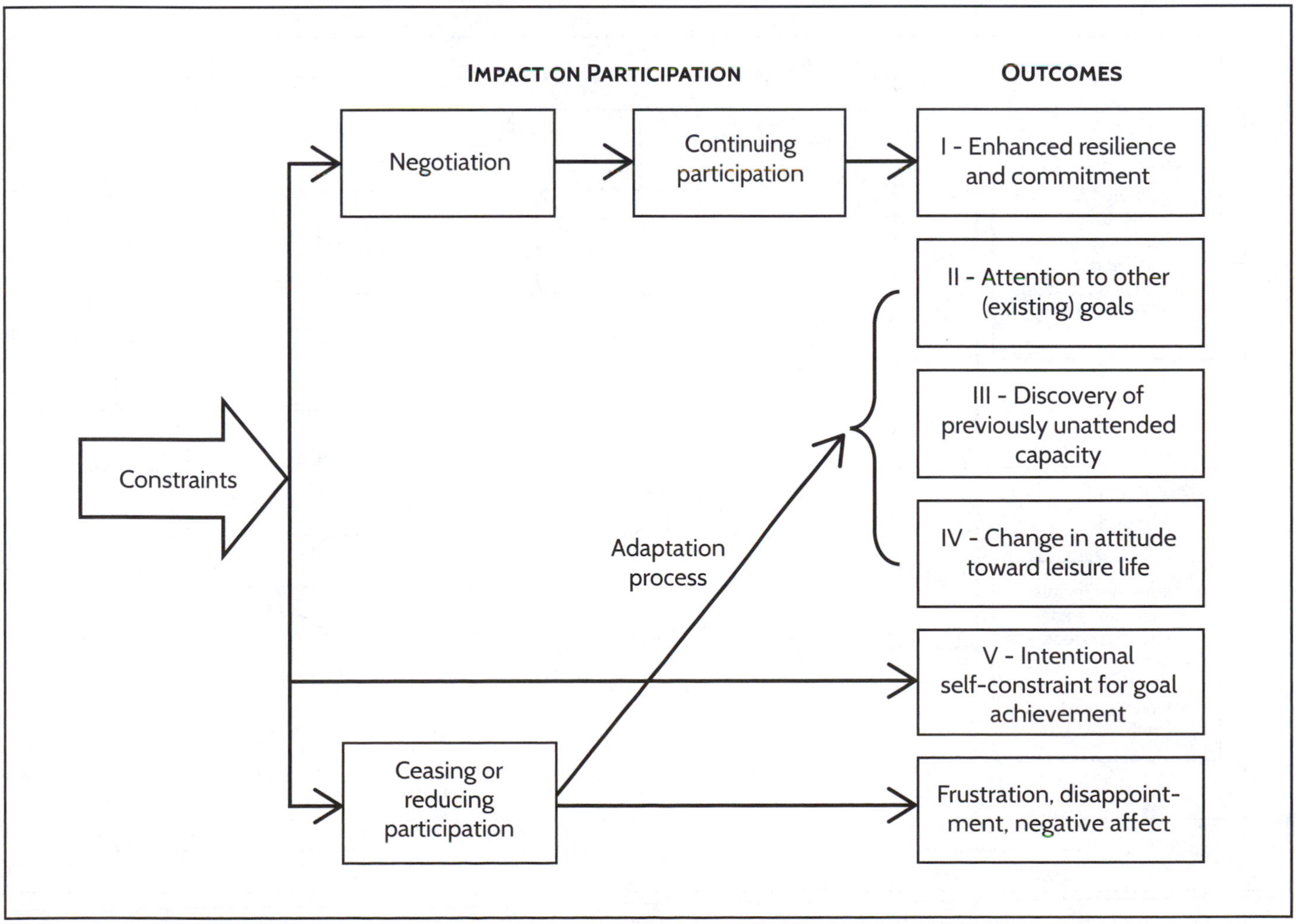

Figure 18.4. Five Types of Constraint Benefits (Kleiber et al., 2004)

post-participation evaluation of the recreation experience, and the decision to negotiate. Schneider and Wilhelm Stanis (2007) presented an iterative coping model which also integrated individual and social factors, three appraisal processes and feedback loops to consider if and how coping addresses the stresses that constrain leisure. An integrated model was proposed by Walker (2007b) (Figure 18.5) which showed significant conceptual promise to address the hierarchical issue with initial models, personal and environmental factors, and the actual process of negotiation/coping.

In contrast and in response to calls for a more sociological focus (Jackson, 2000), Crawford and Stodolska (2008) developed a model with the use of grounded theory (Figure 18.6). Based on interviews with athletes with disabilities from a non-Western country, this model explicitly recognized culturally-grounded attitudes and values as a fundamental constraint, sparking interest and answering the call to consider culture in future examinations of leisure constraints (Chick & Dong, 2005). Additional assessments of its validity and transferability beyond the sample used to generate it remain necessary. Also with a sociological bent, Jun and Kyle (2011) maintained identity conflict (i.e., the conflict of having multiple identities, such as mother, teacher, yogi, soccer mom) is the primary motivation for a person's negotiation. Jun and Kyle's multi-method investigation affirmed the role of identity in constraints research and also showed promise for future studies.

CONCEPTUAL CONVERSATIONS

Conceptually, several conversations occupy the academic discussions related to constraints and negotiation and include a: (a) theoretical absence; (b) cross-cultural relevance; (c) need to assess outcome variables beyond participation; and (d) an all-encompassing view of leisure constraints and negotiation.

An absence of theory within leisure constraints and negotiation research is a concern and a topic of an ongoing discussion. Crawford and Jackson (2005) assessed constraints work as "largely consistent with the demands of 'good' theory' . . . although there is doubtless much to be done" (p. 162; see also Walker, Kono, & Dieser, Chapter 36). Also in 2005, Jackson asserted that atheoretical constraints research was no longer dominant and Godbey et al. (2010) maintained that a constraints theory existed and that it evolved from the

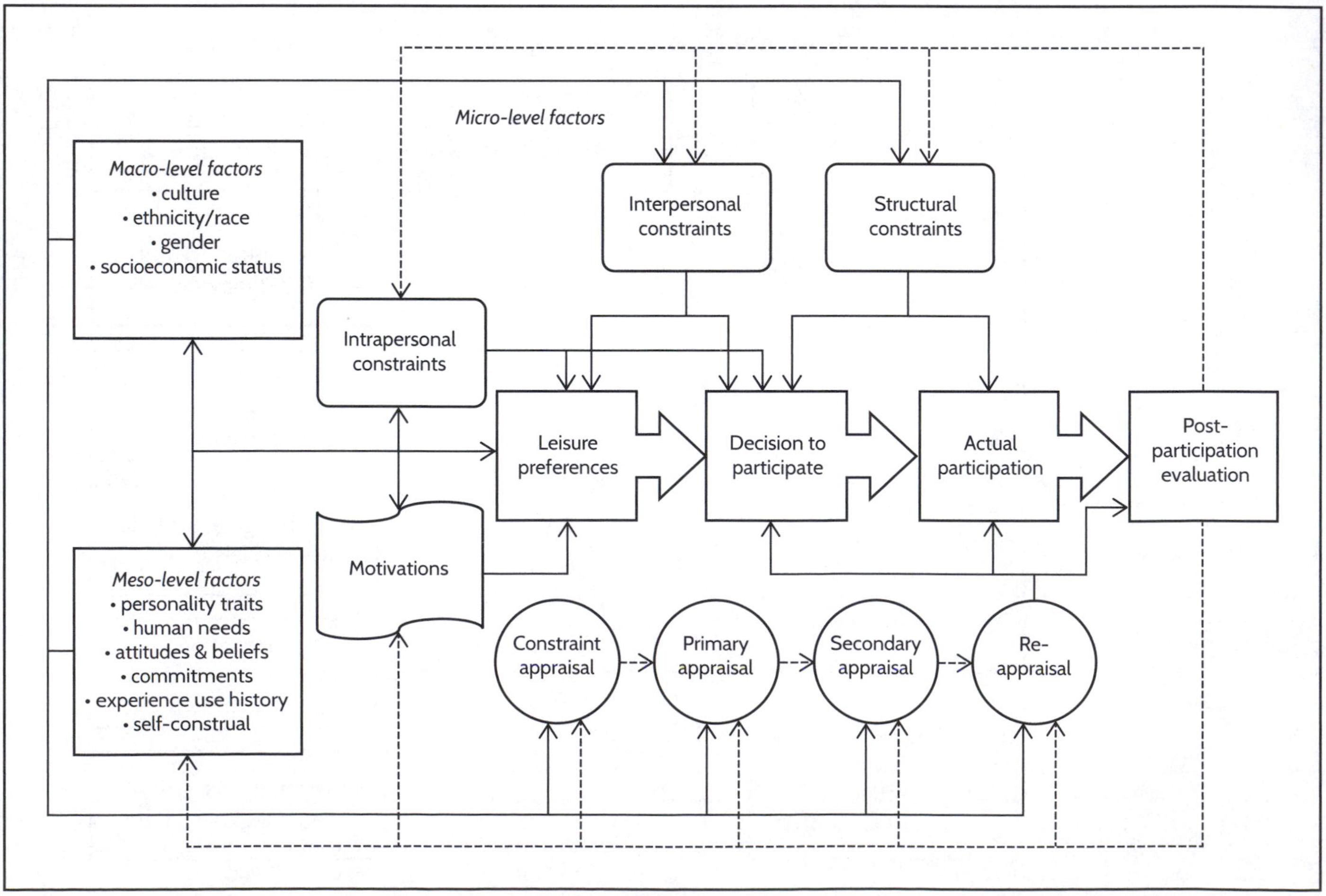

Figure 18.5. Integrative Leisure Constraints Model (Adapted from, in alphabetical order: Crawford, Jackson, & Godbey, 1991; Lazarus & Folkman, 1984; Schneider & Hammitt, 1995; Schneider & Wilhelm Stanis, 2007; and Walker & Virden, 2005)

work in the 1990s. However, divergent views exist regarding the presence of a constraints theory (Henderson, 1997; Jun & Kyle, 2011; Samdahl, 2005; Samdahl & Jekubovich, 1997) and even a constraints theory purpose (Crawford & Jackson, 2005; Godbey et al., 2010). Samdahl (2005) suggested a model is simply a conceptual tool that should be abandoned when something else is found that more effectively serves its purpose. Since the turn of the twenty-first century, a number of explicit theoretical orientations have been presented to explain constraints and negotiation: the theory of planned behavior and self-determination theory (Walker et al., 2007), efficacy theory (Son et al., 2008), selective optimization (Kleiber et al., 2004), multiple stratification hierarchy theory (Shores, Scott, & Floyd, 2007), and stress-coping theory (Schneider & Wilhelm Stanis, 2007). Based on the arguments and theoretical discussions, to assert that a single constraints theory exists seems inappropriate and inaccurate as of 2014: there is not a single constraints theory at this time.

The position of culture within the constraints framework remains important, but has also been debated. At least two perspectives exist: (a) culture exists as a separate construct that conditions constraints or in which constraints are embedded (Chick & Dong, 2005; Crawford & Stodolska, 2008) or (b) culture is considered within the intrapersonal constraint (Godbey et al., 2010; Walker et al., 2007). Beyond the role of culture, Godbey et al. contended the hierarchical model "is cross-culturally relevant . . ." (p. 111), while Chick and Dong (2005) suggested the model may have relevance but needs a more explicit treatment of culture.

Within constraints research, calls persist to study outcomes other than participation (Godbey et al., 2010; Kleiber et al., 2004, 2005, 2008; McGuire & Norman, 2005; Nadirova & Jackson, 2000; Raymore, 2002; Samdahl & Jekubovich, 1997). Expanded models include outcomes other than participation such as emotional responses, displacement, and a lack of support for the recreation area. These expanded models either need empirical testing overall (Schneider & Wilhelm Stanis, 2007) or testing with more diverse samples (Kleiber et al., 2008). Qualitative assessments of these outcomes beyond participation will aid in expanding their utility toward a greater understanding of constraints and negotiation.

Since the 1990s, concerns regarding an overextended constraints utility have been raised (Jackson, 1997; Jackson & Scott, 1999; Samdahl, 2005; Samdahl & Jekubovich, 1997). Samdahl and Jekubovich (1997) cautioned of

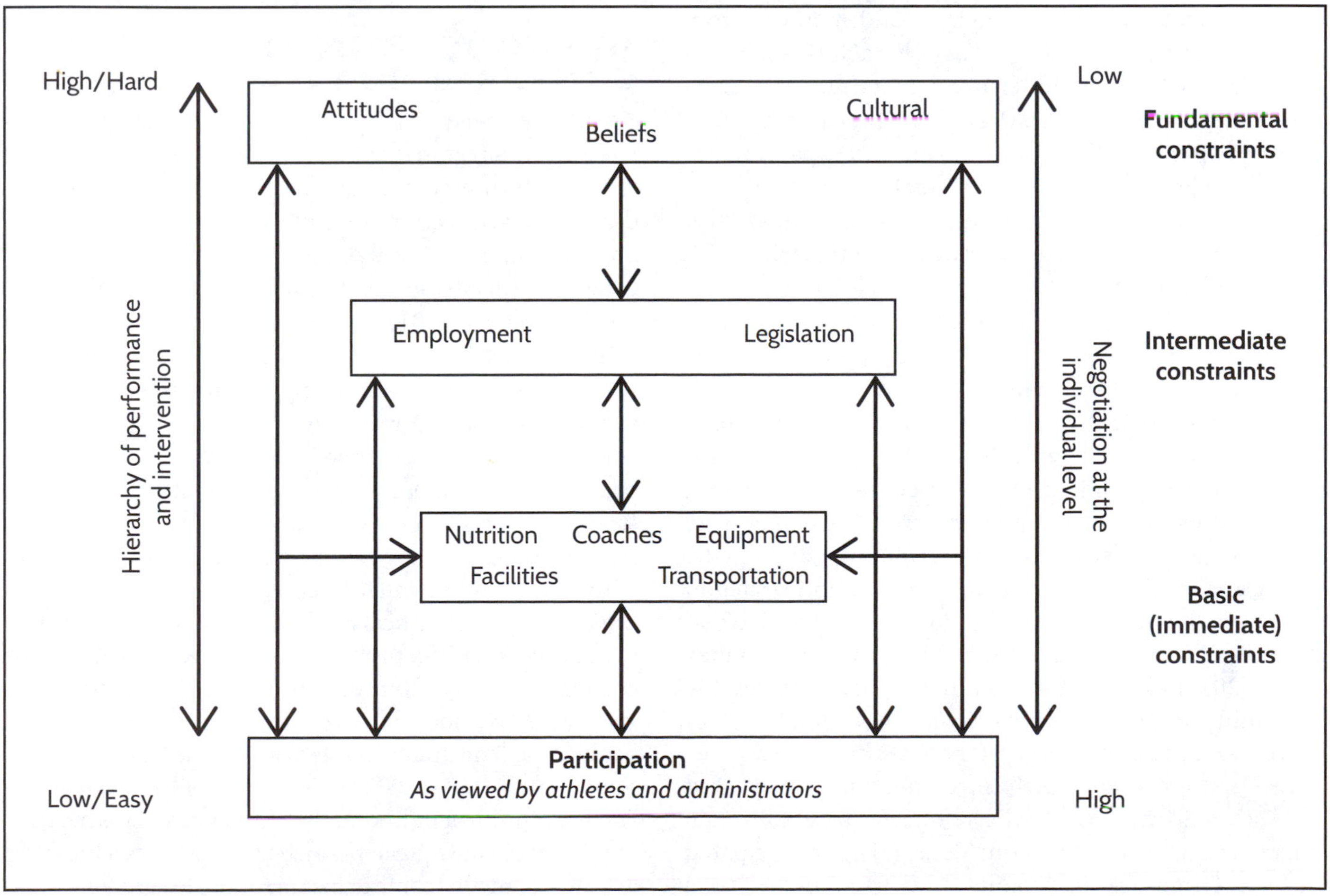

Figure 18.6. Social Issues as Constraints (Crawford & Stodolska, 2008)

adoption of the constraints concept without more critical questioning. Jackson (1997) similarly cautioned the field to beware of constraints becoming an end-all to everything, able to explain all of leisure and consuming everything in its path (likening it to a 1980s video game of wild popularity, Pac-Man). While current conversations continue to question the breadth of constraints and negotiation research, we must acknowledge the criticisms and take the challenge to push forward. For, as Henderson (2006) suggested, ". . . all theory is incomplete, yet leisure researchers must continue to ascertain how theory and research contribute to a better understanding than existed previously and how knowledge is always evolving" (p. 394). In 1999, Jackson and Scott suggested much work remained in leisure constraint negotiation research and, as of 2014, their statement still stands.

METHODOLOGICAL ADVANCES AND STATUS

In 1999, Jackson and Scott characterized leisure constraints research as dominated by "a positivist, quantitative, survey-based approach...and that any future changes in focus....will represent not just a change of topic but will also demand different research methods and the incorporation of concepts and methods from other disciplines" (p. 315). This characterization still holds for the majority of leisure constraints research in the twenty-first century, although qualitative approaches have expanded. The model testing and expansion has been largely quantitative, with qualitative approaches providing richer understandings of constraints. Ellis, Lee, and Satchabut (Chapter 38) documented within the latest published studies "leisure research has been built on correlational and contextual methods". Samdahl (Chapter 37) provides insights into opportunities for more qualitative approaches.

Methodologically, much of the leisure constraints research followed the typical path of describing, categorizing, and modeling. Lists of both constraint and negotiation items were generated to describe them, they were then categorized using simple groupings and finally factor analyzed. Constraints and negotiation strategies remain in the process of being statistically modeled and expanded. A lack of standardized instruments (Godbey et al., 2010; Hubbard & Mannell, 2001) negates the possibility for comparisons across most projects, but leaves the possibility for greater contextual understanding. Although a core of leisure constraints may exist (Jackson & Scott, 1999), the lists continue to grow through purposeful research that considers activity participated in (e.g., Dimmock & Wilson, 2011; Jun & Kyle, 2011) and the social and environmental context of the leisure experience such as group composition and sexual identity (Jordan & Gibson, 2005; Lewis & Johnson, 2011; Wood & Danylchuk, 2012).

Constraints and negotiation modeling has evolved from fairly simple and straightforward processes using single dimension factors (Hubbard & Mannell, 2001) to greater use of more complex solutions (Nyaupene & Andereck, 2008). Similarly, assessing the relationships among constraints and related variables moved from description through prediction with increasing sophistication. Quantitative approaches with complex structural equation models have been heralded as a way "to identify and disentangle complex relationships among many leisure-related variables defining and connected with leisure constraints" (Jackson, 2005, p. 13). Additionally, qualitative approaches provided rich descriptions of constraints (e.g., Dimmock & Wilson, 2011), revealed a greater complexity into constraints models than originally proposed (Henderson & Bialescki, 1993), and addressed the latest calls to expand beyond individualistic approaches (Crawford & Stodolska, 2008). Certainly continued inquiries with both approaches and mixed methods designs will yield greater insights into constraints and negotiation.

METHODOLOGICAL CONVERSATIONS

As in other areas of leisure research, leisure constraints researchers suggested enhancing constraints scholarship through the use of more qualitative approaches, longitudinal data acquisition and analysis (Mowen, Payne, & Scott, 2005), cross-cultural research (Chick & Dong, 2005), gendered considerations (Henderson & Bialeschki, 1993; Lewis & Johnson, 2011) and, most recently, experimental analysis (Ellis, Lee, & Satchabut, Chapter 38). Among and beyond these ideas, compelling methodological conversations include arguments for a greater integration of context, attention to units of analysis and negotiation as process. Each of these deserves greater attention in constraints research.

The social and environmental context associated with leisure constraints is multifaceted and demands both continued complex statistical modeling as well as investigation with the use of qualitative approaches. Operationalizing the context can range from culture (Walker et al., 2007), to gender (Lewis & Johnson, 2011), through adopting a holistic approach as "constraints don't exist separate from socio-cultural context" (Little, 2002, p. 163). The number of qualitative and retrospective studies conducted this century is heartening. They provide a greater understanding of both the social and environmental context that surrounds leisure constraints and their negotiation, as well as the process of how those negotiations occur. These qualitative approaches are "weaving a far richer tapestry of how constraints fit into the context of people's lives and of how these in turn are shaped and affected by the broader ... milieu within which we live" (Jackson, 2005b, pp. 9–10).

For the vast majority of leisure constraints research, the focus has been on the individual. Henderson (1997) suggested that constraints negotiation "problem is ... that the onus is almost always on individuals" (p. 456) and argued societal factors affect people's leisure involvement. However, as the leisure constraint lens expands and calls for sociological approaches become more vociferous, leisure research should address this gap in understanding groups, group interactions, and the social factors that influence them (Samdahl, 2005). Although initiated with group assessments (Scott, 1991), constraints and negotiation attention within a group has been minimal. Wood and Danylchuk (2012) addressed the paucity of work focused on constraints at a group level and encouraged more work in this area. Arguably constraints and negotiation among women as a group have been explored to a significant degree (Goodale & Witt, 1989; Henderson & Bialeschki, 1993; Little, 2002) but group studies remain scant in the published literature. In the twenty-first century, increasing attention has been paid to non-dominant racial and ethnic populations (Stodolska, 1998; Stodolska & Yi-Kook, 2005) which is important as those racially and ethnically diverse groups have attenuated constraints that relate to access to resources, immigration factors, and historical and discrimination issues (Fox, Chapter 27; Schneider, Shinew, & Fernandez, 2013; Stodolska & Floyd, Chapter 28).

Negotiating constraints has been identified as a process where individuals are continually assessing the situation, coping with constraints as necessary, and then reassessing the process. However, constraint negotiation research remains largely focused on a single occurrence or decision. Save a few quantitative designs that capture data across times (Mowen et al., 2005) or stages (Wilhelm Stanis et al., 2009) and several sets of interviews (Dommick & Wilson, 2011; Wood & Danylchuk, 2012), cross-sectional designs dominate the leisure constraints landscapes. One exception is in the area of women's leisure where qualitative interviews have revealed insights about negotiation processes (e.g., Jordan & Gibson, 2005). Longitudinal and even multiple-day research can provide additional insight into the processes of constraint negotiation, compare across life stages, and identify when and where constraints become enabling. Our understanding of the negotiation process remains severely lacking and, as such, Jackson's (2000) call to study the process of negotiation remains relevant.

CONCLUSION

Approaching a base of nearly 40 years of research, the leisure constraints research road is well-traveled. This chapter provided a broad roadmap to leisure constraints research, highlighting key attractions and illuminating opportunity for future travel. As in any trip, cautions arise about which direction is most desirable, which will yield the optimal experience, and how far we should go how fast. While caution should not be thrown to the wind, researchers do need to act on the suggestions that seem to continuously surface for constraints and negotiation such as more qualitative work, longitudinal research, and studying the process of constraints and coping. In a related vein, researchers need to boldly demand resources for the research we need to do rather than continuing to lament the lack of resources available. While these directions are easy to write, they may be more difficult to implement: but how will we know until we try? Regardless of the road selected, constraints and negotiation research will certainly remain full of conceptual and methodological opportunity and challenge.

REFERENCES

Alexandris, K., Funk, D., & Pritchard, M. (2011). The impact of constraints on motivation, activity attachment and skier intentions to continue. *Journal of Leisure Research, 43*(1), 56–79.

Alexandris, K., Tsorbatzoudis, C., & Grouios, G. (2002). Perceived constraints on recreational sport participation: Investigating their relationship with intrinsic motivation, extrinsic motivation and amotivation. *Journal of Leisure Research, 34*, 233–252.

Aybar-Damali, B. Z., & McGuire, F. A. (2013). The enabling potential of constraints. *Journal of Leisure Research, 45*(2), 136–149.

Carroll B., & Alexandris K. (1997). Perception of constraints and strength of motivation: Their relation to recreational sport participation. *Journal of Leisure Research, 29*(3), 279–299.

Chick, G., & Dong, E. (2005). Cultural constraints on leisure. In E. L. Jackson (Ed.), *Constraints to leisure* (pp. 169–183). State College, PA: Venture Publishing, Inc.

Crawford, J., & Godbey, G. (1987). Reconceptualizing barriers to family leisure. *Leisure Sciences, 9*, 119–127.

Crawford, J., & Jackson, E. L. (2005). Leisure constraints theory: Dimensions, directions and dilemmas. In E. L. Jackson (Ed.), *Constraints to leisure* (pp. 153–168). State College, PA: Venture Publishing, Inc.

Crawford, J., Jackson, E. L., & Godbey, G. (1991). A hierarchical model of leisure constraints. *Leisure Sciences, 13*, 309–330.

Crawford, J., & Stodolska, M. (2008). Constraints experienced by elite athletes with disabilities in Kenya, with implication for the development of a new hierarchical model of constraints at the societal level. *Journal of Leisure Research, 40,* 128–155.

Dominguez, L. A. (2003). Constraints and constraint negotiation by women sea kayakers participating in a women-only course. Unpublished Ph.D. dissertation. Michigan State University.

Dimmick, K., & Wilson, E. (2011). "Take a deep breath": How recreation scuba divers negotiate in-water constraints. *Leisure/Loisir, 35,* 283–297.

Ferris, A. L. (1962). *National Recreation Survey, Outdoor Recreation Resources Review Commission* (Study Report No. 19). Washington, DC: US Government Printing Office.

Gilbert, D., & Hudson, S. (2000). Tourism demand constraints: A skiing participation. *Annals of Tourism Research, 27,* 906–925.

Godbey, G., Crawford, D. W., & Shen, X. S. (2010). Assessing hierarchical leisure constraints theory after two decades. *Journal of Leisure Research, 42*(1), 111–134.

Goodale, T. & Witt, P. A. (1989). Recreation non-participation and barriers to leisure. In E. L. Jackson (Ed.), *Understanding leisure and recreation: Mapping the past, charting the future* (pp. 421–449). State College, PA: Venture Publishing, Inc.

Henderson, K. A. (1997). A critique of constraints theory: A response. *Journal of Leisure Research, 29*(4), 453–457.

Henderson, K. A. (2006). False dichotomies and leisure research. *Leisure Studies, 25(*4), 391–395.

Henderson, K. A., & Bialeschki, M. D. (1993). Exploring an expanded model of women's leisure constraints. *Journal of Applied Recreation Research, 18,* 229–252.

Hubbard, J., & Mannell, R. (2001). Testing competing models of the leisure constraint and negotiation process in a corporate employee recreation setting. *Leisure Sciences, 23,* 145–163.

Jackson, E. L. (1997). In the eye of the beholder: A comment on Samdahl and Jekubovich (1997). A critique of leisure constraints: Comparative analyses and understandings. *Journal of Leisure Research, 29*(4), 458–468.

Jackson, E. L. (2000). Will research on leisure constraints still be relevant in the twenty-first century? *Journal of Leisure Research, 32,* 62–68.

Jackson, E. L. (2005a). (Ed.). *Constraints to leisure.* State College, PA: Venture Publishing, Inc.

Jackson, E. L. (2005b). Leisure constraint research: Overview of a developing theme in leisure studies. In In E. L. Jackson (Ed.), *Constraints to leisure* (pp. 3–19). State College, PA: Venture Publishing, Inc.

Jackson, E. L., Crawford, D. W., & Godbey, G. (1993). The negotiation of leisure constraints. *Leisure Sciences, 15,* 1–11.

Jackson, E. L., & Rucks, V. C. (1995). Negotiation of leisure constraints by junior-high and high-school students: An exploratory study. *Journal of Leisure Research, 27,* 85–105.

Jackson, E. L., & Scott, D. (1999). Constraints to leisure. In E. L. Jackson & T. L. Burton (Eds.), *Leisure studies: Prospects for the twenty-first century* (pp. 299–322). State College, PA: Venture Publishing, Inc.

Jordan, F., & Gibson, H. (2005.) "We're not stupid…But we'll not stay home either": Experiences of solo women travelers. *Tourism Review International,* 9, 195–211.

Jun, J., & Kyle, G. (2011). The effect of identify conflict/facilitation on the experience of constraints to leisure and constraints negotiation. *Journal of Leisure Research, 43*(2), 176–204.

Kay, T., & Jackson, E. L. (1991). Leisure despite constraint: The impact of leisure constraints on leisure participation. *Journal of Leisure Research, 23,* 301–313.

Kleiber, D., McGuire, F. A., & Aybar-Damali, B. Z. (2004, September). *The good, the bad and the better.* Paper presented at the World Leisure & Recreation Association Congress, Brisbane, Australia.

Kleiber, D., McGuire, F. A., Aybar-Damali, B. Z., & Norman, W. (2008). Having more by doing less: The paradox of leisure constraints in later life. *Journal of Leisure Research, 40*(3), 343–360.

Kleiber, D., Wade, M., & Loucks-Atkinson, A. (2005). The utility of the concept of affordance for leisure research. In E. L. Jackson (Ed.), *Constraints to leisure* (pp. 233–245). State College, PA: Venture Publishing, Inc.

Lazarus, R. S., & Folkman, S. (1984). *Stress, appraisal and coping.* New York: Springer Publishing Co., Inc.

Lewis, S. T., & Johnson, C. W. (2011). "But it's not that easy": Negotiating (trans)gender expressions in leisure spaces. *Leisure/Loisir, 35*(2), 115–132.

Little, D. (2002). Women and adventure recreation: Reconstructing leisure constraints and adventure experiences to negotiate continuing participation. *Journal of Leisure Research, 34*(2), 157–177.

Loucks-Atkinson, A., & Mannell, R. C. (2007). Role of self-efficacy in the constraints negotiation process: The case of individuals with Fibromyalgia Syndrome. *Leisure Sciences, 29,* 19–36.

McGuire, F., & Norman, W. (2005). The role of constraints in successful aging: Inhibiting or enabling? In E. L. Jackson (Ed.), *Constraints to leisure* (pp. 89–102). State College, PA: Venture Publishing, Inc.

McQuarrie, F. A., & Jackson, E. L. (1996). Negotiation of leisure constraint and serious leisure: Exploring connections in a case study of adult amateur ice skaters. *Leisure and Society, 19,* 459–483.

Mowen, A., Payne, L., & Scott, D. (2005). Change and stability in park visitation constraints revisited. *Leisure Sciences, 27*, 191–204.

Nadirova, A., & Jackson, E. L. (2000). Alternative criterion variables against which to assess the impacts of constraints to leisure. *Journal of Leisure Research, 32*(4), 396–405.

Nyaupane, G. P., & Andereck, K. L. (2008). Understanding travel constraints: Application and extension of a leisure constraints model. *Journal of Travel Research, 46*(4), 433–440.

Nyaupane, G. P., Morais, D. B., & Graefe, A. (2004). Nature tourism constraints: A cross-activity comparison. *Annals of Tourism Research, 31*(3), 540–555.

Raymore, L. A. (2002). Facilitators to leisure. *Journal of Leisure Research, 34*(1), 37–51.

Raymore, L., Godbey, G., Crawford, D., & von Eye, A. (1993). Nature and process of leisure constraints: An empirical test. *Leisure Sciences, 15*, 99–113.

Samdahl, D. (2005). Making room for "silly" debate: A critical examination on leisure constraints research. In E. L. Jackson (Ed.), *Constraints to leisure* (pp. 337–349). State College, PA: Venture Publishing, Inc.

Samdahl, D. M., Hutchinson, S. L., & Jacobson, S. (1999, May). Navigating constraints? A critical commentary on *negotiation* in leisure studies. Paper presented at the 9th Canadian Congress on Leisure Research, Wolfville, Nova Scotia.

Samdahl, D. M., Jacobson, S., & Hutchinson, S. L. (1998, July). When gender is problematic: Leisure and gender negotiation for marginalized women. Paper presented at the Leisure Studies Association 4th International Conference, Leeds, England.

Samdahl, D. M., & Jekubovich, N. (1997). A critique of leisure constraints: Comparative analyses and understandings. *Journal of Leisure Research, 29*, 430–452.

Schneider, I. E., & Wilhelm Stanis, S. (2007). Coping: An alternative conceptualization for constraint negotiation and accommodation. *Leisure Sciences, 29*, 391–401.

Schneider, I. E., Shinew, K. J., & Fernandez, M. (2013). Leisure constraints. In M. Stodolska, K. J. Shinew, M. F., Floyd, & G. J. Walker (Eds). *Race, ethnicity and leisure* (pp.165–176). Human Kinetics: Champaign, IL.

Scott, D. (1991). The problematic nature of participation in contract bridge: A qualitative study of group-related constraints. *Leisure Sciences, 13*, 321–336.

Shaw, S. M., Bonen, A., & McCabe, J. F. (1991). Do more constraints mean less leisure? Examining the relationship between constraints and participation. *Journal of Leisure Research, 23*, 286–300.

Shogan, D. (2002). Characterizing constraints of leisure: A Foucaultian analysis of leisure constraints. *Leisure Studies, 21*, 27–38.

Shores, K. A., Scott, D., & Floyd, M. F. (2007). Constraints to outdoor recreation: A multiple hierarchy stratification perspective. *Leisure Sciences, 29*(3), 227–246.

Son, J. S., Mowen, A. J., & Kerstetter, D. L. (2008). Testing alternative leisure constraint negotiation models: An extension of Hubbard and Mannell's study. *Leisure Sciences, 30*, 198–216.

Stalp, M. C. (2006). Negotiating time and space for serious leisure: Quilting in the modern U.S. home. *Journal of Leisure Research, 38*(1), 104–132.

Stodolska, M. (1998). Assimilation and leisure constraints: Dynamics of constraints on leisure in immigrant populations. *Journal of Leisure Research, 30*, 521–551.

Stodolska, M., & Yi-Kook, J. (2005). Ethnicity, immigration and constraints. In E. L. Jackson (Ed.), *Constraints to leisure* (pp. 55–73). State College, PA: Venture Publishing, Inc.

Wade, M. (1985). (Ed.). *Constraints on leisure*. Springfield, IL: Charles C. Thomas Publishing.

Walker, G. J. (2007a). Multicultural perspectives. In R. McCarville & K. MacKay (Eds.), *Leisure for Canadians* (pp. 155–161). State College, PA: Venture Publishing, Inc.

Walker, G. J. (2007b). Response to coping as an alternative conceptualization for constraint accommodation and negotiation. *Leisure Sciences, 29*(4), 415–418.

Walker, G. J., Jackson, E. L., & Deng, J. (2007). Culture and leisure constraints: A comparison of Canadian and mainland Chinese university students. *Journal of Leisure Research, 39*(4), 567–590.

Walker, G. J., & Virden, R. J. (2003). A traditional and nontraditional examination of outdoor recreation constraints. Refereed abstract from the 2003 Human Dimensions of Natural Resources in the West Conference, Sun Valley, ID. October 2003.

Walker, G. J., & Virden, R. J. (2005). Constraints on outdoor recreation. In E. L. Jackson (Ed.), *Constraints to leisure* (pp. 201–219). State College, PA: Venture Publishing, Inc.

White, D. (2008). A structural model of leisure constraints negotiation in outdoor recreation. *Leisure Sciences, 30*(4), 342–359.

Wilhelm Stanis, S. A., Schneider, I. E., & Russell, K. (2009). Leisure time physical activity of park visitors: Retesting constraint models in adoption and maintenance stages. *Leisure Sciences, 31(3)*, 287–304.

Wood, L., & Danylchuk, K. (2012). Constraints and negotiation processes in a women's recreational sport group. *Journal of Leisure Research, 44*(4), 463–485.

Zhang, H., Zhang, J., Cheng, S., Lu, S., & Shi, C. (2012). Role of constraints in Chinese calligraphic landscape experience: An extension of a leisure constraints model. *Tourism Management, 33*, 1398–1407.

19

Leisure and Intensity of Participation

David Scott (Texas A&M University)

Within any given leisure social world, activity participants exhibit a wide range of attachments and commitments. For some participants, the activity dominates their everyday lives and may be a central life interest. These individuals seek out other devotees, organize activity on behalf of others, hone their skills through practice and study, and negotiate constraints in order to maintain regular patterns of participation (Hubbard & Mannell, 2001; Scott & Godbey, 1994; Stalp, 2006; Stebbins, 2007). Other participants, in contrast, are far less attached to the leisure activity, participate infrequently, and have little interest in developing their skills. For these "casual" participants, activity choices are often based on their ability to nurture relationships with friends and/or family (Scott, Cavin, & Shafer, 2007).

Leisure researchers and practitioners have long recognized that that an understanding of how recreationists differ in intensity of participation and how involvement changes over time can enhance leisure service delivery and policy (Bryan, 1977; Scott, 2012; Selin & Howard, 1988). Numerous studies have documented that participants' experience, knowledge, and commitment influence several facets of leisure involvement, including motivations and expected rewards; attitudes about management practices; substitution decisions; place attachment; destination preferences; use of information to make trip decisions; perceived crowding and conflict; and physical and social setting preferences (Manning 2011; Scott & Shafer, 2001). Understanding these relationships can help practitioners create programs and services that will be relevant to a multiplicity of activity participants.

There is less agreement, however, about how best to define and measure participants' intensity of participation. Several interrelated concepts and frameworks have been advanced over the last 40 years to study the attachments and meanings people assign to leisure activities. Two frameworks—recreational specialization and serious leisure—have come to dominate how investigators study variability among activity participants. Other concepts and ideas, however, have also been proposed, including experience use history, activity loyalty, commitment, and ego involvement. The purpose of this chapter is to summarize how researchers have conceptualized and used these perspectives in leisure research. I begin by summarizing ideas about experience use history, loyalty, involvement, and commitment. I then turn to providing a summary of serious leisure and recreational specialization. I complete this chapter by putting forward some suggestions for future research.

Conceptualizing Intensity of Participation

Over 40 years ago, Elwood Shafer (1969) warned researchers and practitioners against indiscriminately lumping survey data collected from campers collected at different campgrounds and across different months of the year: "If you study campers by sampling at random at several campgrounds, you may find that your data describe an 'average' camper who simply does not exist" (p. 1). Shafer observed that policies and decision making based on an "average" camper would be invariably flawed as they fail to take into account diversity among participants.

Since the publication of Shafer's (1969) classic work, several empirical and theoretical investigations have been put forward to study variability among activity participants. Much of this literature has been devoted to explaining patterns of leisure (e.g., social and setting preferences) in light of *intensity of participation*. I use intensity of participation as an umbrella term for characterizing the affective and behavioral attachments people exhibit toward specific leisure activities[1]. Three preliminary points about this definition are in order. First, as will become apparent, this

[1] A similar term—high-investment activities—was put forward by Mannell (1993).

definition is a hybrid of several concepts proposed by researchers to depict participants' varying interest and experience in leisure activities. It is presented simply to orient readers to this area of research. Second, my focus here is on the meaning recreationists assign to *specific leisure activities*. We might ask, for example, what proportion of people attending a birdwatching festival are serious, intermediate, or casual birders? This leads to a third point: recreationists can generally be arranged along a continuum of participation from casual to highly serious. As noted by Hobson Bryan (1979), the complexity of the activity largely dictates the amount of variability along the recreation continuum. Participants in complex activities, such as hunting, birdwatching, chess, and contract bridge, manifest a wide range of styles of participation and commitments.

One of the initial attempts to operationalize intensity of participation was in the form of experience use history (EUH). Schreyer, Lime, and Williams (1984) conceived EUH as "an indicator of the extent and type of information available to the individual obtained through participation in differing circumstances" (p. 35). Although EUH was conceived as an indicator of *cognitive complexity*, Schreyer et al. and other investigators have measured the concept by creating a composite index that combines participants' responses to multiple *behavioral* variables. For example, Schreyer et al. had river users indicate: (a) the number of times they had floated the study river, (b) the number of rivers they had floated, and (c) the total number of river trips they had made. Based on their responses to these three questionnaire items, river users were then classified into one of six categories along a continuum of involvement ranging from novice to veteran. Researchers have used since EUH as a segmentation tool to predict motivations, satisfactions, perceptions of conflict, and other facets of involvement among backpackers (Hammitt, McDonald, & Hughes, 1986), horseback riders (Hammitt, Knauf, & Noe, 1989), and golfers (Petrick, Backman, Bixler, & Norman, 2001).

Intensity of participation has also been operationalized via activity loyalty. Backman and Crompton (1991) borrowed the concept from the consumer behavior literature to assess the factors that bind participants to golf and tennis. Their measure of activity loyalty included attitudinal (people's attachment to an activity) and behavioral (proportion of time devoted to tennis and golf) dimensions. Not surprisingly, the attitudinal measure was strongly related to a measure of social psychological involvement, while the behavioral measure was negatively related to frequency of participation in other leisure activities. Activity loyalty has been scantly used over the last 20 years to measure intensity of participation to leisure activities. Instead, it has been primarily used to measure participants' allegiance to services and tourism destinations (e.g., Chi & Qu, 2008).

Selin and Howard (1988) broke important ground in the conceptualization of intensity of participation by introducing ego involvement (or simply activity involvement) to the leisure literature. They defined activity involvement as "the state of identification existing between an individual and a recreational activity, at one point in time, characterized by some level of enjoyment and self-expression being achieved through the activity" (p. 237). Havitz and Dimanche (1997) put forward an alternative, but similar, definition: "An unobservable state of motivation, arousal or interest toward a recreational activity or associated product" (p. 246). As with the concept of loyalty, activity involvement was borrowed from the consumer behavior literature (see Rothschild, 1984) but was originally derived from social judgment theory in social psychology (Sherif & Cantril, 1947). The underlying idea is that when attitudes become aroused they give direction to a person's behavior. Stated differently, recreation participants who are highly attached (involved) to a given activity are more likely than others to behave and make lifestyle decisions that are congruent with their high level of involvement.

While some studies have employed behavioral measures to assess activity involvement (see Kim, Scott, & Crompton, 1997), attitudinal measures have dominated the literature. Some studies (e.g., Backman & Crompton, 1991; Kim et al., 1997) have used Zaichkowsky's (1985) Personal Involvement Inventory (PII) to measure involvement. The PII is a single dimension scale comprised of 20 pairs of semantic differential items. Most studies in the literature, however, treat activity involvement as multidimensional. Many researchers have borrowed and/or modified the Consumer Involvement Profile (CIP) developed by Laurent and Kapferer (1985). The CIP was composed of 15 items and was purported to measure five dimensions of activity involvement: importance, pleasure, sign, risk probability, and risk consequences. Some researchers have questioned the utility of using all five dimensions (e.g., Havitz & Dimanche, 1997) to measure activity involvement. Still others have conceived activity involvement as including enjoyment, importance, self-expression, and centrality (McIntyre, 1989). Despite definitional and measurement differences, activity involvement has been used extensively to measure intensity of participation across a broad array of leisure activities (Havitz & Dimanche, 1997) and to predict various facets of participation, including loyalty to service providers (Iwasaki & Havitz, 2004; Kyle & Mowen, 2005), place attachment (Kyle, Graefe, Manning, & Bacon, 2004; Moore & Graefe, 1994), perceptions of constraints and negotiation of constraints (Lee & Scott, 2009), motivations (Kyle, Absher, Hammitt, & Cavin, 2006), and flow and enjoyment (Havitz & Mannell, 2005).

In many ways, activity loyalty and ego involvement are similar to the concept of commitment. Buchanan (1985) provided leisure researchers one of the first definitions of commitment: "the pledging or binding of an individual to behavioral acts which result in some degree of affective attachment to behavior or the role associated with the behavior and which produce side bets as a result of that behavior" (p. 402). Three dimensions of commitment are implied by Buchanan's definition: (a) consistent or focused behavior and a concomitant rejection of alternative behavior, (b) affective attachment, and (c) side bets. In the leisure literature, affective attachment and side bets have been treated as antecedents of consistent or focused behavior. These two forms of commitment warrant further explanation.

Among sociologists, affective attachment is identical to personal commitment (Kim et al., 1997). Scott and Shafer (2001) described personal commitment as an inner conviction that a leisure activity is superior and worth doing for its own sake. Personal commitment goes beyond simply regarding the activity as enjoyable and interesting—it involves identifying and defining oneself in terms of the pastime (Shamir, 1988; Yair, 1990). It also entails espousing the values and culture of the social world in which one is involved (Buchanan, 1985). In contrast, side bets (which have been called behavioral commitment) are those outside interests and activities that become implicated when people pursue a particular behavior (Becker, 1960). Stated differently, side bets are those penalties or costs associated with discontinuing leisure participation. Some penalties associated with ceasing participation are loss of friends, loss of financial investments, loss of personal identity, and lack of alternative leisure interests.

A few studies have used commitment as a stand-alone indicator of intensity of participation and found it to be correlated with activity involvement, frequency of participation, behavioral intentions, and reported skill and perceived competence (Kim et al., 1997; Shamir, 1988; Yair, 1990). However, commitment is increasingly used in the conceptualization and measurement of recreational specialization. More will be said about commitment and recreational specialization below.

Two observations are in order before introducing ideas about serious leisure and recreational specialization. First, leisure scholars have generally shied away from debating whether or not the concepts reviewed thus far are more alike than they are different. Studies in fact have shown that measures representing the above concepts are moderately correlated with one another (Backman & Crompton, 1991; Kim et al., 1997; Shamir, 1988). That the concepts overlap with one another may stem from the fact that researchers introduced them independently from different disciplines. Some effort, however, has been made to reconcile these differences. Iwasaki and Havitz (1998), for example, argued that people's involvement or attachment to activities was antecedent to commitment and loyalty. Iwasaki and Havitz (2004) subsequently modified their model and argued that activity involvement contributes to participants developing commitments and loyalty to agencies and services. Similar linkages have been proposed between activity involvement and participants' attachments to outdoor recreation environments (Kyle et al., 2004). These studies are unique in their efforts to partition intensity of participation indicators and to link them causally.

Second, the above concepts provide snapshots of recreationists' intensity of participation at a *given point in time*. They say relatively little about how recreationists' attitudes and behavior change and/or evolve over time. EUH comes closest in capturing these changes as the perspective assumes recreationists' cognitions become increasingly complex with increasing experience (Williams, Schreyer, & Knopf, 1990). However, because EUH is constructed by combining a handful of behavioral variables, it provides an indirect measure of participants' cumulative knowledge and familiarity with a leisure activity. Likewise, the four concepts are mute about how skill and knowledge differences impact leisure involvement. For many recreationists, skill acquisition is integral to their participation and leisure and lifestyle choices are made accordingly. The next sections of this chapter summarize ideas about serious leisure and recreational specialization. Change and skill development are central to how these frameworks have been conceptualized.

SERIOUS LEISURE

The serious leisure framework is nearly synonymous with the name of Robert Stebbins. A sociologist by training, Stebbins' (1979) early work focused on documenting the careers and commitments of amateur actors, archeologists, and baseball players. He would expand his focus to other leisure activities which would eventually lead to a formal definition of serious leisure: "The systematic pursuit of an amateur, hobbyist, or volunteer core activity that people find so substantial, interesting, and fulfilling that, in the typical case, they launch themselves on a (leisure) career centered on acquiring and expressing a combination of its special skills, knowledge, and experience" (Stebbins, 1992, p. 3). Stebbins (1982, 1992, 2007) put forward six defining characteristics of serious leisure: participants identify strongly with chosen pastimes, persevere and overcome setbacks, have careers, display effort based on specialized knowledge and training, pursue activity within leisure social worlds, and experience durable (long-term) benefits.

Stebbins' serious leisure framework includes two other important concepts: casual leisure and project-based leisure. Stebbins (1997) described casual leisure as activity that is inherently less substantial than serious leisure and offers little in the way of career development. He added that it is "immediately, intrinsically rewarding, relatively short-lived pleasurable activity requiring little or no special training to enjoy it" (p. 18). Examples of casual leisure include watching television, taking a nap, and reading the paper. Stebbins (2007) defined project-based leisure as "a short-term, moderately complicated, either one-shot or occasional, though infrequent, creative undertaking carried out in free time" (p. 43). Stebbins cited elaborate surprise parties and preparations for holidays as examples of project-based leisure. In sum, compared to serious leisure, casual leisure and project-based leisure lack complexity and do not offer the same opportunities for careers and skill development.

It is important to note that Stebbins' (1979, 1982) early research on serious leisure was directed at elucidating an *intense* style of leisure participation. His definition of serious leisure and exposition of its six distinguishing qualities were created with this style of leisure participation in mind. Although Stebbins (2012) acknowledged that participants in complex activities varied in seriousness—he distinguished among devotees (highly serious), participants (moderately serious), and dabblers (unserious)—his focus has primarily been on describing patterns of participation of devotees (i.e., participants who are highly serious). Stebbins' "dabblers" are similar to casual participants in that neither are highly invested and lack interest in developing their skills. However, he reserves the term "casual leisure" for describing activities that are inherently simple (i.e., not complex) and can be pursued without advanced training. In recent years, a new cadre of scholars have emerged who recognize that recreation participants do in fact vary in seriousness (Shen & Yarnal, 2010; Tsaur & Liang, 2008). A newly created Serious Leisure Inventory (Gould, Moore, McGuire, & Stebbins, 2008) seeks to measure the six distinguishing qualities of serious leisure. This instrument may help researchers and practitioners better study degrees of seriousness along a continuum of participation.

Stebbins (1992) emphasized that people have careers and serious participants go through typical stages of involvement. These stages were a beginning, development, establishment, maintenance, and decline. Stebbins noted that movement from one stage to another is far from automatic and is *contingent* on a variety of factors that are sometimes outside the control of the individual. Children's progression, for example, is contingent on parental support. Mentors and coaches may also provide participants instruction and confidence to persevere. Having requisite skills and being collegial may facilitate and/or inhibit progression. Stebbins noted that participants judged to be unskilled, lacking knowledge, or unfriendly are likely to "find others being hired or invited into a group before themselves" (pp. 82–83). Mastery and display of appropriate skills and knowledge appear to be essential for long-term participation in serious leisure.

Serious leisure has become a "construct of choice" (Scott, 2012) to study intense forms of leisure. It has been used to study a wide array of pastimes, including Taekwondo (Kim, Dattilo, & Heo, 2011), football spectating (Gibson, Willming, & Holdnak, 2002), and Civil War re-enacting (Hunt, 2004). Serious leisure has also been studied across diverse groups, including immigrants, people with disabilities, older adults, and women. These and other studies have shown that participation in serious leisure activities contributes to positive outcomes, including successful aging (Brown, McGuire, & Voelkl, 2008) and challenging traditional gender roles (Dilley & Scraton, 2010). Participation in serious leisure can also contribute to ethnic identity and ethnic boundary maintenance (Lee, Scott, & Dunlap, 2011). In this case, immigrant groups use "serious leisure to highlight how they are culturally different from non-immigrant groups" (p. 305). In summary, the serious leisure perspective has proven to be a useful conceptual framework for describing how participants strive to create identity in contemporary societies and the behaviors and attitudes of participants involved in intense and complex forms of activities.

RECREATIONAL SPECIALIZATION

Hobson Bryan (1977, 1979) introduced the recreational specialization (or simply specialization) framework into the literature to explain within-activity differences among outdoor recreation participants. Although its use continues to be primarily applied to outdoor pursuits, some researchers have used the framework to study indoor pastimes (Scott & Godbey, 1994) as well as tourism activities (Kerstetter, Confer, & Graefe, 2001). Bryan defined specialization as "a continuum of behavior from the general to the particular, reflected by equipment and skills used in the sport, and activity setting preferences" (1977, p. 175). This definition is a bit ambiguous but the idea is that participants within any activity can be arranged along a continuum from "casual" to "serious" as reflected by their level of commitment, frequency of participation, skill and knowledge, and equipment preferences.

The specialization framework goes beyond the serious leisure framework by describing characteristic styles of participation along a continuum of involvement. According to Bryan (1977), these styles of participation can be represented in the form of a typology (a system of classification). Bryan contended, for example, that trout fishermen could be grouped into four classes of anglers: occasional fishermen, generalists, technique specialists, and technique setting specialists. These angler types provide researchers and practitioners a "comparative tool for examining typical behaviors and attitudes along a "continuum of fishing specialization" (p. 184). Stated differently, the four categories of anglers can be distinguished on the basis of their equipment preferences, skills, social and setting preferences, and history of participation. Other researchers have developed similar specialization typologies of boaters (Donnelly, Vaske, & Graefe, 1986), contract bridge players (Scott & Godbey, 1994), birdwatchers (McFarlane, 1994), and scuba divers (Todd, Graefe, & Mann, 2002).

Similar to Stebbins' ideas about serious leisure, Bryan (1977) argued that people have *careers* in their leisure pursuits. His typology of fishing participation, thus, constituted a framework for explaining the typical stages through which recreationists advance the longer they fished. He theorized that anglers "typically start with simple, easily mastered techniques which maximize chances of a catch, then move to more involved and demanding methods the longer they engage in the sport" (p. 182). Specialization, thus, is more than an analytic scheme for differentiating participants along a continuum of involvement—it constitutes a *developmental process* that entails a progression in how people participate in and view the activity over time (Scott & Shafer, 2001). As recreationists move from one stage of participation to another, their motivations, social and setting preferences, and attitudes about management practices and policies change as well.

To recap, research on specialization seeks: first, to classify activity participants along a continuum of involvement from casual to serious, and second, to explain how participants' interests and skills change over time. Both of these applications converge on a sticky point: exactly how should specialization be measured? Although researchers agree that specialization is multidimensional, they have put forward multiple overlapping dimensions and variables (Scott, Ditton, Stoll, & Eubanks, 2005; Scott & Shafer, 2001), including frequency of participation, past experience, general experience, recent experience, commitment, economic investments, centrality to lifestyle, enduring involvement, purism values, media involvement, skills, and resource use. Definitional challenges are exacerbated by whether or not specific measures reflect one dimension of specialization or another (Kuentzel & McDonald, 1992). For example, ability to identify birds has been conceived as both an indicator of skill and an indicator of past experience.

After surveying existing research, Scott and Shafer (2001) concluded that specialization should be conceived and measured using three dimensions: (a) a focusing of behavior, (b) the acquiring of skills and knowledge, and (c) personal and behavioral commitments. Behavioral indicators include years of involvement and frequency of participation. Skill indicators are activity-specific and might include skill at navigating white water rapids and ability to identify bird songs. As noted, personal commitments include affective attachment and personal identity, while behavioral commitments include potential penalties (e.g., loss of friends) associated with ceasing participation. These three dimensions are quite similar to ones put forth by McIntyre and Pigram (1992) who argued that specialization included a behavioral dimension (e.g., prior experience and familiarity), a cognitive dimension (e.g., skills and knowledge), and an affective dimension (e.g., enduring involvement and centrality). Clearly, both of these approaches to operationalizing specialization borrowed a great deal from other intensity of participation concepts.

Researchers studying specialization have also debated how best to classify recreationists along a continuum of involvement. Two approaches have been dominant. One approach is to create a composite (or additive) index by adding a recreation participant's responses to multiple questionnaire items (e.g., Salz, Loomis, & Finn, 2001). Recreationists are then divided into three or more groups that range from low (least specialized) to high (highly specialized). This approach has been criticized because specialization dimensions do not always co-vary and have different levels of relationship to other facets of involvement (Kuentzel & McDonald, 1992). Researchers have avoided this problem by using *cluster analysis*. This statistical procedure takes into account the multidimensionality of the specialization construct and classifies respondents into homogenous groups. This second approach has been used extensively across a variety of activities, including fishing (Chipman & Helfrich, 1988), hunting (Needham & Vaske, 2013), birdwatching (McFarlane, 1994), and camping (McIntyre & Pigram, 1992).

An alternative approach for classifying participants has been tested in studies of birdwatchers (Scott et al., 2005) and Ultimate Frisbee (Kerins, Scott, & Shafer, 2007). These studies had respondents self-identify themselves as either a casual, active, or committed (serious) participant. The three categories of participation included elements of behavior, skill, and commitment and were designed to reflect unique styles of participation along the specialization continuum. In both studies, the self-classification measure was compared with an additive index and cluster analysis measure in predicting participants' motives. Results from both studies indicated that the self-classification measure performed as well, if not better, than the two traditional approaches in predicting participants' motives. Likewise, in both studies there was a strong association between the self-classification measure and individual specialization indicators.

Dozens of studies have used the specialization framework to effectively document differences among activity participants in regards to a wide range of variables, such as motives, substitution decisions, place attachment and dependence, attitudes toward resource management, socialization influences, equipment preferences, and perceptions of crowding (see Manning, 2011 for a more complete summary of variables studied by researchers). Before putting forward some conclusions and recommendations for future research, it is important to emphasize that scholars continue to grapple with how best to measure specialization. A lack of consensus has compromised their ability to generalize findings. Even with this limitation, the specialization framework provides researchers and practitioners an invaluable tool for exploring characteristic styles of participation along a continuum of involvement.

CONCLUSIONS AND SUGGESTIONS FOR FUTURE RESEARCH

Several concepts have been reviewed that purportedly measure intensity of participation. Two of these, serious leisure and recreational specialization, have come to dominate how researchers think about and study variability among activity participants. A question arises: Just how different from one another are the concepts and frameworks used to study intensity of participation? For example, specialization is frequently measured using indicators of experience use history, commitment, and involvement. Likewise, serious leisure implies commitment and a high degree of affective attachment. Are researchers guilty of reinventing the wheel or are the different concepts measuring different facets of participation? Arguments have been made that the concepts have more in common than not (Scott, 2012), but others scholars have argued they are different (Iwasaki & Havitz, 2004; Stebbins, 2007). Research is needed to understand better the linkages among the concepts reviewed in this chapter. It could be that the concepts can be combined to provide a more complete assessment of people's participation in complex forms of leisure.

Although researchers agree that positive outcomes can accrue for individuals who advance to higher stages of involvement, progression can have a dark side. Stebbins (2007) used the term "uncontrollability" to refer the "desire to engage in an activity beyond the time or the money (if not both) available for it" (p. 17). Another term for this is "addiction," which can be defined as a recurring and unhealthy behavior the individual has difficulty ending (Yee, 2002). Taken to an extreme, serious leisure can have negative consequences for participants' health, school and work, and relationships with significant others (Holt & Kleiber, 2009; Partington, Partington, & Olivier, 2009; Wu, Scott, & Yang, 2013). To date, researchers have focused primarily on the positive aspects of serious leisure, involvement, and specialization. More research is needed to understand the costs and negative consequences of serious leisure and progression.

Increasingly, researchers are questioning the conventional wisdom that participants naturally progress to higher stages of involvement over time. Panel data from boaters and birdwatchers suggest that while some individuals do in fact progress over time, most participants follow a pattern of stability or decline (Kuentzel & Heberlein, 2006; Scott & Lee, 2010). Studies also suggest that most recreation participants are clustered toward the casual end of the specialization continuum (McFarlane, 1994). At least one study shows that many participants actually eschew progression and are content to participate in a leisure activity at a rudimentary level (Scott & Godbey, 1994). The truth is we are only beginning to understand the contingencies and various life course events impacting people's interest and attachment to leisure activities over time. Additional studies using panel data will shed insight into how intrapersonal, interpersonal, and structural factors both facilitate and constrain people's movement to different stages of participation. Such studies should examine the extent to which people desire to progress to higher stages of participation, and the factors that contribute to patterns of regression. It is also important to examine how performance standards contribute to progression, stability, and decline. Competitive sports, for example, tend to stymie participants' desire and ability to progress, whereas outdoor recreation activities provide participants more opportunities for both stability and progression over time.

A related and final area of research that is needed pertains to how different population groups think about intensity of participation. An argument could be made that ideas about serious leisure and specialization are male-centric. In many societies, opportunities for progression and advancement are more restricted for women than they are for men. Scott and Shafer (2001) noted that married women who participate in serious leisure go to great lengths to ensure that time spent in the activity does not interfere with family obligations. Simultaneously, the vast majority of studies on serious leisure and specialization have skirted issues related to race, ethnicity, and social class. Research clearly shows that discrimination and status group barriers are major constraints to leisure among people of color and people who are poor (Stodolska & Floyd, Chapter 28). At the same time, research shows that immigrants use leisure to insulate themselves from nonimmigrants. Extending investigations into the lived experiences of different population groups will enhance our understanding of serious leisure, specialization, and related concepts. This research will require using phenomenological and ethnographic methods to study intensity of participation.

REFERENCES

Backman, S. J. (1991). The usefulness of selected variables for predicting activity loyalty. *Leisure Sciences, 13*, 205–220.

Becker, H. S. (1960). Notes on the concept of commitment. *American Journal of Sociology, 66*(1), 32–40.

Bryan, H. (1977). Leisure value system and recreational specialization: The case of trout fishermen. *Journal of Leisure Research, 9*, 174–187.

Bryan, H. (1979). *Conflict in the great outdoors.* Birmingham, AL: The Birmingham Publishing Co.

Brown, C. A., McGuire, F. A., & Voelkl, J. (2008). The link between successful aging and serious leisure. *The International Journal of Aging and Human Development, 66*, 73–95.

Buchanan, T. (1985). Commitment and leisure behavior: A theoretical perspective. *Leisure Sciences, 7*, 401–420.

Chi, C. G., & Qu, J. (2008). Examining the structural relationships of destination image, tourist satisfaction and destination loyalty: An integrated approach. *Tourism Management, 29*, 624–636.

Chipman, B. D., & Helfrich, L. A. (1988). Recreation specialization and motivations of Virginia river anglers. *North American Journal of Fisheries Management, 8*, 390–398.

Dilley, R. E., & Scraton, S. J. (2010). Women, climbing and serious leisure. *Leisure Studies, 29*, 125–141.

Donnelly, M. P., Vaske, J. J., & Graefe, A. R. (1986). Degree and range of recreation specialization: Toward a typology of boating related activities. *Journal of Leisure Research, 18*, 81–95.

Gibson, H., Willming, C., & Holdnak, A. (2002). "We're Gators . . . not just gator fans": Serious leisure and University of Florida football. *Journal of Leisure Research, 34*, 397–425.

Gould, J., Moore, D., McGuire, F., & Stebbins, R. (2008). Development of the serious leisure inventory and measure. *Journal of Leisure Research, 40*, 47–68.

Hammitt, W. E., Knauf, L. R., & Noe, F. P. (1989). A comparison of user vs researcher determined level of past experience on recreation preference. *Journal of Leisure Research, 21*, 202–213.

Hammitt, W., McDonald, C., & Hughes. (1986). Experience level and participation motives of winter wilderness users. *Proceedings—National Wilderness Research Conference: Current Research*. USDA Forest Service General Technical Report INT-212, 269–277.

Havitz, M. E., & Dimanche, F. (1997). Leisure involvement revisited: Conceptual conundrums and measurement advances. *Journal of Leisure Research, 29*, 245–278.

Havitz, M. E., & Mannell, R. C. (2005). Enduring involvement, situational involvement, and flow in leisure and non-leisure activities. *Journal of Leisure Research, 37*, 152–177.

Holt, N. A., & Kleiber, D. A. (2009). The Sirens' song of multiplayer games. *Children, Youth and Environments, 19*, 223–244.

Hubbard, J., & Mannell, R. C. (2001). Testing competing models of the leisure constraint negotiation process in a corporate employee recreation setting. *Leisure Sciences, 23*, 145–163.

Hunt, S. J. (2004). Acting the part: "Living history" as a serious leisure pursuit. *Leisure Studies, 23*, 387–403.

Iwasaki, Y., & Havitz, M. E. (1998). A path analytic model of the relationships between involvement, psychological commitment, and loyalty. *Journal of Leisure Research, 30*, 256–280.

Iwasaki, Y., & Havitz, M. E. (2004). Examining relationships between leisure involvement, psychological commitment and loyalty to a recreation agency. *Journal of Leisure Research, 36*, 45–72.

Kerins, A. J., Scott, D., & Shafer, C. S. (2007). Evaluating the efficacy of a self-classification measure of recreation specialization in the context of Ultimate Frisbee. *Journal of Park and Recreation Administration, 25*(3), 1–22.

Kerstetter, D. L., Confer, J. J., & Graefe, A. R. (2001). An exploration of the specialization concept within the context of heritage tourism. *Journal of Travel Research, 39*, 267–274.

Kim, J. H., Dattilo, J., & Heo, J. M. (2011). Taekwondo participation as serious leisure for life satisfaction and health. *Journal of Leisure Research, 43*, 545–559.

Kim, S. S., Scott, D., & Crompton, J. L. (1997). An exploration of the relationships among social psychological involvement, behavioral involvement, commitment, and future intentions in the context of birdwatching. *Journal of Leisure Research, 29*, 320–341.

Kuentzel, W. F., & Heberlein, T. A. (2006). From novice to expert? A panel study of specialization progression and change. *Journal of Leisure Research, 38*, 496–512.

Kuentzel, W., & McDonald, C. D. (1992). Differential effects of past experience commitment, and lifestyle dimensions on river use specialization. *Journal of Leisure Research, 24*, 269–287.

Kyle, G., Absher, J., Hammit, W., & Cavin, J. (2006). An examination of the motivation-involvement relationship. *Leisure Sciences, 28*, 467–485.

Kyle, G., Graefe, A., Manning, R., & Bacon, J. (2004). Predictors of behavioral loyalty among hikers along the Appalachian Trail. *Leisure Sciences, 26*, 99–118.

Kyle, G. T., & Mowen, A. J. (2005). An examination of the leisure involvement-agency commitment relationship. *Journal of Leisure Research, 37*, 342–363.

Laurent, G., and Kapferer, J. N. (1985). Measuring consumer involvement profiles. *Journal of Marketing Research, 22*, 41–53.

Lee, K. J., Dunlap, R., & Scott, D. (2011). Korean immigrants' serious leisure experiences and their perceptions of different play styles in recreational sports. *Leisure Sciences, 33*, 290–308.

Lee, S., & Scott, D. (2009). The process of celebrity fan's constraint negotiation. *Journal of Leisure Research, 41*, 137–156.

Mannell, R. C. (1993). High-investment activity and life satisfaction among older adults: Committed, serious leisure, and flow activities. In J. R. Kelly (Ed.), *Activity and aging: Staying involved in later life* (pp. 125–145). Newbury Park, CA: Sage Publication.

Manning, R. E. (2011). *Studies in outdoor recreation* (3rd ed.). Corvallis: University of Oregon Press.

McFarlane, B. L. (1994). Specialization and motivations of birdwatchers. *Wildlife Society Bulletin, 22*, 361–370.

McIntyre, N. (1989). The personal meaning of participation: Enduring involvement. *Journal of Leisure Research, 21*, 167–179.

McIntyre, N., & Pigram, J. J. (1992). Recreation specialization reexamined: The case of vehicle-based campers. *Leisure Sciences, 14*, 3–15.

Moore, R. L., & Graefe, A. R. (1994). Attachments to recreation settings: The case of rail-trail users. *Leisure Sciences, 16*, 17–31.

Needham, M. D., & Vaske, J. J. (2013). Activity substitutability and degree of specialization among deer and elk hunters in multiple states. *Leisure Sciences, 35*, 235–255.

Partington, S., Partington, E., & Olivier S. (2009). The dark side of flow: A qualitative study of dependence in big wave surfing. *The Sport Psychologist, 23*, 170–185.

Petrick, J. F., Backman, S. J., Bixler, R., & Norman, W. C. (2001). Analysis of golfer motivations and constraints by experience use history. *Journal of Leisure Research, 33*, 56–70.

Rothschild, M. L. (1984). Perspectives on involvement: Current problems and future directions. *Advances in Consumer Research, 11*, 216–217.

Salz, R. J., Loomis, D. K., & Finn, K. L. (2001). Development and validation of a specialization index and testing of specialization theory. *Human Dimensions of Wildlife, 6*(4), 239–258.

Schreyer, R., Lime, D. W., & Williams, D. R. (1984). Characterizing the influence of past experience on recreation behavior. *Journal of Leisure Research, 16*, 34–50.

Scott, D. (2012). Serious leisure and recreation specialization: An uneasy marriage. *Leisure Science, 34*, 366–371.

Scott, S., Cavin, D. A., & Shafer, C. S. (2007). Toward a new understanding of recreational specialization. *Annals of Leisure and Recreation Research, 1*(2), 1–24.

Scott, D., Ditton, R. B., Stoll, J. R., & Eubanks Jr., T. L. (2005). Measuring specialization among birders: Utility of a self-classification measure. *Human Dimensions of Wildlife, 10*(1), 53–74.

Scott, D., & Godbey, G. (1994). Recreation specialization in the social world of contract bridge. *Journal of Leisure Research, 26*, 275–295.

Scott, D., & Lee, J. H. (2010). Progression, stability, or decline? Sociological mechanisms underlying change in specialization among birdwatchers. *Leisure Sciences, 32*, 180–194.

Scott, D., & Shafer, C. S. (2001). Recreational specialization: A critical look at the construct. *Journal of Leisure Research, 33*, 319–343.

Selin, S. W., & Howard, D. R. (1988). Ego involvement and leisure behavior. *Journal of Leisure Research, 20*, 237–244.

Shafer, E. L., Jr. (1969). *The average camper who doesn't exist.* USDA Forest Service Research Paper (NE-142). Upper Darby, PA: Northeastern Forest Experiment Station.

Shamir, B. (1988). Commitment and leisure. *Sociological Perspective, 31*, 238–258.

Shen, X.S., & Yarnal, C. (2010). Blowing open the serious leisure-casual leisure dichotomy: What's in there? *Leisure Sciences, 32*, 162–179.

Sherif, M., & Cantril, H. (1947). *The psychology of ego-involvement*. New York: John Wiley & Sons, Inc.

Stalp, M. (2006). Negotiating time and space for serious leisure: Quilting in the modern U.S. *Journal of Leisure Research, 38*, 104–132.

Stebbins, R. A. (1979). *Amateurs: On the margin between work and leisure*. Beverly Hills, CA: Sage.

Stebbins, R. A. (1982). Serious leisure: A conceptual statement. *Pacific Sociological Review, 25*, 251–272.

Stebbins, R. A. (1992). *Amateurs, professionals and serious leisure.* Montreal, QC: McGill-Queen's University Press.

Stebbins, R. A. (1997). Casual leisure: A conceptual statement. *Leisure Studies, 16*, 17–25.

Stebbins, R. A. (2007). *Serious leisure: A perspective for our time*. New Brunswick, NJ: Transaction Publishers.

Stebbins, R. A. (2012). Comments on Scott: Recreation specialization and the CL-SL continuum. *Leisure Sciences, 34*, 372–373.

Todd, S. L., Graefe, A. R., & Mann, W. (2002). Differences in diver motivation based on level of development. *Proceedings of the 2001 Northeastern Recreation Research Symposium* (pp. 107–114). General Technical Report

NE 289. Newtown Square, PA: US Forest Service, Northeastern Research Station.

Tsaur, S.-H., & Liang, Y.-W. (2008). Serious leisure and recreation specialization. *Leisure Science, 30*, 325–341.

Williams, D. R., Schreyer, R., & Knopf, R. C. (1990). The effect of the experience use history on the multidimensional structure of motivations to participate in leisure activities. *Journal of Leisure Research, 22*, 36–54.

Wu, T., Scott, D., & Yang, C. (2013). Advanced or addicted? Exploring the relationship of recreation specialization to flow experiences and online game addiction. *Leisure Sciences, 35*, 203–217.

Yair, G. (1990). The commitments to long distance running and levels of activity: Personal or structural? *Journal of Leisure Research, 22*, 213–227.

Yee, N. (2002). *Ariadne: Understanding MMORPG addiction.* Retrieved June 8, 2012 from http://www.nickyee.com/hub/addiction/home.html.

Zaichkowsky, J. L. (1985). Measuring the involvement construct. *Journal of Consumer Research, 12*, 341–352.

20

From Purple Roots to Dark, Sexy, and Diverse: The Past, Present, and Future of Deviant Leisure

D J Williams (Idaho State University, Pocatello; and the Center for Positive Sexuality, Los Angeles)

People have always been, and probably always will be, fascinated with deviance. Deviance is consumed in large doses by the masses via popular culture, and it is not surprising that the recent book series *50 Shades of Grey* (by E. L. James; Vintage Books) and *Twilight* (by Stephanie Meyer; Little, Brown & Company) have been international bestsellers. Central to such fascination with deviance are questions involving "what," "who," and "why." There is a broad spectrum of experiences that may be classified as deviant at any given time, and of course, many scholars have been, and still are, curious about deviance. Social and behavioral scientists of all varieties have long sought to explain it, and, simultaneously, often control it.

Deviant leisure, sometimes referred to as *purple leisure* or *taboo recreation* (Russell, 2013), is the focus of this chapter. There has been some excellent initial work on this topic conducted primarily by Chris Rojek and Robert Stebbins during the 1990s (i.e., Rojek, 1997, 1999a, 1999b; Stebbins, 1996, 1997), along with a special issue on deviant leisure in *Leisure/Loisir* (Stebbins, Rojek, & Sullivan, 2006). Nevertheless, deviant leisure remains underexplored and undertheorized. Despite this observation, the concept is starting to draw interest from scholars formally outside of leisure science but in related fields. The phenomenon of deviant leisure extending beyond the borders of leisure science is likely to continue, for important reasons, well into the future.

In this chapter I will quickly review a few key studies in the development of the concept of deviant leisure. A basic understanding of deviant leisure is important to learn, but it seems to be somewhat restrictive in that it draws heavily from traditional deviance discourses rooted in psychology and sociology. So, in considering current scholarship and important social issues, I plan to get just a little bit deviant in writing the remainder of the chapter! Specifically, I will discuss an emerging need to emphasize the "leisure" in deviant leisure. Emphasizing the leisure in understanding deviant leisure seems to hold considerable promise in substantially contributing, theoretically and practically, to addressing current and future social issues. Such potential will be illustrated through highlighting recent research on unconventional sexuality (specifically consensual sadomasochism) and discussing the world of contemporary human vampires. In short, approaching deviant leisure from multiple perspectives remains vitally important, and leisure scholars are poised to be major contributors in helping to understand and address key social issues.

Some Basics of Deviant Leisure

Fifteen years ago, Rojek (1999b) pointed out that leisure has been viewed as an unequivocal good for over a hundred years. Rojek traced the pairing of leisure with the social good during early modernization and the more recent medicalization of society. He then explained that leisure can also have abnormal (deviant) forms: *invasive, wild,* or *mephitic.* Invasive leisure occurs when an individual cannot build satisfying relationships with others, thus turns to solitary leisure interests, such as recreational drug use. Wild leisure, according to Rojek, is somewhat spontaneous, opportunistic, and based around social limits in everyday life. He noted that wildness, to a degree, is built into social order in the form of celebratory events, such as New Year's Eve. Rojek discussed serial killing as a notable example of mephitic (meaning poisonous stench) leisure. Some leisure scholars are uncomfortable with the idea that serial killing resembles a form of leisure, as Rojek suggested, but others have also discussed this similarity (Gunn & Cassie, 2006; Williams & Walker, 2006).

Also during the 1990s, Stebbins (1996) discussed *tolerable* and *intolerable* forms of deviance, which are differentiated largely according to beliefs and reactions concerning community welfare. Stebbins further noted that both tolerable and intolerable forms of deviance can be leisure, and either may be criminal (for example, forms of tolerable deviant leisure may be technically illegal but not enforced). Stebbins (1997) has also described a continuum of *casual* versus *serious* leisure. While casual leisure tends to be somewhat spontaneous, immediate, and requires little or no formal training (Stebbins, 1997), serious leisure is characterized by (a) the need to persevere; (b) having stages of progression (career-like); (c) effort to acquire knowledge, training or skill; (d) providing durable benefits or rewards (i.e., belongingness, self-expression); (e) identifying with or having an identity based on the activity; and (f) having a unique ethos and social world (Stebbins, 1999; see also Scott, Chapter 19).

Williams and Walker (2006) explored the complex relationships of leisure, deviant leisure, and crime and constructed a basic typology of deviant leisure based on Stebbins' (1996, 1997) work. Deviant leisure activities seem to have dimensions of tolerability (tolerable to intolerable), criminality (legitimate, non-criminal or criminal), and intensity (casual to serious). Although deviant leisure may be classified according to these dimensions (see Table 20.1), these authors acknowledge that linkages of deviance, leisure and crime are complex and interpretations of deviance can vary based on the social contexts of observers.

GETTING "DEVIANT" WITH DEVIANT LEISURE!

Virtually all recent studies on deviant leisure have roots in the important groundbreaking work conducted by Rojek and Stebbins. Furthermore, much of the existing work on deviant leisure has roots in traditional theories relating to deviance from sociology and psychology. From these theories, deviance is usually flavored as something negative or bad. Crime as deviance, or deviant leisure, is an obvious example. While deviance is often socially undesirable, sociologists are aware that deviance can be functionally beneficial (a social good), and that a person once labeled as a negative deviant can later be understood as being a very positive influence on society. Heckert (2003) cited the French Impressionists, Galileo, and various civil rights leaders as being positive deviants. Of course, the reverse can also be true. A person perceived as being a hero during one particular time and place may later be judged to have been a negative deviant. A cliché example of this is Hitler in Nazi Germany. Numerous people that were once idealized, such as several religious leaders, celebrities, and sports figures, later have been found to have engaged in unethical or criminal conduct. Thus, once again, we are reminded that deviance is contextual. Similarly, Galloway (2006) suggested that deviant leisure is also contextual and has positive forms, which need to be recognized and considered.

Table 20.1. Deviant Leisure Typology

Dimensions			Examples
Tolerability	Criminality	Intensity	
Tolerable	Legitimate	Casual	Erotic literature
Tolerable	Legitimate	Serious	Religious cult (i.e., Scientology)
Tolerable	Non-criminal	Casual	Social nudism
Tolerable	Non-criminal	Serious	Being a "Trekkie"
Tolerable	Criminal	Casual	Marijuana use, flashing, public sex
Tolerable	Criminal	Serious	Street racing
Intolerable	Legitimate	Casual	Flag burning
Intolerable	Legitimate	Serious	Religious cult (i.e., Satanism)
Intolerable	Non-criminal	Casual	Hiring a prostitute
Intolerable	Non-criminal	Serious	Motorcycle gang
Intolerable	Criminal	Casual	Shoplifting, vandalism, nudity, indecent exposure, child and violent pornography, murder
Intolerable	Criminal	Serious	Computer hacking, serial murder

All dimensions are continuums. Adapted from Williams & Walker (2006) from *Leisure/Loisir* (with permission).

Indeed, we may better understand deviant leisure by approaching it from a broad and diverse range of disciplines, methods, and theories (Williams, 2009).

Deviant Leisure: From Risky to Normal in Leisure Studies

My personal experience is that, to date, deviant leisure perhaps has been a risky topic of study for leisure scientists. Echoing Rojek (1999b), if leisure is generally assumed by scholars to be inherently good, then studying deviant leisure, wherein the "deviant" is flavored with negativity, quickly becomes problematic, and perhaps even risky to one's career. By combining the face value of "deviance" and "leisure," deviant leisure would appear to be somewhat of a contradiction, though this is not necessarily the case. From such a precarious position, those who study deviant leisure would, understandably, be inclined to study it as detached observers using traditional research methods. Thus, participant-observation studies of deviant leisure are quite rare.

However, similar to other social and behavioral sciences, the field of leisure has welcomed newer epistemological and methodological approaches as acceptable forms of inquiry. Years ago, well-known scholars recognized that leisure, like deviance, is highly contextual (Kelly, 1997; Roberts, 1997; Rojek, 1997). Besides positivist and post-positivist methods, postmodern and poststructuralist approaches, which emphasize contexts, narratives, and subjectivities, are now commonly utilized in helping to understand a wide range of leisure topics (see Henderson, 2011; Henderson, Presley, & Bialeschki, 2004; Snelgrove & Havits, 2010). It has been pointed out that many current research approaches that are now mainstream within leisure and sport sciences were once considered to be deviant (Strean & Williams, 2011).

Despite the many ways to learn about most leisure topics, we have yet to explore deviant leisure via this same intellectual and theoretical breadth. More thorough and diverse analyses, as with any topic, are sure to yield unique insights and a fuller understanding. Furthermore, there has been very little examination of the implications of deviant leisure interpretations in the real-world lives of people (Williams, 2009).

What if certain forms of deviant leisure are (mis)interpreted due to cultural norms and common socialization, thus participants face marginalization and discrimination? What if laws are passed or existing laws interpreted such that asymptomatic, nonviolent people are prosecuted and convicted based on narrow interpretations? These questions help illustrate the direct connections between deviant leisure, human diversity, and social justice. Recently, leisure scholars have realized the importance of conducting research from critical approaches that are connected to social justice (Parry, Johnson, & Stewart, 2013). My scholarship on deviant leisure utilizes such an approach, which includes spending considerable time with specific alternative communities, critically examining assumptions of deviant practices, emphasizing ethical implications, and considering contextual factors.

Not only is there a critical need to explore thoroughly the "deviant" in deviant leisure, but an emphasis on its "leisure" can add a new perspective to matters involving human diversity and social justice. In other words, a leisure perspective is capable of explaining certain deviant practices, where other popular discourses currently cannot. Consensual sadomasochism and contemporary vampirism are two good examples that I shall now discuss.

REMEMBERING THE "LEISURE" IN DEVIANT LEISURE: SADOMASOCHISM AND VAMPIRES

In the special issue of *Leisure/Loisir* on deviant leisure (Stebbins, et al., Eds., 2006), three papers (Bowen & Daniels, 2006; Byrne, 2006; Franklin-Reible, 2006) focused on forms of deviant leisure directly associated with sex and eroticism. Indeed, atypical sexual practices and various types of criminal behavior are commonly acknowledged as forms of deviant leisure.

The topics of consensual sadomasochism, or bondage-discipline, dominance-submission, sadism-masochism (BDSM) and self-identified vampirism are commonly perceived to be rather extreme forms of deviant leisure and perhaps even dangerous, and for the past several years I have had the unique opportunity to interact extensively with people in these communities. Both communities commonly have been assumed to be motivated by an underlying psychopathology, and both are frequently negatively labeled and marginalized by outsiders.

Getting Beyond Pathology: Is BDSM Positive Deviant Leisure?

From the time of *Psychopathia Sexualis,* published by Richard von Krafft-Ebing (1886/1978), sexual deviations, including sadism (sexual gratification from inflicting pain) and masochism (arousal from receiving pain), were interpreted as perversions. von Krafft-Ebing's work was shaped by "sexual ideals" of his time, and deviations from those were considered pathological. *Psychopathia Sexualis* has had significant and lasting impact on how medicine and psychiatry have interpreted sexuality, and sadism and masochism continue to be officially designated as disorders by the American Psychiatric Association.

Despite psychiatric interpretations, there is tremendous variation in "normal" sexuality across times, places, and cultures (see Popovic, 2006). However, in considering sexual diversity, it has been observed that often researchers give cultural forces "lip service" but not serious attention in understanding sexual behavior (Bhugra, Popelyuk, & McMullen, 2010). Sexuality is also much more fluid among individuals than is commonly believed (Diamond, 2009), and greater overall openness to discussing sexuality should help resolve major social problems, such as sexual violence, ineffective sex education, and discrimination against minorities (Williams, Prior, & Wegner, 2013).

Over the past three decades, there has been a growing scholarly literature on the topic of BDSM. Potential BDSM activities are diverse and many, and may include spanking, whipping, bondage, temporary piercings or cuttings, application of hot wax, various forms of sensory stimulation, role play, catheters, fisting (carefully inserting a hand into the vagina or anus), and various other possibilities. Emphasis is placed on communication and consent of participants and learning relevant technical skills in order to perform specific activities safely.

Research from several different countries consistently shows that BDSM participation cannot be explained by psychopathology. Using a battery of psychological tests, Connolly (2006) found that BDSM participants in her study in the U.S. did not show high levels of depression, anxiety, obsessive-compulsion, or posttraumatic stress disorder. Canadian researchers Cross and Matheson (2006) utilized psychological testing to assess stress, neuroticism, somatic complaints, anxiety, hostility, dissociation, self-esteem, and sexual guilt among BDSM participants. They found no evidence that BDSM participation could be explained from psychopathology.

A national study in Australia (N = 19,307) found that about 2% of all respondents reported being involved in BDSM during the previous year (Richters, de Visser, Rissel, Grulich, & Smith, 2008). BDSM participation was not related to sexual difficulties, unhappiness, or anxiety. Interestingly, males that participated in BDSM scored significantly lower on psychological distress than other men. Most recently, in the Netherlands Wismeijer and van Assen (2013) compared 902 BDSM participants with 434 matched control participants. These researchers compared measures pertaining to personality dimensions, attachment styles, rejection sensitivity, and subjective well-being. Compared to controls, BDSM participants were less neurotic, more extraverted, more open to new experiences, more conscientious, less rejection sensitive, and reported higher subjective well-being, but were less agreeable. Overall, BDSM participants were significantly healthier, psychologically, than controls.

Several scholarly reviews show that participation in BDSM is not pathological or harmful (i.e., Kleinplatz & Moser, 2007; Powls & Davies, 2012; Weinberg, 2006; Williams, 2006), nor is participation motivated by antifeminist attitudes (Cross & Matheson, 2006; Prior, 2013). Despite such research, marginalization and discrimination toward BDSM participants remains common including among mental health professionals (Hoff & Sprott, 2009; Kolmes, Stock, & Moser, 2006). This is unfortunate, and it needs to change.

BDSM participation is often highly erotic, but it is not necessarily always about sex. Sexology discourses are relevant to BDSM, yet these, too, are limited. Many participants engage in BDSM activities for sensory experiences and power exchange (Newmahr, 2010; Prior, 2013). Interestingly, the work of professional dominatrices seems to be psychotherapeutic, and sex itself is taboo within professional BDSM (Williams & Storm, 2012). If BDSM is not psychopathological nor is it necessarily sexual, then what is it? How are we to make sense of it?

Leisure science could provide the answer. Freedom, a necessary criterion for leisure, seems to be met in BDSM, including for those who enjoy extensive submission (Prior, 2013; Taylor & Ussher, 2001). Scholars realize that regular BDSM participation is a form of serious leisure; BDSM seems to have durable benefits and rewards, requires learning specific skills, reflects a specific identity, requires effort, and has a unique ethos (Franklin-Reible, 2006; Newmahr, 2010; Williams, 2006, 2009). BDSM as serious leisure poses interesting new challenges to understanding, however, because potential marginalization comes in at least two forms. First and foremost, is the obvious marginalization based on assumptions discussed above that BDSM is psychopathological. However, BDSM participants, like other serious leisure enthusiasts, may also experience to some degree what Stebbins (2001) calls leisure marginalization. Stebbins observed that serious leisure participants are not dabblers or professionals, yet they pursue their interests with intentness and considerable time and money are often needed. Because of these realities, those who enjoy serious leisure pursuits may be judged by others who may not understand the rationale for such an investment.

While regular BDSM participation clearly has qualities of serious leisure, it also seems to reflect a few important attributes of casual leisure. Taylor and Ussher (2001) found that BDSM participation was described as being pleasurable, playful and fun, an escape from the ordinariness of life, and having a spiritual quality. Thus, on a continuum of casual to serious leisure, it appears to be skewed to the serious side, but perhaps not at the exclusion of some casual attributes. Or, perhaps the training and skill (serious leisure) needed for many BDSM activities subsequently allows for characteristics of casual leisure (i.e., play and fun) to emerge during participation.

It is exciting that leisure science is capable of providing an understanding of BDSM that is consistent with numerous recent scholarly studies, whereas other popular explanations are lacking. Clearly, psychopathological explanations do not fit the evidence. In fact, the Nordic countries no longer acknowledge sadism and masochism as psychiatric disorders, and some researchers in those nations continue to lobby the World Health Organization to remove these terms from the International Classification of Diseases. Sexology discourses, while appropriate and somewhat useful to particular aspects of BDSM, remain limited. Leisure scholars know that sex can also be a form of leisure (Meaney & Rye, 2007), yet a leisure perspective allows for a wide range of diverse activities and experiences that may or may not be sexual. For many participants, BDSM seems to be a form of deviant, tolerable, serious, and healthy leisure.

Human Vampires: Unconventional Identities and Deviant Leisure

Few topics can rival the popularity of vampires in popular culture. Books, movies, and television shows about vampires continue to attract huge audiences. Vampires as presented in popular culture have become more sexualized over the past few decades. At the same time, there are likely thousands of ordinary people across many different countries that secretly self-identify, in one way or another, as vampires. How such people identify as a vampire seems to impact, at least to some degree, their leisure preferences and experiences.

There are vastly different types of human vampires that can be roughly divided into "lifestyle" or "real" vampires (Laycock, 2009). The former designation includes those who live a lifestyle that is patterned after images of the vampire (i.e., sleeping in coffins and/or wearing fangs), various social or religious entities formed around mystical and spiritual beliefs, and the large number of vampire role-playing enthusiasts. Lifestyle vampirism is diverse, yet its essence seems to be deviant leisure. For example, Stebbins (1996) suggested that engaging in unconventional religious belief systems may be deviant leisure; or dressing in vampire-style clothing, attending vampire clubs and parties, and participation in role-playing games also would seem to qualify as deviant leisure activity. Like other forms of deviant leisure, lifestyle vampirism may be interpreted as positive or negative (or a combination) depending on the form, its functions, and the legal and ethical issues associated with it.

In contemporary vampire communities, the term "real vampire" is used to distinguish members from various forms of lifestyle vampirism (Laycock, 2009; Williams, 2008). Real vampires may or may not have interest in vampire imagery, myths, and lifestyle practices. The essential feature of real vampirism is a perceived need to take in "subtle human energy" in order to maintain physical, psychological, and spiritual health (Laycock, 2010). According to Laycock (2010), such vampirism is an identity that is formed around a commonly understood (among fellow vampires) chronic and immutable condition of needing extra energy. Some vampires claim to take energy through consensually drinking tiny amounts of blood from their "donors" (often the partner of the vampire), while others "feed" psychically from donors. Unlike lifestyle vampires, real vampires apparently do not choose their vampirism. For real vampires, the preferred term "vampirism" seems to accurately describe a process of taking energy (Belanger, 2004).

Whereas the diverse forms of lifestyle vampirism may be understood directly as deviant leisure, real vampirism primarily concerns an unconventional identity rather than leisure behavior. However, such an identity, like other common identities, influences various leisure preferences. Vampire social groups and events, which may be types of (deviant) leisure, have developed based on the real vampire identity. An obvious leisure benefit of such groups and events is social support. Additionally, a vampire identity, along with more common identities, may also influence other deviant leisure experiences, including erotic and sexual practices (Williams, 2015).

Self-identified vampires reflect rich social diversity, including ethnicity, religious and spiritual beliefs, education levels, occupations, and gender and sexual orientations (Atlanta Vampire Alliance, 2007). Like BDSM participation, common traditional discourses from medicine, psychiatry, and Judeo-Christian religion tend to psychopathologize self-identified vampires (Williams, 2008), yet there is no available evidence that simply identifying as a vampire is inherently harmful, dangerous, or blatantly unethical. Thus, there remains a strong need for professionals to examine critically widespread assumptions about deviant communities, and to act ethically and responsibly when working with vulnerable people (Williams, 2013).

Professionals should be aware that claiming a vampire identity can mean vastly different things. The real vampires whom I know and have worked with seem to be decent, responsible, law-abiding citizens. However, there have been several violent criminals throughout history that are associated with extreme blood fetishism and/or vampirism, including Countess Erzsebet Bathory, John Haigh, Fritz Haarmann, and Richard Ramirez (Newton, 2000). Based on such extreme cases and associated high visibility via the media, it is sometimes tempting to generalize that all self-identified vampires are psychologically unwell, immoral, and/or potentially dangerous or threatening. Nevertheless, such generalization is unfair and irresponsible.

Similar to understanding BDSM, it would be unwise to discard existing knowledge from psychology and forensics and various other disciplines when exploring the phenomena of various forms of vampirism. At the same time, it is also unwise to accept these explanations exclusively and uncritically. It seems that leisure science is capable of contributing to a richer, and in many cases, a more relevant understanding of such phenomena when other explanations are limited. Indeed, there is much yet to learn about leisure among those with alternative identities and lifestyles.

CONCLUSION

Deviant leisure has strong roots primarily based on the pioneering work of Rojek (1997, 1999a, 1999b) and Stebbins (1996, 1997). However, an understanding of deviant leisure among many leisure scholars and practitioners seems to remain embedded in academic discourses that focus on deviance (particularly psychiatry and psychology, sociology, and forensics). These discourses are important and should be carefully considered, yet they are also limiting and in some instances seem to lack sufficient explanatory power. Deviant leisure will be greatly enriched, and may contribute substantially in understanding unusual practices and experiences, by remembering and refocusing on leisure. However, to do this, we may need to widen the range of what constitutes "healthy leisure."

Noting that the concept of positive deviance already exists in sociology, I propose that deviant leisure may be interpreted as positive, meaningful, and healthy (i.e., BDSM for many participants and leisure for many vampires) or perhaps psychopathological, detrimental, and sometimes criminal and even blatantly immoral (i.e., violent crime as leisure), or a complex combination depending on the activity. Regardless of the activity or experience, the field of leisure seeks to explain who, why, and how people are motivated to engage in certain forms of leisure and associated benefits, constraints, risks, and rewards. Such scholarship can add a richer understanding of all varieties of deviance, and it can also lead to helping resolve various related social issues.

Of course, it is imperative to be able to assess accurately dangerousness and potential violence from what might first appear to be so, but is not. With a background in leisure science and criminology, I sometimes deal with such cases where much is at stake. Furthermore, the issue of accurate assessment is becoming increasingly more difficult and pressing given that we live in the age of technology. Besides real-time forms of deviant leisure, numerous online chat rooms, forums, and interactive games exist that involve deviance, including BDSM and fetish-related activities, cannibalism, torture, and vampirism. Unlike much of real-time deviant leisure, online activities are anonymous and impersonal, yet communication between players can be highly detailed and specific. How do we know who is truly sociopathic compared to those who are harmlessly acting out fantasy? And, what exactly constitutes a legitimate threat or bullying (in a legal sense)? Where exactly are other important legal and ethical boundaries pertaining to deviance-focused chat rooms and online role-playing games? These are extremely difficult issues that judicial and law enforcement personnel are beginning to face, yet leisure science eventually may be prove to be helpful in understanding and addressing them.

Though still somewhat neglected by scholars, deviant leisure is complex, rich, and fascinating. Deviant leisure provokes curiosity, yet its depth and breadth remain largely unexplored. I believe that as we move toward the future, both its theoretical and practical value will become far more apparent. After all, widespread interest in crime, vampires, and sex from social and behavioral researchers and the general public is not going to go away.

REFERENCES

Atlanta Vampire Alliance. (2007). *The vampire and energy work research survey: An introspective examination of the real vampire community.* Atlanta, GA: Author.

Belanger, M. (2004). *The psychic vampire codex.* Boston, MA: Weiser Books.

Bhugra, D., Popelyuk, D., & McMullen, I. (2010). Paraphilias across cultures: Contexts and controversies. *Journal of Sex Research, 47,* 242–256. doi: 10.1080/00224491003699833

Bowen, H. E., & Daniels, M. (2006). Beyond body: Buying and selling attitude and fantasy. *Leisure/Loisir, 30,* 87–109.

Byrne, R. (2006). Beyond lovers' lane—the rise of illicit sexual leisure in countryside recreational space. *Leisure/Loisir, 30,* 73–85.

Connolly, P. H. (2006). Psychological functioning of bondage/domination/sado-masochism (BDSM) practitioners. *Journal of Psychology and Human Sexuality, 18*(1), 79–120. doi: 10.1300/J056v18n01_05

Cross, P. A., & Matheson, K. (2006). Understanding sadomasochism: An empirical examination of four perspectives. *Journal of Homosexuality, 50*(2/3), 133–166. doi: 10.1300/J082v50n02_07

Diamond, L. M. (2009). *Sexual fluidity: Understanding women's love and desire.* Cambridge, MA: Harvard University Press.

Franklin-Reible, H. (2006). Deviant leisure: Uncovering the "goods" in transgressive behaviour. *Leisure/Loisir, 30,* 55–71.

Galloway, S. (2006). Adventure recreation reconceived: Positive forms of deviant leisure. *Leisure/Loisir, 30,* 219–231.

Gunn, L., & Cassie, L. T. (2006). Serial murder as an act of deviant leisure. *Leisure/Loisir, 30,* 27–53.

Heckert, D. M. (2003). Positive deviance: A classificatory model. In E. H. Kelly & E. J. Clarke (Eds.), *Deviant Behavior* (pp. 20–32). New York: Worth Publishers.

Henderson, K. A. (2011). Post-positivism and the pragmatics of leisure research. *Leisure Sciences, 33*, 341–346. doi: 10.1080/01490400.2011.583166

Henderson, K. A., Presley, J., & Bialeschki, M. D. (2004). Theory in recreation and leisure research: Reflections from the editors. *Leisure Sciences, 26*, 411–425. doi: 10.1080/01490400490502471

Hoff, G., & Sprott, R. A. (2009). Therapy experiences of clients with BDSM sexualities: Listening to a stigmatized sexuality. *Electronic Journal of Human Sexuality, 12.*

Kelly, J. (1997). Leisure as life: Outline of a poststructuralist reconstruction. *Society and Leisure, 20*, 401–418.

Kleinplatz, P. J., & Moser, C. (2007). Is SM pathological? In D. Langdridge & M. Barker (Eds.), *Safe, sane and consensual: Contemporary perspectives on sadomasochism* (pp. 55–62). New York: Palgrave Macmillan.

Kolmes, K., Stock, W., & Moser, C. (2006). Investigating bias in psychotherapy with BDSM clients. *Journal of Homosexuality, 50*(2/3), 301–324. doi: 10.1300/J082v50n02_15

Laycock, J. (2009). *Vampires today: The truth about modern vampirism.* Westport, CT: Praeger.

Laycock, J. (2010). Real vampires as an identity group: Analyzing causes and effects of an introspective survey by the vampire community. *Nova Religio, 14*, 4–23. doi: 10.1525/nr.2010.14.1.4

Meaney, G. J., & Rye, B. J. (2007). Sex, sexuality, and leisure. In R. McCarville & K. MacKay (Eds.), *Leisure for Canadians* (pp. 131–188). State College, PA: Venture Publishing, Inc.

Newmahr, S. (2010). Rethinking kink: Sadomasochism as serious leisure. *Qualitative Sociology, 33*, 313–331. doi: 10.1007/s11133-010-9158-9

Newton, M. (2000). *The encyclopedia of serial killers.* New York: Checkmark Books.

Parry, D. C., Johnson, C. W., & Stewart, W. (2013). Leisure research for social justice: A response to Henderson. *Leisure Sciences, 35*, 81–87. doi: 10.1080/01490400.2013.739906

Popovic, M. (2006). Psychosexual diversity as the best representation of human normality across cultures. *Sexual and Relationship Therapy, 21*, 171–186. doi: 10.1080/14681990500358469

Powls, J., & Davies, J. (2012). A descriptive review of research relating to sadomasochism: Considerations for practice. *Deviant Behavior, 33*, 223–234. doi: 10.1080/01639625.2011.573391

Prior, E. E. (2013). Women's perspectives of BDSM power exchange. *Electronic Journal of Human Sexuality, 16.*

Richters, J., de Visser, R. O., Rissel, C. E., Grulich, A. E., & Smith, A. M. A. (2008). Demographic and psychosocial features of participants in bondage and discipline, "sadomasochism" or dominance and submission (BDSM): Data from a national survey. *Journal of Sexual Medicine, 5*, 1660–1668. doi: 10.1111/j.1743-6109.2008.00795.x

Roberts, K. (1997). Why old questions are the right responses to new challenges. The sociology of leisure in the 1990s. *Society and Leisure, 20*, 369–381.

Rojek, C. (1997). Leisure theory: Retrospect and prospect. *Society and Leisure, 20*, 383–400.

Rojek, C. (1999a). Deviant leisure: The dark side of free-time activity. In E. L. Jackson & T. L. Burton (Eds.), *Leisure studies: Prospects for the twenty-first century* (pp. 83–97). State College, PA: Venture Publishing, Inc.

Rojek, C. (1999b). Abnormal leisure: Invasive, mephitic, and wild forms. *Society and Leisure, 22*, 21–35.

Russell, R. V. (2013). *Pastimes: The context of contemporary leisure.* Urbana, IL: Sagamore.

Snelgrove, R., & Havitz, M. E. (2010). Looking back in time: The pitfalls and potential of retrospective methods in leisure studies. *Leisure Sciences, 32*, 337–351. doi: 10.1080/01490400.2010.488199

Stebbins, R. A. (1996). *Tolerable differences: Living with deviance.* Toronto: McGraw-Hill Ryerson Limited.

Stebbins, R. A. (1997). Casual leisure: A conceptual statement. *Leisure Studies, 16*, 17–25.

Stebbins, R. A. (1999). Serious leisure. In E. L. Jackson & T. L. Burton (Eds.), *Leisure studies: Prospects for the twenty-first century* (pp. 70–82). State College, PA: Venture Publishing, Inc.

Stebbins, R. A. (2001). *New directions in the theory and research of serious leisure.* Queenston, ON: Edwin Mellen Press.

Stebbins, R. A., Rojek, C., & Sullivan, A.-M. (2006). Deviant leisure. *Leisure/Loisir, 30*, 3–5.

Strean, W. B., & Williams, D J (2011). Playful deviance. In D. Gilbourne & M. B. Andersen (Eds.), *Critical essays in applied sport psychology* (pp. 129–143).Champaign, IL: Human Kinetics.

Taylor, G. W., & Ussher, J. M. (2001). Making sense of S&M: A discourse analytic account. *Sexualities, 4*, 293–314.

von Krafft-Ebing, R. (1886/1978). *Psychopathia sexualis.* New York: Stein & Day/Scarborough.

Weinberg, T. S. (2006). Sadomasochism and the social sciences: A review of the sociological and social psychological literature. *Journal of Homosexuality, 50*(2/3), 17–40. doi: 10.1300/J082v50n02_02

Williams, D J (2006). Different (painful!) strokes for different folks: A general overview of sexual sadomasochism and its diversity. *Sexual Addiction and Compulsivity, 13*, 333–346. doi: 10.1080/10720160601011240

Williams, D J (2008). Contemporary vampires and (blood-red) leisure: Should we be afraid of the dark? *Leisure/Loisir, 32*, 513–539.

Williams, D J (2009). Deviant leisure: Rethinking "the good, the bad, and the ugly." *Leisure Sciences, 31*, 207–213. doi: 10.1080/01490400802686110

Williams, D J (2013). Social work, BDSM, and vampires: Toward understanding and empowering people with nontraditional identities. *Canadian Social Work, 15*, 10–24.

Williams, D J (2015). Intersections of vampirism and sexuality: A narrative description of a vampire feeding. In S. Newmahr & T. S. Weinberg (Eds.), *Selves, symbols and sexualities: An interactionist anthology* (pp. 265–274). Thousand Oaks, CA: Sage.

Williams, D J, Prior, E. E., & Wegner, J. (2013). Understanding social problems associated with sexuality: Can a "sex positive" approach help? *Social Work*. doi: 10.1093/sw/swt024

Williams, D J, & Storm, L. E. (2012). Unconventional leisure and career: Insights into the work of professional dominatrices. *Electronic Journal of Human Sexuality, 15*.

Williams, D J, & Walker, G. J. (2006). Leisure, deviant leisure, and crime: Caution: Objects may be closer than they appear. *Leisure/Loisir, 30*, 193–217.

Wismeijer, A. A. J., & van Assen, M. A. L. M. (2013). Psychological characteristics of BDSM practitioners. *Journal of Sexual Medicine*. Advance online publication. doi: 10.1111/jsm.12192

21
YOUTH AND LEISURE

Linda L. Caldwell (The Pennsylvania State University)

This chapter explores the importance of leisure during the period of adolescence, which is characterized by transitions and social-psychological-physical change. Adolescence is generally considered the period between puberty and adulthood. Over the past two decades researchers, practitioners, and policymakers have devoted increased attention to this critical period of human development because of the recognition that patterns and habits established during adolescence are associated with success and health as an adult. This chapter begins with a brief discussion about adolescent development and then describes research that focuses on how and why leisure matters to adolescent development. The chapter concludes with a discussion on current and future considerations and possible directions from a neuroscience perspective.

UNDERSTANDING THE PERIOD OF ADOLESCENCE

To begin, it may be useful to recognize the way adolescents have been viewed historically compared with how they are viewed contemporaneously. Historically, development was something that adults did to youth because they lacked adult characteristics. The thought was that in order for youth to develop into functioning adults, they had to be taught, managed and molded by adults and were generally considered as problems (e.g., they are too emotional or always getting into trouble) and something to be "fixed." This adult-driven model had origins in the perspectives and theories of Skinner (e.g., 1953). Recent research and thought has radically revised this version of youth development to recognize that development is not something done to a youth but a process in which they are active participants.

In this contemporary perspective, youth are seen as *co-producers* of their own development, where development stems primarily from an interaction between young people and their environment. This reciprocal interaction or dialectical perspective is based on work by Vygotsky (e.g., 1978) where youth develop by exerting influence on and being influenced by others and their environments.

From a meta-theoretical perspective, ecological systems theory, which later evolved into the bioecological model (see Bronfenbrenner & Morris, 2006), provides a foundation for understanding the reciprocal and multilayered influences on human development. Bronfenbrenner's models put "meat on the bones" of Vygotsky's dialectical perspective. These models describe, explain and predict human development across time, taking into consideration the individual, social, community, and cultural factors that influence (and are influenced by) individuals. The evolution of the ecological systems theory to place more emphasis on the biological perspective was borne of increased understanding of the biological bases of behavior.

From a practical perspective, these theoretical perspectives have been operationalized by the positive youth development movement (PYD). This movement is important because it has elevated the status of young people who are now recognized as valuable assets who even as young people can be contributing members of society.

Implicated in both the PYD perspective and the bioecological model of human development is the notion that in order to develop, youth need a constellation of human services, adult supports, and contextual opportunities from which to learn and grow. Much of the research over the past two decades has embraced this perspective and has attempted to unpack the relations within and across individual, social, community, and cultural factors that shape and are shaped by interactions that either support or detract from positive and healthy adolescent development.

Scholars generally agree that there are a fairly robust set of developmental events or "tasks" that young people go through during the period of adolescence. I will briefly describe the central developmental tasks as distinct processes, but as with all human development, these tasks are mutually influencing.

- *Identity.* Perhaps the major task in adolescence is developing a sense of one's unique self. During identity formation, adolescents attempt to answer the question such as, "Who am I?" or "What do I stand for?"
- *Civic engagement.* Being engaged with and connected to school or to one's community and developing as sense of being something bigger than is an important developmental task.
- *Developing a moral compass.* Adolescents learn to develop a sense of what is right and what is wrong.
- *Social connections, social capital, and relatedness.* Peer relationships begin to compete with family relationships and adolescents have a strong need for affiliation with one or more peer groups and for a sense of belonging.
- *Sexuality and changing bodies.* Adolescents must learn to deal with pubertal changes, including learning to deal with their sexuality. Navigating romantic relationships is also an important process in adolescence.
- *Autonomy development and self-determination.* At the same time youth are learning who they are and how to interact with peers and live in various communities (e.g., school, neighborhood), they also need to develop behavioral and emotional autonomy from parents and family in order to make their own decisions and regulate their own behavior.
- *Initiative and goal setting.* Adolescents must learn to take initiative for their actions and understand consequences; they become more future-oriented and are better able to set goals.
- *Achievement and competence.* Adolescents have a strong need for believing that they are competent and can achieve their own, or externally placed (e.g., schoolwork), goals.
- *Experimentation, risk taking, and sensation seeking.* Learning how to deal with this list of tasks coupled with biophysical changes lends itself to a period of experimentation, possible risk taking, and an affinity for sensation seeking. This topic will be discussed subsequently.

LEISURE AND ADOLESCENT DEVELOPMENT

What an adolescent does, or does not do, in his or her leisure matters a great deal in terms of human development. This is especially true since a large proportion of an adolescent's day is considered free time and therefore conducive to leisure experiences. That is, there are distinct and empirically demonstrated developmental benefits to filling this free time with positive experiences of play, recreation and leisure engagement. At the same time, if youth do not engage in these activities, they miss a significant opportunity to reap these health and developmental benefits. Finally, youth can also fill their free time in unhealthy or unproductive ways, such as vandalism or using substances such as alcohol or other drugs.

The Leisure Activities-Context-Experience (LACE) model (Caldwell, 2005) presents a vehicle by which to understand how a combination of activity, context, and experiential quality interact to produce positive and healthy outcomes or negative and risky outcomes. In addition, this model provides a frame for specifying causal pathways from a bioecological perspective. Each of these elements contributes to, or detracts from, adolescents getting as much out of their leisure as possible.

Activity

Leisure activities contain inherent characteristics that contribute to adolescent development. Finding a consensus on outcomes associated with activity participation is challenging because it is difficult to classify leisure activity engagement. Activities have been categorized in many ways, including active and passive, healthy and unhealthy, and duration and frequency. The bulk of the literature has focused on the importance of organized or structured activity and the problems associated with unstructured activity. Previous research shows that adolescents who participate in structured extracurricular activities are less likely to engage in antisocial behavior (e.g., Mahoney, Larson, & Eccles, 2005; Zaff, Moore, Papillo, & Williams, 2003) and more likely to have a higher level of academic achievement (Bartko & Eccles, 2003; Mahoney, Cairns, & Farmer, 2003) and positive psychosocial functioning (Bartko & Eccles). There are some mixed findings about the developmental benefits of structured activities, however. For example, some researchers have found that participation in sports was related to lower levels of anxiety/depression but *higher* levels of delinquency and substance use (Fauth, Roth, & Brooks-Gunn, 2007).

Participation in unstructured activities is typically linked to negative outcomes when "unstructured" is defined as being sedentary, hanging out, and having no supervision. For example, hanging out is positively related to alcohol initiation and misuse (Strycker, Duncan, & Pickering, 2003) and sedentary activities such as watching TV and playing video games are related to outcomes such as declines in physical activity (Motl, McAuley, Birnbaum, & Lytle, 2006) and related weight gain (Koezuka et al., 2006).

Some researchers, however, have argued that unstructured time is important for healthy development and self-expression because too many children and adolescents are overscheduled and stressed with the array of activities in which they are involved (e.g., Elkins, 2003; Kleiber, 1999). Unstructured activities that include engaging in pursuits like learning a new hobby, painting, playing music on one's own, and other such endeavors may contribute to the development of creativity, persistence, competence, social belonging, and identity as well as help alleviate the stress often associated with a constant menu of structured and organized activities. Thus, there is reason to believe that positive experiences and outcomes may result from adolescents' participation in unsupervised leisure activities, although much more research is needed in this area.

Whether structured or unstructured, social activities are among the most commonly pursued forms of leisure among adolescents (Kleiber, Caldwell, & Shaw, 1993). They are also the most commonly desired form of leisure as adolescents crave the feeling that they belong. The social context of leisure is important to adolescent development in that it provides opportunities to learn empathy and develop deep relationships as well as to negotiate with peers, resolve conflict, and work together for communal goals. Developmentally, social leisure activities allow for both differentiation and integration and facilitate youth's abilities to exert personal control over their environments.

Experience

Engagement in any leisure pursuit evokes an emotional response, if not multiple responses, that may differ over the course of the activity. This response, be it positive or negative, and its valence, are important factors in the matrix of developmental outcomes associated with an activity. From a simplistic perspective, activities or engagements that produce joy or stress release are far more likely to produce positive benefits that those that produce anger, stress, or boredom.

Joy, fun, interest, and happiness are hallmarks of leisure; fortunately most adolescents report positive emotional experiences in leisure (Caldwell, 2005). These leisure-related emotions contribute to positive psychological adjustment, stress release, and well-being (Mock, Mannell, and Guttentag, Chapter 6). In addition, leisure is a rich context in which to experience flow, which is a state of consciousness in which one loses track of time and becomes merged with the activity (Csikszentmihalyi, 1990). Research has suggested that the happiest adolescents tend to be more often engaged in flow-producing situations (Csikszentmihalyi & Hunter, 2003).

Adolescents may also experience negative emotions in their leisure. Stress, embarrassment, boredom, and loneliness are among a number of negative emotions that can be associated with leisure pursuits (Caldwell, 2005). Boredom in leisure is a common complaint among adolescents. Being bored during leisure is particularly troubling because leisure is "supposed" to be intrinsically motivating, self-directed, fun, and enjoyable. If an adolescent is bored during leisure, it should trigger the need to identify the sources of boredom and deal with that. For example, youth could change aspects of participation (e.g., changing rules to make it more fun) or find something more interesting to do.

Thus, boredom can be a staging area for creative action; unfortunately, many times boredom leads to risky or deviant behavior. Youth who experience consistently high rates of boredom and disengagement during their leisure time or report just "hanging out" in their leisure are at greater risk for engaging in substance use and delinquency behaviors (Mahoney, et al., 2005; Osgood, Anderson, &Shaffer, 2005). For example, the National Center on Addictions and Substance Abuse (2003) surveyed close to 2,000 12- to 17-year-olds and found that high stress, boredom and/or disposable income were associated with higher risk of substance use. Some recent longitudinal work also suggests that high school youth who experience high levels of leisure boredom are more likely to engage in risky sexual behaviors (Miller, Caldwell, Weybright, Smith, Vergnani, & Wegner, 2014).

In addition to emotional responses that occur during leisure engagement, it is also important to consider the degree to which adolescents act out of internal or external compulsion to engage in the activity. In fact, this is one of the most important ways leisure can contribute to positive youth development. Leisure is one of the few contexts in adolescents' lives where they have the opportunity to exercise free choice and self-determination. The more an adolescent experiences feelings of freedom and choice, the more likely he or she is to reap important developmental benefits. This is one of the reasons leisure is an ideal context for autonomy development and identity formation. It is also an ideal context to learn how to self-regulate the various emotions one might experience in a leisure activity, thus contributing to social-emotional competence and psychological health (Johnson & Johnson, 2004).

Autonomy development and self-determination are intricately linked with being intrinsically motivated, developing initiative, and goal setting skills (Walker, Chapter 17). For example, youth with higher levels of internal motivation for after-school activities set more goals for themselves (Beiswenger & Grolnick, 2009). Research also suggests that intrinsically motivated activities are related to health and well-being (Csikszentmihalyi & Hunter, 2003; Larson, 2000). These intrinsic types of activities include those that are pursued purely for their own enjoyment (such as singing in the shower) and those that are pursued to achieve a personally meaningful and self-endorsed goal (such as getting the lead in a local drama production). It is these types of meaningful and internally driven activities that provide the material, time, and space for youth to reflect on what makes them unique and part of something bigger than themselves (Dworkin, Larson, & Hansen, 2003). Thus, self-determined and intrinsically motivated activities promote identity development and provide adolescents with a sense of meaning and personal fulfillment.

Another important aspect of internally motivated pursuits is that they are more likely to be sustained over time. When internally motivated, adolescents are more likely to remain focused and stick to a personally desired activity even when faced with challenges (for example, transportation difficulties or lack of initial skill). Undertaking internally motivated leisure pursuits leads to the development of initiative which is important to fostering the transition from adolescence to adulthood.

Outcomes are less positive when behavior is externally compelled, although this is a complex topic, especially during adolescent years, and a full discussion is beyond the scope of the chapter. Research has indicated that adolescents who perceive that their parents have too much control over their leisure activities are less likely to have positive outcomes such as lower levels of initiative lower levels of autonomy, and higher levels of boredom and amotivation (Sharp, Caldwell, Graham, & Ridenour, 2006; Watts & Caldwell, 2008). Other research has found that early adolescents who choose their friends for external rewards (e.g., to be popular) have poorer relationship quality six months later (Ojanen, Sijtsema, Hawley, & Little, 2010). Substance use and sexual activity have also been linked with extrinsic motivation (Williams, Cox, Hedberg, & Deci, 2000); conversely, having higher levels of intrinsic motivation has been linked with lower levels of substance use (Caldwell, Bradley, & Coffman, 2009).

The process of helping an adolescent become internally motivated (called internalization) in an activity is an under-studied area of research. A recent study by Dawes and Larson (2011) provides some particularly compelling evidence of how to facilitate internalization. Interviews from a diverse sample of youth overwhelmingly suggested that developing a personal connection with an adult led to higher levels of personal engagement and meaning associated with the activity.

Context

Activities and experiences take place in contexts, which contain elements embedded in the environment that contribute to how adolescents experience the activity. Most of the research on contextual factors has focused on elements of organized or structured activities associated with positive outcomes. The National Research Council and Institute of Medicine (2002) presented eight context or program features of structured activities necessary to produce these outcomes: physical and psychological safety; appropriate structure; supportive relationships; opportunities to belong; positive social norms; support for efficacy and mattering; opportunities for skill building; and integration of family, school, and community efforts. Specifically, research has concluded that:

- Leadership, guidance and facilitation from competent and caring adults are critical.
- Adolescents should be given authentic opportunity to make decisions and be self-determined.
- Adults should appropriately scaffold opportunities for youth to learn, be challenged, and be supported through success and failure.
- Ample opportunities should exist for youth to belong and be recognized as being valued and important.
- Opportunities to develop social capital should be available and facilitated (see also Glover, Chapter 32).
- Positive social norms should be present and recognized.
- There should be ample opportunities for skill building and adults should provide specific feedback in order to improve performance.
- Adolescents should perceive they are in a safe place physically and psychologically.
- Adults should provide appropriate structure regarding consistent and clear rules and boundaries, and age- and task-appropriate supervision is provided.

To summarize thus far, there are a number of powerful health and developmental benefits that may be associated with leisure participation. As well, a number of negative outcomes may be associated with leisure participation. Although these positive and negative outcomes may be realized by all human beings, they are particularly salient for young people given their unique developmental period. As previously noted, one such normative developmental behavior is risk taking, which will be highlighted in the next section.

RISK TAKING, SENSATION SEEKING, LEISURE, AND THE ADOLESCENT BRAIN: A PROMISING PERSPECTIVE

A line from a song by the rock music group Greenday (2000) "Warning, live without warning" is emblematic of a great deal of adolescent behavior. Despite that this age group, compared to other age groups, is characterized by vitality and resilience, it is also characterized by an increased level of morbidity and mortality (Dahl, 2004). For example, rates of death by injury between ages 15 to 19 are about six times that of the rate between ages 10 and 14 (National Institute of Mental Health, 2011). Noteworthy to this chapter is that much of this risk behavior takes place in free time and it is often considered leisure by those who engage in it (Williams & Walker, 2006).

Much has been written about adolescent impulsivity and propensity to engage in risk-taking behaviors such as substance use, unprotected sex, and vandalism from sociological, psychological, and criminal justice perspectives. These perspectives have been insightful but not very helpful in providing guidance on how to help adolescents deal with impulsivity toward risk behavior. Recently, a neurobiological model, sometimes called the dual systems model, offers a promising perspective for understanding adolescent risk-taking behavior. This model helps explain why adolescents engage in more risk-taking behavior even though there is growing empirical evidence that there are no age differences in being aware of and assessing risk and one's vulnerability to such risk (Steinberg, 2007).

It is critical to underscore that developmental psychologists and neurobiologists do not consider the brain to be the *only* driver of adolescent behavior. In keeping with the bioecological model, the brain is just one factor that helps explain and predict behavior (see McCormick, Chapter 2). It is also important to note that up to 80% of adolescents have little or no problems with stress or risk-taking behavior as they mature (Dahl, 2004). Nevertheless, this stage of development sets patterns for adult behavior and the evolution of neuroscience promises to provide better guidance in terms of scaffolding youth through this developmental period.

As the adolescent brain matures from about age 12 there are two developing networks that that govern behavior: cognitive-control and socioemotional networks. The interaction of these two systems may explain the propensity toward risk taking among adolescents (Steinberg, 2010). These two systems develop at different times and at different rates. The cognitive-control network, in the prefrontal cortex, controls executive functions such as planning, future orientation, and self-regulation. This system matures gradually, reaching maturation during later adolescence, and is independent of puberty.

The socioemotional network is located in the paralimbic areas of the brain and is responsive to emotion and novelty. It is the command center for reward processing. As adolescents move from childhood to adolescence, this network becomes increasingly activated resulting in a heightened sensitivity to social and emotional stimuli and a greater need for and propensity to seek out excitement and crave intense feelings. This system matures in early adolescence.

Researchers theorize that it is the rapid and dramatic increase of dopaminergic activity in the socioemotional network in early adolescence without a corresponding increase in the "brakes" from the prefrontal cortex that elevates the possibility of risk-taking behavior in the name of reward-seeking behavior. The inability to inhibit impulsivity to act emotionally is heightened in a social context (Albert, Chein, & Steinberg, 2013). Furthermore, when there is less emotionality the cognitive-control system can provide regulatory control and the two systems are in balance. In this case, adolescents are as competent as adults as decision makers in the absence of intense psychosocial factors. The differential influence these two systems have in the face of "emotionally-laden contexts diminishes as adolescents mature.

The processes by which the two neurobiological networks develop and interact provide insight into why leisure is important. Initial cell proliferation of gray matter results in the overproduction of neurons and their interconnections. This proliferation results in synaptic pruning and selective elimination of infrequently used cells and connections; approximately 50% of neurons are eliminated during the process of pruning (Low & Cheng, 2006).

A related process is myelination, which is the development of myelin (a fatty coating) that insulates nerve fibers and speed neural processing between regions of the brain's gray matter. Myelination is slower in the frontal lobes that connect the cognitive-control and socioemotional networks, resulting in the cognitive-control system being unable to handle the socioemotional system under emotionally-laden and/or social conditions.

The process of pruning is thought to be associated with learning and is associated with establishing precursors to adult behavior. It is during this time of pruning and myelination that the brain can be customized by taking advantage of the early activation of emotions. This activation is what leads to developing passions in leisure activities such as music, art, and hobbies. Because of the pruning that takes place in the brain, youth can actually sculpt their abilities to control impulses and "ignite their passions" by developing interests and goal setting behavior (Dahl, 2004). Consequently, adolescent brains are primed to become hardwired for developing leisure activity preferences, setting the stage for continued participation throughout adulthood.

NEUROSCIENCE, LEISURE, AND YOUTH DEVELOPMENT: CHALLENGES AND OPPORTUNITIES

Research on adolescents' brain plasticity, early propensity toward sensation seeking and passion, and the later evolution of the cognitive-control and goal setting system presents opportunities for leisure researchers to better understand the role of activities, experiences, and contexts in promoting healthy growth and development during adolescence. In simple terms, the leisure context is uniquely situated to promote brain development in order to help youth develop passions, learn socioemotional regulation in a social context, and prevent unsafe risky behavior.

In retrospect, some of the research on adolescent leisure and positive youth development can be reframed using a neuroscience perspective. The dual systems model may help explain why leisure contexts that promote appropriate adult supervision, provide leadership opportunities, and expect self-regulate behavior is critical to adolescent development. It also helps understand why adolescents seem more engaged and energized in social situations and why they enjoy thrills and excitement. The model also provides rationale for paying more attention to the emotional and experiential qualities associated with leisure activities. More research could be conducted on how these qualities may be leveraged to facilitate positive risk and thrill that are not subject to impulsive behavior, but at the same time sate the need for sensation seeking.

Besides offering deeper insight into why things might work the way they do, neuroscience research also suggests potential research topics that are particularly relevant for leisure. One cluster of potential research questions has to do with the temporal trajectory and clustering of behaviors and emotion. As longitudinal research methods and analyses continue to evolve, it becomes easier to address issues such as how does engagement in leisure pursuits, and related experiences, change over time? For example, research suggests that adolescents become less intrinsically motivated (Eccles &Midgley, 1991; Sharp et al., 2006) and report being less interested (Sharp et al.; Hunter & Csikszentmihalyi, 2003) as they age.

The decline in intrinsic motivation and interest as youth age seems to contradict the notion that adolescence is a time for developing passions and interests. Because research in this area is still in its infancy, one could consider this apparent contradiction as a piece of the biosocial puzzle that needs solved. For example, research might identify when these declines occur in relation to the changing brain and under what conditions the changes take place. One might ask if there are there specific points of intervention through leisure activity that may be more productive than others to stave the decline of motivation and interest and maximize the brain's propensity to develop leisure interests.

Other questions might address why boredom occurs so regularly or intensely in adolescents. Is it because there is juxtaposition with the need for thrills and excitement that any lower level of engagement is perceived as boring? Does it have to do with the presence of peers? Likewise, can "structured leisure risk" take the place of the need for thrills and excitement and reduce risky impulsivity?

Research has suggested that youth's brains can be sculpted. This implies intentionality and begs the question of how leisure might play a deliberate role. A possible line of inquiry might address whether regular exposure to leisure activities would strengthen myelin development of "good" synapses and prune the "bad" synapses? Under what conditions would this strengthening and pruning occur? What does the reward processing system in the brain have to do with it? Is it possible that the right matrix of leisure activities and experiences within contexts can promote earlier development or strengthening of the cognitive-processing system while at the same time helping to regulate the socioemotional system in order to help prevent risky adolescent behavior?

Further questions about the reward processing system include whether different activities activate the reward processing system uniquely? For example, are there different regions of the brain more or less activated by sport, nature-based activity, computer games, or expressive activities? What is the role of peers in this type of reward activation? Are peers always necessary for greater experiences of pleasure (as indicated by brain activation) or does it depend on the activity, experience, or contextual elements? Do the peers need to be *in situ* or via some mediated technology? Can the brain be trained to find pleasure in solitary activities?

Another set of questions has to do with within-person and between-person changes over time and the developing brain. For example, in some of our work we found that youth who became more bored in their leisure between the eighth grade and tenth grade had the highest odds of smoking and use of alcohol and marijuana (Sharp, et al., 2011). Weybright, Caldwell, Ram, Smith and Wegner (submitted) studied how state (experienced in the moment) and trait (general personality) boredom in leisure was associated with substance use. State, but not trait, boredom in leisure was associated with higher levels of substance use. Perhaps more importantly, they found that this association was stronger for individuals with high levels of trait boredom. Similarly, Weybright (2013) found that higher levels of trait healthy leisure were associated with a tendency to use fewer substances, and on occasions when individuals experienced higher than normal levels of healthy leisure, they tended to use fewer substances.

Understanding why youth drop in and out of activities, and related developmental outcomes, is also an area where more research is needed. Tibbits, Caldwell and Smith (2008) reported that males and females who drop out of sports have higher odds of substance use than those who do not participate or those who participate consistently. Whether and how the developing brain is implicated in these changes across time and within individual may provide a deeper understand of leisure and risk behavior.

Steinberg (2010) suggested that prevention efforts should not focus on cognitive messages because risk activity is more social and emotionally instigated. He suggested that efforts should focus on the context under which risky behavior takes place, which clearly implicates considering the activity, experience and contextual elements of leisure. Currently most prevention efforts are school-based and lack an experiential component. Steinberg's suggestion squares firmly with much of adventure-based and other types of leisure programs that help youth take lessons learn during the experience and apply them to real-world challenges and problems. Further, this would suggest that it might be powerful to embed prevention messages in types of activities, such as sports (e.g., Tibbits et al., 2011) if the context was appropriate.

CONCLUSION

The leisure and developmental and research reviewed in this chapter suggests that we know that leisure contributes to healthy youth development. Although Steinberg (2008) cautioned that much of what is known about the neural underpinnings of adolescent behavior is "reasonable speculation" (p. 81), the additional knowledge gained by neuroscience research may lead to a refinement of what we know to contribute to continued research and practical efforts to promote healthy youth development and reduce risk. From an ecological systems perspective, it is clear that leisure activity, context, and experiences are critical to healthy youth development. It is also clear, however, that the brain alone is only one system in the complex constellation of dialectic processes and mechanisms that promote healthy behavior or facilitate risk behavior.

Despite the understanding current research provides, more research is needed that brings a transdisciplinary approach combining neuroscience, developmental science, and leisure science together to better understand causal pathways and specific points of development that are more or less open for intervention (broadly conceptualized). Although this chapter attempted to highlight possible areas of future research, it only scratched the surface. The role of parents, for example, was only briefly mentioned and the role of family was not even addressed (but see also Trussell, Chapter 22). Specific contexts such as camps or after-school and the entire burgeoning area of technology-based leisure were omitted only due to space restrictions. Furthermore, an entire age group (children up to age 12) was omitted. These are only a few examples of the shortcomings of this chapter.

Although there are many omissions in this chapter, and the complexities of various developmental, social-psychological, and neurobiological processes were not examined to the extent they could have been, I hope that the chapter has provided some knowledge of how leisure is important to healthy adolescent development and sparked some possible ideas for further research.

REFERENCES

Albert, D., Chein, J., & Steinberb, L. (2013). Peer influence on adolescent decision-making. *Current Directions in Psychological Science, 22*, 80–86.

Bartko, W. T., & Eccles, J. S. (2003). Adolescent participation in structured and unstructured activities: A person-oriented analysis. *Journal of Youth and Adolescence, 32*, 233–242.

Beiswenger, K. L., & Grolnick, W. S. (2009). Interpersonal and intrapersonal actors associated with autonomous motivation in adolescents' after-school activities, *Journal of Early Adolescence, 30*, 369–394.

Bronfenbrenner, U. & Morris, P. A. (2006). The bioecological model of human development. *Handbook of Child Psychology, 1*, 793–828.

Caldwell, L. L. (2005). Recreation and youth development. In P. Witt & L. Caldwell (Ed.), *Recreation and youth development* (pp. 169–189). State College, PA: Venture Publishing, Inc.

Caldwell, L. L., Bradley, S., & Coffman, D. (2009). A person-centered approach to individualizing a school-based universal prevention intervention. *American Journal of Alcohol and Drug Addictions, 35*, 214–219.

Csikszentmihalyi, M. (1990). *Flow: The psychology of optimal experience*. New York: Harper and Row.

Csikszentmihalyi, M., & Hunter, J. (2003). Happiness in everyday life: The uses of experience sampling. *Journal of Happiness Studies, 4*, 185–199.

Dahl, R. (2004). Adolescent brain develepoment: A period of vulnerabilities and opportunities. *Annals of New York Academies of Science, 1021*, 1–22.

Dawes, N. P., & Larson, R. (2011). How youth get engaged: Grounded-theory research on motivational development in organized youth programs. *Developmental Psychology, 47*, 259–269.

Dworkin, J. B., Larson, R., & Hansen, D. (2003). Adolescents' accounts of growth experiences in youth activities. *Journal of Youth and Adolescence, 32*, 17–26.

Eccles, J. S., and Midgley, C. (1990). Changes in academic motivation and self-perception during early adolescence. In G. R. Adams and R. Montemayor (Eds.), *From childhood to adolescence: A transition period? (pp. 134-155)*. Thousand Oaks, CA: Sage.

Elkins, D. (Jan./Feb. 2003). The overbooked child: Are we pushing our kids too hard? *Psychology Today, 36*(1), 64–69. Retrieved from http://proquest.umi.com.ezproxy.librarieis.psu.edu

Fauth, R. C., Roth, J., & Brooks-Gunn, J. (2007). Does the neighborhood context alter the link between youth's after-school time activities and developmental outcomes? A multilevel analysis. *Developmental Psychology, 43*(3), 760–777.

Hunter, J. P., & Csikszentmihalyi, M. (2003). The positive psychology of interested adolescents. *Journal of Youth and Adolescence, 32*, 27–35.

Johnson, D. W. & Johnson, R. T. (2004). The three Cs of promoting social and emotional learning. In J. E. Zins, R. P. Weissberg, M. C. Wang, & H. J. Walberg (Eds.), *Building academic success on social and emotional learning* (pp. 40–58). New York: Teachers College Press.

Kleiber, D. A. (1999). *Leisure experience and human development: A dialectical interpretation*. New York: Basic Books.

Kleiber, D. A., Caldwell, L. L., & Shaw, S. A. (1993). Leisure meanings among adolescents, *Loisir & Société/Leisure and Society, 16*, 99–114.

Koezuka, N., Koo, M., Allison, K. R., Adlaf, E. M., Dwyer, J. J. M., Faulkner, G., et al. (2006). The relationship between sedentary activities and physical inactivity among adolescents: Results from the Canadian Community Health Survey. *Journal of Adolescent Health, 39*(4), 515–522.

Larson, R. W. (2000). Toward a psychology of positive youth development. *American Psychologist, 55*, 170–183.

Low, L., K., & Cheng, H. J. (2006). Axon pruning: An essential step underlying the developmental plasticity of neuronal connections. *Philos Trans R Soc Lond B Biol Sci, 361*, pp. 1531–1544.

Mahoney, J.L., Cairns, B.D., & Farmer, T.W. (2003). Promoting interpersonal competence and educational success through extracurricular activity participation. *Journal of Educational Psychology, 95*, 409–418.

Mahoney, J., Larson, R., & Eccles, J. (Eds.). (2005). *Organized Activities as Contexts of Development: Extracurricular Activities, After-school and Community programs* (pp. 45–64). Mahwah, NJ: Lawrence Erlbaum Associates, Publishers.

Miller, J. A., Caldwell, L.L., Weybright, E. H., Smith, E.A., Vergnani, T., & Wegner, L. (2014). Was Bob Seger right? Relation between free time boredom and [Risky] sex. *Leisure Sciences, 36*, 52–67.

Motl, R. W., McAuley, E., Birnbaum, A. S., & Lytle, L. A. (2006). Naturally occurring changes in time spent watching television are inversely related to frequency of physical activity during early adolescence. *Journal of Adolescence, 29*(1), 19–32.

National Center on Addiction and Substance Abuse. (2003). *National survey of American attitudes on substance abuse VIII: Teens and Parents*. National Center on Addiction and Substance Abuse at Columbia University.

National Institute of Mental Health (2011). *The teen brain: Still under construction*. http://www.nimh.nih.gov/health/publications/the-teen-brain-still-under-construction/index.shtml

National Research Council and Institute of Medicine. (2002). Features of positive developmental settings. Committee on community-level programs for youth. In J. Eccles & J. A. Gootman (Eds.), *Community programs to promote youth development* (pp. 86–120). Washington, D. C.: National Academy Press.

Ojanen, T., Sijtsema, J. J., Hawley, P. H., & Little, T. D. (2010). Intrinsic and extrinsic motivation in early adolescents' friendship development: Friendship selection, influence, and prospective friendship quality. *Journal of Adolescence, 33*, 837–851.

Osgood, D. W., Anderson, A. L., & Shaffer, J. N. (2005). Unstructured leisure in the after-school hours. In J. Mahoney, R. Larson & J. Eccles (Eds.), *Organized Activities as Contexts of Development: Extracurricular Activities, After-school and Community programs* (pp. 45–64). Mahwah, NJ: Lawrence Erlbaum Associates, Publishers.

Sharp, E., Caldwell, L. L., Graham, J., & Ridenour, T. (2006). Individual motivation and parental influence on adolescents' experiences of interest in the free time context: A longitudinal examination. *Journal of Youth and Adolescence, 35*, 359–372.

Sharp, E. H., Coffman, D. L., Caldwell, L. L., Smith, E. A., Wegner, L., Flisher, A. J., Vergnani, T., Mathews, C. (2011). Predicting substance use behavior among South African adolescents: The role of free time experiences. *International Journal of Behavioral Development, 35*, 343–351

Skinner, B. F. (1953). *Science and human behavior*. New York: Macmillan.

Steinberg, L. (2007). Risk-taking in adolescence: New perspective from brain and behavioral science. *Current Directions in Psychological Science, 16*, 55–59.

Steinberg, L. (2008). A social neuroscience perspective on adolescent risk-taking. *Developmental Review, 28*, 78–106.

Steinberg, L. (2010). A dual systems model of adolescent risk-taking. *Developmental Psychobiology, 52*, 216–224.

Strycker, L. A., Duncan, S. C., & Pickering, M. A. (2003). The social context of alcohol initiation among African American and White youth. *Journal of Ethnicity in Substance Abuse, 2*(1), 35–42.

Tibbits, M., Caldwell, L. L., Smith, E. Flisher, A., Vergnani, T., & Wegner, L. (June, 2011). *Are sports a protective context for South African youth? Gender differences in the relationships between sports and sexual behavior and substance use*. Paper presented at the Society for Prevention Research Conference, Washington, DC, May 31–June 3.

Tibbits, M. K., Caldwell, L. L., & Smith, E. A. (2008). *The developmental implications of sports participation among*

South African youth. Paper presented at the Leisure Research Symposium, 15 October, 2008, Baltimore, MD.

Vygotsky, L. S. (1978). *Mind and society*. Cambridge: Harvard Press.

Watts, C., & Caldwell, L. L. (2008). Self-determination and free time activity participation as predictors of initiative. *Journal of Leisure Research, 40,* 156–181.

Weybright, E. (2013). *Healthy leisure and its relationship to substance use in South African adolescents: A variable and person centered approach.* Unpublished dissertation, The Pennsylvania State University.

Weybright, E. H., Caldwell, L. L., Ram, N., Smith, E. A. & Wegner, L. L. (submitted). Boredom prone or nothing to do? Distinguishing between state and trait leisure boredom and its association with substance use in South African adolescents.

Williams, G. C., Cox, E. M., Hedberg, V. A., & Deci, E. L. (2000). Extrinsic life goals and health-risk behaviors in adolescents. *Journal of Applied Social Psychology, 30,* 1756–1771.

Williams, D. J., & Walker, G. J. (2006). Leisure, deviant leisure, and crime: 'Caution: Objects may be closer than they appear'. *Leisure/Loisir, 30,* 193–218.

Zaff, J. F., Moore, K. A., Papillo, A. R., & Williams, S. (2003). Implications of extracurricular activity participation during adolescence on positive outcomes. *Journal of Adolescent Research, 18*(6), 599–630.

22
Family Leisure

Dawn E. Trussell (Brock University)

Families, for many people, provide the primary context for their leisure, and yet, until the end of the twentieth century, family leisure was a relatively neglected area of research within leisure studies (Kelly, 1997; Shaw, 1997). This lack of attention was due, in part, to the belief that "leisure was best explained from its relation to work" (Kelly, 1997, p. 132), the prominence of social psychological models that focused on individual experiences and patterns of behavior (Shaw, 1997), and an emphasis on couples and marital leisure patterns without consideration of other family forms or the broader family system (Zabriske & McCormick, 2003). Moreover, early research on family leisure focused primarily on the benefits of family activities (Shaw, 2008), and although this research provided an important beginning, it did not reflect the reality of lived experiences that includes both positive and negative attributes. As Kelly (1997) argued, "In family there is both community and alienation. In relationships there is both bonding and violence. In nurture there is both love and exploitation. Consequently we should avoid any simple models or assumptions" (p. 134).

In recent years, a more critical lens has highlighted the contradictory aspects of family leisure and the multiplicity of meanings that may be experienced by individual family members as well as among diverse family forms. This chapter strives to present some of the salient issues in family leisure scholarship and draws upon research from leisure studies as well as family studies. It begins with a critical discussion of what constitutes a family, followed by current research on family leisure, and then concludes with a discussion of future considerations that reflect an ever-changing society.

What Constitutes a Family?

Families shape our everyday lives and for many individuals are a primary source of companionship and psychological gratification (Freysinger, 1994). However, what exactly constitutes a "family" is characterized by multiple meanings and contexts and has been a subject of ongoing debate and disagreement (Allen, 2000; Shaw, 1997). As a result, numerous definitions have been developed, that promote specific political and ideological perspectives. For example, the most traditional and idealized definition is the Standard North American Family (SNAF) (Smith, 1993). The traditional SNAF is a legally married heterosexual couple with an ideology rooted in an era of industrialization. As Mestdag and Vandeweyer (2005) explained:

> Industrialization promoted an ideology that identified work and the wider public area with the male and the private, domestic area with the female. The home was the place a man could come home to, where the private, caring family could protect itself against the heartless, competitive world. (p. 304)

Yet, the nuclear family model is largely associated with idealized middle-class values, and was not a lived-reality for many families, even during the era of industrialization. Consequently, the SNAF definition has been challenged as ideological, mythical, and a romanticized notion of a reality that never existed (Coontz, 1992).

Several researchers in leisure and family studies have called for the recognition of cultural variations in family types that are more representative of the diverse family forms that exist. An inclusive conceptualization of family would include family forms such as childless couples, lone parents, separated and divorced families, remarried and stepfamilies, cohabiting families, gay and lesbian families, and extended families (Ambert, 2006; Shaw, 2010). The meaning of family is deeply embedded within legal, educational, religious, and social policies (Allen, 2001). Omission of these family forms from the socially constructed definition of family can have negative implications on their everyday lives (Luxton, 2001). Consequently, many marginalized families encounter economic and legal difficulties in successfully functioning as a family unit (e.g., health benefits) and the ongoing emotional struggle of being "different" and "less legitimate" in mainstream society. In response to the rights of non-SNAF families, Baker (2001) noted that:

> Increasingly, researchers and advocacy groups are arguing that definitions of family should be broadened to encompass caring and enduring intimate relationships regardless of legal or blood ties. In other words, they argue that the structure of the unit or its legality is less important in defining family than the functions fulfilled by the unit or the services provided. (p. 9)

Thus, how the family unit is conceptualized is complex and embedded within political and sociocultural ideologies in a particular moment in time.

WHAT IS FAMILY LEISURE AND HOW DO FAMILY MEMBERS EXPERIENCE IT DIFFERENTLY?

Research has identified the value and significance of leisure on family life. Family leisure is valued as an important way to build and strengthen the family unit, in that, the potential of family leisure to foster togetherness and intra-familial communication is particularly idealized (Daly, 2001; Shaw, 2008). Family leisure research has paid significant attention to the role that leisure plays in the lives of families with young children. Parents organize family leisure activities to build and strengthen family relationships through encouraged togetherness and child socialization (Harrington, 2013). Parents also believe that family leisure activities provide a range of other benefits as well, including the inculcation of life lessons and moral values as well as the promotion of children's physical development (Shaw, 2008). The preteen stage has heightened value for family leisure activities, as there is "a sense of urgency to do things together before the children reached adolescence and might drift away from the family or get involved in negative activities" (Shaw & Dawson, 2001, p. 224). Moreover, some parents hope that family leisure will provide important learning opportunities to aid their children when they become parents and have a family of their own (Shaw & Dawson, 2001; Shaw, 2008). Family leisure is thought to establish a *sense of family* and is deliberately used to provide opportunities for positive interactions.

However, facilitating the family's leisure activities may not be freely chosen or intrinsically motivated by parents, as there is often a sense of duty or responsibility associated with organizing and participating in these activities (Harrington, 2013; Shaw & Dawson, 2001; Trussell & Shaw, 2012). Women, in particular, may experience the facilitation of family leisure as an obligatory part of their parental role and in many cases organize family leisure activities around the needs of their children and/or husband, rather than around their own personal needs (Harrington, 2006, 2013; Parry, Chapter 24; Shaw, 2008; Such, 2009; Trussell & Shaw, 2009).

The obligatory nature of family leisure, and the expectation that facilitating and organizing such activities is part of the parental role led Shaw and Dawson (2001) to suggest that family leisure should be seen as *purposive leisure*, rather than pure, or freely chosen leisure. Shaw and Dawson argued that the current social psychological definitions of leisure as freedom of choice, intrinsic motivation, and the quality of enjoyment or experiences might not always be applicable to family leisure activities. The authors suggested that socially oriented conceptualizations of leisure that put more emphasis on the social obligations and motivations for involvement or the concept of serious leisure may be more applicable; however, they too have shortcomings that do not adequately describe the meanings of family leisure.

In light of the existing definitional shortcomings, Shaw and Dawson (2001) posited that family leisure "should be seen as a form of purposive leisure, which is planned, facilitated, and executed by parents in order to achieve particular short- and long-term goals" (p. 228). Since the original conceptualization of purposive leisure, other studies have adopted this concept and applied it to a variety of family contexts. For example, Trussell and Shaw (2012) examined the purposive nature of family leisure experiences related to youth sport involvement and Shannon and Shaw (2008) examined mothers' roles as leisure educators and what their daughters learned about leisure from their mothers. Palmer, Freeman, and Zabriskie (2007) used the concept of purposive leisure to examine the familial impact of volunteering on family service expeditions. Hebblethwaite and Norris (2010) also expanded the conceptualization of purposive leisure to include the "experience of time spent together by grandparents and [their adult] grandchildren in free time or recreational activities" (p. 490).

Another area of family research, originating from a seminal study by Zabriskie and McCormick (2001), has influenced a line of inquiry focused on the Core and Balance Model of Family Leisure Functioning. This model argued that there are two general patterns or categories of leisure activities that families participate in to meet family functioning needs. According to the model, core activities "address a family's need for familiarity and stability by regularly providing predictable family leisure experiences that foster personal relatedness and feelings of family closeness" (p. 283). Core family leisure activities are common, everyday, low-cost, and often home-based activities that families do together frequently, require little planning and are often spontaneous (e.g., watching television, playing board games, playing in the yard). "Balance family leisure patterns address a family's need for novelty and change by providing new experiences that provide the input necessary for family systems to be challenged, to develop, and to progress as a working unit" (p. 283). Balance activities are less frequent than core activities, require greater investment of resources (e.g., time, effort, and money), involve substantial planning and organization, and usually occur outside of the home (e.g., family vacations, special events, day trips). The authors contend that both forms of activities are essential to foster feelings of cohesion and adaptability for families within today's society.

Over the last decade, a group of family leisure scholars from the United States have built on this model and the corresponding measurement tool of family leisure involvement. Researchers have consistently reported a positive relationship between different types of family leisure activities and aspects of family functioning (specifically family cohesion and adaptability). Different types of family samples have been examined such as adoptive families (Freeman & Zabriskie, 2003), single-parent families (Hornberger, Zabriskie, & Freeman, 2010), and Mexican-American families (Christenson, Zabriskie, Eggett, & Freeman, 2006).

Family leisure has also been positively related to family life satisfaction (Agate, Zabriskie, Agate, & Poff, 2009; Zabriskie & McCormick, 2003). Findings by Agate et al. argued: "the satisfaction with their leisure involvement together is clearly the best predictor of overall satisfaction with family life, even when accounting for family income, marital status, age, history of divorce, and family leisure involvement" (p. 218). Moreover, Agate et al. suggested that "more is not necessarily better" (p. 218); that is, the *quality* of the family leisure experiences and finding activities that are individually satisfying and meaningful are also significant.

Some of the studies that have used the Core and Balance Model have examined data at the parent, child, and family level and divergent perspectives within the family unit have been reported. For example, Zabriske and McCormick (2003) argued that youth who have greater involvement in core family leisure activities reported higher levels of family satisfaction. In contrast, for parents who participated in the same study, both core and balance family leisure activities were significantly related to family satisfaction. Building on this earlier research, Agate et al. (2009) reported: "particularly from the youth perspective, family involvement, and satisfaction with frequent, simple home-based activities such as reading together, eating dinners together, playing board games . . . and attending family member's games or performances, is absolutely essential to satisfaction with family life" (p. 219).

Divergent perspectives between parents and children have also been emphasized in other studies that have adopted a more critical approach. For example, Shaw, Havitz, and Delemere (2008), found that for parents family vacations were seen as a form of escape from everyday life (i.e., for the fathers their employment-related activities and for the mothers an escape from everyday household responsibilities and children's scheduled activities). The parents valued the purposive nature of the vacations as an opportunity for family togetherness and enhanced communication. Long-term goals emphasized memory-making as well as strengthening the family unit before the children became teenagers. And yet, drawing from the same data set, Hilbrecht, Shaw, Delamere, and Havitz (2008) reported that the children were more focused on fun as being central to the experience, the novelty and uniqueness of the activities, and a sense of belonging to family and other social groups. Unlike their parents, children did not notice "a purposive component to the vacation other than simply having fun" (p. 567).

The motivations for shared family time and family leisure activities may also be different between parents. For example, Shaw and Dawson (2001) argued that mothers were found to have a keen interest in the short-term goals of their children getting along better. Fathers seemed to place more emphasis on family leisure as a long-term investment, with future goals of family cohesiveness and maintaining close relationships, when the children were older. Further support for diverse parental perspectives comes from research by Harrington (2013). In this study, mothers' motivation for organizing family time activities was to enhance immediate and long-term interpersonal relationships and emotional bonding. In comparison, fathers were motivated to enjoy shared family activities that emphasized teaching skills, technical knowledge, and "more instrumental values rather than bonds per se" (p. 333).

Different roles and meanings for shared couple time may also create conflict between family members. For example, Dyck and Daly (2006) in their research on couple time found that it was almost always fathers who had the initial idea to instigate time without the children, whereas the mothers would maintain their role as the family organizer by scheduling and implementing a couple outing and looking after details such as child-care arrangements. However, what was perceived as quality couple time, and how the time would be spent, could become a source of conflict. As Dyck and Daly argued:

> Several interviews indicated that partners sometimes held different views regarding couple time, although they did not always seem to realize this. Different and unclear meanings for couple time, perhaps hopes for sexual intimacy that were not communicated or not heard, might explain the resentment some fathers expressed about wives' scheduling of couple time. (pp. 208–209)

Thus, although there may be many shared qualities, rather than assuming that family members experience family leisure involvement similarly, it is important to recognize that at times their motivations and meanings may diverge. One such reason for divergent perspectives is often the *idealization* of family leisure involvement.

THE IDEALIZATION OF FAMILY LEISURE ACTIVITIES AND ITS CONNECTION TO PARENTING IDEOLOGIES

Research has shown that it is taken for granted and expected that women are typically responsible for the organization and production of everyday family leisure activities as well as special events such as family vacations, holidays, birthdays, and Christmas celebrations (Bella, 1992; Shaw, 2008). For women, the organization of family time special events can bring contradictory meanings and experiences as they provide the emotional support and energy to ensure its success. Women organize these family activities with high expectations for positive interactions and experiences. When conflict between family members occurs and the activity does not turn out as planned, there are often high levels of disappointment, frustration, and lack of enjoyment (Shaw 2008; Shaw & Dawson, 2001). And yet, as Daly (2003) pointed out, "Emotions are rarely foregrounded in our theories about families, and yet much of the everyday rhetoric of living in families is about love, jealousy, anger, disappointment, hurt, tolerance, and care" (p. 775). In researching family life, understanding both the positive and negative emotions that are felt by family members may deepen our understanding of the meanings of family experiences beyond inventory types of description (Daly, 2003).

It is clear that the idealization of family leisure can create mixed emotions of satisfaction and frustration as there is a "gap between parental ideals and reality" (Shaw & Dawson, 2003/4, p. 179). This gap is socially constructed with nostalgic and ideological assumptions that alter the context and meanings of family experiences. As Daly (2003) argued, "everyone lives in two families: one they live with (in everyday reality) and one they *live by*" (p. 778). Parents who perceive that there is never enough family time commonly express disillusionment and guilt and describe most of their time together as characterized by obligation, conflict, and service of children, rather than romanticized ideals (Daly, 2001). This discourse has emerged around the idea of time famine and perceived neglect of time spent with children due to paid employment and/or domestic work (Daly, 2004).

In part, the idealization, motivation, and expectations for family leisure activities might be connected to broader parenting ideologies (Shaw, 2008, 2010). Moreover, many parents see organized youth sport as a significant component of their family leisure activities and a way to achieve the parenting ideal (Trussell & Shaw, 2009, 2012). As Coakley (2009) theorized, there are now important cultural connections between organized youth sport and ideologies of parenting and gender. For most of the twentieth century, a father's employment status and ability to provide financially for his family, underpinned strong ideological assumptions about masculinity and the fatherhood role (Brannen & Nilsen, 2006). However, a contemporary ideal to a more *involved* style of fathering expects fathers to share in the physical and emotional care of their children, and sport and leisure fosters a context in which they can meet these new parenting ideals (see Kay, 2009). As the ideology of *involved fathering* has emerged, so has a culture of *intensive mothering*. Contemporary mothering arguably entails more involved and deliberate practices (Arendell, 2001). Mothers are expected to be child-centered and actively manage and direct their children's lives in organized extracurricular activities.

Trussell and Shaw (2012) examined the connection of organized youth sport to cultural beliefs, values, and practices of contemporary parenting ideologies (i.e., involved fathering and intensive mothering). They posited, "parenting goes beyond the home environment and becomes a public act that is observed by other parents, with these observations creating the bases of what is deemed to be a good parent" (p. 377). That is, children's extracurricular participation and their family leisure engagements may reflect and contribute to broader and complex sociocultural changes in contemporary parenting ideologies and provide not only an idealization of childrearing practices, but also a set of criteria by which they are judged.

DIVERSE MEANINGS AND EXPERIENCES AMONG FAMILIES

Daly (2003) called family researchers to task in recognizing the diversity, complexity, and richness of shared meanings and understanding. Kelly (1997) and Shaw (1997) also pointed to the significance of recognizing diversity among families. Many scholars have responded to this call and advanced the understanding of the multiplicity and diversity of family experiences.

Parents' employment can shape family forms and the everyday experiences of family time and family leisure activities even for families that fit the SNAF model (two heterosexual, married parents and their children). For example, truckers, resource extraction industries, migrants, and military personnel may be gone for periods of time, and their work schedules can interrupt family life with extended absences and then reintegration back into family life. The temporary absences of one family member can be particularly disruptive to family relationships and time spent together. To promote family unity during a partner's absence, shared family time and leisure activities become all that more important and heightened (Werner & Shannon, 2013).

Although there is limited research on nontraditional family structures such as families of same-sex parents, we can garner a sense of the potential significance of diverse insights and how it might affect parental labor and family leisure experiences and meanings. For example, seminal work by Bialeschki and Pearce (1997) revealed how a sense of freedom or liberation may be found as lesbian mothers "redistribute power and responsibilities based on factors other than gender difference" (p. 116). The authors argued that the couples negotiated household and child-care roles and responsibilities based on interests, time, and structured agreements. In turn, these responsibilities had direct implications for their leisure practices. Through family leisure activities the lesbian mothers were able to bond with each other and their children, while creating the opportunity to reinforce and validate feelings of being a family, counter and resistant to traditional societal views.

Mactavish, MacKay, Iwasaki, and Betteridge (2007) examined family caregivers of individuals with intellectual disabilities, and reported findings similar to Shaw et al. (2008), in that, central to family vacations was the sense of "getting away from routine" and "doing and learning new things" (p. 144). However, their family leisure experiences had altered meanings whereby the "strong influence of disability and health-related needs" (p. 145) influenced destination choice. Parents also had to contend with the tension of bringing aides/respite workers and the financial and emotional implications of such decisions and their impact on the quality of the families' experiences. Mactavish and Schleien (2004) reported that parents with a child who has a developmental disability also valued family leisure interactions as beneficial for enhancing quality of family life and the development of life-long skills, and yet, family leisure was particularly valued for the child with the disability as they had fewer opportunities for leisure engagements outside of the family unit (see Dattilo, Chapter 26).

Family leisure may also play an important role for families facing different forms of adversity. For example, facing rising costs, diminishing revenues, and a work-driven lifestyle, Trussell and Shaw (2009) found that rural farm families thought of their family leisure activities (i.e., 4-H shows/community fairs and youth sport programs) as a "medium to preserve traditional farm values while preparing future generations for a life outside of agriculture" (p. 443). Werner and Shannon (2013) examined the role of leisure during the deployment of a partner in the military during a time of war. The women in their study revealed that shared family time between mother and child(ren) was seen to be all that more valuable to meet their needs for distraction and enjoyment during the fathers' temporary absence. It also provided the women with a sense of control and was a helpful coping strategy. Hutchinson, Afifi, and Krause (2007) reported that shared family time following divorce, provided much-needed humor and distractions as a way to cope and diffuse immediate and enduring stress. Deliberate efforts were also made by parents to create new special family events and memories and (re)create a sense of being a family. Family leisure engagements also became a venue in which new partners/stepparents were able to connect with the children and facilitate relationship-building opportunities.

Finally, family leisure scholars, to date, have paid scant attention to issues of social class and race/ethnicity; however, we can garner a sense of the potential diverse meanings and experiences. For example, sociologist, Lareau (2002) investigated the effects of social class on family interactions inside the home, and children's consequent participation in organized and informal leisure activities within their community. Lareau argued that social differentiation does matter—it shapes parenting practices and the consequent meanings and experiences of family time and shared leisure activities. Middle-class parents (White and Black) engage in what Lareau termed "concerted cultivation" (p. 748). Parents sought out opportunities to foster their children's talents, skills, and abilities through organized leisure activities. In contrast, working-class and poor parents (White and Black) engage in what she termed "natural growth" (p. 748). Parents provided the necessary conditions under which children can grow (comfort, food, shelter, and other basic support), but left leisure activities to the children themselves. Compared to middle-class children, Lareau argued that, "working-class and poor children participate in few organized activities and have more free time and deeper, richer ties with their extended families" (p. 749). Recent work by Harrington (2013) tentatively suggested similar class-based values, in that, middle-class participants used family leisure to foster values of discipline, achievement, and confidence. In contrast, the individual achievement orientation associated with the middle class was absent with working-class families who sought out a sense of "family togetherness and a sense of security in an uncertain world" (p. 335). As Harrington pointed out, this research is a start to family leisure scholars' analysis of social class—and further questions might arise when class becomes the central context of investigation.

Moreover, the limited research that has examined family leisure and race/ethnicity highlights the diversity, complexity, and richness of shared meanings and understanding *among* families. For example, family leisure for intercultural unions among Korean-American and East European-American married couples pointed to the significance of family leisure to facilitate opportunities for quality time, healthy communication, and the opportunity to learn about each other's culture (Sharaievska, Kim, & Stodolska, 2013; Stodolska & Floyd, Chapter 28). At the same time, unique problems were revealed such as language-related frustrations or cultural differences such as communication styles and social behavior. Research on Mexican-American families and the acculturation process found that family leisure involvement in core activities played an important role for bicultural youth (i.e., a person who is acculturated to dominant culture, but still retains aspects of her or his origin) (Christenson et al., 2006). In comparison, high-acculturated Mexican-American youth (i.e., a person who integrates well into the dominant culture while giving up her or his culture of origin) placed importance on balance family leisure activities. (See above discussion on Core and Balance Model.)

Despite the advancements that have been made over the past decade in understanding families and their leisure involvement, these studies (and others not cited in this chapter) represent only a beginning in understanding the rich complexity and divergence of meanings and experiences between family members as well as among different family forms. As Werner and Shannon (2013) pointed out, "there is value in continuing to explore the role and meaning of family leisure in different family structures and with families experiencing different circumstances" (p. 76).

FUTURE CONSIDERATIONS FOR FAMILY LEISURE INVOLVEMENT

Overall, the literature presents a picture of family leisure as highly valued and a central component to family life, but also stress-inducing. That is, family members have high expectations about the positive outcomes of family activities, but often have divergent perspectives and expectations, and organizing and facilitating these activities takes time and effort, particularly for women. Because of these conflicting perspectives on family leisure, it has been suggested that family time should be conceptualized as inherently contradictory (Shaw, 1997). Framing the family leisure paradigm in a contradictory lens helps to capture the conflicting realities of family members' experiences as they seek to enhance family life. Also, the perspective can be seen to provide a more holistic understanding of family leisure and may help to sensitize researchers to both the positive and negative aspects of family life.

Globalization and post-industrial economies have changed the meanings of family time (Daly, 2001). Neo-liberal government paradigms, a shrinking middle class, the rising costs of home ownership, and the changing nature of the workplace culture, have serious implications on family life. Daly (2003) called attention to the importance of globalization and consumption-related meanings and activities that have come to dominate much of our everyday lives. As Daly (2003) suggested, "Things shape values and beliefs in families, mediate family relationships, create conflicts in families, and are part of the process of identity work and dream management in families" (p. 778). Material goods can strengthen family relations through shared leisure resources. However, consumerism and material products can also create much conflict and dissention within the family unit with individual interests, priorities, and goals in what goods the family should own and use for their research endeavors (Daly, 2003). Moreover, a paradox of consumption-related activities might be their financial cost and the loss of family time to work time to afford the material products (Daly, 2003). This may exacerbate the discourse that has emerged around the idea of time famine, and in turn, the value of such recreational material products and their consequent meanings to the family unit might be one future area of study.

A culture of consumerism and technological advancements have also changed family life with a higher priority given to bigger homes, smaller backyards, and more private and individual spaces within the home. The popularity of personal computers, smartphones and other electronic devices has altered the way that families communicate with each other and how they attain and organize information for their leisure pursuits. These technological advances and their private location in the home (i.e., offices, bedrooms) have also played a major role in constraining, mediating, and altering everyday family interactions and time spent together (Daly, 2003).

Although family leisure scholars, to date, have paid scant attention to the impact of technological advancements on family life, we can garner a glimpse of its potential significance. For example, Hodge et al. (2012) reported that "higher levels of youth media use were associated with significantly lower levels of family functioning" (p. 298) and that shared media connection (e.g., cell phones, text messages, social networks, and watching TV or movies together) positively correlated with family functioning. Sharaievska (2012) reported that the use of social network sites could decrease time spent together and the quality of family interactions while creating conflicts over privacy issues. Yet, at the same time, social network sites provided an important mechanism to foster shared interests and enhance social connections between immediate family members as well as extended family members. Future technological advances are difficult to predict—but a continued and enhanced understanding of how the advancement of technology dramatically alters our society (see Nimrod, Chapter 30), and in turn, influences the dynamics of family life is essential to future scholarship and practice.

Moreover, in family leisure research we often consider only the core family unit, with little consideration for the significance of extended family members. Studies by Hebblethwaite and Norris (2010), Trussell and Shaw (2009), Havitz (2007), and Hilbrecht et al. (2008) suggest that future research should include extended family members such as grandparents, aunts, uncles, and cousins in the analysis for a more holistic understanding of family leisure experiences. Further, with North America's increasingly diverse culture, consideration should also be given to the value of multigenerational households and how it might alter the perspectives and context of family leisure experiences (e.g., Tirone & Shaw, 1997) as well as intercultural marriages (e.g., Sharaievska et al., 2013). Moreover, as Freysinger (1997) argued, "What of the leisure and families of older adults who soon will comprise the largest proportion of households in North America?" (p. 2). How might their perspectives and experiences differ from families with young children? Clearly, it will be important in future research and professional practice to give consideration to the multiple family forms that may co-exist, for a more inclusive and diverse conceptualization of family time and leisure experiences.

Definitions and models of family leisure are needed to provide shared understanding and communication; however they can also reduce the complexity, diversity, and richness of a social construct to a monolithic entity. Definitions and models also reflect the phenomenon of family leisure in a particular moment in time. The future will require shifting conceptualizations of family units and their leisure involvement that examines their similarities, the divergences among families, the different social dynamics that exist within families, as well as the connection to broader sociocultural ideologies. Globalization, economic instability, and changing social beliefs have shaped the everyday lives of family members—and changing cultural processes and values will continue to do so in the future.

REFERENCES

Agate, J., Zabriskie, R., Agate, S., & Poff, R. (2009). Family leisure satisfaction and satisfaction with family life. *Journal of Leisure Research, 41*(2), 205–223.

Allen, K. (2000). A conscious and inclusive family studies. *Journal of Marriage and the Family, 62*, 4–17.

Allen, K. (2001). Finding new paths to family scholarship: A response to James White and Sheila Marshall. *Journal of Marriage and Family, 63*, 899–901.

Ambert, A.M. (2006). *Changing families: Relationships in context*. Toronto, ON: Pearson Education Canada.

Arendell, T. (2001). The new care work of middle class mothers: Managing childrearing, employment, and time. In K. Daly (Ed.), *Minding the time in family experience: Emerging perspectives and issues* (pp. 163–204). London: Elsevier Science Press.

Baker, M. (2001). Definitions, cultural variations, and demographic trends. In M. Baker (Ed.), *Families: Changing trends in Canada* (4th ed., pp. 3–27). Toronto, ON: McGraw-Hill Ryerson.

Bella, L. (1992). *The Christmas imperative*. Halifax, NS: Fernwood.

Bialeschki, D., & Pearce, K. (1997). "I don't want a lifestyle—I want a life": The effect of role negotiations on the leisure of lesbian mothers. *Journal of Leisure Research, 29*(1), 113–131.

Brannen, J., & Nilsen, A. (2006). From fatherhood to fathering: Transmission and change among British fathers in four-generation families. *Sociology, 40*(2), 335–352.

Christenson, O., Zabriskie, R., Eggett, D., & Freeman, P. (2006). Family acculturation, family leisure involvement, and family functioning among Mexican-Americans. *Journal of Leisure Research, 38*(4), 475–495.

Coakley, J. (2009). The good father: Parental expectations and youth sports. In T. Kay (Ed.), *Fathering through sport and leisure* (pp. 40–50). New York: Routledge.

Coontz, S. (1992). *The way we never were: American families and the nostalgia trap*. New York: HarperCollins.

Daly, K. (2001). Deconstructing family time: From ideology to lived experience. *Journal of Marriage and Family, 63*, 283–294.

Daly, K. (2003). Family theory versus the theories families live by. *Journal of Marriage and Family, 65*, 771–784.

Daly, K. (2004). *The changing culture of parenting*. Retrieved from http://www.vanierinstitute.ca/include/get.php?nodeid=1144&format=download

Dyck, V., & Daly, K. (2009). Rising to the challenge: Fathers' roles in the negotiation of couple time. In T. Kay (Ed.), *Fathering through sport and leisure* (pp. 183–199). New York: Routledge.

Freeman, P., & Zabriskie, R. (2003). Leisure and family functioning in adoptive families: Implications for therapeutic recreation. *Therapeutic Recreation Journal, 37*(1), 73–93.

Freysinger, V. (1994). Leisure with children and parental satisfaction: further evidence of a sex difference in the adult roles and leisure. *Journal of Leisure Research, 26*, 212–226.

Freysinger, V. (1997). Redefining family, redefining leisure: Progress made and challenges ahead in research on leisure and families. *Journal of Leisure Research, 29*(1), 1–4.

Harrington, M. (2006). Family leisure. In C. Rojek, S. Shaw, & A. J. Veal (Eds.), *A handbook of leisure studies*, pp. 417–432. New York: Palgrave Macmillan.

Harrington, M. (2013). Families, gender, social class, and leisure. In V. J. Freysinger, S. M. Shaw, K. A. Henderson, & M. D. Bialeschki (Eds.), *Leisure, women, and gender* (pp. 325–341). State College, PA: Venture Publishing, Inc.

Havitz, M. (2007). A host, a guest, and our lifetime relationship: Another hour with grandma Havitz. *Leisure Sciences, 29*, 131–141. doi: 10.1080/01490400601160754

Hebblethwaite, S., & Norris, J. (2010). "You don't want to hurt his feelings ...": Family leisure as a context for intergenerational ambivalence. *Journal of Leisure Research, 42*(3), 489–508.

Hilbrecht, M., Shaw, S., Delamere, F., & Havitz, M. (2008). Experiences, perspectives, and meanings of family vacations for children. *Leisure/Loisir, 32*(2), 541–571. doi: 10.1080/14927713.2008.9651421

Hodge, C., Zabriskie, R., Fellingham, G., Coyne, S., Lundberg, N., Padilla-Walker, L., & Day, R. (2012). The relationship between media in the home and family functioning in context of leisure. *Journal of Leisure Research, 44*(3), 285–307.

Hornberger, L., Zabriskie, R., & Freeman, P. (2010). Contributions of family leisure to family functioning among single-parent families. *Leisure Sciences, 32*, 143–161. doi: 10.1080/01490400903547153

Hutchinson, S., Afifi, T., & Krause, S. (2007). The family that plays together fares better: Examining the contribution of shared family time to family resilience following divorce. *Journal of Divorce & Remarriage, 46*(3/4), 21–48. doi: 10.1300/J087v46n03_03

Kay, T. (Ed.). (2009). *Fathering through sport and leisure.* New York, NY: Routledge.

Kelly, J. (1997). Changing issues in leisure-family research—again. *Journal of Leisure Research, 29*, 132–134.

Lareau, A. (2002). Invisible inequality: Social class and childrearing in black families and white families. *American Sociological Review, 67*(5), 747–776.

Luxton, M. (2001). Conceptualizing "families": Theoretical frameworks and family research. In M. Baker (Ed.), *Families: Changing trends in Canada* (4th ed.) (pp. 28–50). Toronto, ON: McGraw-Hill Ryerson.

Mactavish, J., MacKay, K., Iwasaki, Y., & Betteridge, D. (2007). Family caregivers of individuals with intellectual disability: Perspectives on life quality and the role of vacations. *Journal of Leisure Research, 39*(1), 127–155.

Mactavish, J., & Schleien, S. (2004). Re-injecting spontaneity and balance in family life: Parents' perspectives on recreation in families that include children with developmental disability. *Journal of Intellectual Disability Research, 48*(2), 123–141.

Mestdag, I., & Vandeweyer, J. (2005). Where has family time gone? In search of joint family activities and the role of the family meal in 1966 and 1999. *Journal of Family History, 30*(3), 304–323.

Palmer, A., Freeman, P., & Zabriskie, R. (2007). Family deepening: A qualitative inquiry into the experience of families who participate in service expeditions. *Journal of Leisure Research, 39*(3), 438–458.

Shannon, C., & Shaw, S. (2008). Mothers and daughters: Teaching and learning about leisure. *Leisure Sciences, 30*, 1–16. doi: 10.1080/01490400701544659

Sharaievska, I. (2012). *Family and marital satisfaction and the use of social network technologies.* Unpublished doctoral dissertation, University of Illinois at Urbana-Champaign.

Sharaievska, I., Kim, J., & Stodolska, M. (2013). Leisure and marital satisfaction in intercultural marriages. *Journal of Leisure Research, 45*(4), 445–465.

Shaw, S. (1997). Controversies and contradictions in family leisure: An analysis of conflicting paradigms. *Journal of Leisure Research, 29*, 98–112.

Shaw, S. (2008). Family leisure and changing ideologies of parenthood. *Sociology Compass, 2*(2), 688–703.

Shaw, S. (2010). Diversity and ideology: Changes in Canadian family life and implications for leisure. *World Leisure, 52*(1), 4–13.

Shaw, S., & Dawson, D. (2001). Purposive leisure: Examining parental discourses on family activities. *Leisure Sciences, 23*, 217–231.

Shaw, S., & Dawson, D. (2003/4). Contradictory aspects of family leisure: Idealization versus experience. *Leisure/Loisir, 28*(3–4), 179–201.

Shaw, S., Havitz, M, & Delemere, F. (2008). "I decided to invest in my kids' memories": Family vacations, memories, and the social construction of the family. *Tourism, Culture & Communication, 8*, 13–26.

Smith, D. (1993). The standard north American family: SNAF as an ideological code. *Journal of Family Issues, 14*(1), 50–65.

Such, E. (2009). Fatherhood, the morality of personal time and leisure-based parenting. In T. Kay (Ed.), *Fathering through sport and leisure* (pp. 73–87). New York: Routledge.

Tirone, S., & Shaw, S. (1997). At the center of their lives: Indo Canadian women, their families and leisure. *Journal of Leisure Research, 29*(2), 225–244.

Trussell, D., & Shaw, S. (2009). Changing family life in the rural context: Women's perspectives of family leisure on the farm. *Leisure Sciences, 31*(5), 434–449.

Trussell, D., & Shaw, S. (2012). Organized youth sport and parenting in public and private spaces. *Leisure Sciences, 34*(5), 377–394. doi: 10.1080/01490400.2012.714699

Werner, T., & Shannon, S. (2013). Doing more with less: Women's leisure during their partners' military deployment. *Leisure Sciences, 35*, 63–80. doi: 10.1080/014900400.2013.739897

Zabriskie, R., & McCormick, B. (2001). The influences of family leisure patterns on perceptions of family functioning. *Family Relations, 50*(3), 281–289.

Zabriskie, R., & McCormick, B. (2003). Parent and child perspectives of family leisure involvement and satisfaction with family life. *Journal of Leisure Research, 35*(2), 163–189.

23
LEISURE AND AGING (WELL)

Douglas A. Kleiber (University of Georgia)

As leisure is generally considered the realm of opportunity for self-expressive activity, it would seem to be enhanced by the reduction of work and family obligations that typically comes in later life. On the other hand, the losses associated with aging, especially around declining health and physical capacity, would naturally be expected to diminish such opportunities. Both sets of influence are real and describe the experiences of most older people in a general sense, perhaps balancing each other out to some extent. Indeed, rather than reduction or expansion of activity, continuity of interest and activity tends to be the most descriptive and characteristic pattern through the transition of retirement, and particularly for the "third age" folks most recently retired.[1] These trends may change, however, as an increasingly larger portion of people in North America are living longer and in better health and as newer cohorts, particularly boomers, move into later live with higher expectations about being and staying active, adventurous, and socially engaged.[2] The focus of this chapter, however, is on the question of what difference such activity changes and choices make to the *quality* of later life.

SUCCESSFUL AGING

Successful aging is a controversial subject, fraught with conflicting and competing interpretations (cf. Bowling, 2007). For some researchers and writers (e.g., Rowe & Kahn, 1998) those with physical limitations that constrain leisure activity are by definition aging unsuccessfully, as are those whose activities are high on engagement but short on meaning and "productivity." For many others, happiness and subjective well-being must be taken into account. And one of the most common problems is that some of the qualities and activity patterns used to define or indicate successful aging, such as good health or activity engagement, are also used as predictors or antecedents of successful aging.

There is evidence that leisure activity contributes at least to the subjective well-being dimensions of successful aging (see Adams, Leibbrandt, & Moon, 2011, for a critical review). Generally, small but significant and positive relationships have been found between amount of leisure participation and life satisfaction (e.g., Fernandez-Ballesteros, Zamarron, & Ruiz, 2001). Although a few studies have found that socially- and psychologically-involving pursuits such as hobbies, sports, and outdoor recreation may be more strongly related to life satisfaction than participation in passive pursuits (e.g., Butrica & Schaner, 2005), these relationships appear to differ according to gender, age, and stage in the life course (e.g., Brown, Frankel, & Fennell, 1991). Some of the strongest support for the link between leisure participation and life satisfaction comes from research on successful aging and life satisfaction, even suggesting that leisure activity levels may be better predictors of life satisfaction in later life than health and income (see Mannell & Dupuis, 1994). However, since most of this research has been cross-sectional and correlational, we are left with the possible interpretation that subjective well-being may lead to more active participation rather than the opposite (see also Mock, Mannell, & Guttentag, Chapter 5).

Turning back to theory for interpretation offers some help. Perhaps the most recognized view of "successful aging" is that offered by Rowe and Kahn (1998) in their book by that title, identifying three factors as essential: (a) avoiding disease; (b) maintaining high cognitive and physical function; and (c) engagement with life. In the last of these, the authors do invoke leisure potentially in referring to "happy activities," but these are confined in the

---

[1] For related research and reviews, see Harahousou, 2006; Roberts, 2013; Singleton & Gibson, 2011.

[2] For views on changing demographics and their measured and expected impacts on leisure activity, see Harahousou, 2006.

authors' analysis to those associated with productivity, accomplishment, and connecting with others. Their general view might suggest that physical leisure activity would be critical to avoiding disease and maintaining good health and that volunteer work or other forms of *serious* leisure (Stebbins, 1992) would be the best ways to "engage with life" since they are most likely to bring about accomplishment, productivity, and connection with others. But the model circumscribes leisure as only being valuable in those ways. More important, this model sees "success" as unavailable to those with disabilities or chronic health issues in later life. When considering the value of leisure for *compensation* for such difficulties, we often look first to whether it will offer some solace for the loss of work after retirement, or for some of the other burdensome aspects of life. But we also look to leisure for the expansion of a repertoire of possibilities that may keep individuals engaged with significant others and the community. Even from a purely psychological perspective, a repertoire of competencies is protective when one or more are lost due to illness, accident, relocation, or the debilitating aspects of aging (Linville, 1987). Evidence supports the value of a breadth of activities for identity development, self-actualization, and adaptation, whether it is in the context of work or leisure. In a study of leisure activity predictors of well-being in later life, Dupuis and Smale (1995) found that having a breadth of interests, whether they be active or passive, was associated with lower levels of depression.

An arguably more applicable and appropriate model of successful aging is the Selective Optimization with Compensation (SOC) Model (Baltes & Baltes, 1990; Baltes & Carstensen, 1996) that acknowledges loss and illness as a part of aging and the ability to *adapt* as being critical to the feelings of aging successfully. Furthermore their model incorporates *disengagement*, as long as it is selective and within one's control, as a vital part of that process. (More will be said shortly about disengagement as well as engagement as important contributors to successful aging.) SOC is also the broader umbrella for Cartensen's Socio-emotional Selectivity (SES) theory (Carstensen, Fung, & Charles, 2003) that regards close meaningful relationships as an essential part of the "optimization" of later life. Others, such as George Vaillant (2002), also regard intimate relationships, particularly marriage and close friendships, as central. It seems reasonable to assume that when participation in various leisure activities is associated with life satisfaction and other indicators, it may be as much about *with whom* one participates as with the activity itself and that the experience of shared participation strengthens the emotional bonds that are so critical to living later life well and successfully.

ENGAGEMENT

The contribution of leisure engagement to successful aging may be best reflected in persistent activity in the face of loss of work and other roles. The idea of staying active compensates for some of the activity losses associated with ending work roles through retirement, but, again, the theory that most accurately describes the patterned activities of later life is the continuity theory (Atchley, 1999) where people maintain their favorite activities and associated companionships, as a familiar convoy for enduring the losses associated with later life. Atchley hastens to point out that the activities need not be exactly the same to provide a sense of continuity; indeed new activities may be substituted for older activities—and for lost work tasks and roles—while being familiar enough to preserve a sense of self. Atchley refers to this as maintaining *inner continuity* where external activities may be changed in some respects but the underlying meaning is preserved, while others have talked about this as preservation of self (Nimrod & Kleiber, 2007).

Continuity is about enduring personal meaning, and enduring personal meaning is also often reflected in one's attachment to leisure places (Kyle, Graefe, & Manning 2004). Personal identity is reinforced and restored simply by being in a preferred place at times, whether in the woods and mountains of a particular state or province or in one's hometown library. There is even a spirituality associated with special places for some that adds to one's personal connection (Heintzman & Mannell, 2003).

Finally, the function of self-preservation and continuity in leisure activities is important to group solidarity and cultural preservation (e.g. Kim, Kleiber, & Kroft, 2001). Regular events such as festivals, holidays, and parades not only contribute to social and community connectedness but may also be personally reassuring and stabilizing (Kyle & Chick, 2007).

Retirement may present special challenges to the vitalizing aspects of enduring meaning and continuity, especially those associated with work. Retirement is eagerly anticipated and mostly welcomed, particularly for those with adequate resources (Weiss, 2005), but the loss of work through retirement can be as problematic and stressful as when one is laid off and unemployed earlier in adult life, especially where resources are inadequate. Loss of professional identity and work-based associations are part of the picture, but the chief loss for many is a loss of engagement, that is, sustained and meaningful activity. Losses associated with retirement beg for some kind of compensation to make later life agreeable, satisfying and "successful." Of course work does not always provide that experience, and serious leisure activities (Stebbins, 1992) may offer more of a sense of competence and well-being throughout adult life than comes through work that is meaningless, boring or lacking in intrinsic value and satisfaction.

As suggested by Rowe and Kahn (1998), however, unless an activity like chess, collecting, etc. brings a sense of meaning and social integration, it may contribute relatively little to subjective well-being. Indeed, those oriented to leisure simply for relaxation, pleasure, and self-indulgence may have little to gain from such activity beyond simple diversion. And this may explain why outside of leisure studies there is relatively little consideration of the value of leisure activities for successful aging, unless they contribute to physical health.

A perspective on engagement that is somewhat more sympathetic to the value of leisure activity for successful aging more generally, however, takes both the benefits of deep absorption and the symbolic qualities of the activity for personal meaning into account. Nakamura and Csikszentmihalyi's (2003) concept of "vital engagement" recognizes both as a function of enduring interest, whether it be in work or leisure. Interests (or at least enduring interests) have person-object relationships beyond either one alone, considerable complexity, positive emotion and even passion, as well as value. The interests of childhood, while being enduring in many cases, are not typically tied to values, remote ends, and elaborated meanings to the extent that they are in adulthood. Thus, refreshing a rose garden, participating in political discussions at a local coffee shop once a week with familiar friends, or fundraising for a local community center are activities that are voluntary, enjoyable, and still substantial in ways that would contribute the most to successful aging.

Some of the more positive ways in which leisure experience can lead to self-expansion, however, may occur where least expected. People faced with difficult life circumstances and stressful life events—rather than giving into helplessness and relying on leisure only for escape—may take their conditions and circumstances as catalysts for change. Research on the role of leisure in coping with negative life events suggests that not only are leisure activities sources of distraction, they also can become emblematic of the opening of a new chapter in one's life story (Kleiber, Hutchinson, & Williams, 2002). For example, a young man whose auto accident deprived him of the sports that he loved so much turned to writing and found that he had a special talent for narrative and the short story. Researchers studying response to traumatic events have judged such changes as "post-traumatic growth," and have observed that among the changes made by people who have experienced injuries—or lost a child, suffered life-threatening illness like cancer or heart attacks, or sexual assault, or other traumatic events—are changes in perspective about living in and enjoying the present and turning to new expressive activities (Tedeschi & Calhoun, 2004). Self-renewal is an important part of life, and although not everyone responds to challenges in a way that sees them as opportunities or even takes advantage of what is afforded for personal change, many do, including those in their post-retirement years.

Using leisure for self-renewal occurs throughout the life course (e.g., Grafanaki et al., 2005); the spark of possibility continues to be considered in the selection of activities of the healthiest older people even as they have had to give up many of the activities that have interested them previously. Indeed, healthy aging and adaptation may be best reflected in the ongoing evaluation of optional activities (Baltes & Carstensen, 1996; Burnett-Wolle & Godbey, 2007; Kleiber, McGuire, Aybar-Damali, & Norman, 2008; Liechty & Genoe, 2013; Nimrod & Kleiber, 2007; Vaillant, 2002), and new interests are often triggered by life events, even negative ones.

One of the most obvious conveyors of engagement in later life—whether as an enduring interest or a new one—is volunteerism. Volunteerism is most often a mixture of work and leisure in that its productive outcomes define its purpose while the fact that it is voluntary and intrinsically motivated to a great extent brings it into the realm of leisure as well. In fact, as noted before, it is one of the three forms of serious leisure according to Stebbins (1992), the other two being amateurism and hobbies. Although not all occasions of volunteer work are associated with the continuing commitment associated with serious leisure, it is often true that identification with social causes and local purposes can take on career-like characteristics (e.g., working for the local soup kitchen or food bank).

In such cases the benefit to the organizations served is obvious. But what is sometimes missed in these outcome assessments is the benefit to the individuals involved. Volunteering is associated with life satisfaction (Aquino et al., 1996), self-efficacy, happiness and contentment, lower negative affect, lower depression (Morrow-Howell, Hinterlong, Rosario, & Tang, 2003), and sense of community. Community initiatives may even be *created* to elicit community participation. Arai and Pedlar (1997) reported on the organization in Kitchener, Ontario of "Healthy Communities," an initiative intended to involve people in various voluntary service activities. The initiative led to five positive outcomes for participants: (a) learning and developing new skills, (b) becoming more vocal, (c) balance and renewal, (d) group accomplishment and ability to influence change, and (e) development of community.

DISENGAGEMENT

The disengagement associated with giving up activities and "retiring" in a psychological sense from activities in pursuit of little more than "peace and quiet," solitude, and relaxation, would seem to be of far less value to aging well; but there are at least theoretical justifications for the value of leisure in that sense. The personal reconstruction of leisure as openness to experience and a more relaxed appreciation for life in the present (Kleiber, 1999, 2013) is associated with a kind of acceptance that is necessary for ego-integration in Erikson's terms. It is even associated with a special kind of psychological growth and wisdom that Tornstam (2005) refers to as "gerotranscendence.. It is the psychological "letting go" of the inclination to acquire things, social acquaintances, and experiences that may have been important for becoming established in life and for adult accomplishment, but toward the last stages of life acts as a disquieting "busyness" that is ultimately distressing. There will be more to say about this in the next section on adaptation, but research is needed to distinguish the idle, degenerative, dissipative aspects of leisure and disengagement that are inconsistent with successful aging from those that are more positive, just as healthy engagement is distinguished from neurotic activity and busyness.

ADAPTATION AND COPING THROUGH LEISURE

Among the ways that leisure activities compensate for needs unmet in other domains of life, is in maintaining a sense of self *regardless of the difficulties and losses* that come about. This is true across the lifespan, but since difficulties and losses accumulate with age, there is more call on opportunities and experiences of leisure to serve in this way in later life. We are often forced to abandon activities—to meet the demands of circumstances such as leaving one's job or moving to a new location—that are disruptive to a sense of self, especially when favored leisure activities may be lost in the process. The ability to draw on other activities in a repertoire or to substitute activities for those that are lost can preserve a sense of self and a sense of personal continuity. Indeed, to the extent that activity involvement is associated with personal identity, then maintaining that activity in some way is crucially important to emotional stability.

Research on emotion indicates that positive emotions lead to a variety of effects that strengthen general psychological capacity (Fredrickson, 2003). Joy, especially, seems to endure, to spill over in some ways, and to make one more resilient. This effect is true throughout life, but studies of aging in particular have been revealing. For example, interviews with members of a "Red Hat Society" demonstrated that the joy, contentment, and love that is experienced in playful interactions with others—with the intention of having fun and being "outrageous"—empowered older participants and made them feel happier and stronger in the other aspects of their lives (Yarnal, 2006).

Sometimes leisure experience and activity may have the greatest impact in the *protection* of feelings of well-being rather than in the production of them. People turn to leisure to reduce stress related to frustration and fatigue. Activities, whether physical or mental, that lead to relaxation and the refreshment of capacities are important antidotes to the pressures of everyday life. Physically active leisure has been found to help older adults decrease anxiety and symptoms of depression (King, Barr Taylor, & Haskell, 1993).

Preoccupying activities have the virtue of keeping one's mind diverted from distressing thoughts that may be triggered by stressful life events, such as the death of a spouse. By keeping the mind busy, people may temporarily avoid or escape the stress of these event. Television programs, exercise, and other activities that distract are among a wide range of diversionary actions that have the value of substituting positive feelings for negative ones. This kind of coping is referred to as "emotion-focused," or palliative, coping (Lazarus & Folkman, 1984). Using leisure to keep busy is then a very common palliative strategy in coping with stress and loss. But if such actions are primarily escapist, they may only have short-term value, without enabling a person to adjust more completely to the problem. More complete adjustment requires some *reappraisal* of the situation, "reframing" of a sort, that leaves a person with a new view. Such reframing may be made more likely with relaxing leisure that allows one to "breathe deeply" and get perspective, and it may use the enjoyment created through the activities to restore an element of faith and hopefulness about life after the troubling events (Kleiber et al., 2002). And while serious leisure (Stebbins, 1992) and flow experiences (Csikszentmihalyi, 1990) may offer the preoccupying activity that keeps a person's mind off the trouble, the humor-generating aspects of casual, relaxing, and social leisure situations can be "relativising" in a way that puts the problem into some manageable perspective. In a study comparing humor (watching a video of stand-up comedy) with a bout of exercise, the former was found to be more effective in reducing anxiety (Szabo, 2003).

Leisure in the Management of Injury and Illness

Illnesses have a variety of forms. Some are slow in coming and long enduring while others are sudden, shocking, and immediately debilitating. They may be chronic or acute. Serious injuries fit more commonly into the latter, though injuries also produce chronic illness effects sometimes. As was noted earlier, the loss of leisure may be among the most immediate casualties of such events and may be part of the illness itself. Studies of negative life events such as spinal cord injury, the sudden onset of illness, or the loss of a loved one suggest that a loss of leisure abilities, leisure opportunities, and leisure companions are regularly part of the "illness experience" that people endure (Kleiber, Brock, Lee, Dattilo, & Caldwell, 1995). And yet leisure activities and experiences do appear to play a prominent role in adjusting and adapting to those circumstances in many cases as well (Dattilo, Chapter 26; Kleiber et al., 2002).

In studies of *spinal cord injury* (e.g., Loy, Dattilo, & Kleiber, 2003) many of the patterns referred to earlier have been found. As devastating as the loss of mobility is, finding alternative skills and interests and even recovering one's old skills appear to have therapeutic effects (Chun, Lee, & Heo, 2008). Diversity, frequency, and intensity of leisure engagement are all associated with adjustment. Leisure engagement also contributes indirectly through building social support. But initially, as with other trauma, the more attractive activities are more often those that take one's mind off the pain. The fact that these injuries are acute and dramatic in their impact for physical activity, however, does seem to make the recovery of old physical functions and the identification of new physical activities an urgent priority in most cases. On the other hand, the possibilities for change and self-expansion may also open up. In the case of those who were more body-oriented in their interests and activities, the life of the mind may be the new focus. Studies of people with traumatic brain injury show similar patterns and outcomes (cf. Hutchinson, Loy, Kleiber, & Dattilo, 2003); leisure has been found to be a source of self-preservation and continuity (recovering valued aspects of past self), escape, hope and optimism, structure and a sense of purpose, sense of belonging and acceptance, and competence.

On the more chronic side, middle age may bring on the occurrence of seriously debilitating and chronic diseases like *arthritis*. These illnesses lack the dramatic blows that a spinal cord or traumatic brain injury inflicts, but they require adjustment and adaptation nonetheless. In a study of a group of older adults with arthritis, leisure-based social interaction was found to be a significant hedge against declines in mental health (Payne, Mowen, & Montoro-Rodriguez, 2006). *Cancer* also becomes chronic over time, but the initial awareness of it—life-threatening as it can be—often has much the same effect as more acutely dramatic and debilitating injuries. It may even be transformative as how best to use the life left to be lived becomes the critical, existential question. And some of the answers show themselves to be intimately associated with leisure (e.g., Glover & Parry, 2008). Finally, we must recognize *depression* as amenable to the influence of leisure. An interview study with 48 women with depression in Australia revealed the use of leisure practices in their experience of coping and recovery, building on friendships to overcome feelings of lack of entitlement (to just lay and rest on the couch, for example), and developing feelings of vitality through exercise and gardening (Fullagar, 2008).

Losing a Spouse

Losing one's spouse has a variety of effects according to the research, but it can be the most significant event in one's life, especially for relationships that have endured for a long time. As with many other negative life events leisure is often immediately implicated in the "illness" experience of widowhood; a spouse is often a companion for leisure activities and that loss changes the opportunity to participate and the experience itself in many cases. Certainly home-based leisure is different as well. But according to research, widows often increase involvement in activities for two reasons: (a) they feel the need to "keep busy" (Sharpe & Mannell, 1996); in other words, to use activities for their palliative distraction value to reduce the grieving and distress; and (b) they take the opportunity to do new things that their previous marital status—often as a caregiver—did not afford them. In the latter case, usually occurring somewhat after an initial adjustment period, there may be a "blossoming" effect, where widows discover new aspects of themselves (Lopata, 1993), often in expressive leisure activities such as joining the Red Hat Society described earlier. There is considerable evidence now that widows who stay engaged or increase engagement in satisfying leisure activities, particularly social activities, exercise, and religious activities, have higher life satisfaction and less depression than those who reduce such activities (e.g., Janke, Nimrod, & Kleiber, 2008). On the other hand, the importance of being selective about leisure activities was also born out in the Janke et al. studies; participation in some activities (maintaining membership in clubs for one) was negatively associated with subjective well-being in this national sample.

Losses Associated with Retirement

A longitudinal study of 44 older men who had retired at least five years before (Chiriboga & Pierce, 1993) demonstrated how leisure behavior may play a role in successful retirement and psychological well-being. The respondents' participation in solitary activities, sports, social activities, and contemplative activities was measured early in retirement and about five years later. Measures of the stressful life events they had experienced during the previous year, psychological distress symptoms, happiness, and self-reported health were also collected. Participation levels in the various leisure activities were not related to self-esteem at or soon after retirement. After five years, however, the situation had changed.

Activity involvement was significantly related to self-esteem. Specifically, those retired individuals who were more positive about themselves were also more likely to be engaged in outdoor and social activities, and tended to participate less in contemplative activities which were characterized as solitary and passive.

The onset of retirement does represent a major transition point that has the potential to alter lifestyle, but again, the accumulated evidence shows that most have few problems in adjusting to retirement, though there is still substantial variation in the degree of adjustment and the subsequent quality of life experienced (e.g., Vaillant, 2002; Weiss, 2005) Consistent with activity and continuity theories, research has also shown that those people who use their free time to continue to participate in similar types of social activity at about the same level as they did prior to retirement, and who have positive attitudes toward leisure, adjust better and are more satisfied with their lives (e.g., Nimrod, 2007a, b; Nimrod & Adoni, 2006; Nimrod, Janke & Kleiber, 2007) And as noted earlier, there are also indications that those who begin new leisure activities after retirement benefit substantially from the adventure (Nimrod, 2008b; Nimrod & Kleiber, 2007; Vaillant, 2002) However, as with adjustment to widowhood, there is also evidence that being selective is important, that activities must be meaningful to contribute to life satisfaction, and that giving up some less meaningful activities is generally warranted (Kleiber et al., 2008; Kleiber & Nimrod, 2009). Finally, losses associated with retirement, as with other negative life events and illnesses, can be the occasion for selecting other action alternatives for optimization that may have otherwise been ignored or neglected (see Kleiber et al., 2008).

CONCLUSION

The foregoing should suggest that easy conclusions about the relationship between leisure and aging well are rather elusive. But if successful aging is as much a matter of adapting well to challenging circumstances as avoiding them all together, then the value of leisure expands considerably. To the extent that an individual maintains control of her or his options, losses and limitations may be accepted and managed with some equanimity. The more prevalent view, however, is that activities will be maintained as long as possible, even if they have to be modified or reinvented to some extent, and that such patterns are associated with effective coping and aging well. Increasing tendencies to experiment and innovate in later life, especially in the "third age" period just after retirement, reflect significant demographic and generational changes and may require revision of some of our assumptions about aging and leisure, even those that are well-supported by evidence from the past. Finally, though, the idea that leisure may itself be reconstructed around the peace associated with selective disengagement also deserves further consideration.

REFERENCES

Aquino, J. A., Russell, D. W., Cutrona, C. E., & Altaier, E. M. (1996). Employment status, social support and life satisfaction among the elderly. *Journal of Counseling Psychology, 43*, 480–489.

Adams, K. B., Leibbrandt, S. & Moon, H. (2011). A critical review of the literature on social and leisure activity and wellbeing in later life. *Ageing & Society, 31*, 683–712.

Arai, S. M., & Pedlar, A. M. (1997). Building communities through leisure: Citizen participation in a healthy communities initiative. *Journal of Leisure Research, 29*, 167–182.

Atchley, R. (1999). *Continuity and adaptation in aging.* Baltimore, MD: The John Hopkins University Press.

Baltes, P., & Baltes, M. (1990). Psychological perspectives on successful aging: The model of selective optimization with compensation. In P. Baltes & M. Baltes (Eds.), *Successful aging* (pp. 1–34). New York: Cambridge University Press.

Baltes, M. M., & Carstensen, L. L. (1996). The process of successful aging. *Aging and Society, 16*, 398–404.

Bowling, A. (2007), Aspirations for older age in the 21st century: What is successful aging? *International Journal of Aging and Human Development, 54*, 263–297.

Brown, B. A., Frankel, B. G., & Fennell, M. (1991). Happiness through leisure: The impact of type of leisure activity, age, gender and leisure satisfaction on psychological well-being. *Journal of Applied Recreation Research, 16*, 368–392.

Burnett-Wolle, S., & Godbey, G. (2007). Refining research on older adults' leisure: Implications of selection, optimization and compensation and socioemotional selectivity theories. *Journal of Leisure Research, 39*, 498–513.

Butrica, B. A., & Schaner, S. G. (2005). Satisfaction and engagement in retirement. *Perspectives on Productive Aging (No. 2).* Washington, DC: The Urban Institute.

Chun, S., Lee, Y., & Heo, J. (2008, October). *The benefits of serious leisure following traumatic spinal cord injury.* Paper presented at the 12th Canadian Conference on Leisure Research. Montreal, QC.

Carstensen, L. L., Fung, H. H., & Charles, S. T. (2003). Socioemotional selectivity theory and the regulation of emotion in the second half of life. *Motivation and Emotion, 27*, 103–123.

Chiriboga, D. A., & Pierce, R. C. (1993). Changing contexts of activity. In J. R. Kelly (Ed.), *Activity and aging: Staying involved in later life* (pp. 42–59). Newbury Park, CA: Sage Publications.

Csikszentmihalyi, M. (1990). *Flow: The psychology of optimal experience*. New York: Harper Perennial.

Dupuis, S. L., & Smale, B. J. A. (1995). An examination of the relationship between psychological well-being and depression and leisure activity participation among older adults *Loisir et Société/Society and Leisure, 18*, 67–92.

Fernandez-Ballesteros, R., Zamarron, M. & Ruiz, M. (2001). The contribution of socio-demographic and psychosocial factors to life satisfaction. *Ageing and Society, 21*, 25–43.

Fredrickson, B. (2003). The value of positive emotions. *American Scientist, 91*, 330–335.

Fullagar, S. (2008). Leisure practices as counter-depressants: Emotion-work and emotion-play within women's recovery from depression. *Leisure Sciences, 30*(1), 35–52.

Glover, T., & Parry, D. (2008). Friendship developed subsequent to a stressful life event: The interplay of leisure social capital and health. *Journal of Leisure Research, 40*, 208–230.

Grafanaki, S., Pearson, D., Cini, F., Godula, D., McKenzie, S., Nason, S., & Anderegg, M. (2005) Sources of renewal: A qualitative study on the experience and role of leisure in the life of counselors and psychologists. *Counseling Psychology Report, 18*, 31–40.

Harahousou, Y. (2006). Leisure and ageing. In C. Rojek, S. Shaw & A. Veal. (Eds.), *A handbook of leisure studies*. (pp. 231–249). New York: Palgrave Macmillan.

Heintzman, P., & Mannell, R. C. (2003). Spiritual functions of leisure and spiritual well-being: Coping with time pressure. *Leisure Sciences, 25*, 207–230.

Hutchinson, S. L., Loy, D. P., Kleiber, D. A., & Dattilo, J. (2003). Leisure as a coping resource: Variations in coping with traumatic injury and illness. *Leisure Sciences, 25*, 143–161.

Janke, M., Nimrod, G., & Kleiber, D. A. (2008). Leisure patterns and health among recently widowed adults. *Activities, Adaptation and Aging, 32*, 19–39.

Kim, E., Kleiber, D., & Kropf, N. (2001). Social integration and ethnic preservation in the leisure activities of older Korean immigrants. *Journal of Gerontological Social Work, 36*, 107–109.

King, A. C., Barr Taylor, C., & Haskell, W. L. (1993). Effects of differing intensities and formats of 12 months of exercise training on psychological outcomes in older adults. *Health Psychology, 12*, 292–300.

Kleiber, D. A. (1999). *Leisure experience and human development*. New York: Basic Books.

Kleiber, D. A. (2013). Redeeming leisure in later life. In T. Freire (Ed.), *Positive leisure science: From individual experience to social contexts*. London: Springer.

Kleiber, D. A., Brock, S., Lee, Y., Dattilo, J. & Caldwell, L. (1995). The relevance of leisure in an illness experience: Realities of spinal cord injury. *Journal of Leisure Research, 27*, 283–299.

Kleiber, D. A., Hutchinson, S., & Williams, R. (2002). Leisure as a resource in transcending negative life events: Self-protection, self-restoration and personal transformation. *Leisure Sciences, 24*, 219–235.

Kleiber, D. A., McGuire, F., Aybar-Damali, B., & Norman, W. (2008). Having more by doing less: The paradox of leisure constraints in later life. *Journal of Leisure Research, 40*, 343–359.

Kleiber, D. A., & Nimrod, G. (2009). "I can't be very sad": Constraints and adaptations in the leisure of a 'learning in retirement' group. *Leisure Studies, 28*, 67–83.

Kyle, G., & Chick, G. (2007). The social construction of a sense of place. *Leisure Sciences, 29*, 209–225.

Kyle, G., Graefe, A., & Manning, R. (2004). Satisfaction derived through leisure involvement and setting attachment. *Leisure/Loisir, 28*(3–4), 277–306.

Lazarus, R. S., & Folkman, S. (1984). *Stress, appraisal, and coping*. New York: Springer.

Liechty, T & Genoe, M. R. (2013). Older men's perceptions of leisure and aging. *Leisure Sciences, 35*, 438–454.

Linville, P. W. (1987). Self-complexity as a cognitive buffer against stress-related illness and depression. *Journal of Personality and Social Psychology, 52*, 663–676.

Lopata, H. J. (1993). Widows: Social integration and activity. In J. R. Kelly (Ed.), *Activity and aging* (pp. 99–105). Newbury Park, CA: Sage Publications.

Loy, D. P., Dattilo, J., & Kleiber, D.A. (2003). Exploring the influence of leisure on adjustment: Development of the leisure and spinal cord injury adjustment model. *Leisure Sciences, 25*, 231–255.

Mannell, R. C., and Dupuis, S. (1994). Leisure and productive activity. In M. P. Lawton & J. Teresi (Eds.), *Annual review of gerontology and geriatrics*, Vol. 14 (pp. 125–141). New York, NY: Springer Publishing.

Morrow-Howell, N., Hinterlong, J., Rosario, P. A., & Tang, F. (2003). Effects of volunteering on the well-being of older adults. *Journal of Gerontology, Social Sciences, 58B*, S137–S145.

Nakamura, J., & Csikszentmihaly, M. (2003). The construction of meaning through vital engagement. In C. L. Keyes & J. Haidt (Eds.), *Flourishing: Positive psychology and the life well-lived.* Washington, DC: American Psychological Association.

Nimrod, G. (2007a). Retirees' leisure: Activities, benefits and their contribution to life satisfaction. *Leisure Studies, 26*, 65–80.

Nimrod, G. (2007b). Expanding, reducing, concentrating and diffusing: Post retirement leisure behavior and life satisfaction. *Leisure Sciences, 29*, 91–111.

Nimrod, G. (2008a). In support of innovation theory: Innovation in activity patterns and life satisfaction among recently retired individuals. *Aging & Society, 28*, 831–846.

Nimrod, G. (2008b). Time for old friends and grandchildren? Post retirement get-togethers and life satisfaction. *Leisure/Loisir, 32*, 21–46.

Nimrod G., & Adoni, H. (2006). Leisure styles and life satisfaction among recent retirees in Israel. *Aging and Society, 26*, 607–630.

Nimrod, G., Janke, M., & Kleiber, D. A. (2007). Retirement, activity, and subjective well-being in Israel and the Unites States. *World Leisure Journal, 49*(4), 18–32.

Nimrod, G., & Kleiber, D. (2007). Reconsidering change and continuity in later life: Toward an innovation theory of successful aging. *International Journal of Aging and Human Development, 65*,1–22.

Payne, L., Mowen, A., & Montoro-Rodriguez, J. (2006). The role of leisure style in maintaining the health of older adults with arthritis. *Journal of Leisure Research, 38*, 20–45.

Roberts, K. (2013). Leisure and the life course. In T. Blackshaw (Ed.), *Routledge handbook of leisure studies* (pp. 257–265). London: Routledge.

Rowe, J. W., & Kahn, R. L. (1998) *Successful aging.* New York: Pantheon Books.

Sharpe, A., & Mannell, R. C. (1996). *Participation in leisure as a coping strategy among bereaved women.* In Proceedings of the Eighth Canadian Congress on Leisure Research. (pp. 241–244). Ottawa, ON: University of Ottawa.

Singleton, J., & Gibson, H. (Eds.). (2011). *Leisure, aging and well-being.* Champaign, IL: Human Kinetics.

Stebbins, R. A. (1992). *Amateurs, professionals, and serious leisure.* Montreal, PQ: McGill-Queen's University Press.

Szabo, A. (2003). The acute effects of humor and exercise on mood and anxiety. *Journal* of *Leisure Research, 35*, 152–162.

Tedeschi, R. G., & Calhoun, C. G. (2004). Posttraumatic growth: Conceptual foundatio and empirical evidence. *Psychological Inquiry, 15*,1–18.

Tornstam, L. (2005). *Gerotranscendance: A developmental theory of positive aging.* New York: Springer.

Vaillant, G. (2002). *Aging well.* New York: Little Brown.

Weiss, R. S. (2005). *The experience of retirement.* Ithaca, NY: Cornell University Press.

Yarnal, C. (2006). The Red Hat Society: Exploring the role of play, liminality, and communitas in older women's lives. *Journal of Women and Aging, 18*, 51–73.

24

The Relational Politics of Gender and Leisure

Diana C. Parry (University of Waterloo)

Gender is a powerful influence in the lives of people and societies. Often confused with the word sex and associated mostly with women, gender is a consideration that *everyone* must negotiate (Freysinger, Shaw, Henderson, & Bialeschki, 2013). Indeed, gender is so pervasive that it often takes a deliberate disruption to draw attention to the gendered nature of society. Given the pervasive nature of gender in society, it follows that leisure is also influenced by gender. Over the past three decades, a large body of literature has revealed the important ways that *gender* influences leisure, but also the ways that *leisure* influences gender. The purpose of this chapter is to draw upon recent theoretical contributions and empirical research to discuss the interplay between gender and leisure, including an analysis of women's and men's leisure experiences, attitudes, constraints, challenges, and behaviors. I emphasize the ways in which gender relations and gender role expectations affect, and are affected by, leisure.

WHAT IS GENDER?

The words "sex" and "gender" are two distinct, but overlapping terms. Typically, sex refers to the assignment of male or female based on biological features (Lorber, 2006) such as genitalia, chromosomes, and secondary sex characteristics. In Western society we commonly consider there to be only two sexes, although some researchers argue there are as many as five. To unpack the male/female duality, Fausto-Sterling (2006) uses the term intersex to refer to those who embody a mixture of male and female characteristics including hermaphrodites, male pseudohermaphrodites, and female pseudohermaphrodites.

In contrast to sex, which is biologically driven, gender is a social and cultural construct. Gender refers to societal *expectations* for roles and behavior based upon one's assigned biological sex. Freysinger et al. (2013) explained, "one's biological sex leads to a lifetime of relationships and expectations, opportunities and constraints, based upon gender…[it] is an ongoing process rather than an inborn biological trait. People learn and transform gender, they *do* or *perform* gender, in every context of their lives" (p. 12, original emphasis). Indeed, social and cultural notions of gender inform our conceptualizations of masculinity (e.g., tough, aggressive, strong, unemotional) and femininity (caring, supportive, nurturing, compassionate), which translate into gender role expectations. For example, understandings of masculinity translate into roles such as fatherhood and economic provider (Freysinger et al., 2013). Similarly, notions of femininity translate into roles such as motherhood and the acceptance of household and emotional responsibility. With this in mind, Lorber (2006) explains gender is not "in our genes," but rather is a social process constantly created and recreated through human interaction and social life. In this sense, gender is commonly referred to as a social construction that humans produce, reproduce, and resist in their social interactions. For these reasons we can think of gender as relational, "constructed and reconstructed in relation to and interaction with other individuals within the contexts of society, culture, and history" (Freysinger et al., 2013, p. 4).

Given its relational nature, we often think of gender differences as occurring between groups of men and women. However, there are also differences among and within groups of women and men depending on age, life stage, sexual identity, socioeconomic status, abilities, and race/ethnicity among others. Freysinger et al. (2013) explained:

> although the concept of gendered lives implies some commonality of experience among women, other dimensions of power and ideological constructions such as racism, heterosexism, and discourses surrounding obesity and appearance, also differentially affect women of colour, older women, and women and girls who do not conform to the ideal body weight, body shape or functioning.

> Similar processes also affect men in marginalized groups such as men who do not conform to the dominant norm of heterosexism. (p. 12)

Either way, between group differences or within group differences, there is plenty of evidence that society is gendered for everyone. At the social or macro level, we see the influence of gender in our societal structures including the family, work, institutions, and public policies. Similarly, on an individual or micro scale, the influence of gender is evident in daily routines and practices, including childrearing practices, leisure choices, television shows, and sports (Schmalz, 2013; Scraton & Watson, 2013). In short, gender remains a salient practice that informs and shapes lives and societies (Freysinger et al., 2013).

FEMINIST SCHOLARSHIP WITHIN LEISURE STUDIES

Within leisure studies, much of the research exploring the influence of gender is conducted from a feminist theoretical perspective. Feminism is enormously diverse and dynamic as it represents both an individual and collective identity of complex political and personal ideologies (Zucker & Bay-Cheng, 2010). Indeed, there are as many variations of feminism as there are feminists, which leads many to suggest the term of reference should be "feminisms" (Braithwaite, 2002). Despite the diversity in feminisms, most feminists share a consciousness about women's distinct and shared disadvantages within patriarchal society, the political nature of everyday life, and link these everyday experiences to larger social injustices (Rupp & Taylor, 1999). One recent definition of feminism proposed by DeVault and Gross (2012) offers feminism as "a set of practices and perspectives that affirms differences among women and promotes women's interests, health, and safety, locally and abroad" with a goal of well-being and social justice (p. 207). Similarly, Lather (1998) posits, "through the questions that feminism poses and the absences it locates, feminism argues the centrality of gender in shaping our consciousness, skills, and institutions as well as in the distribution of power and privilege" (p. 571). From a feminist perspective, power and privilege is linked to the patriarchy.

Patriarchy refers to a social system in which power rests with men and privileges them through greater access to institutional power, higher incomes, higher labor force participation, and greater access to social and cultural resources, public and private spaces, and other beneficial arrangements (Hibbins, 2013; Kirkley, 2000). Toward this end, Snyder-Hall (2010) argued, feminism is "fundamentally about transforming patriarchal culture and society" (p. 256). Consequently, many feminists focus on patriarchy (as opposed to women), which makes the movement inclusive of both women *and* men. As leisure scholars have identified, patriarchy does not serve marginalized groups of men well (gay men, poor men, racialized men, men with mental health challenges, etc.) (Hibbins, 2013; Johnson, 2013; Johnson, Chapter 25). Feminism enables men to challenge the social construction of masculinity and break free of traditional ideals about what it means to be a man (Johnson, 2013). Feminists (female and male) can work together to expose, analyze, and ultimately deconstruct the patriarchal system of domination and oppression, thereby creating a more just society for women and men (Snyder-Hall, 2010; Reid, 2004). Feminism is thus inherently activist.

Feminist scholars bring an activist lens to their work by challenging "taken-for-granted beliefs about women and about the naturalization of gender and gendered lives within society" (Freysinger et al., 2013, p. 63). In doing so, feminist scholars argue for social change, seek ways to empower women, and advance gender equity by changing attitudes and behaviors, but also social, economic, and political practices (Freysinger et al., 2013). In their efforts, feminist scholars use a combination of epistemology, methodology, and methods (Hesse-Biber, 2012). There is no single or monolithic method, methodology, or theoretical base of feminist scholarship; in fact, there are competing theoretical foundations and varied methodologies that reveal sexist, racist, homophobic, and colonialist points of view (Hesse-Biber, 2012). Despite this diversity, there are several dominant tendencies of feminist research: (a) values underpin all research; (b) the personal is political; (c) women's lived experiences are an important source of knowledge; (d) relational approaches to research and their inherent subjectivity is valued; and (e) truth and objectivity may not exist (Thompson, 1992). These tendencies reveal that the *process* of research is just as important as the *outcomes* of research (Hesse-Biber & Piatelli, 2012). Moreover, these tendencies speak to the ways that feminist scholarship takes up issues of power, authority, ethics, and reflexivity while seeking to challenge the patriarchy in all forms and permutations with the goal of advancing a more just society (Reid, 2004; Hesse-Biber, 2012).

AN INTERACTIVE RELATIONSHIP: THE INTERPLAY BETWEEN GENDER AND LEISURE

Over the past three decades, feminist scholarship has informed leisure studies while evolving through a variety of phases or stages (Henderson 1994; Parry, 2003). Initially, leisure research ignored women and focused solely on men assuming a universal leisure experience. This "male scholarship" evolved into what Henderson (1994) coined the compensatory phase wherein women's experiences were recognized as an important consideration, commonly referred to as the "add women and stir" phase. Next, leisure studies benefited from "bifocal scholarship" that focused on gender differences between groups of men and women. Following this phase, leisure studies moved into a "woman-centered" stage that brought to the fore the gendered forms of oppression that women faced in their daily lives, specifically leisure. Research during this stage focused on gendered ideological influences, such as womanhood and motherhood (Shaw, 1994). Following this woman-centered approach, a fifth stage coined "gender scholarship" emerged. Henderson (1994) noted "a premise underlying this phase of scholarship is that all of us live in a heavily gendered society so behavior can be better understood by examining the experiences of women *and* men within that framework (pp. 3–4). Gender scholarship extended feminist work by proposing that women's leisure could not be universalized and by asserting that no one female or male voice existed. A sixth phase of feminist leisure scholarship purports it is not enough to *interpret* the gendered nature of the world, but that it be *changed* as well (Parry, 2003). Social change and justice can be accomplished when research is undertaken for critical, strategic, and political purposes. This sixth phase of feminist leisure scholarship exposes and transforms subtle and deep-rooted causes of oppression moving the field closer towards what Denzin (2000) referred to as a 'politics of hope' (p. 262). Thus, the sixth phase of leisure research is grounded in social justice, advocacy, and a hopeful optimism.

Collectively, these phases have revealed that the relationship between gender and leisure is interactive (Freysinger et al., 2013), meaning leisure is a context in which people can embody and/or resist gendered discourses (Shaw, 2001). More specifically, three decades of feminist leisure scholarship has demonstrated that *gender* influences leisure, but so too does *leisure* influence gender.

The Influence of Gender on Leisure

One of the main contributions of the feminist leisure literature has been to illustrate that gender has an important influence on leisure opportunities, experiences, and meanings. The influence of gender can be seen in the extent to which leisure pursuits and activities are gender stereotyped. This research dates back to Metheny (1967) a sport sociologist who studied the gender stereotyping of sports, which she argued is linked to gendered roles and expectations. Metheny's research revealed that sports can be categorized as either "masculine" or "feminine" depending upon physicality, bodily contact, and aesthetics. Decades later, Wiley, Shaw, and Havitz (2000) noted football, ice hockey, and boxing are considered as socially appropriate sports for men while dance, gymnastics, figure-skating, and other non-contact sports are considered as socially appropriate for women. Based upon their findings, Wiley et al. concluded gender:

> stereotyping of activities clearly affects participation choices, with most men restricting their participation to masculine activities that conform to male gender role expectations, and the majority of women participants also conforming by choosing activities that are thought of as feminine. (p. 22)

Most recently, Riemer and Visio (2003) concluded that gendered stereotypes of sport participation persist. For example, gymnastics and aerobics are considered female sports whereas football and wrestling are seen as men's. In short, men are channeled towards contact sports whereas women are encouraged to participate in graceful, aesthetically pleasing activities that do not involve physical contact or aggression (Shaw, 1994).

Although women and men face gender stereotyping of leisure activities some research suggests men may face more restrictive choices because, as a society, we tend to be more accepting of women crossing over into nontraditional gender activities (Schmalz, 2013). That is, the "opportunities for girls in so-called 'masculine' activities increased in Western societies in particular in recent years," but not with equal opportunity (Freysinger et al., 2013, p. 9). For example, it tends to be more socially acceptable for women to participate in a nontraditional leisure pursuit such as riding motorcycles (Roster, 2013). In contrast, boys and men who pursue leisure interests that fall outside of dominant expectations of masculinity are particularly likely to be stigmatized (Johnson, 2013; Schmalz, 2013). In particular, there is significant pressure for boys to play sports as a context for learning/developing/practicing/displaying (hegemonic) masculinity (Messner, 1998; Schmalz, 2013). Messner notes how boys learn to be men—tough, aggressive, competition—through sport and leisure. Unfortunately, research illustrates that most people do not cross traditional gender lines in their leisure because "conforming activities that are deemed to be gender-appropriate provides females and males with higher social status compared with participation in nonconforming or gender inappropriate sports" (Wiley, et al., 2000, p. 22). In short, the influence of gender on leisure is evident in the reproduction of pursuits considered gender appropriate.

A second area where the research reveals a strong influence of gender on leisure is with respect to leisure constraints. Constraints are personal and situational factors that impact upon access to, and enjoyment of, desired leisure pursuits (Samdahl, 2013; Schneider, Chapter 18). Constraints are often categorized as structural (lack of resources or external forces), intrapersonal (within an individual) or interpersonal (between groups of people) (Crawford & Godbey,

1987; Shaw, 1994). Research in this area reveals that women experience all three types of constraints including time and money (structural), an ethic of care that socializes women to sacrifice personal desires for the sake of others (intrapersonal), and family responsibilities/commitments (interpersonal) (Samdahl, 2013).

Indeed, a number of studies have demonstrated that women are constrained by not feeling entitled to personal leisure (Henderson, 1994) and by household and child-care responsibilities that serve as a second shift of work after paid employment (Hochschild, 1989). For example, Miller and Brown (2005) found that women, and especially women with young children, were less likely to participate in physically active leisure despite being aware of the health benefits of such participation. They explained, "household norms relating to gender-based time negotiation and ideologies regarding an ethic of care were important determinants of active leisure among women with young children" (Miller & Brown, 2005, p. 405).

Notably, interpersonal and intrapersonal constraints are often harder to identify and negotiate then structural ones (Samdahl, 2013). As a result, gendered constraints—such as family responsibilities and an ethic of care—result in a major gap between men's and women's leisure time and experiences (Freysinger et al., 2013). Men, however, are also constrained in their leisure by paid employment responsibilities, social pressure to be successful, and gendered expectations around activity participation (Freysinger et al., 2013). Kay (2006) studied men's experiences with fatherhood and noted that males are often constrained by the role expectations of breadwinner, limiting their time for family leisure. Taken together, constraints research demonstrates how gender impacts both access to and enjoyment of leisure (Shaw, 1994).

However, leisure itself can also be constraining because of the potential to reinforce and reproduce oppressive gender structures or relations (Shaw, 1994). Du (2013) explained, "Leisure activities are often a re-embodiment of stereotyped gender roles and further reproduces inequity in the relationships between men and women" (p. 180). For example, Berbary (2013) explored leisure pursuits within sororities demonstrating how the activities produced and reproduced stereotyped gender roles, behavior, and expectations. That is, stereotyped gender behavior was reproduced through leisure in sororities. For example, through leisure the sorority girls learned to how act like a "lady" including being respectful, modest, gracious, and reserved, which reproduced hyper-feminine gendered behavior. Berbary (2013) explained, "within sororities, leisure spaces, where individual gendered performances are watched, judged, and restricted, often become discursively disciplined" (p. 153). Sororities, Berbary reveals, are important contexts in which girls learn about gendered behavior through their involvement in leisure activities that reproduce stereotyped gender roles. Similarly, Delamere and Dixon (2013) found women's behavior was strictly governed according to gendered ideologies in their study of women's experience of digital game play. They found game culture and the behavior of some male gamers created a hostile environment for females. More specifically, female gamers experienced overt sexism from male players including name calling (bitch, whore, slut), damage to their gaming equipment, and being asked to perform sexual acts both outside and inside the game (Delamere & Dixon, 2013). In a study of Civil War re-enacting, Hunt (2004) reported that males did not want women intruding on their space—they justified this on the basis that their presence would undermine authenticity.

It happens for men too! Johnson (2013) expressed feeling as though his masculinity was under attack when he took off his shoes and socks at a spring picnic with his friends to reveal his toenails painted hot pink, which is not expected or socially sanctioned as appropriate for men. Collectively, these areas of research demonstrate that constraints are influenced by "networks of sociocultural beliefs that shape expectations and opportunities," but also enjoyment of leisure based upon gendered ideologies (Samdahl, 2013, p. 120).

An important body of leisure research focuses on the negotiation of gendered leisure constraints. From a gender perspective, constraint negotiation occurs when people accept certain aspects of cultural discourse, but reject or redefine others (Samdahl, 2013). Constraint negotiation is an important line of research as it "contested the image of women as helpless victims of discrimination and emphasized, instead, how women can be active agents who creatively response to inequity" (Samdahl, 2013, p. 117). For example, James (2000) found young girls utilize a variety of strategies to negotiate body consciousness and a fear of the public gaze at public swimming pools. While this has been an important line of feminist research, the individual focus of constraint negotiation also has its critics. Samdahl (2013) argued, "It is no longer sufficient to study how individuals overcome constraints on their own; focusing only on individuals ignores the cultural factors that placed constraints in their paths in the first place" (p. 120). Her statements clearly indicate a new direction for future leisure research.

Taken collectively, feminist scholarship has revealed that gender has a powerful influence on the type of leisure pursuits people select (or feel channeled towards) and their levels of enjoyment. Thus, leisure may be considered constrained or constraining to both women and men given its role in reinforcing and reproducing oppressive gender structures or relations (Shaw, 1994).

The Influence of Leisure on Gender

While it is important to understand the ways that leisure serves to reproduce gendered ideologies, roles, and expectations, it is equally important to understand leisure as a context for resistance. Resistance refers to "questioning, challenging, and seeking to change processes and circumstances that are disempowering" (Freysinger et al., 2013, p. 91). This line of research emerged in the literature when women were found to gain a sense of empowerment from their leisure. Shaw (2001) explained, women use their leisure to "challenge their own lack of power or their dissatisfaction with societal views about women's expected roles and behaviors" (p. 187). The notion of leisure as resistance is based on the idea that leisure practices, experiences, satisfactions, choices, and activities are linked to power and power relations in the social world (Shaw, 2001). Leisure when conceptualized as resistance, is seen as a site for people, either individually or in groups, to challenge unequal power distributions or the ways that power is implemented. Under this premise, leisure becomes one arena where power is gained, maintained, reinforced, diminished or lost (Shaw, 2001). In this sense, women's leisure as resistance is based on two theoretical assumptions: "first, the idea of agency… which allows for the view that women are social actors who perceive and interpret social situations and actively determine, in each setting, how they will respond" (Shaw, 1994, p. 15). Second, the notion that leisure experiences are relatively freely chosen. Specifically, two key characteristics of leisure, personal choice and self-determination, are associated with resistance to traditionally prescribed gender identities, stereotypes, and roles propagated through dominant patriarchal culture by enabling women to exert personal control and power (Shaw, 2001).

Resistance can manifest, for example, in women challenging the aforementioned constraints on their time by asserting a sense of entitlement to leisure despite caregiving roles (Freysinger et al., 2013). This form of resistance was evident in Wearing's (1990) study of first-time mothers who resisted an ideology of motherhood that perpetuated the belief that "good" mothers did not prioritize themselves or claim personal time by asserting their entitlement and carving out space for leisure. Resistance is also evident in challenges to gendered expectations for activity participation. For example, Roster (2013) studied women involved in motorcycling, which remains a male dominated pursuit. The women in her study "embraced the positive attributes of strength, independence, freedom, adventure, and power that were associated with the masculine biker culture, but rejected stereotypes that suggested women riders were passive, sexually promiscuous, drug addicts, or rebellious members of society" (p. 199). A similar form of resistance was revealed by Dionigi (2013) who studied senior women participating in competitive sports. She argued by choosing competitive sport activities "that go against the *cultural grain*, these older women are using leisure as a site for resistance" (p. 168, original emphasis). Men also use leisure as a context to resist the patriarchy. Johnson (2013), for example, outlined how gay men resist heterosexism at gay bars by feeling free to "openly challenge and/or create a new gendered meaning… where they perceive freedom from heterosexual ideologies" (p. 252). Leisure, therefore, is an important context for women and men to resist gendered ideologies grounded in the patriarchy.

Two important conceptual issues have emerged with respect to leisure as resistance. The first is regarding the intentionality of resistance. Shaw (2001) explained:

> since empowerment and resistance are seen to be associated with self-expression and self-determination, this would seem to be imply that resistance is a deliberate or conscious choice made by the participant or actor. This idea, though, has not been fully explored. (p. 192)

Recent research exploring this important aspect of resistance demonstrates at least some degree of intentionality is behind many acts of resistance within leisure contexts. For example, Roster (2013) found that female motorcycle riders were attracted, at least in part, to the nontraditional leisure pursuit precisely because of the challenges they faced partaking in an unconventional gender choice. Berbary (2013) also found intentionality in the acts of resistance within sororities. She argued, "a few women began to see how they were disciplined and started to reconstitute themselves as something other than what had always been expected" (p. 164). This led Berbary to conclude "even in strictly disciplined leisure spaces, women were able to penetrate boundaries, signify new meanings, and create spaces for alternative possibilities" (p. 164). Similarly, in my own research, I found women dealing with infertility made intentional decisions around leisure pursuits, activities, and experiences based upon resisting a pronatalist ideology (Parry, 2005). However, there are other acts that demonstrate an unintentional resistance. For example, a female hockey player who plays on a men's team because there are no teams for women could be seen as resisting, but she might argue she just wants to play the game. Intentionality, therefore, is an important conceptual issue with respect to resistance and this area warrants our further investigation.

The second important conceptual issue with respect to resistance is the individual versus collective nature of the act and the outcomes (Shaw, 2001). The research in this area demonstrates there are both individual *and* collective acts of resistance. Yet, even our individual acts can have collective outcomes. For example, a woman who, through her leisure choices and pursuits presents herself as strong, independent, and athletic challenges traditional conceptualizations of femininity—her individual action. Yet, her actions can then encourage other women (maybe men too), serving as a collective outcome (Freysinger et al., 2013). One example from the literature is Roster's (2013) study of female motorcycle riders, which represents both individual and collective acts of resistance. More specifically, a decision to ride motorcycles represents an individual act of resistance to gendered activity participation. Yet, Roster also revealed a central theme of girl power in the women's participation. In her words, "by banding together, these women riders sought to put a new attractiveness to other women. Many women felt like pioneers forging a path for other women to follow. These female motorcyclists relished opportunities to demonstrate their collective power and display positive gender role models" (p. 197). Thus, Roster's study demonstrates both individual and collective acts and outcomes of resistance. In contrast, Berbary's (2013) study of sororities detailed only individual acts of resistance. However, such individual acts of resistance had collective outcomes as "their small resistances created cracks in the discursive foundation and provided insight into or illuminated the discipline and resistance of dominant discourse within leisure spaces" (p. 164). Similarly, Lewis and Johnson (2011) detail how leisure can be a safe site for individuals to perform preferred gender expression, which can have implications for the way others understand and appreciate transfolks. Clearly, even individual acts of resistance have the potential to create collective outcomes for women (and other marginalized populations) as a social group.

Moreover, individual acts of resistance in one leisure context have the potential to spill over and influence other aspects of a woman's life. Resistance, therefore, has implications for the individual involved, but also for others and large scale social change (Freysinger et al., 2013). Given that the notion of resistance respects each woman's agency, but also recognizes the existence of oppression, inequities, and constraints, individual *and* collective outcomes of resistance with the potential for spillover are an important outcome (Shaw, 2001).

The literature clearly demonstrates that leisure is an important context for people to resist societal views about socially sanctioned, appropriate, and expected roles and behaviors based upon traditional gender ideologies (Shaw, 2001). Given this important role of leisure, we need to ask, how might leisure contexts be *created* to promote resistance (Berbary, 2013)?

FUTURE DIRECTIONS: FEMINIST RESEARCH IN THE CONTEMPORARY ERA

The body of feminist scholarship demonstrates that "gendered ideologies and discourses influence what is seen as appropriate and what is seen as possible. Although these discourses can be challenged, systemic inequity persists in subtle and overt ways, influencing time use, leisure involvement, and leisure experiences" (Freysinger et al., 2013, p. 542). Given the salience of gender to leisure choices, experiences, and pursuits, there are a number of important areas for our future inquiry.

One important consideration for future feminist leisure scholarship will be "the growing interest in thinking about gender identities, experiences, diversity, and interconnections" (Parry & Fullagar, 2013, p. 577). *Interconnections*, argue Parry and Fullagar (2013) move beyond the concept of intersectionality and "connotes more movement and fluidity than lies in the metaphor of intersection, as well as offering a way of thinking about how not only race and gender, but also nation, sexuality, and wealth all interconnect, configure, and reshape each other" (Bhavnani & Talcott, 2012, p. 137). Interconnectivity reveals how the leisure literature can bring a "feminist consciousness that opens up intellectual and emotional spaces for all [people] to articulate their relations to one another and the wider society—spaces where the personal transforms into the political" (Hesse-Biber, 2012, p. 2). Indeed, interconnectivity enables the proliferation of feminisms so that each individual can articulate her or his own feminist lens and bring that perspective to the literature. Hopefully, this type of proliferation will ensure underrepresented groups will be given appropriate feminist attention.

For example, Grossman, O'Connell, and D'Augelli (2005) noted trans people have received scant attention in the leisure literature or elsewhere. Trans people "challenge recreation and leisure professionals because their gender identity and expressions differ from society's role expectations of what it means to be male or female. These . . . people confront traditional 'girl-boy' activities associated with gender stereotyping" (Grossman et al., 2005, p. 5). Clearly this is an area of gender research that deserves more attention, which could be addressed through a focus on interconnectivity. In short, interconnectivity would help ensure the feminist leisure literature benefits from a robustness of substantive, theoretical, epistemological, and methodological diversity that will further the understanding of this complex phenomena of leisure with the goal of creating a more just society.

Social justice is also another area for future feminist research. Given the activist orientation of much feminist leisure research, social change and social justice are key areas of interest. Stewart (in press) noted there are several streams of leisure research focused on various forms of oppression and marginalization related to gender, race, ethnicity, sexual identity, ability, and socioeconomic status within leisure-related contexts. Interestingly, even though many areas of leisure research explicitly work toward a social change and social justice agenda, they have largely done so in isolation from one another (Stewart, in press). An opportunity exists, therefore, for these multiple strands to explore common themes across otherwise distinct areas of leisure literature. Stewart (in press) explained "with a focus on critiquing the philosophy and practice of research, rather than on the particular injustices, the cross-cutting themes emerge as bridges across traditionally isolated strands of research." Along with taking up the theme of interconnectivity described above, feminist scholars could also create the "bridges" with other leisure researchers focused on exposing oppression and marginalization with the goal of advancing social justice.

CONCLUSION

The purpose of this chapter was to demonstrate a clear link between gender and leisure that has implications for the lives of all individuals. Opportunities for a variety of leisure experiences are needed and our attention should be directed towards *creating* environments that empower people to resist traditional gender roles, expectations, and relations (Berbary, 2013). Indeed, feminist leisure scholars and professionals are in the unique positions of being able to contribute to social justice—either on an individual or broader level—in regard to gender roles, expectations, and relations through the provision of leisure pursuits that are not divided along gender lines, but support the lives of both men and women. Recognizing the influence of gender helps people understand their leisure choices and think critically about the type of choices they make and why. Problematizing gender is a responsibility that we all need to face and embrace to bring about a more equitable society (Sandberg, 2013).

REFERENCES

Berbary, L. (2013). Sorority spaces: Discipline of gendered reputation in public leisure. In V. Freysinger, S. Shaw, K. Henderson, & D. Bialeschki (Eds.), *Leisure, women, and gender* (pp. 151–166). State College, PA: Venture Publishing, Inc.

Bhavnani, K., & Talcott, M. (2012). Interconnections and configurations: Toward a global feminist ethnography. In S. Hesse-Biber (Ed.), *Handbook of feminist research: Theory and praxis* (pp. 135–153). Thousand Oaks, CA: Sage.

Braithwaite, A. (2002). The personal, the political, third-wave and postfeminisms. *Feminist Theory, 3*(3), 335–344.

Crawford, D. W., & Godbey, G. (1987). Reconceptualizing barriers to family leisure. *Leisure Sciences, 9*, 119–127.

Delamere, F.M., & Dixon, S. (2013). Gender and digital-game situated play: Women, girls, and the multiple constructions of play. In V. Freysinger, S. Shaw, K. Henderson, & D. Bialeschki (Eds.), *Leisure, women, and gender* (pp. 491–502). State College, PA: Venture Publishing, Inc.

Denzin, N. K. (2000). Aesthetics and the practices of qualitative inquiry. *Qualitative Inquiry, 6*, 256–265.

DeVault, M. L., & Gross, G. (2012). Feminist qualitative interviewing. In S. Hesse-Biber (Ed.), *The handbook of feminist research: Theory and praxis* (2nd ed.) (pp. 206–236). Thousand Oaks, CA: Sage.

Dionigi, R. A. (2013). Older women and competitive sports: Resistance and empowerment through leisure. In V. Freysinger, S. Shaw, K. Henderson, & D. Bialeschki (Eds.), *Leisure, women, and gender* (pp. 167–176). State College, PA: Venture Publishing, Inc.

Du, J. (2008). Women's leisure as reproduction and resistance. *Affilia, 23*, 179–189.

Fausto-Sterling, A. (2006). The five sexes: Why male and female is not enough. In K. E. Rosenblum & T. C. Travis (Eds.), *The meaning of difference: American constructions of race, sex and gender, social class, and sexual orientation* (pp. 87–90). New York: McGraw-Hill.

Freysinger, V., Shaw, S., Henderson, K., & Bialeschki, D. (Eds.). (2013). *Leisure, women, and gender*. State College, PA: Venture Publishing, Inc.

Grossman, A. H., O'Connell, T. S., & D'Augelli, A. R. (2005). Leisure and recreational "girl-boy" activities: Studying the unique challenges provided by transgendered young people. *Leisure, 29*, 5–26.

Henderson, K. A. (1994). Broadening an understanding of women, gender, and leisure. *Journal of Leisure Research, 26*, 1–7.

Hesse-Biber, S. N. (Ed.). (2012). *The handbook of feminist research: Theory and praxis*. Thousand Oaks, CA: Sage.

Hesse-Biber, S. N., & Piatelli, D. (2012). The synergistic practice of theory and method. In S. Hesse-Biber (Ed.), *The handbook of feminist research: Theory and praxis* (2nd ed.) (pp. 176–186). Thousand Oaks, CA: Sage.

Hibbins, R (2013). Reconstructing masculinities, migration, and transnational leisure spaces. In V. Freysinger, S. Shaw, K. Henderson, & D. Bialeschki (Eds.), *Leisure,*

Women, and Gender (pp. 451–463). State College, PA: Venture Publishing, Inc.

Hochschild, A. (1989). *The second shift: Working parents and the revolution at home*. New York: Viking.

Hunt, S. J. (2004). Acting the part: "Living history" as a serious leisure pursuit. *Leisure Studies, 23*, 387–403.

James, K. (2000). "You can feel them looking at you": The experiences of adolescent girls at swimming pools. *Journal of Leisure Research, 32*, 262-280.

Johnson, C. W. (2013). Feminist masculinities: Inquiries into the leisure, gender, and sexual identity. In V. Freysinger, S. Shaw, K. Henderson, & D. Bialeschki (Eds.), *Leisure, women, and gender* (pp. 245–258). State College, PA: Venture Publishing, Inc.

Kay, T. (2006). Where's Dad? Fatherhood in leisure studies. *Leisure Studies, 25*, 133–152.

Kirkley, D. (2000). Is motherhood good for women? A feminist exploration. *Journal of Obstetric, Gynecologic and Neonatal Nursing, 29*, 459–464.

Lather, P. (1998). Feminist perspectives on empowering research methodologies. *Women's Studies International Forum, 11*, 569–581.

Lewis, S. T., & Johnson, C. (2011). "But it's not *that* easy": Negotiating (trans)gender expressions in leisure spaces, *Leisure/Loisir, 35*, 115–132.

Lorber, J. (2006). The social construction of gender. In T. E. Ore (Ed.), *The social construction of difference and inequality: Race, class, and gender* (3rd ed.) (pp. 112–119). New York: McGraw-Hill.

Messner, M. A. (1998). Boyhood, organized sports, and the construction of masculinities. In M. S. Kimmel & M. A. Messner (Eds.), *Men's lives* (4th ed.) (pp. 109–121). Boston, MA: Allyn and Bacon.

Metheny, E. (1967). *Connotations of movement in sport and dance*. Dubuque, IA: William C. Brown.

Miller, Y. D., & Brown, W. J. (2005). Determinants of active leisure for women with young children—an 'ethic of care' prevails. *Leisure Sciences, 27*, p. 405–420.

Parry, D. C. (2003). Towards a 'Politics of Hope': Advocating a sixth phase of feminist leisure research. *Leisure and Society, 26*, 49–67.

Parry, D. C. (2005). Women's leisure as resistance to pronatalist ideology. *Journal of Leisure Research, 37*, 133–151.

Parry, D. C., & Fullagar, S. (2013). Feminist leisure research in the contemporary era: Introduction to the Special Issue. *Journal of Leisure Research, 45*(5), 571–582.

Reid, C. (2004). Advancing women's social justice agenda: A feminist action research framework. *International Journal of Qualitative Methods, 3*, 1–15.

Riemer, B. A., & Visio, M. E. (2003). Gender typing of sports: An investigation of Metheny's classification. *Research Quarterly for Exercise and Sport, 74*, 193–204.

Rupp, L. J., & Taylor, V. (1999). Forging feminist identity in an international movement: A collective identity approach to Twentieth-Century Feminism. *Journal of Women in Culture and Society, 24*, 363–386.

Roster, C. A. (2013). Women's transcendental experiences with motorcycling. In V. Freysinger, S. Shaw, K. Henderson, & D. Bialeschki (Eds.), *Leisure, women, and gender* (pp. 193–202). State College, PA: Venture Publishing, Inc.

Samdahl, D. M. (2013). Women, gender, and leisure constraints. In V. Freysinger, S. Shaw, K. Henderson, & D. Bialeschki (Eds.), *Leisure, women, and gender* (pp. 109–126). State College, PA: Venture Publishing, Inc.

Sandberg, S. (2013). *Lean in: Women, work, and the will to lead*. New York, NY: Alfred Knopf.

Schmalz, D. L. (2013). Girls, gender, and recreational sport. In V. Freysinger, S. Shaw, K. Henderson, & D. Bialeschki (Eds.), *Leisure, women, and gender* (pp. 127–136). State College, PA: Venture Publishing, Inc.

Scraton, S., & Watson, B. (2013). Older age, family and leisure. In V. Freysinger, S. Shaw, K. Henderson, & D. Bialeschki (Eds.), *Leisure, women, and gender* (pp. 383–396). State College, PA: Venture Publishing, Inc.

Shaw, S. M. (1994). Gender, leisure, and constraint: Towards a framework for the analysis of women's leisure, *Journal of Leisure Research, 26*, 8–22.

Shaw, S. M. (2001). Conceptualizing resistance: Women's leisure as political practice. *Journal of Leisure Research, 33*, 186–201.

Stewart, W. (2014). Leisure research to enhance social justice. *Leisure Sciences, 36*(4), 325–339.

Snyder-Hall, R. C. (2010). Third-wave feminism and the defense of "Choice." *Perspectives on Politics, 8*, 255–261.

Thompson, L. (1992). Feminist methodology for family studies. *Journal of Marriage and the Family, 54*, 3–18.

Wearing, B. (1990). Beyond the ideology of motherhood: Leisure as resistance. *Australian and New Zealand Journal of Sociology, 26*, 36–58.

Wiley, C. G. E., Shaw, S. M., & Havitz, M. E. (2000). Men's and women's involvement in sports: An examination of the gendered aspects of leisure involvement. *Leisure Sciences, 22*, 19–31.

Zucker, A. N., & Bay-Cheng, L. Y. (2010). Minding the gap between feminist identity and attitudes: The behavioural and ideological divide between feminists and non-labellers. *Journal of Personality, 78*, 1895–1924.

25

More Equitable Moments: The Changing Nature of Leisure for the LGBQ Community

Corey W. Johnson (University of Waterloo)

> *It is now our generation's task to carry on what those pioneers began...Our journey is not complete until our gay brothers and sisters are treated like anyone else under the law -- for if we are truly created equal, then surely the love we commit to one another must be equal as well.*
>
> Barack Obama (Office of the Press Secretary, 2013)

Lesbian, Gay, Bisexual, and Queer (LGBQ)[1] people and their allies have scored decisive and historic victories on LGBQ rights, both in the United States as well as around the globe. Even since the remarks made by President Obama we have seen the elimination of "don't ask, don't tell" which asked U.S. military service men and women to conceal their identity, we have added federal protections in immigration and federal employment, and seen two important decisions on same-sex marriage from the Supreme Court. The first ruling struck down Defense of Marriage Act, a 1996 federal law that denied federal benefits to same-sex couples married in states that permit such unions. The second decision found Proposition 8, California's voter-approved ban on same-sex marriage unconstitutional, making same-sex marriage now legal in 15 states.

Globally, same-sex marriage is also becoming more commonplace following Denmark's radical 1989 achievement. Progress with same-sex marriage has followed in Canada, England, New Zealand, France, Israel and Mexico, among others joining during the last decade. We have also seen the United Nations introduce a resolution in the Human Rights Council requesting a report detailing the situation of LGBT citizens worldwide. As a result of this report, the High Commissioner Navi Pillay called for the repeal of laws criminalizing homosexuality; equitable ages of consent; comprehensive laws against discrimination based on sexual orientation; prompt investigation and recording of hate crime incidents; and other measures to ensure the protection of LGBQ rights globally. It is apparent we are living in radically changing times in relation to the equality and equity of LGBQ rights.

In an effort to inform others about the lives of LGBQ populations and drawing on previous research, I detail the politics of sexual identity, discuss appropriate terminology, and give the context for how LGBQ people have been treated differently both historically and in contemporary times, specifically in North America. Finally, I detail four leisure contexts of particular importance to illustrate how non-inclusivity and inclusivity play out in leisure as we move from inequality to what I believe are more equitable moments of our history.

THE POLITICS OF SEXUAL IDENTITY

Gender and sexuality are entangled in our culture. The dominant ideological messages around gender and sexuality are created, perpetuated, maintained, and enforced in the social institutions and social structures of society, making the dominant (or popular) categories seem natural

[1] I am intentionally leaving out the "T" typically found in the acronym LGBTQ because the Transgender individuals who are such a valuable and important part of the LGBTQ community are so often lumped in to the larger discussions around sexual identity. However, their issues are those primarily of gender identity and expression. Consequently, that community and the challenges they face are both similar to, yet also distinctly different from, those who identify as Lesbian, Gay, Bisexual, and/or Queer. I also acknowledge that the acronym can also take on many other "sexual minority" groups, but I have chosen, deliberately here to talk only about LGBQ.

and/or unproblematic. Amid competing theories regarding sexual identity, most social scientists support Foucault's (1978) thinking that the term homosexuality was a modern invention created by the medical profession to define people by the sexual acts in which they participated. Notwithstanding arguments over language use, homosexuality has commonly and widely been used to describe same-sex sexual behavior in humans, though that behavior occurs in all mammals.

Regardless, the goal of deciding what *makes up homosexuality* or *who is a homosexual* is much more ambiguous. In fact, historical arguments indicate that the designation of homosexuality, and consequently the identity categories of gay, lesbian, bisexual, queer, and straight have only been constructed during the past century (Jagose, 1996). While there is ongoing debate over the exact historical (trans) formation of the "modern homosexual," and alongside the mounting biological and genetic research on the cause of the behavior, homosexuality continues to remain categorically elusive. Researchers have used a variety of determinants in an attempt to identify "homosexuals" (Laumann, Gagnon, Michael, & Michaels, 1994/1997). These determinants include behavior, desire, and self-identification, just to name a few. Traditionally, homosexual behavior has been used to categorize specific actions conducted with a partner of the same sex. These actions include, but are not limited to, active and receptive oral sex, active and receptive anal sex, and other forms of genital stimulation. Although research exists regarding leisure behaviors of people who merely "engage" in homosexual behaviors, this chapter focuses primarily on the leisure experiences of those people who "identify" as lesbian, gay, bisexual, and/or Queer.

What Does It Mean to Be Lesbian, Gay, Bisexual, or Queer?

Fairly common in our contemporary vernacular and more appropriate than the outdated use of the term "homosexual" is the terminology Lesbian, Gay, and Bisexual. Lesbian, gay, or bisexual "identity" indicates the ability of the individual to self-report that he or she ascribes to some label of same/both-sex sexual orientation: Lesbians are commonly women who have an affinity for other women; gay[2] is used to describe men who have an affinity for other men; and bisexual is used to describe either men or women who have an affinity for both genders.

Queer is decidedly promiscuous. In its pejorative heyday, in the years before the late-1980s, queer served to denigrate perverts and men who fancied other men (Beemyn & Eliason, 1996; Eaklor, 2008; Marinucci, 2010). In the time that has passed, queer has traveled a varied and harried terrain, finding at times contempt and at others a warm reception. At every turn, "queer" evades definition (Jagose, 1996). As an affirming personal identity, or worldview, queer takes many forms. One form is a personal refusal to adhere to or identify with static, essentialist categories such as woman/man, gay/straight, or feminine/masculine. Rather than adopt or appropriate these labels, a person might instead identify as queer. Identifying as queer, however, does not entail or suggest other identity categories "below the surface;" instead, queer serves as a decidedly ambiguous category. As an identity, queer is fluid, malleable, and transgresses boundaries as a way of establishing agency and unity. Queer refuses to be locked into any permanent state of identification. As a term, queer has mostly been engaged to describe those who transgress sex and gender categories (Cavanagh, 2010), but many also appropriate queer as an identity for anyone who refuses normative ways of being and interacting in the world. In this way, queer-as-identity allows individuals to transcend or outright reject normative labels, or to carve out an identity that more accurately represents who they are and how they relate to others.

However, the use of queer as an identity category is not without contestation. Because of its historically pejorative use, some do not understand or appreciate the more recent reclamation of the term (Eaklor, 2008). In addition to adopting queer as a personal identity, many claim a queer political identity. Additionally, queer's deliberate ambiguity provides a framework for building coalitions rallying around a diverse swath of social issues spanning race, class, gender, and sexual orientation.

LGBQ People as *Othered*

Since the advent of sexuality categories in the late 1800s, three beliefs have remained prevalent: (a) heterosexuality is normal and natural, and (b) homosexuality (or LGBQ people) is the opposite of heterosexuality, and (c) other non-normative sexual identity groups are further marginalized and/or invisible. This split of heterosexuality and homosexuality creates mutually exclusive categories with a considerable perceived need to identify as straight or lesbian, gay bisexual or queer. Since heterosexuality is believed to be normal and natural, non-heterosexuals have been damned, criminalized, medicalized, regulated, and reformed throughout history. The tension between heterosexuality and homosexuality is evident when examining heterosexism and homophobia in today's society.

Adrienne Rich (1993) coined the term *compulsory heterosexuality* indicating, "however we choose to identify ourselves, however we find ourselves labeled, [heterosexuality] flickers across and distorts our lives" (p. 244). Com-

[2] Although historically it was also applied to women before the term lesbian became more central.

pulsory heterosexuality is the portrayal or enactment of a heterosexual identity. It is perceived as the only correct or normal way to be, coercively encouraging individuals to live their existence according to the choices that heterosexuality and a heterosexual gender order expect. Female athletes, for instance, often perform compulsory heterosexuality by wearing makeup, dresses, and ribbons, having long hair, and perhaps being seen with a boyfriend in order to not be mistaken for a lesbian.

Related to compulsory heterosexuality, heteronormativity refers to the "principles of order and control that position heterosexuality at the cornerstone of the American sex/gender system and obligate the personal construction of sexuality and gender in terms of heterosexual norms" (Leap, 1999, p. 98). Not only does heteronormativity assume two genders and two sexualities, but it also leads to dichotomies of heterosexuality/homosexuality and male/female. The notion that being straight is correct, normal, and desired in our society, constrains LGBQ individuals, particularly in their sexual identity development. With the pressure to conform to the heterosexual norm, gays, lesbians, bisexuals, and queer people may struggle with their same/both-sex desires. These struggles could even postpone their sexual identity development and lead to isolation, low self-esteem, depression, and anger.

The two largest factors that contribute to the delays in sexual identity development are homophobia and heterosexism. *Homophobia* refers to an irrational fear or hatred of non-heterosexuals, which often leads to discrimination and violent acts, such as physical and verbal abuse, but also things such as being denied employment and housing (Johnson, Singh, & Gonzalez, 2014). *Heterosexism*, on the other hand, is "the individual, institutional, and societal/cultural beliefs and practices based on the belief that heterosexuality is the only normal and acceptable sexual orientation" (Adams, Bell, & Griffin, 1997, p. 146). Eventually these unquestioned heterosexist behaviors lead to heterosexists policies, procedures, and practices apparent when LGBQ individuals are not afforded the rights that heterosexuals enjoy. This includes things such as health insurance for partners, marriage[3], adoption, tax breaks, hospital visitation, or even family membership privileges at the local recreation center. Although grounded in heterosexism, these practices become naturalized and unquestioned, otherwise known as heteronormative.

With heterosexuality being the norm in our society, LGBQ identified individuals have to develop an identity that runs counter to the heteronormative culture in which they are socialized. This identity development process can last a lifetime and usually requires the LGBQ person to "come out." Although it is helpful to think of coming out as developmental, it is a life-long process that is never complete, given the fact that heterosexist assumptions and heternormative practices persist.

In addition to the subversive structural inequality, LGBQ individuals often experience prejudice, discrimination, and even violence (Johnson et al., 2014). Additionally, these oppressive experiences may be more pronounced for individuals based on intersecting identities such as gender, race, ethnicity, socioeconomic class, and disability. And while these oppressive experiences can occur in any domain of life (e.g., home, work, education), they increase the potential for negative outcomes in leisure too. Homophobia and heterosexism in leisure settings frequently influence the accessibility and utilization of services and the quality of services rendered (Johnson, 2003; Johnson et al., 2014).

Due to the heterosexism and discrimination encountered directly or indirectly, many LGBQ individuals anticipate being stigmatized and expect rejection. Therefore, many engage in chronic vigilance to evade these encounters either avoiding leisure settings and/or creating self-segregated environments (Johnson, 2008). When faced with negative encounters, some individuals may not have the skills to be able to manage the situation. Experiencing, or the threats of experiencing, these discriminatory situations, often result in LGBQ individuals concealing or not disclosing their identity as an LGBQ person. Even when individuals have developed their sexual identity and are living out and proud, some situations may still arise where they choose not to do so. When an LGBQ individual cannot share of themselves freely in the leisure setting, the very characteristic that defines leisure—freedom—is diminished.

As a coping strategy, concealment or "staying in the closet" shields many from injury and harm; however, the vigilance required to conceal one's identity is also a source of stress. The incessant monitoring of behaviors has been related to decreased wellness, including lowered self-esteem, increased depression, increased suicide attempts, and increased substance abuse (Williamson, 2000). Concealing one's LGBQ identity, as compared to disclosing it, has been associated with a number of negative health outcomes, weakened relationships, and poor leisure choices (Williamson, 2000).

Some LGBQ individuals also internalize the negative, homophobic, and heteronormative encounters and messages they receive from society (e.g., internalized homophobia), leading to even greater consequences. Internalized homophobia is the most insidious form of stress and signifies the inability to integrate sexual orientation into self-identity (Boehmer, Bowen, & Bauer, 2007). Those

[3] 15 states plus the District of Columbia have legalized same-sex marriage as of November 13, 2013. By the time this book went to publication, same-sex marriage became legalized federally in the U.S.

experiencing internalized homophobia often have cognitions of self-devaluation and self-hatred. Although internalized homophobia is within the individual, it is anchored in societal norms of homophobia and heterosexism (Dean et al., 2000; Williamson, 2000).

Yet, in spite of the perceived or real outcomes of homophobia and heterosexism, many LGBQ people are able to lead productive lives and enjoy their leisure (Johnson, 2005, 2008). By coming out, LGBQ individuals are able to garner social support from others resulting in positive leisure experiences. When they disclose their sexual identity to close friends, they are able to share fully about their life and build stronger relationships. By participating in the LGBQ community, individuals can engage in environments where they are not stigmatized and are able to acquire support given their oppressive, heteronormative experiences (Johnson, 2008; Johnson et al., 2014; Kivel, 1997; Williamson, 2000). Given the unique challenges faced by LGBQ people living in a heterosexually privileged world we can see the implications play out in four major leisure contexts: bars and nightclubs, sports, youth camps, and scouting.

FOUR LEISURE CONTEXTS FOR LGBQ PEOPLE

Bars and Nightclubs

The gay bar has been an important leisure site for LGBQ people since the gay liberation movement began. Since the Stonewall riots, and perhaps even before the riots, the bar served as a pivotal site for LGBQ social life, providing a cultural environment where release and enjoyment can occur away from heterosexualized spaces that dominate social life. By far the most common leisure spaces studied in queer communities have been the bars and dance clubs that offer an after-dark home for the gay and lesbian population in that geographic region (Barnett & Johnson, 2013; Hindle, 1994; Johnson, 2005, 2008). Bars and dance clubs are also often the singular space within a larger community where queer people can meet and engage intimately with one another with minimal fear of being attacked by homophobic citizens.

My intent is not to imply that the bar is a leisure context for all LGBQ people, nor to speak about gay bars as monolithic sites that are always positive. However, given the growing acceptance of LGBQ people in mainstream society, the segregated space of the gay bar may lose some of the significance as a necessary place away from heterosexuals, resulting in a decreased financial stability from a LGBQ target community it enjoyed previously (Barnett & Johnson, 2013). In addition, social media applications such as Grindr, Scruff, Jacked, Lesbian Social, and Brenda may allow LGB people to meet in alternative ways, via the computer or smartphone. These alternative forms of socially mediated meeting spaces are yet to be explored in detail.

Sports

For many decades in the United States, LGBQ athletes were subjected to terror, victimization, silence, and blatant homophobia while attempting to undertake activities in the forced closet atmosphere of sports. In his studies about homophobic attitudes in sport, Messner (2003) confirmed the overwhelmingly homophobic disposition present in male sport, stating that young boys learn that being gay or even merely being suspected of being gay is unacceptable and comes with harsh penalties.

Elling and Janssens (2009) described sports spaces as being symbolically connected to sexuality in gender-specific ways. Specifically, they claimed constant gendered and sexualized images strongly influence young adults' choices in leisure and sports activities. Hegemonic gender norms are significant in both female and male sports, as the most popular male sports promote the assertion of dominant heterosexuality through violence and the idea of "playing hard," while hegemonic masculinity is mirrored by "privileged femininity" among women (Elling & Janssens, 2009; Kivel & Kleiber, 2000; Messner & Sabo, 1994). Male homosexuality has long been associated with femininity, and because mainstream competitive sports are associated with hegemonic masculinity, there is an unspoken assumption that gay men are mostly unsuited for sports, especially team sports like football, rugby, and hockey (Connell, 1995; Laberge & Albert, 1999; Plummer, 2006). Lesbians, on the other hand, have been viewed as more "masculine" than heterosexual women and therefore have been viewed as more likely to play "masculine" sports (Elling & Janssens, 2009; Griffin, 1992; Palzkill, 1990).

Many athletes coming out of the closet in recent years, including the first overall Women's National Basketball Association pick Brittney Griner, U.S. soccer player Robbie Rogers, World Wrestling Entertainment wrestler Darren Young, and 21 openly gay athletes in the 2012 Olympic Games are all standing proud in the athletic spotlight. However, even with increasing support for LGBQ rights in legislation, popular media, and with a majority of the population, there has been only one active gay male athlete to come out in a major sport in the United States, which occurred in 2013 when Jason Collins came out as a gay National Basketball Association player. To this date, there have been no active LGBQ players to come out in the National Football League or Major League Baseball, two of the most-watched and successful American sports.

Conversely, in some women's sports, homophobia still exists in the marketing of female athletes as sexual beings, which runs contrary to the marketing of male sports stars.

Further complicating matters, the female athletes that represent a threat to traditional gender norms and hegemonic masculinity may fall victim to the threat of the "lesbian" label (Fink, 2012). The label of "lesbian" has been used politically as a weapon against women who speak up against sexism, and as a result, female athletes are repeatedly given the message that their appearance, mannerisms, and behavior should remain in line with hegemonic masculinity in order to avoid the lesbian stereotype and lose financial marketability (Fink, 2012; Griffin, 1992). The promotion of "heterosexy" female sports stars such as automobile racer Danica Patrick, tennis player Maria Sharapova, and soccer player Hope Solo serves to reassure fans and corporations that females can be successful and competitive in sports while remaining feminine in a non-threatening way (Fink, 2012; Kane, 2011).

In addition, leisure studies scholars such as Anderson and Mowatt (2013) have explored less commercialized environments to expand the nature of our understanding of LGBQ participation. Focusing in on intercollegiate club and recreational sports they examined how homophobia and heterosexism permeate athletic participation across individual and team sports, in club and recreational leagues. In addition, they examined variables such as gender, race, and previous contact with LGBQ persons to arrive at powerful recommendations for leisure scholars and practitioners alike. Studies like these are important steps for understanding sports participation for LGBQ people in everyday leisure situations.

Youth Camp

Youth camps for boys can be dated back as early as the late 1800s, while camps for girls and co-ed camps did not become available until the early 1900s. As time progressed, residential summer camps were established providing for a less rustic experience in order to accommodate many interests (Thurber & Malinowski, 2009). Camps continue to evolve and develop to provide opportunities for new and challenging experiences for adolescent boys and girls, but not until recently have camps become available to meet the needs of LGBTQ youth and children of LGBQ families.

The establishment of LGBQ specific youth camps is also a fairly new concept beginning in the late 1990s and early 2000s. LGBQ specific youth camps allow participants to enjoy the camp experience that so many American youth take for granted. LGBQ youth leave camp feeling empowered and often more educated on issues facing the LGBQ community (Mok, 2006). For example, founded in 2001, Camp Ten Trees is a camp for LGBQ children and youth or children with LGBQ family members. By creating a space where participants feel valued for who they are, Camp Ten Trees provides an opportunity for campers to meet others like themselves, build community, and be accepted (Acain, 2010).

Due to the lack of accessibility to the handful of LGBQ youth camps, youth camps in general need to become focused on providing a safe and inclusive environment for LGBQ campers. This is also important for non-LGBQ youth to interact with LGBQ youth in a positive way. As bullying remains salient against LGBQ youth in schools, educating others is an important step in assisting youth to interact positively with one another and transferring knowledge gained at camp to their community.

In essence, the importance of creating a safe space for LGBQ youth in camp is an increasing need. Funding needs to be available and accessible to develop more LGBQ camps with more sessions. Awareness of issues surrounding LGBQ youth and a willingness to include LGBQ youth will also assist all camps in creating a safe and open space for youth of all backgrounds to interact and grow together. One investigation instrumental in these efforts is Oakleaf's (2013) study of heteronormativity and homophobia encountered by camp staff in youth camp settings. What they found is that most LGBQ staff did not feel that they could be "out" at camp, but instead had to depersonalize themselves in an effort to acquiesce to the heteronormativity of camp life and policy. Consequently, we can discern from their findings that if adult staff are unable to feel safe and comfortable in the camp environment, it is logical youth will also find it challenging and like their adult role models, minimize that aspect of their identity over others.

Scouting

The Boy Scouts of America (BSA), founded in 1910, exist to provide avenues for young boys to build character, develop personal fitness, and become trained in responsibilities of participating citizenship (Boy Scouts of America Statement, 2013). In 1980, 17-year-old scout Timothy Curran took a male date to his senior prom and a picture of the couple was published in the local newspaper. Consequently, he was called to appear in front of the Boy Scouts' Council office, only to be expelled from scouting, under the guise that "homosexuality and Boy Scouting are not compatible." Curran sued, seeking an injunction that would keep him as a scout and troop leader (Donohue, 1994). In 1998, California Supreme Court ruled in favor of the Boy Scouts of America, ruling that Curran could not continue to serve as assistant scoutmaster in the BSA, and that the BSA did not infringe on anti-discrimination laws as applicable. The Boy Scouts of America's official position was to "not grant membership to individuals who are open or avowed homosexuals" as scouts or as adult scout leaders.

In 1990, James Dale, a scout leader for the BSA, became the co-president of the Lesbian/Gay student alliance at

Rutgers University. When the Local BSA Troop found out his sexual orientation, he was promptly expelled from the BSA, on the grounds that his homosexual lifestyle was inconsistent with the values of the BSA. Dale, an Eagle Scout himself, filed suit alleging that the BSA violated the state's public accommodation law prohibiting discrimination of memberships based on sexual orientation. The case was initially ruled against the Boy Scouts of America, who appealed the judgment to the U.S. Supreme Court. In 2000, the Supreme Court delivered a five-to-four ruling in favor of the BSA, arguing that the opposition to homosexuality is part of the organization's "expressive message" and that the government could not constitutionally prohibit the Boy Scouts of America from discrimination.

The response to the Dale judgment has been overwhelmingly in support of LGBQ membership and leadership. In particular, as many as 100 Eagle Scouts have returned their Eagle Scout badges in protest (which cannot be returned), while some Boy Scout troops completely ignored the ban on openly Gay scout leaders by crossing out the promise to abide by the BSA policies when they renew their charter. Thousands of public and private organizations, as well as private individuals, have withdrawn longstanding support due to the anti-LGBQ discrimination.

In May 2013, the BSA approved a resolution to remove the restriction that denies scouting membership to openly gay youth, but elected to still prohibit openly gay scout leaders. In contrast, the Girl Scouts of America (GSA) policy states, "Girl Scouts of the USA and its local councils and troops value diversity and inclusiveness and do not discriminate or recruit on the basis of race, religion, ethnicity, sexual orientation, socioeconomic status, national origin, or physical or developmental disability." In fact, the GSA welcomes LGBQ rights activists to speak at GSA events, be featured in Girl Scout materials, and promote LGBQ rights websites. Moreover, in October 2011, a Colorado Girl Scouts troop admitted a 7-year old transgender girl, Bobby Montoya, after initially rejecting her. Unfortunately, despite the ripe opportunity for research related to LGBQ young people's involvement in scouting, there is no current empirical work to document the influence or impact of this discrimination on their lives short or long term.

BEYOND OUR BINARIES: FUTURE RESEARCH

The scholarship on LGBQ people in leisure studies remains sparse. Only a small number of North American leisure researchers in the past 20 years examined sexual minorities, and based on the emerging scholarship, there are only a few currently interested in this work. Regardless, the mainstreaming of LGBQ identity should have scholars turn our eyes to those places where heterosexuals have already been studied in leisure including the outdoors, the family, tourism, and other recreational activities.

In addition, the complexity of sexual (and gender) identity raised over the past 15 to 20 years of our scholarship has changed how we think about emancipation for LGBQ people. We certainly believe in striving for equality and first-class citizenship rights for all people through institutional policies and/or the effective training of leisure service professionals. However, considering the tensions and additional questions raised in my own leisure studies scholarship, I believe researchers are often just managing shifts in discourses that create a *virtual equality* (Vaid, 1995). I believe to escape the confining and oppressive structures of gender and sexual identity we need both intellectual and political mobility grounded firmly in the communities where people live, so that hegemony (and power) are situated and understood as contextual and contingent. I see this intellectual and political mobility entering into leisure studies, and leisure in general, through conceptualizations inspired by *Queer*. The concept of Queer helps explore and interrogate the discourses where, in contexts such as gay bars, sports, camp, and scouting, gender and sexual identity are simultaneously produced by and in those leisure contexts.

In addition, we need to expand our umbrella of sexual minorities to include others that remain invisible. The most notable absence in our literature is studies of those who identify as asexual. According to most scholars, asexuality is defined as a lack of sexual attraction (Asexuality Visibility & Education Network 2012; Bogaert, 2004). For many asexuals (frequently referred to as "aces" in their community), the journey to acceptance of their own unique sexuality begins with isolation and confusion. Described in the DSM-IV as causing "marked distress or interpersonal difficulties" due to a lack or an absence of "sexual fantasies and desire for sexual activity," most medical professionals consider asexuality as a sexual dysfunction that should be treated with medication and therapy (Mosbergen, 2013). However, Bogaert (2006) clarified that society has claimed that sexual feelings and a sexual orientation is essential to the human condition, and that asexuality stands to challenge the idea that humans are biologically determined to feel sexual feelings towards others. He claimed that knowledge about sexual orientation development is limited, and therefore it is unfair to claim that there is no biological predisposition to asexuality. Furthermore, asexuals do not commonly report "personal distress" over their lack of sexual desires, which raises questions over the legitimacy of the claim for asexuality as a mental "disorder" (Brotto, Knudson, Inskip, Rhodes, & Erskine, 2010; Prause & Graham, 2007).

Further complicating matters, asexuality has been found to be as susceptible to discrimination and bias as other sexual minorities, and that people of all sexual orientations are more likely to discriminate against asexuals (MacInnis & Hodson, 2012). Because of the lack of understanding, and seemingly due to the prior association with mental disorders, asexuals are frequently met with denial that asexuality actually exists, or they are mocked and slandered by characterizations of abnormality, unhappiness, and in some cases, "cure" via threats of corrective rape (Mosbergen, 2013). Currently, asexuals are also fighting for inclusion within the sexual minority, LGBT, and queer communities (Mosbergen, 2013). Some asexuals draw parallels to the trans community's fight for inclusion within the LGBT spectrum of sexual minorities, meaning that the leisure studies community should begin to pay more attention to this invisible sexual minority.

CONCLUSION

Significant progress is being made in the U.S. and around the globe related to LGBQ rights and there is no doubt that leisure serves as a context for both exploring and celebrating that identity. However, leisure can also be a place where discrimination and marginalization occur. In this chapter we have explored the roots and politics of sexual identity, come to understand the detrimental effects of compulsory heterosexuality and explored four relevant leisure contexts where LGBQ people are beginning to see more equitable moments. I have also forwarded what I see as the future of research on sexual and gender minorities in leisure studies. There is much for us to do on a number of fronts!

> The only thing [LGBQ people] have to look forward to is hope. And you have to give them hope. Hope for a better world, hope for a better tomorrow, hope for a better place to come to if the pressures at home are too great. Hope that all will be all right. Without hope, not only gays, but the blacks, the seniors, the [disabled], the us'es, the us'es will give up . . . It means hope to a nation that has given up, because if a gay person makes it, the doors are open to everyone. (Milk, 1978)

REFERENCES

Asexuality Visibility & Education Network. (2012). *Overview*. Retrieved from http://www.asexuality.org/home/overview.html

Acain, A. (2010, March–April). Camp Ten Trees for children and youth of the LGBTQ community. *Gay Parent Magazine*, 18–21.

Adams, M., Bell, L. A., & Griffin, P. (Eds.). (1997). *Teaching for diversity and social justice*. New York: Routledge.

Anderson, A. R., & Mowatt, R.A. (2013). Heterosexism in campus recreational club sports: An exploratory investigation into attitudes toward gay men and lesbians. *Recreational Sports Journal, 37*(2), 106–122.

Barnett, J. T., & Johnson, C. W. (2013). We are all royalty: Narrative comparisons of a drag queen and king. *Journal of Leisure Research, 45*(5), 677–694.

Beemyn, B., & Eliason, M. (Eds.). (1996). *Queer studies: A lesbian, gay, bisexual, and transgender anthology*. New York: New York University Press.

Boehmer, U., Bowen, D. J., & Bauer, G. R. (2007). Overweight and obesity in sexual-minority women: Evidence from population-based data. *American Journal of Public Health, 97*(6), 1134–1140.

Bogaert, A. F. (2004). Asexuality: Prevalence and associated factors in a national probability sample. *Journal of Sex Research, 41*(3), 279–287.

Bogaert, A. F. (2006). Toward a conceptual understanding of asexuality. *Review of General Psychology, 10*(3), 241.

Boy Scouts of America Statement. (2013, May 23). *Boy Scouts of America*. Retrieved from http://www.scouting.org/sitecore/content/MembershipStandards/Resolution/results.aspx

Brotto, L. A., Knudson, G., Inskip, J., Rhodes, K., & Erskine, Y. (2010). Asexuality: A mixed-methods approach. *Archives of Sexual Behavior, 39*(3), 599–618.

Cavanagh, S. L. (2010). *Queering bathrooms: Gender, sexuality, and the hygienic imagination*. Toronto, ON: University of Toronto Press.

Connell, R. W. (1995). *Masculinities*. Berkeley: University of California Press.

Dean, L., Meyer, I. H., Robinson, K., Sell, R. L., Sember, R., Silenzio, V. M., Wolfe, D., Bowen, D. J., Bradford, J., Rothblum, E., Scout, M. A., White, J., & Dunn, P. (2000). Lesbian, gay, bisexual, and transgender health: Findings and concerns. *Journal of the Gay and Lesbian Medical Association, 4*(3), 102–151.

Donohue, W. A. (1994). Culture wars against the boy scouts. *Society, 31*(4), 59–68.

Eaklor, V. L. (2008). *Queer America: A GLBT history of the 20th century*. Westport, CT: Greenwood Press.

Elling, A., & Janssens, J. (2009). Sexuality as a structural principle in sport participation negotiating sports spaces. *International Review for the Sociology of Sport, 44*(1), 71–86.

Fink, J. S. (2012). Homophobia and the marketing of female athletes and women's sport. In G. B. Cunningham (Ed.), *Sexual orientation and gender identity in sport: Essays from activists, coaches, and scholars* (pp. 49–60). College Station, TX: Center for Sport Management Research and Education.

Foucault, M. (1978). *The history of sexuality, Vol. 1*. New York, NY: Pantheon Books.

Griffin, P. (1992). Changing the game: Homophobia, sexism and lesbians in sport. *Quest, 44*, 251–265.

Hindle, P. (1994). Gay communities and gay space in the city. In S. Whittle (Ed.), *The margins of the city: Gay men's urban lives* (pp. 7–25). Brookfield, VT: Ashgate Publishing Company.

Jagose, A. (1996). *Queer theory: An introduction*. Washington Square, NY: New York University Press.

Johnson, C. W. (2003, March). Speaking the unspeakable: A decade of research on sexual minorities. Research Update. *Parks & Recreation, 38*(3), 21–34.

Johnson, C. W. (2005). "The first step is the two-step": Hegemonic masculinity and dancing in a country-western gay bar. *International Journal of Qualitative Studies in Education, 18*(4), 445–464.

Johnson, C. W. (2008). "Don't call him a cowboy": Masculinity, cowboy drag, and a costume change. *Journal of Leisure Research, 40*(3), 385–403.

Johnson, C. W., Singh, A. A., & Gonzalez, M. (2014). "It's complicated": Collective memories of transgender, queer, and questioning youth in high school. *Journal of Homosexuality, 61*(3), 419–434, doi: 10.1080/00918369.2013.842436

Kane, M. J. (2011, July 27). *Sex sells sex, not women's sport*. Retrieved from http://www.thenation.com

Kivel, B. D. (1997). Leisure, narratives and the construction of identity among lesbian, gay and bisexual youth. *Journal of Leisurability, 24*(4), 31–38.

Kivel, B. D., & Kleiber, D. A. (2000). Leisure in the identity formation of lesbian/gay youth: Personal, but not social. *Leisure Sciences, 22*, 215–232.

Laberge, S., & Albert, M. (1999). Conceptions of masculinity and of gender transgressions in sport among adolescent boys: Hegemony, contestation, and social class dynamic. *Men and Masculinities, 1*(3), 243–267.

Laumann, E., Gagnon, J., Michael, R., & Michaels, S. (1994/1997). The social organization of sexuality. In W. Rubenstein (Ed.), *Cases and materials on sexual orientation and the law*. (pp. 19–28). St. Paul, MN: West Publishing Co.

Leap, W. (1999). Language, socialization, and silence in gay adolescence. In K. E. Lovaas & M. M. Jenkins (Eds.), *Sexualities and communication in everyday life: A reader* (pp. 95–106). Thousand Oaks, CA: SAGE Publications, Inc.

MacInnis, C. C., & Hodson, G. (2012). Intergroup bias toward "Group X": Evidence of prejudice, dehumanization, avoidance, and discrimination against asexuals. *Group Processes & Intergroup Relations, 15*(6), 725–743.

Marinucci, M. (2010). *Feminism is queer: The intimate connection between queer and feminist theory*. London and New York: Zed Books.

Messner, M. A. (2003). *Taking the field: Women, men, and sports*. Minneapolis, MN: University of Minnesota Press.

Messner, M. A., & Sabo, D. F. (Eds.). (1994). *Sex, violence & power in sports: Rethinking masculinity*. Freedom, CA: The Crossing Press.

Mok, F. (2006, July 4). A love of camp. *Advocate, 966*, 25–26.

Milk, H. (1978). The hope speech—Harvey Milk. Retrieved from http://www.danaroc.com/guests_harvemilk_12208

Mosbergen, D. (2013, August). Asexuality: The 'x' in a sexual world. *Huffington, 63*. Retrieved from http://www.huffingtonpost.com/2013/06/17/asexuality-the-x-in-a-sexual-world_n_3444417.html

Oakleaf, L. (2013). "Having to think about it all the time": Factors affecting the identity management strategies of residential summer camp staff who self-identify as lesbian, gay, bisexual, or transgender. *Leisure/Loisir, 37*(3), 251–266.

Office of the Press Secretary. (2013, January 21). *Inaugural address by President Barack Obama* [Online press release]. Retrieved from http://www.whitehouse.gov/the-press-office/2013/01/21/inaugural-address-president-barack-obama

Palzkill, B. (1990). Between gymshoes and high-heels—The development of a lesbian identity and experience in top class sport. *International Review for the Sociology of Sport, 25*(3), 221–234.

Plummer, D. (2006, May). Sportophobia: Why do some men avoid sport? *Journal of Sport and Social Issues, 30*(2), 122–137.

Prause, N., & Graham, C. A. (2007). Asexuality: Classification and characterization. *Archives of Sexual Behavior, 36*(3), 341–356.

Rich, A. (1993). Compulsory heterosexuality and lesbian existence. In G. Rubin, H. Abelove, M. A. Barale, & D. M. Halperin (Eds.), *The lesbian and gay studies reader* (pp. 227–254). New York: Routledge.

Thurber, C., & Malinowski, J. (2009). *Summer camp handbook*. Retrieved from http://www.summercamphandbook.com

Williamson, I. R. (2000). Internalized homophobia and health issues affecting lesbians and gay men. *Health Education Research, 15*(1), 97–107.

Vaid, U. (1995). *Virtual equality: The mainstreaming of gay and lesbian liberation* (1st Anchor Books hardcover ed.). New York: Anchor Books.

26

LEISURE AND PEOPLE WITH DISABILITIES

John Dattilo (The Pennsylvania State University)

Advances for people with disabilities have occurred in various countries across the globe. For example, it has been over 20 years since the Americans with Disabilities Act was signed into law in the United States. Similar legislative acts have occurred in other countries. These civil rights legislative acts have helped to advance opportunities for people with disabilities in many different arenas of life, including leisure. Although progress has been made, much research is needed to move people who have disabilities from being members of an oppressed group to the mainstream.

This chapter contains a summary of research studies associated with people with disabilities and their leisure participation within their communities. In addition, some general themes of research findings are identified. These themes are acknowledged in the initial portion of the chapter and identified as (a) leisure and inclusion as a human right, and (b) restrictions experienced by people with disabilities. These themes then were used to help generate some operative assumptions on which the chapter is based. This foundation is followed by a description of research that has identified issues and techniques that may be helpful to consider when providing leisure services. The final section contains considerations when attempting to conduct research that is respectful and meaningful to people with disabilities, their families and friends, leisure service providers, and other members of the community. This chapter includes material from writings published elsewhere (e.g., Dattilo, 2012, 2013; Dattilo & Rusch, 2012; Dattilo & Williams, 2012).

LEISURE AND INCLUSION AS HUMAN RIGHTS

LEISURE AS A HUMAN RIGHT

Across the world, many people consider leisure a human right (e.g., Cohen-Gewerc & Stebbins, 2007). The United Nations' (1948) *Universal Declaration of Human Rights* identifies leisure and cultural life within the community as two basic human rights. In addition to general human rights proclamations, documents specific to people with disabilities highlight their right to leisure. As an example, Article 30 of the Convention on the Rights of People with Disabilities (United Nations, 2006) states that people with disabilities should have full access to cultural, sport, and leisure opportunities.

INCLUSION AS A HUMAN RIGHT

Inclusion involves people living together in the same community so that they share experiences and develop an appreciation for one another. The practice of inclusion promotes valuing differences and recognizing that each person has an important contribution to make to society. Inclusion implies that all people, including people with disabilities, deserve to be given a chance to be a part of a community from the beginning of their lives. True inclusion goes beyond tolerance toward embracing and recognizing the value of diversity and difference. Inclusion affirms that all people bring value to a group or, more generally, society.

Inclusion does *not* mean we are all the same, we all agree, and we are oblivious to individual differences; rather, inclusion means that we celebrate our diversity and differences with respect. There is extensive research highlighting the many benefits of inclusion for people with and without disabilities (Ryndak, Ward, Alper, Storch, & Montgomery, 2010). In sum, inclusion is positive and involves people living together in the same community, sharing experiences, and developing an appreciation for each other.

RESTRICTIONS EXPERIENCED BY PEOPLE WITH DISABILITIES

DISCRIMINATION

Consistently across various cultures the characteristic of disability has and does result in extreme acts of discrimination. Julie Smart (2009) speaks to this issue:

> In spite of the long history and the universality of disability, almost without exception, people with disabilities have been discriminated against, with that discrimination ranging from minor embarrassment and inconvenience to relegation to a life of limited experience and reduced social opportunity and civil rights.... No other racial, cultural, ethnic, linguistic, religious, political, national, sexual orientation, or gender group has experienced this degree of pervasive and generalized prejudice and discrimination, which included killing babies ... [who have] disabilities, forced sterilization, institutionalization, and mass murder. (pp. 177–118)

The American with Disabilities Act of 1990 identified the pervasive oppression facing people with disabilities:

> Individuals with disabilities are a discrete and insular minority who have been faced with restrictions and limitations, subjected to a history of purposeful unequal treatment, and relegated to a position of political powerlessness in our society, based on characteristics that are beyond the control of such individuals and resulting from stereotypic assumptions not truly indicative of the individual ability of such individuals to participate in, and contribute to, society.

People without disabilities can experience stress when interacting with people with disabilities. This discomfort stems from ignorance or perceptions that people with disabilities do not look or act the way most other people might. Stress can create major barriers to inclusion for people with disabilities. According to Pivik, McComas, and LaFlamme (2002), negative attitudes comprise the most devastating barriers facing people with disabilities. Attitudinal barriers may be intentional (e.g., isolation and bullying) and unintentional (e.g., lack of knowledge or understanding).

As a result of discrimination, societies have historically isolated and segregated individuals with disabilities. Despite some improvements, discrimination against individuals with disabilities continues to be pervasive. Inclusive practices can potentially combat historical discrimination in ways that acknowledge and celebrate individual differences.

Restrictions to Leisure

A barrier to inclusion occurs when people with disabilities do not have the opportunity to use their free time in personally satisfying ways or to build meaningful social relationships. Research has documented that many people who have a disability experience loneliness, boredom, and anxiety brought on by an abundance of unstructured free time and a lack of knowledge and skills needed to experience leisure (Duvdevany, 2008). For many people with disabilities, leisure participation is often solitary and sedentary (Oates, Bebbington, Bourke, Girdler, & Leonard, 2011).

After an extensive review of the choice and preference assessment literature for individuals with more severe disabilities, Tullis et al. (2011) surmised that even though people with disabilities express a desire to increase engagement in leisure pursuits, many are not given an opportunity to do so and do not possess skills required to adapt to new challenges and solve related problems. Likewise, Solish, Perry, and Minnes (2010) reported that there have been limited gains in leisure involvement and social adjustment of people with disabilities.

Limited leisure engagement by individuals with disabilities is a global phenomenon. For example, Azaiza, Croitoru, Rimmerman, and Naon (2012) conducted a secondary analysis of Jewish and Arab adults with disabilities and concluded that they rarely participate in inclusive leisure. This finding reflects a lack of inclusion and illustrates the point that living in the community does not guarantee that individuals with disabilities "will have a real opportunity to be part of the community" (p. 387). In a related study of adolescents with disabilities residing in Taiwan, participants reported limited diversity and intensity of participation in enjoyable activities (Wuang & Su, 2012). Worldwide, people with disabilities continue to encounter barriers to inclusive leisure.

OPERATIVE ASSUMPTIONS

There are some operative assumptions which guide research related to leisure and people with disabilities. As noted, people with disabilities have been oppressed and represent a marginalized group. Inclusive leisure services result in positive outcomes for all involved. Also, leisure service professionals are placed in positions of power that give them the capacity to control and influence other people's actions. Dattilo and Williams (2012) reflected on the mantra of Spider-Man as shared with him by his Uncle Ben, *with great power comes great responsibility*, and concluded that researchers and practitioners must acknowledge how they impact others. Combatting oppression can be done by considering our common humanity, exhibiting respect, and valuing others. Acting in these ways provides others pride and dignity. Also, to avoid being paternalistic, it is helpful to consider that everyone has the right to autonomy. Broadly, human rights involves reconfiguring how people with disabilities have been viewed, regarding them as people first, and foremost, affirming they are human beings who have legal and moral rights as well as responsibilities that are the same as anyone else.

LEISURE PARTICIPATION

Applied research studies have been implemented to examine the lives of people with disabilities and the effects of various interventions designed to empower them and the people around them to experience meaningful and enjoyable leisure. This research can guide public policy decisions regarding inclusion, self-determination, and empowerment (Schalock, Verdugo, & Gomez, 2011). Research supporting the following suggestions for facilitating leisure are highlighted in this chapter: (a) leisure education; (b) promoting self-determination; (c) social supports for and through leisure participation facilitated by family, peers, and staff members; (d) physically active leisure that reduces obesity and encourages healthy living; and (e) use of technology that facilitates leisure engagement.

Leisure Education

According to Cohen-Gewerc and Stebbins (2007), leisure education is "a lifelong process through which people can better understand themselves and the role of leisure in their life and act upon this understanding to bring about desirable changes to their use of leisure" (p. 53). The term *leisure education* describes a multifaceted, dynamic process promoting exploration of perspectives and opportunities intended to develop an ethic of positivity and savoring conducive to leisure, flow, and arousal and is designed to stimulate self-awareness, promote acquisition of leisure-related knowledge, and encourage skill development; leisure education is provided to meet needs for autonomy, competence, and social connections that contribute to self-determination and the ability to manage challenges that create conditions for intrinsic motivation and opportunities to experience meaningful and enjoyable leisure, happiness, and the ability to flourish (Dattilo, 2015).

After reviewing relevant research, Duvdevany (2008) concluded that when services are not designed to facilitate supportive relationships and leisure for individuals with disabilities, full inclusion is not achieved. Duvdevany also noted that life-long learning associated with leisure for individuals with disabilities is invaluable and that leisure education should receive high priority in policymaking, service delivery, and research. Chang (2011) examined the interaction effect of leisure, self-determination, and leisure competence and recommended that opportunities be provided for adults to continue to learn about ways to engage in leisure as they transition into later life.

People engage in leisure casually or they approach their involvement with a strong commitment; both can be addressed via leisure education. A strong commitment of time, resources, and energy to a leisure experience is akin to *serious leisure* which involves systematic pursuit of an enjoyable activity that is substantial, interesting, fulfilling, and provides a context that can contribute to a person's sense of identity (Stebbins, 2008).

Serious leisure has been found to have positive outcomes for people with disabilities. Fesko, Hall, Qujinlan, and Jockell (2012) found that serious volunteering by individuals with intellectual and developmental disabilities provided opportunities for social interaction, community engagement, and a feeling of accomplishing something worthwhile. Azaiza et al. (2012) likewise reported that serious volunteering promoted a feeling of inclusion among Jewish and Arab adults with disabilities. Also, when Badia, Orgaz, Berdugo, and Ullan (2013) asked youth and adults with disabilities about social activities in which they were most interested, volunteering with its positive effects on community involvement and satisfaction topped the list. Another example of a type of serious leisure pursuit that potentially engages individuals in their community is religious activities. Novak Amado, Degrande, Boice, and Hutcheson (2012) observed that many religious activities occur at regular intervals and provide multiple opportunities for meaningful interactions and serious leisure experiences.

Even though creating a context for people to pursue serious leisure is valuable, there is merit in developing situations conducive to more casual engagement that foster relaxation, connections with others, and a level of introspection. Kleiber (2012) underscored the importance of "learning to appreciate the world at large, learning to relax and be open and curious, learning about one's own interests and possibilities, and responding to the collective activities of others" (p. 8). As a result, leisure can be an educational context for people with disabilities that meets multiple needs associated with becoming self-determined (McGuire & McDonnell, 2008). According to Kleiber, leisure with its associated freedom and openness provides an optimal environment for indulging curiosity, communing with nature, connecting with people, and realizing one's potential more fully.

Self-Determination

Verdonschot, Witte, Reichrath, Buntinx, and Curfs (2009a) conducted a review of the impact of environmental factors associated with community participation, and identified several environmental factors that positively influence community engagement among people with disabilities. Some of these were opportunities to be autonomous and to make choices. Both of these factors are thought to be integral to self-determination among people with disabilities (Smith, Polloway, Smith, & Patton, 2007). Autonomy and the ability to make choices are also inextricably connected to leisure.

Leisure, as used in this chapter, is an experience that results from being intrinsically motivated to participate in freely chosen, meaningful activity that when engaged in competently is a form of self-expression, contributes to a sense of identity and connectedness, and results in positive emotions. Consequently, leisure is connected to our sense of happiness and our ability to flourish. McGuire and McDonnell (2008) examined the relationship between recreation and levels of self-determination of adolescents and young adults with disabilities. They established that the amount of time individuals with disabilities spend experiencing leisure is predictive of higher levels of self-determination. In general, research supports the idea that the positive impact of self-determined instruction is connected to a range of positive long-range outcomes for people with disabilities (Wehmeyer, Tassé, Davies, & Stock, 2012).

After examining the effect of social and classroom ecological factors on promoting self-determination for children, Cho, Wehmeyer, and Kingston (2012) observed that it is helpful for people with disabilities to develop skills associated with self-determined leisure as they experience a variety of challenges associated with using their free time. Dattilo and Rusch (2012) proposed that self-determination in leisure can be facilitated among people with disabilities by helping them learn to identify different leisure opportunities, pursue those options, and negotiate barriers to leisure participation. Similarly, McGuire and McDonnell (2008) concluded that the time that adolescents and young adults with disabilities spend actively participating in leisure is predictive of higher levels of self-determination. They also reported that leisure could be a useful context for enhancing the selection of activities that individuals regard as enjoyable and meaningful.

Social Supports

Fredrickson (2009) observed that there is a strong connection between flourishing and enjoying good social relations. Flourishing extends beyond happiness to doing something valuable. According to Fredrickson, to *flourish* we must move past self-interest to arrive at a point when we share and celebrate goodness in others and the natural world.

Unfortunately, research by Verdonschot, Witte, Reichrath, Buntinx, and Curfs (2009b) identified that the social network of many people with disabilities is relatively small and the absence of such social supports can inhibit inclusive leisure engagement and prevent flourishing. Lippold and Burns (2009) examined social networks of adults with disabilities and concluded that despite living in everyday communities, these individuals often do not have meaningful relationships with people other than paid staff. In general, the social relationships of people with disabilities are shaped by family members, peers, and leisure service personnel (Mahy, Shields, Taylor, & Dodd, 2010).

According to researchers (Dyson, 2010; Resch et al., 2010), family participation has significant effects on development. Research consistently demonstrates that families strongly influence a person's inclusion (Edwards & Da Fonte, 2012) and are a primary outlet for leisure for individuals with disabilities (Dodd, Zabriskie, Widmer, & Eggett, 2009; Eisenman, Tanverdi, Perrington, & Geiman, 2009). Greater family involvement and availability of social support are associated with increased community and leisure participation among people with disabilities (Verdonschot et al., 2009a).

Research conducted by Worcester Nesman, Raffaele-Mendez, and Keller (2008) indicate it is important to include parents' voices in designing interventions for youth with disabilities. After examining effects of a caregiver-delivered home-based intervention, Batu (2008) concluded that when parents are involved, youth with disabilities are better able to generalize their skills. Likewise, findings from Agate, Zabriske, Agate, and Poff (2009) provided support that family leisure involvement is a critical component of family satisfaction (see also Trussell, Chapter 22). Using participatory action research, Walmsley and Mannan (2009) found that family-centered approaches supporting people with disabilities contribute to positive outcomes and feelings of acceptance and recommended that leisure service providers strive to promote regular communication with families.

Research also shows that peers are another source of support for leisure engagement. Carter, Moss, Hoffman, Chung, and Sisco (2011) designed a peer support intervention based on the observation that youth are willing to interact with youth with disabilities as long as they are initially encouraged to do so and that adults are not continuously present. The intervention facilitated sustained proximity by relocating peers, decreasing continuous adult proximity, providing initial information and guidance, encouraging support staff to use social facilitation strategies, and establishing interaction opportunities. Carter and colleagues found that their intervention was successful in increasing peer interactions.

Considering that peer interactions are often critical in creating a context conducive for leisure participation, it is valuable to examine effects of programs designed to establish and maintain supportive relationships that occur within the context of leisure (Duvdevany, 2008). Using focus group discussion, Jones and Goble (2012) identified key components for creating and improving effective partnerships, which were providing orientations, developing effective systems for communication and collaboration, establishing equal relationships, maintaining high expectations, having individuals act as natural supports, prioritizing fun and socialization, and focusing on inclusion. Research also suggests a small number of prolonged social relationships tend to provide an important level of intimacy and protection (Lippold & Burns, 2009). According to Duvdevany, these types of intimate relationships and valued social contexts tend to be highly correlated with rewarding leisure engagement.

Researchers have begun to recognize the importance of people whose role is specifically devoted to facilitating inclusion. After conducting a series of interviews and focus groups, Miller, Schleien, and Bowens (2010) identified the importance of having an *inclusion facilitator*, an employee with specialized training in providing leisure service to people with disabilities (i.e., certified therapeutic recreation specialist), and *inclusion support staff*, such as employees, volunteers, family members, or peers who help facilitate inclusion. Miller et al. recommend that leisure service providers "invest more heavily in the hiring, preparing, and support of highly qualified inclusion facilitators" (p. 47).

Physically Active Leisure

Rimmer, Wang, Yamaki, and Davis (2010) identified obesity as a major global health problem and noted that although this epidemic cuts across groups, it is people with disabilities who appear to have the highest propensity for obesity. Likewise, Murphy, Carbone, and the Council on Children with Disabilities, (2008) reported that children with disabilities are more restricted in their physical activity and have lower levels of fitness and higher levels of obesity than their peers without disabilities. Rimmer and colleagues concluded that chronic and secondary conditions associated with obesity undermine physical independence and limit opportunities for community engagement in leisure and physical activity. Mahy et al. (2010) found that the incidence of obesity is directly related to limited physical activity (see also Bocarro & Edwards, Chapter 8). Promoting physical activity is a critical issue for people with disabilities.

Studies show that people with disabilities have limited engagement in physically active leisure across the lifespan. Oates et al. (2011) reported that children with disabilities are extremely sedentary, with less than one-fourth of them meeting national standards for physical activity. Wuang and Su (2012) reported that people with disabilities do not participate in a high number of physically based, enjoyable activities and worried that their ". . . sedentary lifestyle might trigger the development of obesity, which may lead to a self-perpetuating vicious cycle of less activity, low energy expenditure, and limited lifestyle" (p. 846). In a study of youth and adults with developmental disabilities, Badia and colleagues (2013) noted that although respondents reported that they rarely engage in physically active leisure, they expressed an interest in becoming involved in a variety of physical activities. Given that many people with disabilities have low socioeconomic levels, Cohen-Gewerc and Stebbins (2007) encouraged practitioners to provide low-cost activities such as walking and cycling.

To further explore engagement in physically active leisure, Taylor and Yun (2012) studied factors influencing after-school program staffs' inclusion of youth with disabilities. Based on their results, the authors recommend that after-school personnel develop clear expectations of inclusion by detailing and communicating the importance of inclusive leisure services in their program philosophy and mission statement. They also identified the importance of staff members' attitudes to the success of inclusive leisure services and suggested that agencies provide training designed to encourage staffs' positive attitudes toward youth with disabilities participating in physical activity. These findings echo research reported by Verdonschot et al. (2009a) who found that constructive staff attitudes are positively correlated with community integration.

Research supports the conclusion that staff members play a key role in both facilitating and creating barriers to physical activity among people with disabilities. For example, Mahy et al. (2010) found that physical activity among people with disabilities is better facilitated when employees actively participate with them. They surmised from their research that practitioners should instruct staff members about the importance of physical activity and encourage them to be more physically active themselves.

Unfortunately, little research has been conducted on benefits of sport participation among people with disabilities (Murphy et al., 2008). One exception is a study of inclusive sports for adolescents with disabilities reported by Grandisson, Tetreault, and Freeman (2012). Their findings indicate that sports can increase social participation, promote health, and develop important skills for adolescents with disabilities and their families. Given these benefits, they recommended that municipalities "continue working on providing universal access to services, such as sports, by removing architectural and social barriers" (p. 227). More research is needed to understand the benefits that accrue for individuals with disabilities who participate in active sports.

Technology

Research has documented that technology can increase opportunities for people with disabilities to connect with their community and vice versa (Luckasson & Schalock, 2012; Wehmeyer et al., 2012). After a review of the literature, Wehmeyer et al. (2011) determined that use of technology can facilitate self-determination. Walser, Ayers, and Foote (2012) observed that some individuals with disabilities tend to have limited access to such digital technology. They also reported that video modeling was effective in encouraging individuals with intellectual disabilities to use cell phones.

RECOMMENDATIONS FOR RESEARCH AND THE RESEARCH PROCESS

Using a multiple case design study of 15 agencies providing inclusive services, Miller, Schleien, and Lausie (2009) concluded that while many agencies offer strictly segregated programs as an option for people with disabilities, the number of agencies adopting inclusive support practices is on the rise. Unfortunately, Miller et al. also recognized that ". . . there remains a paucity of good science, effective model building, and a comprehensive and coherent view of the inclusive recreation landscape" (p. 39).

Verdonshot et al. (2009b) concluded there is a need for more research to identify barriers and facilitators that guarantee the fundamental right of people with disabilities to experience leisure. Echoing this, Garcia-Villamisar and Dattilo (2010) recommend that researchers examine effects of leisure education programs on individuals with disabilities. A question arises as to how to conduct such research. The following are suggestions that may help to create and analyze contexts conducive for experiencing leisure by people with disabilities through the process of participatory action research and collaborative research teams.

There is a need for active involvement of people with disabilities in the research process. This will promote accessible and meaningful information (Garcia-Iriarte, Kramer, Kramer, & Hammel, 2009). Participatory action research is one way to examine issues associated with leisure participation among people with disabilities. According to Northway (2010), this approach to research involves an assurance to include participants, their families and friends, and community leisure providers in all aspects of research design, implementation, and analysis. Consequently, it is helpful to work to achieve representation of multiple viewpoints and to confirm participants' awareness of other perspectives and associated motives and how research can operate as a catalyst for change (McIntyre, 2008).

It is important for a research community to also engage in reflexivity to facilitate critical examination of how researchers interact and influence data related to beliefs about disabilities, information accessibility, and levels of participation and control (Garcia-Iriarte et al., 2008; Newton, Rothlingova, Gutteridge, LeMarchand, & Raphael, 2012). *Reflexivity* is the active acknowledgement of researchers that their actions and decisions impact meaning and context of the studied experience (Horsburgh, 2003).

CONCLUSION

The bad news is that research shows that people with disabilities continue to experience restrictions to their leisure because of negative attitudes and acts of discrimination. More research is needed on ways to reduce barriers, constraints, and overall restrictions to leisure that they experience. The good news is that there is some research that has begun to identify important considerations that help empower people with disabilities and their communities. Leisure service providers are in an excellent position to facilitate leisure for *all* community members. Research findings highlight the value of leisure education, self-determination, social support, physically active leisure, and technology to empower people with disabilities to experience leisure. Inclusive leisure services can be a major avenue for promoting inclusion and a sense of community. There is also agreement among educational experts that inclusion enhances social justice (Moberg, 2003).

Since participation in leisure can be argued to be a human right, it is helpful to set goals to have people with disabilities experience inclusive leisure. To achieve inclusion goals, we must strive to respect the inherent rights of people with disabilities and create networks that provide them with manageable challenges during their free time. There is value in researching how to create an environment that is conducive for people with disabilities to engage in leisure within their communities that brings them meaning, enjoyment, and, ultimately, satisfaction.

REFERENCES

Agate, J. R., Zabriskie, R. B., Agate, S. T., & Poff, R. (2009). Family leisure satisfaction and satisfaction with family life. *Journal of Leisure Research, 41*, 205–223.

Azaiza F., Croitoru T., Rimmerman A., & Naon D. (2012). Participation in leisure activities of Jewish and Arab adults with intellectual disabilities living in the community. *Journal of Leisure Research, 44*, 379–391.

Badia M., Orgaz M. B., Verdugo M. A., & Ullan A. M. (2013). Patterns and determinants of leisure participation of youth and adults with developmental disabilities. *Journal of Intellectual Disabilities Research, 54*, 319–332.

Batu, S. (2008). Caregiver-delivered home-based instruction using simultaneous prompting for teaching home skills to individuals with developmental disabilities. *Education and Training in Developmental Disabilities, 43*, 541–555.

Carter, E. W., Moss, C. K., Hoffman, A., Chung, Y., & Sisco, L. (2011). Efficacy and social validity of peer support arrangements for adolescents with disabilities. *Exceptional Children, 78*, 107–125.

Chang, L. (2011). An interaction effect of leisure self-determination and leisure competence on older adults' self-rated health. *Journal of Health Psychology, 17*, 324–332.

Cho, H., Wehmeyer, M. L., & Kingston, N. M. (2012). The effect of social and classroom ecological factors on promoting self-determination in elementary school. *Preventing School Failure, 56(1)*, 19–28.

Cohen-Gewerc, E., & Stebbins, R. A. (2007). *The pivotal role of leisure education: Finding personal fulfillment in this century*. State College, PA: Venture Publishing, Inc.

Dattilo, J. (2012). *Inclusive leisure services* (3rd ed.). State College, PA: Venture Publishing, Inc.

Dattilo, J. (2013). Inclusive leisure and individuals with intellectual disability. *Inclusion, 1*(1), 76–88.

Dattilo, J. (2015). *Leisure education program planning* (4th ed.). State College, PA: Venture Publishing, Inc.

Dattilo, J., & Rusch, F. (2012). Teaching problem solving to promote self-determined leisure engagement. *Therapeutic Recreation Journal, 46*, 91–105.

Dattilo, J., & Williams, R. (2012). Some thoughts about leisure education, therapeutic recreation, and the philosophy of Spider-Man. *Therapeutic Recreation Journal, 46*, 1–8.

Dodd, D. C. H., Zabriskie, R. B., Widmer, M. A., & Eggett, D. (2009). Contributions of family leisure to family functioning among families that include children with developmental disabilities. *Journal of Leisure Research, 41*, 261–286.

Duvdevany, I. (2008). Do persons with intellectual disabilities have a social life? The Israeli reality. *Salud Publica Mex, 50*, S222–S229.

Dyson, L. (2010). Unanticipated effects of children with learning disabilities on their families. *Learning Disabilities Quarterly, 33*, 43–55.

Edwards, C. C., & Da Fonte, A. (2012). Fostering successful partnerships with families of students with disabilities. *Teaching Exceptional Children, 44*(3), 6–13.

Eisenman, L. T., Tanverdi, A., Perrington, C., & Geiman, A. (2009). Secondary and postsecondary community activities for youth with significant intellectual disabilities. *Education and Training in Developmental Disabilities, 44*, 168–176.

Fesko, S. L., Hall, A. C., Quinlan, J., & Jockell, C. (2012). Active gaining for individuals with intellectual disabilities: Meaningful community participation through employment, retirement, service and volunteerism. *American Journal of Intellectual and Developmental Disabilities, 117*, 497–508.

Fredrickson, B. (2009). *Positivity: Top-notch research reveals the 3 to 1 ratio that will change your life*. New York: Crown Publishing.

Garcia-Iriarte, E., Kramer, J. C., Kramer, J. M., & Hammel, J. (2009). 'Who did what?': A participatory action research project to increase group capacity for advocacy. *Journal of Applied Research in Intellectual Disabilities, 22*, 10–22.

Garcia-Villamisar, D., & Dattilo, J. (2010). Effects of a leisure programme on quality of life and stress of individuals with ASD. *Journal of Intellectual Disabilities Research, 54*, 611–619.

Grandisson, M., Tetreault, S., & Freeman, A. R. (2012). Enabling integration in sports for adolescents with intellectual disabilities. *Journal of Applied Research in Intellectual Disabilities, 25*, 217–230.

Horsburgh, D. (2003). Evaluation of qualitative research. *Journal of Clinical Nursing, 12*, 307–312.

Jones M. M., & Goble Z. (2012). Creative effective mentoring partnerships for students with intellectual disabilities on campus. *Journal of Policy and Practice in Intellectual Disabilities, 9*, 270–278.

Kleiber, D. A. (2012). Taking leisure seriously: New and older considerations about leisure education. *World Leisure Journal, 54*, 5–15.

Lippold, T., & Burns, J. (2009). Social support and intellectual disabilities: A comparison between social networks and adults with intellectual disabilities and those with physical disabilities. *Journal of Intellectual Disabilities Research, 53*, 463–473.

Luckasson, R., & Schalock, R. L. (2012). Human functioning, supports, assistive technology, and evidence-based practices in the field of intellectual disabilities. *Journal of Special Education Technology, 27*(2), 3–10.

Mahy, J., Shields, N., Taylor, N. F., & Dodd, K. J. (2010). Identifying facilitators and barriers to physical activity for adults with Down syndrome. *Journal of Intellectual Disabilities Research, 54*, 795–805.

McGuire, J., & McDonnell, J. (2008). Relationships between recreation and levels of self-determination for adolescents and young adults with disabilities. *Career Development for Exceptional Individuals, 31*, 154–163.

McIntyre, A. (2008). *Participatory action research*. Los Angeles: Sage.

Meadan, H., Stoner, J. B., & Angell, M. E. (2009). Review of literature related to the social, emotional, and behavioral adjustment of siblings of individuals with autism spectrum disorder. *Journal of Developmental and Physical Disabilities, 22*, 83–100.

Miller, K. D., Schleien, S. J., & Lausier, J. (2009). Search for best practices in inclusive recreation: Programmatic findings. *Therapeutic Recreation Journal, 43*, 27–41.

Miller, K. D., Schleien, S. J., & Bowens, F. (2010). Support staff as a best practice in inclusive recreation services. *Therapeutic Recreation Journal, 44*, 35–50.

Moberg, S. (2003). Education for all in the North and South: Teacher's attitudes towards inclusive education in Finland and Zambia. *Education and Training in Developmental Disabilities, 38*, 417–428.

Murphy N. A., Carbone P. S., & the Council on Children with Disabilities. (2008). Promoting the participation of children with disabilities in sports, recreation and physical activities. *American Academy of Pediatrics, 121*, 1057–1061.

Newton, B. J., Rothlingova, Z., Gutteridge, R., LeMarchand, K., & Raphael, J. H. (2012). No room for reflexivity? Critical reflections following a systematic review of qualitative research. *Journal of Health Psychology, 17*, 866–885.

Northway, R. (2010). Participatory research. Part 1: Key features and underlying philosophy. *International Journal of Therapy and Rehabilitation, 17*, 174–179.

Novak Amado, A., Degrande, M., Boice, C., & Hutcheson, S. (2012). Accessible Congregations Campaign: Follow-up survey of impact on individuals with intellectual/developmental disabilities (ID/DD). *Journal of Religion, Disabilities, & Health, 16*, 394–419.

Oates A., Bebbington A., Bourke J., Girdler S., & Leonard, H. (2011). Leisure participation for school-aged children with Down syndrome. *Disabilities and Rehabilitation, 33*, 1880–1889.

Pivik, J., McComas, J., & LaFlamme, M. (2002). Barriers and facilitators to inclusive education. *Exceptional Children, 69*, 97–107.

Resch, J. A., Mireles, G., Benz, M. R., Grenwelge, C., Peterson, R., & Zhang, D. (2010). Giving parents a voice: A qualitative study of the challenges experienced by parents of children with disabilities. *Rehabilitation Psychology, 55*, 139–150.

Rimmer, J. H., Wang, E., Yamaki, K., & Davis, B. (2010). Documenting disparities in obesity and disabilities. *FOCUS Technical Brief Number 24*. Austin, TX: SEDL.

Ryndak, D. L., Ward, T., Alper, S., Storch, J. F., & Montgomery, J. W. (2010). Long-term outcomes of services in inclusive and self-contained settings for siblings with comparable significant disabilities. *Education and Training in Autism and Developmental Disabilities, 45*, 38–53.

Schalock, R. L., Verdugo, M. A., & Gomez, L. E. (2011). Evidence-based practices in the field of intellectual and developmental disabilities: An international consensus approach. *Evaluation and Program Planning, 34*, 274–282.

Smart, J. (2009). Disability, society, and the individual (2nd ed.) Austin, TX: Pro-Ed.

Smith, T. L., Polloway, E. A., Smith, J. D., & Patton, J. R. (2007). Self-determination for persons with developmental disabilities: Ethical considerations for instructors. *Education and Training in Developmental Disabilities, 42*, 144–151.

Solish, A., Perry, A., & Minnes, P. (2010). Participation of children with and without disabilities in social, recreational and leisure activities. *Journal of Applied Research in Intellectual Disabilities, 23*, 226–236.

Stebbins, R. A. (2008). *Serious leisure: A perspective for our time*. New Brunswick, NJ: Transaction Publishers.

Taylor, J., & Yun, J. (2012). Factors influencing staff inclusion of youth with disabilities in after-school programs. *Therapeutic Recreation Journal, 46*, 301–325.

Tullis, C. A., Cannella-Malone, H. I., Basbigill, A. R., Yeager, A., Fleming, C. V., Payne, D., & Wu, P. (2011). Review of the choice and preference assessment literature for individuals with severe to profound disabilities. *Education and Training in Autism and Developmental Disabilities, 46*, 576–592.

United Nations. (1948). *The universal declaration of human rights.* Available at: http://www.un.org/

United Nations (2006). Convention of the rights of persons with disabilities. Retrieved from http://www.un.org/disabilities/convention/conventionfull.shtml

Verdonschot, M. M. L., Witte, L. P., Reichrath E., Buntinx, W. H. E., & Curfs, L. M. G. (2009a). Impact of environmental factors on community participation of persons with an intellectual disability: A systematic review. *Journal of Intellectual Disabilities Research, 53*, 54–64.

Verdonschot, M. M. L., Witte, L. P., Reichrath, E., Buntinx, W. H. E., & Curfs, L. M. G. (2009b). Community participation of people with an intellectual disabilities: A review of empirical findings. *Journal of Intellectual Disabilities Research, 53*, 303–318.

Walmsley J., & Mannan H. (2009). Parents as co-researchers: a participatory action research initiative involving parents of people with intellectual disabilities in Ireland. *British Journal of Learning Disabilities, 37*, 271–276.

Walser, K., Ayres, K., & Foote, E. (2012). Effects of a video model to tech students with moderate intellectual disabilities to use key features of an iphone. *Education and Training in Autism and Developmental Disabilities, 47*, 319–331.

Wehmeyer, M. L., Palmer, S. B., Williams-Diehm, K., Shogren, K. A., Davies, D. K., & Stock, S. (2011). Technology and self-determination in transition planning: the impact of technology use in transition planning on student self-determination. *Journal of Special Education Technology, 26*, 13–24.

Wehmeyer, M. L., Tassé, M. J., Davies, D. K., & Stock, S. (2012). Support needs of adults with intellectual disabilities across disabilities: The role of technology. *Journal of Special Education Technology, 27*(2), 11–22.

Worcester, J. A., Nesman, T. M., Raffaele-Mendez, L. M., & Keller, H. R. (2008). Giving voice to parents of young children with challenging behaviors. *Exceptional Children, 74*, 509–525.

Wuang, Y., & Su, C., (2012). Patterns of participation and enjoyment in adolescents with Down syndrome. *Research in Developmental Disabilities, 33*, 841–848.

27

How Does Leisure Studies Respond to the Needs and Requests of Indigenous People?

Karen M. Fox (University of Alberta)

I moved to Alberta the same year that *Dead Dog Café Comedy Hour* began on Canadian Broadcasting Corporation Radio. Despite its name, the show was only 15 minutes of politically rich, dark humor by three Indigenous actors intermixing political and social critique, the mocking of cultural stereotypes, and irreverent comedy. The show borrowed numerous elements from the award-winning novelist Thomas King. King, of Cherokee, Greek, and German-American descent, played himself on the show. One of my favorite sketches was *Ask Tonto*:

> because you can't expect unbiased answers from a White guy riding around in a black mask shooting people with silver bullets...and don't forget the Lone Ranger is an American who has been making the world safe for democracy and multi-national corporations; whereas Tonto is a Mohawk from Six Nations. (1997 Season)

I was reminded of this show as I reviewed the literature on leisure[1*] and Indigenous peoples[2]. Most of this research occurred as responses by predominantly non-Indigenous[3] leisure scholars (of whom I am one) to requests or perceived urgent needs for "solutions or programs" in Indigenous communities. Time would expose these well-intentioned efforts to being typically contrary to traditional Indigenous values and self-determination as well as divorced from the political realities of Indigenous treaties, governance, and land-claims.

For example, the *Journal of Applied Recreation Research* (now *Leisure/Loisir*) published a special issue on "Recreation and First Nation Communities" in 1993. Four articles were by non-Indigenous scholars, whereas only two were by Mohawk recreation professionals documenting how Indigenous communities preserved traditional values through Aboriginal-based recreation programming. Since then, other scholars have addressed Indigenous peoples from particular leisure lenses (i.e., tourism, sports, health, or recreation) in major North American leisure journals. Additionally, there have been several extensive reviews summarizing the research about leisure and Indigenous peoples (e.g., Fox, McAvoy, Wang, & Henhawk, 2014; McDonald & McAvoy, 1997); however, these have predominantly focused on non-Indigenous-authored, English-language articles published in North America. The three main areas of leisure scholarship that address, or include the concerns of, Indigenous peoples are: community recreation and physical activity (including urban leisure), natural areas and outdoor recreation/education, and tourism. Each of these will be described, key articles will be identified, and how Indigenous worldviews, land-based knowledge, and self-determination have been included or ignored will be discussed.

Community Recreation and Physical Activity

Community recreation and physical activity research has been connected to Indigenous community and individual health since the previously-mentioned special issue of the *Journal of Applied Recreation Research*. Common underlying assumptions in this research include activity as a central focus, competition and volunteerism as culturally neutral, and recreation leads to positive benefits. Paraschak's (1995) historical research provided one of the few political analyses of how Canadian sport and recreation associations, programming, and governmental policies prescribed social and healthy behaviors irrespective of, if not harmful to, traditional Indigenous practices and beliefs. The bulk of this research was, and is, typically structured around resolving a problem or "deficiency" such as: (a) reducing crime, delinquency, truancy, or disease (e.g., Fox, Ryan, van Dyck, Chivers, Chuchmach, & Quesnel, 1998),

* Footnotes for this chapter are located on page 241.

(b) exploring tensions between Indigenous and non-Indigenous approaches (e.g., Rousell & Giles, 2012), or (c) documenting specific programs (e.g., Rose & Giles, 2007). Recent trends in this area have included: (a) building cases for more Indigenous voices and culturally sensitive models (e.g., Iwasaki, Bartlett, Gottlieb, & Hall, 2009); (b) documenting Aboriginal athletes and their stories (e.g., Forsyth, 2002) or Indigenous games (e.g., Forsyth & Wamsley, 2006); and (c) helping Indigenous peoples adapt to non-Indigenous sport (e.g., Schinke et al., 2010).

Absent from most scholarly discussions is the large population of Indigenous people who live in urban areas. This gap belies an image of reservations and tribal lands created as "Native spaces" and the lands in between as "empty" and thus available for settlement (Baloy, 2011). In point of fact, urban areas are located on lands that were *originally* home to Indigenous peoples. The leisure literature has followed this pattern and said little about leisure practices of urban Indigenous peoples. The existing research either focuses on recreation as a way to correct criminal behavior or address deficiencies such as poor health or addiction, or arts-based qualitative research, such as Lashua and Fox (2006). Expressive arts, whether Aboriginal hip-hop or traditional dance, storytelling, popular culture, and crafts, replicate and reimagine various Indigenous histories of the city and alternative performances for inhabiting and cohabiting urban spaces (Buffam, 2009). Given the increasing urban Indigenous populations in North America and worldwide, as well as the political and economic tensions surrounding the resources to support them, this area deserves far more attention.

Natural Areas and Outdoor Recreation/Education

Although the establishment of national parks and outdoor recreation areas are located on traditional Indigenous lands, the history of parks and outdoor recreation is based upon the erasure of, and negative effects upon, Indigenous peoples (Callier, 2012). The first serious leisure research about and with Indigenous people began in the 1990s, primarily in the areas of park management. This research still privileged non-Indigenous frameworks of management, conservation, and ecology, with some discussion of the tension between the different paradigms (e.g., Simpson, 2004). Eagles' (2009) assessment of government models highlighted the lack of attention to Indigenous historical struggles. The Aboriginal governmental model, as viewed by settlers, was elite, self-centered, and lacked openness to broad consultation. However, this analysis left invisible generations of broken treaties, exclusion by federal and provincial governments, and rejection of Indigenous needs and rights.

McAvoy, McDonald, and Carlson (2003) and McAvoy, Shirilla, and Flood (2004) provided the foundational work on differences between Indigenous and non-Indigenous peoples' views of parks and natural areas. This research also highlighted the tension between the two groups' perspectives on outdoor recreation management; even though non-Indigenous practices are designed to protect and sustain natural areas, they are often contrary to relational practices based on traditional Indigenous knowledge.

Few pieces have considered the debt outdoor recreation[4] owes to Indigenous practices—from the "quintessential Canadian icon," the canoe, which was endemic to Indigenous culture in North America (Raffan, 1999), to the kayak of the Inuit, Yup'ik, and Aleut (Walls, 2012), to locales of outdoor recreation. Recent critical scholarship highlighted the difference between Indigenous and non-Indigenous approaches to outdoor recreation. Lowan (2009) interviewed Aboriginal students in an Outward Bound (OB) program. The OB fundamental assumptions of a "hostile wilderness" that required team building activities and human stewardship were contrary to "wilderness" as home to be entered through ceremony and elder guidance. The curriculum of OB unintentionally overruled Indigenous worldviews and practices.

Tourism

The initial support for tourism as sustainable, ecologically sound, and culturally respectful was naïve, idealistic, and optimistic (McLaren, 1999) given current critiques and Indigenous political movements. The original conception of "Indigenous tourism" was defined as any activity "in which indigenous people are directly involved either through control and/or by having their culture serve as the essence of the attraction" (Butler & Hinch, 1996, p. 4). Butler and Hinch (2007) revisited the discussion and complicated Indigenous tourism with layers of political, cultural, environmental and economic concerns. However, they also stated: "Western-based economic rationale remains the primary motivation for engaging in the business of indigenous tourism" (p. 3). The neo-liberal policies (that emphasize privatization, individualism, decreased public expenditure, prioritization of profit over collective good and social, ecological and spiritual values) underpinning most of the work in this area have rarely been questioned. Furthermore, non-Indigenous tourism scholarship has paid little attention to successful American Indian tourism initiatives (Wiedman, 2010), such as the Miccosukee and Seminole examples that have spanned a century.

Summary

To date, research in these three main areas has paid scant attention to: (a) Indigenous scholarship by Indigenous authors generally, (b) critiques of non-Indigenous research and frameworks relevant to Indigenous peoples, and/or (c) integration of Indigenous worldviews and research methods into leisure research. These trends are of particular concern given that leisure-relevant research conducted by Indigenous scholars and published in Indigenous-focused journals does exist. Additionally, to date no substantive survey of the literature that addresses leisure and Indigenous people worldwide has been undertaken.

YOU CAN'T EXPECT UNBIASED ANSWERS FROM A WHITE GUY

Leisure research is framed in a non-Indigenous paradigm that presumes humans are separate from and superior to other living entities and natural forces. Consequently, knowledge that divides entities, natural forces, and processes into separate parts to be analyzed is valued, as is expertise, control, and predictability. This differs from Indigenous worldviews of humans as part of the cosmos or even as "younger siblings" to animals and plants. Knowledge, in this case, is holistic, and entities, natural forces, and processes are to be respected and nourished. The dominance and power of settler views undermine the relationship Indigenous peoples have with each other and the world.

Paradigms shape what counts as knowledge, what can be seen and experienced; it is not clear how well humans can understand across these differences. There are practical and survival necessities for Indigenous people to "walk in two worlds," or adopt *Etuaptmunk* the Mi'kmaw word meaning "two-eyed seeing" (Marshall, 2004). They must also find creative ways to redefine notions of identity and community by manifesting Indigenous culture through a globalized, high-tech world (Martinez, 2013).

In a complex and global world, it is time settlers master walking in multiple worlds as well. The loss of Indigenous ways of knowing and being in the world not only affects Indigenous peoples, but non-Indigenous people through the loss of wisdom relevant to being in the world differently. Recent empirical research has verified ancient Indigenous knowledge about the brain's ability to heal the body (Rankin, 2013), and confirmed traditional Indigenous knowledge about animal behavior, navigating skills, and ecological changes (Finney, 1994).

This is not to romanticize "an" Indigenous identity or worldview. Rather, it is to think carefully about how Indigenous peoples strive to stay interrelated within particular spaces and how diversity may be crucial for addressing global problems. This can be contrasted with non-Indigenous strategies that structure space—and the entities within them—as objects to be used in service of human desires. These different spatial practices (Lefebvre, 1991) have led to alternative understandings and ethics about being in the world. As Alfred (2009) noted, many Indigenous peoples have a nagging sense that something is wrong with the "supposed solutions" of the modern world. They have a sinking feeling that the time, effort, and resources invested into political and economic ventures within non-Indigenous systems will not liberate them from their present realities. Therefore, leisure itself cannot be seen as separate from non-Indigenous paradigms that lead to the destruction of Indigenous lands, rights, and ways of life. How Indigenous ways of knowing and being in the world could inform leisure studies is described in detail in the remainder of this chapter.

WHEREAS TONTO IS A MOHAWK FROM SIX NATIONS

As I reflect on scholarship emerging from Indigenous scholars and practitioners, I am convinced that we begin with listening carefully to Indigenous words and insights, forming collaborative relationships while accounting for the inability to measure and rectify the difference in power and privileges between Indigenous peoples and settlers. This listening sustains a scholarship that requires change and transformation from non-Indigenous leisure scholars and practitioners. Profound listening calls for engaging with Indigenous languages. As Davis (2009) argued, language is:

> a flash of the human spirit. It's a vehicle through which the soul of each particular culture comes into the material world. Every language is an old-growth forest of the mind, a watershed, a thought, an ecosystem of spiritual possibilities. (p. 3)

Some familiarity if not fluency with specific Indigenous languages will be necessary for leisure scholarship in the future. Based on the above, five related steps are proposed.

Step 1: Deep Listening, Attending, and Responding

Corntassel (2012), from the Cherokee Nation, stated: "Being Indigenous today means struggling to reclaim and regenerate one's relational, place-based [both land- and ocean-based] existence by challenging the ongoing, destructive forces of colonization" (p. 88). This approach is different from or in addition to a cognitive, rational framework; it involves spatial practices that are lived daily so the world is experienced in a particular way. Deeply, profoundly listening, attending, and responding to the struggles, visceral realities and desires of how Indigenous peoples address today's world lay a foundation for seeing them not as ideological or fictionalized ideals but on their own terms (King, 2012).

Listening leads to actively challenging "colonialism" because of its ongoing detriment to Indigenous peoples.

Tuck, a member of the Aleut Tribal Government of St. Paul Island, Alaska, described three forms of colonialism: (a) external processes where Indigenous plants, animals, human beings, and knowledge are extracted and transported by others for use and profit in their world; (b) internal processes of using particularized modes of control (e.g., prisons, schools, policing) to ensure the ascendancy of a non-Indigenous nation and its elite; and (c) settler processes where people come to a land to stay, forcibly displace original inhabitants, and use the land, plants, and original people and knowledge for their own benefit (Tuck & Yang, 2012). All three forms of colonialism are woven throughout leisure scholarship and practice—historically and currently; examples include: (a) the use of Indigenous ceremonies, crafts, and other products to support settler recreation or commercial exploitation of Indigenous spiritual traditions (Aldred, 2000); (b) the design of recreation programs to "rehabilitate" Indigenous peoples; and (c) the appropriation, designation, and use of Indigenous lands for national parks, summer camps, and recreation areas.

"Decolonizing" processes focus on the return of Indigenous land and life. Decolonizing is different from the concept of "social justice" (Walker, 2004). The elements of social justice (e.g., treaties, reconciliation) belong to non-Indigenous systems and are associated with laws and legal structures that sanctioned the illegal taking of Indigenous lands and the attempted annihilation of Indigenous peoples' ways of knowing and being. Decolonizing processes allow for the resurgence of traditional Indigenous ways of knowing and being by defending Indigenous peoples' heritages and existence and questioning the assumptions and practices of settler societies (Alfred, 2009).

Alfred (2009), who resonates with many young Indigenous scholars, activists, and leaders, described the task of today's "warrior" as a: "journey of making meaningful change in lives and to transform society by recreating Onkwehonwe [Mohawk meaning "original people"] existence, regenerating Onkwehonwe cultures, and surging against the forces that keep Onkwehonwe bound to Onkwehonwe colonial past" (p. 19). It is not a call to a "mythical past," a rejection of the modern world, or to war. It is the resurgence of Onkwehonwe practices that can help Indigenous peoples (and I would suggest non-Indigenous peoples as well) live a sustainable life and nourish relationships with all living beings and forces.

Step 2: Accountability by Non-Indigenous Leisure Scholars

The history and practice of non-Indigenous leisure and recreation, especially for nations involved in exploring and developing trade routes and colonizing new lands, has focused almost exclusively on the positive benefits for and by settlers. This focus has obscured the harms and costs born by Indigenous peoples. Although the experience and history of Indigenous peoples is central to world history, it has predominantly been written by non-Indigenous people fascinated with the "imagined" Indigenous person of the past and grounded in written records crafted by settlers in the service of political and economic self-interests (Chaat Smith, 2009). For example, although there were some 125,000 pages of Hawaiian language newspapers documenting the Kanaka Maoli (i.e., Native Hawaiian) daily life between 1834 and 1948, most settlers saw no need to access these original documents or learn the Hawaiian language (Nogelmeier, 2010). Across North America, First Nations, Métis, Inuit and American Indian wayfaring skills were used to develop trade routes as they themselves were removed from lands and erased from historical records so settlers could build homesteads and towns. Likewise, mainstream naturalist and park policies revolved around "terra nullius" (i.e., "land belonging to no one"), and territories traditionally occupied by First Nations and American Indians were appropriated as national parks (Cook-Lynn, 1996).

The move to see commonalities between Indigenous and non-Indigenous worldviews is often at the expense of recognizing the significant differences essential to the well-being and survival of Indigenous peoples. This may also undermine the decolonizing processes while leaving non-Indigenous people comfortable with existing behaviors of exclusion and inequality (Simpson, 2004; Tuck & Yang, 2012). Decolonizing requires collaboration, accountability, and restitution for harms *already* committed. Specifically, decolonizing may lead to reassessing conservation frameworks, food harvesting in national parks, or the creation of recreation programs that support Indigenous-led goals and values.

Step 3: Rethinking Indigenous Culture and Everyday Life

Although I, and others, have theorized "leisures" (Fox & Klaiber, 2006) as a pluralistic concept, I am persuaded by Henhawk (2012), a Haudenosaunee scholar from Six Nations of the Grand River reserve, and Meyer, (2004), a Kanaka Maoli scholar, that "leisure" or "leisures" might not apply to Indigenous peoples. Given the lack of scholarly research and discussion around this question and the problematic nature of settler research for Indigenous peoples, I suggest future research, at a minimum, needs to: (a) honor Indigenous methodologies, worldviews, and collaborative processes, (b) use more original language resources, and (c) employ decolonizing frameworks.

The use of leisure across cultural differences is problematic. Leisure is an abstract category that presumes paradigmatic assumptions about space and time, the individual and community, and relationships between humans and non-humans. In many Indigenous worldviews these assumptions begin in different embodied relationships with local ecological and ethnocultural systems. Early anthropological research by Culin (1903) on American Indian games hinted that his descriptions were abstracted from such patterns, but he never completed this work. The *pachitle* (or "potlatch" ceremony) of the Pacific Northwest First Nations and the *Makahiki* (four-month celebration of the rainy season and distribution of harvest) season of the Kanaka Maoli also highlight the complexity and interconnection of games, dance, ceremony, economics, politics, celebrations, spiritual, and natural spaces. These examples underscore ways of being and knowing that differ from the emphasis on the rational, logical, and dualistic leisure concept. Leisure, as currently defined, obscures the interrelatedness of Indigenous practices as well as the people from the lands, oceans, waters, community, cultural practices, and spirits.

A key initiative among Indigenous peoples is revitalizing their languages. Languages shape the way people interact with the world, how they think, perceive, and communicate. English is a language that favors nouns, where many Indigenous languages highlight verbs or processes. These differences are not, necessarily, inherent in the language but a function of alliances of political, philosophical, and economic regimes (Coleman et al., 2012). Very few Indigenous languages have words or a worldview that can be connected with leisure as an object or thing to be manipulated, measured, produced, or consumed (i.e., free choice, free time, or state of mind).

North American missionaries did translate the Hawaiian phrase *manawa walea* with the English word leisure (Schütz, 1994), which in the 1800s was related to idleness and sinfulness. Literally, *manawa walea* means "lying in a shallow lagoon with water flowing over you while relaxing" (according to my translation). The literal connotations suggest an embodied, sensuous relationship with one's cosmos (including animals and natural forces) as well as mind-body-spirit. This sharply contrasts with a non-Indigenous sensibility of leisure grounded in a liberal humanist interpretation of the self as disembodied, rational, liberated, and autonomous.

Beginning with the attributes of the Hawaiian language (i.e., multiple and hidden meanings, supporting word play, and, valuing specific references to natural entities and local places), the reduction of the literal translation to leisure is curious. *Manawa* refers to time as "the ebb and flow of water in a lagoon" or space-time. *Wale* refers to the sap that binds the plant material and bark to make tapa (bark cloth) for clothing. The hints within the literal translation suggest *manawa walea* was part of a complete cycle or ebb and flow of life, where various elements of life and society (humans and non-humans) are co-mingled. Although we have no definitive evidence at this time, it is interesting to contemplate what activities would fit or would be structured under *manawa walea* as a category.

Step 4: Re-evaluating the Effect of Non-Indigenous Decisions on Indigenous Peoples' Lives

Non-Indigenous political, economical, cultural, and religious forces circumscribe all aspects of Indigenous lives including education, health, governance, burial of their bones, control of their historical sites and lands, and adoption of their children. Within non-Indigenous legal structures and programs, Indigenous people receive less for health and education than their non-Indigenous counterparts, are more likely to live in poverty, watch their lands being destroyed by corporations or in the service of other peoples' desires, and are denied access to the basic necessities of life (Jones, 2006). Programs designed to "bring them into the modern world" are predominantly designed to "integrate" or "assimilate" traditional cultures and practices without regard for the costs to traditional practices, their lands, or the larger ecosystems that support traditional Indigenous practices.

On average, leisure scholarship and practice has been mostly silent about how mainstream leisure and its resource needs negatively impact Indigenous peoples. Because leisure pursuits and activities combined are one of the largest economic sectors, the demands on goods and resources are substantial (Ben-Shabat, Moriarty, Chandra, & Sojkowska, 2012). These include everything from transportation for pleasure, entertainment, specialized gear and clothing, infrastructure to meet specific requirements, skilled professionals and guides, as well as service people. Leisure is not directly connected, but it is not unconnected, to the controversy over the oilsands in Canada and associated pipelines. These interconnections are painfully clear to Indigenous peoples. The effects of the oilsands continue to emerge: heavy metals in river systems near First Nation communities threaten fish and water habitat, higher rates of cancer occur in nearby First Nations communities, and reclamation plans are questionable for returning natural habitat for hunting and gathering (Parajulee & Wania, 2014). Their lands are being seized or damaged to provide the resources that partially go to make leisure equipment, fuel leisure vehicles, or create leisure spaces. If non-Indigenous leisure is truly relevant for Indigenous peoples, serious consideration must be given to how leisure is more than an activity or a segregated human sphere, and can address the fundamental needs and challenges facing Indigenous peoples.

Tourism is a globalizing force of capitalism and commodification of cultures, practices, and experiences. Alfred

(2009) and Corntassel (2012) suggested that decolonizing must occur in everyday acts of resurgence that disrupt the colonial physical, social, and political boundaries designed to impede actions to restore nationhood. Such a response in tourism might be "Indigenous tourism" as described by Native Alaskan Bunten (2010) along with Nelson Graburn (2009) as "any service or product that is (a) owned and operated at least in part by an Indigenous group and (b) results from a means of exchange with outside guests" (p. 3). Indigenous tourism attempts to negotiate the crosscurrents of global neo-liberal forces and Indigenous values to provide prosperity and stability for Indigenous communities. The pathways to Indigenous tourism begin with cultural perpetuation as part of a strategy to employ identity politics to retain or reclaim history, control representation, land rights, and political sovereignty. In addition, Indigenous tourism involves social and cultural issues, potential for increased political power, and the possibility of widened future options as well as material expansion, and increased income and employment (Bunten, 2010).

Step 5: Begin with Indigenous Perspectives and Support Indigenous Leisure Scholars and Practitioners.

Most current research and support have been focused on dominant non-Indigenous leisure and delivery systems (Fox et al., 2014; Lashua & Fox, 2006). This focus obscures the diversity and innovation occurring within Indigenous communities and emerging from their dreams for their children. Although there are growing numbers of Indigenous scholars in some areas of the world, their presence within the ranks of leisure scholars is woefully few. This is somewhat understandable given our small field and the few universities that support doctoral programs. On the other hand, Indigenous people consistently bear the burden of "walking in two worlds" and adjusting to settler systems. In North America, the legacy of residential schools and the objectification and harm done by research haunts all Indigenous peoples. Māori scholar Smith's (1999) pivotal work on decolonizing methodology graphically describes the harm of research as "the dirtiest words in the indigenous world's vocabulary," "implicated in the worst excesses of colonialism," and "offends our sense of who and what we are" (p. 1).

Maybe a starting point is to listen carefully to the experiences of Indigenous people in leisure programs. Henhawk's (2013) *My Critical Awakening* described the intersection of personal experience, ongoing colonial effects, and the struggles of decolonizing while pursuing a graduate degree in leisure studies. Western leisure and recreation provides "calm eddies" for Indigenous people as well as undercurrents of harm and discrimination that affect health and well-being. Even as scholarship seeks multiple perspectives, it often places the burden of accommodation on Indigenous peoples rather than require changes within dominant society.

Lowan-Trudeau's (2013) discussion of a métissage approach opens space for non-Indigenous researchers and practitioners. To avoid exploitation of Indigenous peoples, non-Indigenous people must begin with self-decolonizing processes, developing collaborative and reciprocal relationships among other strategies for working across power differentials and within problematic and oppressive systems. Indigenous people can engage with education and research when these become acts of honoring multiple ways of knowing, questioning, searching for answers, creating knowledge, and voicing counter-stories. It is *as important* for non-Indigenous people to embark on decolonizing journeys and rethink the assumptions of leisure if it is to be a mutual and reciprocal relationship and journey.

There has been little research or focus on how non-Indigenous scholars, professionals and systems need to change, to employ decolonizing processes that will support Indigenous peoples and their journeys of decolonizing, self-expression, and self-determination. Even when Indigenous peoples successfully negotiate settler educational or recreational systems, they leave because they find the atmosphere hostile to their values and well-being, or they seek to establish Indigenous systems (Kahakalau, 2003). From a professional and practice level, the need for significant Indigenous voices is crucial if: (a) non-Indigenous leisure programs are, in fact, to be relevant beyond certain settler groups and practices, and (b) non-Indigenous leisure is to benefit from Indigenous insights and wisdom.

CONCLUSION

The *Dead Dog Café* always ended with Gracie, Jasper, and Tom signing off with "Stay calm, be brave, and wait for the signs." In one episode, Tom asked Jasper: "What is that supposed to mean?"

> Jasper: Boy, it would be hard to translate into English.
>
> Tom: It is in English.
>
> Jasper: No, that is the translation.

This exchange captures the experience of communication for Indigenous people with non-Indigenous people. The translation across paradigms is still not necessarily heard nor understood. So much of the non-Indigenous approach to Indigenous people is grounded in settler worldviews about goals, objectives, changing the world to meet settler needs and ideas, or an imagined, constructed image of "the Native." These flawed presuppositions have not turned out well for

Indigenous peoples (and maybe not even for settlers). If I understand the emerging Indigenous literature correctly, it is a call for different strategies that do, indeed, challenge the status quo, chart new pathways, and re-sing or re-chant traditional songs in today's world. The role for non-Indigenous leisure scholars and practitioners may be to understand the world as, in the words of Bringhurst (2007), a Canadian poet and recorder of Haida myths, "everywhere being is dancing." The questions for non-Indigenous leisure are: How does leisure address Indigenous needs? Is leisure relevant to the political, economical, and spiritual needs of Indigenous peoples? And, ultimately, can leisure sing and dance with Indigenous peoples and the world?

REFERENCES

Aldred, L. (2000). Plastic shamans and astroturf Sun Dances. *American Indian Quarterly, 24*(3), 329–354.

Alfred, T. (2009). *Wasáse: Indigenous pathways of action and freedom*. Toronto, ON: University of Toronto Press.

Baloy, N. J. K. (2011). "We can't feel our language": Making places in the city for Aboriginal language revitalization. *The American Indian Quarterly, 35*(4), 515–548.

Ben-Shabat, H., Moriarty, M., Chandra, V., & Sojkowska, E. (2012). *Consumer wealth and spending: The $12 trillion opportunity*. Calgary, AB: A.T. Kearny.

Bringhurst, R. (2007). *Everywhere being is dancing: Twenty pieces of thinking*. Berkeley, CA: Counterpoint Press.

Buffam, B. (2009). Can't hold us back! Hip-hop and the racial motility of Aboriginal bodies in urban spaces. *Social Identities, 17*(3), 337–350.

Bunten, A. C. (2010). More like ourselves: Indigenous capitalism through tourism. *American Indian Quarterly, 34*(3), 285–311.

Bunten, A. C., & Graburn, N. (2009). Current themes in Indigenous tourism. *London Journal of Tourism, Sport and Creative Industries, 2*(1), 3.

Butler, R., & Hinch, T. (1996). Indigenous Tourism: A Common Ground for Discussion. In R. Butler and T. Hinch (Eds.), *Tourism and Indigenous peoples* (pp. 3–19). London: International Thomson Business Press.

Butler, R., & Hinch, T. (2007). *Tourism and Indigenous peoples: Issues and implications*. Boston, MA: Elsevier/Butterworth-Heinemann.

Callier, D. M. (2012). But where were they? Race, Era(c)sure, and the imaginary American west. *Cultural Studies <=> Critical Methodologies, 12*(6), 502–505.

Chaat Smith, Paul. (2009). *Everything you know about Indians is wrong*. Minneapolis, MN: University of Minnesota Press.

Coleman, D., Battiste, M., Henderson, S., Findlay, I. M., & Findlay, L. (2012). Different knowings and the Indigenous humanities. *English Studies in Canada, 38*(1), 141–159.

Cook-Lynn, E. (1996). *Why I can't read Wallace Stegner and other essays*. Madison WI: The University of Wisconsin Press.

Corntassel, J. (2012). Re-envisioning resurgence: Indigenous pathways to decolonization and sustainable self-determination. *Decolonization: Indigeneity, Education & Society, 1*(1), 86–101.

Culin, S. (1903). American Indian games. American Anthropologist. n.s., 5, 58-64. Reprinted in E. M. Avedon & B. Sutton-Smith (Eds.). (1971). *The study of games*. (103–108). New York: John Wiley & Sons, Inc.

Davis, W. (2009). *The wayfinders: Why ancient wisdom matters in the modern world*. Toronto, ON: House of Anansi Press Inc.

Eagles, P. F. J. (2009). Governance of recreation and tourism partnerships in parks and protected areas. *Journal of Sustainable Tourism, 17*(2), 213–248.

Finney, B. (1994). *Voyage of discovery: A cultural odyssey through Polynesia*. Berkeley, CA: University of California Press.

Fixico, D. (2003). *The American Indian mind in a linear world: American Indian Studies and traditional knowledge*. New York: Routledge.

Forsyth, J. (2002). "Strong, proud, and true"—the 2002 North American Indigenous Games. *FastForward, 9*(1), 10–13.

Forsyth, J., & Wamsley, K. B. (2006). 'Native to native . . . we'll recapture our spirits': The world indigenous nations games and North American indigenous games as cultural resistance. *International Journal of the History of Sport, 23*(2), 294–315.

Fox, K.M., Ryan, S., van Dyck, J., Chivers, B., Chuchmach, L., & Quesnel, S. (1998). Cultural perspectives, resilient Aboriginal communities and recreation. *Journal of Applied Recreation Research, 23*(2), 147–192.

Fox, K., & Klaiber, E. (2006). Listening for a leisure remix. *Leisure Sciences, 28*(5), 411–430.

Fox, K., McAvoy, L., Wang, X., & Henhawk, D. A. (2014). Leisure among Alaskan Natives, American Indians, First Nations, Inuit, Métis, Native Hawaiians, and other Pacific Islanders. In M. Stodolska, K. J. Shinew, M. F. Floyd, & G. J. Walker (Eds.), *Race, ethnicity, and leisure: Perspectives on research, theory, and practice* (pp. 111–128). Champaign, IL: Human Kinetics.

Henhawk, D. (2013). My critical awakening: A process of struggles and decolonizing hope. *International Review of Qualitative Research, 6*(4), 510–525.

Iwasaki, Y., Bartlett, J. G., Gottlieb, B., & Hall, D. (2009). Leisure-like pursuits as an expression of Aboriginal cultural strengths and living actions. *Leisure Sciences, 31*(2), 158–173.

Jones, D. S. (2006). The persistence of American Indian health disparities. *American Journal of Public Health, 96*, 2122–2134.

Kahakalau, K. (2003). *Kanu o ka 'āina—Natives of the land generations back: A pedagogy of Hawaiian liberation*. Unpublished doctoral thesis. Union Institute.

King, T. (2012). *The Inconvenient Indian: A curious account of Native People in North America*. Toronto, ON: Doubleday Canada.

Lashua, B. D., & Fox, K. M. (2006). Rec needs a new rhythm cuz rap is where we're livin'. *Leisure Sciences, 28*(3), 267–283.

Lefebvre, H. (1991). *The production of space*. Trans. Donald Nicholson-Smith. Oxford, UK: Blackwell.

Lowan, G. (2009). Exploring place from an Aboriginal perspective: Considerations for outdoor and environmental education. *Canadian Journal of Environmental Education, 14*, 42–58.

Lowan-Trudeau, G. (2013). Methodological Métissage: An interpretive Indigenous approach to environmental education research. *Canadian Journal of Environmental Education, 17*, 113–130.

Marshall, A. (2004). Two-eyed seeing. Retrieved from http://www.integrativescience.ca/Principles/TwoEyedSeeing/

Martinez, D. (2013). From off the rez to off the hook! Douglas Miles and Apache Skateboards. *The American Indian Quarterly, 37*(4), 370–394.

Mason, C. W. (2009). The Buffalo Nations/Luxton Museum: Tourism, regional forces and problematising cultural representations of Aboriginal peoples in Banff, Canada. *International Journal of Heritage Studies, 15*(4), 355–373.

McAvoy, L., McDonald, D., & Carlson, M. (2003). American Indian/First Nation place attachment to park lands: The case of the Nuu-chah-nulth of British Columbia. *Journal of Park and Recreation Administration, 21*(2), 84–104.

McAvoy, L., Shirilla, P., & Flood, J. (2004). American Indian gathering and recreation uses of national forests. In K. Bricker (Compiler and Ed.), *Proceedings of the 2004 Northeastern Recreation Research Symposium*. General Technical Report NE-326. (pp. 81–87). Newtown Square, PA: USDA Forest Service, Northeastern Research Station.

McDonald, D., & McAvoy, L. (1997). Native Americans and leisure: State of the research and future directions. *Journal of Leisure Research, 29*(2), 145–166.

McLaren, D. R. (1999). The history of Indigenous peoples and tourism. *Cultural Survival, 23*(2). Retrieved from http://www.culturalsurvival.org/ourpublications/csq/article/the-history-indigenous-peoples-and-tourism

Meyer, M. A. (2004). *Ho'oulu Our Time of Becoming: Collected early writings of Manulani Meyer.* Honolulu, HI: 'Ai Pōhaku Press.

Nogelmeier, M. P. (2010). *Mai Pa'a I Ka Leo: Historical voice in Hawaiian primary materials, looking forward and listening back*. Honolulu, Hawai'i: Bishop Museum Press/Awaiaulu.

Paraschak, V. (1995). The Native Sport and Recreation program, 1972–1981: Patterns of resistance, patterns of reproduction. *Canadian Journal of History of Sport, 26*(2), 1–18.

Parajulee, A., & Wania, F. (2014). Evaluating officially reported polycyclic aromatic hydrocarbon emissions in the Athabasca oil sands region with a multimedia fate model. *Proceedings of the National Academy of Sciences of the United States of AmericaI*. doi: 10.1073/pnas.1319780111. Retrieved from http://www.pnas.org/content/early/2014/01/29/1319780111.full.pdf+html

Raffan, J. (1999). *Bark, skin and cedar: Exploring the canoe in Canadian experience*. Toronto, ON: HarperCollins

Rankin, L. (2013). *Mind over medicine*. Carlsbad, CA: Hay House.

Rose, A., & Giles, A. R. (2007). Alberta's Future Leaders Program: A case study of Aboriginal youth and community development. *The Canadian Journal of Native Studies, XXXVII*(2), 425–450.

Rousell, D. D., & Giles, A. R. (2012). Leadership, power and racism: Lifeguards' influences on Aboriginal people's experiences at a Northern Canadian aquatic facility. *Leisure Studies, 31*(4), 409–428.

Schinke, R. J., Blodgett, A. T., Yongblut, H. E., Eys, M. A., Battochio, R. C., Wabano, M. J., Peltier, D., Ritchie, S., Pickard, P., & Recollet-Saikonnen, D. (2010). The adaptation challenges and strategies of adolescent Aboriginal athletes competing off reserve. *Journal of Sport & Social Issues, 34*(4), 438–447.

Schütz, A. J. (1994). *The voices of Eden: A history of Hawaiian language studies*. Honolulu, HI: University of Hawai'i Press.

Simpson, L. R. (2004). Anticolonial strategies for the recovery and maintenance of Indigenous knowledge. *American Indian Quarterly, 28*(3/4), 373–384.

Smith, L. T. (1999). *Decolonizing methodologies: Research and Indigenous Peoples*. Dunedin, New Zealand: University of Otago Press.

Tuck, E., & Yang, K. W. (2012). Decolonization is not a metaphor. *Decolonization: Indigeneity, Education & Society, 1*(1), 1–40.

Walker, P. O. (2004). Decolonizing conflict resolution: Addressing the ontological violence of Westernization. *American Indian Quarterly, 28*(3/4), 527–549.

Walls, M. (2012). Kayak games and hunting enskilment: An archaeological consideration of sports and the situated learning of technical skills. *World Archaeology, 44*(2), 175–188.

Wiedman, D. (2010). Global marketing of Indigenous culture: Discovering Native America with Lee Tiger and the Florida and Miccosukee. *American Indian Culture and Research Journal, 34*(3), 1–26.

FOOTNOTES

[1] I use leisures or leisure to refer to Euro-North American concepts and practices. I use *manawa nanea* to refer to the colonial translation for practices in Indigenous cultures that may resonate with Euro-North American leisure.

[2] I generally use the term Indigenous, because it comes from the United Nations Charter for Indigenous peoples. However, Alfred (2009), from Kahnawà:ke in the Mohawk Nation, argues that these labels: (a) create identities (i.e., Indigenous, Native American, or Aboriginal) associated with non-Indigenous legal and social constructions that sanction violence and economic oppression against Indigenous peoples; (b) belong to the history of residential schools; and (c) reflect the state's efforts to homogenize and erase individual tribal histories and languages. Most of them are not descriptions chosen by Indigenous peoples or reflective of their languages that speak to political, cultural, spiritual, and ecological realities. Beatrice Medicine, a Sioux anthropologist, asserts that homogeneous labels support offensive and even racist stereotypes of Indigenous peoples by overlooking the diversity of North American Indigenous languages and sovereign groups. On the other hand, the emergence of pan-Indianism or intertribal organizations created the ability for Indigenous people to position themselves politically and economically within Western and globalized political economies (Fixico, 2003). However, the use of homogenizing labels and categories must make visible the multiple possibilities or only the destructive homogenizing effects will stay in play (Mason, 2009). An overwhelming number of Indigenous scholars request that they be identified by place, tribe, band names, or their preferred categories (i.e., in Canada the appropriate terms are First Nations, Inuit, and Métis, and in the United States it is American Indian, Alaskan Natives and Native Hawaiians). This request, in fact, is acknowledged in the *Publication Manual of the American Psychological Association* (6th ed.), which states: "…authors are encouraged to name the participants' specific groups, recognizing that some groups prefer the name for their group in their native language (e.g., *Dine* instead of *Navajo*, *Tohono O'odham* instead of *Papago*)" (p. 75).

[3] I use non-Indigenous or settler for those authors who are not Indigenous, and are most likely part of a long history of settling the land in North America and associated territories that were/are home to Indigenous people. My choice of words references the political influences that bind us all to colonizing forces and their continuing presence. Some authors use Western to refer to Eurocentric or Euro-North American traditions grounded in Greek, Roman, and Enlightenment scholarly tradition.

[4] Environmental philosophy and ethics have a substantial history exploring the differences between Indigenous and non-Indigenous views about the environment.

28

Leisure, Race, Ethnicity, and Immigration

Monika Stodolska (University of Illinois at Urbana-Champaign)
and Myron F. Floyd (North Carolina State University)

In the second decade of the twenty-first century, the United States is more diverse than it has been at any time in recent history. According to the 2010 U.S. Census, more than one-third of the American population was classified as racial or ethnic minorities (U.S. Census, 2013). In 2012, Non-Hispanic Whites accounted for 63% of the population, Hispanics for 16.9% (53 million), African Americans for 13.1% (41 million), Asians for 5.1% (16 million), and American Indians and Alaskan Natives for 1.2% (3.8 million) (U.S. Census, 2013). Similar patterns exist in Canada, where between 1981 and 2011, the number of visible minorities increased fivefold, from 1.1 million (5% of the total population) to over 6 million (19% of the total population) (Statistics Canada, 2013). Between 2000 and 2010, racial and ethnic minorities accounted for 91.7% of the U.S. population growth (Passel, Livingston, & Cohn, 2012) and, if the current trends continue, in 2050 non-Hispanic Whites will comprise slightly less than half (47%) of U.S. citizens (Humes, Jones, & Ramirez, 2011). Similarly, in Canada, visible minorities are projected to comprise nearly one in three citizens by 2031 (Statistics Canada, 2010).

Ethnic minorities contribute to cultures, economies, and politics of their host countries and are indispensable parts of the rich tapestry that are the United States and Canadian societies. At the same time, issues of legalization of undocumented immigrants and concerns about border security, jobs, bilingual education, health-care costs, and cultural change are at the forefront of political debates and everyday conversations in the receiving countries (PEW Research Center, 2013). Moreover, despite the U.S. and Canada being built and strengthened by the contributions of people of color and immigrants, both countries continue to struggle with the painful history of interracial conflict, genocide of the local native populations (Fox, Chapter 27) and, especially in the case of the U.S., slavery.

Leisure among ethnic and racial minorities[1] has been the subject of research for over 40 years. While the early studies documented the differences in recreation participation among non-Hispanic Whites and African Americans (e.g., Mueller & Gurin, 1962), more contemporary scholarship has examined interracial relations in the context of leisure, constraints on leisure faced by minorities, the roles of leisure in the adaptation of immigrants, as well as their unique meanings and motivations for leisure. This chapter is intended to explore selected topics addressed in the existing literature on race, ethnicity, and leisure[2]. We will begin by providing an overview of theoretical frameworks employed in studies of race, ethnicity, and leisure. We will then describe extant research on leisure meanings and motivations, the roles of leisure in the lives of ethnic and racial minorities, and constraints on leisure experienced

---

[1] Defining race and ethnicity has been a contentious subject. Race is usually considered to be a socially-constructed concept "grounded in ideological and cultural discourses" and related to "relations of power and processes of struggle" (Kivel, Johnson, & Scraton, 2009, pp. 478–479). Ethnic group has been defined as a group of people possessing "Ties of cultural homogeneity; a high degree of loyalty and adherence to certain basic institutions such as family patterns, religion, and language; distinctive folkways and mores; customs of dress, art, and ornamentation; moral codes and value systems; patterns of recreation; some sort of object to which the group manifests allegiance, such as a monarch, a religion, a language, or a territory; a consciousness of kind, a we feeling; common descent (perhaps racial), real or imagined; and a political unit" (Anderson & Frideres, 1981, p. 36).

[2] For a more complete examination of the subject, please see: Stodolska, M., Shinew, K. J., Floyd, M. F., & Walker, G. J. (2014). *Race, ethnicity, and leisure: Perspectives on research, theory, and practice.* Champaign, IL Human Kinetics.

by members of minority populations. We will end this chapter by discussing possible topics for future study.

THEORETICAL FRAMEWORKS

Marginality-Ethnicity

Significant theoretical developments in the area of race, ethnicity, and leisure have occurred over the past four decades. The marginality-ethnicity framework was the earliest theoretical perspective employed in the leisure literature that focused on understanding racial differences in leisure behavior (Washburne, 1978). This approach guided much of the empirical work in the field in the 1970s and 1980s. Washburne offered two perspectives to explain differences in rates of wildland recreation participation between Whites and African Americans. The marginality hypothesis held that low participation rates among Blacks were a result of limited access to socioeconomic resources, which in turn resulted from past discrimination[3]. The marginality hypothesis was commonly tested by comparing rates of recreation participation between Whites and African Americans while controlling for income, education, or other socioeconomic variables (Johnson, Bowker, English, & Worthen, 1998). If any observed differences disappeared, it was considered evidence of marginality effects. The ethnicity hypothesis (also known as the subcultural hypothesis) explained intergroup variations as a result of cultural factors, such as cultural norms, values systems, and socialization practices. It was concluded that the ethnicity perspective was supported if differences in participation remained after controlling for socioeconomic factors (Johnson et al., 1998). The shortcomings of the marginality-ethnicity approach were explicated by Floyd (1998) who argued that the concepts of race and ethnicity often had been confounded and used interchangeably, that measurements of culture were often lacking or imprecise, and that diversity within racial and ethnic groups was neglected.

Multiple Hierarchy Stratification Perspective

With few exceptions (e.g., Floyd, Gramann, & Saenz, 1993), studies on race and ethnicity did not consider how multiple sources of stratification (e.g., class, gender, age), along with race/ethnicity, affect leisure behavior. In response, a number of studies adopted the multiple hierarchy stratification perspective (Markides, Liang, & Jackson, 1990) to examine how combined sources of disadvantage (e.g., low income, female, minority, older adult) condition various domains of leisure. For example, the multiple hierarchy stratification perspective has been applied to analyze leisure activity preferences and participation (Shinew, Floyd, McGuire, & Noe, 1995), leisure benefits (Philipp, 1997), visitation to local and state parks (Lee, Scott, & Floyd, 2001), and constraints to park use (Shores, Scott, & Floyd, 2007).

Adaptation Theories

Several theoretical perspectives have been used to explain how the adaptation process to new cultural environments influences leisure among immigrants. Four specific concepts have been applied in this regard: assimilation, acculturation, segmented assimilation, and selective acculturation. Much of the research in the 1990s on leisure and ethnicity was informed by Gordon's (1964) theory of assimilation (e.g., Floyd & Gramann, 1993). This traditional assimilationist approach stemmed from the works of the Chicago School of Sociology (Park & Burges, 1921/1969) and argued that immigrants follow a one-directional path where, with time, they shed their ethnic traits and replace them with the traits of the mainstream, Anglo population. Among the key sub-processes of assimilation outlined by Gordon (1964) were cultural assimilation (or acculturation) and structural assimilation. Gordon's (1964) assimilation theory attracted much criticism over the years, in response to which other models characterizing adaptation processes of immigrant groups have been developed (Alba & Nee, 1997). The more recent research has argued that the contemporary ethnic groups are very diverse, and consist of people with various personal histories, goals, and distinct social endowments who follow different trajectories when it comes to their adaptation to the host country (Portes & Zhou, 1993). For instance, the concept of segmented assimilation suggested that because of socioeconomic and racial stratification in the U.S., multiple "assimilation outcomes" are possible (Portes & Zhou, 1993). Selective acculturation referred to the strategic retention of core cultural values and practices among minority groups (Keefe & Padilla, 1987). The segmented assimilation and selective acculturation theories were used in studies on race and ethnicity by Shaull and Gramann (1998) and Stodolska and Alexandris (2004).

Transnationalism

A few studies have examined the concept of transnationalism and its influence on leisure behaviors of immigrants (e.g., Li & Stodolska, 2006). Transnationalism refers to sustained interaction and exchanges across borders through which immigrants maintain social networks in the home and host society (Glick Schiller, Basch, & Blanc-Szaton, 1992). This perspective was introduced by Stodolska and

---

[3] Discrimination has also been used as a separate framework guiding studies in the field of ethnic/racial leisure. Literature in this area has been described later in the chapter.

Santos (2006), who proposed the concept of transnational leisure—defined as leisure maintained by temporary migrants to "foster their ties with their countries and communities of origin" (p. 162)—to describe how immigrants used their leisure to stay connected to their families and home country.

Self-Construal

The concept of self-construal has guided much of the research on Chinese-Canadians' leisure behavior conducted by Walker and his co-investigators (e.g., Walker, Deng, & Dieser, 2001). Self-construal refers to how a person thinks about her or himself in relation to others. Markus and Kitayama (1991) proposed that there are two main types of self-construal: (a) independent (or individualistic), where people endorse being unique, asserting oneself, expressing one's inner attributes, and promoting one's own goals; and (b) interdependent (or collectivistic), where people endorse belonging, fitting in, maintaining harmony, restraining oneself, and promoting others' goals. Research has indicated Asian Americans are higher in collectivism compared with European Americans (Coon & Kemmelmeier, 2001), while other studies suggested that Latinos are also more likely to endorse this type of self-construal than European Americans (Freeberg & Stein, 1996).

Emerging Frameworks

Two theoretical frameworks have been developed within the field of leisure with the study of racial and ethnicity minorities in mind. First, the Conditioned Attitude Model of Discrimination (Stodolska, 2005) focused on the decision-making process leading to discrimination against minorities. According to the model, the mechanism which determines whether discrimination occurs and what form it takes consists of three stages. First, people use their information set to derive beliefs about a group or an evaluation of its characteristics. Then they combine these beliefs with new information input to form an attitude toward the group members. Finally, they weigh the benefits and consequences of discrimination and decide whether or not to engage in the behavior. Second, the Ethnicity and Public Recreation Participation Model (EPRP) (Gómez, 2002) was based on a review and synthesis of theories and models applied to recreation and leisure participation among racial and ethnic minority groups. Gómez (2002) distilled five major concepts that were incorporated into the EPRP: acculturation, socioeconomic status, subcultural identify, recreation benefits, and perceived discrimination.

Recent work in the field has also been informed by the theory of planned behavior (Walker, Courneya, & Deng, 2006), social and cultural capital theories (Shinew, Glover, & Parry, 2004), and critical race theory (Arai & Kivel, 2009). Stewart (2014) argued that the new paradigms linked to the critical race theory in particular have a transformative potential as they "problematize whiteness as an ethnic category (rather than the norm from which others deviate) and connect it with hegemonic power that racializes spaces, institutions, and research processes" (p. 332).

One could argue that significant progress has been made in the theoretical sophistication of our subfield, but much work remains to be done. In particular, the next decade seems to be conducive to incorporating, or perhaps developing, novel theoretical frameworks to study ethnicity, race, and leisure, as increased globalization, realignment of the existing racial and ethnic hierarchy, and shifting migration patterns will call for new ways of understanding the dynamics of leisure behavior among minority populations.

EMPIRICAL RESEARCH

Beginning in the 1960s and continuing to the 1990s, research on leisure among ethnic and racial minorities focused primarily on examining and explaining differences in activity participation patterns and styles between majority and minority groups. While the early studies examined leisure behaviors among African Americans, research conducted during the 1980s and 1990s expanded its focus to Latinos and Asian Americans[4]. This line of research was later criticized by Floyd (1998), Stodolska, and Walker (2007), and Arai and Kivel (2009), who argued that research needs to move beyond the descriptive frameworks to examine more complex issues related to sources of power and inequality; individual, group and societal-level factors that condition leisure behaviors; as well as outcomes of leisure participation among minorities. Much of the research on leisure meanings, motivations, and benefits, as well as leisure constraints, and the roles of leisure in the lives of ethnic and racial minorities belongs to this tradition.

Meanings, Motivations, and Benefits

Although early studies sought to identify and catalog basic needs leisure activities could satisfy (Walker, Kono, & Dieser, Chapter 36), these efforts did not consider potential variation by race or ethnicity. Later research showed that there are patterns of similarity and difference in leisure motivations and perceived benefits among ethnic and racial groups. For instance, Hunt and Ditton (2001) observed that escaping stress and being in a natural environment was more important to Anglo American anglers while Hispanic

---

[4] For a review of this line of research see Gramann, J. H. & Allison, M. T. (1999). Ethnicity, race, and leisure. In: Jackson, E. L., & Burton, T. L. (Eds.), *Leisure Studies: Prospects for the twenty-first century.* State College, PA: Venture Publishing, Inc., pp. 283–297.

American anglers rated achievement as more important. Toth and Brown's (1997) study showed that among White and Black anglers fishing held similar meanings, but that Whites placed greater emphasis on "sport" aspects of the activity, while subsistence was of greater importance to Blacks. These studies reveal that even when activity participation or settings are similar, motivations and perceived benefits are affected by diverse cultural patterns among racial and ethnic groups.

Motivations and perceived benefits associated with leisure may also vary *within* ethnic groups. Shaull and Gramann (1998) analyzed perceived benefit domains (nature enjoyment and family cohesiveness) among Anglo Americans and Mexican Americans of different acculturation level. They found that bicultural Mexicans rated family cohesion more highly than the other acculturation groups and the Anglos. Winter, Jeong, and Godbey (2004) compared three motive domains associated with visiting natural areas (consumption, nature, and social interaction) among Chinese, Japanese, Korean, and Filipino residents in the San Francisco area. Consumptive reasons and social interaction were rated higher among Chinese and Filipino respondents, while Chinese respondents had the highest ratings on nature-related motivations. An important contribution of this study was its comparison of four different Asian origin groups and its demonstration of significant heterogeneity within this population. In a study of motivations for outdoor recreation among Euro-North Americans and Chinese in Canada, Walker et al. (2001) found that self-construal (Markus & Kitayama, 1991) mediated the effect of ethnicity on nature-related experience preference and two motives related to social interdependence. Their conceptual approach and findings showed the need to consider foundational culture in understanding the meanings and motivations for leisure of different ethnic groups.

In view of immigration trends, potential differences between Western and non-Western cultures should be considered. Cultures can differ in terms of perceptual orientation to nature (Gudykunst & Kim, 1984), as well as concept of time and orientation toward past, present, and future (Samovar, Porter, & Jain, 1981). Moreover, patterns and values related to decision making and initiating behavior, as well as extent of individualism and collectivism may vary (Simcox, 1993). Leisure in Western cultures is marked by activity, rationality, and efficiency with emphasis on individual and personal needs, while non-Western cultures place more value on passive use, as well as familial and group-level benefits and collectivism (Simcox, 1993). Given the influence of culture on leisure and immigration trends, ethnic differences in leisure motivations, meanings, and perceived benefits are likely to endure (Floyd & Gramann, 1993).

The Roles of Leisure in the Lives of Ethnic and Racial Minorities

Adaptation.

Some of the questions that drive the research on race, ethnicity, and leisure have to do with the strategies immigrants employ to adapt to life in the new country and with the roles that leisure can play in the process. Research has shown that leisure activities that incorporate traditions of the home and host countries help to build bridges between ethnic and mainstream communities and promote cultural understanding (Tirone & Goodberry, 2011). Leisure and sport are also convenient ways immigrants use to familiarize themselves with the local environment and culture, learn the language, establish initial contacts with people in the U.S., and to interact with them in non-stressful settings (Kim, Kleiber, & Kropf, 2001).[5] Sport in particular plays an important role in the adaptation process among youth by allowing them to develop new contacts and to feel accepted by the peer group (Stodolska & Alexandris, 2004). Leisure also provides an important communication platform in interracial/interethnic marriages (Sharaievska, Kim, & Stodolska, 2013), a mechanism to release tension in a prejudicial environment (Hibbler & Shinew, 2002), and an opportunity to bond with children who struggle with acculturative stress (Stodolska & Yi, 2003).

Retention of ethnic traits.

Leisure activities not only facilitate intra and intergroup contacts, but also provide a sense of familiarity after arrival, help to retain desired cultural elements and achieve an optimum level of arousal. In an environment where everything is new, where work is stressful and people struggle to rebuild their lives, it is through leisure that they maintain contact with their traditional culture, families back home, keep up with news from the home country, and celebrate their heritage (Kim et al., 2001; Stodolska, 2000). Stress reduction, improvement in self-esteem and self-confidence, feeling of security, and increased life satisfaction are important benefits of participation in familiar activities and associating with people who can understand and sympathize with one's experiences (Kim et al., 2001). Leisure activities are also crucial to preserving ethnic culture among second and subsequent generations as they allow for celebrating ethnic traditions and maintaining contact with family and other members of the ethnic community (Tirone & Goodberry, 2011). Ethnic clubs and associations and

5 It needs to be noted, however, that sport also promotes competition and introduces a possibility of interethnic/racial conflict which may negatively contribute to interethnic interactions (Walker, Halpenny, & Deng, 2011).

ethnic churches often play an important role as carriers of such traditions and help to strengthen community bonds through leisure, sport, and cultural events (Price & Whitworth, 2004).

Identity development.

Leisure activities can play an important role in helping ethnic and racial minority members develop and maintain ethnic and national identities. Kelly (1983) argued that leisure is the "life space in which identity is most fully expressed and developed" (p. 116) as, unlike work, it is the realm of freedom that allows people to "play" with different identities. Leisure also facilitates entry into new "communities of commonality" (p. 117) and development of social ties. A study by Kim and Kleiber (2001) on cultural integration and ethnic preservation of older Korean immigrants found that leisure activities contributed to maintaining Koreans' cultural bonds, restoring their sense of ethnic identity, reinforcing their Koreanness and maintaining traditions. Stodolska and Yi (2003) indicated that ethnic identity among first generation teenage immigrants from Mexico, Korea, and Poland was shaped by self-discovery of their cultural differences vis-à-vis mainstream Americans and other minorities, by comparisons with other members of their in-group, and by outside labeling. In another study, Stodolska and Tainsky (2015) showed that sport spectatorship helped immigrants to discover their common Latino traits and to embrace ethnic designations imposed by others. Ethnic identity may also be shaped by genealogical travel to ancestral homelands that allows people to reconnect with their heritage and reexamine their cultural values (Day-Vines, Barker, & Exum, 1998).

Physical activity and health.

Research has shown that although the attitudes toward leisure-time physical activity (LTPA) among ethnic minority members are often positive (Skowron, Stodolska, & Shinew, 2008), involvement in LTPA is significantly below that of the Anglo mainstream (National Center for Health Statistics, 2013). Such low rates of LTPA contribute to high overweight and obesity rates among African Americans and Mexican Americans and other negative health outcomes. Older minority members and those with low socioeconomic status are at a greatest risk for inactive lifestyles (Whitt-Glover, Taylor, Heath, & Macera, 2007), although some groups, such as Latinos, are less active across the entire lifespan (Crespo, 2000). Low LTPA among ethnic minorities has been attributed to a number of factors, including different perceptions of body and health (Airhihenbuwa, Kumanyika, Agurs, & Lowe, 1995), and constraints such as fatigue, lack of time, lack of family support, lack of role models, lack of partners, child-care responsibilities, as well as gender role expectations related to family and household duties (Skowron et al., 2008). Public spaces, such as urban parks, have been shown to be the primary contexts for physical activity, although the use of natural environments in minority communities for LTPA is often constrained by overcrowding, poor maintenance, safety concerns, and racial tensions (Stodolska & Shinew, 2010).

Leisure Constraints

Socioeconomic status.

Research on socioeconomic constraints can be traced to Washburne's (1978) marginality thesis that attributed minorities' underparticipation in wildland recreation to inequality in resource allocation. Although ethnic minorities have achieved a remarkable economic progress in the last several decades, they are still predominantly clustered in lower-status occupations, earn less, and exhibit higher poverty rates than non-Hispanic Whites (Macartney, Bishaw, & Fontenot, 2013). Lower wages make it difficult for people to afford costly recreation equipment and program fees (Trussell, Chapter 22). Strenuous employment also leads to lack of time, exhaustion, and restricts minorities' participation in some pastimes, including LTPA (Crespo, 2000). Lack of set work hours prevents people from taking part in organized sport or recreation, and the low-skill work they perform (and resulting lack of job stability) make them unable or unwilling to take extended time off. Such constraints are particularly pronounced among immigrants in the immediate period after arrival, among international students with limited means of financial support, as well as undocumented and transnational migrants (Stodolska & Alexandris, 2004).

Despite recent declines in residential segregation (Iceland, Weinberg, & Steinmetz, 2002), place of residence is still one of the key factors shaping leisure opportunities among minorities. Average living costs tend to be higher in cities where minorities are concentrated, worsening the economic burden they experience. Moreover, minorities make up a disproportionately large share of residents of central-city communities that offer less access to recreational facilities and quality natural environments (Garcia, 2013).

Culture-related constraints.

Cultural differences can constrain recreation participation among minority groups. Specific gender role expectations, lack of culturally appropriate child-care services, religious restrictions on mixed-gender interactions, and religiously-prescribed clothing that limits body movements have been shown to restrict leisure options (Stodolska & Livengood, 2006). Language problems and broken social networks due to emigration are also important constraints faced by many ethnic minorities (Doherty & Taylor, 2007). Immigrants not fluent in the langue of the host country may have difficulties establishing social contacts, finding out about recreation opportunities, communicating with staff of recreation centers, and signing up for programs (Stodolska, Shinew, Acevedo, & Izenstark, 2011). Many activities to which immigrants were used to in their home country may also not be available in the U.S. or Canada, while others may be offered in a different form.

Two other factors related to culture that may constrain leisure are acculturative stress and intergenerational conflict. Walker et al. (2011) defined acculturative stress as "behaviors and experiences that are disruptive to a person after he or she immigrates" (p. 227) and isolated four types of acculturative stress experienced by Chinese immigrants to Canada: language difficulties, not feeling at home, loss/nostalgia, and perceived discrimination. Intergenerational conflict can affect leisure opportunities when parents (often first generation immigrants) disapprove of the lifestyle choices of their children and of their children's moving too far away from the traditional culture (Tirone & Godberry, 2011). Interethnic dating/ marriage, engaging in leisure pursuits deemed unacceptable by the ethnic community and devoting too much time to leisure have been shown to lead to conflict in immigrant families (Stodolska & Yi, 2003).

Access to natural environments.

Natural environments provide a number of benefits to ethnic and racial minorities, including the opportunity to express cultural values, get away from urban life, relax, improve intergroup relations, and promote social interaction (Gómez, 2002; Shinew et al., 2004; Stodolska et al., 2011). Many of these benefits, however, are unrealized as access to natural environments is often severely restricted for ethnic and racial groups. Minority communities with higher poverty rates are less likely to have access to parks and green spaces, and public spending on parks in communities of color is usually lower than in more affluent neighborhoods (Garcia, 2013). Parks and facilities that are available are often overcrowded and poorly maintained (Stodolska et al., 2011). Problems with park access are exacerbated by interracial conflict and discrimination (Fernandez & Witt, 2013). The perceptions of "unwelcomeness" come not only from deliberate discrimination, but also from exclusion due to lack of information about programs and services in the native language of local residents, inability of the staff to communicate with recreationists, and lack of understanding among the staff of the needs of the local population (Fernandez & Witt, 2013; Stodolska et al., 2011). These perceptions may worsen if the place or the leisure activity is labeled in a particular way (e.g., "African American park," "White sport") (Philipp, 1999; West, 1989). Access to more distant, suburban natural environments or national parks may be additionally hindered by cost, problems with transportation, or historical issues tied to those places (Erickson, Johnson, & Kivel, 2009; Stodolska et al., 2011; West, 1989). Fear for personal safety due to high crime and gang activity has also been shown to disproportionately affect minorities' participation in leisure activities in public spaces (Stodolska, Acevedo, & Shinew, 2009).

Discrimination.

Discrimination has been reported as a constraint on leisure among minorities since the early 1970s (Lindsay & Ogle, 1972), although it was the seminal article by West (1989) that brought renewed attention to this topic. Since then, numerous studies have documented that racial and ethnic minority groups experience discrimination in parks, campgrounds, recreation areas, pools, beaches, golf courses, and forests (e.g., Floyd et al., 1993). Discrimination in leisure has been shown to affect quality of recreation experience, recreation site choices, and to force minorities to isolate themselves during their leisure engagements or, conversely, to recreate in larger groups (Hibbler & Shinew, 2002; Johnson et al., 1998). Discrimination also makes people restrict their leisure activities in terms of timing (people would not go out after dark) and location (they would avoid parks, campgrounds and other areas where they feel they may be unwelcome) (Flood & McAvoy, 2007). Within recreation settings, studies have documented instances of discrimination from other recreationists such as physical attacks, verbal confrontations, and hate stares (e.g., Hibbler & Shinew, 2002). Minority recreationists have also been denied service or offered a substandard service by the staff of recreation centers, and have been followed by the staff, park rangers, or the police (Fernandez & Witt, 2013; Flood & McAvoy, 2007). Past racist practices that led to some recreation resources being associated with poverty, hard manual labor, and lynchings have also been reported to shape current leisure behavior of people of color (Erickson et al., 2009; Johnson et al., 1998). It is only recently that studies considered institutional and structural forms of discrimination (Scott, 2014).

CONCLUSION

Although research on leisure, race, and ethnicity has significantly expanded and matured in recent years, it still occupies a relatively small place in the general body of leisure research (Floyd, Bocarro, & Thompson, 2008). In particular, a number of areas have been unexplored or underexplored and require further attention. Research should focus more on the globalization issues and on the mobility of minority populations. While most research in our field has concentrated on minority groups in Western developed countries, migrations and diversity are global phenomena. Thus, it would be desirable to explore leisure behaviors among minorities outside of the traditional receiving countries of the West. Researchers also need to consider significant economic, social, and cultural changes taking places in the traditional immigrant sending countries such as China, India, and Mexico, and the effects of globalization on leisure behaviors of immigrants even *before* they arrive to their destination (Floyd, Walker, Stodolska, & Shinew, 2014). The growing minority population in the U.S. and Canada is also likely to create a major realignment of racial and ethnic hierarchies in these countries, which may have significant implications for research on leisure among people of color and for the provision of leisure programs and services to minority groups. Future research needs to place more emphasis on social change, resistance, "mobilization of power" (Arai & Kivel, 2009, p. 460), and trajectories of success and advancement within racial and ethnic groups. An important outcome of research on race and ethnicity should be a lasting change and reduction of oppression among the individuals and communities that we study.

Future research also needs to pay closer attention to the heterogeneity *within* minority populations, both when it comes to socioeconomic status, as well as acculturation level, identity, urban-rural residence, immigration experiences, and other possible markers of difference (Henderson & Walker, 2014). Simultaneously, researchers need to acknowledge the similarities *across* ethnic groups that may be overlooked by those used to investigating intergroup differences in leisure (Floyd et al., 2014). Considering the youthful age structure of the U.S. African American and Latino populations, future research should examine the provision of leisure services to children residing in disadvantaged communities and to the roles leisure can play in the positive development of immigrant youth. Also, while sport behavior among ethnic and racial minorities has been investigated extensively (Harrison & Bimper, 2014), tourism and travel among immigrants as well as people of color remains almost completely unexplored (Philipp, 1994). Finally, as Scott (2014) pointed out, "inequality in service delivery is deeply embedded in the everyday functioning of how public park and recreation agencies do business" (p. 47). As the literature on race, ethnicity and leisure continues to expand, how to best translate and disseminate research findings in systematic ways and how to best provide leisure services to diverse groups should be a priority.

REFERENCES

Airhihenbuwa, C., Kumanyika, S., Agurs, T., & Lowe, A. (1995). Perceptions and beliefs about exercise, rest, and health among African-Americans. *American Journal of Health Promotion, 9*, 426–429.

Alba, R. D., & Nee, V. (1997). Rethinking assimilation theory for a new era of immigration. *International Migration Review, 31*, 826–874.

Anderson, A. B., & Frideres, J. S. (1981). *Ethnicity in Canada. Theoretical perspectives.* Toronto, ON: Butterworths.

Arai, S., & Kivel, B. D. (2009). Critical race theory and social justice perspectives on whiteness, difference(s) and (anti)racism: A fourth wave of race research in leisure studies. *Journal of Leisure Research, 41*, 459–473.

Coon, H., & Kemmelmeier, M. (2001). Cultural orientations in the United States: (Re)Examining differences among ethnic groups. *Journal of Cross-Cultural Psychology, 32*, 348–364.

Crespo, C. J. (2000). Encouraging physical activity in minorities. *The Physician and Sports Medicine, 28*, 36–51.

Day-Vines, N. Barker, J. M., & Exum, H. A. (1998). Impact of diasporic travel on ethnic identity development of African American college students. *College Student Journal, 32*(3), 463–471.

Doherty, A., & Taylor, T. (2007). Sport and physical recreation in the settlement of immigrant youth. *Leisure/Loisir, 31*, 27–55.

Erickson, B., Johnson, C. W., & Kivel, B. D. (2009). Rocky Mountain National Park: History and culture as factors in African-American park visitation. *Journal of Leisure Research, 41*, 529–545.

Fernandez, M., & Witt, P. (2013). Attracting Hispanics to a public recreation center: Examining intergroup tension and historical factors. *Journal of Leisure Research, 45*, 423–444.

Flood, J. P., & McAvoy, L. H. (2007). Use of National Forests by Salish-Kootenai tribal members: Traditional recreation and a legacy of cultural values. *Leisure/Loisir, 31*, 191–216.

Floyd, M. F. (1998). Getting beyond marginality and ethnicity: The challenge for race and ethnic studies in leisure research. *Journal of Leisure Research, 30*(1), 3–22.

Floyd, M. F., Bocarro, J. N., & Thompson, T. D. (2008). Research on race and ethnicity in leisure studies: A review of five major journals. *Journal of Leisure Research, 40*, 1–22.

Floyd, M. F., & Gramann, J. H. (1993). Effects of acculturation and structural assimilation in resource-based recreation: The case of Mexican Americans. *Journal of Leisure Research, 5*, 6–21.

Floyd, M. F., Gramann, J. H., & Saenz, R. (1993). Ethnic factors and the use of public outdoor recreation areas: The case of Mexican Americans. *Leisure Sciences, 15*, 83–98.

Floyd, M. F., Shinew, K. J., McGuire, F. A., & Noe, F. P. (1994). Race, class, and leisure activity preferences: Marginality and ethnicity revisited. *Journal of Leisure Research, 26*(2), 158–173.

Floyd, M. F., Walker, G. J., Stodolska, M., & Shinew, K. J. (2014). Conclusions: Emerging issues. In M. Stodolska, K. J. Shinew, M. F. Floyd, & G. J. Walker. (Eds.), *Race, ethnicity and leisure: Perspectives on research, theory, and practice.* Champaign, IL: Human Kinetics.

Freeberg, A., & Stein, C. (1996). Felt obligation toward parents in Mexican-American and Anglo-American young adults. *Journal of Social and Personal Relationships, 13*, 457–471.

Garcia, R. (2013). The George Butler leisure social justice and leisure: The usefulness and uselessness of research. *Journal of Leisure Research, 45*, 7–22.

Glick Schiller, N., Basch, L., & Blanc-Szanton, C. (1992). *Towards a transnational perspective on migration: Race, class, ethnicity and nationalism reconsidered.* New York: New York Academy of Science.

Gómez, E. (2002). The Ethnicity and Public Recreation Participation Model. *Leisure Sciences, 24*(2), 123–142.

Gordon, M. M. (1964). *Assimilation in American life.* New York: Oxford University Press.

Gramann, J. H., & Allison, M. T. (1999). Ethnicity, race, and leisure. In E. L. Jackson & T. L. Burton (Eds.), *Leisure studies: Prospects for the twenty-first century* (pp. 283–297). State College, PA: Venture Publishing, Inc.

Gudykunst, W. B., & Kim, Y. Y. (1984). *Communicating with strangers: An approach to intercultural communication.* New York: Random House.

Harrison, L., & Bimper, A. (2014). Race, ethnicity and sport. In M. Stodolska, K. J. Shinew, M. F. Floyd, & G. J. Walker. (Eds.), *Race, ethnicity and leisure; Perspectives on research, theory, and practice.* Champaign, IL: Human Kinetics.

Henderson, K. A., & Walker, G. J. (2014). Ethnic and racial research methods. In M. Stodolska, K. J. Shinew, M. F. Floyd, & G. J. Walker. (Eds.), *Race, ethnicity and leisure: Perspectives on research, theory, and practice* (pp. 21–36). Champaign, IL: Human Kinetics.

Hibbler, D., & Shinew K. (2002). Interracial couples' experience of leisure: A social network approach. *Journal of Leisure Research, 34*, 135–156.

Humes, K. R., Jones, N. A., & Ramirez, R. R. (2011). Overview of race and Hispanic origin: 2010. 2010 Census Briefs. http://www.census.gov/prod/cen2010/briefs/c2010br-02.pdf

Hunt, K. M., & Ditton, R. B. (2010). Perceived benefits of recreational fishing to Hispanic-American and Anglo anglers. *Human Dimensions of Wildlife: An International Journal, 6*(3), 153–172.

Iceland, J., Weinberg, D. H., & Steinmetz, E. (2002). *Racial and Ethnic Residential Segregation in the United States: 1980–2000,* U.S. Census Bureau, Series CENSR-3. Washington, DC: U.S. Government Printing Office. Retrieved from http://www.census.gov/hhes/www/housing/housing_patterns/pdftoc.html

Johnson, C. Y., Bowker, J., English, D. B. K., & Worthen, D. (1998). Wildland recreation in the rural South: An examination of marginality and ethnicity theory. *Journal of Leisure Research, 30*(1), 101–120.

Keefe, S. E., & Padilla, A. M. (1987). *Chicano ethnicity.* Albuquerque, NM: University of New Mexico Press.

Kelly, J. R. (1983). *Leisure identities and interactions.* Boston, MA: Allyn & Unwin.

Kim, E., & Kleiber, D. A. (2001). *Leisure activity, cultural integration & ethnic preservation of older Korean Americans in the U.S.* Proceedings from the 2001 NRPA Leisure Research Symposium.

Kim, E., Kleiber, D., & Kropf, N. (2001). Social integration and ethnic preservation in the leisure activities of older Korean immigrants. *Journal of Gerontological Social Work, 36*, 107–129.

Kivel, B., Johnson, C. W., & Scraton, S. (2009). (Re)Theorzing race, experience, and leisure: Using critical ethnography and collective memory work. *Journal of Leisure Research, 41*(4), 471–492.

Lee, J., Scott, D., & Floyd, M. F. (2001). Structural inequalities in outdoor recreation participation: A multiple hierarchy stratification perspective. *Journal of Leisure Research, 33*(4), 427–449.

Li, M. Z., & Stodolska, M. (2006). Transnationalism, leisure, and Chinese graduate students in the United States. *Leisure Sciences, 28*, 39–55.

Lindsay, J. J., & Ogle, R. A. (1972). Socioeconomic patterns of outdoor recreation use near urban areas. *Journal of Leisure Research, 4*, 19–24.

Macartney, S., Bishaw, A., & Fontenot, K. (2013). *Poverty rates for selected detailed race and Hispanic groups by state and place.* Retrieved from http://www.census.gov/prod/2013pubs/acsbr11-17.pdf

Markides, K., Liang, J., & Jackson, J. (1990). Race, ethnicity, and aging: Conceptual and methodological issues. In R. H. Binstock & L. K. George (Eds.), *Handbook of aging and the social sciences* (pp. 112–129). San Diego, CA: Academic Press.

Markus, H., & Kitayama, S. (1991). Culture and the self: Implications for cognition, emotion, and motivation. *Psychological Review, 98*, 224–253.

Mueller, E., & Gurin, G. (1962). *Participation in outdoor recreation behavior: Factors affecting demand among American adults. Outdoor Recreation Resources Review Commission (ORRRC) Study Report 20.* Washington, DC: U.S. Government Printing Office.

National Center for Health Statistics. (2013). *Health, United States, 2012: With Special Featureon Emergency Care.* Retrieved from http://www.cdc.gov/nchs/data/hus/hus12.pdf

Park, R. E., & Burges, E. (1921/1969). *Introduction to the science of sociology.* Chicago, IL: University of Chicago Press.

Passel, J. S., Livingston, G., & Cohn, D. (2012). Explaining why minority births now outnumber white births. *PEW Research Center Social & Demographic Trends.* Retrieved from http://www.pewsocialtrends.org/2012/05/17/explaining-why-minority-births-now-outnumber-white- births/?src=hispanic-footer

PEW Research Center. (2013). *Immigration: Key data points from Pew Research.* Retrieved from http://www.pewresearch.org/key-data-points/immigration-tip-sheet-on-u-s-public-opinion/

Philipp, S. F. (1994). Race and tourism choice: A legacy of discrimination? *Annals of Tourism Research, 21*, 479–488.

Philipp, S. F. (1997). Race, gender, and leisure benefits. *Leisure Sciences, 19*(3), 191–207.

Philipp, S. F. (1999). Are we welcome? African American racial acceptance in leisure activities and the importance given to children's leisure. *Journal of Leisure Research, 31*, 385–403.

Portes, A., & Zhou, M. (1993). The second new generation: Segmented assimilation and its variants. *The Annals of the American Academy of Political and Social Science, 530*, 74–96.

Price, M., & Whitworth, C. (2004). Soccer and Latino cultural space. Metropolitan Washington Fútbol Leagues. In D. Arreola (Ed.), *Hispanic spaces, Latino places: Community and cultural diversity in contemporary America.* Austin, TX: University of Texas Press, pp. 167–186.

Samovar, L. A., Porter, R. E., & Jain, N. C. (1981). *Understanding intercultural communication.* Belmont, CA: Wadworth.

Scott, D. (2014). Race, ethnicity and leisure services practice: Can we hope to escape the past? In M. Stodolska, K. J. Shinew, M. F. Floyd, & G. J. Walker (Eds.), *Race, ethnicity and leisure: Perspectives on research, theory, and practice.* Champaign, IL: Human Kinetics.

Sharaievska, I., Kim, J., & Stodolska, M. (2013). Leisure and marital satisfaction in intercultural marriages. *Journal of Leisure Research, 46*, 445–465.

Shaull, S. L., & Gramann, J. H. (1998). The effect of cultural assimilation and the importance of family-related and nature-related recreation among Hispanic Americans. *Journal of Leisure Research, 30*(1), 47–63.

Shinew, K. J., Floyd, M. F., McGuire, F. A., & Noe, F. P. (1995). Gender, race and subjective social class and their association with leisure preference. *Leisure Sciences, 17*(2), 75–89.

Shinew, K. J., Glover, T. D., & Parry, D. C. (2004). Leisure spaces as potential sites for interracial interaction: Community gardens in a segregated urban area. *Journal of Leisure Research, 36*(3), 336–355.

Shores, K. A., Scott, D., & Floyd, M. F. (2007). Constraints to outdoor recreation: A multiple hierarchy stratification perspective. *Leisure Sciences, 29*(3), 227–246.

Simcox, D. E. (1993). Cultural foundations for leisure preference, behavior, and environmental orientation. In A. W. Ewert, D. J. Chavez, & A. W. Magill (Eds.), *Culture, conflict and communication in the wildland-urban interface* (pp. 267–280). Boulder, CO: Westview Press.

Skowron, M.A., Stodolska, M., & Shinew, K. J. (2008). Determinants of leisure time physical activity participation among Latina women. *Leisure Sciences, 30*(5), 429–447.

Statistics Canada. (2010). *Projections of the diversity of the Canadian population, 2006 to 2031.* Retrieved from http://www.statcan.gc.ca/pub/91-551-x/91-551-x2010001-eng.pdf

Statistics Canada. (2013). *Immigration and ethnocultural diversity in Canada.* Retrieved from http://www12.statcan.gc.ca/nhs-enm/2011/as-sa/99-010-x/99-010-x2011001-eng.cfm

Stewart, W. (2014). Leisure research to enhance social justice. *Leisure Sciences, 36*(4), 325–339.

Stodolska, M. (2000). Changes in leisure participation patterns after immigration. *Leisure Sciences, 22*, 39–63.

Stodolska, M. (2005). A Conditioned Attitude Model of Individual Discriminatory Behavior. *Leisure Sciences, 27*(1), 1–20.

Stodolska, M., Acevedo, J. C., & Shinew, K. J. (2009). Gangs of Chicago: Perceptions of crime and its effect on the recreation behavior of Latino residents in urban communities. *Leisure Sciences, 31*, 466–482.

Stodolska, M., & Alexandris, K. (2004). The role of recreational sport in the adaptation of first generation immigrants in the United States. *Journal of Leisure Research, 36*, 379–413.

Stodolska, M., & Livengood, J. S. (2006). The effects of religion on the leisure behavior of American Muslim immigrants. *Journal of Leisure Research, 38*, 293–320.

Stodolska, M., & Santos, C. (2006). Transnationalism and leisure: Mexican temporary migrants in the U.S. *Journal of Leisure Research, 38*(2), 143–167.

Stodolska, M., & Shinew, K. J. (2010). Environmental constraints on leisure time physical activity among Latino urban residents. *Qualitative Research in Sport and Exercise, 2*, 313–335.

Stodolska, M., Shinew, K. J., Acevedo, J. C., & Izenstark, D. (2011). Perceptions of urban parks as havens and contested terrains by Mexican-Americans in Chicago neighborhoods. *Leisure Sciences, 33*, 103–126.

Stodolska, M., & Tainsky, S. (2015). Soccer spectatorship and identity discourses among Latino immigrants. *Leisure Sciences, 37*, 142–159.

Stodolska, M., & Walker, G. J. (2007). Ethnicity and leisure: Historical development, current status, and future directions. *Leisure/Loisir, 31*, 3–26.

Stodolska, M., & Yi, J. (2003). Impacts of immigration on ethnic identity and leisure behavior of adolescent immigrants from Korea, Mexico, and Poland. *Journal of Leisure Research, 35*, 49–79.

Tirone, S., & Goodberry, A. (2011). Leisure, biculturalism, and second-generation Canadians. *Journal of Leisure Research, 43*, 427–444.

Toth Jr., J. F., & Brown, R. B. (1997). Racial and gender meanings of why people participate in recreational fishing. *Leisure Sciences, 19*(2), 129–146.

U.S. Census. (2013). *State and County QuickFacts.* http://quickfacts.census.gov/qfd/states/00000.html

Walker, G. J., Courneya, K. S., & Deng, J. (2006). Ethnicity, gender, and the theory of planned behavior: The case of playing the lottery. *Journal of Leisure Research, 38*, 224–248.

Walker, G. J., Deng, J., & Dieser, R. (2001). Ethnicity, acculturation, self-construal, and motivations for outdoor recreation. *Leisure Sciences, 23*, 263–283.

Walker, G. J., Halpenny, E. A., & Deng, J. (2011). Leisure satisfaction and acculturative stress: The case of Chinese-Canadian immigrants. *Journal of Leisure Research, 43*, 226–245.

Washburne, R. F. (1978). Black under-participation in wildland recreation: Alternative explanations. *Leisure Sciences, 1*, 175–189.

West, P. C. (1989). Urban region parks and black minorities: Subculture, marginality, and interracial relations in park use in Detroit metropolitan area. *Leisure Sciences, 11*, 11–28.

Whitt-Glover, M. C., Taylor, W. C., Heath, G. W., & Macera, C. A. (2007). Self-reported physical activity among Blacks: Estimates from national surveys. *American Journal of Preventive Medicine, 33*(5), 412–417.

Winter, P., Jeong, W., & Godbey, G. (2004). Outdoor recreation among Asian Americans: A case study of San Francisco Bay area residents. *Journal of Park and Recreation Administration, 22*, 114–136.

29

TRENDS IN TIME FOR LEISURE

Geoffrey Godbey (The Pennsylvania State University)

This chapter discusses various concepts of time, past and present free time use, and potential free time use in the future and what this could mean for the field of leisure studies.

INTRODUCTION

To have free time has been one of the oldest dreams of humans. Gains in productivity have historically resulted in some increase in material possessions and some increase in time not devoted to necessary labor. Usually, when the basis of an economy changed from, for instance, hunting and gathering to farming, there has been, at first, an increase in time spent working and then a gradual decline. The same is true of industrialization (Rifkin, 1996). In Southeast Asia, for example, hours of labor in urban areas are coming down from 14 hours a day to 12 to 10. The number of holidays is also increasing—although many employers make employees "make up" the hours missed due to these holidays (Venture Outsource, 2011).

In the modern and postmodern worlds, time has often been thought of as the primary constraint to leisure (see Schneider, Chapter 18). Time constrains how long we live and every aspect of participation in leisure activity, including time to undertake an activity, how often it can be done, how much time can be devoted to it during each occasion, when it can be done, the pace at which it is done, and how much time can be spent preparing for it or recovering from it (Robinson & Godbey, 1997). Time may also constrain our ability to experience leisure as a state of mind. Feeling rushed, feeling that everything is "necessary," and the inability to let go and drift in the direction the world takes us are assuredly constraints, perhaps of a more severe nature.

"Time is what keeps everything from happening at once" (Cummings, 1922, p. 46). Time constraints make intentionality necessary, and without intention there can be no leisure. It is the very fact of temporal constraint that makes leisure possible. Leisure involves choice: the willing sacrifice for that which might be desirable for that which clearly, intuitively, is desirable. Leisure demands sacrifice, as does all free choice. Constraints of time are therefore both constraints to leisure and a necessary condition for leisure to occur. When this is not understood, there is no leisure.

CONCEPTS OF TIME

Every living thing on the earth has its own sense of time as a part of its genetic endowment. The way humans think about time, however, is based largely on their way of life and how they view the world. There is now more evidence that the brain is changed by cultural practices which become, in effect, automatic. Sense and meaning of time is likely among such cultural understandings. Kitayama and Uskul (2011), for example, developed a model of neuro-culture interaction that addressed this conceptual gap by:

> hypothesizing that the brain serves as a crucial site that accumulates effects of cultural experience, insofar as neural connectivity is likely modified through sustained engagement in cultural practices. Thus, culture is "embrained," and moreover, this process requires no cognitive mediation. (p. 419)

If these researchers are correct, then concepts of time—which are a function of culture—would similarly be absorbed and "embrained."

Although all notions of time relate in some way to change, vastly different concepts historically conditioned the individual to behave in a certain way and affected his or her understanding of others. In ancient and traditional societies, time had to do with the ebb and flow of tides, the orbits of sun and moon, and the passing of seasons. Time was a circle within which humans lived. The Chinese have historically had a preference for organic naturalism in which time and nature are conceived as aspects of dynamic, living systems to be qualitatively explored. Both the Hindu judgment of time as unimportant and the Chinese preference for thinking of time in natural, qualitative terms, however, are systematically changed when a culture begins to "modernize." If "modern" means anything, it means our sense of time becomes more ordered by human activity than by the acts of nature (Robinson & Godbey, 1997).

Viewing time as a line with a beginning and an end made it a finite commodity. As an expert in the study of time, philosopher J. T. Fraser (1987), pointed out:

> With the meteoric advance of science and technology—made possible by the linear view of time and history—the relationship between God-the-timer and man-the-timed has changed. In our epoch, carrying out the promise of salvation history became a responsibility of the created and not the Creator. (p. 48)

Little by little, humans became runners on the straight line of time. From the Middle Ages through industrialism, the pace of life began an unprecedented process of speeding up, not only the speedup of work in factories but also related changes that reflected the new values of speed and efficiency: standardization of hours during which pubs could be open, mass production of watches, the imposition of laws against loitering. Slowly, time became the ultimate organizing mechanism of the modern world—the ultimate scarce commodity.

While industrialization and the clock profoundly altered life and sped up its pace dramatically, Frederick Taylor, the creator of scientific management, may have been responsible more than anyone else for the time famine in American culture (Kanigel, 1997). In 1899, Taylor established a company whose product was advice on how to make enterprises more efficient. Taylor's techniques controlled each of six temporal dimensions on the shop floor—sequence, duration, schedule, rhythm, synchronization, and time perspective—stripping the individual worker of control of the processes of work and making him a servant of the machine. Taylor unwittingly reshaped the use of time in every aspect of our lives. Modern homemaking began to reflect these values and processes: kitchens were designed in increasingly standardized ways based on the same time-and-motion studies that Taylor helped introduce. Leisure, too, was affected. The methods of coaching many sports became indistinguishable from the methods employed by Henry Ford to produce the Model T automobile. Largely because of the economic success of scientific management in the workplace, time and attitudes toward time have slowly been reorganized in the rest of life, with the ultimate result being a general scarcity of time.

THE INDUSTRIALIZATION OF FREE TIME

As work became more ordered and time became the ordering device, for many the rest of life became "free time"—an empty container that could no longer be filled with the old forms of play and holy days, which characterized peasant life. New work patterns, the emergence of capitalism, and the urban environment—the last a largely unplanned phenomenon accompanying the factory system—made former ways of life and leisure obsolete. If the factory system was a catastrophe for peasant culture, peasant culture was initially a catastrophe for the factory system. Peasants often preferred idleness, drink, working when the mood struck them, and the pleasures of the body over the pleasures of the mind. In both Europe and North America, gambling and drinking either accompanied or had been the source of most leisure activity of adult males and some females. Such preferences led to a series of attempts to reform the leisure of the peasants, since employers and managers believed it was necessary to change such habits for industrialism to succeed (Cross, 1990; Hemingway, Chapter 4).

By the 1830s, reformers understood new work patterns were harming non-work experiences. Modern sport, for instance, was born in the nineteenth century during the transformation of work to the industrial system. Athletics were increasingly measured, timed, specialized, and synchronized in ways that would have made Taylor proud. Play in sport began to disappear in favor of industrial efficiency.

To reform the habits of working-class women, the "rational domesticity" movement featured visits to their homes by upper-class females to teach ways of improving housework, handicrafts, and childrearing; increasing hygiene; and becoming more efficient, punctual, and productive (Cross, 1993). "Work" and "free time" existed as separate spheres of life—at least for males. For females, those who married and stayed at home to raise children found the distinction between work and free time less meaningful. "Housework" has an elasticity about it; it can be done in more or less time depending on how much it is valued and the other work-related duties of females (Walker, 1969). For society as a whole, industrial cycles of work and leisure also became more identifiable across the day, week, and year.

Post-industrial society changed this dynamic. When an economy based primarily on manufacturing goods in factories became automated and most people began to make their living as teachers, salespeople, hospitality workers, medical occupations and others, free time and work became more entangled. Individuals were often at work and experiencing free time in the same sequence of events. More often, two activities were going on at once. The sequencing of work and free time became more flexible and customized. Weekly rhythms of life changed so that the idea of free time coming on Saturdays and Sundays and week days devoted primarily to work made little sense. Work became more difficult to disengage from as the smart phone, laptop, and tablet brought the issues of work to those on vacation or simply relaxing in the back yard. Even the idea of doing one activity at a time became obsolete for many, as multitasking became more common and admired.

WHAT MEASURES OF FREE TIME ARE USEFUL?

To find out how much free time people have, a number or questions must be answered—some of which are simply unanswerable. The broadest query is: "What percentage of life is spent in free time activity?" Answering this question requires knowing the age of entering and exiting the labor force, years of retirement in relation to life expectancy, hours spent in housework, paid work, personal care, school, transportation to and from obligated activities, etc. There must also be some judgments made about what parts of "school" can be classified as free or discretionary. Since pace of activity may be an indicator of "leisurely" activity, it is difficult to code the eating of a meal as always work or leisure, voluntary or discretionary. Further, the sequencing of paid work, housework, personal care, leisure, and other uses of time are critical. A long weekend (i.e., 72 consecutive hours) is far different than 144 one-half hour segments of free time. Finally, we must also know about secondary activity (and even, on occasion, tertiary activity). For example, is a person eating dinner, watching television, talking to their spouse, or a combination thereof?

Free Time Use in Modern Nations

There are several generalizations that can be made about time use in modern nations. While the precise numbers vary somewhat from nation to nation, the following appears to be true (Goodin, Mahmud Rice, Parpo, & Eriksson, 2008):

- People have more freedom to choose how they use their time than is popularly imagined. Those who have children have much less such choice and those who have children but do not have a partner to help them raise children have even less choice in their time use.
- Women in modern nations have less, but only slightly less, "temporal autonomy" than men. Stay at home moms, however, have much more free time than their employed husbands.
- The amount of free time varies greatly from country to country. Swedes, for example, average nine hours of free time per week more than the French.
- Countries which are "social-democratic/female friendly welfare gender regimes" provide an average of five more hours of free time per week than those that are either "liberal/individualist or corporatist/traditionalist regimes" (p. 261).
- Divorce leads to less free time and the loss is greater for females than for males. Government policies play some role in how much this loss is.
- The majority of free time takes place in and around the home and much of that involves social media.
- Doing more than one thing at once has become normal behavior for younger people.
- Physically active uses of leisure constitute a small part of free time.

Thus, modern nations are not alike in their use of time or amount of free time. Social policies shape who gets free time and how much. So, too, does the portion of the population raising young children. Single-parent families have substantially less free time than others (Goodin et al., 2008).

Free Time Use in the United States

The 2012 American Time Use Survey (Bureau of Labor Statistics, 2013a, 2013b) found that, during an average day, nearly everyone (96%) age 15 and over engaged in some sort of leisure activity. Considerable variation existed, however, by age, gender, race/ethnicity, and parental and employment status. For example:

- Men spent more time engaged in leisure activities (5.8 hours) than did women (5.0 hours).
- Men were more likely than women to participate in sports, exercise, or recreation on any given day (22.5% vs. 17.6%, respectively). On the days that they participated, men also spent more time in these activities than did women (2.0 hours vs. 1.5 hours, respectively).
- On an average day, adults age 75 and over spent 7.7 hours engaged in leisure activities, more than any other age group. In contrast, 25- to 34-year-olds spent 4.4 hours and 35- to 44-year-olds spent 4.3 hours engaged in leisure and sports activities; less than any other age groups.
- Watching TV was the leisure activity that occupied the most time (2.8 hours per day), accounting for about half of leisure time, on average, for those age 15 and over.
- Time spent reading for personal interest and playing games or using a computer for leisure varied greatly by age. Individuals age 75 and over averaged 1.0 hour of reading per weekend day and 20 minutes playing games or using a computer for

leisure. Conversely, individuals ages 15 to 19 read for an average of 7 minutes per weekend day while spending 1.0 hour playing games or using a computer for leisure.

- Employed adults living in households with no children under age 18 engaged in leisure activities for 4.7 hours per day, about an hour more than employed adults living with a child under age six.
- Hispanic or Latinos spent 4.8 hours engaged in leisure each day, less than both Whites and African Americans (5.3 hours and 6.1 hours, respectively).

Just as Americans may think they have less free time than they actually do, there may also be a tendency to think that more time is spent in socially desirable uses of free time than is the case. There are some surprises from other data reported in the 2012 American Time Use Survey that focuses on time spent on leisure on weekdays versus weekends (Bureau of Labor Statistics, 2013a, 2013b). First, for instance, if holidays are excluded, the majority of free time comes during the five week days, not the two weekend days. Second, watching TV continues to account for more than half of all free time use. Part of the reason for this is that most "free time" comes in small increments, 45 minutes here and there. When you add them up, you get around 35 hours per week but the usefulness of these small increments is limited. Watching TV fits right in to these small segments of free time, since it can be accessed almost instantly and requires no travel.

As well, according to the American Time Use Survey (Bureau of Labor Statistics. (2013a), less than one out of five Americans is participating in sports, exercise, or recreation on any given day (see also Bocarro & Edwards, Chapter 8). While TV shows sports events non-stop, time spent in actual participation is much rarer in daily life. In terms of sport, for instance, time spent participating in sport and fitness is generally less than might be expected. Dedicated walking is the most prevalent activity, engaged in by 5% of Americans on an average day for about 53 minutes per walker, leading to an average of about 2.6 minutes per day. In terms of more physically active team sports, basketball is by far the most popular, followed by football, soccer, baseball, and hockey. These numbers still highlight how rare participation in a given sport really is. On a given day, only one about out of 500 Americans plays baseball, one out of 300 goes bowling, and one out of 60 goes swimming or engages in other water sports. Health officials and fitness enthusiasts may be dismayed to find these daily participation figures to be at such low levels. However, when combined, they add up to about 2 hours a week, almost three times higher than was found in the first U.S. national diary study conducted in 1965.

WHY INCREASED FREE TIME HAS OCCURRED

We have more free time than 50 years ago for many reasons, including later entry into the labor force, fewer children in an average family, and longer life after retirement. In terms of the second, the U.S. birth rate has fallen to a record low and fewer or no children mean more free time for parents (Livingstone & Cohn, 2012). In terms of the last, it is easy to forget that Social Security in the U.S. and comparable government social insurance plans in other countries originally set the age for qualifying for retirement at 65, because that was the average age of life expectancy. At that time, most people worked all their lives, with retirement limited to a few wealthy folks (Pearson, 2011). More specifically, while life expectancy was 65.5 years in 1950—and so, on average, no years spent in retirement, life expectancy was 75.2 years in 2005—with, on average, 13.5 years being spent in retirement.

Noteworthy, however, is evidence exists that suggests the great increase in years of retirement is now stopping and, in fact, may even be reversing. Reasons for this trend include: a much higher portion of the pre-retirement population with no savings or company retirement plan to make retirement possible, legal changes which steadily increase the age at which an individual is eligible for Social Security, and the decline of unions. Also, life expectancy may actually decline in the U.S. due to the obesity epidemic. Moreover, while women currently live 5 to 8 years longer than men, this gap may close since a higher percentage of women are negatively affected by obesity in later life and more women smoke. In combination, all these factors seem to imply the huge gains of leisure in retirement will at least level off and possibly decline (see also Kleiber, Chapter 23).

HOW FREE TIME HAS CHANGED: THE RISE IN MULTITASKING

American children and teens are spending an increasing amount of time using "new media" like computers, the Internet, and video games, without cutting back on the time they spend with "old" media like TV, print, and music (see also Caldwell, Chapter 21). According to Rideout, Foehr, and Roberts (2010), young people's total media use each day increased by over an hour between 2004 and 2009 (from 6.21 to 7.38 hours, respectively). Even more importantly, however, the total amount of media content they were exposed increased by more two hours (i.e., from 8:33 hours in 2004 to 10.45 hours in 2009). The latter increase occurred across four different media forms, including: television content (to 4.29 from 3.51 hours), music/audio (to 2.31 hours from 1.44 hours), computers (to 1.29 hours from 1.02 hours), and video games (to 1.13 hours from 0.49 hours).

Rideout and associates (2010) also found that 29% of the time American children and teens were using media, they were using two or more forms concurrently (a rise from 26% in 2004). The increased prevalence in multitasking is perhaps the most important trend in time use in modern nations. Multitasking may be thought of as one form of "time deepening." Time deepening, an attempt to increase the "output" on a unit of time, may involve doing an activity faster, substituting a faster activity for a slower one or doing more than one thing at a time (Godbey, 1976).

Multitasking has changed the notion that a person is doing one activity or the other—now they are thought to be doing two (or more) things at once. In reality, what is happening is they are doing one thing for a tiny period of time and then switching to another. This way of behavior, while increasingly popular, raises questions of safety, efficiency, and even happiness. In terms of safety, driving a car and texting or talking on a cell phone appears to be as dangerous as driving drunk. Using a handheld electronic device while crossing a street increases the chances of getting hit by a car. Studies also show that multitaskers are less efficient than those doing only one activity (Sullivan & Thompson, 2013). The consequences of this may be a lower quality of communication, failure to grasp important visual or audio signals, and a general loss of quality in performing the function. Noteworthy here is that research suggests older people may have slightly less of an ability to multitask than younger people, possibly because they cannot refocus as well after getting interrupted (Dotinga, 2011). Finally, there is also the issue of multitasking being a misnomer. Sullivan and Thompson (2013) state that:

> in most situations, the person juggling e-mail, text messaging, Facebook and a meeting is really doing something called "rapid toggling between tasks," and is engaged in constant context switching. As economics students know, switching involves costs. But how much? When a consumer switches banks, or a company switches suppliers, it's relatively easy to count the added expense of the hassle of change. When your brain is switching tasks, the cost is harder to quantify. (p. SR12)

FREE TIME IN THE FUTURE

If people in modern nations have less time for leisure than they think, it may be partially due to the desirability of showing that one is busy (Gershuny, 1992, 2005). Being busy implies that one is important, needed, useful. It is no surprise, then, that people overestimate their hours of paid work and underestimate how much free time they have. The free time they do have has been greatly shaped by electronic media—TV, computers, handheld devices of communication. These instruments of communication and entertainment have changed the idea of what one is doing—from one activity to multitasking. Multitasking is the opposite of all classical concepts of leisure, in which an individual gives full attention to an activity thought to be intrinsically worth doing—at the expense of doing another activity. TV, the cell phone, and other instruments are almost completely controlled by corporations and they are used for huge amounts of advertising. Thus, as much as one-fourth of our use of these instruments is receiving advertising of products and services. It may be that newer innovations, such as the 3D printer, will begin to reshape the use of leisure in ways that cannot yet be predicted (see also Nimrod, Chapter 30).

Additionally, while gender has historically been among the best predictor of access to leisure and how it is used, this has changed dramatically and continues to do so. In terms of leisure, the first stage of change was females becoming more like males in their overall time use and use of free time. In the next stage, males are becoming more like women in their overall time use. Differences remain, of course, and are likely to remain. The policies of government shape how much difference exists between males and females in important ways (Goodin et al., 2008).

Leisure studies has generally not paid much attention to time use research. Indeed, most time use researchers are in other academic units of universities or government. The International Association of Time Use Researchers publicizes research concerning time use in dozens of countries. Leisure studies needs to make more use of time data since the amount of free time, its sequencing across the day, week, and life cycle help predict and explain the use and meaning of leisure behavior. In particular, the sequencing of work and leisure into short segments rules out participation in many forms of serious leisure (Stebbins, 1992) which involve skill and a challenge.

Leisure studies came into being mostly due to concern about the consequences for society of increasing free time. Understanding the amount, distribution, and use of free time is the foundation upon which other topics in leisure studies must be built.

REFERENCES

Bureau of Labor Statistics. (2013a). *American Time Use Survey—Leisure and sports*. Retrieved from http://www.bls.gov/tus/current/leisure.htm

Bureau of Labor Statistics. (2013b). *American Time Use Survey—2012 results*. Retrieved from http://www.bls.gov/news.release/pdf/atus.pdf

Cross, G. (1990). *A social history of leisure since 1600*. State College, PA: Venture Publishing, Inc.

Cross, G. (1993). *Time and money—The making of consumer culture*. London, England: Routledge.

Cummings, R. K. (1922). *The girl in the golden atom*. Lincoln, NE: University of Nebraska Press.

Dotinga, R. (2011). Multitasking just a bit tougher for older people: Study. Retrieved from http://health.usnews.com/health-news/family-health/brain-and-behavior/articles/2011/04/11/multitasking-just-a-bit-tougher-for-older-people-study

Fraser, J. T. (1987). *Time—The familiar stranger*. Redmond, WA: Microsoft Press.

Gershuny, J. (1992, January/February). Are we running out of time? *Futures*, 1–18.

Gershuny, D. (2005). Business as the Badge of Honor for the new superordinate working class. *Social Research, 72*, 287–314.

Godbey, G. (1976). Time deepening and the future of leisure. *Journal of Physical Education and Recreation, 47*(8), 40–42.

Goodin, R., Mahmud Rice, J., Parpo, A., & Eriksson, L. (2008). Discretionary time: A new measure of freedom. Cambridge, UK: Cambridge University Press.

Kanigel, R. (1997). *The one best way: Fredrick Winslow Taylor and the enigma of efficiency*. New York: Viking.

Kitayama, S., & Uskul, A. (2011). Culture, mind, and the brain: Current evidence and future directions. *Annual Review of Psychology, 62*, 419–49.

Livingstone, G., & Cohn, D. (2012). *U.S. birthrate falls to a record low: Decline is greatest among immigrants*. Retrieved from http://www.pewsocialtrends.org/2012/11/29/u-s-birth-rate-falls-to-a-record-low-decline-is-greatest-among-immigrants/

Pearson, C. (2011). *Life expectancy declining in large parts of US*. Retrieved from http://www.voanews.com/content/life-expectancy-declining-in-large-parts-of-us-124128694/171521

Rideout, V., Foehr, U., & Roberts, D. (2010). *Generation M^2: Media in the life of 8- to 18-year olds. A Kaiser Family Foundation Study*. Retrieved from http://kaiserfamilyfoundation.files.wordpress.com/2013/04/8010.pdf

Rifkin, J. (1996). *The end of work*. New York: Penguin.

Robinson, J., & Godbey, G. (1997). *Time for life: The surprising ways Americans use their time*. (Rev. ed.). University Park, PA: Penn State Press.

Stebbins, R. (1992). *Amateurs, professionals and serious leisure*. Montreal, QC: McGill-Queen's University Press.

Sullivan, B., & Thompson, H. (2013, May 7). *Brain, Interrupted*. New York Times.

Venture Outsource. (2011, April 17). *Report: China manufacturing hourly labor rate, compensation costs impact EMS*. Retrieved from http://www.ventureoutsource.com/contract-manufacturing/2011-china-manufacturing-hourly-labor-rate-compensation-costs-ems

Walker, K. (1969). Homemaking still takes time. *Journal of Home Economics, 61*, 621–624.

30

The Roles Technology Plays in Twenty-First Century Leisure

Galit Nimrod (Ben-Gurion University of the Negev, Israel)

Technology has shaped leisure since the early days of human history, although its progress has been rather slow. Technological development only began to accelerate after the Industrial Revolution—and even more so during the twentieth century (Basalla, 1989), bringing about the rapid progress we have been witnessing since the turn of the millennium (Kurzweil, 2005). Consequently, understanding the various impacts of technology on leisure and the roles it plays therein has become a key research issue to be explored thoroughly as part of the broader discipline of leisure studies.

Technology exerts a threefold effect on leisure, addressing all of its core defining aspects, namely time, action, and experience (Katz et al., 2000; Kelly, 1996). First, technology clearly affects the *amount* of free time individuals have. The past century provided many technological advances that increased individual free time, including medical technologies that significantly extended longevity, workplace machinery that decreased working hours and home appliances (such as dishwashers and washing machines) that freed many people, especially women in developed countries, from long hours of sisyphean work. Some (e.g., Schor, 1991) argued that the latter development had the opposite effect on women, as it promoted women's involvement in the labor force and eventually decreased their free time. Moreover, technological developments may be considered as catalysts of longer working hours, when consumers are motivated to earn more in order to upgrade their lifestyle. Still, people have the alternative to downshift by working less, earning less, and living their lives much more deliberately (Hodgkinson, 2006; Schor, 1997).

Second, technology impacts *what* people do in their free time, as it provides both greater access to leisure and new options for leisure activities. Examples from the past century include mobility technologies (e.g., motor vehicles and aircraft) that made travel and tourism accessible and widespread and media technologies (e.g., radio, television) that provided new forms of leisure activity. In the past two decades, it was computer technologies that dramatically affected what people did in their free time. The impact was particularly strong for children and adolescents. In the U.S., for example, the average 8- to 18-year-old spends three hours a day using computers and video games (Kaiser Family Foundation, 2010; see also Godbey, Chapter 29).

The third aspect, that is somewhat more complex to demonstrate, concerns technology's effect on *how* people experience leisure. Listening to music, for example, is a common leisure activity and one of the oldest documented in human history. Originally, one had to be in the same time and space in which the music was played. It was only in 1877, after Thomas Edison invented the phonograph, that one could listen to music in a different time and place. Twentieth-century technological advances (such as commercial radio—launched in the 1920s—and the widespread use of vinyl records during the 1950s) increased accessibility to music and enhanced the control people had over the time and type of music listening they preferred. Subsequently, portable electronic devices (e.g., Walkman, Discman) enabled them to listen to music everywhere and digital devices (MP3 players and cell phones, for example) substantially increased the sound quality, supported downloading and offered massive music libraries that allowed for much greater diversity. Thanks to these advances, music lovers now experience more freedom of choice and control than ever before. As these two qualities are intrinsically correlated with the essence of leisure, we may say that the leisure experience of listening to music was enhanced by technology.

Technology embodies numerous such potential impacts on leisure, whether direct or indirect, positive or negative. Studying the various effects of technology on leisure behavior and the leisure experience is highly relevant to the leisure studies discipline, bearing potential for both theoretical and practical implications. Nevertheless, until recently this topic was rather neglected by leisure scholars and thus the literature on technology and leisure is still limited.

This chapter seeks to provide a conceptual framework for understanding the various roles technology plays in twenty-first century leisure. It contends that under current technological realities, technology may simultaneously enhance leisure, function as leisure and constrain leisure. Furthermore, it argues that one should differentiate between "low" and "high" (i.e., computer-based) technology when exploring these roles. Rather than providing answers, this chapter outlines the type of questions leisure researchers should ask in an increasingly technological world.

WHAT IS TECHNOLOGY AND WHAT IS LEISURE TECHNOLOGY?

Dictionary definitions of the term "technology" cover a wide range of meanings. Such definitions tend to stress two aspects characterizing technology, namely its knowledge-based status and its utility. For example, the Merriam-Webster Dictionary defines technology as "the practical application of knowledge" and the Oxford Dictionary as "the application of scientific knowledge for practical purposes." Hence, technology may be defined broadly as any tool, machine, or technique created by the application of knowledge for achievement of some practical value. Drawing on this general definition, leisure technology may be defined as any tool, machine, or technique created by the application of knowledge that helps individuals and societies achieve leisure goals.

Two terms often used in discussing technology are "high tech" and "low tech." High-tech (or high technology) refers to the latest developments in technology; consequently, technologies currently referred to as "low tech" may have been "high tech" in the past. Contemporary high tech is also characterized by sophisticated production processes that involve a large number of individuals, significant specialization and compartmentalization, as well as considerable capital investment. Most often, this term is used in reference to microelectronics, especially computer hardware and software (Eurostat, 2013). Thus, in this chapter, the discussion of high tech will focus primarily on Information and Communication Technology (ICT).

Leisure technology may be "high" (e.g., digital games) or "low" (e.g., bicycles). Although nominally intended for the leisure sector, many leisure technologies were originally developed for commercial, scientific, or military purposes and were simply extended and modified for leisure-time use by organizations active in the leisure sector or by end users themselves (Poser, 2011; Russell, 2013), especially in the ICT sphere. For example, the first computer was designed to calculate artillery firing tables for the U.S. Army. Similarly, first computer network was created by the U.S. Department of Defense for use by its projects at universities and research laboratories (Cortada, 2000; Robins & Webster, 1999). Once the World Wide Web took shape in the 1990s, however, mass use of ICT became common; at present, leisure use accounts for a sizable share of network activity.

Leisure technologies can play three different roles: as an instrument supporting participation in leisure activities and deriving benefit from them, as an activity in itself, and— in a somewhat negative role—as a constraint to leisure. The following section will discuss each of these roles. Differentiating between low technology (non-ICT) and high technology (ICT), it will also demonstrate the various roles and underscore the rationale for referring to the type of technology when studying the associations between technology and leisure in contemporary realities.

THE ROLES TECHNOLOGY PLAYS IN LEISURE

Technology as an Instrument Supporting Leisure

Various technologies facilitate participation in leisure activities and/or benefits that can be derived from the involvement. Some of these technologies are essential for participation in leisure activities, such as those supporting aids for people with disabilities. These devices may be the same as the ones people with disabilities use in other activities (e.g., hearing aids, walkers), but many technological developments were designed specifically for leisure (e.g., flotation devices in swimming pools, larger game pieces for children with motor coordination difficulties). Such technologies may turn non-participants into participants and enhance autonomy and self-efficacy among participants (Capio, Mascolo, & Sit, 2012; Ripat & Woodgate, 2012).

An increase in the use of non-mandatory technology (i.e., gadgets) for leisure activity is evident as well. For example, people may travel without using technology, but a variety of items, from special clothing and footwear to sophisticated binoculars and cameras, may help travelers optimize their tourism experience. Unlike such aids that support participants *during* leisure activity, ICT is primarily used as a supporting technology *before* and *after* participation in offline activities. As a pre-participation tool, ICT may serve as an instrument for learning, planning, and purchasing leisure services. For example, when planning a vacation, people can learn about various locations they consider visiting and the attractions they offer. They can also read previous visitors' recommendations, visit the websites of resorts and hotels, compare prices, and make transportation and hotel reservations (Buhalis & Law, 2008). Such uses of technology may support decision-making processes regarding almost every leisure product or service.

ICT may also constitute a post-participation instrument for savoring the leisure experience and sharing it with others. For example, after returning from a vacation, people may use ICT to post photos and reflections about their experiences (Sigala, Christou, & Gretzel, 2012). As wireless and cellular access to Internet becomes more common, ICT may also support participants during activity. For example, when independently visiting a tourist site with historical or cultural value, people can use online information to learn more about it (MacKay & Vogt, 2012). However, ICT use during the activity can damage the leisure experience, as explained later in this chapter.

Technology can also be employed by recreation agencies to better serve their customers. Again, this may be done before, during, and after participation, or, in other words, in each stage of the programming cycle (Jordan, DeGraaf, & DeGraaf, 2005). ICT may be particularly useful in the pre and post-implementation stages. For example, in the need-assessment stage agencies may follow discussions in online communities and use online surveys to understand users and non-users' attitudes and expectations (Gupta, Sleezer, & Russ-Eft, 2011). In the pre-program stage they may use ICT for promotion and sales management (Christou, 2011; Mowen & Havitz, Chapter 34), and in the evaluation stage they may re-contact consumers to assess satisfaction and improve the program. Non-ICT technology (e.g., equipment, lighting, music) may mainly be used in the implementation stage. Such usages of technology promote consumer satisfaction and eventually increase effectiveness and profitability (Demirkan et al., 2008).

Technology Use as a Leisure Activity in Itself

Besides supporting participation in and benefit from leisure activities, technology use may also be an activity in itself. To differentiate between the use of technology as an instrument supporting leisure and the use of it as an activity in itself, one should examine the centrality of technology to the various activities. For example, although there are a variety of technologies supporting runners, people can run without any technology. In cycling, however, the technology (i.e., the tool itself; such as the bicycle) is central, if not essential, to the activity. Hence, when discussing technology use as an activity, we refer to activities that are *dependent* on technology, such as various arts and crafts (e.g., carpentry), media use (e.g., TV viewing and computer use) and extreme sports (e.g., skydiving).

The distinction between high and low technology is particularly important when discussing technology as an activity in itself. Studying non-ICT technology-based activities is quite different from studying activities made possible by ICT. The latter are often described as "digital leisure," "online leisure," "cyber leisure," or simply "E-leisure." The numerous E-leisure activities may be grouped into six major categories:

Social activities.

Interpersonal communication is one of the chief leisure uses of ICT. Users are offered a wide range of technological platforms to communicate with others, from email and instant messaging software to social network services (SNS) such as Facebook, online communities, blogs, online dating websites, and so forth. Offering three types of communication (one-to-one, one-to-many, and many-to-many) and allowing for both synchronous and asynchronous communication, these platforms enable users to maintain existing relationships and form new contacts (Jensen & Helles, 2011), using them is becoming increasingly interwoven with users' social lives (Papacharissi, 2010).

Games.

ICT offers a wide range of digital games, varying dramatically in terms of complexity, competitiveness, realism vs. imaginary worlds, skills activated (e.g., cognitive, creative, social, physical), number of players (from playing alone or against the computer to playing against millions—as in the case of certain massively multiplayer online games), level of engagement and impact on life satisfaction (Boyle, Connolly, Hainey, & Boyle, 2012). Players' emotional connection to these games may shift over time from carefree escapism to bitter and self-destructive compulsion (Bissell, 2010).

Entertainment.

All forms of entertainment we used to consume offline are now offered online. Movies, TV shows, radio programs, newspapers and magazines, music, video clips and even art exhibitions are available via the World Wide Web. Perhaps more than anything else, this trend represents the process of media convergence (Jenkins, 2006), in which common interfaces on a single medium merge most types of old media and communication services. Often, such entertainment is offered for free (legally or illegally), allowing for greater accessibility to cultural goods (Healy, 2002). In addition, consumers may frequently comment, discuss, and even affect the contents via complimentary social media (cf. Chau, 2010). This turns them from passive to active audience, which not only consumes but also produces media contents.

Hobbies.

The Internet enables development of new hobbies and interests via activities such as online courses, blog writing, and volunteer activities. In addition, it supports intensification of involvement in existing hobbies through acquisition of knowledge, communicating with others with similar interests, and using online applications (e.g., photo albums). These opportunities are particularly exciting for individuals experiencing many constraints to leisure such as people with disabilities, older adults, immigrants, and those residing in remote places, as they allow them to be socially active in spite of limiting factors (Khvorostianov, Elias, & Nimrod, 2012; Mukherjee, 2010).

Physical activities.

The Internet offers a growing number of online gyms in which, for a very low monthly fee, one may attend online classes (i.e., follow at home what the instructor demonstrates on screen). Furthermore, a growing number of digital games promote physical activity. These games—sometimes called "exergames" or "exertainment"—involve various forms of physical activity and exertion as a means of interaction (Lieberman, 2006), and there is considerable evidence demonstrating that their physical effects are similar to traditional light- to moderate-intensity offline physical activities (Peng, Lin, & Crouse, 2011).

Online shopping.

Like its offline counterpart, online shopping should be considered semi-leisure (i.e., an activity in which there is some degree of obligation or purpose, perceived as leisure by some and as duty by others). There is a continuous increase in the number of people involved in online shopping and accompanying activities (e.g., information searches for company and/or product details, consumer social networking). These activities are often experienced as enjoyable and generate feelings of control and freedom (Rose, Hair, & Clark, 2010). Moreover, consumers may experience the optimal experience of *flow*. This experience is characterized by full involvement, intense and focused concentration, merging of action and awareness, and a loss of reflective self-consciousness (Nakamura & Csikszentmihalyi, 2009). Flow has been acknowledged to be a useful variable for explaining online consumer behavior (Lee & Chen, 2010).

To a great extent, all these categories have offline parallels and one may argue that traditional leisure spaces and activities are simply reproduced in virtual leisure spaces (Bryce, 2001). To gain a more comprehensive understanding of the experience that E-leisure provides, however, we should note that not all dimensions used in studying offline activities (including non-ICT technology-based activities) are equally relevant in the study of E-leisure. Specifically, the *distinctiveness* of leisure as time, the importance of *physical place and space*, and the division between *formal* and *informal* leisure lose relevance significantly in E-leisure (Nimrod & Adoni, 2012).

In the realities of a wired world, the traditional boundaries between work and leisure hardly exist any longer (Lightman, 2005). Individuals enjoy E-leisure during their working and commuting activity and follow up on work-related issues while at leisure. Moreover, most E-leisure activities are informal (i.e., flexible, with no clear constraints on time, place and participants) and people may take part in them almost anywhere, with the external environment having little to no impact on the experience (Hampton, Livio, & Sessions-Goulet, 2010).

At the same time, however, E-leisure has introduced four new and unique dimensions that were not commonly applied in traditional leisure research (Nimrod & Adoni, 2012). These dimensions may have some relevance to offline leisure as well, but they are primarily significant in understanding E-leisure experiences.

1. **V**irtual reality—A sense of being present or existing in a place that is different from the place in which the physical body is situated at the time.
2. **I**nteractivity—Reciprocal computer-mediated communication exchanges that involve either *user-to-system* or *user-to-user* interaction.
3. **S**ynchronicity—E-leisure enables asynchronous social activities and interactions that have virtually no equivalent in offline leisure.
4. **A**nonymity—Although one can be anonymous when participating in traditional leisure activities, total anonymity and invisibility in social activities is possible only in cyberspace.

Briefly stated, **VISA** is required for the study of E-leisure. In order to fully understand the leisure experience provided by ICT-based technologies, we should explore the effects of these four dimensions on users and online dynamics.

Technology as a Leisure Constraint

The abovementioned roles may be regarded as positive, as in both roles technology promotes leisure participation and expands the variety of activities people may choose from. Nevertheless, technology may also play a somewhat negative role, which may be described as posing constraints to leisure (see also Schneider, Chapter 18). Leisure constraints are often divided into *intervening* and *antecedent* (Jackson, 2005). Intervening constraints may be interpersonal or structural factors affecting participation and the ability to benefit from it by intervening between leisure preferences and participation. Antecedent constraints are intrapersonal factors affecting the preferences and interests of an individual. This chapter argues that both low and high technologies may act as leisure constraints—and as both intervening and antecedent constraints when technophobia (a fear of modern technology) is involved.

It is estimated that technophobia affects 30% of the general population, depending on gender, age, education, personality, culture, and ideology (Anthony, Clarke, & Anderson, 2000; Gilbert, Lee-Kelley, & Barton, 2003; Weil & Rosen, 1995). Technophobia is associated primarily with ICT use. In fact, in the past two decades, this term was mainly mentioned as a dominant factor explaining Digital Divides, namely, inequalities between groups in terms of ICT access, use, and knowledge. Research has found, for example, that technophobia may explain limited ICT use among women (Johnson, 2012), older adults (Curran, Walters, & Robinson, 2007), ethnic minorities, and/or people with low educational level (Zickuhr & Smith, 2012). Such limited ICT use may constrain participation not only in E-leisure but also in offline leisure activities. This is particularly true when most of the information about the offline activity is provided via online channels, and when registration involves online forms and payment methods.

It should be noted, though, that people may also avoid participation in certain activities—or derive less benefit from them—if they fear low technology. For example, people who distrust the technology required for scuba diving may either develop no interest in this activity (antecedent constraint) or avoid it despite great interest (intervening constraint). If they do decide to try scuba diving at some point, constant concern about the technology will decrease their enjoyment compared with that of non-technophobes (intervening constraint). If they do not develop trust and gain confidence with time, they will likely quit the activity for that reason. The same is true regarding ICT: Technophobes will either not use it or experience some discomfort when using it, especially in the early stages or following technological upgrades.

Except in cases of technophobia, where low and high technologies have similar effects, these two types of technology act as leisure constraints in different ways. Low technology may be a leisure constraint when acquiring it, learning how to use it and/or when using it involve high costs. Returning to the example of scuba diving, it is probable that the fee for scuba diving classes (mandatory in most countries), along with the costs of buying or renting the equipment required, are significant constraints for many people who are interested in this activity. Costs may be a constraint for the use of ICT as well, especially in developing countries. However, in most developed countries costs lose their significance as a constraining factor. In recent years, the cost of computers has significantly decreased. In addition, if one does not insist on purchasing the latest technology (or is willing to acquire used products), the expenditure on hardware is rather low. Furthermore, the monthly fee for Internet access is declining in many developed and developing countries and ICT is also available at schools and community centers at little to no cost to the consumer.

ICT may function as a leisure constraint, however, in cases of technostress—"a modern disease of adaptation caused by an inability to cope with ICT in a healthy manner" (Brod, 1984, p. 16). Technostress is associated with high physiological arousal and various psychosomatic symptoms and manifests itself in overidentification with technology and compulsiveness about being connected, sharing constant updates, responding to others in real time, and constant multitasking (Arnetz & Wiholm, 1997). Its chief causes are work overload, our increasing dependence on ICT, and the decline in differentiation between work and leisure that keep us "switched on" constantly (Ayyagari, Grover, & Purvis, 2011; Ragu-Nathan, Tarafdar, Ragu-Nathan, & Tu, 2008).

Technostress may be work-related or leisure/social-related, and have various negative effects. Work-related technostress significantly reduces employees' job satisfaction, commitment, innovation, and productivity (Tarafdar, Tu, Ragu-Nathan, & Ragu-Nathan, 2011). Similarly, social-related technostress, manifested in social interaction overload via SNS, affects users' satisfaction and continuous usage intention (Laumer, Maier, & Weinert, 2013). At its worst, technostress and excessive use of ICT may turn into Internet addiction, or formally, Internet Use Disorder (defined as "condition for further study" at the latest Diagnostic and Statistical Manual of Mental Disorders [DSM], published by the American Psychiatric Association). This disorder is associated with depression, anxiety, attention deficit hyperactivity disorder, and social isolation (Byun et al., 2009; Shaw & Black, 2008; Weinstein & Lejoyeux, 2010).

Even without becoming an addiction, but particularly when it does, technostress may turn ICT use into an intervening leisure constraint. First, it may affect participation in various leisure activities, as ICT use, regardless of its purpose, takes time. Second, compulsive use of ICT may affect the ability to benefit from leisure by preventing flow, the optimal experience in which action and awareness merge (Nakamura & Csikszentmihalyi, 2009). It is quite probable that a person who keeps answering his or her cell phone while spending time with friends, or feels the urge to post messages and photos during a rock concert, does not experience flow in the same frequency or to the same degree as a person who is able to "switch off."

RESEARCH ON TECHNOLOGY IN THE FIELD OF LEISURE STUDIES

As we proceed into the twenty-first century, people are spending more and more of their free time using technology—and ICT in particular. They play, socialize, shop, blog, read the news, listen to music, watch videos, date, and enjoy many other technology-based activities. Furthermore, they use technology before, during and after participation in various non-technology-based leisure activities to gain information, plan and share their experiences with others. This chapter argues that technology plays three main roles in the twenty-first leisure: An instrument supporting participation in and derivation of benefits from leisure activities, an activity in itself, and a constraint to leisure. Moreover, it suggests that these roles vary considerably between low (non-ICT) and high technology (ICT). Table 30.1 provides a summary of that discussion and presents the various roles played by each type of technology.

Over the past two decades, numerous studies have explored various psychological, sociological and cultural aspects of technology-based activities. Dozens and even hundreds of articles on specific activities such as using SNS and online games have been published in journals in the fields of sociology, psychology, communication, education, social work, nursing, computer sciences, and other disciplines. More general discussions of the technological trends in leisure and their various implications, however, are rare. Furthermore, and quite surprisingly, leisure studies is the only relevant discipline in which research on leisure use of technology is only developing.

Every new technology tends to elicit varying responses, from sheer enthusiasm to suspicion and doubt. In particular, utopian and dystopian visions of ICT have given rise to some extremely polarized academic discussions from the time the Internet became accessible to mass society in the early 1990s (Fisher & Wright, 2001). Examples include long-lasting discussions of the Internet's impact on democracy and society (e.g., Barber, 1999), social relationships (e.g., Tufekci, 2010), identity (e.g., Nach & Lejeune, 2009), privacy (e.g., Solove, 2011) and individual well-being (e.g., Nimrod, 2013).

Table 30.1. The Roles Technology Plays in Leisure

	Technology Supporting Activity	Technology as an Activity in Itself	Technology as Activity Constraint
Low Tech (non-ICT)	Technology-supported leisure (e.g., aids, gadgets)	Technology-based leisure (e.g., TV)	Technophobia Costs
High Tech (ICT)	Pre- and post-activity support (e.g., planning, sharing)	E-Leisure (e.g., online games, SNS)	Technophobia Technostress

Note: ICT–Information and Communication Technology; SNS–Social Network Services

Technology may have many positive impacts on leisure. It provides new activities for everyone, as well as some promising opportunities for negotiation of leisure constraints. It also promotes access to vital information on leisure services and products, facilitates pre- and post-activity processes and may enhance well-being in various ways. At the same time, however, technology may have negative effects on leisure participation and experience and may also create a social divide between those who have access to technology and those who do not (and/or technophobes). Moreover, technostress may have negative effects on psychological well-being, and technology use may have negative influence on physical health by reducing participation in physically active and health-enhancing leisure activities (Mannell, Kaczynski, & Aronson, 2005; see also Bocarro & Edwards, Chapter 8). While most leisure scholars agree that technology affects the amount of free time that people have and what they do with it (Russell, 2013), an in-depth discussion of the positive and negative effects of technology on leisure is missing from our literature.

One possible explanation for the neglect of such discussion on technology in leisure studies is that leisure scholars do not have any contradictory visions of technology. A more probable explanation, however, may be found in the origin and tradition of leisure studies as a discipline. Rooted in the parks and recreation heritage, it appears that many leisure scholars do not perceive technology use as leisure and even perceive it as a threat to traditional leisure. Such scholars prefer focusing on outdoor recreation, physical activities, and so forth, and ignore this crucial topic altogether. This neglect is troubling, as it overlooks not only the opportunities that technology offers to communities, individuals, and recreation agencies but also its potential risks. Moreover, ignoring the topic leaves the discussion on leisure and technology to scholars from other disciplines, who do not necessarily understand the *essence* of leisure.

Fortunately, research on technology in the field of leisure studies is currently developing, and some leisure scholars have already examined (or currently explore) various aspects of the subject. Holt (2012), for example, explored serious leisure in virtual world involvement, Wu, Scott, and Yang (2013) investigated relationships between flow experiences and online game addiction, and the author (Nimrod, 2014) studied the benefits of and constraints to participation in seniors' online communities. Unlike most studies conducted in other fields, these explorations integrated basic concepts of leisure studies with the study of leisure-use of technology. Such integration holds a great potential to deepen the understanding of leisure-use of technology.

Future research should further explore the three roles technology plays in leisure and the various positive and negative effects of technology on leisure. Referring to individuals, research should explore how technology affects leisure participation, experiences, and psychological and physical well-being. With regard to recreation agencies, studies should explore how technology can optimize their functioning and help them better serve their customers. In addition, studies should explore the social, cultural, economic, and political effects of leisure-use of technology on communities and society at large.

Such future research may apply a micro-level approach, namely, focus on a specific role, activity, group of participants and/or type of agency. Alternatively, they may use a macro-level approach and explore general topics such as differences between low and high technologies and the effects of the VISA on attitudes, behavior, and experiences of E-leisure participants. Both types of research, as well as longitudinal studies that will follow changes in technology use and the role it plays in leisure, are required to enhance the existing body of knowledge. As technology also offers a variety of advanced research methods and tools, from online surveys and ethnography to experience sampling method (ESM) and Global Positioning System (GPS) that help monitor participants' behaviors and experiences, future studies may be quite innovative and exciting.

CONCLUSION

The discussion presented in this chapter, examining the roles technology plays in twenty-first century leisure, is inevitably limited and may only serve as a springboard for scholarly debate on the topic. Hopefully, this preliminary discussion will promote understanding among leisure scholars and students with regard to the centrality of technology in the field of leisure studies and the essentiality of studying the various roles and impacts technology has on individuals and communities, as well as on the leisure sector and its services.

REFERENCES

Anthony, L. M., Clarke, M. C., & Anderson, S. J. (2000). Technophobia and personality subtypes in a sample of South African university students. *Computers in Human Behavior, 16*(1), 31–44.

Arnetz, B. B., & Wiholm, C. (1997). Technological stress: Psychophysiological symptoms in modern offices. *Journal of Psychosomatic Research, 43*(1), 35–42.

Ayyagari, R., Grover, V., & Purvis, R. (2011). Technostress: Technological antecedents and implications. *MIS Quarterly, 35*, 831–858.

Barber, B. (1999). Three scenarios for the future of technology and strong democracy. *Political Science Quarterly, 113*(4), 573–589.

Basalla, G. (1989). *The evolution of technology*. Cambridge, UK: Cambridge University Press.

Bissell, T. (2010). *Extra lives: Why video games matter*. New York: Pantheon Books.

Boyle, E. A., Connolly, T. M., Hainey, T., & Boyle, J. M. (2012). Engagement in digital entertainment games: A systematic review. *Computers in Human Behavior, 28*(3), 771–780.

Brod, C. (1984) *Technostress: The human cost of the computer revolution*. Reading, MA: Addison Weslety.

Bryce, J. (2001). The technological transformation of leisure. *Social Science Computer Review, 19*(1), 7–16.

Buhalis, D., & Law, R. (2008). Progress in information technology and tourism management 20 years on and 10 years after the Internet: The state of eTourism research. *Tourism Management, 29*(4), 609–623.

Byun, S., Ruffini, C., Mills, J. E., Douglas, A. C., Niang, M., Stepchenkova, S., et al. (2009). Internet addiction: Meta-synthesis of 1996–2006 quantitative research. *CyberPsychology & Behavior, 12*, 203–207.

Capio, C. M., Mascolo, G., & Sit, C. H. P. (2012). Methods and technologies for leisure, recreation and an accessible sport. In S. Federici & M. J. Scherer (Eds.), *Assistive technology assessment handbook*, pp. 421–433. Boca Raton, FL: Francis & Taylor.

Chau, C. (2010). YouTube as a participatory culture. *New Directions for Youth Development, 2010*(128), 65–77.

Christou, E. (2011). Exploring online sales promotions in the hospitality industry. *Journal of Hospitality Marketing & Management, 20*(7), 814–829

Cortada, J. W. (2000). Progenitors of the information age. In A. D. Chandler, Jr. & J. W. Cortada (Eds.), *A nation transformed by information: How information has shaped the United States from colonial times to the present* (pp. 177–216). Oxford and New York: Oxford University Press.

Curran, K., Walters, N., & Robinson, D. (2007). Investigating the problems faced by older adults and people with disabilities in online environments. *Behavior and Information Technology, 26*(6), 447–453.

Demirkan, H., Kauffman, R. J., Vayghan, J. A., Fill, H-G., Karagiannis, D., & Maglio, P. P. (2008). Service-oriented technology and management: Perspectives on research and practice for the coming decade. *Electronic Commerce Research and Applications, 7*(4), 356–376.

Eurostat. (2013). *Glossary: High-tech*. Retrieved from: http://epp.eurostat.ec.europa.eu/statistics_explained/index.php/Glossary:High-tech

Fisher, D. R., & Wright, L. M. (2001). On utopias and dystopias: Toward an understanding of the discourse surrounding the Internet. *Journal of Computer Mediated Communication, 6*(2). Retrieved from: http://jcmc.indiana.edu/vol6/issue2/fisher.html

Gilbert, D., Lee-Kelley, L., & Barton, M. (2003). Technophobia, gender influences and consumer decision-making for technology-related products. *European Journal of Innovation Management, 6*(4), 253–263.

Gupta, K., Sleezer, C. M., & Russ-Eft, D. F. (2011). *A practical guide to needs assessment*. San Francisco, CA: Jossey-Bass Pfeiffer.

Hampton, K. N., Livio, O., & Sessions-Goulet, L. (2010). The social life of wireless urban spaces: Internet use, social networks, and the public realm. *Journal of Communication, 60*(4), 701–722.

Healy, K. (2002). Digital technology and cultural goods. *The Journal of Political Philosophy, 10*(4), 478–500.

Hodgkinson, T. (2006). *How to be free*. London, UK: Penguin.

Holt, N. (2012). "Calgon, take me away": Identifying qualities of serious leisure in virtual world involvement inside World of Warcraft. *Loisir et Société/Society and Leisure, 35*(1), 57–77.

Jackson, E. L. (2005). (Ed.). *Constraints to leisure*. State College, PA: Venture Publishing, Inc.

Jenkins, H. (2006). *Convergence culture*. New York: New York University Press.

Jensen, K. B., & Helles, R. (2011). The internet as a cultural forum: Implications for research. *New Media & Society, 13*, 517–533.

Johnson, V. (2012). The gender divide: Attitudinal issues inhibiting access. In R. Pande & T. Van der Weide (Eds.), *Globalization, technology diffusion and gender disparity: Social impacts of ICTs*, pp. 110–119. Hershey, PA: IGI Global Snippet.

Jordan, D. J., DeGraaf, D. G., & DeGraaf, K. H. (2005). *Programming for parks, recreation, and leisure services: A servant leadership approach* (2nd ed.). State College, PA: Venture Publishing, Inc.

Kaiser Family Foundation. (2010). *Generation M2: Media in the lives of 8- to 18-year-olds. Retrieved from http://kaiserfamilyfoundation.files.wordpress.com/2010/01/mh012010presentl.pdf*

Katz, E., Hass, H., Weitz, S., Adoni, H., Gurevitch, M., Schiff, M., & Goldberg-Anabi, D. (2000). *Tarbut hapnai beIsrael: Tmurot bedfusei hapeilut hatarbutit 1970–1990* [Leisure patterns in Israel: Changes in cultural activity 1970–1990]. Tel Aviv, Israel: The Open University.

Kelly, J. R. (1996). *Leisure* (3rd ed.). Boston, MA: Allyn & Bacon.

Khvorostianov, N., Elias, N., & Nimrod, G. (2012). 'Without it I'm nothing': The Internet in the lives of older immigrants. *New Media and Society, 14*(4), 583–599.

Kurzweil, R. (2005). *The singularity is near*. New York: Viking Books.

Laumer, S., Maier, C., & Weinert, C. (2013). The negative side of ICT-enabled communication: The case of social interaction overload in online social networks, *Proceeding of ECIS* (2013), Retrieved from http://works.bepress.com/christian_maier/12

Lee, S. M., & Chen L. (2010). The impact of flow on online consumer behavior. *Journal of Computer Information Systems, 50*(4), 1–10.

Lieberman, D. E. (2006). *Dance games and other exergames: What the research says*. Retrieved from http://www.comm.ucsb.edu/faculty/lieberman/exergames.htm

Lightman A. (2005). Prisoner in a wired world. In *A Sense of the mysterious: Science and the human spirit* (pp. 183–208). New York: Random House.

MacKay, K., & Vogt, C. (2012). Information technology in everyday and vacation contexts. *Annals of Tourism Research, 39*(3), 1380–1401.

Mannell, R. C., Kaczynski, A. T., & Aronson, R. M. (2005). Adolescent participation and flow experience in physically active leisure and electronic media activities: Testing the displacement hypothesis. *Loisir et Société/Society and Leisure, 28*, 653–675.

Mukherjee, D. (2010). An exploratory study of older adults' engagement with virtual volunteerism. *Journal of Technology in Human Services, 28*(3), 188–196.

Nach, H., & Lejeune, A. (2009). The impact of information technology on identity: Framing the research agenda. *Proceedings of the Administrative Sciences Association of Canada (ASAC) Conference, 2009*. Retrieved from http://papers.ssrn.com/sol3/papers.cfm?abstract_id=1713332

Nakamura, J., & Csikszentmihalyi, M. (2009). Flow theory and research. In C. R. Snyder & S. J. Lopez (Eds.), *Handbook of positive psychology* (pp. 195–206). Oxford and New York: Oxford University Press.

Nimrod, G. (2013). Challenging the Internet paradox: Online depression communities and well-being. *International Journal of Internet Science, 8*(1), 30–48.

Nimrod, G. (2014). The benefits of and constraints to participation in seniors' online communities. *Leisure Studies, 33*(3), 247–266.

Nimrod, G., & Adoni, H. (2012). Conceptualizing E-leisure. *Loisir et Société/Society and Leisure, 35*(1), 31–56.

Papacharissi, Z. (2010). *The networked self: Identity, community and culture on social network sites*. New York: Routledge.

Peng, W., Lin, J. H., & Crouse, J. (2011). Is playing exergames really exercising? A meta-analysis of energy expenditure in active video games. *Cyberpsychology, Behavior, and Social Networking, 14*(11), 681–688.

Poser, S. (2011). *Leisure time and technology*. Retrieved from http://www.ieg-ego.eu/en/threads/crossroads/technified-environments/stefan-poser-leisure-time-and-technology

Ragu-Nathan, T. S., Tarafdar, M., Ragu-Nathan, B., & Tu, Q. (2008). Consequence of technostress in end users: Conceptual development and empirical validation. *Information Systems Research, 19*(4), 417–433.

Ripat, J. D., & Woodgate, R. L. (2012). The role of assistive technology in self-perceived participation. *International Journal of Rehabilitation Research, 35*(2), 170–177.

Robins, K., & Webster, F. (1999). The long history of the information revolution. In K. Robins & F. Webster (Eds.), *Times of the Technoculture: From the information, communication society to the virtual life* (pp. 89–110). London: Routledge.

Rose, S., Hair, N., & Clark, M. (2010). Online customer experience: A review of the business-to-consumer online purchase context. *International Journal of Management Reviews, 13*(1), 24–39.

Russell, R. V. (2013). Leisure and technology. In *Pastimes: The context of contemporary leisure* (5th ed.) (pp. 127–144). Urbana, IL: Sagamore.

Schor, J. B. (1991). *The overworked American*. New York: Basic Books.

Schor, J. B. (1998). *The overspent American*. New York: Basic Books.

Shaw, M., & Black, D. W. (2008). Internet addiction: Definition, assessment, epidemiology and clinical management. *CNS Drugs, 22*(5), 353–365.

Sigala, M., Christou, E., & Gretzel, U. (2012). *Social media in travel, tourism and hospitality: Theory, practice and cases*. Surrey, UK: Ashgate.

Solove, D. J. (2011). *Nothing to hide: The false tradeoff between privacy and security*. New Haven and London: Yale University.

Tarafdar, M, Tu, Q., Ragu-Nathan, T. S., & Ragu-Nathan, B. S. (2011). Crossing to the dark side: Examining creators, outcomes, and inhibitors of technostress. *Communications of the ACM, 54*(9), 113–120.

Tufekci, Z. (2010). Who acquires friends through social media and why? "Rich get richer" versus "Seek and ye shall find." In *Proceedings of the 4th International AAAI Conference on Weblogs and Social Media (ICWSM, 2010)*, 170-177. AAAI Press. Retrieved from http://www.aaai.org/ocs/index.php/ICWSM/ICWSM10/paper/viewFile/1525/1850

Weil, M. M., & Rosen, L. D. (1995). A study of technological sophistication and technophobia in university students from 23 countries. *Computers in Human Behavior, 11*(1), 95–133.

Weinstein A, & Lejoyeux, M. (2010). Internet addiction or excessive Internet use. *American Journal of Drug and Alcohol Abuse, 36*, 277–283.

Wu, T-C, Scott, D., & Yang, C-C. (2013). Advanced or addicted? Exploring the relationship of recreation specialization to flow experiences and online game addiction. *Leisure Science, 35*(3), 203–217.

Zickuhr, A., & Smith, K. (2012). *Digital differences*. Retrieved from http://www.pewinternet.org/~/media//Files/Reports/2012/PIP_Digital_differences_041312.pdf

31
Place and Leisure

Gerard Kyle (Texas A&M University)

In their discussion of place attachment almost 30 years ago, Shumaker and Hankin (1984. p. 60) noted that "few fields of inquiry are so clearly interdisciplinary in nature" as investigations of humans feelings about places. Hummon (1992) further noted that the theoretical complexity was "inevitable, for the emotional bonds of people and places arise from locales that are at once ecological, built, social, and symbolic" (p. 253). Interestingly, the theoretical diversity that has informed our understanding of leisure behavior is, until recently, not evidenced in leisure researchers' explorations of place. Further, the implications stemming from an understanding of the relationships people share with place for understanding behavior has a much briefer history in the leisure literature compared to many of the other social sciences. This is surprising given that "space and place are fundamental means through which we make sense of the world and through which we act" (Sack, 1992, p. 1). In the context of leisure, a context that is more often characterized by perceived freedom and intrinsic motivation (Kleiber, Walker & Mannell, 2011), Sack's sentiments more strongly resonate given the potential for more meaningful experience. Given the role of experience in the shaping of meaning and sentiment (Tuan, 1974), I feel the context of leisure is fertile for the exploration of place phenomena as it contributes to both our understanding of leisure behavior and human's relationship with the physical environment. With this in mind, the purpose of this chapter is to provide insight on the potential of place research to inform our understanding of leisure behavior. In so doing, my discussion begins with a review of issues related to the vernacular of place research and modes of enquiry that underlie place scholarship. I then turn my attention to the presence of place within the context of leisure studies. The chapter concludes with discussion of issues warranting further inquiry.

WHAT IS PLACE AND PLACE ATTACHMENT?

If I were to ask a human geographer, an environmental sociologist, a cultural anthropologist, and an environmental psychologist to define "place attachment," it is quite likely I would be offered several definitions that share some similarity but also hold critical distinction. While there is general consensus that the study of "place" is inclusive of its material form in addition to the meanings humans ascribe to the setting, the ontological and epistemological assumptions that govern these disciplines' conception of reality and processes for exploring reality, gird this nuance. The differing research traditions have spurned a variety of place-related concepts that characterize the human-place relationship. For scholars beginning their exploration of place, the vernacular of place scholarship can be quite daunting—if not frustrating. Developing an appreciation for the nuance, vagaries, and congruence in definition can take some time and requires a grasp of the breadth of place research. In the context of the discussion provided in this chapter, the review and interpretation of the literature is a reflection of my biases anchored within positivist environmental psychology. In this vein, I consider the concept of place attachment integrating, primarily referring to the emotional bonds people share with meaningful environments (Low & Altman, 1992). While emotion and sentiment have been central to researchers' understandings of attachment, the concept is also overarching with attention given to understanding cognition, behavior, and social phenomena that underlie individual attachments to the landscape.

As I noted, one of the challenging issues for scholars beginning the study of place is developing an understanding of the diversity in terminology. A review of this diversity is beyond the scope of this chapter, but there are several terms of importance for understanding humans' attachment to place that warrant discussion. For concepts such as place identity and place dependence, there is general consensus on their distinction. The oft-cited definition provided by Proshansky, Fabian, and Kaminoff (1983) suggests that *place identity* is a "sub-structure of self identity . . . consisting of, broadly conceived cognitions about the physical world . . . [where] these cognitions represent memories, ideas, feelings, attitudes, values, preferences, meanings, and conceptions of behavior and experience" (p. 59). While some scholars have questioned this definition (e.g., Dixon & Durrheim, 2000; Korpela, 1989), with some subtle variation, there is broad acknowledgement that place has important implications for understanding individual and collective identity in addition to revealing the character of place.

For *place dependence*, the human place-bond references different processes. Another commonly cited conceptualization offered by Stokols and Shumaker (1981) suggests that this mode of attachment is driven by an individual's perception that the target setting will satisfy their needs better than other settings. Most conceptualizations of place attachment also include an affective or emotional component (*affective attachment*) in addition to place identity and dependence (e.g., Jorgensen & Stedman, 2001). This component of attachment refers to people's emotional attachment to the setting (Low & Altman, 1992).

A fourth facet of attachment that has received some attention in environmental psychology literature refers to the social bonds that bind people to place (Hidalgo & Hernández, 2001; Kyle, Graefe, & Manning, 2005). Like the identity, dependence, and affective bases of attachment, *social attachment* has also been considered a sub-dimension. This form of attachment is based on the relationships people share with friends and relatives that are maintained in place. Social attachments can also be manifested in two ways. For example, Kyle and Chick (2007) observed that their informants' attachments to settings of varied in scale and was both a product of the affection they held toward significant friends and family in addition to the memories of past experience with those friends and family. For the former, the prospect of severing ties drives the place bond. For the latter, the meanings informants ascribed to their experiences with friends and family became embedded in the settings where those experiences were shared.

Finally, a concept that is often used interchangeably with place attachment by both leisure researchers and environmental psychologists is *sense of place* (SOP). While a number of different conceptualizations have been offered in the literature, the most salient distinction appears to rest on the extent to which emotion and affect are emphasized. As noted above, emotion and affect lie at the heart of definitions of place attachment. For SOP, in addition to emotional attachment and identification, scholars have also referenced place satisfaction (Brown, Altman, & Werner, 2012), place aesthetics (Hay, 1998), and ancestral ties (Lippard, 1997). Sense of place research, within the interpretivist research tradition of human geography, is also seen as being more holistic, involving meaning, memory, experience, and symbolism (Buttimer, 1980; Seamon, 1987).

WHAT IS THE OBJECT OF PEOPLE'S ATTACHMENT?

Assessing the object of recreationists' attachment would, as first glance, seem relatively simple. Most place research has been conducted with respondents (or informants) who live, work, or recreate within the setting of interest. One might assume, then, the object of attachment would be a physical environment; the "stage" on which human action and experience unfolds. While there can be general consensus on the characteristics of the physical attributes (e.g., size, shape, color, texture) that constitute the setting, individual and collective interpretation of these attributes and the setting whole, can vary considerably. The meanings assigned to these attributes can often differ based on individual and collective histories. In this way, the physical environment is symbolic; textured by memory, history, and experience. Thus, settings can hold multiple values independent of physical form. This is not to say the physical form is irrelevant. Most scholars would acknowledge place attributes are integral to the way in which people interact with the landscape and one another. Beach, mountain, and desert environments impact us physically, emotionally, and socially. Their impact, however, is not uniform. Our interpretation of the attributes that constitute these settings is rooted in our ancestry, experience, and memory (Stokowski, 2002, 2008).

While extreme social constructivist perspectives on place meaning have been criticized (Crist, 2004; Proctor, 1998), the interpretation implies that the importance of place for both individuals and collectives can be anchored in a diverse array of factors, some which are shaped by setting attributes (e.g., exceptional kayaking, surfing, climbing) and some independent of form (e.g., childhood memory, experience with family/friends). Most important, the attraction (or aversion) of people to place is based on the meanings they associate with the setting. This phenomenon is clearly evidenced in the way in which different cultural groups interact with natural environments. For example, Johnson (1998) suggested that African Americans' aversion to natural landscapes could be attributed to their "collective memories" of these landscapes. It was within "natural landscapes" that 200 years of slavery, violence, and extreme oppression was perpetrated. Consequently, these landscapes, for some, are symbolic of a dark past. Also, for Hispanic groups, research has shown their use of urban-proximate protected areas differs considerably from historical White uses. Hispanic use of picnic areas within these settings often appears incompatible with present design; designed 30 years prior for the preferences of a White America. White visitors have traditionally preferred small picnic areas isolated from others within the park or recreation area. These settings were originally designed to support experiences of solitude and privacy with immediate family and friends. Hispanic users, however, have tended to visit these areas in large groups of extended family (Chavez, 2002). Their preference and use is a manifestation of meaning ascribed to the picnic area—that is, settings valued for their ability to support large family gatherings.

Aligned with the question concerning the object of attachment is the distinction between place meaning and place attachment. I see the distinction being an epistemological artifact that is evidenced in researchers' chosen mode of enquiry. While related, the other side of the same coin, place attachment has generally been considered an evaluative concept evidenced in affective, cognitive, and behavioral intent. In the psychometric tradition, efforts to measure place attachment have provided insight on the *extent* to which people bond with a specific setting and less so on *why* people bond with place (Smale, 2006). This line of scholarship most often employs quantitative designs where concerns about measurement are paramount. To understand humans' attachment to place, these scientists attempt to reduce the phenomena to what are perceived to be its constituent elements or attributes. The product of such efforts typically yields a numerical indication of respondent(s) intensity of attachment across however many dimensions of attachment chosen by the researcher. While these dimensions of place attachment (e.g., *affective attachment, place dependence, social bonding*) have been conceptualized in an attempt to provide some insight on *why*, it does so in ways that abstract many of elements interpretivist scholars exploring place meaning consider integral. For these scholars, the process of measurement reflects a false abstraction of the human-place experience that does not adequately account for the *lived* experience of place. Driven by questions of *why* and *how*, phenomenological or humanistic understandings of place meaning (often explored using the concept of sense of place) foreground the dynamic processes involving the interplay of experience, actors that shape experience, cultural and political forces, and the language and symbolic representation of place.

PLACE RESEARCH IN LEISURE STUDIES

Recognition of the importance of place for understanding leisure behavior was first reported in the leisure literature over 40 years ago by Robert Lee (1972). Adopting a symbolic interactionist orientation for the construction and maintenance of meaning, Lee reported that the character of various outdoor settings—neighborhood, district, regional, and remote outdoor places—was evidenced in the identity of actors who dwell within the setting. Lee suggested the meanings people ascribed to place were derived from the meaning they associated with the identity of those actors. As such, the places of interest were gendered, racialized, and marked by social standing. Consequently, movement and action were shaped by individuals' perception of what was appropriate and was dependent on their cultural affiliation. Lee was one of the first scholars to acknowledge that people's interpretation and understanding of place and the physical attributes that constitute setting, territory, and structure, are not absolute or universal. Rather, they are social constructions where meaning is shaped and filtered through cultural lenses (see also Stodolska and Floyd, Chapter 28). For place research, Lee's investigation was pioneering; highlighting the significance of place for understanding leisure behavior in addition to presenting an array of compelling questions that could have guided several streams of leisure research for decades to come. Unfortunately, it was another 20 years before leisure researchers would once again be reminded of the importance of place for understanding the leisure experience.

In 1992, Williams, Patterson, Roggenbuck, and Watson (1992) expressed concern with U.S. public land management policy governing natural resource management. They likened current agency efforts "to an engineering like emphasis on the manipulation and control" (p. 30) of setting attributes to offer preferred experiential outcomes. They argued that this commodification of the resource neglected the emotional and symbolic values recreationists might also ascribe to the resource. Findings from their investigation of visitors to wilderness areas within the U.S. illustrated that the intensity of respondents' attachment was key in distinguishing variation in a variety of indicators related to their personal characteristics, behavior, and management preferences related to the setting. Since then, a large body of literature has been published illustrating the utility of place research for natural resource management and conservation (e.g., Farnam, Hall, & Kruger, 2005; Kruger, Hall, & Stiefel, 2008; Stewart, Williams, & Kruger, 2013). This understanding—that people's interpretation, relationship, and interaction with nature is not solely defined by the physical form—is becoming a prominent feature of natural resource and protected area management across the globe. The approach acknowledges that, in many contexts, humans are part of the ecosystem with cultures shaping and being shaped by its physical form. For application, place-based planning for natural resource conservation helps to democratize decision processes and is more collaborative in nature. In contrast to centralized decision-making structures that are prevalent within public land management agencies, place-based conservation is more sensitive to the historical, cultural, and symbolic significance of the landscape to relevant stakeholders.

Following from Williams et al. (1992), place research within the context of leisure has most often explored the nature and intensity of recreationists' attachment to natural landscapes and settings varying in scale. Most of this work has fallen within the domain of the construct "place attachment"—defined as the emotional ties people share with a specific setting or structure (Brown et al., 2012). While the focus of this work has been on humans' emotional and positively valenced attachments to natural landscapes, the concept also encapsulates other elements of the human-place bond embodied in other place-related constructs. Drawing from several streams of place research, Williams et al.'s (1992) conceptualization of place attachment was comprised of two dimensions: place identity and place dependence. Differing from Proshansky et al.'s (1983) original conceptualization, they defined place identity in terms of both the emotional ties people share with place and the extent to which identity was inextricably linked to place. For place dependence, the human-place bond was derived from an evaluation of how well the place met individual needs in comparison to other settings. This conceptualization and associated measure has been the dominant framework employed by leisure researchers conducting quantitative work in the context of natural resource recreation. While there has been some refinement, such as the separation of the emotional and affective components from identification processes (Jorgensen & Stedman, 2001) along with the inclusion of social ties (Kyle, Graefe & Manning, 2005), Williams et al.'s work continues to be adopted by many researchers today.

Beyond the myopic focus on natural environments, leisure research has addressed three broad questions: (a) What are the factors that shape recreationists' attachments to place? (b) How do attachments vary among recreationists/stakeholders? and (c) How does attachment influence recreationists' sentiments toward the environment and issues of managerial concern? For the first question, research has identified three systems underpinning people-place bonds: (a) biological or evolutionary tendencies that underlie people's preference for natural landscapes (Brown, Kaplan, & Quarderer, 1999; Kaltenborn & Bjerke, 2002) and the physical attributes that constitute natural landscapes (Appleton, 1996; Kaplan & Kaplan, 1989); (b) individualized experiential processes where place sentiment develops over time and is the product of place interaction, personal meaning, and memory (Hammitt, Backlund, & Bixler, 2004; Moore & Scott, 2003); and (c) sociocultural processes where place meanings are shared, shaped, and in some instances, imposed by cultural groups (Gieryn, 2000; Lee, 1972).

For the second question concerning variations in attachment across different types of recreationists, resource proximity (e.g., "local" vs. "nonlocal") has been a compelling factor contributing not only the intensity of attachment among recreationists but also the mode of attachment. For example, both Bonaiuto, Carrus, Martorella, and Bonnes (2002) and Beckley (2003) reported that locals expressed stronger place attachment than non-locals owing to economic and social dependencies. Each of these studies also indicated that the settings were more intimately ingrained in local respondents' identities. Locals' stronger ties can be attributed to their extended tenure leading to the steady accretion of sentiment and their proximity to the setting which allows for more frequent interaction and familiarity. Other research has also shown that the intensity of leisure engagement directly contributes to recreationists' place attachments. Consistent with the tenets of specialization, as recreationists become involved and engaged with a specific activity, they also develop more specific setting preferences. These preferences are evidenced not just in terms of greater dependence on the resource to facilitate desired leisure experiences, but also in terms recreationists' emotional ties to the landscape (Bricker & Kersetter, 2000; Kyle, Bricker, Graefe, & Wickham, 2004).

Finally, for the third question examining recreationists' views on the environment and a range of issues concerning the management of protected areas, the research has shown that an understanding of recreationists' attachment to the landscape is revealing of their disposition toward these issues. For example, work has shown that place attachment is a significant predictor of visitors' perceptions of entrance fees to public protected areas, with attachments anchored in emotion as opposed to setting dependence, engendering greater opposition to fee programs (Kyle, Absher, & Graefe, 2003). Other work also reveals that those most attached to a particular setting, particularly those expressing stronger emotional bonds, are also most sensitive to human-influenced impact (Kyle, Graefe, Manning, & Bacon, 2004). Place research has also revealed how recreationists' or stakeholders' attachment can be used to address issues related to conflict. This has been a popular theme in the natural resource recreation literature. The strength of place-based approaches for examining these issues lies in their ability to shed light on the question of "why" the conflict exists. Often it is more complex than one group's behavior impinging on the experience of another (i.e., goal interference). It can also be considered in terms of stakeholders' value orientation. Given that those with stronger emotional and symbolic attachments are most sensitive to anthropogenic impacts on the environment, some recreation uses (e.g., off-road vehicle use, snowmobiles, jet skis) represent both a threat to the environment and to others' values related to nature. For example, Hawkins and Backman (1998) reported an asymmetrical conflict between horseback riders and boaters along the Chattooga River in the Nantahala National Forest. Their analysis revealed that horseback riders considered themselves more appreciative and attached to the area than the boaters. In a different context, McAvoy (2002) explored conflict in the meanings American Indians and recreational climbers ascribed to Devils Tower National Monument in Wyoming. While the Monument is a resource that is highly valued by both groups, the reasons for its significance differ markedly. For American Indians, the Monument is of spiritual significance whereas for climbers, the Monument afforded them a unique opportunity to enjoy climbing. While an understanding of recreationists' place meanings and attachments does not offer an immediate resolution to the conflicts such as these, it does offer insight on *why*, from which dialogue among the affected groups can be anchored.

In the 20-plus years since Williams et al.'s (1992) influential piece (at the time of writing, it remains the most cited paper published in the journal *Leisure Sciences*), a number of studies have recently been conducted that draw from diverse ontological and epistemological traditions. While my focus throughout this discussion has been on studies of place attachment cast within the psychometric tradition, in many ways, leisure researchers' study of place is becoming more reflective of the broader place literature. The interdisciplinary nature of leisure studies is now evidenced in conceptual frameworks and research designs. Where the leisure literature sharply departs from the broader place literature, however, has been its almost exclusive exploration of recreationists' attachment to nature. This includes both the natural environment and communities situated within close proximity to natural amenities. Williams et al. and later Greider and Garkovich (1994) provided compelling arguments for adopting place as a lens to explore human dimensions issues impacting natural resource and protected areas. As discussed above, the research has shown that an understanding of recreationists' attachments to the landscape (and reasons for attachment), provides insight on their disposition toward specific issues impacting the resource.

While this work has contributed tremendously toward understanding the nature and intensity of recreationists' attachments to natural landscapes, contributing to both the leisure and broader place literatures, it does not reflect the full potential of place for informing behavior within the diversity of contexts in which leisure is experienced. While a few exceptions exist (Henderson & King, 1999; Kyle & Chick, 2007), one could be mistaken for believing the concept only had utility for understanding issues confronting the human dimensions of natural resources. It is a given that the relevance of incorporating place within explorations of the leisure experience will vary according to the investigator's research purpose/objectives. As the broader place literature illustrates, however, I feel its versatility remains to be fully understood. Turning to this issue, I conclude the chapter with some thoughts on issues that remain elusive for place and leisure researchers alike.

PLACE, LEISURE, AND SO MANY QUESTIONS

If space and place are fundamental means through which we view and experience the world (Sack, 1992), then it seems logical that place research holds strong potential for informing our understanding of leisure behavior in a broad array of contexts. In this regard, there are a number of areas of enquiry that remain poorly understood within both the place and leisure literatures. First, while it is understood that the processes underlying the creation of meaning and sentiment are fluid and dynamic, meaning and sentiment are also said to accrue over time. Given this, what happens in contexts where place interaction is punctuated by seasonality, place disruptions (e.g., limited access owing to natural occurrences or changes in policy), or life-stage events? Is sentiment maintained or even magnified owing to the time's ability to distort autobiographical memory (Braun, Ellis, & Loftus, 2002). While the "steady accretion of sentiment" (Tuan, 1977, p. 33) implies a certain linearity, questions remain over meaning and attachment's stability, growth, or decline. This not unlike the "progression hypotheses" that early work on specialization once claimed and is now considered to be the exception (Backlund & Kuentzel, 2013). For example, how are the constraints (see Schneider, Chapter 18) that impinge upon recreationists' access to settings throughout different life stages evidenced in the bonds people share with leisure settings?

Another fertile area of inquiry concerns the normative expectations governing behavior within leisure settings. As I mentioned, Lee (1972) reported that the identity of places also has implications for action within these settings. Referring to similar phenomena, Gieryn (2000) noted that "acceptable" behavior within place is often a product of the normative expectations determined by the extant culture with territorial claims to the locale. An understanding of normative landscapes give rise to questions over morality (e.g., what actions are appropriate?), the politics of place (e.g., who determines what is normative?), and the territorial distinctions that can "gate keep" access to the landscape (e.g., gendered and racialized territories). While leisure is a context that facilitates self-determined action (see Walker, Chapter 17), it is also situated within the confines of societal structure. Alternately, research has shown that leisure is also a context where societal norms can be resisted (Theberge, 2000). Place and the attachments recreationists express toward leisure settings provide a unique lens through which to view these phenomena. Otherwise subtle and obscure, the phenomena are revealed in very distinct spatial manifestations (Spain, 1992).

Where the benefits of leisure have been well-documented, the benefits of place have received less attention in the leisure literature. A number of authors have commented on functions of place attachment in the context of nature (Kahn & Kellert, 2002; Kaplan & Kaplan, 1989; Korpela, 1989), but few leisure researchers have formally explored outcomes, particularly those related to physical and mental health. Given the role of place, as depicted in Breakwell's (1986) identity process theory (e.g., continuity, distinctiveness, self-efficacy, self-esteem), there is reason to believe that place would have important implications for mental and physical health. Research has also documented the social benefits that can be derived through civic activities such as community gardens (Glover, 2004; Glover, Chapter 32) and urban greening (Jorgensen & Gobster, 2010). Given these activities are place-focused, often considered leisure by those who participate, it would seem ripe for enquiry by leisure researchers.

REFERENCES

Appleton, J. (1996). *The experience of the landscape*. New York: John Wiley and Sons.

Backlund, E., & Kuentzel, W. (2013). Beyond progression in specialization research: Leisure capital and participation change. *Leisure Sciences, 35*, 293–299.

Beckley, T. M. (2003). The relative importance of sociocultural and ecological factors in attachment to place. In L. E. Kruger (Ed.), *Understanding community forest relations* (pp. 105–125; PNW-GTR-566). Portland, OR: USDA Forest Service, Pacific Northwest Research Station.

Bonaiuto, M., Carrus, G., Martorella, H., & Bonnes, M. (2002). Local identity processes and environmental attitudes in land use changes: The case of natural protected areas. *Journal of Environmental Psychology, 23*, 631–653.

Braun, K. A., Ellis, R., & Loftus, E. F. (2002). Make my memory: How advertising can change our memories of the past. *Psychology & Marketing, 19*, 1–23.

Breakwell, G. M. (1986). *Coping with threatened identity*. London: Methuen.

Bricker, K. S., & Kerstetter, D. L. (2000). Level of specialization and place attachment: An exploratory study of whitewater recreationists. *Leisure Sciences, 22*, 233–257.

Brown, B. B., Altman, I., Werner, C. M. (2012). Place attachment. In S. Smith (Ed.), *International encyclopedia of housing and home* (pp. 183–188). Oxford, UK: Elsevier.

Brown, T. J., Kaplan, R., & Quaderer, G. (1999). Beyond accessibility: preference for natural places. *Therapeutic Recreation Journal, 33*, 209–221

Buttimer, A. (1980). Home, reach, and sense of place. In A. Buttimer & D. Seamon (Eds.), *The human experience of space and place* (pp. 73–85). London: Croom Helm.

Chavez, D. J. (2002). Adaptive management in outdoor recreation: Serving Hispanics in Southern California. *Western Journal of Applied Forestry, 17*(3), 129–133.

Crist, E. (2004). Against the social construction of nature and wilderness. *Environmental Ethics, 26*, 5–26.

Dixon, J., & Durrheim, K. (2000). Displacing place-identity: A discursive approach to locating self and other. *British Journal of Social Psychology, 39*, 27–44.

Farnum, J., Hall, T., & Kruger, L. E. (2005). *Sense of place in natural resource recreation and tourism: An evaluation and assessment of research findings* (PNW-GTR-660). Portland, OR: USDA Forest Service, Pacific Northwest Research Station.

Gieryn, T. F. (2000). A space for place in sociology. *Annual review of Sociology, 26*, 463–466.

Glover, T. (2004). Social capital in the lived experiences of community gardeners. *Leisure Sciences, 26*, 143–162.

Greider, T., & Garkovich, I. (1994). Landscapes: The social construction of nature and the environment. *Rural Sociology, 59*, 1–24.

Hammitt, W. E., Backlund, E. A., & Bixler, R. D. (2004). Experience use history, place bonding and resource substitution of trout anglers during recreation engagements. *Journal of Leisure Research, 36*, 356–378.

Hawkins, G., & Backman, K. F. (1998). An exploration of sense of place as a possible explanatory concept in nature-based traveler conflict. *Tourism Analysis, 3*, 89–102.

Hay, R. B. (1998). Sense of place in a developmental context. *Journal of Environmental Psychology, 18*, 5–29.

Henderson, K. A., & King, K. (1999). Youth spaces and places: Case studies of two teen clubs. *Journal of Recreation and Park Administration, 17*(2), 28–41.

Hidalgo, M. C., & Hernández, B. (2001). Place attachment: Conceptual and empirical questions. *Journal of Environmental Psychology, 21*, 273–281.

Hummon, D. M. (1992). Community attachment: Local sentiment and sense of place. In I. Altman & S. Low (Eds.), *Human behavior and environments: Advances in theory and research. Volume 12: Place attachment* (pp. 253–278). New York: Plenum Press.

Johnson, C. Y. (1998). A consideration of collective memory in African American attachment to wildland recreation places. *Research in Human Ecology, 5*(1), 57–68.

Jorgensen, A., & Gobster, P. H. (2010). Shades of green: Measuring the ecology of urban green space in the context of human health and well-being. *Nature and Culture, 5*, 338–363.

Jorgensen, B. S., & Stedman, R. C. (2001). Sense of place as an attitude: Lakeshore owners' attitudes toward their properties. *Journal of Environmental Psychology, 21*, 233–248.

Kahn, P. H., & Kellert, S. R. (2002). *Children and nature: Psychological, sociological, and evolutionary investigations*. Cambridge, MA: Massachusetts Institute of Technology.

Kaltenborn, B. P., & Bjerke, T. (2002). Associations between landscape preferences and place attachment: A study in Røros, southern Norway. *Landscape Research, 27*, 381–386.

Kaplan, R., & Kaplan, S. (1989). *The experience of nature: A psychological perspective*. New York: Cambridge University Press.

Kleiber, D. A., Walker, G. J., & Mannell, R. C. (2011). *A social psychology of leisure* (2nd ed.). State College, PA: Venture Publishing, Inc.

Korpela, K. (1989). Place-identity as a product of environmental self-regulation. *Journal of Environmental Psychology, 9*, 241–256.

Kruger, L. E., Hall, T. E., & Stiefel, M. C. (2008). *Understanding concepts of place in recreation research and management* (PNW-GTR-744). Portland, OR: USDA Forest Service, Pacific Northwest Research Station.

Kyle, G. T., Absher, A. R., & Graefe, A. R. (2003). The moderating role of place attachment on the relationship between attitudes toward fees and spending preferences. *Leisure Sciences, 25*, 33–50.

Kyle, G. T., Bricker, K. S., Graefe, A. R., & Wickham, T. D. (2004). An examination of recreationists' relationship with activities and settings. *Leisure Sciences, 26*, 125–142.

Kyle, G. T., & Chick, G. E. (2007). The social construction of a sense of place. *Leisure Sciences, 29*, 209–225.

Kyle, G. T., Graefe, A. R., & Manning, R. E. (2005). Testing the dimensionality of place attachment in recreation settings. *Environment and Behavior, 21*, 233–248.

Kyle, G. T., Graefe, A. R., Manning, R. E., & Bacon, J. (2004). The effect of place attachment on users' perception of social and environmental conditions encountered in a natural setting. *Journal of Environmental Psychology, 24*, 213–225.

Lee, R. G. (1972). The social definition of outdoor recreation places. In W. R. Branch, N. H. Cheek, & L. Taylor (Eds.), *Social behavior, natural resources, and the environment* (pp. 68–84). New York: Harper and Row Publishers.

Lippard, L. R. (1997). *The lure of the local: Sense of place in a multicentered society*. New York: New Press.

Low, S. M., & Altman, I. (1992). Place attachment: A conceptual inquiry. In I. Altman & S. Low (Eds.), *Human behavior and environments: Advances in theory and research. Volume 12: Place attachment* (pp. 253–278). New York: Plenum Press.

McAvoy, L. (2002). American Indians, place meanings and the Old/New West. *Journal of Leisure Research, 34*, 383–396.

Moore, R. L., & Scott, D. (2003). Place attachment and context: Comparing a park and trail within. *Forest Science, 49*, 877–884.

Proctor, J. D. (1998). The social construction of nature: Relativist accusations, pragmatist and critical realist responses. *Annals of the Association of American Geographers, 88*, 352–376.

Proshansky, H. M., Fabian, A. K., & Kaminoff, R. (1983). Place identity: Physical world socialization of the self. *Journal of Environmental Psychology, 3*, 57–83.

Sack, R. D. (1992). *Place, modernity, and the consumer's world*. Baltimore, MD: Johns Hopkins University Press.

Seamon, D. (1987). Phenomenology and environment-behavior research. In E. H. Zube & G. T. Moore (Eds.), *Advances in environment and behavior design* (Vol. 1, pp. 3–27). New York: Plenum Press.

Shumaker, S. A., & Hankin, J. (1984). The bonds between people and their residential environments: Theory and research. *Population and Environment, 7*, 59–60.

Smale, B. (2006). Critical perspectives on place in leisure research. *Leisure/Loisir, 30*, 369–382.

Spain, D. (1992). *Gendered spaces*. Chappell Hill, NC: University of North Carolina Press.

Stewart, W. P., Williams, D. R., & Kruger, L. E. (2013). *Place-based conservation: Perspectives from the social sciences*. New York: Springer.

Stokols, D., & Shumaker, S. A. (1981). People in places: A transactional view of settings. In J. H. Harvey (Ed.), *Cognition, social behavior, and the environment* (pp. 441–488). Hillsdale, NJ: Lawrence Earlbaum Associates.

Stokowski, P. A. (2002). Languages of place and discourses of power: Constructing new senses of place. *Journal of Leisure Research, 34*, 368–382.

Stokowski, P. A., (2008). Creating social senses of place: New directions for sense of place research in natural resource management. In L. E. Kruger, T. E. Hall, & M. C. Stiefel (Eds.), *Understanding concepts of place in recreation research and management* (pp. 31–60; PNW-GTR-744). Portland, OR: USDA Forest Service, Pacific Northwest Research Station.

Theberge, N. (2000). *Higher goals: Women's ice hockey and the politics of gender*. Albany, NY: State University of New York Press.

Tuan, Y. (1974). Space and place: Humanistic perspective. *Progress in Geography, 6*, 211–252.

Tuan, Y. (1977). *Space and place: The perspective of experience*. Minneapolis, MN: The University of Minnesota Press.

Williams, D. R., Patterson, M. E., Roggenbuck, J. W., & Watson, A. E. (1992). Beyond the commodity metaphor: Examining emotional and symbolic attachment to place. *Leisure Sciences, 14*, 29–46.

32
Leveraging Leisure-Based Community Networks to Access Social Capital

Troy D. Glover (University of Waterloo)

Community is ironically one of the most palpable comforts and anxieties of our time. As Christenson and Levinson (2006, p. xxxi) pointed out, "we live in a time when our desire for community seems to grow in proportion to our sense that it is declining." Recent concerns about the loss of community stem from the work of Robert Putnam, the Harvard political scientist who drew the world's attention to the concept of social capital. Like other forms of capital, social capital is premised upon the notion that an investment (in social relations) will result in a return (some benefit or profit) to the individual (Lin, 2001). It refers to ". . . the consequence of investment in and cultivation of social relationships allowing an individual access to resources that would otherwise be unavailable to him or her" (Glover, Shinew, & Parry, 2005, p. 87). Putnam (2000) cited an impressive quantity of evidence to demonstrate how an increasing erosion of social and civic engagement has led to a serious decline in social capital in United States. This decline, he surmised, has had a damaging effect on the social fabric of American society. To describe this trend, Putnam applied the provocative title *Bowling Alone* (1995, 2000) to his work, having observed that Americans are steadily become less likely to bowl in organized leagues. The leisure metaphor was deliberate, for he argued associational memberships bring relative strangers together routinely and frequently, thus building and sustaining a larger set of social networks that nurture values like generalized trust and reciprocity, values that in turn facilitate social cooperation.

Not surprisingly, criticisms of Putnam's interpretations abound. Chief among these is the notion that Putnam is simply lamenting the death of old-style community bonds. Florida (2003) argued people desire quasi-anonymity and prefer weak ties to the stronger tight-knit communities that Putnam favors. Accordingly, Bruhn (2011, p. 22) wrote, "Communities exist, but they are less likely to be warm and fuzzy places, and what holds them together are the common interests of their members and not their deep emotional ties." Many critics bemoan this shift toward communities of interest. As Glover and Hemingway (2005) noted, skepticism regarding Putnam's work is highest regarding the consequences of memberships in leisure-based voluntary associations. While Etzioni (2000) agreed leisure is a context that reinforces friendships, he was less confident it encourages people to ". . . shore up their moral commitments, talk about basic moral questions, such as what is right and wrong, or encourage each other to be better than they would be otherwise—things that are essential prerequisites of a good society." Thus, Putnam's work raises the question: *What role, if any, does leisure play in advancing community?*

This question has spurred unprecedented interest in community and social capital, twin subjects whose appearance has grown remarkably in leisure studies in recent years. Within the last decade alone, all streams of inquiry in our field have seen examples of research focused on leisure as a potential site for building community or generating social capital. This explosion of interest signals an appropriate time to step back and reflect on what we know about community and social capital in leisure studies, what direction this literature is taking, and what questions remain unanswered.

Thus, the purpose of this chapter is to provide an overview of our current understanding of the relationship between community and social capital in leisure studies and offer suggestions for future research. The chapter begins by disentangling community and social capital, two concepts frequently conflated. Next, it moves onto reviewing the relationship between leisure and its role in building community and generating social capital. Finally, I discuss future directions in community and social capital research by exploring inequality in access to social capital and the need to examine the implications of liminality and durability in leisure networks.

DISENTANGLING COMMUNITY AND SOCIAL CAPITAL

Community and social capital are different, albeit complementary. Community is a *source* of social capital, and social capital represents the *value* of community. This distinction may not sit well with some people. Detractors may infer, perhaps fairly, that I am privileging social capital over community, thereby undermining the inherent value of community. To be sure, there are many intrinsic benefits of community, including sense of belonging, common affective union, and commitment to a set of shared values, norms, and history. Studies in our field have certainly underscored these features (see Glover, 2003, 2004a). However, this limited perspective, in Blackshaw's (2010) words, is "... burdened by a romantic sensibility" (p. 1) that colors our conceptualization.

Many leisure researchers are seemingly uncomfortable with the notion that community built through leisure would be used for instrumental gain. As a result, social solidarity is often privileged without acknowledging what makes community valuable, namely its routine appropriation to facilitate social support, personal advancement, and group desires (Glover, 2006). However, we must fight the seductive tendency to fetishize community and critically examine it in all of its complexity, including its appropriation for personal and collective benefit (Cook, 2006). This chapter boldly points us in such a direction.

While Putnam (2000) was correct to refer to community as social capital's "conceptual cousin" (p. 21), the literature too often conflates the two social constructs (Colclough & Sitaraman, 2005). Social capital is routinely confused with its sources (e.g., social connections) and its outcomes (social support) (see Portes, 1998). Similarly, community is often mixed up with its by-products, namely its bounded solidarity or intentional organization (forms of social capital identified by Coleman, 1990). Accordingly, distinguishing among sources, forms, and outcomes is a useful framework to explore the interplay of community, leisure, and social capital.

COMMUNITY AS A SOURCE OF SOCIAL CAPITAL

Common among the numerous ways to study community is the notion of groups of people whose lives are linked together in various ways (Glover & Stewart, 2006). Whether intentional, imagined, or connected by a common interest, a particular place or ties of shared social identity, community in its various networked forms links people together. These linkages are particularly relevant in contemporary society in which community has become less *place-based* and more *connection-based*. While complex social networks have always existed, recent developments in communication technology have afforded their emergence as a dominant form of social organization, thereby leading scholars to increasingly operationalize contemporary communities as social networks (see Bauman, 2001; Wellman, 2001). These networks of interpersonal ties provide a sense of belonging, social identity, and access to support and information (Wellman, 2001).

The notion of community as a "portfolio of networks" (Bruhn, 2011, p. 45) contrasts sharply with its more traditional operationalization as aggregates of small-scale, geographically based populations. Not surprisingly, given its roots in public recreation, leisure studies has historically treated community as a vague descriptor to represent the audience for whom leisure is provided (Glover & Stewart, 2006). However, in this contemporary age, connections stretch well beyond geographic boundaries, thereby necessitating an expansion of our definition of community.

What makes community in the form of social networks so valuable is its role as a conduit to access necessary resources. No matter how many resources we may personally own, we depend on the generosity and support of others to achieve our aims. We *need* to build our social capital. As Hemingway (2006) clarified, social capital originates from the relationships we build *within* our community networks. Thus, the resources of our networks are not made available to just anyone; they are available through the exclusivity of our network membership. The notion that certain communities are inclusive, therefore, is misleading because network membership is ultimately finite. The very exclusiveness of community increases the currency of community membership. This currency amounts to social capital. Building community networks, then, is crucial to the development of social capital. Germane to leisure research is the idea that networks have the potential to be built, maintained, enhanced, or changed through leisure.

GETTING TOGETHER THROUGH LEISURE: BONDING, BRIDGING, AND LINKING

Because individuals are unlikely to come together without a purpose, leisure plays a fundamental role in attracting people to socialize together and encourages them to build meaningful relationships that can lead to the development of durable community networks. Leisure is adept at drawing people together as a community because of its intrinsic value. It promotes sociability, which is alluring to individuals, making it crucial to the development of community relationships. The sense of freedom leisure affords opens up lines of communication and allows us to transcend the boundaries of our various social identities. In so doing, it serves as an indispensable vehicle for the realization of community (Cook, 2003) and access to necessary resources.

Relationships form and social capital develops within what Glover and Parry (2008) called the "sphere of sociability." To maintain our stocks of social capital, we must routinely re-invest in our relationships by continuing to be social, otherwise those relationships and the resources accessible through them are likely to wither. Leisure becomes a meaningful domain of everyday life in which we connect and renew our social bonds. For this reason, Glover, Parry et al. (2005) described leisure as "the social lubricant" for social capital production.

Various studies have showcased leisure and its role in forging community networks that lead to the development of social capital. These studies can be organized according to three types of relationship building known in the social capital literature as: (a) bonding, (b) bridging, and (c) linking. Bonding refers to "trusting and co-operative relations between members of a network who see themselves as being similar in terms of their shared social identity" (Szreter & Woolcock, 2004, p. 654). More often than not, researchers find that leisure draws together individuals who share a common identity. For example, play groups connect young mothers who help each other cope through the experience of motherhood (Mulcahy, Parry, & Glover, 2010); social clubs, like the Red Hat Society, forge a "sisterhood" among members, which give middle-aged and older women access to social support (Son, Yarnal, & Kerstetter, 2010); and festivals involve residents in rituals that support strong intra-group ties (Arcodia & Whitford, 2007; Misener & Mason, 2006). In each case, leisure facilitates strong community connections among people who share a common bond.

Leisure can also facilitate the formation of community relationships among people who see themselves as different. *Bridging social capital* refers to "relations of respect and mutuality between people who know that they are not alike in some sociodemographic (or social identity) sense (differing by age, ethnic group, class, etc.)" (Szreter & Woolcock, 2004, p. 655). Achieving this outcome is admittedly challenging because most people prefer to associate with others similar to themselves (McPherson, Smith-Livin, & Cook, 2001) and will sometimes clash (see Glover, Parry, & Mulchay, 2012) or "hunker down" (see Putnam, 2007) when faced with the prospect of interacting with dissimilar people. Even so, the sometimes liminal quality of leisure—leisure's temporary state of being—releases its participants ". . . from day-to-day structural necessities and obligatoriness" (Turner, 1973, p. 217) by giving them permission to embrace the moment, share the experience, and dispense with pre-existing social structures (see Sharpe, 2008). Accordingly, the literature reveals leisure can be a focal point in bridging racial and ethnic groups (Shinew, Glover, & Parry, 2004), cultures (Moscardo, 2012), persons with and without disabilities (Devine & Parr, 2008), among others.

In still other ways, leisure connects individuals vertically. Szreter and Woolcock (2004) defined linking social capital as "norms of respect and networks of trusting relationships between people who are interacting across explicit, formal or institutionalized power or authority gradients in society" (p. 655). Arcodia and Whitford (2007) found festival administrators, by interacting directly with local businesses and the public to make arrangements for the festival, raised their awareness of community resources, produced social links between previously unrelated groups, and generally encouraged a stronger interaction between existing community organizations. In short, leisure and its delivery enable individuals to forge relationships with others across institutionalized statuses.

SOME CAVEATS

Three caveats are necessary to mention before moving on. First, *the specific strength of ties involved in each scenario is open to interpretation*. Whether individuals bond or bridge is a subjective judgment. Glover (2003, 2004b) studied a community garden project in the American Midwest that brought together residents of a diverse neighborhood to reclaim a corner lot and displace undesirable groups, a scenario that could be interpreted as neighbors bonding. But perhaps it is an illustration of different racial or ethnic groups bridging. Which identity stands out to claim participants as members? The intersectionality of our multiple identities makes it challenging to nail down definitively whether bonding or bridging took place. Putnam (2000, p. 23) acknowledged this quandary by observing, "Many groups simultaneously bond along some social dimensions and bridge across others," which led him to add, ". . . bonding and bridging are not 'either-or' categories into which social networks can be neatly divided, but 'more or less' dimensions along which we can compare different forms of social capital." For this reason, it is fair to say that people share some form of social identity when coming together to form a community, whether interest-based (Scott, Chapter 19), place-based (Kyle, Chapter 31), or sociodemographic (e.g., Stodolska and Floyd, Chapter 28). Ultimately, leisure researchers ought to be careful when making outright claims of bonding or bridging.

Second, *social capital can be facilitated through leisure, but its creation is never guaranteed*. Sociability makes leisure a powerful context in which community relationships can be built, maintained, and sustained. While leisure gets people together, however, it does not necessarily *keep* them together. For a variety of reasons, sometimes people just do not get along, they do not click, they have no interest in continuing to connect or they are excluded from joining. Graham and Glover (2014) found owners of certain breeds of dogs thought to be aggressive were discriminated against, shunned, or left out of group formations by other dog park users. Mulcahy et al. (2010) found mothers who belonged to playgroups were often subjected to "mummy judgment," a review and policing of their parenting experiences and decisions, and subsequently, in some cases, pushed out of groups. Getting together, in other words, is never enough. While leisure plays a crucial role in getting people together to create community networks, there's no guarantee those individuals will build meaningful relationships that generate social capital. Ultimately, all leisure can do is provide a context in which people connect. The rest is up to people themselves.

The way leisure is experienced appears to make a difference, though. Hemingway (1999) argued the more autonomy people have during leisure and the more leisure contributes to fuller development of individual capacities, the more social capital will be generated and transferable. He went on to speculate that, to the extent individuals participate in creating their own leisure, rather than simply consuming it passively, the more likely the resulting social capital will contribute to strong citizenship. Hemingway's propositions hold up well upon empirical investigation (see Doherty & Misener, 2008; Glover, 2002). Relatedly, Yuen and Glover (2005) distinguished between leisure that encourages people to *socialize* (i.e., interact casually) and *mobilize* (i.e., act collectively to achieve a common goal), noting the former is effective at facilitating bonding, whereas the latter is effective at facilitating bridging and linking. In both cases, social capital is likely to be generated, so "the question is not if leisure is associated with civically relevant social capital, but what kinds of leisure in what kinds of settings" (Glover & Hemingway, 2005, p. 395).

Third, *community networks that represent sources of social capital do not necessarily have to be face-to-face.* Glover and Parry (2008) stressed the role of leisure in facilitating the *ongoing maintenance* of community networks. As Nahapiet and Ghoshal (1998) noted, "social relationships generally, though not always, are strengthened through interaction but die out if not maintained" (p. 258). In what I suspect he would now view as a dated argument, Putnam (2000) privileged face-to-face interactions in the formation of social capital. He figured connecting from a distance is more impersonal and less effective as a strategy to invest meaningfully in relationships, something that resonates for those in long-distance relationships. However, the ubiquity of communications technology in everyday life has made online connections, at the very least, complementary with "offline" connections (Wellman et al., 2001). Parry et al. (2013), in their exploration of Momstown.ca, a membership-based social networking site for mothers of young children, showed how the site provided a portal for "friend-shopping" by helping users find new friends through access to profiles of members and facilitating face-to-face interactions. Face-to-face interactions combined with continued electronic correspondence to enable "friend-shipping," the building of successful friendships. Thus, online interactions proved to be as important as face-to-face interactions. The topic of online connections and their implications for building community and generating social capital warrants greater attention in leisure research (see also Nimrod, Chapter 30).

All told, the literature on leisure and social capital shows leisure is not trivial, but rather essential to enabling individuals to build, maintain, and sustain community networks that will give them access to resources for purposive actions. Leisure has *social value* that can be leveraged for individual and collective benefit (Chalip, 2006). And so, understanding the forms social capital and the actions they facilitate is important to better appreciating the value of community networks.

FORMS OF SOCIAL CAPITAL AND THE ACTIONS THEY FACILITATE

Coleman (1990) identified six forms of social capital individuals appropriate from their community networks. First, *obligations and expectations* provide incentives for individuals to invest in community networks and accrue obligations, which investors trust will be reciprocated and repaid. Simply being a member of a leisure-oriented group necessitates the presence of obligation to ensure the group continues to meet routinely and function as intended. If everyone decided not to show up, it would not be much of an experience. This necessity has led Stebbins (2000) to argue that *agreeable obligation* accompanies positive attachment to an activity and is framed by participants in satisfying terms.

Second, *information potential* entails the use of community networks to access specialized information without having to obtain the information directly. In separate studies, Mulcahy et al. (2010) and Parry et al. (2013) found mothers they interviewed were granted access to advice of other more seasoned mothers through their leisure-based networks. Similarly, Graham and Glover (2014) found dog owners who belonged to a network of dog park users exchanged dog-related information concerning their favorite veterinarians, groomers, and pet stores. In addition to all things dog, some participants even found employment, housing, or dating arrangements through their interactions.

Third, *norms and effective sanctions* persuade members to work for the collective good of the network and in its members' interests. In Glover and Parry's (2008) research on the friendship networks of women experiencing infertility, research participants who remained infertile felt compelled to support friends who conceived or adopted children, even though such support confronted them with their own infertility. Activities that generated stress in participants were, more often than not, child-centered (e.g., baby showers) that reminded participants of their own childlessness, thereby creating further stress in their lives. The social norms and sanctions embedded in their friendships compelled them to support their friends under stressful circumstances.

Fourth, *authority relations* occur when a social network transfers "rights of control" to one individual who then has access to an extensive network of social capital that can be directed toward a specific goal. Johnson et al. (2009) showed how community representatives worked with municipal officials to build trusting partnerships within their city. Though being representatives led these residents to feel caught between neighbors they represented and the city officials with whom they negotiated, their role enabled them to speak on behalf of the neighborhood and work toward desired improvements.

Fifth, an *appropriable social organization* is an organization developed for one purpose, but appropriated for another. Glover (2003) discussed how a community garden became a symbol of residents' efforts to reclaim their neighborhood and was appropriated deliberately by the neighborhood association to enhance the association's credibility with external audiences. The story of the community garden was further used to unite the neighborhood and elicit emotional affirmations of community identity.

Finally, *intentional organizations* join individuals together to create an entity that will benefit members, but also others. Glover (2004a) found volunteers described their community center as an ongoing project that warranted continued investment, thereby making it an intentional organization that benefited volunteers directly, yet profited other users, too.

These forms of social capital are valuable because they facilitate action. Exploring the actions they enable is crucial to demonstrating the social relevance of social capital. There are four types of action exhibited in the literature, all of which are found in the examples above: First, *expressive action* (or getting by) refers to emotional support. Examples above reveal how networks assist individuals in coping with their life situations, whether dealing with infertility or the challenges of parenting young children, through the receipt of empathetic support. Second, *instrumental action* (or getting ahead), the material dimension of community networks, gives members access to resources that help them advance their social position. Acquiring valuable information, as noted above, is a common example. Third, *collective action* (or working together) refers to an effort by more than one person to improve their shared conditions and achieve change through joint organization, mobilization, and negotiation. Community formation in whatever shape or form is aimed at advancing collective interests. Fourth, *obstructive action* (or falling behind) refers to actions taken by network members that do themselves harm. Glover and Parry (2008) identified this form of action to acknowledge the potential ill-effects of community networks. Obstructive action represents a set back or keeps an individual from getting ahead.

The inclusion of obstructive action alerts us to the potential costs of social capital. Portes and Sensenbrenner (1993) recognized the very same social structures "that give rise to appropriate resources for individual use can also constrain action or even derail it from its original goals" (p. 1338). Correspondingly, Portes and Landlot (1996) argued social capital is contingent on a high degree of conformity within the group, and nonconformists can be ostracized. Any attempt by a member to achieve something outside the network may be seen as a threat to group solidarity and discouraged. With this in mind, it is no surprise that research participants in Glover and Parry's (2008) study of women who experienced infertility felt compelled to support their friends, even though their participation was detrimental to their own well-being. Social capital has a dark side, which warrants further investigation by leisure researchers.

INEQUALITY IN ACCESS TO AND RETURNS FROM SOCIAL CAPITAL

A growing area of leisure research on social capital that aligns well with examining the dark side of social capital is the subject of access and return. Access to resources is fundamental to the presence of social capital, yet resources are not made available to just anyone. While community networks can be appropriated by more than one network member for personal gain, such resources often are denied to outsiders. The "old boys' network," for example, represents the use of exclusive connections for professional advantage at the expense of the social mobility of women. The benefits that accrue to community networks are no less evident in many leisure contexts wherein non-membership means group benefits are often inaccessible to outsiders. As Glover (2006, p. 360) wrote, "social capital has value precisely because it is exclusive." While a network can expand, membership remains restricted. Moreover, within a community network, benefits are distributed differentially based upon the unique social positions community members occupy. As a result, the returns of social capital differ, too. Leisure research must focus on how social capital both enables *and* denies (Glover, 2006).

Focusing on the actual distribution within and between community networks by examining the extent to which *individuals* can actually *appropriate* social capital from their networks is crucial to better understanding who benefits from social capital. The extent to which social capital is actually appropriable is relevant here because it is premised upon the notion that people have differential access to and returns from social capital. As Glover (2006) outlined, access and return are dependent upon at least three factors. First, certain individuals, because of their social standing, are differentially rewarded for their investment in network relationships, despite making the same investment as other members of the network. Lin (2001) identified this form of inequality as a *return deficit*. Glover (2004b) found that, despite being pleased with their efforts to revitalize their neighborhood, non-White renters, in comparison to White homeowners, had limited access to the community garden they helped to build, even though they put an equal effort into the project. *Within group* inequalities, such as this, are important to consider in any analysis of social capital.

Second, the broader socioeconomic context shapes the ways specific networks link their members to resources (Foley & Edwards, 1999). This factor acknowledges that, while an individual may have extensive access to resources in a community network, the network as a whole may be embedded in an oppressed constituency. Lin (2001) referred to this form of inequality as a *capital deficit*. Hunter (2010) revealed the importance of night clubs as spaces that help poor urban African Americans get ahead, get by, and negotiate their isolation from opportunities and spaces in the city that their White counterparts readily access. In so doing, club-goers generated social ties that connected them to job opportunities, partner selection, and social support. Ultimately, however, these individuals were able to get ahead only so far because of the limited resources accessible within their club networks. Appreciating this capital deficit acknowledges how certain social groups initially enter a relationship with different resources at their disposal. Leisure researchers need to acknowledge inequality (racial or otherwise) as a feature enmeshed with the production and use of social capital.

Third, access to social capital is contingent on *the quantity* and *quality of relationships*. It is generally accepted that the more an individual *bonds* with social actors who share a similar social identity and *bridges* with others to diversify his or her social identity, the more social capital the individual will have at his or her disposal. By concentrating exclusively on quantity of relationships formed, however, there is a tendency to ignore quality. More ties are presumably better, yet one tie may suffice to gain access to a crucial resource (Foley & Edwards, 1999).

While a strong support network made up of family and friends is generally considered paramount to coping with health-related issues, some relationships can be detrimental to well-being. Halpern (2005) noted, close relationships with abusive, depressed, or disturbed individuals can have damaging effects on mental health, adding that when support shifts into dependence, it can bring with it feelings of helplessness and resentment. The simple fact of knowing someone is not enough; the relationship must be supportive and positive to have beneficial impacts. Accordingly, leisure researchers need to consider the quality, as well as the quantity, of relationships in their examinations of social capital.

LIMINALITY AND DURABILITY

I referred earlier to the notion that leisure can have a liminal feature to it (e.g., moments out of time and social structure). Its temporary nature means contact among participants is short-lived. Thus, questions rightly persist about the durability of relationships. If social capital requires ongoing investments in social relationships, do liminal leisure activities make a difference in terms of accessing resources? Perhaps some leisure is trivial after all.

Bauman (2001) described collectivities developed in and through leisure as "peg" communities—that is, ". . . communities formed by the act of hanging individual concerns on a common 'peg' . . . Just like the overcoats in the theatre cloakroom, so the concerns are hung on the peg only for the duration of the spectacle, remaining the whole time the private property of their rightful individual owners" (Bauman, 2000, p. 19). Populated by people who never meet again, Bauman argued peg-communities do not create ethical responsibilities or long-term commitments, but rather "carnival bonds" (Bauman, 2001, p. 72). Heimtun (2007), a tourism scholar, took issue with Bauman's framing of tourists whom Bauman described as wanting real community, but are left to settle for transitory and mobile experiences that last for limited time beyond the actual holiday itself. This criticism can be applied to other leisure experiences, too (see Chalip, 2006). The question of durability remains.

Social capital is not embodied in any particular person, but rather is embedded in social relationships, even though it is *realized* by individuals. If the relationship fails to endure, social capital, presumably, diminishes, perhaps even disappearing altogether. Thus, there is a question about the enduring nature of social capital and whether it continues to exist after the "peg community" is dispersed. This question is a serious matter for leisure scholars.

Interestingly, Heimtun (2007) countered Bauman's criticisms by arguing tourists build social capital. She cited her research on the tourist experiences of Norwegian midlife single women and reported their proclivity to bond with significant others during their travels. Evidence in the leisure literature, as cited in the many examples above, further supports Heimtun's observations that meaningful relationships develop in leisure contexts. How long these relationships endure is tantamount to asking the question "How long is a piece of string?" We just do not know. Ultimately, leisure scholars recognize leisure is more than rudimentary pleasure-seeking; it plays a critical role in community building and the generation of social capital. Even so, investigating the matter of durability, perhaps through longitudinal analyses, warrants greater attention from our field.

CONCLUSION

I used this chapter to make the case that leisure plays a vital role in the formation and maintenance of community networks. These networks have value because they serve as important sources of social capital, which gives their members access to resources they would otherwise be without. Not all social capital is good, however. And not all members have the same access to it. Accordingly, I have called on leisure researchers to explore the distribution of social capital in terms of access and return. Doing so applies a necessarily critical lens on leisure, community, and social capital research. Moreover, there is an urgent need for leisure researchers to address the consequences, if any, of the liminality of leisure for the generation of durable social capital. The field remains silent on this matter, yet it is fundamental to positioning leisure as a meaningful domain in which networks are formed and social capital is accessed. Too often leisure is dismissed by critics as trivial. Leisure researchers need to respond to the critiques and demonstrate the value of leisure to community and social capital.

REFERENCES

Arcodia, C., & Whitford, M. (2007). Festival attendance and the development of social capital. *Journal of Convention & Event Tourism, 8*(2), 1–18.

Bauman, Z. (2001). *Community. Seeking safety in an insecure world.* Cambridge, UK: Polity Press.

Bauman, Z. (2000). As seen on TV. *Philosophical Perspectives, 7*(2-3), 107–122.

Blackshaw, T. (2010). *Key concepts in community studies.* Washington, DC: Sage.

Bourdieu, P. (1986). The forms of capital. In J. Richardson (Ed.), *Handbook of theory and research for the sociology of education* (pp. 241–258). New York: Greenwood.

Bruhn, J. G. (2011). *The sociology of community connections* (2nd ed.). New York: Springer.

Chalip, L. (2006). Towards social leverage of sport events. *Journal of Sport & Tourism, 11*(2), 109–127.

Christensen, K., & Levinson, D. (2003). Introduction. In K Christensen & D. Levinson (Eds.), *Encyclopedia of Community* (pp. xxxi–xlii). Thousand Oaks, CA: Sage.

Colclough, G., & Sitaraman, B. (2005). Community and social capital: What is the difference? *Sociological Inquiry, 75*(4), 474–496.

Coleman, J. S. (1990). *Foundations of Social Theory.* Cambridge, MA: Belknap Press.

Cook, D. T. (2003). Recreation. In K. Christensen & D. Levinson (Eds.), *Encyclopedia of Community* (pp. 1146–1149). Thousand Oaks, CA: Sage.

Cook, D. T. (2006). Problematizing consumption, community, and leisure: Some thoughts on moving beyond essentialist thinking. *Leisure/Loisir, 30*(2), 455–466.

Devine, M. A., & Parr, M. G. (2008). "Come on in, but not too far": Social capital in an inclusive leisure setting. *Leisure Sciences, 30*(5), 391–408.

Doherty, A., & Misener, K. (2008). Community sport networks. In M. Nicholson & R. Hoye (Eds.), *Sport and social capital* (pp. 113–142). New York: Butterworth-Heinemann.

Etzioni, A. (2000). *Book review: Community as we know it.* Retrieved from http://speakout.com/activism/opinions/2865-1.html

Florida, R. (2003). Cities and the creative class. *City & Community, 2*(1), 3–19.

Foley, M. W., & Edwards, B. (1999). Is it time to divest in social capital? *Journal of Public Policy, 19*(2), 141–173.

Glover, T. D. (2002). Citizenship and the production of public recreation: Is there an empirical relationship? *Journal of Leisure Research, 34*(2), 204–231.

Glover, T. D. (2003). The story of the Queen Anne Memorial Garden: Resisting a dominant cultural narrative. *Journal of Leisure Research, 35*(2), 190–212.

Glover, T. D. (2004a). The 'community' center and the social construction of citizenship. *Leisure Sciences, 26*(1), 63–83.

Glover, T. D. (2004b). Social capital in the lived experiences of community gardeners, *Leisure Sciences, 26*(2), 143–162.

Glover, T. D. (2006). Toward a critical examination of social capital within leisure contexts: From production and maintenance to distribution. *Leisure/Loisir: Journal of the Canadian Association for Leisure Studies, 30*(2), 357–367.

Glover, T. D., & Hemingway, J. L. (2005). Locating leisure in the social capital literature. *Journal of Leisure Research, 37*(4), 387–401.

Glover, T. D., & Parry, D. C. (2008). Friendships developed subsequent to a stressful life event: Links with leisure, social capital, and health. *Journal of Leisure Research, 40*(2), 208–230.

Glover, T. D., Parry, D. C., & Mulcahy, C. M. (2012). At once liberating and exclusionary? A Lefebvrean analysis of Gilda's Club of Toronto. *Leisure Studies*. doi: 10.1080/02614367.2012.677057

Glover, T. D., Parry, D. C., & Shinew, K. J. (2005). Building relationships, accessing resources: Mobilizing social capital in community garden contexts. *Journal of Leisure Research, 37*(4), 450–474.

Glover, T. D., Shinew, K. J., & Parry, D. C. (2005). Association, sociability, and civic culture: The democratic effect of community gardening. *Leisure Sciences, 27*(1), 75–92.

Glover, T. D., & Stewart, W. P. (2006). Rethinking leisure and community research: Critical reflections and future agendas. *Leisure/Loisir: Journal of the Canadian Association for Leisure Studies, 30*(2), 315–327.

Graham, T. M., & Glover, T. D. (2014). On the fence: Dog parks in the (un)leashing of community and social capital. *Leisure Sciences, 36,* 217–234.

Halpern, D. (2005). *Social capital*. Cambridge, UK: Polity Press.

Heimtun, B. (2007). Depathologizing the tourist syndrome: Tourism as social capital production. *Tourist Studies, 7*(3), 271–293.

Hemingway, J. L. (1999). Leisure, social capital, and democratic citizenship. *Journal of Leisure Research, 31*(2), 150–165.

Hemingway, J. L. (2006). Leisure, social capital and civic competence. *Leisure/Loisir, 30*(2), 341–355.

Hunter, M. A. (2010). The nightly round: Space, social capital, and urban black nightlife. *City & Community, 9*(2), 165–186.

Johnson, A. J., Glover, T. D., & Yuen, F. (2009). Supporting effective community representation: Lessons from the Festival of Neighbourhoods. *Managing Leisure, 14*(1), 1–16.

Lin, N. (2001). *Social capital: A theory of social structure and action*. New York: Cambridge University Press.

McPherson, M., Smith-Livin, L., & Cook, J. (2001). Birds of a feather: Homophily in social networks. *Annual Review of Sociology, 27*, 415–444.

Misener, L., & Mason, D. (2006). Creating community networks: Can sporting events offer meaningful sources of social capital? *Managing Leisure, 11*(1), 39–56.

Moscardo, G. (2012). Building social capital to enhance the quality-of-life of destination. In M. Uysal, R. R. Purdue, & M. J. Sirgy (Ed.), *Handbook of tourism and quality-of-life research: Enhancing the lives of tourists and residents of host communities* (pp. 402–421). New York: Springer.

Mulcahy, C. M., Parry, D. C., & Glover, T. D. (2010). Playgroup politics: A critical social capital exploration of exclusion and conformity in mummies groups. *Leisure Studies, 29*(1), 3–27.

Nahapiet, J., & Ghosal, S. (1998). Social capital, intellectual capital, and the organization advantage. *Academy of Management Review, 23*(2), 242–266.

Parry, D. C., Glover, T. D., & Mulcahy, C. M. (2013). From "stroller-stalker" to "momancer": Courting friends through a social networking site for mothers. *Journal of Leisure Research, 45*(1), 23–46.

Portes, A. (1998). Social capital: Its origins and applications in modern sociology. *Annual Review of Sociology, 24*, 1–24.

Portes, A., & Landlot, P. (1996). The downside of social capital. *American Prospect, 26*, 18–21, 94.

Portes, A. & Sensenbrenner, J. (1993). Embeddedness and immigration: Notes on the social determinants of economic action. *American Journal of Sociology, 98*(6), 1320–1350.

Putnam, R. D. (1995). Bowling alone: America's declining social capital. *Journal of Democracy, 6*(1), 65–78.

Putnam, R. D. (2000). *Bowling alone: The collapse and revival of American community*. New York, NY: Simon & Schuster.

Putnam, R. D. (2007). E Pluribus Unum: Diversity and community in the Twenty-first Century. *Scandinavian Political Studies, 30*(2), 137–174.

Sharpe, E. K. (2008). Festivals and social change: Intersections of pleasure and politics at a community music festival. *Leisure Sciences, 30*(3), 217–234.

Shinew, K. J., Glover, T. D., & Parry, D. C. (2004). Leisure spaces as potential sites for interracial interaction: Community gardens in a segregated urban area. *Journal of Leisure Research, 36*(3), 336–355.

Son, J., Yarnal, C., & Kerstetter, D. (2010). Engendering social capital through a leisure club for middle-aged and older women: Implications for individual and community health and well-being. *Leisure Studies, 29*(1), 67–83.

Stebbins, R. A. (2000). Obligation as an aspect of leisure experience. *Journal of Leisure Research, 32*(1), 152–155.

Szreter, S., & Woolcock, M. (2004). Health by association? Social capital, social theory, and the political economy of public health. *International Journal of Epidemiology, 33*(4), 650–667.

Turner, V. (1973). The center out there: Pilgrim's goal. *History of religions, 12*(3), 191–230.

Wellman, B. (2001). Physical place and cyberspace: The rise of personalized networking. *International Journal of Urban and Regional Research, 25*(2), 227–252.

Wellman, B., Haase, A. Q., Witte, J., & Hampton, K. (2001). Does the Internet increase, decrease, or supplement social capital? Social networks, participation, and community commitment. *American Behaviorial Scientist, 45*(3), 436–455.

Yuen, F., & Glover, T. D. (2005). Enabling social capital development: An examination of the Festival of Neighbourhoods in Kitchener, Ontario. *Journal of Park and Recreation Administration, 23*(4), 20–38.

33
Public Policy and Planning Frameworks

A. J. Veal (University of Technology, Sydney)

This chapter begins with brief discussions of the nature and political context of policymaking and planning for leisure, followed by an examination of a range of approaches to planning which have been recommended and used in the leisure sector in recent years. Finally, a view is expressed on the most valid policymaking and planning framework for the public leisure sector to adopt for the future.

PUBLIC POLICYMAKING, PLANNING, AND LEISURE

Public policymaking can be seen as the process by which governmental bodies formulate broad goals and principles which frame their subsequent actions, while planning can be seen as the development of specific programs to pursue goals and apply principles over a specific period of time. For example, a government might decide on a *policy* to seek to reduce obesity in the community and then, to implement the policy, it might develop a five-year *plan* to increase the proportion of the population engaging in regular physical activity in leisure time by ensuring greater access to fitness facilities and programs.

Public policymaking and planning for leisure can involve supra-government bodies, such as the European Commission, national, state/provincial and local governments, statutory agencies, and other independent bodies, such as trusts and charities, which perform public functions, often with partial or total government funding. Government involvement in the field may imply direct government *provision* of services but can also involve various forms of *regulation* or *indirect support*. For example, governments control the allocation of broadcasting wavelengths to broadcasters but may or may not be direct providers of broadcasting services, and they license venues for gambling and for the sale of alcohol without themselves being involved in provision for these leisure activities. Furthermore, there is a long tradition of government providing financial support for not-for-profit service provision organizations. In the terms used by Burton and Glover (1999), governments may play the roles of: legislator and regulator; patron and arm's length provider; coordinator; direct provider; and/or enabler. More recently, Giddens (2011) has coined the term "ensuring state" which is similar to the "enabling state," but places more emphasis on the realization of specific outcomes.

PUBLIC POLICYMAKING, LEISURE, AND THE POLITICAL CONTEXT

Public policymaking is *political* because it involves, explicitly or implicitly, adopting an overall stance on: the type and extent of government activity in society; the raising of tax revenue and its expenditure on the provision of particular services; and/or the exercise of direct control over the activities of individuals and organizations. Different societies have differing views on the roles and consequent size of government. Thus, in the United States it is generally believed that government should be minimal, while in European countries a greater role for government is expected. Paralleling these differences is a range of values and attitudes concerning the acceptability of direct involvement in people's lives. While leisure rarely features in the major debating arenas in which political ideologies and perspectives on policymaking and planning are fought out, it is not immune to political consideration. Thus, when more conservative "small government" parties win power from left-leaning "big government" parties, and proceed to reduce the role of government by cutting public expenditure, leisure facilities and programs are typically affected along with other service areas. Furthermore, such matters as the control of gambling or of the use of recreational drugs can be politically highly controversial, as can legislating to protect certain natural areas from development.

APPROACHES TO PLANNING

Since early in the twentieth century, leisure planning has been characterized by a slow accretion of diverse frameworks and approaches, often coexisting and finding favor with different groups of practitioners at various times. Eight such frameworks and approaches, identified from an analysis of over 80 sets of planning guidelines published since the 1950s by governments, professional bodies, and academics from a number of countries (Veal, 2011), are evaluated in turn below.

1. Meeting Provision Standards

While the leisure sector is subject to a number of types of standards, dealing with such matters as safety and the design of facilities, we are here concerned with *fixed provision standards* promulgated by an external, typically national, authoritative organization, generally expressed as a required level of provision of facilities per 1000 population. The attractions of this approach lay in its simplicity in understanding and application, which offered a form of accountability. However, while still promoted by some, it has been subject to substantial criticism for at least 40 years (Sports Council, 1968; Veal, 2010), on the grounds that a "one-size-fits-all" approach is not appropriate and determination of leisure service requirements should take account of local conditions. Furthermore, their technical basis was often in doubt. For example, the precise original basis of one of the most well-known American standards, the National Recreation and Parks Association (NRPA) standard for the provision of open space, is not known, even by the NRPA itself (Wilkinson, 1985) and it was abandoned in 1996 (Mertes & Hall, 1996). In the case of the playing fields component of the British-based playing space standard, promulgated by Fields in Trust, the required area was originally based on estimates of sporting participation rates in Britain in the 1920s (Fields in Trust, 2008) and has remained substantially unchanged ever since (Veal, 2012). While promulgators of standards often recognize their limitations and indicate that they may need to be modified in light of local conditions (e.g. Fields in Trust, 2008), they typically provide little or no guidance regarding how such modifications should be undertaken. Furthermore, if it is admitted that there are overriding factors which require the standards to be modified, the question arises as to why such factors are not the basis of provision requirements in the first place.

2. Meeting Needs

Leisure plans and planning guidelines often claim to assess "community needs," but few define what is meant by "need." One of the difficulties in doing so is is that the word need is used in different senses. Taylor (1959) identified four different uses of the term, as follows.

1. Something required to satisfy a law or rule—for example, the need to have a license to drive a vehicle.
2. A means to an end (specified or implied)—for example, the need for a racquet to play tennis.
3. Certain "conscious or unconscious wants, motivations, drives, desires"—for example, the "need" for excitement or for the taste of chocolate. Taylor suggests: "Needs in this sense constitute conative dispositions."
4. Recommendations or normative evaluations (for example, in relation to nutrition).

The first two uses are technical in nature and do not concern us here. The third meaning is typically used in the commercial sector and in marketing in relation to all types of consumer products, and can be seen as equivalent to demand. The fourth type tends to be used by leisure policymakers in the public sector who seek to align leisure with mainstream social services, such as health or education. An Australian state government, for example, declared that: " . . . cultural amenities can be seen not as something remote or apart from everyday life but as fundamental to people's needs" (New South Wales Department of Local Government, 2004, p. 2).

There is an enormous theoretical literature on the concept of need, in various disciplines, but two sources stand out in the leisure context: Maslow's (1954/1987) well-known 'hierarchy of needs' and the typology of need put forward by Mercer (1973), based on the work of Bradshaw (1972).
Despite criticism over the years (e.g., Rowan, 1998), references to Maslow continue to appear in some research publications (e.g., Ravenscroft, 1993) and in numerous textbooks, in the fields of tourism (Kotler, Bowen, & Makens, 2006), leisure (Taylor, 2011) and the arts (Bernstein, 2007; Black, 2005), while Hall and Page (2006) observe that Maslow's research has shaped "much of the recreation and tourism demand work" (p. 37). In this theory, needs are arranged in a hierarchy of saliency, from survival, through security, affinity and esteem to self-actualization. However, the feature which is invariably ignored is that Maslow's hierarchy applied to *basically important needs*, defined in his statement: "Thwarting of unimportant desires produces no psychopathological results: thwarting of basically important needs does produce such results" (Maslow, 1954/1987, p. 30). So the hierarchy refers not to "unimportant desires" but to "basically important needs" which, if denied, result in harm to the individual. The harm-related definition of need has been endorsed by later authors (e.g., Doyal &

Gough, 1991; Walker, Chapter 17). Such a definition corresponds with Taylor's (1959) fourth type, since a normative position has to be adopted as to what constitutes harm, which Maslow did, based on his work in psychotherapy. Applying this conception of need to leisure is therefore to argue that certain forms of leisure activity, if denied, would, other things being equal, result in harm to the individual or the community. This idea is implicit in the government statement quoted above and in widely accepted arguments for public provision of leisure services, such as the prevention of poor health through exercise and the belief, despite the paucity of firm evidence (Nichols, 2007), in the crime-prevention qualities of certain forms of leisure provision.

Desires which are *not* needs in Maslow's (1954/1987) sense might be referred to as "wants." But, as Paddick (1982) put it:

> The inclination to call a great many things 'needs' is not difficult to appreciate. At least part of the answer is that 'need' is a particularly powerful planning concept, because we are much more likely to gain acceptance for giving people what they need, than for giving them what they want. (p. 41)

In practice, however, public leisure services do not *only* meet needs in this sense, they cater to needs and wants together; people may make use of services to satisfy a variety of desires and those whose desires do not satisfy the criterion of "need" cannot be excluded. Thus, despite policymakers often adopting the rhetoric of normative need the services to which they refer typically cater also, and even mostly, to conative dispositions, or wants.

The Bradshaw (1972)/Mercer (1973) typology comprises: (a) *expressed need* (what people currently do, or actively seek to do by, for example, putting their names on a waiting list); (b) *felt need* (what people say they would like to do); (c) *comparative need* (deficiencies indicated by comparison with others); and (d) *normative need* (based on normative criteria as defined by experts, an elected body, pressure group or the general public). As with the Maslow's (1954/1987) theory, this typology is also referred to in textbooks (e.g., Pigram & Jenkins, 2006) and the terminology is sometimes used in policy documents. However, neither Bradshaw nor Mercer actually *define* need. It was not necessary for Bradshaw to do so, since he was writing in the context of the mainstream social services in Britain, the needs-based status of which was not in question. Mercer recognizes that this is an issue in relation to leisure, querying the basis of normative claims at the time, but then going on to simply assume that leisure is a *social need*, but without defining it. It is therefore reasonable to conclude that: "expressed need" is no different from demand; "felt need" corresponds approximately to latent demand; "comparative need" refers to current effective demand; and "normative need" remains undefined.

This conclusion reflects the reality of planning practice based on the needs concept: community "recreation needs" surveys do not ask respondents specifically about "needs," but about current participation, preferences, and aspirations: no distinction is made between needs and wants. Furthermore, with the possible exception of children's play and some sport/exercise activity, no considered program of research has been conducted to establish the status of various forms of leisure activity as needs in the harm prevention sense.

3. Providing Opportunity

Expressing the goals of a leisure plan in terms of "providing opportunity" has seemed to provide a suitable "bottom up" alternative to the "top down" approach of standards and has been suggested in a number of sets of planning guidelines; for example, the goal: "To provide recreation opportunities for all people regardless of age, sex, religion or culture" (British Columbia Recreation and Sport Branch, 1980, p. 10). However, while all leisure service providers inevitably do provide opportunities, this is a means to an end and not the end itself. Thus, if an organization provides an outdoor recreation opportunity in the form of a park and it attracts no users, the provision will be judged a failure: there is no point in providing opportunities which are not taken advantage of by the people for whom they were intended. The "end" is not provision of opportunity but people engaging in recreational activity.

4. Satisfying Stakeholder Groups

Consulting stakeholder groups is another "bottom up" approach which has come to prominence in place of the use of standards. Of course, stakeholder consultation has a role to play in all planning, and for some situations it is a statutory requirement. It produces factual information on demand and supply, which feeds into demand analysis, but here we are concerned with information on individuals' leisure activity aspirations and perceived constraints, and requests from individuals and organizations regarding service provision. This information is typically gathered by means of surveys, focus groups, and public meetings. In some plans and planning guidelines, the amount of emphasis given to the gathering of this type of information and the fact that it refers specifically to the desire to participate and to requests for facilities and services and seems to feed directly into policy recommendations, suggests that it is the main approach to planning being adopted or recommended. However, this level of reliance is unjustified.

Stakeholder groups can be divided into two types: organized and non-organized. Organized groups are generally consulted via representatives and questions must be raised regarding consistency in the quality of the information collected, in that: response rates from some sectors, such as local sports clubs, are often very low; the views of group representatives may not be typical of those of the group membership, let alone of non-member participants (Lord & Elmendorf, 2008); representatives vary in their advocacy skills and level of knowledge and expertise regarding the activity they represent and the policymaking/planning process; and representatives are, by definition, biased in favor of their own activity to varying degrees. So, while the information may have considerable utility in the planning process, it is unlikely to provide the main basis for decision making.

Non-organized members of the community are generally consulted via questionnaire-based survey or focus group and sometimes by other means such as public meetings. Questionnaire-based surveys are generally representative if they are professionally conducted. Focus group and public meeting attendees may be representative in a broad way, but not sufficiently to enable findings to be quantified. Typically, survey respondents are asked to indicate what activities they would like to take part in, and the constraints preventing them from doing so. However, the relationship between such responses and actual behavior when or if the constraints are removed is poorly understood (see Schneider, Chapter 18). Indeed, market researchers have for decades cautioned against relying on declared intentions or aspirations as a straightforward guide to future behavior (e.g., Packard, 1957).

One problem common to consultation with both organized and non-organized stakeholders is how to analyze the "shopping lists" from various sources, comprising: quantitative or qualitative information on activities in which people would like to participate; constraints preventing participation; and views on what facilities/services should be provided. With few exceptions (e.g., Grogan & Mercer, 1995), planning guidelines which place great emphasis on stakeholder consultation provide no advice on how such information should be analyzed to formulate project proposals, even though this process could be said to enshrine the core of the stakeholder consultation-based planning approach. It is, in effect, a "black box."

5. The Benefits Approach to Leisure (BAL)

Planning for the provision of benefits involves developing plans based on their efficacy in producing outcomes considered to be desirable by the decision-making body. Benefits are *net*, in the sense that the total benefits produced should exceed the public and private costs of provision. The benefits of leisure which public policy seeks to secure or enhance are numerous and varied and have been spelled out on a number of occasions (e.g., Driver, Brown, & Peterson, 1991; Crompton, 2008). In the case of tourism, they are generally seen as the generation of local jobs and incomes, but in other leisure sectors they are more diverse. To use leisure benefits as a basis for planning requires some system for assessing, measuring and comparing different bundles of benefits likely to be generated by different policy measures. One such system is the non-economic Benefits Approach to Leisure (BAL) system, developed by Driver (2008) and his associates in the U.S. Forest Service.

The BAL system seeks to base the planning of leisure facilities/services on research evidence about users' assessments of a wide range of specified benefits or satisfactions enjoyed, typically based on responses to Likert-type scales gathered by means of questionnaire-based surveys. Later versions have introduced other stakeholders and such features as 'economic benefits' and 'environmental benefits' (Driver & Bruns, 1999), but these appear not to have been operationalized within the system. While this approach relates particularly to the management of natural areas, it has also been promoted as being applicable in wider leisure planning situations (e.g., Tucker & Allen, 2008).

The BAL system is most understandable when applied to enhancement of existing facilities or services, which is in the realm of management rather than planning, but it could also provide the basis for some modification to the pattern of supply of facilities, with decision making being based on the predicted level of user satisfaction at new facilities, although the system does not appear to explicitly deal with visit numbers and costs. Despite the extensive literature on the development of the system, there are few published examples of its application as a complete planning approach, and even less in urban settings, and questions arise as to the practicality of dealing with the more than 200 types of benefit/satisfaction utilized in the system (Driver & Bruns, 2008).

6. Natural/Heritage Resource-Based

Resource-based planning has as long a history in the leisure sector as the use of standards. It is clear that if natural or heritage resources are involved in a planning project, then conservation values and decision-making criteria come into play, and in many cases they may be dominant. But these are distinct from leisure considerations, as is indicated by the fact that substantial parts of the collections of most museums and galleries are conserved for research purposes rather than public display and access to natural areas is regulated in the interests of conservation. Assessing the leisure potential of such resources requires a set of skills and procedures which are different from those required to assess their conservation values. Once the two forms of assessment have been carried out, planners and decision makers must juggle the conservation and leisure requirements to arrive at decisions. This may be relatively easy or difficult, depending on whether the two are complementary or in conflict. Thus the well-known Recreation Opportunity Spectrum (ROS), devised by Clark and Stankey (1979; Stankey, McCool, Clark, & Brown, 1999), classifies areas, or "settings," in which people might seek outdoor recreation along a continuum from the totally undeveloped, such as pristine wilderness (i.e., "primitive"), to the highly developed, such as a fully serviced camping site and recreation area (i.e., "modern").

7. Meeting Demand

Demand-based planning has been used particularly in relation to tourism and countryside recreation but less so in other sectors. Demand has generally been viewed as an economic relationship which, in its simplest form, refers to the way the amount of a good or service which a consumer is willing to purchase varies according to the price. This has caused some confusion among a number of commentators. For example, Evans (2001) rejects its use in cultural planning because he sees "demand" as being equated with "current effective demand," concluding therefore, that "latent, excess, or unrealized demand" is ignored. But this fails to recognize that knowledge of the *relationship* between supply conditions, price, and quantities purchased (as illustrated by the familiar price/demand curve of economic theory) indicates that current effective demand is just one point on the demand curve and that if policy measures are taken to reduce prices or improve supply conditions (in terms of capacity, access, quality), effective demand can be predicted to increase, thus satisfying "latent, excess or unrealized demand."

A second source of confusion is the perception that the economic definition of demand implies that the only policy lever available is price, and this is associated with the private sector and such concepts as 'user pays' and privatization. However, demand analysis seeks to understand demand dynamics in relation not only to variable pricing (including a zero price) but also to user characteristics and a range of other supply conditions, such as quality, size, and access, the very variables upon which policy operates (see Hanley, Shaw, & Wright, 2003; Wicker, Hallmann, & Breuer, 2013).

8. Setting and Pursuing Participation Targets

The setting of participation targets, in the area of sport/physical exercise and cultural activity has emerged recently in practice. For example, in its 2008 strategic plan, Sport England (2008) set a national target of one million more people participating in sport over five years. In Australia, the New South Wales 2006 State Plan (NSW Dept of Arts, Sport, and Recreation, 2007) set participation targets for sport/physical activity, arts participation and parks visits. One version of the participation-based approach involves the setting of participation targets for generic groups of activity, such as sport/physical activity and arts/cultural activity, both overall and for different geographical areas or planning zones and/or different socioeconomic groups (Veal, 2010). Participation rates are measured by social survey at the start of the planning period, at its conclusion, and possibly at points in between. Detailed work is then undertaken to establish the most effective way of achieving the targets in particular local contexts—for example, by considering the types of activity most likely to be successful and whether to: provide additional capacity by means of new facilities or expanded existing facilities; develop targeted programs; offer grants to organizations; or conduct educational or publicity campaigns.

The question arises as to how the targets should be set. In the policy examples referred to above, the targets are quite modest and no particular rationale is published. In the Veal (2010) example social or spatial equity is used as the criterion; that is, targets are set to bring low participant groups or areas up to the average, which, if achieved, would gradually increase the overall average participation rate. Over the longer term, the setting of higher targets would involve arguments similar to those applying to demand-based planning; that is, it would require the input of the results of cost-benefit-based research, which would provide justification for higher targets in terms of net benefits gained.

9. Cost-Benefit Analysis

Cost-benefit analysis has a long history but is frequently misunderstood by non-economists: in particular, it is often thought that the technique considers only user benefits and the financial aspects of a project, but this is not the case. In a full cost-benefit-based planning exercise, decisions are based on estimates of *all* the identifiable social and environmental, as well as financial, costs, and benefits which arise throughout the life of a proposed project. Cost-benefit ratios, or internal rates of return on capital invested, are used to rank proposed projects in order of priority. Where possible, all costs and all benefits are identified, and assigned money values, but those which cannot be measured in this way should, ideally, be clearly identified and then assessed by decision makers against the aggregate net costs or net benefits of the items which *can* be measured. Assessment can extend well beyond financial matters to capture the effects of market failure, such as externalities and public goods components. For example, in a cost-benefit study of the Adelaide Grand Prix automobile race (Burns et al., 1986) a money value was calculated for the cost of the noise intrusion suffered by some residents and for the "psychic benefit" of the event to the Adelaide population; that is, the sense of pride and excitement of hosting the event.

Cost-benefit studies are increasingly being demanded in the public sector, as indicated by government directives (HM Treasury, 2003; U.S. Government, 1993). However, conducting bespoke cost-benefit studies for individual plans or projects would be prohibitively costly. In other sectors, however, this is avoided by using "value transfer" or "benefit transfer"; for example, in the planning of major road investments, national transport agencies fund research to develop generic values of benefits, such as the value per hour of saved travel time (including leisure time) and the value to society of the prevention of death and injury, for application in local cost-benefit studies. This approach could conceivably be developed for leisure planning, based on a database of research findings of the sort assembled by Rosenberger and Loomis (2001) in the United States, the UK Cultural and Sport Evidence (CASE) (2010) program, and Kaval and Yao (2010) in New Zealand, but further research would be needed to establish, and keep up-to-date, a much wider range of values.

FUTURE DIRECTIONS

Crompton (2008) blames the low, and declining, political profile of the public leisure services sector in the U.S. on the tendency, among those professionally, politically, and academically involved, to adopt a narrow service-delivery and user-benefits stance to policymaking. In doing so, they fail to recognize, promote, and exploit, the community-wide economic, environmental, and social benefits arising from the provision of public leisure services, thus failing to "position" leisure services appropriately within the wider polity (see also Mowen and Havitz, Chapter 34). To reposition the sector he outlines a "community benefit paradigm," which involves the shaping of leisure policies based on broader economic, environmental, and social goals of the community and governments.

The reform of leisure planning methods can be seen as part of this process. Of the nine planning approaches discussed in this chapter, it has been argued that six are inappropriate as the core basis for planning for leisure. *Standards*, because of their limitations and questionable validity, have been largely abandoned in practice. *Needs* may have been a useful concept in past efforts to gain acceptance for the establishment of public leisure services but, since planning-related research has generally failed to distinguish between wants and needs, and most recreation services cater to both wants and needs, the concept of need alone does not provide a firm analytically basis for planning for leisure (but see also Walker, Chapter 17). *Resource-based systems*, such as the Recreation Opportunity Spectrum, suggest ways of distributing different types of demand in suitable settings, but do not deal with the generation of that demand and its overall level and so do not constitute a widely applicable leisure planning approach. *Provision of opportunity* must ultimately be judged by the extent to which opportunities provided are actually taken advantage of; that is, by some measure of participation. *Stakeholder consultation* is a key component of planning, but cannot form its core because it typically presents a 'black box' problem in regard to the evaluation of the data gathered and relies on an unknown relationship between aspirational data and likely actual future behavior. *The BAL system* has yet to be operationalized outside of public land management, and not fully even in this context.

The other three approaches—*demand-based*, *cost-benefit methods*, and the *setting and pursuing of participation targets*—can, however, be combined to provide the basis for a valid approach.

Demand studies can model how participation levels will respond to different supply conditions, including the quantity, distribution, quality, and pricing of facilities/services. However, this does not *of itself* determine what those supply conditions, and associated demand levels, should be. The level of demand can be almost open-ended, depending on the generosity of the supply conditions offered. To determine acceptable limits within the economic demand framework requires the use of cost-benefit analysis, which sets limits based on the point at which the value of total economic, social, and environmental benefits generated by a project no longer exceed the costs of supply. This in turn requires the consideration of benefits and their valuation and comparison with costs.

A proposed framework designed to take these matters into account is summarized in Figure 33.1. The framework is a version of the traditional demand approach, but with two important modifications. First, it will be noted that certain of the connecting arrows are two-way, indicating that the process is iterative: it is not a one-way process in which a quantum of "demand" is determined by external forces and must, by implication, be met in full by the agency concerned. Instead, it is recognized that the agency, through its ability to intervene and manipulate supply conditions, influences the level and pattern of demand. The term "participation" is therefore used to emphasize that the level and pattern of activity to be facilitated is itself the focus of the policymaking process. Second, the framework accepts, in a traditional way, that the generation of benefits must be assessed in relation to costs but recognizes that it is impractical for every leisure project and plan to embark on an

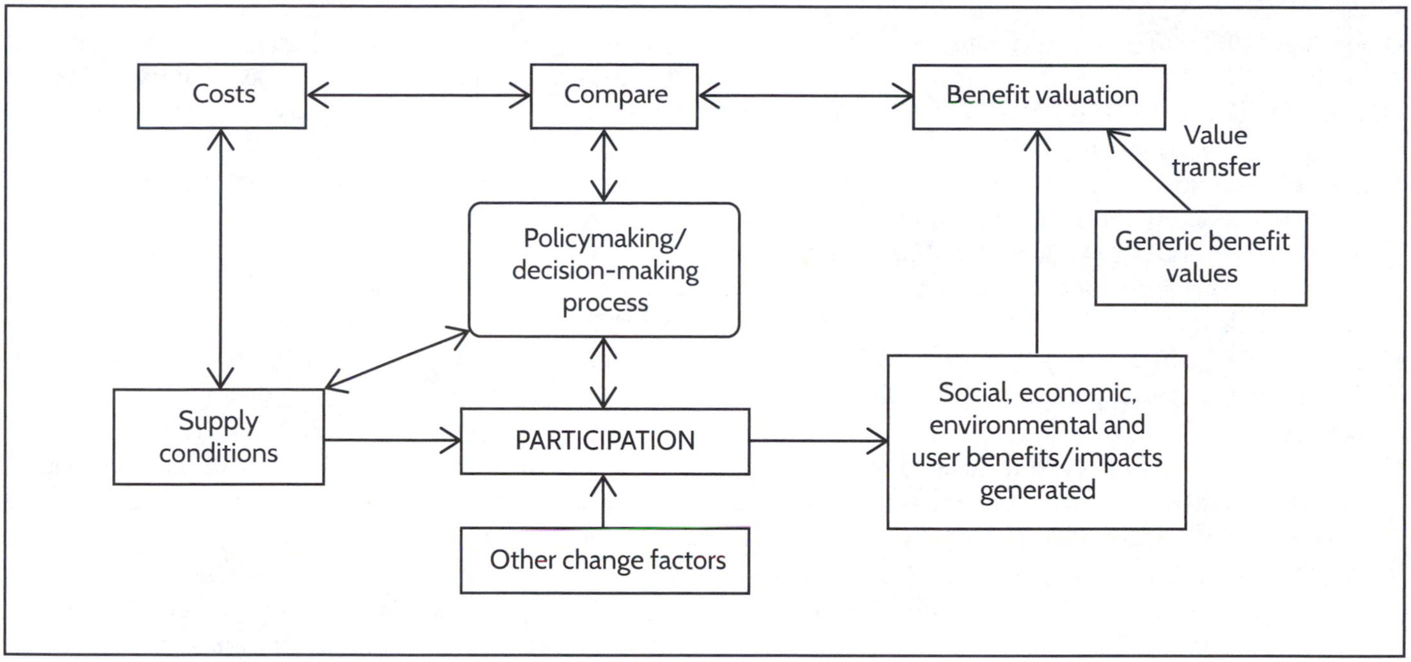

Figure 33.1. Proposed Planning for Leisure Framework

original, bespoke, cost-benefit study. This work must be undertaken generically, providing a database of benefit values to be drawn on by local planners and applied through the process of value transfer. This, then, is the practical challenge for the leisure provider and research community: to establish a process to generate and maintain such a database and provide guidance for its use into the future.

If the leisure sector is to be repositioned to align with wider social policy concerns, it requires a policymaking and planning framework which speaks a common language with other public policy areas. Setting participation targets which generate specified and evaluated net social, economic, and environmental benefits, as well as direct user benefits, is suggested as a basis for such a framework.

REFERENCES

Bernstein, J. S. (2007). *Arts marketing insights.* San Francisco, CA: Jossey-Bass.

Black, G. (2005). *The engaging museum.* London: Routledge.

Bradshaw, J. (1972). The concept of social need. *New Society, 30*, 640–643.

British Columbia Recreation and Sport Branch. (1980). *A guide to recreation planning in British Columbia.* Victoria, BC: Ministry of Provincial Secretary and Government Services.

Burns, J. P. A., Hatch, J., & Mules, T. J. (Eds.). (1986). *The Adelaide Grand Prix: The impact of a special event.* Adelaide, AUS: Centre for South Australian Economics Studies.

Burton, T. L., & Glover, T. D. (1999). Back to the future: Leisure services and the reemergence of the enabling authority of the state. In E. L. Jackson & T. L. Burton (Eds.), *Leisure studies: Prospects for the twenty-first century* (pp. 371–383). State College, PA: Venture Publishing, Inc.

Clark, R., & Stankey, G. (1979). *The Recreation Opportunity Spectrum.* General Technical Report PNW-98, Seattle, WA: U.S. Department of Agriculture Forest Service.

Crompton, J. L. (2008). Evolution and implications of a paradigm shift in the marketing of leisure services in the USA. *Leisure Studies, 27*, 181–206.

Culture and Sport Evidence (CASE) Programme (2010). *Understanding the value of engagement in culture and sport: Technical report.* London: Department for Culture, Media and Sport, available at http://www.gov.uk/case-programme

Doyal, L., & Gough, I. (1991). *A theory of human needs.* London: Macmillan.

Driver, B. L. (Ed.). (2008). *Managing to optimize the beneficial outcomes of recreation.* State College, PA: Venture Publishing, Inc.

Driver, B. L., Brown, P. J., & Peterson, G. L. (Eds.). (1991). *Benefits of leisure.* State College, PA: Venture Publishing, Inc.

Driver, B. L., & Bruns, D. (2008). Implementing OFM on public nature-based recreation and related amenity resources. In B. L. Driver (Ed.), *Managing to optimize the beneficial outcomes of recreation* (pp. 39–73). State College, PA: Venture Publishing, Inc.

Evans, G. (2001). *Cultural planning: An urban renaissance?* London: Routledge.

Fields in Trust. (2008). *Planning and design for outdoor sport and play.* London: Fields in Trust.

Giddens, A. (2011). *The politics of climate change*. Cambridge: Polity.

Grogan, D., & Mercer, C. (1995). *The cultural planning handbook*. St. Leonards, NSW: Allen and Unwin.

Hall, C. M., & Page, S. J. (2006). *The geography of tourism and recreation* (3rd ed.). London: Routledge.

Hanley, N., Shaw, W. D., & Wright, R. E. (Eds.). (2003). *The new economics of outdoor recreation*. Cheltenham, UK: Edward Elgar.

HM Treasury. (2003). *The green book: Appraisal and evaluation in central government*. London: Stationery Office.

Kaval, P., & Yao, R. (2010). A New Zealand outdoor recreation benefit database for benefit transfer studies. *Annals of Leisure Research, 13*, 709–715.

Kotler, P., Bowen, J. T., & Makens, J. C. (2006). *Marketing for hospitality and tourism* (4th ed.). Upper Saddle River, NJ: Pearson Education.

Lord, B. E., & Elmendorf, W. F. (2008). Are recreation organizations representative of all participants? *Journal of Park and Recreation Administration, 26*, 87–96.

Maslow, A. (1954/1987). *Motivation and personality* (3rd ed.). New York: Longman.

Mercer, D. (1973). The concept of recreational need. *Journal of Leisure Research, 5*, 37–50.

Mertes, J. D., & Hall, J. R. (1996). *Park, recreation, open space and greenway guidelines*. Ashburn, VA: National Recreation and Park Association.

New South Wales (NSW) Department of Arts, Sport and Recreation. (2007). *Corporate plan: 2007–11*. Sydney: DASR.

NSW Department of Local Government. (2004). *Cultural planning guidelines for local government*. Sydney: Department of Local Government. Retrieved from http://www.dlg.nsw.gov.au/dlg/dlghome/documents/information/CPG-final.pdf

Nichols, G. (2007). *Sport and crime prevention*. London: Routledge.

Packard, V. (1957). *The hidden persuaders*. London: Longman.

Paddick, R. J. (1982). The concept of need in planning for recreation. In M. L. Howell & J. R. Brehaut (Eds.), *Proceedings of the VII Commonwealth and international conference on sport, physical education, recreation and dance: vol. 4 (Recreation)* (pp. 39–47). Brisbane, AUS: University of Queensland.

Pigram, J., & Jenkins, J. (2006). *Outdoor recreation management* (2nd ed.). London: Routledge.

Ravenscroft, N. (1993). Public leisure provision and the good citizen. *Leisure Studies, 12*, 33–45.

Rosenberger, R. S., & Loomis, J. B. (2001). *Benefit transfer of outdoor recreation use values*. Gen. Tech. Rep. RMRS-GTR-72, Fort Collins, CO: U.S. Department of Agriculture, Forest Service, Rocky Mountain Research Station. Retrieved from http://www.fs.fed.us/rm/pubs/rmrs_ gtr72.pdf

Rowan, J. (1998). Maslow amended. *Journal of Humanistic Psychology, 38*, 81–93.

Sports Council. (1968). *Planning for sport*. London: Central Council for Physical Recreation.

Sport England. (2008). *Sport England strategy*. London: Sport England. Retrieved from http://www.sportengland.org/about_us/what_we_do.aspx

Stankey, G., McCool, S., Clark, R. N., & Brown, P. J. (1999). Institutional and organizational challenges to managing natural resources for recreation: a social learning model. In E. L. Jackson & T. L. Burton (Eds.), *Leisure studies: Prospects for the twenty-first century* (pp. 435–450). State College, PA: Venture Publishing, Inc.

Taylor, P. (Ed.). (2011). *Torkildsen's sport and leisure management* (6th ed.). London: Routledge.

Taylor, P. W. (1959). 'Need' statements. *Analysis, 19*, 106–111.

Tucker, T. W., & Allen, L. R. (2008). Implementing OFM in municipal parks and recreation departments. In B. L. Driver (Ed.), *Managing to optimize the beneficial outcomes of recreation* (pp. 75–94). State College, PA: Venture Publishing, Inc.

U. S. Government (1993). *Government Performance and Results Act, 1993*. Retrieved from http://govinfo.library.unt.edu/npr/library/misc/s20.html

Veal, A. J. (2010). *Leisure, sport and tourism, politics, policy and planning*. Wallingford, UK: CABI.

Veal, A. J. (2011). Planning for leisure, sport, tourism and the arts: Goals and rationales. *World Leisure Journal, 53*, 119–48.

Veal, A. J. (2012). FIT for the purpose? Open space planning standards in Britain. *Journal of Policy Research in Tourism, Leisure and Events, 4*, 375–79.

Wicker, P., Hallmann, K., and Breur, C. (2013). Analyzing the impact of sport infrastructure on sport participation using geo-coded data: Evidence from multi-level models. *Sport Management Review, 16*, 54–67.

Wilkinson, P. F. (1985). The golden fleece: The search for standards. *Leisure Studies, 4*, 189–204.

34

Marketing Public Leisure Services: Key Concepts, Approaches, and Emerging Trends

Andrew J. Mowen (The Pennsylvania State University)
and Mark Havitz (University of Waterloo)

This chapter begins with a brief description of marketing and its historical evolution in leisure services. We focus our message on unique characteristics of the public sector that beg for more contextualized marketing approaches and highlight specific models to advance the provision of public leisure marketing. We then conclude by identifying emerging marketing trends and their potential implications for public leisure.

Marketing has been understood as a philosophy, a planning process, or a series of activities (McCarville, 1999). For example, Crompton and Lamb (1986) defined it as: (a) a philosophy, attitude, or perspective and (b) a set of activities used to fulfill that philosophy. Marketing focuses primarily on understanding and meeting the needs of customers/constituents rather than solely the needs of organizations. As a philosophy, it emphasizes an outward way of thinking. Instead of convincing people to purchase historical offerings, the emphasis shifts toward understanding client needs as the principal basis for organizational products/services.

Beyond philosophical perspectives, marketing has also been understood as a planning process. Kotler, Armstrong, Cunningham, and Warren (1996, p. 6) characterized marketing as "a social and managerial process by which individuals and groups obtain what they need and want through creating and exchanging products and value with others." As part of this process, marketing offers a set of neutral tools and activities which can be applied appropriately to achieve a number of organizational and participant objectives (Kaczynski & Potwarka, 2007). These tools include market segmentation and marketing research as well as a marketing mix of promotions, pricing, product, and placement (commonly known as the "4 P's"; see Figure 34.1). A widespread perception is that marketing is synonymous with promotions (e.g., advertising, sales promotions), but these activities are merely the most visible part of the marketing mix and philosophies that support their use. Pricing decisions sometimes enter public discussion as well, especially if they are controversial and an agency or business is seen as pushing a hard sell. In fact, most marketing activities (such as segmentation, distribution, program development) occur "behind the scenes," which is why marketing and its most visible activity, promotion, are often erroneously confused as being one and the same (Kaczynski & Potwarka, 2007). A detailed account of the marketing mix is beyond the scope of our chapter, and we encourage readers to refer to other existing works (e.g., Janes, 2006; Kaczynski & Potwarka, 2007) that offer more detailed discussions of their application in leisure contexts.

Products–refers to anything that can be offered to a market for attention, acquisition, use, or consumption that satisfies a want or need (Kotler, McDougall, & Armstrong, 1988). Products can be tangible goods and, as typical for leisure services, intangible experiences.

Place–refers to the process for presenting or distributing products or services to clients and addresses the questions of where, when, how, and by whom a program or service will be offered (Tew, Havitz, & McCarville, 1999).

Price–any cost an individual must forego to consume/experience a product or service, including both monetary and non-monetary costs (e.g., travel time, opportunity cost; McClosky, 1982).

Promotion–a set of activities that communicate the merits of a product/service and persuades target audiences to use it (Kotler, Armstrong, & Cunningham, 2005). These activities are designed to inform, educate, persuade, and remind target audiences about offerings (Crompton & Lamb, 1986) and include mechanisms such as advertising, personal contact, public relations, publicity, and sales promotions.

Figure 34.1. Core Elements of the Marketing Mix: The 4 P's

While the marketing concept has resonated with many public and nonprofit agencies, confusion about the inherent neutrality of the concept and distaste for its use by public agencies, whose purpose is to fulfill social needs for "the greater good," persists (McCarville, 1999). Critics argue that marketing philosophies, language, and practices are inconsistent with social service operating systems (Jacobs, 1994; McLean & Johnson, 1993). These criticisms have some degree of merit given the widespread misapplication of marketing principles and tools across public leisure services (McCarville, 1999). Studies of public leisure marketing (McCarville & Smale 1991) found that, while marketing was reported as a common practice, evidence of rudimentary marketing principles were absent. Naïve and ill-guided implementation of the marketing mix provides ammunition for marketing critics, but they do not necessarily negate marketing's potential value to public leisure service.

THE HISTORICAL EVOLUTION OF MARKETING

The rationale for marketing (e.g., understanding what consumers want and figuring out how to provide it) seems commonsensical today. However, this was not always the case. The late nineteenth century ushered in new inventions and products, which stimulated consumer demand. Companies' marketing efforts were minimal. They focused on increasing mass production capabilities to provide products to a seemingly endless pool of consumers ready to purchase whatever was offered on the marketplace. During this "production era," client preferences were perceived as secondary to companies' specific products and production needs. However, as more competitors joined the marketplace, supply caught up to and exceeded demand. Instead of figuring out different ways to differentiate or redesign products to meet changing consumer needs, companies focused on more aggressive promotion of existing product lines. This new phase, characterized by a selling focus, was simply a variant of the product era (McCarville, 1999). Businesses did not markedly change their offerings and put little emphasis on understanding changing consumer needs/tastes. Companies knew what their products were, believed in them, and employed numerous advertising and sales tactics to sell them (McCarville, 1999).

Widespread dissatisfaction with aggressive and questionable sales practices led to a new way of thinking. In his seminal article, Levitt (1960) suggested that too many companies were focusing on promoting existing products and improving production efficiencies. He believed them to be short-sighted and doomed to failure because consumer needs were not central in their product design or promotional decisions. Levitt and others argued that looking through customers' eyes, identifying their needs, and producing products to meet those needs was a much more sustainable business model. The business community responded favorably to this "new" philosophy, departed from their supply orientation, and ushered in the marketing era that continues to today. Over time, adoption of the marketing concept expanded to service industries as well as nonprofit and public-sector organizations.

Public leisure services' "arrival" at marketing progressed in a similar manner. Crompton (2008) described five stages of leisure services marketing: pre-marketing (custodial focus), promotion/selling, user benefits, community benefits, and repositioning focus. The field's earliest custodial focus centered on creating, quietly taking care of, and operating their existing product (e.g., parks, recreation centers). Programs and facilities were developed and offered on a "take it or leave it" basis, and standards were commonly applied without regard for characteristics of communities or their inhabitants.

With the emergence of fiscal conservatism in the 1970s and 1980s, leisure service agencies began to more aggressively promote and justify their services. In this era of declining public tax resources, focus shifted to internal needs by increasing participation levels and generating new revenue streams, without consideration of benefits desired (Crompton, 2008). Over time, limitations of this "selling" orientation became apparent, much as it did for their corporate counterparts. Progressive leisure agencies began to shift to a more customer-centered approach, which sought to satisfy key user benefits and provide services adapted to deliver individual benefits. While laudable, these efforts had a limited effect on changing perceptions of the value of leisure services to the general public and elected officials (Crompton, 2008).

Nonprofit and public-sector marketers acknowledge that strict adoption of a pure marketing philosophy and its associated practices (serving individual needs and wants) are inconsistent with the social mandates of their organizations. For example, Havitz (2000) argued that pure marketing approaches ignore potential negative consequences to individuals and long-term interest of community and society. More contextualized or refined marketing approaches that embraced relationships (Berry, 1995; Kaczynski & Havitz, 2001), experiences (O'Sullivan & Spangler, 1998), and social marketing principles (Kotler, Roberto, & Lee, 2002) began to take root. Scholars, activists, and progressive professionals are now identifying contextualized approaches to better advance public leisure through community benefits and repositioning strategies. Today's leisure professionals should understand the unique conditions that beg for these contextualized approaches *and* why such marketing approaches are more viable for public-sector leisure.

Societal (or Tempered) Marketing

Societal (or tempered) marketing is similar to traditional marketing in that it maintains its focus on delivering client value by satisfying their individual needs/wants, but aims to do this in such a manner that maintains or improves societal well-being (Kotler et al., 1996). Crompton and Lamb (1986) further clarified this approach by stating that, "the justification for an agency's existence is the satisfaction of clients' wants and the preservation or enhancement of the community's well-being" (p. 13). With tempered marketing, individual needs are a starting point for designing services. However these needs are balanced against long-term community interests, which include considerations of health, well-being, and environment, as well as underserved and non-participant population segments (Kaczynski 2008). Havitz (2000) held that most of what constitutes public-sector recreation delivery entering the new millennium could be classified as societal or tempered marketing. Critics of societal marketing approaches purport that it is not different enough from pure marketing, particularly because an organization's focus is still directed toward fiscal responsibility and customer satisfaction rather than greater social needs (Crane & Desmond, 2002; Gaski, 1985). While public leisure services generally recognize that "profit-first" orientations should not be the sole goal of marketing, many still focus on serving individual needs, measured primarily through utilization and customer satisfaction metrics (Crompton & Lamb, 1986).

Social Marketing

To address societal marketing's shortcomings for public leisure, Kaczynski (2008) proposed social marketing as a more tenable framework from which to operate. Social marketing places its primary emphasis on improving society at large and gives secondary consideration to individual wants or needs (Kotler et al., 2002). Andreason (2003, p. 296) defined social marketing as, "the application of commercial marketing technologies to the analysis, planning, execution, and evaluation of programs designed to influence the voluntary behavior of target audiences in order to improve their personal welfare and that of the society of which they are a part." Leisure scholars have noted that, unlike traditional or societal marketing, social marketing is more centrally aligned with public leisure agencies' social service philosophies (Bright, 2000). Social marketing approaches are often about giving an individual or the community at large something that it needs, but not always something it necessarily desires. However, it is still done with as much attention given to marketing philosophy, and its central tenets, as possible (Kaczynski & Potwarka, 2007). Social marketing, in essence, seeks to influence voluntary behavior rather than using coercion or other non-voluntary measures (Andreason, 1994).

Marketing to Whom?

Before addressing the emerging push to reposition public leisure services, it is appropriate to acknowledge a fundamental tension of public-sector marketing: Public-sector marketers encounter a fundamental segmentation dilemma not faced by private-sector marketers in that governments exist to serve all citizens, not just customer segments. However, no program or service can effectively appeal to everyone, so most public agencies offer a smorgasbord of services/activities in the hope of eventually reaching everyone in some way. Compounding the public-sector dilemma, especially in social marketing contexts, is the reality that small percentages of the population account for the lions' share of participation (Barber & Havitz, 2001; Chalip, Chapter 10; Howard, 1992). Some mass activities such as walking, swimming, and bicycling generate participation rates approaching or exceeding 50% of the population, but rates for most common leisure activities (such as tennis, hockey, skiing, and so forth) hover at less than 15 or 20%. Even more discouraging are within-activity participation rates. For example, Barber and Havitz found that nearly 11% of the adult Canadian population age 12 and up were "active" hockey players, but 84% of hockey was played by only 4% of the population. The net result is that public leisure service agencies consistently find themselves building and staffing facilities that appeal to relatively small portions of the population. To whom should they market—the 4% who are avid participants, the 4% who are regular participants, the 3% who are occasional participants, or the 89% who do not participate at all? Crompton (2008) argued that leisure service agencies must focus on narrower constituencies and suggested a short list including retirees, at-risk youth, people who are unemployed, etc., as possible group segments. While Crompton's point is valid and consistent with basic market segmentation principles, it is fundamentally inconsistent, as noted earlier in this paragraph, with the traditional public-sector mandate to serve *all* citizens. We also must acknowledge diversity and the fact that consensus is virtually impossible in large, multicultural communities whose needs and constituencies inevitably evolve over time.

Taking a Modified Social Marketing Approach: A Case for Repositioning

Successful leisure-based social marketing approaches consider a broader cross-section of stakeholders beyond current users. In the case of public leisure, they expand their focus to include elected officials as well as non-users. Crompton (2008) provided a comprehensive assessment of the marketing concept as it related to public leisure services and suggested a modified paradigm, consistent with a social marketing perspective, to move the field forward. Like other leisure researchers (e.g., Havitz, Kaczynski, McCarville), Crompton asserted that key assumptions of traditional marketing (e.g., open-systems, voluntary exchange, self-interest motivation) are inconsistent with the operating system in which many public leisure service organizations operate. He argued that the field has failed to contextualize marketing approaches when delivering or communicating public leisure (and its benefits) to a broader constituency.

According to Crompton (2008), because public leisure misconceived what marketing actually was, it adopted marketing concepts inappropriately. In essence, it used marketing as a way to pursue business-centric objectives (e.g., enhanced user-based revenues/sales, increased user satisfaction levels) within leisure's social service milieu. These efforts focused on efficient/direct offerings to responsive client groups, but at the expense of non-responsive or apathetic stakeholders. While increased self-generated funds have been realized through these efforts, they are dwarfed by the amount of "revenues" provided through publically-supported tax funds (Crompton & Kaczynski, 2003). Over the course of time, leisure offerings that provided widespread social merit, but did not provide revenue, were cut leading to reduced justification for public tax support and hence lower overall agency operating budgets. This circular process creates a downward spiral of diminished support (Crompton, 2008).

From User to Community Benefits

Novatorov and Crompton (2001) asserted that many of today's public leisure agencies still operate under an inappropriate "user benefit paradigm" when their mission should actually be to serve a broader constituency. This paradigm is based on traditional marketing principles used by the private sector (e.g., an open-systems model, voluntary exchange, self-interest motivation); none of which are consistent with the community benefits paradigm of public leisure. In an open system, organizations are able to provide quick and direct response to the needs of various market segments because they have the independence to do so. However, public leisure professionals know they must often confer first with elected officials before they employ key strategic/tactical marketing decisions to respond to emerging constituent needs. This closed system limits the degree to which an agency's response to market trends is quick and direct. Furthermore, the notion of voluntary exchange suggests that agencies provide benefit-delivering services to recipients who provide financial resources to agencies in the form of fees and taxes (Crompton, 2008). While user fees, travel costs, and opportunity costs (e.g., time) are voluntarily provided by users to participate in an agency's services, such revenues typically go to the larger jurisdiction's general fund and taxes exacted are involuntary, legal obligations that are redistributed across various public services (Crompton, 2008, p. 192). Finally, the user benefits paradigm assumes self-interest is an essential motivation, grounded by the notion of reciprocity between user and service provider. However, leisure service agencies cannot and should not always give users everything they ask for and must balance diverse needs for the greater good. They must also reconcile individual needs against their organizational mandates (e.g., community health, environmental preservation, recreation opportunities for all). Collectively, these three conditions (e.g., closed system, involuntary redistribution, mutually agreed coercion) characterize the predominant environment that public leisure agencies operate in and beg for a new marketing paradigm, which addresses community benefits across a wider stakeholder audience.

Crompton (2008) proposed an expanded marketing exchange model to guide this paradigm shift. His model emphasizes that legislative bodies are primary constituents because, in most leisure service contexts, they set agency goals, collect and distribute fiscal resources, and make rules governing their use. In Crompton's expanded marketing model, the onus is on leisure service agencies to first understand key needs of both user and non-user residents and use the existing evidence-base to persuade legislative bodies to direct funds toward public leisure agencies as a way of fulfilling community/political mandates. In doing so, agencies can better *position* their services to a place of higher value relative to other tax-supported services (e.g., police, fire, public health services). Positioning is a central marketing concept in that it maintains its focus on consumers and asks what position the organization or brand holds in their minds (Ries & Trout, 2001). Crompton contended that public leisure services' current position is characterized as a series of discretionary, non-essential services, and he pushed leisure agencies to better position themselves in the minds of elected officials using the politics of seduction rather than political confrontation.

One way for public leisure agencies to influence legislative and non-user perceptions is through user-generated marketing content, which provides compelling stories as well as recent/relevant scientific evidence linked to a consistent benefit position. If elected officials and non-users are thoroughly briefed on the merits of public leisure and specific investments that go into them they may be more inclined to champion these projects as their own (Crompton, 2008; Mowen, Hickerson, & Kaczynski, 2013).

RECENT MARKETING DEVELOPMENTS AND THEIR IMPLICATIONS FOR PUBLIC LEISURE SERVICES

There have been more changes in marketing over the last five years than in the previous 30 years; with technological advancements being the driving force behind these changes (Liodice, 2007). While it is difficult to project the diffusion, longevity, and relevance of emerging marketing trends for public leisure, it is important to acknowledge them and consider their implications. What follows is a brief overview of four emerging trends—real-time mobile communications, inbound marketing, marketing content, and marketing decentralization—gleaned from contemporary marketing literature, along with some ways they could be used to better market public leisure services.

GETTING WIRED UP: ESTABLISHING REAL-TIME AND CUSTOMIZED SOCIAL CONNECTIONS

Society's adoption of and expectations for online content, social media, and constant connectivity have profound impacts on the way we communicate and behave. We live in a world that is wired 24/7 and our leisure behaviors and lifestyles are no exception (Nimrod, Chapter 30). Combined with mobile shopping and payment, leisure marketers have more options to reach audiences and drive real-time behavior. What this means is more channels, more data, and more options to engage with constituents (Graham, 2012). In fact, we have never had more opportunity to connect with constituents, but the sheer messaging possibilities and volume is overwhelming for organizations constrained by limited technological prowess and hierarchical decision-making structures.

Future leisure professionals must be both technologically and socially savvy if public leisure is to survive in this fast-paced world. Constant connectivity and social media has changed the nature of public agency-constituent relationships by flattening communication chains and stimulating real-time, direct two-way exchanges. Recent evidence suggests that municipal leisure agencies tend to treat their websites as extensions, in both form and substance, of historically tried and true seasonal program brochures (Gillies, 2008). Static websites or agency program guides alone are insufficient in reaching and persuading the next generation of leisure stakeholders. Successful agencies will not necessarily discard traditional promotional tools, but rather expand and integrate them with other forms of online content and social media. These new approaches can be used to reinforce a consistent message or benefit position as suggested by Crompton (2008) and could stimulate increased agency engagement and support among broader constituencies.

In 2012, more people purchased smartphones than PCs (Forbes, 2013). These purchases reflect a desire for constant connectivity. Large segments of the population are increasingly inclined to abandon organizations if they cannot easily engage them from a mobile device. For-profit organizations understand that the future of their online content rests with mobile platforms and are optimizing their emails and web pages for fast mobile viewing (Gallaher, 2013). These shifts have compelled public agencies to design mobile applications that not only provide basic information on leisure services and facilities, but also location-specific and real-time data on current and future programs/events at nearby public leisure settings. Purchasing options are also being integrated into leisure agencies' mobile applications (Hannan, 2013).

Online platforms can utilize data-driven personalization or dynamic content to examine users' past patterns and suggest other agency-provided activities and experiences that might be of interest to them. Personalization is best illustrated by Amazon's "recommended for you" links on their web pages and is similar to the concept of mass customization (e.g., tailoring services to individual preferences rather than generic packages to large market segments).

Other types of constituent engagement, such as volunteer opportunities and public participation/input, could be "distributed" through an agency's mobile platform. Public leisure agencies' young and tech savvy employees are an important resource to be tapped for ideas (e.g., how to best implement mobile technology, ways to distribute online content). Partnerships with non-profits (e.g., friends groups) or businesses (e.g., through corporate partnerships) may be another way for public leisure professionals to experiment and familiarize themselves with mobile platforms and communication strategies.

INBOUND MARKETING

Marketing promotion is experiencing a shift from outbound approaches such as advertising toward inbound approaches such as blogs, white papers, and social media sites. The term *inbound marketing* was presented as a strategy to get an organization spotted or found (Halligan & Shah, 2009). It is based on the concepts of earning constituent attention, making organizations easy to find, and drawing constituents to the organization's online presence by producing informative and valuable content. Inbound marketing approaches differ from outbound marketing approaches in that they "pull" rather than "push" constituents to the brand. Inbound marketing is not an entirely new concept for public leisure service agencies, yet by creating their own blogs and participating in social media sites and "news feeds," agencies may be able to broaden their visibility, clarify their agency position (e.g., economic development, health promotion, environmental sustainability) and expand their constituency. A necessary ingredient of inbound marketing is the relevance and quality of the content generated; by both organizations and their end users.

King Content

Society has learned to cope with and shut out traditional marketing promotions and techniques such as advertising. With limited advertising budgets and a relatively small user base (comparatively speaking), public leisure agencies are seeking more efficient and targeted ways to reach and retain core users. Content-based marketing is an increasingly popular technique to do this. In 2013 alone, $118 billion was projected to be spent on content marketing and roughly a quarter of businesses' marketing budgets were devoted to it (Wishpond Technologies, 2013). Simply put, content marketing is an inbound approach for creating and distributing both relevant and valuable information for the purpose of attracting, acquiring, and engaging clearly defined and understood target audiences and constituencies—with the objective of driving profitable customer action (Content Marketing Institute, n.d.).

Instead of expensive advertising and media purchases, organizations are increasingly creating and distributing their own content through blogs, podcasts, videos, educational guides, case studies, how-to guides, white papers, studies, games, and photos to generate and distribute this content though social channels and websites (Johnson, 2013). Content marketing is not an entirely new concept as several companies pioneered its use in the early twentieth century. What is new, however, are the diversity, interactivity, and speed of message channels from which to deliver this content. Experts claim that content marketing is no longer a fad as 80% of chief marketing officers believe it is the future of marketing (Slaughter, 2013).

While content marketing is all the rage in today's corporate world, public and nonprofit organizations have long used content to influence constituent behavior, partially because of limited advertising budgets. Content marketing is attractive for public leisure agencies because it can communicate the benefits of leisure services to broad constituencies *and* can suggest ways to realize those benefits by directing readers to local leisure opportunities. However, developing good content is seldom easy in a message saturated world. Today's consumers expect online content to be new, fresh, and unique to their own community. Regular updates are essential and individual stories about specific places/programs matter. As people become more accustomed to online content, they could be more purposely directed toward public leisure services and advocacy. For example, a park agency could disseminate online content that describes one or two benefits of parks for specific audiences and provide tips for that target audience on how to better utilize local services to realize these benefits. By doing this, marketing content and the stories that go with it, remain both relevant and original. Public leisure agencies can develop/distribute their own content through inbound approaches or could establish content distribution partnerships with businesses and nonprofit organizations.

Content can also be user-generated. The emergence of social media has increased the number of bloggers, online conversations, opinion pieces, and reviews from end users themselves. More people are having a voice through these channels and are using online search and social media platforms to learn about and speak to each other about products and services. In doing so, they self-market organizations and brands through Facebook pages, blogs, Twitter, and Yelp (Rishad, 2013). While self-marketing poses a challenge for leisure agencies by abdicating direct control of the message, user-generated content cannot be ignored. Successful organizations will figure out how to ensure that their brands are easily accessible, responsive, and broadly distributed in these user-generated conversations.

Marketing Decentralized

It is often said that marketing is everyone's responsibility, yet the role of market planning and practice has historically either been the dominion of an agency's marketing department or a staff member skilled enough to be assigned such duties. However, the rise of social media and user-generated content (coupled with an expectation for instantaneous, real-time communication) have compelled leisure agencies to educate, equip, and empower employees throughout the entire organization to engage in marketing activities in real time. In such an environment, rationale for a separate marketing department is considerably diminished. Every interaction, real and virtual, that staff have with constituents will be an opportunity to position and promote the agency. In short, employees will turn into inbound marketers who will be responsible for understanding, creating, and distributing agency content (Meher, 2012). Instead of focusing on controlling every piece of branded content that leaves the agency, executives should focus on training staff at all levels of an organization to actively proselytize the brand (Dimitrova, 2013). For public leisure, this means that each employee's personal and virtual interactions make explicit connections between their organization's offerings and key community benefits (e.g., economic prosperity, health). In this new environment, public leisure agencies that allow their employees, friends groups, or affiliate organizations to have a voice can usher in a state of highly effective, habitual storytelling that, in turn, creates unique and relevant marketing content.

CONCLUSION

Evidence suggests that we are at the cusp of realizing marketing's potential within public leisure services. However diffusion will be slow unless we adopt a more contextualized approach to marketing public services to a broader constituency. Our historical understanding and use of marketing had been too narrow and had focused primarily on participants and specific marketing activities (e.g., the 4 P's). Leisure scholars are urging the field to embrace new marketing paradigms to increase support for public leisure and strengthen its impact across multiple constituencies.

A central tenet of marketing is to maintain an outward, as opposed to inward, organizational focus. Today's leisure service professional must push boundaries by responding to emerging marketing trends outside of their organizational and disciplinary silos. This is not to say that we blindly adopt every new marketing fad, buzzword, or practice that comes along. Rather, we must be aware of what marketing opinion leaders are saying and what innovative businesses are doing before deciding whether these ideas/practices have merit for public leisure. We believe that the future of leisure marketing will be characterized by increasingly sophisticated and tailored approaches, decentralization of marketing activities, increased integration of promotional efforts, and growing customer (or constituent) control over message content. These same innovations and developments might also facilitate wider diffusion of social marketing, both philosophically and practically, across a wider cross-section of public leisure contexts. We live in an increasingly digital and virtual world, which has expanded the diversity of connections (or relationships) that can be established and the speed with which they can be accessed. Through technology, we have an unprecedented opportunity to market our services and our brand position among users, non-users, and elected officials. However, to date our response to these and other marketing trends seems to have been reactionary, slow, and incremental. The silver lining in this is that personal relationships (whether face-to-face or virtual) are still as important as ever in today's society. The personal connections that leisure professionals and organizations make across broader constituencies using emerging technologies might ultimately be the key to better positioning leisure services, enhancing public support, and maximizing beneficial societal outcomes.

REFERENCES

Andreasen, A. R. (1994). Social marketing: its definition and domain. *Journal of Public Policy & Marketing, 13*(1), 108–114.

Andreasen, A. R. (2003). The life trajectory of social marketing: Some implications. *Marketing Theory, 3*(3), 293–303.

Barber, N., & Havitz, M. E. (2001). Canadian participation rates in ten sport and fitness activities. *Journal of Sport Management, 15*(1), 51–76.

Berry, L. L. (1995). Relationship marketing of services—growing interest, emerging perspectives. *Journal of the Academy of Marketing Science, 23*(4), 236–245.

Bright, A. D. (2000). The role of social marketing in leisure and recreation management. *Journal of Leisure Research, 32*(1), 12–17.

Content Marketing Institute. (n.d.). What is content marketing? *Contenmarketinginstitute.com*. Retrieved from http://contentmarketinginstitute.com/what-is-content-marketing/

Crane, A., & Desmond, J. (2002). Societal marketing and morality. *European Journal of Marketing, 36*(5/6), 548–569.

Crompton, J. L. (2008). Evolution and implications of a paradigm shift in the marketing of leisure services in the USA. *Leisure Studies, 27*(2), 181–205.

Crompton, J. L., & Kaczynski, A. T. (2003). Trends in local park and recreation department finances and staffing from 1964–65 to 1999–2000. *Journal of Park and Recreation Administration, 21*(4), 124–144.

Crompton, J. L., & Lamb, C. W. (1986). *Marketing government and social services*. New York: John Wiley & Sons.

Dimitrova, I. (2013, July 25). Three strategies to help start-ups survive the age of content marketing. *Huffingtonpost.com*. Retrieved from http://www.huffingtonpost.com/ilina-dimitrova/three-strate gies-to-help-_b_3562952.html

Forbes. (2013, January 23). Five surprising marketing trends for 2013. *Forbes.com*. Retrieved from http://www.forbes.com/sites/thesba/2013/01/23/5-surprising-marketing-trends-for-2013/

Gallaher, C. (2013). Four keys to capitalizing on today's most relevant marketing trends. *Jacobs & Clevenger*. Retrieved from http://www.jacobsclevenger.com/blog/four-keys-to-capitalizing-on-todays-most-relevant-marketing-trends/

Gaski, F. (1985). Dangerous territory: The societal marketing concept revisited. *Business Horizons, 28*, 42–47.

Gillies, A. (2008). *Online communication of public leisure services*. Unpublished MA thesis, Department of Recreation and Leisure Studies, University of Waterloo.

Graham, M. (2012, November 8). Ten trends to define 2013 in marketing. *Sourcelink.com*. Retrieved from http://www.sourcelink.com/blog/matt_graham/matt-graham/2012/11/08/10-trends-to-define-2013-in-marketing

Halligan, B., & Shah, D. (2009). *Inbound marketing: get found using Google, social media, and blogs*. New York: John Wiley & Sons.

Hannan, M. (2013, February 1). Here to stay. *National Recreation and Parks Association*. Retrieved from http://www.parksandrecreation.org/2013/February/Here-to-Stay/

Havitz, M. E. (2000). Marketing public leisure services: Some (temporarily) pessimistic perspectives from an unrepentant optimist. *Journal of Leisure Research, 32*, 42–48.

Howard, D. R. (1992). Participation rates in selected sport and fitness activities. *Journal of Sport Management, 6*(1), 191–205.

Jacobs, J. (1994). *Systems of survival*. New York: Vintage Books.

Janes, P. C. (2006). *Marketing in leisure and tourism: Reaching new heights*. State College, PA: Venture Publishing, Inc.

Johnson, P. (2013, July 25). Content marketing, the next pyramid scheme and how to avoid being a sucker. *Forbes.com*. Retrieved from http://www.forbes.com/sites/philjohnson/2013/07/25/content-marketing-the-next-pyramid-scheme-and-how-to-avoid-being-a-sucker/

Kaczynski, A. T. (2008). A more tenable marketing for leisure services and studies. *Leisure Sciences, 30*(3), 253–272.

Kaczynski, A. T., & Havitz, M. E. (2001). Relational benefits in recreation services: examining differences between operating sectors. *Journal of Park and Recreation Administration, 19*(2), 20–42.

Kaczynski, A. T., & Potwarka, L. R. (2007). Marketing recreation and leisure services. In R. E. McCarville & K. MacKay (Eds.), *Leisure for Canadians* (pp. 289–297). State College, PA: Venture Publishing, Inc.

Kotler, P., Armstrong, P., & Cunningham, P. H. (2005). *Principles of marketing, sixth Canadian edition*. Scarborough, ON: Prentice Hall.

Kotler, P., Armstrong, G., Cunningham, P. H., & Warren, R. (1996). *Principles of marketing, third Canadian edition*. Scarborough, ON: Prentice Hall.

Kotler, P., McDougall, G., & Armstrong, G. (1988). *Marketing, Canadian edition*. Scarborough, ON: Prentice Hall.

Kotler, P., Roberto, E., & Lee, N. (2002). *Social marketing: Strategies for changing public behavior*. Thousand Oaks, CA: Sage Publications.

Levitt, T. (1960). Marketing myopia. *Harvard Business Review, 38*, 24–47.

Liodice, R. (2007). Continuous marketing reinvention. *Advertising Educational Foundation*, Retrieved from http://www.aef.com/on_campus/classroom/speaker_pres/data/7001

McCarville, R. (1999). Marketing public leisure services. In E. L. Jackson & T. L. Burton (Eds.), *Leisure studies: Prospects for the twenty-first century*, (pp. 415–433), State College, PA: Venture Publishing, Inc.

McCarville, R. E., & Smale, B. J. (1991). Involvement in pricing by municipal recreation agencies. *Journal of Applied Recreation Research, 16*(3), 200–219.

McClosky, D. (1982). *The applied theory of price*. New York: MacMillan.

McLean, D., & Johnson, R. C. A. (1993). The leisure service delivery dilemma: The professional versus the marketing model. *Journal of Applied Recreation Research, 18*(4), 253–264.

Meher, J. (2012). Twenty marketing trends and predictions for 2013 and beyond. *HubSpot.com*. Retrieved from http://cdn1.hubspot.com/hub/53/2013-Marketing-Trends-HubSpot-02.pdf

Mowen, A. J., Hickerson, B. D., & Kaczynski, A. T. (2013). Beyond the ribbon cutting: The impact of a neighborhood park renovation on visitor experiences, behaviors, and evaluations. *Journal of Park and Recreation Administration, 31*(1), 57–77.

Novatorov, E. V., & Crompton, J. L. (2001). A revised conceptualization of marketing in the context of public leisure services. *Journal of Leisure Research, 33*(2), 160–185.

O'Sullivan, E. L., & Spangler, K. J. (1998). *Experience marketing: Strategies for the new Millennium*. State College, PA: Venture Publishing, Inc.

Ries, A., & Trout, J. (2001). *Positioning, The battle for your mind* (20th anniversary ed.). New York: McGraw-Hill.

Rishad, T. (2013, April 25). Six current and six rapidly expanding trends marketers should focus on. *WordPress.com*. Retrieved from http://rishadt.wordpress.com/2013/04/25/six-current-and-six-rapidly-expanding-trends-marketers-should-focus-on/

Slaughter, S. (2013, July 12). Stop linkbait before it ruins content marketing. *Mashable.com*. Retrieved from http://mashable.com/2013/07/12/linkbait-content-marketing/

Tew, C. P. F. J., Havitz, M. E., & McCarville, R. E. (1999). The role of marketing in municipal recreation programming decisions: a challenge to conventional wisdom. *Journal of Park and Recreation Administration, 17*(1), 1–20.

Wishpond Technologies. (2013). The state of content marketing. *Visually*. Retrieved from http://visual.ly/state-content-marketing-2013.

35
Contemporary Views of Management and Leadership in Leisure Studies

Debra J. Jordan (East Carolina University)

As professionals in parks, recreation, and leisure services, we will engage in managerial and leadership roles, tasks, and relationships throughout our careers. Thus, this chapter will present a brief overview of twenty-first century views of management and leadership, and then examine the research as it relates to understanding leadership, leadership competencies, and the importance of culture in leadership relationships. The final section of the chapter is intended to challenge current thinking about the future of leadership in the parks, recreation, and leisure services profession.

MANAGEMENT AND STRUCTURE

Management and leadership are terms that are often used interchangeably when referring to practices, behaviors, or processes related to working within an agency or organization to provide leisure experiences and products for various constituents. In addition, management refers to the inner workings related to agency functioning within a particular organizational structure. Those inner workings include legal status, reporting structures, budgeting and finance, human resource policies and practices, planning, and service delivery.

Management as Structure

In the field of leisure studies, agencies are categorized by the organizational and legal structures (e.g., tax status, governance, sources of revenue) that define them. Eagles (2009) reported that the most prevalent structural categorization of leisure providers is: (a) fully public, (b) private nonprofit, (c) private for-profit, (d) public/nonprofit, and (e) public/for-profit. It is quite common (and in some cases legally mandated) for each of the structures to include an oversight board. These boards play an important role in ensuring that the agency maintains its purpose and operations as legally mandated.

Management is integral to every leisure services provider—management of resources (e.g., people, financial, facilities, and grounds), management of policies and procedures, and management of the organizational culture—all to the end result of producing a quality leisure service, experience, or product for constituents. Thus, management is a system of authority identified with running an organization, and serves to organize internal authority and responsibilities to meet agency objectives. Organizational behaviors (employee relations), internal leadership, effective and efficient processes, and the provision of quality services all fall within the purview of management. Many management functions and tasks are necessary to facilitate the achievement of agency goals.

Management as Tasks

In the early twentieth century, Fayol (1917) theorized what is now considered the classical view of organizational management. He suggested 14 principles of management, which were then collapsed into the five basic functions of management we still utilize today: *Planning* is a basic function of management and requires vision, mission, time management, positioning, and diagnostic skills. *Organizing* is the process of bringing together physical, financial, and human resources in ways that facilitate the achievement of agency-wide goals. *Staffing* involves effective selection, appraisal, development, and assignments of personnel within an agency. *Directing* is the process of motivating staff to work efficiently and effectively toward goals. Finally, *controlling* involves measuring accomplishments against standards or goals and making corrections as necessary. Thus, controlling effectively serves as the assessment and response process for the various elements of an agency.

DeChurch, Hiller, Murase, Doty, and Sala (2010) note that individuals at every level of management engage in the same types of functions with some differences. They note a difference between direction setting or planning at the top and bottom of the organizational chart is related to time orientation. At the lower levels of an organization, a leader may plan only three months ahead while the executive director plans for years ahead. In boundary spanning, a lower level leader focuses on connections between her or his unit and other units within the agency. At higher levels, managers are involved in relationships that link the agency to entities outside the organization.

UNDERSTANDING LEADERSHIP

People have been trying to understand leadership for hundreds, if not thousands, of years. Thus, wide arrays of theories exist to explain the construct; some have been researched and found to be valid, others have not. This chapter examines only a few of the more contemporary leadership models that have been investigated in the parks, recreation, and leisure services field as well as in other professions. Current thinking about leadership emphasizes the nature of the relationships within the leadership construct. Leaders do not lead without followers. For a leader to exist, others must recognize and accept that individual as a leader. Some refer to this as *granting* and *claiming*, whereby an individual grants leadership status to another while claiming the role of followership for oneself (Hoffman & Lord, 2013).

Four views of leadership are most prevalent in contemporary literature: transactional leadership, transformational leadership, servant leadership, and implicit leadership. In addition to these models, several additional concepts have arisen describing leadership skills and competencies for the profession; these are addressed in the following section.

LEADERSHIP AS RELATIONSHIP

Leadership as an Exchange

Transactional leadership is viewed as an exchange between a leader and followers. A common example of this model is the Leader-Member-Exchange (LMX) theory (Sherman, Kennedy, Woodard, & McComb, 2012). LMX focuses on leader-follower relationships and examines how the exchange processes affect that relationship over time. As relationships strengthen, so too does mutual trust and commitment to agency goals. Antonakis and House (2014) noted that the exchange process between leaders and members exhibit three characteristics: (a) the exchange relationship is influenced by personal characteristics of both parties, such as leader/follower prototypes; (b) leaders and group members develop expectations for the exchange based on the characteristics of themselves and others; and (c) the relationship is either reinforced or weakened based on each partner's evaluation of the exchange (i.e., whether or not the exchange meets their expectations of a "fair trade"). Research has demonstrated that followers benefit from high-quality LMX relationships because quality results in increased leader support, challenging work tasks, and opportunities for personal growth and learning. These outcomes lead to higher levels of job satisfaction, loyalty to the leader and agency, and better job performance than when poor LMX behaviors are exhibited.

Leadership that Transforms

A second popular theory of leadership is based on the personal values of the leader who inspires others to commit to a common purpose, empowers others to reach their potential, and promotes nontraditional thinking (Tonkin, 2013). Transformational leadership has four components: *idealized influence,* which explains how leaders serve as role models with a vision and drive; *inspirational motivation* describes how the leader creates bonds with followers and articulates a shared purpose; *individualized consideration* refers to the way that transformational leaders work with followers, treating each one as an individual and celebrating their uniqueness; and *intellectual stimulation*, whereby the leader engages in behaviors that demonstrate intellectual stimulation—that is, they question assumptions, provoke others' thinking in appropriate ways, and help to engage the creative side of followers. As with transactional leadership, transformational leadership has been consistently linked to positive outcomes such as follower satisfaction, motivation, and effectiveness (Hartley & Benington, 2011; Salk & Schneider, 2009).

Leader as Servant

Another theory of leadership that has been in the literature over the past several years is that of servant leadership; some view it as a philosophy or a way of living, rather than a theory. Servant leadership was first conceptualized in the early 1970s by Greenleaf and has been influencing leisure services agency leadership over the past ten years. Greenleaf (1991) captured the essence of servant leadership when he stated:

> The servant leader is servant first. It begins with the natural feeling that one wants to serve, to serve first. Then conscious choice brings one to aspire to lead. The best test is: Do those served grow as persons; do they, while being served, become healthier, wiser, freer, more autonomous, more likely themselves to become servants? And, what is the effect on the least privileged in society; will they benefit or, at least, not be further deprived? (p. 7)

This service orientation is quite compatible with the provision of recreation, park, and leisure services, particularly in the public and nonprofit sectors. According to Hunter, Neubert, Perry, and Witt (2013), leaders' ethical behaviors and the prioritization of followers' concerns are primary characteristics of servant leadership.

Researchers have found that servant leaders are strongest when they exhibit cognitive sophistication (also known as cognitive complexity). These leaders are consistently aware of the personal attributes that define their identity as servants. Further, leaders who demonstrate cognitively complexity are able to differentiate stimuli in a given situation. They quickly understand priorities and relationships between events and future impacts. In addition, cognitively sophisticated leaders are able to see commonalities among the complex dimensions of a given situation. Thus, leaders with this attribute maintain a focus on their service orientation while engaging in complex cognitive processes (Sun, 2013).

DISCERNING THE LEADER AND RECOGNIZING FOLLOWERS

In the earlier section describing LMX as an example of a transactional theory, the idea of leader prototypes was mentioned. A prototype is a standard people hold and use as a benchmark or measurement for future experiences. This has been applied to leadership, and is known as Implicit Leadership Theory (ILT). This theory suggests that each of us has a subconscious mental image of an ideal leader, and we measure potential leaders against that ideal (Whitely, Sy, & Johnson, 2012). Our perceptions and expectations are influenced by the ways we are socialized, previous experiences with leaders, and culture. In addition, our perception of what a leader is "supposed to look like, be, do" may be based partially on physical traits such as gender, height, or ethnicity; and partially on behaviors in which the individual engages (e.g., directs others). Thus, an individual could fail to be perceived as a leader because her or his traits and/or behaviors do not match the expected prototypical leader traits held by the group. Research has demonstrated that in newly formed groups, in particular, if the formal leader does not fit the groups' ILT, she or he may face difficulties in convincing others to follow (Adewoye, 2013; Bellou, 2011; Sy, 2010).

Likewise, Sy (2010) suggests that similar to the ideal leader prototype (ILT) people have in their minds, individuals have preconceived ideas about the ideal follower, which defines the Implicit Follower Theory (IFT). Common and expected traits of a desirable follower include a strong work ethic (i.e., the follower is hardworking, productive, and goes above and beyond), enthusiasm (i.e., the follower is excited, outgoing, and happy), and good citizenship as evidenced by their loyalty, reliability, and being perceived as a team player.

Researchers have shown that leaders more easily recognize potential in followers who fit their implicit idea of the follower prototype than those who do not (Whitely et al., 2012). And, because ILT and IFT are culturally based, leaders may not recognize potential in equally capable followers who do not meet their ideal follower prototype. This means that a leader may not see the follower potential in young, less skilled staff members or those who have a disability, are Hispanic, or female.

Followership and leadership are both active processes; they require individuals to engage and participate throughout the relationship and process. In fact, Uhl-bein, Riggio, Lowe, and Carsten (2014) suggest that leaders and followers are co-producers of the leader-follower relationship. This relationship is dynamic and based on expectations of what people perceive to be an ideal leader and ideal follower. Leader-follower relationships are constantly shifting as each party gains in understanding and experience. Our perceptions are biased by our upbringing, cultural viewpoints, and previous experiences with those in leader and follower positions.

LEADER ATTRIBUTES FOR SUCCESS

The twenty-first century has brought new attention to the study of leadership resulting in newly coined phrases such as authentic leadership, ethical leadership, and transparent leadership. The commonalities among these three constructs are leader self-awareness (e.g., knowing one's strengths and limitations, a willingness to improve), self-regulation (e.g., keeping one's emotions under control, being guided by one's morals and behaving ethically), presenting all of one's self to others (e.g., not trying to hide imperfections, being present in the moment), and engaging in balanced processing (e.g., seeking differing perspectives and utilizing an objective approach to analyzing information prior to making decisions) (Nichols & Erakovich, 2013; Tonkin, 2013).

Other necessary attributes include two internal components of an individual leader: *behavioral repertoire* and *behavioral differentiation* (DeMeuse, Dai, & Hallenbeck, 2010). Behavioral repertoire refers to the collection of leadership skills and behaviors an individual has available (e.g., communication skills, understanding group dynamics). Being capable in a variety of leadership behaviors enhances the likelihood that an individual can meet the expectations of diverse staff, participants, and others. Behavioral differentiation refers to the ability of a leader to utilize appropriate behaviors from their repertoire for a given situation. To demonstrate these skills, a leader must understand how the various parts of the organization relate to each other, how changes in one part of the system affect the other parts, and how changes in the external environment might affect the agency (Eubank, Geffkin, Orzano, & Ricci, 2012). These abilities are those of a leader who is agile, nimble, adaptable, and flexible.

DeMeuse et al. (2010) reported that a successful leader demonstrates several forms of agility—mental agility includes asking questions, being comfortable with ambiguity and complexity, and finding creative solutions to problems. A leader who has *people agility* is open-minded, self-aware, comfortable with diversity and differences of opinion, and has empathy. One who is *politically agile* deals with conflict constructively, is a highly skilled communicator, and understands the nuances of communication behaviors. Those who enjoy experimenting and trying new things, accepting challenges, and taking on responsibility demonstrate *change agility*. Finally, an agile or flexible leader has the characteristic of *results agility*. These individuals strive to build high-performance teams, have a strong drive to accomplish tasks, understand the resources needed, and are able to pull people together to accomplish common goals. With the rapidity of change and challenges in parks, recreation, and leisure services, agility is a must for successful leadership.

THE LATEST RESEARCH: WHAT DOES IT TAKE?

Leadership Tasks and Competencies

In efforts to pre-determine (and develop training for) success in parks, recreation, and leisure services leadership, several investigators have studied leader competencies. They are asking the question, "What skills and knowledge are needed for success in the profession?" This question has been raised related to leadership in public parks and recreation, nonprofit leisure services settings, club management, and within the hospitality industry.

Utilizing a panel of experts, Anderson (2013) reported that essential leader attributes for success in public parks and recreation include: professional knowledge; mental, emotional, and physical health; judgment; efficiency; dependability; considerateness; courage; intelligence; and sociability. These traits carried across four major categories of leadership tasks, the first of which is personnel relations. This category includes public relations, soliciting financial and legislative support for recreation, administration of the recreation program, and representing the department on recreation matters. The second category was identified as management, which entails the supervision of funds, supplies, equipment, and facilities; administration of funds, supplies, equipment, and facilities; and adherence to and enforcement of department regulations.

Program supervision was the third identified category and included administration of staff and volunteer personnel, supervision of the recreation program, supervision of staff and volunteer personnel, organizing and conducting recreation activities, and public relations. Lastly, Anderson (2013) identified a category called activity leadership. This grouping included the administration of recreation programs, supervision of staff and volunteer personnel, organizing and conducting recreation activities, and supervision of recreation programs. Interestingly, while courage was noted as a desirable attribute for public recreation leaders, too much of it was negatively related to leader success.

Hurd and Buschbom (2010) summarized early work related to discerning competencies needed for leaders in parks and recreation. They compared the results of several studies related to nonprofit leadership in leisure services with public parks and recreation leadership. The comparison resulted in eight common competency areas: (a) communication, (b) financial management, (c) understanding the community, (d) partnerships, (e) planning, (f) duty to the mission, (g) knowledge of the sector, and (h) positive public relations. Additional competencies identified included planning and evaluation as well as professionalism (Barcelona, Hurd, & Bruggeman (2011). In a 2015 study, Fultrop and D'Eloia noted the ten most important skills for successful leadership. These include the ability to: make ethical decisions, act professionally, work well with people, clearly communicate with customers, deal with the public, listen, be enthusiastic, clearly communicate with staff, be open to all members of the community, and work in team environments.

In a hospitality-related study, Koenigsfeld, Perdue, Youn, and Woods (2011) investigated the competencies needed for success in club management. They reported that experts rated leadership, interpersonal skills, and accounting and finance competencies as the most important and frequently used managerial competencies. Other competencies included conceptual-creative competencies, the administrative domain (e.g., accounting and finance, human and professional resources, marketing, and external and governmental influences), and technical competencies (e.g., food and beverage, building and facilities, club governance, golf management, and sports and recreation management). Another set of researchers (Suh, West, & Shin, 2012) found that listening skills, tolerance for change, guest interaction, openness to new ideas, personal integrity, interaction with superiors, peer interaction, leadership, interaction with subordinates, staff training, and knowledge in cultural differences were needed for success in the hospitality industry.

Cultural Proficiency: A Vital Leadership Skill

A discussion of leadership in the twenty-first century would be incomplete without a thorough review of the research related to the role of culture in both how individuals lead and how individuals perceive leadership. Unfortunately, space is limited; thus, it is incumbent upon all of us to engage in ongoing personal research and development opportunities in this very important skill area.

Ramthun and Matkin (2012) identified two levels of learning related to culture: (a) cultural knowledge, which describes an individual's awareness, understanding, and appreciation of a specific group's culture or dimensions of culture; and (b) intercultural competence, which focuses on negotiating cultural difference through effective awareness, communication, and interaction with others. Having knowledge of a subject, of course, is a required base for any advancement; personal awareness of a need for knowledge and understanding must precede that.

Leaders who are interculturally competent effectively manage their interactions with those who represent different or divergent affective, cognitive, and behavioral orientations. To do this, Ramthun and Matkin (2012) stated "they must have an understanding of others' world views, cultural self-awareness and capacity for self-assessment, adaptability and adjustment to new cultural environments, listening and observation, a general openness toward intercultural learning and to people from other cultures, and adaptation to varying intercultural communication and learning styles" (Ramthun & Matkin, 2012, p. 305). As can be seen, to be culturally competent is an active, proactive process. It requires action on the part of a learner, an engagement with the information, emotions, and meanings associated with understanding others.

Clearly, becoming interculturally proficient is a lifelong process. One of the most widely used models to describe this process (and included here to facilitate leader development in this area) is the Developmental Model of Intercultural Sensitivity (DMIS) (Bennett, 1993), which is commonly depicted as a continuum. The DMIS describes two stages of perception. The first is the ethnocentric stage during which we assume that our worldview is shared by all, or at least, is superior to any other. In this stage, leaders progress through several phases: a *denial of difference* where we simply do not consider the existence of cultural differences. Next is the *defense* phase when an individual recognizes differences and reacts in a way that suggests their culture is best. The third phase in this stage is *minimization*, and is best illustrated when we say that people are all the same at the core—culture does not matter.

The ethnorelative stage is where we begin to recognize that culture does impact life experiences and that cultural context is important to discerning meaning. The first phase is *acceptance*, when leaders acknowledge and respect cultural differences. Next, *adaptation* occurs when we have empathy for cultures other than our own and act accordingly. At this stage, skills for relating to and communicating with people of other cultures are enhanced. The final phase is *integration*, which occurs when we make continuous conscious efforts to understand our own cultural influences, cultural influences on others, and how identity is born out of these understandings and efforts. And, of course, we act in ways that are congruent with these understandings.

Culture permeates every interaction between leaders and followers—even those interactions that occur through electronic means. Thus, being skilled in virtual leadership is becoming increasingly important to the profession.

Virtual Leadership

The twenty-first century has placed leisure services managers and leaders firmly in the era of technology. This has had a tremendous impact on leadership—definitions, styles, interactions with followers, and other elements vital to the success of an agency and its ability to deliver leisure services are all affected. The virtual environment changes almost every aspect of how leaders work with others. Kelley and Kelloway (2012) noted five primary differences between virtual and face-to-face teams: (a) virtual teams are challenged by a lack of physical interaction (communication is primarily through a two-dimensional medium), (b) working at a distance results in the loss of face-to-face synergies, (c) trust is difficult to create and maintain, (d) virtual followers have a great concern with predictability and reliability of the leader, and (e) a lack of social interaction (especially unplanned) can be problematic to the relationships within the group.

In addition to the challenges noted above, Kelley and Kelloway (2012) found that electronic communication is inferior to face-to-face communication in a variety of ways. Nonverbal cues can contain as much as two-thirds of message content and are reduced or lost in virtual communication. This can result in misinterpretation, increased uncertainty about meaning, and reduced group cohesiveness (which can impact productivity). Further, electronic communications are perceived as less warm than face-to-face interactions. For example, email messages are perceived to contain higher levels of negativity than face-to-face communications. Based on this information, they indicate that one of the most critical aspects of successful virtual leadership is effective and frequent communication. Effective communication includes being clear and consistent in message and making appropriate use of technology (e.g., email, video-conferencing, online collaboration tools) for the task at hand. It also means that virtual leaders and followers should follow up with one another to seek clarity and shared understanding. Frequency of communication, even simply "checking in" with virtual group members is important to develop and maintain trust and a sense of caring.

WHAT DOES THE FUTURE HOLD?

Managers and leaders in the parks, recreation, and leisure services industry are going to continue to be challenged to engage a diverse staff to provide services to a diverse constituency in ways that enhance the quality of life for all. Actions to achieve this may differ based on the organizational structure, legal mandate, mission, and funding sources of an agency. Nonetheless, it will likely entail a conscious awareness of social (including cultural) and environmental issues to set a course for a focus on social justice where leisure is viewed as a human right (Garcia, 2013; Parry, Johnson, & Stewart, 2013). In this way, the leisure services industry will be at the forefront of leading society into a sound and healthy future.

In support of this, Dugan and Komives (2010) suggest that positive social change is the ultimate goal of leadership. Positive social change, then, will likely become an underlying value of leisure providers and may involve realigning mission, vision, and organizational culture with an understanding of the social, environmental, and financial realities of the times. There is no doubt that both leadership and management structures and processes will need to be agile, flexible, and adaptable as change is occurring more and more quickly with technological advances and innovations.

One example of the need for adaptability for public leisure services agencies is the growing pressure to become increasingly efficient in serving various constituencies. Hodgkinson (2012) notes that one common response has been for public agencies to mimic the private sector by implementing a range of market-based reforms. This can be problematic in that the private sector may pick and choose its target market while public agencies are commonly mandated to serve all constituent groups, regardless of their ability to pay, where they live, or any other distinction. Thus, public leisure providers face a dual strategic agenda; they have financial pressures to survive and at the same time, have a social duty to deliver a range of services to all consumer groups (Mowen & Havitz, Chapter 34).

Another ongoing and growing challenge for leisure services leaders and managers is an understanding of cultural influences, not only to ensure the appropriate delivery of services, but to lead effectively within an agency or organization. Ayoko and Konrad (2012) have demonstrated that diversity impacts implicit leader/follower models, the way groups work together, and communication expectations of group members and leaders. Bligh and Kohles (2014) noted that leadership styles reflect cultural nuances, sensitivities, and values. Thus, to be successful leisure professionals will need to enhance their own knowledge of culture, understand their own attitudes and biases, and gain skills to effectively operate in intercultural contexts. Further, they will need to demonstrate the ability to negotiate cultural meanings, beliefs, and values through attitudes, thoughts, and behaviors (Ramthun & Matkin, 2012). This will involve relationships with staff and community members, program innovation and implementation, and continuous and meaningful assessment.

In addition to understanding the importance of the human aspects of leadership and management, leisure services professionals will need to become increasingly skilled in consequential planning, implementation, and assessment. It is quite clear that genuine planning is going be required of managers and leaders in parks and recreation (Karadakis & Kaplanidou, 2010), and that leaders will be held accountable for their actions and follow-through with related activities. Thus, making use of public input, systematic analyses (e.g., cost-benefit; strengths, weaknesses, opportunities, and threats, or SWOT; political, economic, social, and technological factors; or PEST), demonstrating alignment with agency or organizational mandates, and formal means of assessment are all vital skills for successful leaders in the leisure services profession (see also Veal, Chapter 33).

In the United States and many other countries, the profession will continue to be challenged by the conflicting forces of financial sustainability and a social welfare system of service delivery. Thus, being able to advocate for the profession and its benefits will become an increasingly important leadership skill (Shilton, Bull, Del Prete, & Fenton, 2011). Advocacy requires specific knowledge, communication skills, broad networks, and deep understanding of the importance of the profession. Many leaders in parks, recreation, and leisure services are challenging agency leadership to view the field from a public health perspective, which tends to be more understandable to government leaders than does recreation. Thus, understanding the linkages between physical activity, outdoor play, emotional and social gains through leisure engagement, and community health will become an important framework in which to situate parks and recreation in the future (Bocarro & Edwards, Chapter 8).

Finally, leaders in the field will likely see increasing pressures from constituents for high-quality programs and services for all—including those who live in underserved areas of the community and face issues such as poverty, food insecurity, and crime. This will likely require shifts in thinking at the highest levels. Rather than simply providing a basic service, constituents will petition for value-added leisure experiences. They will look to parks, recreation, and leisure agencies and organizations to anticipate and address their needs for out-of-school and out-of-work experiences. The aging of the population will require an enhanced understanding of desirable programs and services, and how to implement them (Dattilo, Chapter 26). The same will hold true to respond to the needs of immigrants, those who speak English as a second language, and the growing populations of racial and ethnic minorities in communities of all sizes (Garcia, 2013; Stodolska & Floyd, Chapter 28).

The challenges for leaders of the future are many and they will continue to evolve as social mores change, expectations for service grow, and the population shifts. Knowledge, skills, understanding, and being able to integrate, synthesize, and assess are all necessary to respond in ways that will further the missions of diverse parks, recreation, and leisure service providers.

REFERENCES

Adewoye, A. (2013). Unique competencies required for female leadership success in the 21st century. Doctor of Business Administration Dissertation. Walden University.

Anderson, J. (2013). The development of personnel standards for leadership duties in public recreation. *Research Quarterly. American Association for Health, Physical Education and Recreation, 20*, 273–295.

Antonakis, J., & House, R. (2014). Instrumental leadership: Measurement and extension of transformational–transactional leadership theory. *The Leadership Quarterly, 25*(4), 746–771.

Ayoko, O., & Konrad, A. (2012). Leaders' transformational, conflict, and emotion management behaviors in culturally diverse workgroups. *Equality, Diversity and Inclusion: An International Journal, 31*, 694–724.

Barcelona, R., Hurd, A., & Bruggeman, J. (2011). A competency-based approach to preparing staff as recreation and youth development leaders. *New Directions for Youth Development*, 130, 121–139.

Bellou, V. (2011). Do women followers prefer a different leadership style than men? *The International Journal of Human Resource Management, 22*, 2818–2833.

Bennett, M. (1993). Towards a developmental model of intercultural sensitivity. In R. M. Paige (Ed.), *Education for the Intercultural Experience* (2nd ed.). Yarmouth, ME: Intercultural Press.

Bligh, M., & Kohles, J. (2014). Comparing leaders across contexts, culture, and time: Computerized content analysis of leader-follower communications. *Leadership, 10*(2), 142–159.

Chung, J., Jung, C., Kyle, G., & Petrick, J. (2010). Servant leadership and procedural justice in the U.S. National Park Service: The antecedents of job satisfaction. *Journal of Park and Recreation Administration, 28*(3), 1–15.

DeChurch, L., Hiller, N., Murase, T., Doty, D., & Sala, E. (2010). Leadership across levels: Levels of leaders and their levels of impact. *The Leadership Quarterly, 21*, 1069–1085.

DeMeuse, K., Dai, G., & Hallenbeck, G. (2010). Learning agility: A construct whose time has come. *Consulting Psychology Journal: Practice and Research, 62*(2), 119–130.

Dugan, J., & Komives, S. (2010). Influences on college students' capacities for socially responsible leadership. *Journal of College Student Development, 51*, 525–549.

Eagles, P. (2009). Governance of recreation and tourism partnerships in parks and protected areas. *Journal of Sustainable Tourism, 17*, 231–248.

Eubank, D., Geffkin, D., Orzano, J., & Ricci, R. (2012). Teaching adaptive leadership to family medicine residents: What? Why? How? *Families, Systems, and Health*, 1–12. doi:10.1037/a0029689

Fayol, H. (1917). *Administration industrielle et générale; Prévoyance, organisation, commandement, coordination, controle* (in French). Paris: H. Dunod et E. Pinat.

Fulthorp, K., & D'Eloia, M. (2015). Managers' perceptions of entry-level job competencies when making hiring decisions for municipal recreation agencies. *Journal of Park & Recreation Administration, 33*(1), 57–71.

Garcia. R. (2013). Social justice and leisure. *Journal of Leisure Research, 46*(1), 7–22.

Greenleaf, R. K. (1991). *The servant as leader*. Indianapolis: The Robert K. Greenleaf Center, 1–37.

Hartley, J., & Benington, J. (2011). *Recent trends in leadership: Thinking and action in the public and voluntary service sectors*. Commission on Leadership and Management in NHS. The King's Fund: London.

Hodgkinson, I. (2012). Are generic strategies 'fit for purpose' in a public service context? *Public Policy and Administration, 28*(1), 90–111.

Hoffman, E., & Lord, R. (2013). A taxonomy of event-level dimensions: Implications for understanding leadership processes, behavior, and performance. *The Leadership Quarterly, 24*, 558–571.

Hunter, E., Neubert, M., Perry, S., & Witt, L. (2013). Servant leaders inspire servant followers: Antecedents and outcomes for employees and the organization. *The Leadership Quarterly, 24*, 316–331.

Hurd, A., & Buschbom, T. (2010). Competency development for chief executive officers in YMCAs. *Managing Leisure, 15*(1–2), 96–110.

Karadakis, K., & Kaplanidou, K. (2010). Event leveraging of mega sport events: A SWOT analysis approach. *International Journal of Event and Festival Management, 1*, 170–185.

Kelley, E. & Kelloway, K. (2012). Context matters: Testing a model of remote leadership. *Journal of Leadership & Organizational Studies, 19*, 437–449.

Koenigsfeld, J., Perdue, J., Youn, H., & Woods, R. (2011). The changing face of competencies for club managers. *International Journal of Contemporary Hospitality Management, 23*, 902–922.

Nichols, T., & Erakovich, R. (2013). Authentic leadership and implicit theory: A normative form of leadership? *Leadership & Organization Development, 34*, 182–195.

Parry, D., Johnson, C., & Stewart, W. (2013). Leisure research for social justice: A response to Henderson. *Leisure Sciences, 35*, 81–87.

Ramthun, A., & Matkin, G. (2012). Multicultural shared leadership: A conceptual model of shared leadership in culturally diverse teams. *Journal of Leadership & Organizational Studies, 19*, 303–314.

Salk, R., & Schneider, I. (2009). Commitment to learning within a public land management agency: The influence of transformational leadership and organizational culture. *Journal of Park and Recreation Administration, 27*(1), 70–84.

Sherman, K., Kennedy, D., Woodard, M., & McComb, S. (2012). Examining the "exchange" in leader-member exchange. *Journal of Leadership & Organizational Studies, 19*, 407–423.

Shilton, T., Bull, F., Del Prete, J., & Fenton, M. (2011). Successful advocacy for physical activity: Moving from evidence to influence. *Journal of Science and Medicine in Sport, 14*(1), e28.

Suh, E., West, J., & Shin, J. (2012). Important competency requirements for managers in the hospitality industry. *Journal of Hospitality, Leisure, Sport & Tourism Education, 11*, 101–112.

Sun, P. (2013). The servant identity: Influences on the cognition and behavior of servant leaders. *The Leadership Quarterly, 24*, 544–557.

Sy, T. (2010). What do you think of followers? Examining the content, structure, and consequences of implicit followership theories. *Organizational Behavior and Human Decision Processes, 113*, 73–84.

Tonkin, T. (2013). Authentic versus transformational leadership: Assessing their effectiveness on organizational citizenship behavior of followers. *International Journal of Business and Public Administration, 10*(1), 40–61.

Uhl-Bien, M., Riggio, R., Lowe, K., & Carsten, M. (2014). Followership theory: A review and research agenda. *The Leadership Quarterly, 25*(1), 83–104.

Vetter, C. (2012). *Leadership competency for the nonprofit leader.* (Ph.D. Dissertation), Gonzaga University, Proquest Dissertations and Theses. (3510692)

Whitely, P., Sy, T., & Johnson, S. (2012). Leaders' conceptions of followers: Implications for naturally occurring Pygmalion effects. *The Leadership Quarterly, 23*, 822–834.

36

METATHEORIZING LEISURE THEORY

Gordon J. Walker (University of Alberta), Shintaro Kono (University of Alberta), and Rodney B. Dieser (University of Northern Iowa)

I never metatheory I didn't like.

(George Ritzer, 1991, p. 21)

We begin this chapter with an overview of what theory and metatheorizing are before outlining the key elements—and continuing relevance—of the first modern leisure theory. We then summarize findings from three investigations that examined current trends in leisure theory usage. Next, we try to attain a deeper understanding of leisure theory by discussing four attributes often used to describe, differentiate, and appraise theories. We conclude by proposing that if leisure theory—and thus the leisure field—is to advance, then the integration of theories into, not grand but rather "grander," theory is essential.

THEORY AND METATHEORIZING

Trying to define theory can result "in some of the same difficulties found in defining leisure. Like leisure, 'finding' theory may be more important than 'defining' it" (Henderson, Presley, & Bialeschki, 2004, p. 412). Despite this definitional dilemma, Henderson et al. held that *theory endeavors to explain relationships among variables in an attempt to provide insight into what can or has been observed.* This perspective largely parallels Kezar's (2006) who, after examining numerous schools of thought, found almost all agreed that theory ordered, systematized, and connected concepts in order to create coherence.

Although the terms theory and model are often used interchangeably they are not identical. Theories involve defined constructs and testable propositions whereas models do not. Models instead often take the form of an analogy (e.g., "The solar system is like a wheel.") or metaphor (e.g., "All the world's a stage.") (Crawford & Jackson, 2005, p. 155). Similarly, Henderson and associates (2004) maintained the purpose of theory was to understand what "is," and this contrasted with philosophy which sought to understand what "ought to be" (see also Babbie, 2003).

When *meta* is used as a prefix it means "beyond, above, at a higher level" (Oxford English Dictionary, 2014). Metatheorizing, therefore, is the process of systematically studying theory (Ritzer, 2001). Ritzer believed social scientists metatheorize for one or more of the following reasons; to: (a) attain a deeper understanding of theory; (b) develop a new and better theory; or (c) create overarching theoretical perspectives. Methatheorizing originates from sociology and, perhaps because sociological approaches are now seldom used to study leisure (Kleiber, Walker, & Mannell, 2011), only one previous investigation has attempted to attain a truly deeper understanding of *leisure* theory. Thus, this chapter builds on and expands upon Crawford and Jackson's (2005) seminal work; albeit after describing the first conventional leisure theory and three contemporary studies of leisure theory usage.[1]

VEBLEN'S THEORY OF THE LEISURE CLASS

The modern era in the study of leisure began with Veblen's (1899/1979) sociological analysis (Burton & Jackson, 1999). Veblen proposed a theory of leisure based on the socially determined ideology of social status, wealth, and privilege. Veblen's important contributions are threefold: (a) developing a theory of leisure; (b) examining leisure empirically;

---

[1] For those less familiar with our field, Dieser's (2013, pp. 16–17) table nicely summarizes some of the major sociological, psychological, anthropological, philosophical, and feminist leisure theories. For more in-depth discussion of these and other leisure theories, readers should peruse, among others: Chick, Chapter 1; Dattilo, Chapter 26; Kleiber, Chapter 23; Parry, Chapter 24; Schneider, Chapter 18; Scott, Chapter 19; Stodolska and Floyd, Chapter 28; Sylvester, Chapter 5; and Walker, Chapter 17.

and (c) suggesting that leisure is not necessarily beneficial for either individuals or societies. From a societal perspective, Veblen posited that leisure for the wealthy class involved three separate, yet overlapping, behaviors that signaled superior social ranking: conspicuous consumption, conspicuous leisure, and conspicuous waste. *Conspicuous consumption* is the visible display of wealth and privilege; *conspicuous leisure* signals wealth and privilege through the non-productive consumption of time; and *conspicuous waste* is the excessive display or disregard of goods. In summary, according to Veblen's theory, "to gain and hold the esteem of men [*sic*] it is not sufficient merely to possess wealth or power. The wealth or power must be put in evidence, for esteem is awarded only on evidence" (p. 36).

Veblen's (1899/1979) theory of the leisure class and its discussion of the display of social status through leisure continue to resonate (e.g., Rojek, 2000, Dunlap, 2010). Scott (2010), for example, outlined how during Veblen's lifetime as well as today, women's clothing provides an example of conspicuous consumption which functions primarily as adornment, and thus signals wealth and privilege (be it the hour-glass corset of the nineteenth, or the red-soled stilettoes of the twenty-first, century). Similarly, Sullivan (2001) and Grybovych and Dieser (2010) underscored that appearance-based cosmetic surgery was also an example of conspicuous consumption, where body display signals social status and privilege.

CONTEMPORARY TRENDS IN LEISURE THEORY

Trends in leisure theory usage have been investigated by Henderson and colleagues, Smith and colleagues, and Walker and colleagues. How each group of researchers conducted their reviews, and what each found, is summarized below.

Henderson and Colleagues

Henderson (1994) and colleagues' (Henderson & McFadden, 2013; Henderson et al., 2004) series of studies reviewed trends in theory use between 1981 and 2012 in American leisure journals. The first two studies reviewed four journals (i.e., *Journal of Leisure Research* [JLR], *Leisure Sciences* [LSc], *Journal of Park and Recreation Administration* [JPRA], and *Therapeutic Recreation Journal* [TRJ]) whereas the last study reviewed only JLR and LSc. The reviews included only original research articles. The first review by Henderson inductively developed the following three categories of theory uses. *Testing* refers to relatively deductive use of theories by explicating *a priori* theory and/or model and testing it with collected data while *Development* refers to relatively inductive use of theories by constructing substantive theory from qualitative data or developing model based on quantitative data. *Application* (originally labeled Conceptual Frameworks) denotes a mixture of deductive and inductive uses of theories to, for example, form research questions or identify relevant variables.

In the first study in this series, Henderson (1994) found that, of 679 articles published between 1981 and 1990, 190 articles (28%) comprised Application; 187 articles (28%) comprised Testing; and 29 articles (4%) comprised Development. In the analysis published a decade later, Henderson et al. (2004) discovered that, of 808 articles published between 1992 and 2002, the largest number still involved Application (n = 329, 41%), followed by Testing (n = 120, 15%) and Development (n = 93, 11%). In the most recent analysis, Henderson and McFadden (2013) did not report the exact number or percentage of articles in each category. However, one of their figures indicated that Application composed the largest proportion (approximately 38%) of articles published in JLR and LSc between 2003 and 2012, followed by Testing and Development (approximately 22% and 20%, respectively). Henderson and McFadden also conducted statistical analyses with data from all three reviews. Their results suggested that while the proportion of Testing-focused articles decreased from the first decade to the latter two timeframes, the proportion of Development-focused articles increased during the same time period.

Overall, the series of reviews by Henderson and colleagues (Henderson, 1994; Henderson & McFadden, 2013; Henderson et al., 2004) indicated that over the past three decades: (a) the percentage of Testing use of theories decreased, (b) the ratio of Development use of theories increased, and (c) the proportion of Application use stayed relatively high. As for the first two trends, Henderson and McFadden suspected this was largely because of the increased use of interpretivist qualitative methods, including certain types of grounded theory. Although this can lead to more leisure-specific theories that reflect life contexts (e.g., meanings of leisure for women on farms; Henderson & Rannells, 1988), we would caution that this trend may also emphasize more low-level theories that explain specific phenomena rather than the "grander" theories advocated for at the end of this chapter. The relatively high percentages of Application-focused articles may have been because this category is more inclusive than the Testing and Development categories, the latter two involving relatively "pure" deductive or inductive theory usage. Combined, these trends suggest that the three different uses of theory became more balanced between Henderson and colleagues' earliest and latest reviews.

Smith and Colleagues

Smith, Xiao, Nunkoo, and Tukamushaba (2013) conducted a review on the trend in use of the *term* theory across three fields: tourism, hospitality, and leisure. The following seven categories were adopted from Smith and Lee (2010): (a) formal theories associated with natural sciences, (b) formal theories often used in social sciences, (c) statistical models without *a priori* theoretical framework, (d) untested/untestable verbal or graphic models, (e) epistemologies or worldviews, (f) grounded theory, and (g) casual or analogical use of theories. Their review included both full-length articles and research notes published between 1989 to 1993 and 2004 to 2008 in three top-tier journals in each fields; with leisure being represented by JLR, LSc, and *Leisure Studies* (LSt). Their review focused on articles whose title, abstract, and/or key words include the term theory or its variations (e.g., theoretical).

Smith et al.'s (2013) findings indicated that while the proportion of articles that met the above criteria to total published articles increased in all three fields (e.g., from 7% in 1989 to 1993, to 15% in 2004 to 2008, for leisure), the average over the two time periods was notably higher in leisure (12%) compared to the tourism (8%) and hospitality (1%) fields. The two most evident uses of the term theory in the leisure field were formal theories often used in social sciences (39%; e.g., Walker, 2008) and epistemologies or worldviews (34%; e.g., Glover & Hemingway, 2005). Whereas the percentages of these two categories stayed relatively high over the two timeframes, the percentages of untested/untestable verbal or graphic models and statistical models without *a priori* theoretical framework "jumped up" (10% to 22% and 0% to 6%, respectively). Interestingly, the absence of grounded theory (0%) seems to contradict the increase in Development-focused articles identified by Henderson and McFadden (2013). A possible explanation for this outcome is that grounded theory-based studies did not meet Smith and colleagues' criteria and thus were excluded from their review. Finally, Smith et al. suggested that the term theory has been used more explicitly in the leisure field than in the tourism and hospitality fields.

Walker and Colleagues

Leisure theory can, of course, also be found in books. Thus, the chapter authors employed Google Books Ngram Viewer (Google Ngram Viewer Team, 2013) to evaluate leisure trends in this medium.[2] What is first evident here is that leisure theory appears to have experienced three "golden" phases: 1983 to 1986, 1990 to 1992, and 1998 to 2000 (see Figure 36.1). Among the books respectively published during each of these periods are, for example: Rojek's (1985) *Capitalism and Leisure Theory*; Stebbins' (1992) *Amateurs, Professionals, and Serious Leisure*; and Wearing's (1998) *Leisure and Feminist Theory*. Also evident in this figure is that the trend from 1985 to 2008 is distinctly downward. Why this has happened is unknown, but we speculate that it may be because leisure theorists began placing greater emphasis on publishing in refereed journals; or as the number of leisure programs declined so did the number of leisure theorists; or publishers became more focused on commercially viable books (e.g., introductory

[2] Google Books Ngram Viewer utilizes a database composed of over five million digitized books, or approximately 4% of all books ever published (Michel et al., 2011). Any time period between 1800 and 2008 can be selected; however, we choose 1975 as our starting point because there were few instances and little fluctuation in our phrase, "leisure theory," before this year. We also specified "English" language books and a smoothing coefficient of 1.

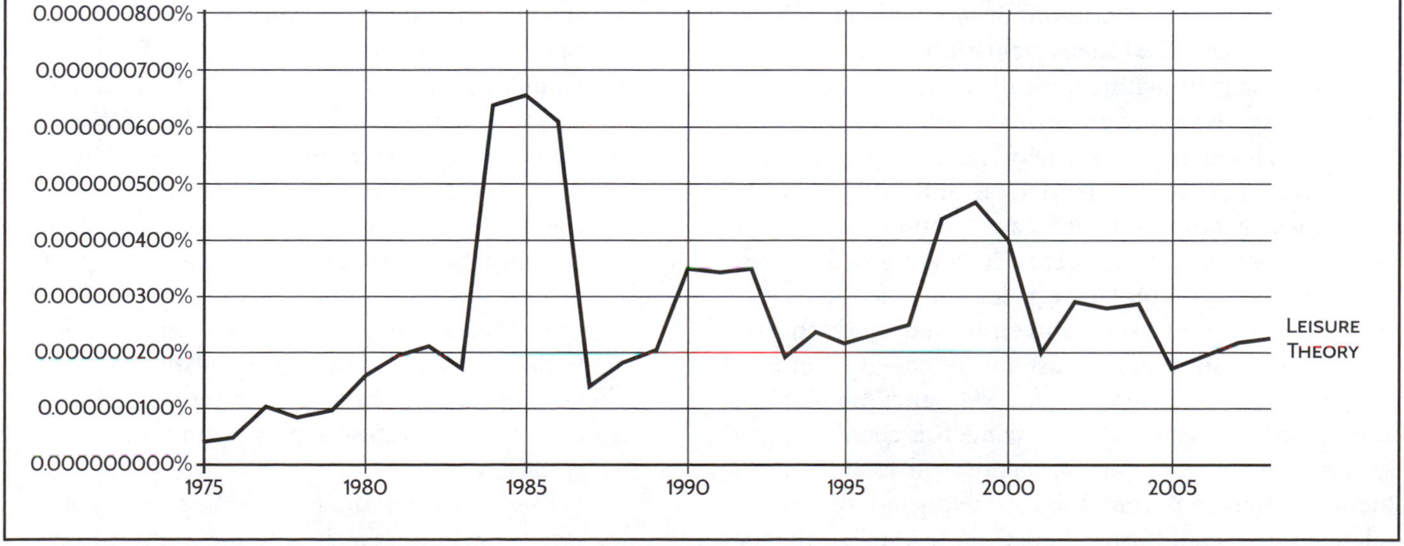

Figure 36.1. Frequency of Term "Leisure Theory" in Google Books (1975 to 2008)

textbooks); or a combination thereof. In summary, although leisure theory has become less common in books over the past decade or two, Henderson and McFadden (2013) and Smith and associates' (2013) findings suggest its frequency continued to increase in leisure journals.

THEORY ATTRIBUTES

The aforementioned studies are useful in that they provide descriptive insight into how often leisure theory has been used, but social scientists have also recognized that theories can exist at different levels, vary across fundamental dimensions, be judged using certain predetermined criteria, and differ in focus depending on a theorist's paradigmatic assumptions. Each of these attributes is described more fully, as well as in regard to leisure theory specifically, as we attempt to attain a deeper understanding of leisure theory through metatheorizing (Ritzer, 2001).

Theory Levels

Theories can range from low-level (or local) to middle-level to grand (or universal). *Low-level* theories explain a specific topic or phenomenon (e.g., urban school organizations and school bullying, respectively); *middle-level* theories explain a broader topic area or phenomenon (e.g., all school organizations and human violence, respectively); and *grand* theory explains an all-encompassing topic or phenomenon (e.g., all organizations and all human behavior, respectively) (Kezar, 2006).

The level most leisure theory is located at remains unclear. For instance, Henderson et al. (2004) held that "most theories used in leisure sciences are middle-range theories, *meaning they are limited and modest in their scope*" (italics added, p. 413). The discrepancy between descriptor and description here is evident, but what is also concerning is that subsequent researchers have framed their work in a similarly conflated fashion. Beaton and Funk (2008), for example, described their evaluation of six theoretical frameworks for studying physically active leisure as being middle-range. However, given this topic and phenomenon's specificity, it seems—as is true of most leisure research—more likely low level. Henderson and colleagues also contended that grand theories are "grandiose" and "may be an impossible task" (p. 413). However, based on some of Kezar's (2006) exemplars (e.g., feminist theories, critical race theory), it is just such universal frameworks that our field has often used in the past and/or called for more of in the future (e.g., Henderson, 1990, and Arai & Kivel, 2009, respectively). On the one hand, this could simply be a case where, to paraphrase Henderson et al., "'finding theory' is more important than 'resolving its level.'" On the other hand, it could prove beneficial to clarify a theory's location for at least two reasons: (a) if we realize we are employing a grand theory to study leisure, we may be more likely to recognize the inherent limitations in doing so; and (b) if we realize we are usually employing low-level theories to study leisure, we may be more likely to act boldly and develop more true, mid-level leisure theories. We will return to the latter point in our conclusion.

Theory Dimensions

Theories have also been described based on their fundamental dimensions. Rychlak's (1968) five, and Corley and Gioia's (2011) two, dimensions are described below.

Rychlak's five dimensions.

Rychlak (1968) identified five dimensions for classifying theories (see Figure 36.2), including:

- *Abstraction*—which ranges from lesser to greater, with an example of the former being "the study of specific behaviors [while] holding many others constant" and an example of the latter being "taking into consideration a broad range of behavior ([and thus] considering the 'whole person')" (p. 15).
- *Realism versus Idealism*—with theorists who gravitate toward the former holding that "perception and cognition has an immutable existence all its own, entirely independent of the perceiver" whereas theorists who gravitate toward the latter holding that "there is no external world of reality apart from, or having an existence independent of the perception and cognition of the perceiver.... [Thus] knowledge is primarily an act of creation" (p. 17).
- *Objective versus Subjective*—with the former indicating that individuals who have similar backgrounds and experiences (e.g., scientific training) can elucidate a shared meaning of the theoretical abstraction in question, whereas the latter indicates that "it is impossible to ever know what goes on in the heads of others" (p. 23), and thus to generalize beyond one's own idiosyncratic behavior.
- *Extraspection versus Introspection*—with theorists who emphasize the former privileging their own frame of reference, whereas theorists who emphasize the latter privilege that of their participants. Noteworthy here is that while Rychlak thought some theories could be construed in terms of both, he added that because extraspection had been overemphasized, "certain blindspots in [psychology's] theoretical sophistication" had resulted (p. 34).
- *Formal versus Informal*—with the former being "theory stated as specifically and uniformly as possible and written to bring together all the

loosely joined tenets, hypotheses, and validate facts into a consistent, interdependent unity" (p. 35), whereas the latter is more ambiguous, intuitive, and speculative.

Noteworthy here is that, although Rychlak thought that certain continuum endpoints were interconnected (i.e., realism, objective, extraspection, and formal; and idealism, subjective, introspection, and informal), he also felt that researchers should, minimally, understand both ends of each continuum and, ideally, be able to cross back and forth between them (p. 457).

The above provides a brief overview of Rychlak's (1968) work, and interested readers can learn more about his theoretical dimensions in Crawford and Jackson (2005). Crawford and Jackson's chapter is also pertinent here as it evaluated leisure constraints theory (LCT; Crawford, Jackson, & Godbey, 1991; see also Schneider, Chapter 18) based on four of Rychlak's dimensions. After doing so, Crawford and Jackson concluded that LCT was quite abstract in scope, objective in nature, and formal in presentation, but equally introspective and extraspective. Oddly, they chose not to evaluate LCT in regard to Rychlak's realism versus idealism dimension.

Corley and Gioia's two dimensions.

Utility is another dimension—one identified after Crawford and Jackson's (2005) chapter was published—that LCT (Crawford et al., 1991) and other leisure theories could be appraised on. Corley and Gioia (2011) contended that, in management studies, there were two dimensions for determining what constituted a theoretical contribution: *originality* (ranging from incremental to revelatory) and *utility* (ranging from scientific to practical). For Corley and Gioia, practical utility arises "when theory can be directly applied to the problems practicing managers and other . . . practitioners face" (p. 18). Unfortunately, they believe, the role of practical utility "in theoretical contribution seems to receive mainly lip service (e.g., several paragraphs on 'practical implications' in the discussion section" (p. 18) of most management studies articles). The same claim could potentially be made in our field; and this might explain why, for instance, Scott (2005) found "there is little indication that [recreation] practitioners are applying findings from constraints research to improve service delivery" (p. 279). Conversely, Stewart (1998) argued that leisure research may have overemphasized managerial applications at the expense of "*conceptual relationships*, say, between gender, willingness-to-pay, and/or satisfaction and aspects of the experience or the environment" (p. 398)—information, he held, recreation practitioners would also benefit from knowing. Stodolska (2000) agreed, noting not only that "the notion that practical applicability is not the only legitimate motivation for leisure research has universal relevance," but also that this supported studying minority groups which, she believed, could provide "a rare opportunity for expanding theory applicable to leisure experience in general" (p. 158).[3]

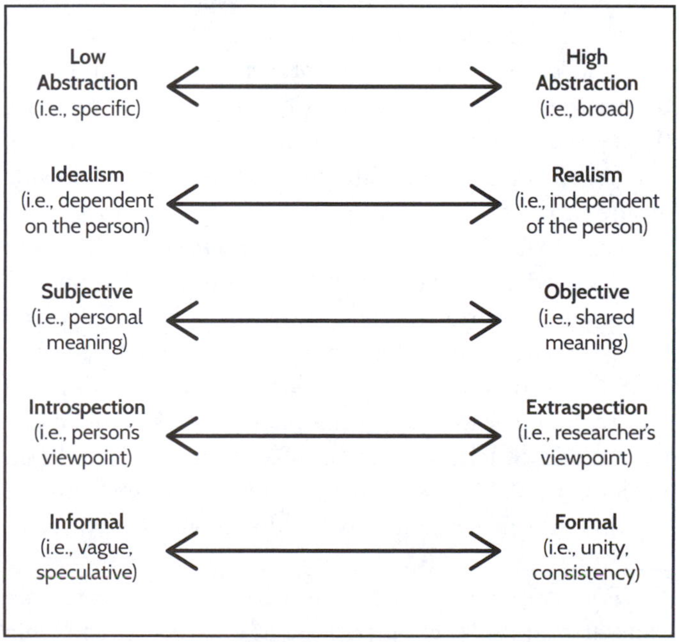

Figure 36.2. Rychlak's (1968) Fundamental Dimensions of Theory

Corley and Gioia (2011) concluded by calling for management theories that displayed greater scientific *and* practical utility, a proposition in line with Kurt Lewin's ideas. Lewin, a preeminent social psychologist, is famous for his saying "there is nothing as practical as a good theory" (1943, p. 118).[4] Unfortunately, much less well known is his statement "a close link with practice can be a blessing for the development of theory. After all, the practitioner is interested in change experiments because he [*sic*] wants to reach certain objectives" (Lewin, 1945, p. 133). Besides championing the inter-relationship between theory and practice, Lewin also advocated for various types of action research. These three combined, he believed, could inform social planning and lead to resolving social conflicts such as the exploitation of minority group members (Adelman, 1993). In summary, the leisure field may now have reached a point in time where we need to

---

[3] Approximately 12% of race/ethnicity and leisure articles are "commentaries/theoretical discussions" (Floyd, Bocarro, & Thompson, 2008), whereas 9% of cross-national/cross-cultural leisure articles are so (Ito, Walker, & Liang, 2014). Greater research attention to both areas, especially theory-based research, is clearly called for.

[4] In point of fact, Lewin gave credit to an anonymous businessman for being the originator of this adage.

determine where we fall along Corley and Gioia's utility dimension and where we best go (cf. Sibthorp & Bocarro, 2014; Tseng, 2014). If correct, then Lewin's integrated approach may be well worth considering.[5]

"Good" Theory Criteria

Crawford and Jackson's (2005) chapter is extraordinary not only because it evaluated leisure constraints theory (Crawford et al., 1991) using four of Rychlak's (1968) dimensions, but also because it assessed LCT on whether it was "good" theory. Popper (1963) was the first to outline characteristics of a "good" theory, proposing that it must be: (a) new, simple, powerful, and unifying; (b) independently testable and predictive of previously unobserved phenomenon; and (c) able to pass new, and severe, empirical tests (pp. 241–242). Others have added to his list, with Wacker's (1998) work often being cited. Wacker's "virtues" and key features of good theories included (p. 365):

- *Uniqueness*—two theories are not identical.
- *Conservatism*—a new theory must prove better than an existing theory.
- *Internal consistency*—all relationships are identified and adequately explained.
- *Parsimonious*—the simpler a theory, the better.
- *Empirical riskiness*—refutation must be possible, with the theory that predicts a less likely event being better.
- *Fecundity*—the more fertile a theory is in terms of generating new hypotheses, the better.
- *Generalizability*—the more widely applicable a theory is, the better.
- *Abstraction*—a theory that integrates more consistent variables and relationships is better than one that integrates fewer.

Crawford and Jackson (2005) did not describe how they selected their criteria for what constitutes good theory, but there is overlap with Popper (1963) and Wacker's (1998) standards. For example, Crawford and Jackson's descriptive function of theory, Popper's unity, and Wacker's internal consistency, as well as Crawford and Jackson's integrative nature of theory and Wacker's abstraction, seem comparable. Conversely, however, Crawford and Jackson's "explanation and prediction" seems less a criterion for assessing what good theory "is" and more part of what defines what a theory actually "is." Regardless of these clarity and transparency issues, these two constraint researchers provide a second example of how we can judge the leisure theories we employ and endorse.

Theory and Paradigmatic Assumptions

Crawford and Jackson (2005) ultimately concluded that LCT (Crawford et al., 1991) largely met their criteria for good theory. They recognized, however, that some leisure scholars might disagree with their positivistic approach and thus, to forestall (or perhaps fan) an academic firestorm, they stated:

> We would nevertheless maintain we see no currently available alternative to positivism. Postpositivism, as a basis for true scientific thought, seems to us to have a grim and joyless future, being much more akin to philosophy or religion than science. (p. 162)[6]

It is interesting to speculate why Crawford and Jackson (2005) instigated this inflammatory assault, but at least one possibility is unfamiliarity with how theory is construed differently and similarly across various schools of thought. Kezar's (2006) in-depth discussion of this topic is exceptional, particularly her summary table (p. 312). In the latter she directly compared and contrasted four paradigms across seven qualities of theory. Kezar proposed, for instance, that the goal of theory development for: (a) *positivists* is "to search for regularities and test to predict and control"; (b) *interpretivists* is "to describe and explain in order to understand"; (c) *critical theorists* is "to describe, critique, and create change"; and (d) *participatory action researchers* (PARs) is "to develop guides for action and change." She posited, for instance, that while both positivists and critical theorists generally consider grand theory to be better, interpretivists typically privilege lower- and middle-level theories, whereas PARs regard all levels to be equally important.

The need for parsimony prevents a more thorough discussion of how paradigmatic assumptions influence theory, but readers are encouraged to peruse Kezar's (2006) chapter in conjunction with, among others, the following leisure scholars' work: Arai and Pedlar (2003), Crawford and Jackson (2005), Hemingway (1999), and Parry and Johnson (2007). In what could best be described as the "after theory" category, also worth reading is Tony Blackshaw's Chapter 7 in this volume, wherein he argues that: "the talent wasted on theorizing contemporary sociological understandings of leisure should be used for the more urgent task of theorizing contemporary leisure" (see also Blackshaw, 2014). Terry Eagleton's (2003) *After Theory* is, of course, the ultimate example of this genre and is highly recommended for its

---

5 For more on this topic, see also Mortensen & Cialdini (2010) and Price & Behrens (2003).

6 For a primer on post-positivism in leisure research, see Henderson (2011). For a critique of post-positivism from a social justice perspective, see Parry, Johnson, & Stewart (2013).

insightful critique of cultural studies' orthodoxies and its humorous asides on leisure (see also Eagleton, 2010).

CONCLUSION

When examined in its entirety, leisure theory has a long and illustrious history; has continued, at least in journals, to increase in usage; and is more common in the leisure field than its counterparts in allied areas (e.g., tourism). Perception (e.g., "What level is most leisure theory at?") and paradigmatic (e.g., "What level should most leisure theory be at?") differences certainly exist; but conflict *can* be a catalyst for growth and progress. Additionally, metatheorizing (Ritzer, 2001) to attain a deeper understanding of leisure theory has now taken place for a second time; although we hope the interval between this chapter and the next such work is shorter than the 10 year gap between Crawford and Jackson's (2005) chapter and our own.

As noted earlier, Ritzer (2001) held that social scientists also metatheorize to create overarching theoretical perspectives. Crawford and Jackson (2005) correspondingly wrote that integration—a criterion of good theory (e.g., Wacker, 1998)—could occur in regard to leisure constraints theory (Crawford et al., 1991). A modest step, Crawford and Jackson suggested (p. 165), would be to link constraint conceptualizations with other areas of leisure scholarship (e.g., motivations; see Walker, Chapter 17), but they also thought it possible that LCT could someday "be completely swallowed up by future theoretical developments, an event that would underscore both the integrative function of theory and the role of theory in science" (p. 161). Merton (1968), as they mentioned, was the first to discuss integrating multiple mid-level theories in the pursuit of grand theory:

> I believe—and beliefs are of course notoriously subject to error—that theories of the middle range hold the largest promise, *provided that* the search for them is coupled with a pervasive concern with consolidating special theories into more general sets of concepts and mutually consistent propositions. Even so, we must adopt the provisional outlook of our big brothers and of Tennyson: "Our little systems have their day; They have their day and cease to be." (pp. 52–53)

Although, as suggested earlier, we consider LCT (Crawford et al., 1991) to be a low-level theory, and that only theoretical frameworks that seek to explain all human leisure behavior are mid-level (and, it follows, that only theoretical frameworks that strive to explain all human behavior are in fact grand), we do concur with Crawford and Jackson (2005) that integration is highly worthwhile—albeit not in the pursuit of grand, but rather "grander," leisure theory. Attempts to do so are not as rare as one might assume. Tinsley and Tinsley (1986), for example, entitled their article *A Theory of the Attributes, Benefits, and Causes of Leisure Experience*, and put forward 21 testable propositions and an equal number of corollaries. Similarly, Driver, Brown, and Peterson (1991) described a comprehensive framework composed of 10 components (e.g., sociodemographic characteristics, preferences, constraints, engagement, experience, experience evaluation, satisfaction/dissatisfaction, and benefits and losses) and multiple interrelationships. Additionally, Walker (2014) and colleagues (Kleiber et al., 2011; Walker & Liang, 2012; Walker & Virden, 2005) have proposed various, interconnected structures, some of which focused more on integrating micro-level psychological theories (e.g., Ajzen's, 1991, theory of planned behavior; Crawford et al's., LCT; Ryan & Deci's, 2000, self-determination theory) whereas others focused more on the potential roles meso- (e.g., self-construal) and macro-level (e.g., ethnicity, culture, social class) factors might play. Finally, Stodolska, Sharaievska, Tainsky, and Ryan (2014) investigated interrelationships among needs, motivations, and facilitators, and how they affected minority youth sport participation.

In conclusion, as Crawford and Jackson (2005) so convincingly wrote a decade ago:

> We may ultimately come to the realization that one of the major issues this line of work faces is not that it has been too brazen, but that it may not have been adventurous enough. Why not be daring and speculate imaginatively now, at this relatively early stage? (p. 165)

We concur, and contend the time has come to replace the "theory shyness" (Kruglanski, 2001) now common in the leisure field with "theory boldness."

REFERENCES

Adelman, C. (1993). Kurt Lewin and the origins of action research. *Educational Action Research, 1*, 7–24.

Ajzen, I. (1991). The theory of planned behavior. *Organisational Behavior and Human Decision Process, 50*, 179–211.

Arai, S., & Kivel, D. (2009). Critical race theory and social justice perspectives on Whiteness, difference(s) and (anti)racism: A fourth wave of race research in leisure studies. *Journal of Leisure Research, 41*, 459–470.

Arai, S., & Pedlar, A. (2003). Moving beyond individualism in leisure theory: A critical analysis of concepts of community and social engagement. *Leisure Studies, 22*, 185–202.

Babbie, E. (2003). *The practice of social research*. Belmont, CA: Wadsworth.

Beaton, A. A., & Funk, D. C. (2008). An evaluation of theoretical frameworks for studying physically active leisure. *Leisure Sciences, 30*, 53–70.

Blackshaw, T. (2014). The crisis in sociological leisure studies and what to do about it. *Annals of Leisure Research, 2*, 127–144.

Burton, T. L., & Jackson, E. L. (1999). Reviewing leisure studies: An organizing framework. In E. L. Jackson & T. L. Burton (Eds.), *Leisure studies: Prospects for the twenty-first century* (pp. xvii–xxiii). State College, PA: Venture Publishing, Inc.

Corley, K. G., & Gioia, D. A. (2011). Building theory about theory building: What constitutes a theoretical contribution? *Academy of Management Review, 36*, 12–32.

Crawford, D., & Jackson, E. (2005). Leisure constraints theory: Dimensions, directions, and dilemmas. In E. Jackson (Ed.), *Constraints to leisure*, (pp. 153–167). State College, PA: Venture Publishing, Inc.

Crawford, D., Jackson, E., & Godbey, G. (1991). A hierarchical model of leisure constraints. *Leisure Sciences, 13*, 309–320.

Dieser, R. B. (2013). *Leisure education: A person-centered, system-directed, social policy perspective*. Urbana, IL: Sagamore.

Driver, B. L., Brown, P. J., & Peterson, G. L. (1991). Research on leisure benefits: An introduction to this volume. In B. L. Driver, P. J. Brown, & G. L. Peterson (Eds.), *Benefits of leisure* (pp. 3–11). State College, PA: Venture Publishing, Inc.

Dunlap, R. (2010). What would Veblen wear? *Leisure Sciences, 32*, 295–297.

Eagleton, T. (2003). *After theory*. London: Penguin Books.

Eagleton, T. (2010, June 15). Football: A dear friend to capitalism. *The Guardian*. Retrieved from http://www.julietdavis.com/COM443/articles/Football%20-%20A%20dear%20friend%20to%20capitalism%20-%20Terry%20Eagleton.pdf

Floyd, M. F., Bocarro, J. N., & Thompson, T. D. (2008). Research on race and ethnicity in leisure studies: A review of five major journals. *Journal of Leisure Research, 40*, 1–22.

Glover, T. D., & Hemingway, J. L. (2005). Locating leisure in the social capital literature. *Journal of Leisure Research, 37*, 387–401.

Google Ngram Viewer Team. (2013). *Google books Ngram Viewer*. Retrieved from https://books.google.com/ngrams/info

Grybovych, O., & Dieser, R. B. (2010). Happiness and leisure: An ethnodrama, Act I. *Leisure/Loisir, 34*, 27–50.

Hemingway, J. L. (1999). Critique and emancipation: Toward a critical theory of leisure. In E. L. Jackson & T. L. Burton (Eds.), *Leisure studies: Prospects for the twenty-first century* (pp. 477–506). State College, PA: Venture Publishing, Inc.

Henderson, K. A. (1990). Anatomy is not destiny: A feminist analysis of the scholarship on women's leisure. *Leisure Sciences, 12*, 229–239.

Henderson, K. A. (1994). Theory application and development in recreation, park, and leisure research. *Journal of Park and Recreation Administration, 12*, 51–64.

Henderson, K. A. (2011). Post-positivism and the pragmatic of leisure research. *Leisure Sciences, 33*, 341–346.

Henderson, K. A., & McFadden, K. (2013). Characteristics of leisure research: Trends over three decades. *International Leisure Review, 2*, 119–134.

Henderson, K. A., Presley, J., & Bialeschki, M. D. (2004). Theory in recreation and leisure research: Reflections from the Editors. *Leisure Sciences, 26*, 411–425.

Henderson, K. A., & Rannells, J. S. (1988). Farm women and the meaning of work and leisure: An oral history perspective. *Leisure Sciences, 10*, 41–50.

Ito, E., Walker, G. J., & Liang. H. (2014). A systematic review of non-Western and cross-cultural/national leisure research. *Journal of Leisure Research, 46*, 226–239.

Kezar, A. (2006). To use or not to use theory: Is that the question? In J. C. Smart (Ed.), *Higher education: Handbook of theory and research* (vol. XXI, pp. 283–344). Houton, Netherlands: Springer.

Kleiber, D. A., Walker, G. J., & Mannell, R. C. (2011). *A social psychology of leisure* (2nd ed.). State College, PA: Venture Publishing, Inc.

Kruglanski, A. (2001). That "vision thing": The state of theory in social and personality psychology at the edge of the new millennium. *Journal of Personality and Social Psychology, 80*, 871–875.

Lewin, K. (1943). Psychology and the process of group living. *The Journal of Social Psychology, SPSSI Bulletin, 17*, 113–131.

Lewin, K. (1945). The Research Center for Group Dynamics at Massachusetts Institute of Technology. *Sociometry, 8*(2), 126–136.

Merton, R. (1968). *Social theory and structure* (Rev ed.). Glencoe, IL: Free Press.

Michel, J-B., Shen, Y. K., Aiden, A. P., Veres, A, Gray, M. K., Brockman, W., The Google Books Team, Pickett, J. P., Hoiberg, D., Clancy, D., Norvig, P., Orwant, J., Pinker, S., Nowak, M. A., & Aiden, E. L. (2011). Quantitative analysis of culture using millions of digitized books. *Science, 331*(6014), 176–182.

Mortensen, C. R., & Cialdini, R. B. (2010). Full-cycle social psychology for theory and application. *Social and Personality Psychology Compass, 4*, 53–63.

Oxford English Dictionary. (2014). *meta-, prefix*. Retrieved from ttp://www.oed.com/view/Entry/117150?rskey=a-0G8Uc&result=4&isAdvanced=false#eid

Parry, D. C., & Johnson, C. W. (2007). Contextualizing leisure research to encompass complexity in lived leisure experience: The need for creative analytic practice. *Leisure Sciences, 29*, 119–130.

Parry, D. C., Johnson, C. W., & Stewart, W. (2013). Leisure research for social justice: A response to Henderson. *Leisure Sciences, 35*, 81–87.

Popper, K. R. (1963). *Conjectures and refutations: The growth of scientific knowledge*. London: Routledge and Kegan Paul.

Price, R. H., & Behrens, T. (2003). Working Pasteur's Quadrant: Harnessing science and action for community change. *American Journal of Community Psychology, 32*, 219–223.

Ritzer, G. (1991). I never metatheory I didn't like. *Mid-American Review of Sociology, 15*(2), 21–32.

Ritzer, G. (2001). *Explorations in social theory: From metatheorizing to rationalization*. London, England: Sage.

Rojek, C. (1985). *Capitalism and leisure theory*. London: Tavistock.

Rojek, C. (2000). Leisure and the rich today: Veblen's thesis after a century. *Leisure Studies, 19*, 1–15.

Ryan, R., & Deci, E. (2000). Self-Determination Theory and the facilitation of intrinsic motivation, social development, and well-being. *American Psychologist, 55*, 68–78.

Rychlak, J. (1968). *A philosophy of science for personality theory*. Boston, MA: Houghton Mifflin.

Scott, D. (2005). The relevance of constraints research to leisure service delivery. In E. Jackson (Ed.), *Constraints to leisure* (pp. 279–293). State College, PA: Venture Publishing, Inc.

Scott, D. (2010). What would Veblen say? *Leisure Sciences, 32*, 288–294.

Sibthorp, J., & Bocarro, J. (2014). Leisure research and the legacy of George Daniel Butler. *Journal of Leisure Research, 46*, 1–5.

Smith, S., & Lee, H. (2010). A typology of "theory" in tourism: In D. Pearce & R. Butler (Eds.), *Tourism research: A 20-20 vision* (pp. 28–39). London: Goodfellow.

Smith, S. L. J., Xiao, H., Nunkoo, R., & Tukamushaba, E. K. (2013). Theory in hospitality, tourism, and leisure studies. *Journal of Hospitality Marketing & Management, 22*, 875–894.

Stebbins, R. A. (1992). *Amateurs, professionals, and serious leisure*. Montreal, PQ and Kingston, ON: McGill-Queen's University Press.

Stewart, W. P. (1998). Leisure as multiphase experience: Challenging traditions. *Journal of Leisure Research, 30*, 391–400.

Stodolska, M. (2000). Looking beyond the invisible: Can research on leisure of ethnic and racial minorities contribute to leisure theory? *Journal of Leisure Research, 32*, 156–160.

Stodolska, M., Sharaievska, I., Tainsky, S., & Ryan, A. (2014). Minority youth participation in an organized sport program. *Journal of Leisure Research, 46*, 612–634.

Sullivan, D. A. (2001). *Cosmetic surgery: The cutting edge of commercial medicine in America*. New Brunswick, NJ: Rutgers University Press.

Tinsley, H. E. A., & Tinsley, D. J. (1986). A theory of the attributes, benefits, and causes of leisure experience. *Leisure Sciences, 8*, 1–45.

Tseng, V. (2014). Forging common ground: Fostering the conditions for evidence use. *Journal of Leisure Research, 46*, 1–5.

Veblen, T. (1899/1979). *Theory of the leisure class*. New York: Penguin.

Wacker, J. G. (1998). A definition of theory: Research guidelines for different theory-building research methods in operations management. *Journal of Operations Management, 16*, 361–385.

Walker, G. J. (2008). The effects of ethnicity and gender on facilitating intrinsic motivation during leisure with a close friend. *Journal of Leisure Research, 40*, 290–311.

Walker, G. J. (2014). The comprehensive leisure participation framework: Theoretical foundation, cross-cultural variation, and practical implications. In S. Elkington & S. Gammon (Eds.), *Contemporary perspectives in leisure: Meanings, motives, and lifelong learning* (pp. 185–196). London: Routledge.

Walker, G. J., & Liang, H. (2012). An overview of a comprehensive leisure participation framework and its application for cross-cultural leisure research. (Published in Chinese.) *Journal of Zhejiang University (Humanities and Social Sciences), 42*, 22–30.

Walker, G. J., & Virden, R. J. (2005). Constraints on outdoor recreation. In E. L. Jackson (Ed.), *Constraints to leisure* (pp. 201–219). State College, PA: Venture Publishing, Inc.

Wearing, B. (1998). *Leisure and feminist theory*. London, England: Sage.

37
QUALITATIVE INQUIRY IN LEISURE STUDIES

Diane M. Samdahl (University of Georgia)

What is the purpose of research? How can you tell if research is any good? According to Laurel Richardson (2000, p. 254), the answer is simple. Key among the criteria she employs for judging research are the following questions: *Does this piece contribute to my understanding of social life? Does it reveal somebody's reality? Does it affect me?* and *Does it generate new questions?*

Central to what Richardson (2000) is saying is a belief that you—the person reading a research report—have within yourself the ability to judge whether or not research has been effective. And again, you—the person tasked with reporting on research you have undertaken—have the freedom as well as the responsibility to represent what you learned in ways that honor the integrity of the people in your study. These are central tenets in the broad field of qualitative inquiry, a form of research that is philosophically quite different from the more familiar science of numbers and statistics. To understand the deeper implications of those differences, it is useful to step back and examine how leisure has been studied over the past several decades.

HOW HAS LEISURE BEEN STUDIED?

Forget for a moment the ancient philosophers such as Aristotle or even the more recent theorists such as Karl Marx, whose writings provide significant insight into possible relationships between leisure and work. More germane to our purpose are leisure theorists such as Josef Pieper (*Leisure as the Basis of Culture*, 1952), or Sebastian deGrazia (*Of Time, Work, and Leisure*, 1962), or Joffre Dumazedier (*Toward a Society of Leisure*, 1967). These authors, who wrote in the middle of the twentieth century, followed the traditions of their time by producing thoughtful, scholarly discussions about society and the ways that modernization was impacting leisure. Their work referenced both the shifting nature of leisure experience as well as the emerging need for society to provide and manage leisure venues, and they backed up their claims with insightful arguments and reference to external facts. There was no "research" the way we have come to understand that term; instead, there was scholarly integrity. Those books, as well as many more contemporary works,[1] offer rich, thoughtful discussions that, using Richardson's (2000) criteria, provide insight into leisure in our society.

The social sciences changed in the 1970s, as did the study of leisure. There was growing interest in applying the scientific method that worked so well in the hard sciences to new fields such as psychology and sociology. This was driven, in part, by a cultural shift that reified a narrow but influential view of what science should look like, and was aided by the advent of computers that opened the door to statistical analyses. During this period, psychology and sociology fought hard to earn the title of *science* and the associated status that presumably would ensue.

Leisure research as we know it today emerged during this era in the 1970s when the social sciences were striving to emulate the hard sciences. Good thinking like the scholarship of Pieper, de Grazia, and Dumazedier was replaced with positivist research (sometimes called *quantitative research*) framed around data collection and hypothesis testing. University departments that had been called parks and recreation changed their names to leisure studies, and new journals such as the *Journal of Leisure Research* and *Leisure Sciences* were established as public repositories to showcase our research. For the past 40 years, this model of positivist inquiry has dominated North American leisure research.

In England and other European countries, traditional forms of scholarship were not replaced with positivism to the same extent as in the United States (Coalter, 1997, refers

[1] Some newer books of comparable scholarship that have been influential in our field include *The Great Good Place* (Oldenburg, 1999), *Bowling Alone* (Putnam, 2000), and *Last Child in the Woods* (Louv, 2005).

to this as a distinction between leisure *studies* and leisure *sciences*). British leisure studies were much more strongly influenced by Marxism and other macro-theories, giving rise to research questions that were not easily answered through experimental designs and surveys. Canada, which did not have its own doctoral program in leisure studies until the mid-1990s, had a mix of scholars trained in the United States and Britain who produced work in both traditions.

The North American allegiance to positivist research was challenged in the 1990s with the introduction of a new form of scholarship termed *qualitative inquiry*. Qualitative researchers rejected many of the central tenets of positivism including reliance on empirical measurement, and aimed to unveil the rich lived experiences of people rather than provide averages and generalizations. After a brief struggle for acceptance during the 1990s, qualitative inquiry became established in many of the social sciences including leisure studies.

When viewed within this historical framework, positivist leisure research can be seen as a cultural phenomenon that replaced prior forms of scholarship like the work of Pieper (1952), deGrazia (1962), and Dumazedier (1967), and is vulnerable itself to being replaced by alternative forms of inquiry at some point in the future. It is fruitless to argue whether one form of research is inherently better than the other; all forms of inquiry are culturally shaped and historically situated. If the goal of research is to contribute to our understanding of social life, to reveal people's lived experience, and to generate new questions, as Richardson (2000) claimed, we can make our own decisions about the relative merit of positivism and/or qualitative inquiry based on how they impact our understandings of the world.

POSITIVIST TRADITIONS IN LEISURE RESEARCH

It is useful to examine some of the central tenets of positivism in order to understand the ways that qualitative inquiry differs. A researcher working within the positivist framework dissects a phenomenon into distinct variables and attempts to obtain valid empirical measurement of those variables.[2] Positivist inquiry is guided by hypotheses that propose expected relationships between variables, and it tests those hypotheses using statistical analysis. For example, a researcher might use a questionnaire to obtain quantitative data that measure the salience of leisure constraints (see Schneider, Chapter 18). Statistical analysis could compare data from women with children to data from women without children in attempt to document a difference in leisure constraints. A good researcher would also take measurement of additional factors such as the mother's age or the number of children in her family in order to statistically control for those confounding factors, and the findings would presumably generalize in a predictable fashion to a wider group of women beyond those who were in the study.

Central to that research design is a belief that experience can be divided up into distinct variables, and that each variable can be empirically measured independent from the influence of other variables. Statistical analysis demands a belief in the integrity of the numbers, requiring you to assume that empirical measurement does indeed reflect the underlying concepts (plus or minus a little measurement error), and multivariate analysis is based on the belief that you can statistically control for the influence of one variable (e.g., age) while examining the influence of another variable (e.g., number of children). A quick examination of any article using statistical analysis will reveal how the researcher focused on specific variables, took measurement of those variables, and discussed the analysis in relation to prior expectations. Positivist researchers believe that rigorous methods will produce results that confirm, modify, or reject what the researcher had proposed at the onset of the research.

When qualitative inquiry first appeared in fields such as leisure studies, some researchers were drawn to the richer data that interviews produced compared to questionnaires. These researchers willingly gave up quantitative data but found it more difficult to step away from other aspects of the positivist tradition. For example, they asked questions in interviews about specific variables and they examined the transcripts looking for relationships they thought would be there, similar to how a questionnaire asks specific questions and statistical analyses look for relationships in accordance with hypotheses. This type of research is referred to as *post-positivism*, reflecting the inclusion of qualitative data but still shaped by a belief in variables or the search for evidence to validate concepts and relationships that were conceived beforehand.

Two studies can be used to highlight aspects of post-positivist leisure research. In a study examining the patterns of leisure within normal daily routines (Samdahl & Jekubovich, 1993), participants filled out a short questionnaire seven times a day when prompted by a beeper that went off at randomly selected times. The questionnaire asked for factual information (e.g., where they were, who they were with, what were they doing, and whether they would call this *leisure*). In addition, the participants engaged in extended interviews that asked about aspects of their daily routines with a special focus on leisure. While the quantitative data confirmed expectations about common patterns of leisure throughout the day and week (for example, people were more likely to report leisure in the evenings and on weekends), the

---

2 Creswell (2014, Chapter 1) offers a good overview and comparison of quantitative and qualitative research designs.

qualitative data added richness and insight into the effort people put into making those patterns possible. As the interviews revealed, these people intentionally structured their days to make room for leisure and had routines that helped them transition into leisure when they got home from work; one woman even changed her job so her free time would correspond to that of her husband. The authors concluded:

> The [quantitative] data alone gave a rather narrow understanding of daily leisure patterns, conveying a static image that was not dissimilar from leisure as empty free time. The interviews, on the other hand, led to a remarkable understanding of the ways in which people actively direct and control their leisure opportunities. Without the qualitative interviews to complement the [quantitative] research design, much of the dynamic nature of leisure would have been missed. (Samdahl & Jekubovich, 1993, p. 146)

A few years later, Samdahl and Jekubovich (1997) returned to the interviews from the previous study with a specific interest in examining leisure constraints. Since the interviews had been conducted before the leisure constraints model was popularized, the concept and terminology of leisure constraints had not been used in the interviews. Samdahl and Jekubovich thought the transcripts were therefore unbiased; if they were able to find evidence of leisure constraints in interviews that had not specifically asked about that topic, this could substantiate the validity of the leisure constraints model. Indeed, the researchers found excellent examples of intrapersonal, interpersonal, and structural constraints in the ways people talked about leisure. However, the authors' immersion into the transcripts left them feeling that their *a priori* focus on constraints did not produce an effective understanding of factors that were shaping these people's leisure. "Thus, we faced the surprising dilemma of finding strong evidence of what we were looking for while progressively losing confidence in the constraints model as an effective tool for understanding leisure behavior" (p. 441). The researchers set aside their interest in the constraints model and reanalyzed the interviews using constant comparative analysis, an analytical process common in qualitative inquiry.[3] This second analysis produced a very different understanding, emphasizing the importance of social relationships and markedly downplaying anything akin to leisure constraints. In presenting these two analyses side-by-side, the authors pointed out that their initial attempt to look for confirmation of leisure constraints "raised the dangerous possibility of reifying the model while preventing new understandings that could emerge from another paradigmatic perspective" (pp. 446–447). That is, they found what they were looking for but missed something else much more significant.

The first paper discussed above (Samdahl & Jekubovich, 1993) highlights the value of qualitative data when used in conjunction with quantitative data, showing how interviews can complement statistical analysis to produce a richer understanding of the phenomenon under examination. This *mixed methods* research design is typical of post-positivist research and illustrates the compatibility of quantitative and qualitative data within the same study. The second paper (Samdahl & Jekubovich, 1997), however, highlights a more important point: simply working with qualitative data is not enough to escape the influence of positivist traditions. As the authors learned, analyzing the transcripts to look for leisure constraints did little more than confirm their *a priori* thinking and blinded them to other factors that were much more meaningful in people's leisure. Only in the last analysis, where the researchers set aside the constraints model and analyzed the interviews in a more grounded fashion, did the study move away from positivist traditions.

POST-POSITIVISM AND INTERVIEW-BASED RESEARCH IN LEISURE STUDIES

The first researchers to use qualitative methods in leisure studies relied upon interviews and small samples of participants; in that sense their work clearly stepped outside the rules of positivism. However, those researchers designed interview questions that let them examine variables or test hypotheses they had proposed ahead of time, as is characteristic of positivism. Because of that dual influence, this early research is best classified as post-positivist rather than true qualitative inquiry.

One of the earliest interview-based studies was by Henderson and Rannells (1988) who interviewed older farm women and asked them to reflect back on work and leisure throughout their lives. It is unclear whether these women would have used that framework, especially the term *leisure*, if the researchers had not specifically asked about it. Nevertheless, the women's stories raised a challenge to the work-leisure distinction that had been prevalent in the literature. Though it seems mild by today's standards, this article was radical at the time because it violated so many tenets of positivist research (e.g., it used a small sample, there was no accompanying quantitative data, and the authors grounded their claims solely in quotes drawn from the interviews). This article opened the door and

---

[3] See Lichtman (2013, Chapter 12) for an easy-to-read overview of qualitative data analysis techniques.

within a decade interview-based research was common in leisure studies.

The use of interview-based methods was particularly attractive for researchers who studied people and topics outside of the normative mainstream including the leisure of people with disabilities (cf. Bedini & Henderson, 1994; McMeeking & Purkayastha, 1995), leisure and gender (cf. Bialeschki & Pearce, 1997; Shaw, 1985), and ethnic diversity (cf. Allison & Geiger, 1993; Tirone & Shaw, 1997). These researchers felt that interviews could better capture the experiences and concerns of people whose stories were not part of our conventional understandings about leisure.

For all its strengths, this form of interview-based research was not exempt from criticism. One concern, reminiscent of the previous example where researchers found evidence of leisure constraints when they specifically went looking for it, had to do with the ways that qualitative researchers subtly and indirectly influence their findings. Hutchinson (see Hutchinson & Samdahl, 2000) illustrated this with a critique of her own earlier research in which she interviewed women who had sustained brain injuries. Hutchinson came to realize that her role as a recreation therapist had shaped the interview questions she asked as well as the interpretations she gave to the women's responses. In one poignant case involving an immigrant woman who lived within a large extended family, Hutchinson had initially judged the success of rehabilitation by whether this woman could pursue independent leisure activities (the woman failed that standard); only later did Hutchinson understand that interdependence and taking care of her extended family was more valued in this woman's culture than independent leisure pursuits. Humbled by that understanding, Hutchinson cautioned that "analyses, even within qualitative research, are limited and filtered through the lens of the researcher" (p. 247) and she spoke of the importance of "decentering" the researcher's voice of authority when reporting qualitative data.

Many of the techniques used in qualitative research are designed to do just that. Especially during this earlier post-positivist phase, researchers believed that steps to ensure rigor could minimize the subjective influence of the researcher.[4] Qualitative researchers often maintain a field journal where they record and analyze their own thoughts and experiences during the research process. They employ rigorous, systematic procedures for coding and analyzing the interview transcripts[5] and establish advisory panels that serve to challenge or confirm the understandings the researcher is forming. Member checking entails returning to the study participants after the researcher has condensed the interviews into preliminary or final results and asking them if they think the researcher "got it right." These and other techniques contribute to the rigor of qualitative inquiry, especially when rigor is defined in terms of minimizing subjectivity.

Like with positivist research, the end product of interview-based research is a summary that condenses the data into a few succinct points. Quite often, this summary takes the form of themes which the researcher extracted through careful analysis of the data. For example, in Henderson and Rannells (1988) study of rural farm women the researchers discussed five themes they felt captured the essence of what these women said about work and leisure: work was never-ending, child care was a necessary responsibility, work was intermingled with social and community responsibilities, work was valued and enjoyed, and the lack of free time was not a problem.

QUALITATIVE INQUIRY IN LEISURE STUDIES

The acceptance of interview-based research was the first movement towards qualitative inquiry in leisure studies. Qualitative data enriched our understanding of people's leisure but there was increasing concern that interviews, especially one-time interviews, left the researcher too far removed from the experiences that the participants were describing. An *interpretive*[6] framework was becoming increasingly popular, built upon a belief that people engage in their own meaning-making; in order to understand the lived (*emic*) experiences of study participants, researchers had to step back and listen more carefully without imposing their own labels and understandings. In response to this interpretivist stance, research questions were revised to avoid mentioning specific variables or interpretations. For example, the research question '*What leisure constraints do new mothers encounter?*' might be reframed as '*What is the nature of leisure during the first year of motherhood?*' Interviews might start with broad questions such as '*Tell me about your life nowadays*' and move toward more specific questions like '*What, if anything, do you miss since*

---

4 See Lichtman (2013, Chapter 8) for a good discussion of reflexivity and subjectivity in qualitative research.

5 Software such as Atlas and NVivo have been developed to assist with the systematic coding of transcripts and other written data. Unlike software for statistical analyses, each step of data reduction is reliant on judgments and decisions by the researcher.

6 In the 1990s, the term *interpretive research* was used interchangeably with qualitative research. However, more recent research has moved away from interpretivism to embrace other theoretical foundations. Thus, the broader term *qualitative inquiry* is used throughout this chapter and the term *interpretive research* is reserved for studies that have specific qualities of research design. See also Sylvester, Chapter 5.

becoming a mother?' while avoiding the term leisure. This new strategy was designed to prevent the researcher from leading the participant towards specific answers. Interpretive researchers often return for a second or third interview as they probe more deeply in attempt to understand the experiences of the participants.

Because it asked researchers to set aside their *a priori* expectations, interpretive research was clearly located outside the realm of positivism and post-positivism. This was not just a shift in research methods but a significant transformation in epistemological beliefs about what constitutes research.[7] For interpretive researchers, the complexity of lived experience is incompatible with things like independent variables and statistical control, and the purpose of research is not to test or confirm the truth of the researcher's predictions but rather to reveal individual truths as they are perceived and experienced by people in the study. Interpretive research was the first step into the broader realm of qualitative inquiry for leisure studies.

Examples of interpretive leisure research from this era[8] include Loeffler's (2004) study of the meanings of participating in an outdoor adventure program for college students, or Uriely and Belhassen's (2005) study of drug-related tourist experiences. These studies began with an interest in what these experiences were like for the participants; there was no attempt to focus on constructs the researchers identified ahead of time. Both studies employed extensive interviews but supplemented them with other techniques: Loeffler asked participants to take photographs during their adventure program then used those photos to elicit stronger memories and more detailed stories during the interviews. Uriely and Belhassen interviewed people engaged in drug-related tourism but complemented that with extensive field notes while observing drug-related tourist venues. This type of interpretive research remains popular today; for example, interviews were used to understand how leisure helped women who were unable to get pregnant negotiate the pro-baby culture that surrounds them (Parry, 2005), and how Mexican-American youth addressed their fears in crime-laden parks (Stodolska, Shinew, Acevedo, & Roman, 2013). The intent of these studies was to unveil the complexity of leisure as experienced by people, not to test ideas proposed by the researcher.

The epistemological revolution that pulled researchers away from positivism also pulled them away from the social psychological framework that focused attention on individual experience, and qualitative researchers began to examine broader social phenomena. This new work sometimes used interview-based data but its purpose extended beyond revealing lived experience. For example, Glover (2004, Chapter 32) used interviews to study the ways that active engagement in a community center fostered social capital and a sense of citizenship. Likewise, MacDonald, Abbott, and Jenkins (2012) interviewed Indigenous women in Australia about messages intended to promote healthy lifestyles, and came to understand those messages as yet another in a long list of post-colonial actions that undermined native culture. This type of research is not aimed at explicating leisure experience; rather, the researchers drew upon critical theory, feminist theory, and other theories to examine the interplay between individuals and broader society.

One form of qualitative inquiry that is not dependent on interviews is ethnography, a research method designed to capture the normative practices and meanings associated with a cultural place. Ethnography relies on the researcher's prolonged immersion in and associated observations of the people and place under study. For example, Johnson (2005) spent a year researching a country-western gay bar, slowly moving from his initial role as outside observer towards a more integrated position as a trusted patron of the bar. By maintaining the intellectual curiosity of a researcher, Johnson was able to "see" the ways that gay men redefined the heterosexual norms of what it means to be masculine (amplified in the lyrics of the country-western music) while creating their own gendered practices for two-step dancing with male partners. Johnson's focus was not on individual experience but on the larger cultural practices that emerged within the bar, particularly against the backdrop of heteronormative masculinity (see also Johnson, Chapter 25).

The further qualitative inquiry moves away from positivism, the less it looks like research as defined by positivist traditions. Two examples can be used to illustrate this point. Rose and Paisley (2012) offered an analysis of white privilege in experiential education, informed not by interviews but by critical reflection on Rose's own experience as the leader of a three-week outdoor education course for youth. Likewise,

---

[7] See Samdahl (1999) for a discussion of epistemological differences between quantitative and qualitative research in leisure studies. Also note that Henderson (2011) takes issue with the distinctions used here and suggests that interpretive research, indeed most qualitative research in leisure studies, should be classified as post-positivist. That claim has been rejected by the authors of the studies she cited in her article (see the rejoinder by Parry, Johnson, & Stewart, 2013) and is not compatible with the term *post-positivism* as used in this chapter.

[8] Some people might argue that post-positivist interview-based leisure research also fits this label of interpretivist research. The distinction being made here is to emphasize an epistemological shift in the approach to research. Some interview-based research comes closer to this interpretivist goal than others, so applying this label is somewhat subjective.

Pavlidis (2012) examined the ways that women embody and reshape gender norms in roller derby, based not on interviews but on Pavlidis' own immersion in that sport. Neither article included a discussion of methods or a separate section for the presentation of data, yet the participatory involvement of Rose and Pavlidis in their respective activities provided a critical framework for their scholarly examination of these leisure venues. This movement away from the standard template of a research report is, in some respects, reminiscent of earlier forms of scholarship that preceded positivism, when books and manuscripts were grounded in insightful observation and critical reflection rather than a discussion of methods and data.

There is another important point to make here. Traditional positivist research establishes rigor by attempting to remove subjectivity (which is termed *bias*) so the data reveal objective facts. Post-positivist research still holds to this standard of objectivity, though it is often discussed as *trustworthiness*; the techniques for working with qualitative data are employed with this goal in mind. There is a growing belief, however, that qualitative researchers *cannot* step away from their subjectivity. This is central to an emerging form of qualitative inquiry termed *post-intentional phenomenology* (Vagle, 2010) which asks researchers to consciously examine how they are intertwined with the research they are conducting. We see this in a study of mothers of young children (Soule, 2013) where the researcher, who is a mother herself, had a colleague interview *her* several times throughout the study using the same interview guides she was using with her participants. Those interviews served to remind Soule of her own experiences and opinions in relation to motherhood, and offered a way to unpack those feelings so that she understood them in relation to her interactions with the participants and with the data.

This acknowledgement of subjectivity and the associated understanding that the qualitative researcher is an active participant in the research process raises one final important point. Some believe there is an arrogance in the positivist stance that the purpose of research is for *us* to learn about *them*. Much has been said about establishing a collaborative attitude that acknowledges research participants as stakeholders in the research and engaging in research that benefits those who are studied (cf. Arai & Pedlar, 2003; Fox, 2006; Pedlar, 1995). However, there is less discussion about the ways the *researcher* is impacted by the research process. In an eloquent examination of this, Lashua and Fox (2006) reflected on the need to become better listeners when studying across a cultural and ethnic divide. Their study involved a recreation center where Aboriginal young people composed rap music; at the end of the project the researchers realized it had "engaged, changed, and challenged [us] to rethink our understandings of leisure and ourselves as leisure scholar-practitioners" (p. 267). They said:

> As practitioners, we often come to provide a "positive experience" for "youth-at-risk." . . . Not only are most urban Aboriginal youth uninterested in [the new downtown recreation centre], these areas do not even begin to support and play with [the youths'] hip-hop world and struggles. In our efforts to better listen to and understand the voices and experiences of young people, we realize that there is much (leisure) work yet to be done. (pp. 280–281)

These researchers remind us of the lessons we might learn once we honor the reality of our study participants (see also Fox, Chapter 27).

DATA REPRESENTATION IN QUALITATIVE INQUIRY

It is important to discuss the ways that data are shared in qualitative research. The traditional positivist researcher "reports" data, trying hard to make sure that tables and analyses are as factual as possible. Post-positivist researchers typically follow this lead, presenting quotes instead of numbers but writing *about* the study participants and using quotes to provide solid documentation for what the researcher is saying. Qualitative researchers, on the other hand, acknowledge their role in selecting and shaping messages drawn from their data. In an effort to highlight the subjective nature of this, qualitative researchers speak about *representing* the data rather than reporting the data.

They also try to foster understandings that come from the participants themselves rather than filtering everything through the voice of the researcher. This desire to *show* rather than to *tell* (Richardson, 1994) is central to qualitative inquiry and has led to a variety of creative practices for data representation (see Parry & Johnson, 2007, for a discussion of this in relation to leisure research). The goal in creative data representation is to make the data come alive and to engage the reader (or listener/observer for non-written reports) in the stories of the participants. This is based in a belief that data representation should not be abstract and theoretical but rather rich in detail in order to parallel the lived experience.

One form of creative analytic practice is to create a *data poem*. Data poems are a compilation of passages extracted from the data that convey important themes. Though the researcher selects specific quotes and arranges them with intentional order, the end result is a poem that allows the participants to speak directly to the reader. Yuen, Arai, and Fortune (2012) used data poems in a study of women in prison. One theme from their analysis was how these women felt about being released back into the community, and they captured that theme in this stanza (p. 288):

I prefer to stay here
I just feel more secure
I don't know what I'm stepping into
I see people walking out of this place crying
Terrified

Each line in the poem was spoken by a woman in the study; pulling the quotes together in this fashion gave emphasis to the women's fears about transitioning out of prison at the end of their terms.

Another form of creative analytic practice is to compose narrative vignettes. Similar to data poems, the researcher first performs a systematic analysis and then constructs stories from the transcripts and field notes that convey specific aspects of that analysis. Johnson (2005) used narrative vignettes when reporting his ethnography of a gay bar, developing stories that provide rich detail so the reader could see the actions and behaviors that illustrated each point in his analysis. Mair (2009) also employed this method in her ethnography of rural Canadian curling clubs, presenting a data-based story that highlighted the ways a curling club fostered shared community leisure. In both cases, the narrative vignettes were drawn from a composite of notes and interviews extending across different days and locales; the stories were data-based but not descriptive of a singular, actual event. In spite of the creativity behind this form of data representation, they differ from true fiction by the rigorous process of observation and analysis upon which the stories are based.

Narrative stories and vignettes can engage the reader in a more effective manner than simple quotes. However, stories themselves are often one-dimensional while the reality of lived experience is a simultaneous mix of confounding feelings and contradictory messages. In attempt to capture this multidimensional aspect of experience, Berbary (2012) used data from her study of sororities to create theatrical scripts that read like a screenplay, with multiple actors on stage at the same time. By intentionally crafting the players to represent different themes from her analysis, Berbary was able to convey the messiness and confusion that sorority women feel when faced with conflicting messages about how to act "ladylike" at a party.

Contemporary qualitative inquiry promotes other forms of data representation beyond the written word. In a study of musicians' experiences writing music, Kumm (2013) used his participant-data to compose a song that illuminated the phenomenon of song writing. In another study, Soule (2013) represented the experiences of new mothers within an elaborate metaphor of gestation, juxtaposing the themes from her analysis upon an artistic rendition of the womb to graphically convey the organic, interconnected factors that contribute to the experience of motherhood.

EFFECTIVE USES FOR QUALITATIVE INQUIRY

As discussed above, qualitative inquiry differs in many ways from quantitative research both in design as well as intent. It is important to remember that research methodologies are simply tools that help us understand the world around us. The trick, therefore, is to match the tool with the task at hand.

In many aspects of leisure service delivery, traditional quantitative research methods are advantageous. We live in a culture where numbers and statistical analyses lend legitimacy to things. Program evaluations, for example, are often most useful when based on numerical counts and quantified assessments. Likewise, agencies that control budgets or provide grants often expect quantitative reports to document need and impact. It is important for everyone in leisure service delivery to have a basic understanding of quantitative research techniques.

The unique niche for qualitative inquiry arises when our interest is in people's experiences, especially people who have been overlooked in mainstream theorizing or programming. We saw this in Parry's (2005) study of women who are attempting to get pregnant, and in Yuen et al.'s (2012) study of women in prison. In addition, qualitative inquiry is often better for examining complex cultural phenomena such as Johnson's (2005) study of a gay bar or Lashua and Fox's (2006) reflections on the ways Aboriginal youth challenge traditional leisure theory and practice. In addition, the focus on reflection and subjectivity that is central to qualitative inquiry has raised awareness among all researchers of the need to be open to new understandings that might emerge when researchers truly listen to their participants.

CONCLUSION

This discussion has attempted to provide an introduction to qualitative inquiry in leisure studies. Obviously, there are additional examples and more complex issues than what has been presented here. But it is important to understand that traditional research as we have come to know it, with quantitative measurement and statistics, is a fairly recent phenomenon, and the emergence of qualitative inquiry is just the newest step in the evolving nature of scholarship.

When focusing our attention on the binary created by quantitative and qualitative research, as this chapter has done, we tend to overlook other forms of scholarship that are pertinent to our field. For example, Mowatt (2012) examined recreational spectatorship at lynchings in the U.S. during the late nineteenth and early twentieth century; this historical, archive-based study does not fit the classification of qualitative research. Neither do many of the scholarly discussions embedded in Marxism, feminism, post-colonialism, cultural studies, and other theoretical frameworks that examine the entanglement of leisure with broader cultural processes (see also Blackshaw, Chapter 7; and Walker, Kono, and Dieser, Chapter 36). When the social sciences adopted positivism in the 1970s, they redefined scholarship as a narrow form of research that required data collection and analysis. Today, contemporary forms of qualitative inquiry are helping us reject that limited view to again define scholarship as critical and insightful thinking.

As the line between research and scholarship becomes blurred, our research might become more interesting to people outside of the academic environment. When researchers are present in their writing rather than removed as an abstract voice of authority, their articles will become more engaging. Imagine a future where data-based fiction is marketed through bookstores, sold as popular bestsellers rather than published in academic journals. Will art and music take the stage alongside peer-reviewed manuscripts as alternative ways to understand and explain experience? As we break away from traditional forms of research, will we become more curious about venues like hip-hop and ethnic foods and *mercados* and churches where people pursue the holistic joy we call leisure? Qualitative inquiry is simply opening the door to possibility.

And if you fear this expansion will move us too far from the "truthfulness" of research, be reminded of Richardson's (2000) criteria: *Does it contribute to my understanding of social life? Does it reveal somebody's reality? Does it affect me?* and *Does it generate new questions?* If so, it has served its purpose.

REFERENCES

Allison, M. T., & Geiger, C. W. (1993). Nature of leisure activities among the Chinese-American elderly. *Leisure Sciences, 15*, 309–319.

Arai, S., & Pedlar, A. (2003). Moving beyond individualism in leisure theory: A critical analysis of concepts of community and social engagement. *Leisure Studies, 22*, 185–202.

Bedini, L. A., & Henderson, K. A. (1994). Women with disabilities and the challenges to leisure service providers. *Journal of Park & Recreation Administration, 12*, 17–34.

Berbary, L. A. (2012). "Don't be a whore, that's not ladylike": Discursive discipline and sorority women's gendered subjectivity. *Qualitative Inquiry, 18*, 606–625.

Bialeschki, M. D., & Pearce, K. D. (1997). 'I don't want a lifestyle—I want a life": The effect of role negotiations on the leisure of lesbian mothers. *Journal of Leisure Research, 29*, 113–131.

Coalter, F. (1997). Leisure sciences and leisure studies: Different concept, same crisis? *Leisure Sciences, 19*, 255–268.

Creswell, J. W. (2014). *Research design: Quantitative, qualitative, and mixed methods approaches*. Thousand Oaks, CA: Sage.

de Grazia, S. (1962). *Of time, work, and leisure*. Garden City, NJ: Anchor Books.

Dumazedier, J. (1967). *Toward a society of leisure*. New York: The Free Press.

Fox, K. (2006). Leisure and indigenous peoples. *Leisure Studies, 25*, 403–409.

Glover, T. D. (2004). The 'community' center and the social construction of citizenship. *Leisure Sciences, 26*, 63–83.

Henderson, K. A. (2011). Post-positivism and the pragmatics of leisure research. *Leisure Sciences, 33*, 341–346.

Henderson, K. A., & Rannells, J. S. (1988). Farm women and the meaning of work and leisure: An oral history perspective. *Leisure Sciences, 10*, 41–50.

Hutchinson, S. L., & Samdahl, D. M. (2000). Reflections on the "voice of authority" in leisure research and practice. *Loisir et Société/Society and Leisure, 23*, 236–250.

Johnson, C. W. (2005). "The first step is the two-step": Hegemonic masculinity and dancing in a country-western gay bar. *International Journal of Qualitative Studies in Education, 18*, 445–464.

Kumm, B. (2013). Finding healing through songwriting: A song for Nicolette. *International Journal of Community Music, 2*, 205–217.

Lashua, B. D., & Fox, K. M. (2006). Rec needs a new rhythm cuz rap is where we're livin'. *Leisure Sciences, 28*(3), 267–283.

Lichtman, M. (2013). *Qualitative research in education: A user's guide*. Thousand Oaks, CA: Sage.

Loeffler, T. A. (2004). A photo elicitation study of the meanings of outdoor adventure experiences. *Journal of Leisure Research, 36*, 536–556.

Louv, R. (2005). *Last child in the woods: Saving our children from nature deficit disorder*. Chapel Hill, NC: Algonquin Books of Chapel Hill.

MacDonald, D., Abbott, R., & Jenkins, D. (2012). Physical activity of remote indigenous Australian women: A postcolonial analysis of lifestyle. *Leisure Sciences, 34*, 39–54.

Mair, H. (2009). Club live: Third place and shared leisure in rural Canada. *Leisure Sciences, 31*, 450–465.

McMeeking, D., & Purkayastha, B. (1995). "I can't have my mom running me everywhere": Adolescents, leisure, and accessibility. *Journal of Leisure Research, 27*, 360–378.

Mowatt, R. A. (2012). Lynching as leisure: Broadening notions of a field. *American Behavioral Scientist, 56*, 1361–1387.

Oldenburg, R. (1999). *The great good place: Cafes, coffee shops, bookstores, bars, hair salons, and other hangouts at the heart of a community* (3rd ed.). New York: Marlowe & Co.

Parry, D. C. (2005). Women's leisure as resistance to pronatalist ideology. *Journal of Leisure Research, 37*, 133–151.

Parry, D. C., & Johnson, C. W. (2007). Contextualizing leisure research to encompass complexity in lived leisure experience: The need for creative analytic practice. *Leisure Sciences, 29*, 119–130.

Parry, D. C., Johnson, C. W., & Stewart, W. (2013). Leisure research for social justice: A response to Henderson. *Leisure Sciences, 35*, 81–87.

Pavlidis, A. (2012). From riot grrrls to roller derby? Exploring the relations between gender, music, and sport. *Leisure Studies, 31*, 165–176.

Pedlar, A. (1995). Relevance and action research in leisure. *Leisure Sciences, 17*, 133–14.

Pieper, J. (1952). *Leisure: The basis of culture*. Translated by A. Dru. New York: Pantheon.

Putnam, R. D. (2000). *Bowling alone: The collapse and revival of American community*. New York: Simon & Schuster.

Richardson, L. (1994). Writing: A method of inquiry. In N. Denzin & Y. Lincoln, *Handbook of Qualitative Research* (1st ed.). Thousand Oaks, CA: Sage.

Richardson, L. (2000). Evaluating ethnography. *Qualitative Inquiry*, 6, 253–255.

Rose, J., & Paisley, K. (2012). White privilege in experiential education: A critical reflection. *Leisure Sciences, 34*, 136–154.

Samdahl, D. M. (1999). Epistemological and methodological issues in leisure research. In E. L. Jackson & T. Burton (Eds.), *Leisure studies at the millennium* (pp. 119–133). State College, PA: Venture Publishing, Inc.

Samdahl, D. M., & Jekubovich, N. J. (1993). Patterns and characteristics of adult daily leisure. *Society and Leisure, 16*, 129–149.

Samdahl, D. M., & Jekubovich, N. J. (1997). A critique of leisure constraints: Comparative analyses and understandings. *Journal of Leisure Research, 29*, 430–452.

Shaw, S. M. (1985). The meaning of leisure in everyday life. *Leisure Sciences, 7*, 1–24.

Soule, K. E. (2013). *Connected: A phenomenology of attachment parenting*. Unpublished dissertation, University of Georgia. Retrieved from http://dbs.galib.uga.edu/cgi-bin/getd.erverno=15&instcode=uga1&query=id:uga_soule_katherine_e_201308_phd

Stodolska, M., Shinew, K., Acevedo, J. C., & Roman, C. G. (2013). "I was born in the hood": Fear of crime, outdoor recreation and physical activity among Mexican-American urban adolescents. *Leisure Sciences, 35*, 1–15.

Tirone, S. C., & Shaw, S. M. (1997). At the center of their lives: Indo-Canadian women, their families and leisure. *Journal of Leisure Research, 29*, 225–234.

Uriely, N., & Belhassen, Y. (2005). Drugs and tourists' experiences. *Journal of Travel Research, 43*, 238–246.

Vagle, M. D. (2010). Re-framing Schön's call for a phenomenology of practice: A post-intentional approach. *Reflective Practice, 11*, 393–407.

Yuen, F., Arai, S., & Fortune, D. (2012). Community (dis) connection through leisure for women in prison. *Leisure Sciences, 34*, 281–297.

38
Experimental Designs in Leisure Studies

Gary Ellis (Texas A&M University), KangJae Jerry Lee (University of Missouri), andThitikan Satchabut (University of the Thai Chamber of Commerce, Thailand)

This book is intended to "be daring and speculative" about the future of leisure studies. In that spirit, we argue that the time has arrived for emergence of distinct strands of focused inquiry in leisure research that are based on experimental designs. Although experimental designs are acknowledged to be the most effective behavioral science research method for confirming cause and effect relationships, those methods have not been widely used by leisure scholars. The goal of this chapter is to evaluate current use of experimental designs in leisure research and describe how those designs can expand our knowledge about leisure and recreation.

We begin with a brief "refresher" on science and experimental designs and illustrate distinctive characteristics of experimental designs. In the next section, we provide a summary of contemporary practice in use of experimental designs in leisure studies. We have classified research designs of all studies published in *Journal of Leisure* Research and *Leisure Sciences* from 2008 to 2012. Finally, we provide two examples of how experimental designs might be used to investigate two different topics in leisure studies.

SCIENCE AND RESEARCH DESIGN REFRESHER

The central position of experimental design in behavioral science research is summarized exceptionally well by Maxwell and Delaney (2004, p. 3) in their innovative and influential text, *Designing Experiments and Analyzing Data*:

> The perspective on science that emerged in the West around 1600 and that profoundly shaped and defined the modern era (Whitehead, 1932) can be identified in terms of its methodology; empirical observation and, whenever possible, experimentation. The essence of experimentation, as Shadish, Cook, and Campbell (2002) note, is an attempt "to discover the effects of presumed causes." It is because of their contribution to the understanding of causal processes that experiments play such a central role in science. As Schmidt (1992) suggests "The major task in any science is the development of theory . . . Theories are causal explanations. The goal in every science is explanation, and explanation is always causal" (p. 1177).

"Causal" is the key word in this passage. Science addresses whether and how specific, well-defined actions affect (cause) specific, well-defined potential outcomes. Experimental designs increase confidence in causal relations because they use protocols that follow from the nature of cause and effect. At a very fundamental level, to conduct an experiment, an investigator changes something and then observes whether something else changes. That which the investigator changes in an experiment is called an "independent variable" and the expected outcome of that change is called the "dependent variable."

Understanding of independent and dependent variables can be achieved by considering a very simple experiment. We might study the effect of the position of a wall switch ("on" or "off") on the degree of illumination emitted from a functional light bulb that is on the same electrical circuit as the switch. If the experimenter changes the switch from the "off" position to the "on" position, we observe greater illumination of the bulb than if we move the switch to the "off" position. In order for the position of a light switch (condition A) to be a cause of the change on illumination level emitted from a bulb on the circuit (condition B), four conditions must be present (Bernard, 2011):

1. "Condition A" must precede "Condition B" in time.
2. "Condition B" must consistently change after "Condition A" changes.

3. Rival (other, perhaps unknown) causes must not intervene.
4. A reasonable explanation (or theory) for Condition A being a causal agent with respect to Condition B must exist. (For more on theory, see Walker, Kono, & Dieser, Chapter 36.) The protocol for the wall switch experiment illustrates attention to these conditions. Illumination from the bulb must not precede the changing of the position of the switch from "off" to "on." The bulb must illuminate following positioning the switch to "on," and electrical current must be flowing through the circuit when the switch is positioned to "on" (absence of sufficient current is an example of a rival cause). The illumination of the bulb can also be explained through knowledge about electricity and heated gases and the like.

"*If, then*" statements can be helpful in further solidifying our understanding connections between causes and effects (i.e., independent and dependent variables). *If* the switch is moved to the "on" position (change in the independent variable), *then* we observe greater illumination (change in the dependent variable).

"If, then" knowledge about leisure has potential to improve the lives of individuals, the cohesiveness of families, the quality of communities, and the success of professionals in parks, recreation, tourism and related professions. Park and recreation professionals, for example, might ask, *If* we build a park with a swimming pool and athletic fields instead of a trail system and a design that highlights natural features, *then* will adjacent property values increase? *If* we stage youth sport programs in ways that reflect prosocial behavior theory, *then* will increased commitment to physical activity and sportsmanship among participants result? Virtually anyone may learn of ways of making her or his life more meaningful and fulfilling through knowledge about leisure behavior-related "if's and then's."

A specific description of a possible leisure studies experiment may be helpful in understanding experimental designs. Imagine an experiment conducted to test the hypothesis that frequency of participation in a certain form of recreation increases subjective quality of life among middle-aged adults. In "if, then" terms, the study would be designed to test the question, if middle-aged adults participate in the specified form of recreation, then will subjective quality of life increase? To conduct this experiment, the researcher might recruit a random sample of middle-aged adults from a defined and accessible population. The researcher could then randomly assign each of these research participants to two (or more) groups. One of these would be a treatment group. Individuals assigned to that group would participate in the recreation activity that is assumed to increase quality of life. Other research participants would be assigned to one or more comparison groups. Those individuals would participate in an activity other than that which the theory suggests will elevate quality of life.

To proceed with a two-group version of this experiment, the researcher would engage participants in the treatment group in the activity, and would ensure that participants in the no-treatment group (sometimes called a "control" group) do not participate in that activity. At the end of the period of recreation participation, all participants in both groups would complete a questionnaire measuring their subjective quality of life. Scores on the subjective quality of life measure could be averaged and these means could be compared across the groups. Statistical analyses could be used to test the hypothesis that the treatment (participation) group will have a higher average score on subjective quality of life than the no-treatment group. If participation does elevate quality of life, the scores of participants in the "treatment" group will, on the whole, be higher than those of the no-treatment group. The mean of the groups prior to the study was assumed to be equal, because all participants were randomly selected from a defined, larger group (a "population").

If the average subjective quality of life score of the "treatment" group is substantially greater than that of the "no-treatment" group, and the difference is "statistically significant," our experiment has yielded good reason to believe that, consistent with our theory, frequency of participation causes a change in subjective well-being. Hypothetical results of this experiment appear in Figure 38.1. Consistent with our hypotheses, the mean of the treatment group is (almost two units) higher than the mean of the control group. The form of recreation investigated does seem to increase quality of life of middle-aged adults.

Note that our experiment modeled all of the necessary conditions of cause and effect. Participation in recreation preceded improvement in quality of life, quality of life changed after participation changed in the treatment group, and, due to random selection and random assignment, rival causes (causes not accounted for in the experiment) are unlikely. A reasonable theory guided our investigation, and our theory was supported by our empirical data.

Despite their utility in uncovering causes and effects, experimental designs are not widely used in leisure studies. Much more common are "correlational designs." In a correlational study, researchers do not assign participants to treatment conditions, but rather take "snapshots" of conditions at given points in time, and compare participants who have had different exposure to the independent variables. Surveys are a popular form of correlational study. We might, for example, use a web-based survey to study of the relation between frequency of participation in rec-

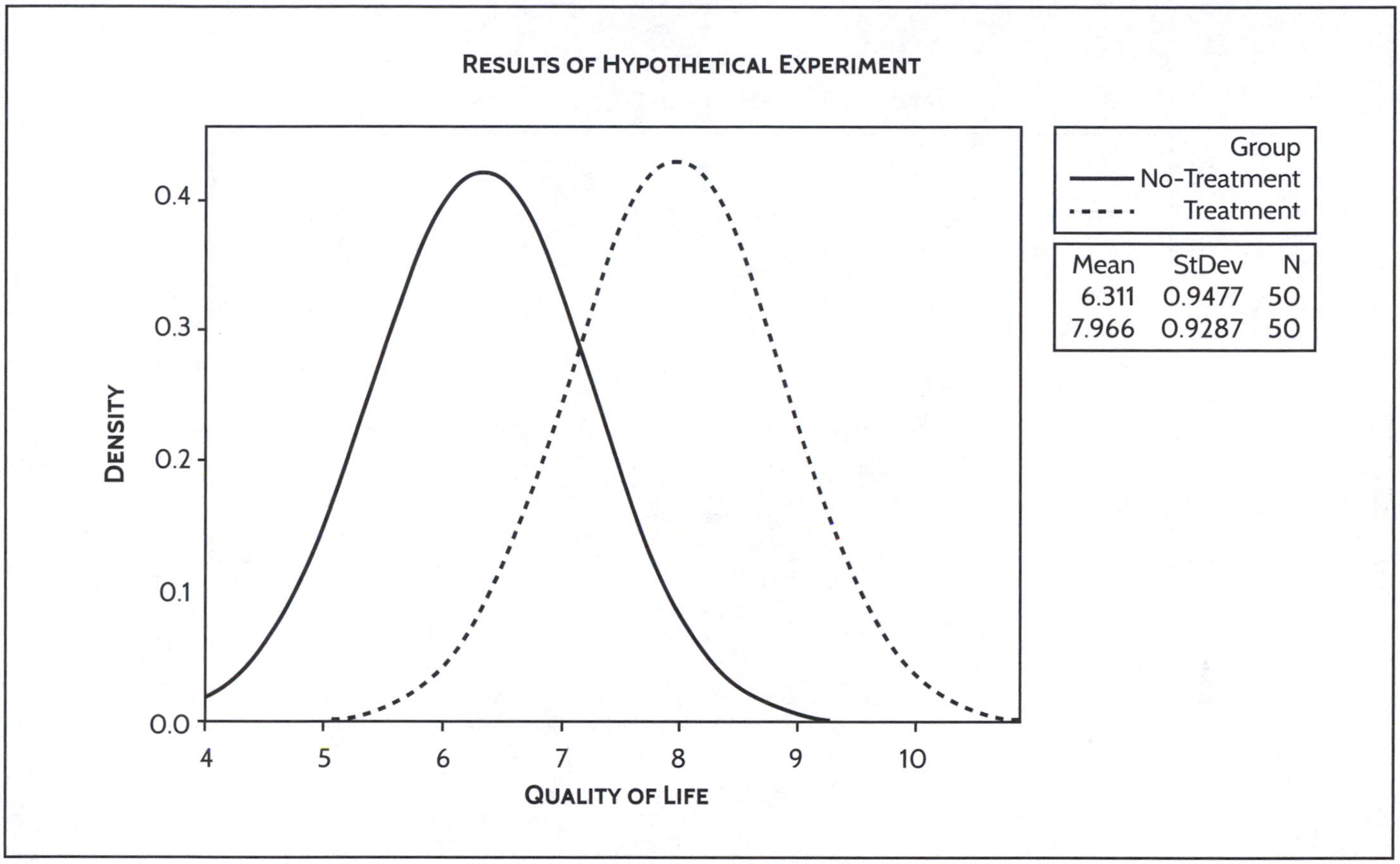

Figure 38.1. Results of Hypothetical Experiment

reation and subjective well-being of middle-aged adults, as described above.

To conduct such a study, the researcher might distribute a web-based questionnaire to a representative sample of our defined population of middle-aged adults. People who received the questionnaire would open the questionnaire from their computers, respond to questions about the frequency of their participation in the recreation behavior of interest, and respond to a second set of questions about their subjective well-being. They would then tap the "enter" key on their computer, and their responses would be sent to the researcher for analysis. Thus, the "snapshot" of each research participant's status on the independent variable (recreation participation) and dependent variable (subjective well-being) would have been taken.

After collecting these snapshots of status with respect to frequency of participation and subjective well-being from a number of participants, the researcher could assemble the data into graphs and calculate statistics to evaluate the statistical significance and strength of relation between the two variables (i.e., frequency of participation and subjective well-being). A scatterplot like Figure 38.2 might be part of this analysis. Each point in the plot is a snapshot of an individual survey respondent showing her or his frequency of participation and subjective quality of life. One respondent, for example, reported participating in the recreation activity one day per week, and that person also scored "70" on the measure of subjective well-being. Note that people who reported more frequent participation in the activity of interest also tended to report greater well-being. As participation increases across people, well-being increases. Based on this result, both of the following hypotheses seem to be reasonable and both are consistent with the data:

- Physical recreation participation yields improved physical well-being
- Subjective well-being yields more frequent participation in recreation.

Thus, the researcher might conclude that the data show that subjective well-being is *associated with* recreation participation among middle-aged adults. Use of the phrase, "is associated with" is pivotal in the previous sentence. Although the researcher's interest is discovering whether recreation behavior *causes* increase in subjective well-being, with a correlational study, we do not have sufficient evidence to warrant this causal relationship. Unlike experiments, correlational studies do not model the critical "time" element that is essential to determining cause. The independent variable does not precede the dependent variable in time. The data were collected as snapshots in time, precluding the opportunity to craft a condition in which the presumed cause (recreation participation) preceded the presumed effect (subjective well-being) in time. Moreover, unlike an experiment, no

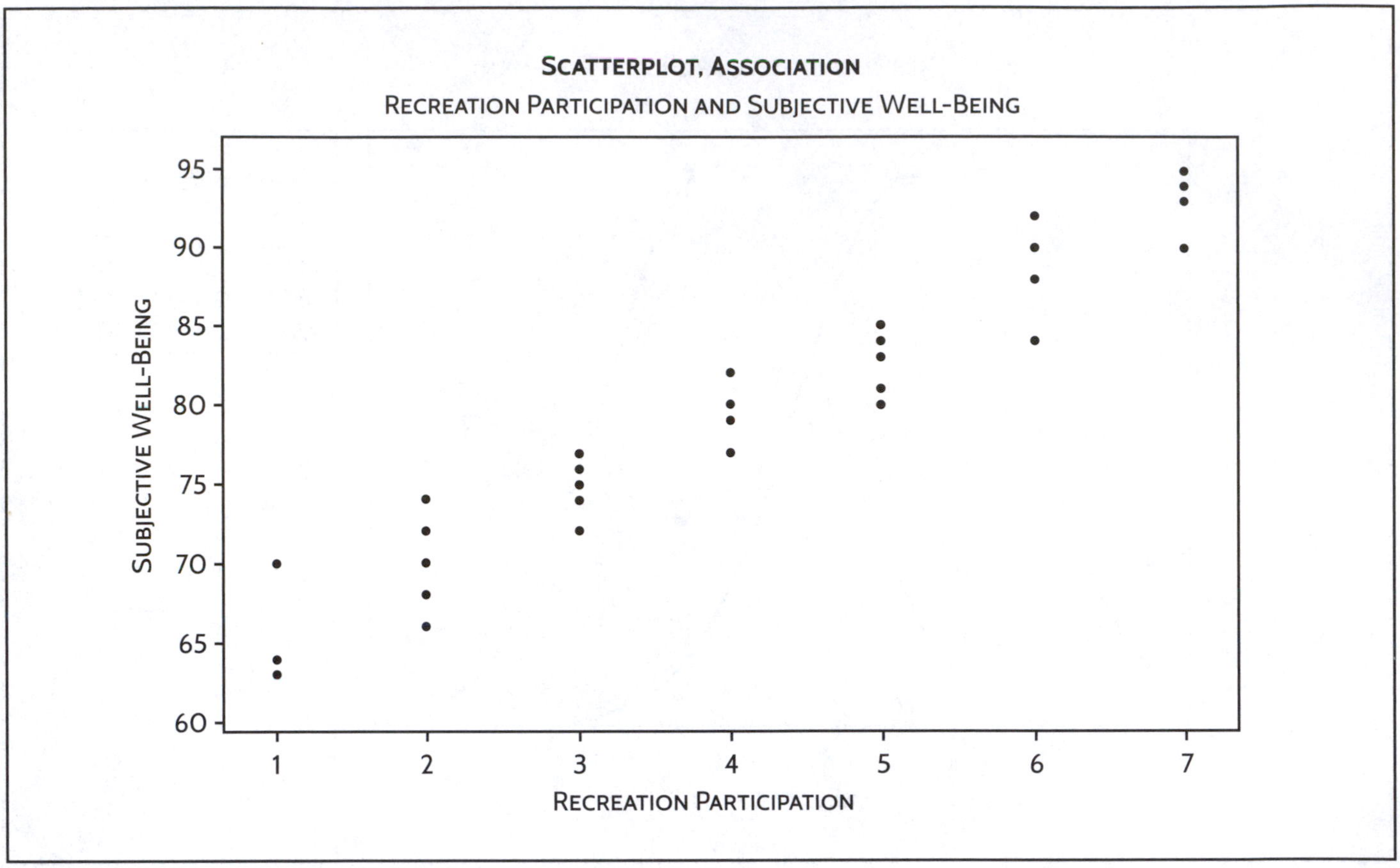

Figure 38.2. Scatterplot of Hypothetical Study

"treatment" occurred in this correlational study. Recreation participation (the independent variable) was assumed to have occurred before the participants received the questionnaire. Some individuals reported having a more extensive history of participation than others. Furthermore, any change in subjective well-being (dependent variable) is also assumed to have occurred prior to the research participants receiving the questionnaires. We have no way of knowing whether or not recreation participation measured in the correlational snapshots is indeed a cause of the well-being of subjects. Thus, in survey research, despite often compelling assumptions about what-causes-what, we really do not know with certainty. To gain a complete picture of the causal relationship between frequency of recreation participation and subjective well-being, we need to conduct experimental research.

TYPES OF EXPERIMENTAL DESIGNS

The experimental design described in the previous section is among the most simple of a vast array of possible experimental designs. Experimental designs can become enormously complex. Most designs involve examination of more than one "presumed cause" (independent variable). These are ordinarily called "factorial designs," signaling that the design includes many independent variables, or factors. Sometimes the design includes all possible combinations of effects of these variables (fully crossed designs) and in other designs only certain combinations of treatment conditions are present (nested effects designs). Independent variables may be "fixed effects" variables or "random effects" variables, depending on whether the levels (categories, attributes) used in the study comprise an entire population of levels that are of interest or if those levels are thought of as being a random sample of a larger population of levels. Some experiments compare effects of independent variables on different groups while others examine how the same people (or other experimental units) respond to different treatment conditions. The former of these are often referred to as between-groups designs, and the latter are within-subjects or repeated measures designs. Multiple dependent variables may be included, resulting in "multivariate designs." The effects of select confounding variables may be controlled through "blocking" designs, and such variables may be controlled statistically through "analysis of covariance" designs. In brief, despite the relatively clear mission of studying the effects of presumed causes (a deceptively complex endeavor in itself), the practice of experimental design is enormously complex. A number of behavioral science research texts provide excellent introductions to experimental design (e.g., Bernard, 2011; Kerlinger & Lee, 2000). More advanced topics are covered in a broad range of books as well (e.g., Kirk, 2013; Maxwell & Delaney, 2004; Myers Well, & Lorch, 2010).

THE STATUS OF EXPERIMENTAL DESIGNS IN LEISURE RESEARCH

If cause and effect is important to science, and the "if, then" knowledge that science reveals is important to people, professionals and society, one would expect widespread use in leisure studies. Is that in fact the case? We reviewed all research methods used by scientists who published in *Journal of Leisure Research* (JLR) and *Leisure Sciences* (LS) from the year of 2008 to 2012. Two journals were selected because of their prominent reputation as leading leisure studies journals. We initially identified 154 articles from JLR, yet we excluded 15 papers from the third issue of volume 41 (2009) devoted to celebrating the journal's fortieth anniversary. To balance the quantity and time period of the two journals, we supplemented six articles from the first issue of 2013. We then excluded 14 articles that are calls for papers, introduction to the special issues, and book reviews. For LS, we identified 153 published articles. Six articles used for either call for papers or introduction to the special issue were excluded from the review. We ultimately evaluated 278 articles from two journals: 131 from JLR and 147 from LS.

We classified those 278 articles into five categories based on their research design: experimental, correlational, contextual, mixed methods, and conceptual/theoretical. Contextual research is inquiry into the "lived experiences" of individuals. Data in these studies are narrative accounts in the form of words, images, gestures, sounds or other information. Mixed methods are those studies that use both correlational and contextual designs. Conceptual/theoretical contributions do not involve data collection and analysis. These papers are based on literature integration and critique.

Figure 38.3 provides the summary of the results of our methodological review. Only two studies (0.7%) used experimental designs. Each journal published one experimental study during the past five years. In contrast, 142 (51%) were correlational studies and 82 (29%) were contextual studies. Ten papers used mixed methods. Forty-two papers were conceptual/theoretical articles. Clearly, leisure research has been built on correlational and contextual methods.

Knowledge about leisure and recreation can grow significantly through experimental research. In the following sections, we provide two specific examples. Both examples illustrate how experimental designs can be used to study topics that have previously been investigated through correlational research.

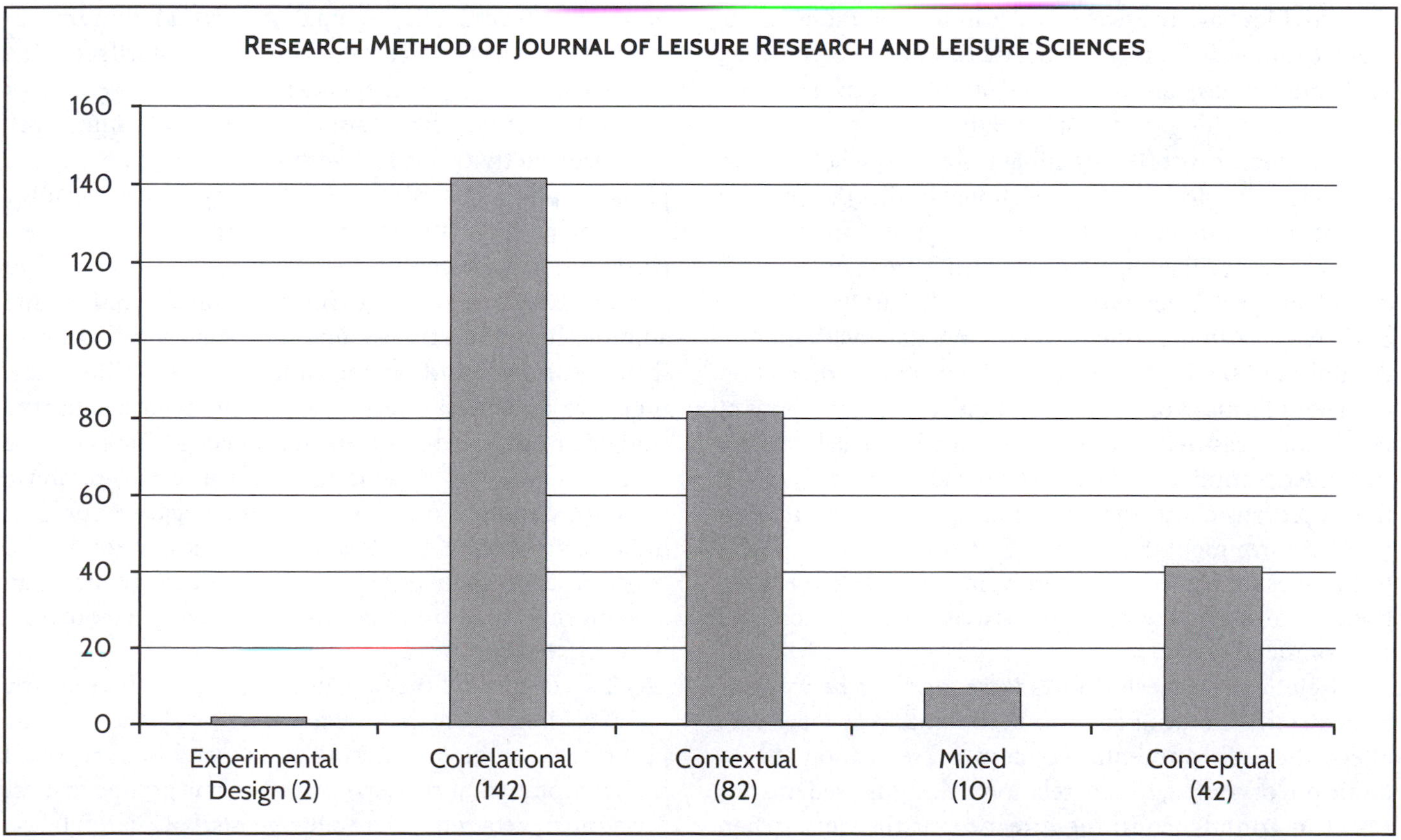

Figure 38.3. Methodological Review on Journal of Leisure Research and Leisure Sciences Published from 2008 to 2012

APPLICATION 1: DOES OUTDOOR RECREATION PARTICIPATION ENHANCE ENVIRONMENTAL CONCERN?

Thitikan Satchabut's (2013) dissertation research was motivated by her passion for the environment. Like increasing numbers of the world's citizens, she found habitat destruction, species extinction, global warming, climate change, and unsustainable development to be troubling. She reasoned that development of environmental concern among citizens, particularly those destined for leadership positions, could be an important step toward resolving those issues. "How," she wondered, "can parks and recreation serve to elevate people's environmental concern?"

Review of literature led her to discover two hypotheses about environmental concern and recreation. Based on "Mere Exposure Theory," Dunlap and Heffernan (1975) hypothesized that outdoor recreation serves to enhance participants' concern for the environment. They reasoned that participation exposes recreationists to "instances of environmental degradation" (p. 18) and thereby "cultivates an esthetic taste" for the natural environment" (p. 18). Dunlap and Heffernan also advanced a second hypothesis, asserting that outdoor recreation activities that are "appreciative" in nature produce greater environmental concern than activities that are "consumptive." Appreciative activities are those that have minimal impact on the environment. In contrast, consumptive activities have relatively greater impact on the environment. Examples of appreciative activities are hiking, birding, and nature photography. Examples of consumptive activities are hunting, fishing, and motor boating.

Consistent with the dominant practice, scholars have conducted descriptive and correlational studies that provide insight into Dunlap and Heffernan's hypotheses (Geisler, Martinson, & Wilkening, 1977; Jackson, 1986; Nord, Lulloff, & Bridger, 1998; Peterson, Hull, Mertig, & Liu, 2008; Pinhey & Michael, 1979; Theordori, Luloff, & Willits, 1998; Van Liere & Dunlap, 1981). The frequency and intensity of participation in various forms of outdoor recreation of different groups of people was measured, along with their environmental concern. In some descriptive studies, participants were simply asked their opinions about the effect their participation had on their environmental concern. Statistical and graphical techniques similar to the scatterplot in Figure 38.2 have been used to measure the relation between participation and environmental concern.

Relations in these studies were found to be weak or nonexistent. Outdoor recreation did not, in fact, seem to affect the environmental concern of recreationists. In addition, of course, the correlational designs used did not result in confidence in the direction of the cause when relations were found to be present. Does outdoor recreation affect environmental concern or do individuals with higher levels of environmental concern tend to participate in specific forms of recreation? The correlational designs used in these studies did not provide support for either of these equally reasonable explanations.

Satchabut (2013) designed an experiment to compensate for the limitations of the correlational studies. She recruited 240 participants. Each participant was randomly assigned to one of four outdoor recreation activity groups: (a) nature photography, (b) birding, (c) motorcycling, and (d) motor boating. Note that the first two activities are "appreciative" and the latter two are "consumptive." Satchabut also noted that interpretation services ("Ranger Talks") are often provided at natural resource-based parks. These services are directly intended to engage visitors in experiences that result in increased understanding of and fascination with natural or heritage features that are the focus of the interpretive program. It is thus reasonable to assume that visitors who receive interpretation services that focus on the natural environment will experience heightened levels of environmental concern. So, Satchabut incorporated interpretation into her experiment. She further divided each activity group into two subgroups. One of these subgroups received interpretation services during their involvement in the activity and the other group did not.

Table 38.1 depicts the full design of the resulting experiment. Technically, Satchabut's (2013) design was "between-subjects factorial, with a nested effect." The "factors" in the design (independent variables) were outdoor recreation activity type (appreciative vs. consumptive), recreation activity nested within activity type (nature photography vs. birding vs. motorcycling vs. motor boating), and interpretation (no interpretation vs. interpretation). The numbers following "*M*" in each cell of Table 38.1 are group averages (means) from a questionnaire administered after the groups finished participating in their respective outdoor recreation activities. The questionnaire measured one of the outcomes in Satchabut's study: "worldwide environmental concern." The data were "standardized" (i.e., z scores, with a mean of 0, and a standard deviation of 1). As such, the negative numbers indicate groups that had lower worldwide environmental concern scores than average, while numbers greater than zero suggest worldwide environmental concern scores that were higher than average.

Two features of the data in Table 38.1 are particularly notable. First, notice that the four groups of students who participated in the "no interpretation" conditions reported less environmental concern than the four groups that received interpretation. This result suggests that interpretation indeed yields environmental concern. But notice also that

Table 38.1. Thitikan Satchabut's Experimental Design

	Appreciative Outdoor Recreation		Consumptive Outdoor Recreation	
	Nature Photography	Birding	Motorcycling	Motor Boating
No Interpretation	*n*=30, *M*=.06	*n*=30, *M*=-.24	*n*=30, *M*=-1.69	*n*=30, *M*=-1.19
Interpretation	*n*=30, *M*=1.07	*n*=30, *M*=-1.19	*n*=30, *M*=.39	*n*=30, *M*=.40

Note: n: numbers of participants; *M*: mean of the measure of worldwide environmental concern

the magnitude of the effect changes for each activity type. For nature photography, for example, interpretation increased the scores by 1.01 units (from .06 to 1.07), but in motorcycling interpretation increased environmental concern by 2.08 units (-1.69 to .39).

This differential effect of one independent variable across different conditions of another independent variable is known as an "interaction effect." Perhaps many readers will recognize this interaction concept as being identical to that which we experience in warnings about pharmaceutical products. "Do not take drug X in combination with drug Y," we are often warned. Taking each drug alone will not harm us, but the joint effect that results from taking the drugs together may be harmful. Common practice is to illustrate interaction effects using a graph, as in Figure 38.4. In addition to plotting the means in this manner, Satchabut (2013) conducted a statistical test (analysis of variance) and found this interaction effect to be "statistically significant."

Satchabut's (2013) study illustrates the potential utility of increased use of experimental designs in leisure research. She advanced knowledge about how outdoor recreation participation may cause a change in environmental concern.

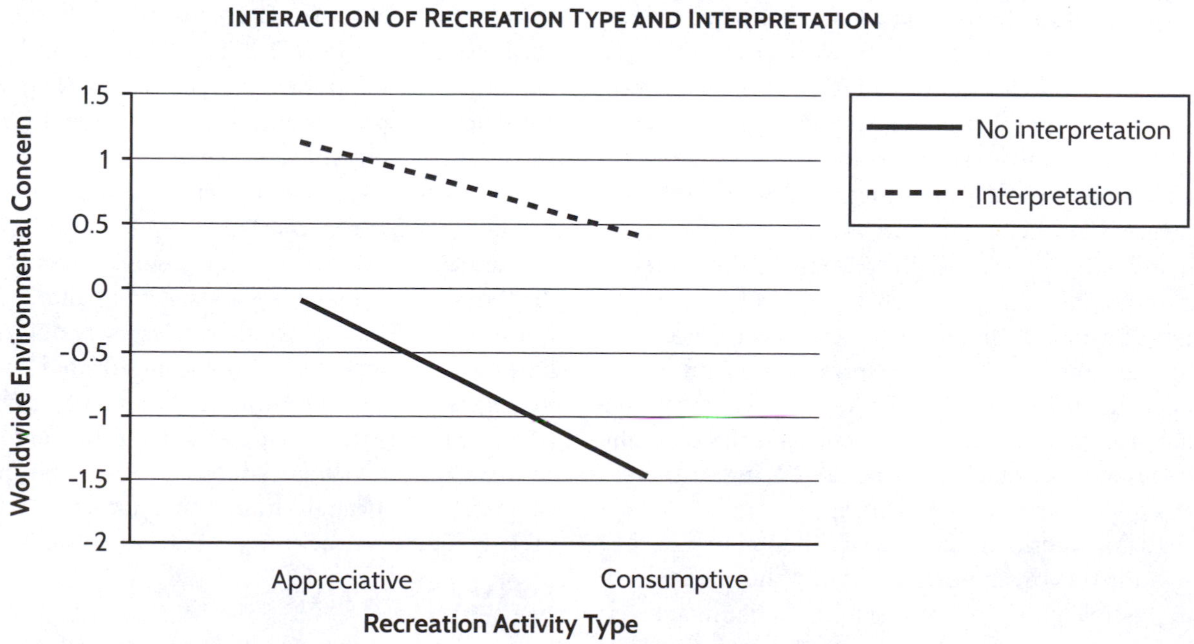

Figure 38.4. Interaction Effect

Her study was a step forward in that it yields confidence in causation. Unlike the correlational studies that preceded her research, the presumed cause (outdoor recreation activity type participation) preceded the observed effect (higher scores in the appreciative and interpretation conditions) in time, other explanations were reasonably well controlled (through random assignment and other mechanisms), and theory suggests that the variables should be related. Other areas of leisure research inquiry can benefit similarly.

APPLICATION 2: LEISURE CONSTRAINTS

Understanding of leisure constraints might also be advanced through experimental research. Leisure constraints have been of interest to leisure studies scholars for over 20 years. Leisure constraints are circumstances that are "... perceived or experienced by individuals to limit the formation of leisure preferences and inhibit or prohibit participation and enjoyment in leisure" (Jackson, 1997, p. 461). In a seminal paper on leisure constraints, Crawford and Godbey (1987) proposed organizing all possible leisure constraints into three categories: Interpersonal, intrapersonal, and structural. *Interpersonal* constraints are circumstances that have to do with relations with others. Examples of interpersonal constraints are lack of co-participants; lack of mentors, coaches, or teachers; and unpleasant relations with potential people who might also participate. *Intrapersonal* constraints are factors that reside within the individual. Examples are poor health, lack of sufficient physical fitness, lack of confidence, lack of interest, and lack of skill. *Structural* constraints have to do with the temporal and spatial circumstances: transportation challenges, distance to the resource needed to participate, work commitments, traffic, inadequate facilities, and the like. Behavioral science knowledge about interpersonal, intrapersonal, and structural leisure constraints has been built on a history of correlational studies (see also Schneider, Chapter 18).

In a recent correlational study on leisure constraints, Lyu, Oh, and Lee (2013) surveyed participants in 20 rehabilitation and welfare centers in urban areas in Korea. These researchers considered "financial constraints" to be an important dimension, in addition to intrapersonal, interpersonal, and structural constraints. Following is a description of how a researcher with access to similar resources might study these four types of leisure constraint using an experimental design known as a "Taguchi experiment."

A Taguchi experiment is an experimental design that allows investigators the opportunity to test the main effects of several possible independent variables. In our imaginary application, we could study interpersonal, intrapersonal, structural, and financial constraints as experimentally manipulated independent variables. Our dependent variable might be participation. In contrast to correlational studies, our experiment would allow us to measure participation through objective observation instead of through subjective self-report procedures.

To conduct the experiment, we would consult with relevant theory to determine an appropriate way to manipulate the constraints. That conceptual work might lead to us choosing the following manipulations:

Independent Variable	Possible Experimental Manipulation
Interpersonal constraints:	Participate with enthusiastic activity leader vs. Participate with unenthusiastic activity leader
Intrapersonal constraint:	Low self-efficacy vs. High self-efficacy
Structural constraint:	Program sessions offered at constant times vs. Program sessions offered at greatly varying times
Financial constraint:	Low fee vs. high fee

We could then randomly assign these "treatments" to 16 facilities according to the "orthogonal array" that characterizes Taguchi experiments (see Table 38.2).

Conducting the experiment would involve several sessions. We would need to find a recreation activity that might be of interest to many people living in the center, and then offer that activity over several sessions. Perhaps it could be a book club, a series of dining events, or maybe an exercise program. We would introduce our experimental manipulations of the four constraints variables through these sessions.

As per the orthogonal design (Table 38.2), participants at sites 1–8 would encounter enthusiastic leaders and participants in sites 9–16 would encounter unenthusiastic leaders (interpersonal constraint). Similarly, we would build self-efficacy promoting mechanisms into the program for participants in facilities 1, 2, 3, 4, 9, 10, 11, and 12, but not use procedures founded in self-efficacy theory to build self-efficacy of participants at sites 5, 6, 7, 8, 13, 14, 15, and 16 (intrapersonal constraint). These self-efficacy mechanisms can be as simple as providing verbal feedback about successes and charting progress (Bandura, 1986, 1997; Wise, Ellis, & Trunnell, 2002). At an initial session, we could announce the times of subsequent sessions. Participants at facilities 1, 2, 5, 6, 9, 10, 13, and 14 would receive a schedule of constant times. Participants at the other facilities would be required to negotiate the structural constraint of varying times (structural constraint). We could charge higher fees at some sites than at others (financial constraint). Participation might be measured through counts of numbers of minutes of participation over the course of the program.

CONCLUSION

In this chapter, we elucidated fundamental characteristics of experimental designs and we evaluated use of experimental designs in leisure studies. We provided examples of

Table 38.2. Taguchi Experiment Design

		Constraint Type			
Pattern	**Participants**	**Interpersonal**	**Intrapersonal**	**Structural**	**Financial**
1	Site 1 & 2	Enthusiastic leader	High self-efficacy	Constant times	Low fee
2	Site 3 & 4	Enthusiastic leader	High self-efficacy	Varying times	High fee
3	Site 5 & 6	Enthusiastic leader	Low self-efficacy	Constant times	High fee
4	Site 7 & 8	Enthusiastic leader	Low self-efficacy	Varying times	Low fee
5	Site 9 & 10	Unenthusiastic leader	High self-efficacy	Constant times	High fee
6	Site 11 & 12	Unenthusiastic leader	High self-efficacy	Varying times	Low fee
7	Site 13 & 14	Unenthusiastic leader	Low self-efficacy	Constant times	Low fee
8	Site 15 & 16	Unenthusiastic leader	Low self-efficacy	Varying times	High fee

how experimental research may be used in leisure studies. We stress that, as compared to much more common approaches to behavioral science research, experimental designs increase our confidence that effects we observe are, in fact, attributable to specific presumed causes. The crux of scientific research is investigation of causes and effects, and experimental designs, though in themselves far from perfect, are behavioral scientists' strongest tool for establishing causal relationships. Despite this strength of experimental designs, our methodological review showed that experimental designs are used very rarely by leisure scientists. More widespread use of experimental designs in leisure studies can result in meaningful contributions to the existing body of knowledge and can lead to knowledge that enriches experiences, lives, and communities.

Why are experimental designs so rare among leisure scholars? A number of explanations are possible. Perhaps one of the more compelling reasons has to do with the knowledge needs of experience industry managers. Managers often need descriptions of people's status on individual variables and survey research is a primary tool for generating these descriptions. Managers use surveys and related techniques to keep their fingers on the pulses of their visitors. Descriptive studies inform planning and resource allocation. How many miles do visitors travel to vacation at specific destinations? What are their overall satisfaction levels? How much money do they spend? Do certain groups feel marginalized at certain attractions? Survey research is effective in generating descriptive knowledge, and the same survey snapshots (data) can be used for both description and for correlational analysis. Survey research is an important tool of park managers, and social scientists who collaborate with managers investigate relations among variables measured in these surveys.

Another explanation for the paucity of experimental studies may be the socialization of leisure researchers. Leisure researchers tend to have been educated in the traditions of disciplines that rely heavily on survey research. Less common are scholars whose backgrounds are in disciplines that emphasize experimental research. A pivotal concern among survey researchers is accurate representation of a defined population through scientific sampling. Generating evidence of possible cause and effect relations is important in such studies, but that concern tends to be overshadowed by questions of the representativeness of the sample to the population from which it was drawn.

Preparation of doctoral students for careers as leisure scientists thus necessitates significant attention to methods of survey research. To help students succeed in careers as scholars who use survey research, coursework must focus on such matters as scientific sampling, questionnaire design, optimizing response rates, and statistical analyses of data sets that include large numbers of variables. If experimentation in leisure studies is to increase, future generations of students will need greater involvement in classes with different foci. They must learn contemporary experimental design options that far exceed those that are briefly introduced through the popular research methods textbooks. More attention will be needed to such topics as small *n* design options; random, nested, crossed and fixed effects; interaction effects, contrasts, and factors that affect validity of inferences made from results of experiments.

Curriculum for budding leisure studies scholars must also emphasize the limitations of both experimental and correlational studies. Neither of these, for example, can provide answers to ethical questions; they can only identify the probable outcomes of decision options. To illustrate, we learn from Satchabut's (2013) study that interpretation service and recreation activity type may work jointly to elevate environmental concern. If we provide interpretation and appreciative forms of recreation, then environmental concern may increase. But, the question, "*Should* park managers direct their efforts at elevating environmental concern?" remains unanswered. Resources for managing parks and attractions are finite. Allocating more resources to the purpose of elevating environmental concern thus results in fewer resources available for other key functions, such as park maintenance, law enforcement, resource management, visitor safety and security, or other visitor services. An even broader ethical question is whether park managers have the right to direct their efforts at elevating environmental concern of their visitors. Should the park focus instead on visitor wants and on market-driven outcomes, such as visitor satisfaction, delight, spending, intention to return, and intention to recommend? Developing answers to such ethical questions is beyond the reach of both experimental and correlational research. (For more on this topic, see Sylvester, Chapter 5.)

Thus, in summary, experimental research provides leisure researchers with a powerful, relatively unbiased, and enormously under-utilized tool for "determining the effects of presumed causes" (Shadish et al., 2002). Experiments are superior to the much more popular correlational studies for that purpose. Results of our review of experimental research in leisure studies suggests substantial opportunity to expand the knowledge base through experiments—designs that allow us to make "if, then" statements with much greater confidence.

REFERENCES

Bandura, A. (1986). *Social foundations of thought and action: A social cognitive theory.* Englewood Cliffs, NJ: Prentice Hall.

Bandura, A. (1997). *Self-efficacy: The exercise of control.* New York: Freeman. Englewood Cliffs, NJ: Prentice Hall.

Bernard, H. R. (2011). *Research methods in anthropology* (5th ed.). Lanham, MD: AltaMira Press.

Crawford, J., & Godbey, G. (1987). Reconceptualizing barriers to family leisure. *Leisure Sciences, 9*, 119–127.

Dunlap, R. E., & Heffernan, R. B. (1975). Outdoor recreation and environmental concern: An empirical examination. *Rural Sociology, 40*, 18–30.

Geisler, C. C., Martinson, O. B., & Wilkening, E. A. (1977). Outdoor recreation and environmental concern: A restudy. *Rural Sociology, 42*, 241–249.

Jackson, E. L. (1986). Outdoor recreation participation and attitudes toward the environment. *Leisure Studies, 5*, 1–23.

Kerlinger, F. N., & Lee, H. B. (2000). *Foundations of behavioral research* (4th ed.). London, UK: Thomson Learning.

Kirk, R. (2013). *Experimental design: procedures for the behavioral sciences* (4th ed.). Thousand Oaks, CA: Sage.

Lyu, S., Oh, C., & Lee, H. (2013). The influence of extraversion on leisure constraints negation process. *Journal of Leisure Research, 45*, 233–252.

Maxwell, S. E., & Delaney, H. D. (2004). *Designing experiments and analyzing data* (2nd ed.). Mahway, NJ: Lawrence Erlbaum Associates.

Myers, J. L., Well, A. D., & Lorch, R. F. (2010). *Research design and statistical analysis.* New York: Routledge.

Nord, M., Luloff, A. E., & Bridger, J. C. (1998). The association of forest recreation with environmentalism. *Environment and Behavior, 30*, 235–246.

Peterson, N., Hull, V., Mertig, A., & Liu, J. (2008). Evaluating household-level relationship between environmental views and outdoor recreation: The Teton Valley case. *Leisure Sciences, 30*, 293–305.

Pinhey, T. K., & Michael D. G. (1979). Outdoor recreation and environmental concern: A re-examination of the Dunlap-Heffernan thesis. *Leisure Sciences, 2*, 1–11.

Satchabut, T. (2013). *Effects of recreation participation and Tildenian Interpretation on tourists' environmental concern* (Unpublished doctoral dissertation). Texas A&M University, College Station, TX.

Schmidt, F. L. (1992). What do data really mean? Research findings, meta-analysis, and cumulative knowledge in psychology. *American psychologist, 47*(10), 1173–1181.

Shadish, W. R., Cook, T. D., & Campbell, D. T. (2002). *Experimental and quasi-experimental designs for generalized causal inference*. Boston, MA: Houghton Mifflin.

Theodori, G. L., Luloff, A., & Willits, F. K. (1998). The association of outdoor recreation and environmental concern: Reexamining the Dunlap-Heffernan thesis. *Rural Sociology, 63*(1), 94–108.

Van Liere, K. D., & Dunlap, R. E. (1981). Environmental concern: Does it make a difference how it is measured? *Environment and Behavior, 13*, 651–676.

Whitehead, A. N. (1932). *Science and the modern world.* Cambridge, UK: Cambridge University Press.

Wise, J., Ellis, G., & Trunnell, E. (2002). Effects of a curriculum designed to generalize self-efficacy from weight training exercises to activities of daily living among adults with spinal injuries. *Journal of Applied Social Psychology, 32*, 500–521.

39

Leisure and the Academy: Curricula and Scholarship in Higher Education

Karla A. Henderson (North Carolina State University)

Compared to many traditional disciplines and fields, leisure and recreation are relatively young. Concerns have been expressed in recent years, however, regarding the future of leisure studies within higher education (e.g., Australian and New Zealand Association for Leisure Studies, 2009; Stebbins, 2011). These concerns relate to institutional as well as intellectual dimensions (Rowe, 2002). Some pertain to administrative and curricular concerns (e.g., professional preparation) while others address the future of leisure research and scholarship. Nevertheless, change is inevitable and managing this change must be considered. The future might be analogous to driving a car toward a cliff in the fog should academics not consider the possibilities and the consequences of ongoing uncertainties.

Although angst has surfaced at the beginning of the twenty-first century, uneasiness about professional curricula and scholarship has been raised from time to time since the field was legitimized over 50 years ago (e.g., Burdge, 1985; Dustin & Goodale, 1999; Pronovost & D'Amours, 1990). Dustin and Goodale, for example, asked in a chapter that was the predecessor to this book whether leisure studies is on course, needs to regain bearings, or is lost at sea. Stebbins (2011) discussed a rough road lying ahead for leisure studies. Based on the history of the field, however, I am not sure the road was ever smooth or ever will be. Nevertheless, the future can be bright if educators recognize the dynamics of this evolving field and, as Rowe (2002) suggested, a fine line exists between a crisis and critical reflection. Critical reflection is essential to a maturing field, and Pronovost and D'Amours argued all fundamental disciplines should continually question their underlying bases.

Some concerns about leisure studies in Western countries seem to be occurring, interestingly, at the same time the field gathers momentum in Asia (see Chapter 14), South America (see Marinho & Reis, Chapter 16), South Africa (see Naidoo, Chapter 12), and areas in the Middle East. This chapter is largely about the evolution of leisure studies in Anglo countries. Lynch (1997) suggested any crisis about leisure is ethnocentric in nature. Many countries do not have the same emphasis on curricula and professional education, as do some Western countries (e.g., U.S., New Zealand, Australia). Non-western countries that have developed professional curricula have relied on Western definitions of leisure and recreation (Roberts, 2010). This reliance on Western models may or may not be fruitful in the future.

The purpose of this chapter is to reflect on the broad field of leisure related to institutional and curricular issues with a concomitant discussion of intellectual and research-based issues. I use references from the literature as well as conversations with colleagues and my experiences of over 38 years in the academy. I am biased by my mentors (e.g., Doug Sessoms) and the circumstances surrounding my career as well as my cultural background as a U.S. citizen. I make no apologies for the interpretations in this article, but I readily acknowledge change is constant and thus, my perceptions are continually evolving.

This chapter is organized into sections beginning with a short background introduction followed by past and present perspectives related to curricula and scholarship in higher education. The final section provides a summary of the ideas by examining possible and preferable futures linking leisure curricula and scholarship.

BACKGROUND

The relationship between careers in recreation-related fields and leisure research has been tenuous over the years. Although professional curricula in leisure studies can be linked to leisure research, this connection is not always evident. Research and teaching are not the same but they are related in many ways. Fullagar (2011) warned about being careful not to conflate changes in leisure studies scholarship with changes in degree programs, similar to what Rowe (2002) called intellectual verses institutional differentiations. Regardless, these philosophical distinctions can be viewed from historical and contemporary perspectives.

In the U.S., parks and/or recreation became a significant a field of *practice* during the mid-twentieth century. Further, the construct of leisure came into existence during the 1960s (Dustin & Goodale, 1999) due partly to assumptions that parks and recreation professionals could address potential problems associated with leisure, and because leisure sciences was thought to provide legitimacy to the field. In addition, leisure had been considered free time or the opposite of work until the 1960s. De Grazia's observations of leisure as a state of mind seemed to elevate the idea of leisure to a more complex notion (Sessoms, 1985). The adoption of leisure as a foundation for parks and recreation, however, was not without controversy.

Burdge (1985) created the first major professional debate in the field when he suggested leisure studies should be separated from parks and recreation. He made an intellectual and institutional distinction, which also implicated a divide between research and professional practice. Burdge argued the preparation of undergraduates for jobs in parks and recreation required a different set of skills than the preparation of graduate students who needed the mastery of leisure philosophy and research methods. He also warned that an applied curriculum often resulted in a failure to ask bigger questions about social issues. He argued an organization such as an American Leisure Studies Association was needed separate from the primary professional organization, the National Recreation and Park Association, and from academic departments fostering curricula aimed at management skills.

Compelling arguments for the continuing cross-pollination of leisure studies with parks and recreation were offered to counter Burdge (1985). Leisure behavior was assumed to be the intellectualizing process for practice according to Godbey (1985). He questioned whether a student could become a parks and recreation professional without understanding the role of leisure in society as well as leisure behavior, motivations, and satisfactions. Smith (1985) suggested bridges should be built between these beliefs and warned if leisure studies and parks and recreation did not travel together, then both would cease to exist, which is a continuing concern expressed today (e.g., Perkins, 2011). Although few other lively debates occurred regarding the divide, other researchers such as Hemingway and Parr (2000) and Williams (2000) provided critical reflections about the unclear relationships between curricula/practice and leisure research/theory.

In 1995, Cushman laid out the growing problems of higher education in New Zealand: dwindling undergraduate enrollments, internal questioning about the essence and definition of the field, the tug of war between professional relevancy and curiosity (i.e., theory-driven) research, the struggle for intellectual rigor and maturity, and striving for academic respectability and legitimacy. He admitted these concerns occurred regularly, but they were becoming institutionally real to scholars in New Zealand.

I agree with Fullagar (2011), who warned against a dominant narrative that equates change in leisure studies with decline. Knowing something about history enables educators to avoid repeating past mistakes. However, knowing something about history runs the risk of clinging too intently to the past. I try to balance these ideas as I explore the past of both professional curricula related to recreation and leisure (i.e., primarily from a U.S. perspective) as well as leisure scholarship.

PROFESSIONAL CURRICULA IN THE UNITED STATES

The Playground Association of America began in 1906 as did the enactment of the Antiquities Act, which resulted in the federal government's protection of public land. Although playground programs and parks existed in the nineteenth century, this formalization marked the beginning of educating and training leaders. Most of the early curricula addressed areas of recreation and parks subsumed in other fields. The traditional field of recreation as well as sports was associated most closely with schools and physical education while park management grew from forestry and natural resources. By 1911, 113 U.S. colleges and universities offered courses in play and playground operations (Sessoms, 1993). In the next five decades professional organizations became well-established to address facets of recreation leadership (e.g., American Recreation Society; American Association of Health, Physical Education, Recreation, and Dance; American Institute of Park Executives; and the Tourism Society).

From programs focused solely on recreation/play and parks/conservation in the U.S. came a merger into a field known as *parks and recreation* in the early 1960s. This merger led to the establishment of the National Recreation and Park Association (NRPA), which occurred largely because the Outdoor Recreation Resources Review Commission (ORRRC) advocated that organized parks and recreation were integral to promoting outdoor opportunities in local communities and beyond (e.g., national parks). Dustin and Goodale (1999) suggested parks and recreation were at their height during the 1960s as was evidenced by President Lyndon B. Johnson addressing the first NRPA Congress (Sessoms & Henderson, 2009).

By the early 1960s, professional recreation and park curricula were established in higher education. To monitor the quality of these programs, the first academic programs in parks and recreation were accredited by the NRPA and American Association of Leisure and Recreation in 1977. At this time, the academic configurations of park and recreation programs varied greatly across the country. The predominant association was with schools of Physical Education and Health, but when a university focused more on natural resources recreation, the configuration was usually in Forestry or Natural Resources.

The early focus of curricula was mainly on public parks and recreation agencies. Other recreation specialties emerged (e.g., therapeutic recreation) along with a change from an emphasis on social service and public good to entrepreneurship and the private sector. The fields of tourism and commercial recreation blossomed in the 1980s with the appearance of a greater focus on sports management in the early 1990s, and event management at the turn into the twenty-first century.

The huge growth in recreation-related units in higher education occurring in the 1960s and 1970s began to decline in the 1990s as the demand for professionals decreased and the once predicted *leisure society* of the twenty-first century did not loom on the horizon. The legitimacy and centrality of leisure and recreation to universities also came under scrutiny and program eliminations began to occur often because these recreation units were perceived as not fitting with the mission of their universities.

The names of units addressing the aspects of recreation changed over the years as well. Many academic departments changed their name to something involving leisure (e.g., recreation and leisure studies) and some community programs also went in that direction (e.g., leisure services). By the end of the twentieth century, however, many units had removed *leisure* from their titles and added new focus areas such as tourism. Leisure was often misunderstood by the public and by university administrators. It connoted *doing nothing* or some other type of inactivity rather than a psychological understanding of a positive *experience* of doing something. For most people, recreation was a more appropriate term since it suggested spaces and opportunities for activity with personal and community benefits.

THE EVOLUTION OF LEISURE SCHOLARSHIP

With important exceptions (e.g., Veblen, 1970 [1899]), the 1960's was the beginning of leisure as a sub-discipline within the International Sociological Association (Roberts, 2011). The proliferation of university curricula focusing on parks and recreation in the U.S. spread rapidly to other Anglo countries. The construct of leisure influenced by the work of de Grazia (1962) opened up a plethora of significant research topics to explore. The *Journal of Leisure Research* (JLR) was established by the NRPA in 1969. As a citizen-advocacy as well as a professional organization, however, the NRPA's focus on leisure was almost always related to its positive benefits and how practitioners could use research to improve recreation delivery and leisure-time activities for community residents (Henderson, 2011). In contrast to the U.S., other English-speaking countries adopted a model of focusing more specifically on leisure phenomena (e.g. the Canadian Association of Leisure Studies, the United Kingdom's Leisure Studies Association) that was often separate from practice.

As professional specialties related to parks, recreation, and leisure in higher education expanded, new journals began such as the *Annals of Tourism Research* (1970s), *Journal of Sport Management* (1980s), *Society and Natural Resources* (1980s), and *Event Management* (formerly *Festival Management & Event Tourism*; 1990s). When these specialty journals emerged, journals such as *JLR* and *Leisure Sciences* moved toward ensuring the intellectual focus was leisure behavior (Henderson, 2011) and not necessarily delivery of recreation services. Research publications linked to specialties were often focused on management issues and were somewhat tangential to the theoretical study of leisure behavior. Intellectual divergence, rather than convergence, was the trend.

In 1989, Jackson and Burton described the "lack of theoretical and conceptual integration and the disciplinary fragmentation" (p. 3) within leisure studies despite its claims of being interdisciplinary research. They suggested leisure studies had little impact in the academy as a result of the low esteem accorded to leisure studies by other social scientists. A survey of researchers conducted by Jackson and Burton indicated the field was perceived as fragmented with conflicting conceptual and methodological development, inconsistent terminology, and intellectual disharmony. However, Burton and Jackson (1990) concluded pluralistic approaches to any topic had great value in offering a broad context to explain leisure behavior. This broad milieu continues in both research and professional education today.

PROFESSIONAL CURRICULA TODAY

Historical perspectives on professional development as well as leisure scholarship have influenced the academy of today. The overt connection of professional curricula to leisure has largely disappeared in most Western countries. Leisure behavior remains an aspect of recreation programs but not necessarily related to specialties such as sports or tourism. Leisure often remains largely misunderstood by students as well as administrators in universities. Fullagar (2011) described how eliminating leisure in department titles and curricula has been rationalized as "no longer a valued signifier" (p. 17).

The interests of faculty related to connections to specialties have also changed. The field related to leisure might be akin to a three generational family (Henderson, 2010), which expands on an analogy Aitchison (2006) first used. The grandparents of the field might be considered the traditional disciplines that nurtured the development of the construct of leisure (e.g., sociology and geography). The parents are the individuals who are firmly focused on leisure studies from interdisciplinary perspectives. The children are the specialty areas such as outdoor recreation management, sports, or therapeutic recreation. Aitchison advocated for subfields working with increasing connections with (grand) parent fields. This suggestion, however, may be more applicable to the United Kingdom than to the U.S. Coalter (1997) noted United Kingdom leisure researchers have only one foot in leisure and one foot in a discipline whereas in U.S., leisure researchers have both feet in *leisure*. I argue today that the interest of many newer faculty members is to have both feet in a specialty (Henderson, 2011). Godbey (2000) argued specialization has been detrimental because it has resulted in separate organizations and journals as well as divisions within academic units.

Specialties are relatively easier to market. Rowe (2002) noted, "Students, teachers and researchers are far more likely to be enthusiastic, even passionate, about a particular art form or sport than about leisure in general" (p. 2). Rowe also noted that students perceived leisure as not employable, but sport and tourism were. Similarly, Chick (1997) suggested potential job opportunities rather than philosophy had greater influence in higher education. Although specializations can offer pluralism within curricula and visible career opportunities, they can fragment the field if commonalities are not evident.

The emphasis of the early leisure and recreation curricula was on social service whereas the forces within universities today relate to both research production as well as student numbers reflecting a market-driven emphasis. Universities and the degree programs they offer, including recreation, appear to be driven by the political economy (Rose & Dustin, 2009; Samdahl, 2000) including the opportunities for employment.

An article appeared in *Parks & Recreation* magazine (Beard, 2011) explored the evolution and necessity of recreation degree programs. The conclusions appeared to be that many areas of expertise are needed in the recreation field. However, professionals must be able to advocate for the value of recreation and must be able to develop strategic partnerships with other fields and organizations. Recreation majors are needed because of their broad understanding, but people from other fields (e.g., landscape architecture, marketing, wildlife biology) are also integral.

LEISURE SCHOLARSHIP TODAY

The intellectual and institutional aspects of leisure studies remain under scrutiny in the twenty-first century. Rojek, Veal, and Shaw (2006) suggested leisure studies has *come of age*. This statement is true to some extent but based on the concerns laid out in this chapter, whether leisure scholars are currently on the right road remains under scrutiny.

Driver (1999) provided an optimistic, but not utopian, summary of the progress made in leisure studies up to 1999. He suggested three states of leisure studies existed: the state of the art (i.e., what is known about leisure), the state of management (i.e., the actual delivery of leisure services), and the state of academic education (i.e., formal education gained in colleges and universities). He noted considerable improvement was occurring in science-based knowledge, but applied research related to management was not as strong as leisure behavior work. He also stated that incrementally, but not sufficiently, leisure was recognized as a legitimate academic area of study. Driver clearly saw the links among research, practice, and higher education. He also stressed the importance of maintaining a positive attitude about the benefits of leisure.

One concern raised is a critique of leisure research as a happy science (Stebbins, 2011). Both Fullagar (2011) and Shaw (2006) illustrated the tension between addressing the positive benefits of leisure without addressing the dark side as it might relate to reproducing social inequities. Some of this tension is a result of an outcome of lingering functionalist approaches to research as contrasted to postmodernism and post-structuralism. Fortunately, more research and discourse is occurring regarding social and environmental justice (Schwab & Dustin, 2013).

In a special issue of *Leisure Sciences*, Mommaas (1997) described the situation regarding leisure studies in Europe at the end of the twentieth century. He concluded the study of leisure, once dominated by sociology, had lost a central focus and salience with the splintering of intellectual areas (e.g., time, play, pleasure, consumption). He asked whether leisure should be re-envisioned or whether this fragmentation was part of the pluralizing of the field and the postmodern condition. Coalter (1997) responded that both leisure sciences in the U.S. and leisure studies in the United Kingdom were at crossroads because of their inability to adequately address the meanings associated with leisure. He acknowledged postmodernism does not mean theory is impossible, but attributed it to the fragmentation of leisure studies, at least in the United Kingdom (see also Blackshaw, Chapter 7).

Rose and Dustin (2009) further challenged the current neoliberalism related to higher education and especially research. They lamented that often leisure research is not fundable, so researchers choose to study topics enabling them to get grants and contracts, which may not always contribute to a larger social good. They contended neoliberalism is a political and economic philosophy exalting privatization and market forces, and leisure scholars were far from immune to this neoliberalism.

DESCRIBING A PREFERABLE FUTURE

The broad field of professional curricula as well as leisure research may thrive with an understanding of the *new normal* and the concept of *homeostasis* (Henderson, 2010). Homeostasis is scientifically defined as any self-regulating process by which biological systems tend to maintain stability while adjusting to conditions optimal for survival. If homeostasis is successful, life continues. If it is unsuccessful, extinction can occur. The stability attained is actually a dynamic equilibrium, in which continuous change occurs yet relatively uniform conditions prevail. When a system is disturbed, the result is to regulate to establish a new balance. Rowe (2002) offered that an applied field like leisure studies will need to transform and change if it is to continue. Leisure is not going to go away, but the associated institutional and intellectual traditions may require adjustments to the previous ways the traditions have been perceived. In response to Stebbins' (2011) rough road analogy, Rowe (2011) suggested academicians may need to go *off road*.

One way to articulate shared vision is through the development of scenarios describing some of the issues. Table 39.1 demonstrates summaries reflecting three possibilities for the future: Downsizing, Extinction, and Re-invention. The potential, probable, and preferable stories reflect the concerns to address in the future.

Talking about the future is always a challenge. No one has a crystal ball. However, thinking about the future related to probable as well as preferable futures is important. Futuring is easiest when the probable and preferable futures are the same. However, they seldom are. Therefore, being knowledgeable about the probable future is important but more important is having a vision of the preferred future. If members of the academy do not know where they want to go, they will likely continue to wander aimlessly down whatever road looks easiest. In this final section of this chapter, I offer some ideas about the preferable future, acknowledging fully these ideas are my interpretations. Although the past has paved the way for now and the future, clinging to the past without acknowledging the necessity for homeostasis will be detrimental.

Acknowledging the concerns or questioning that might occur in any discipline or field is not new, but moving forward with vision and goals is important. Sessom's (1993) summary of 80 years of leadership development in programs of professional education in parks and recreation indicated that throughout the history of the profession, unfinished business and conflicts occurred:

> What is the nature of this enterprise—professional preparation, leisure studies, the promotion of a leisure literate society? What should be the academic base and the content of curricula—an independent academic unit? A division within [some other unit]? . . . What should be the focus: the preparation of specialists? the preparation of graduates for entry level positions? the development of professionals? What should be the relationship between professional education courses and general educational requirements? (p. 123)

I contend the future is not a matter of *either/or* but *both/and* (Henderson, 2006). I do not believe professionals have to choose only one direction, but they should strive to address inevitable change and uncertainties. The challenge is to be strategic and flexible to maintain stability while adjusting to change. Maintaining stability will mean being able to continually change. The answers will evolve with changing social conditions. Just letting the change happen, however, without articulating a preferable future is not acceptable, and will likely result in the extinction of the field.

Describing a preferred future is much easier than facilitating it assuming all can agree on what that future should be. I (Henderson, 2010) offered a vision of what needed to be done: embracing change as inevitable, articulating a clear but flexible collective identity, taking pride in and celebrating the contributions made through leisure analyses as well as enhancing leisure for all, and actively identifying collaborators on all levels. Upon further consideration, I (Henderson, 2011) lamented the difficulty of a collective identity and a shared vision due to the proliferation of specialties.

The NRPA unabashedly advocates for community parks and recreation, and has defined three pillars as the foundation: health and well-being, environmental sustainability, and social justice. No single pillar defines the field and all the specialties, but collectively they seem to offer standpoints for this field of leisure and recreation stands. Visioning the future will be difficult without unifying themes or collective identities.

Table 39.1. Three Scenarios for the Future of Leisure Studies in Higher Education

Three Scenarios for the Future of Leisure Studies in Higher Education

Downsizing Scenario: The year is 2040. Leisure is a topic of study by a small and diverse group of people considering leisure from disciplinary perspectives. The Baby Boomers who had championed the parks and recreation movement in higher education retired. The new generation of faculty was educated in specific areas of practice and did not see recreation and leisure as central to these specialties. Emphasis areas such as sport management, event management, parks and recreation, and therapeutic recreation are now professional education specialties within other departments. Employers in recreation-related fields do not believe a degree in recreation is needed. People who work in community parks and recreation generally receive their training through technical/community colleges or from organizations like the NRPA, which have little to do with university education. The Academy of Leisure Sciences is ineffective as it only appeals to a small number of people associated with the narrow area of leisure research.

Extinction Scenario: The year is 2040. Programs in higher education focusing on parks and recreation gradually disappeared after 2015. Educators continued to try to do business as usual in the university, even though social and employment needs and the interests of both faculty and students had changed. Instead of determining what held their recreation-related units together, faculty continued to make curriculum changes based on what would attract numbers of students. The economy and university administrators define the field. The core is management, which is also a part of the mission of other units in the university. Recreation programs lost their mission and university administrators assumed other related disciplines could educate students just as well as recreation units. Educators pay lip service to the commonalities with other fields and disciplines but do not extend any efforts to collaborate. They apologize for the field and undersell what is offered, while at the same time defending the past importance. Doctoral granting universities across the country have ceased to educate faculty that can work across the specialty areas, which further weakens the core. Professional organizations (e.g., NRPA) do not see the value of involving educators, and the Academy of Leisure Sciences was dissolved because of lack of interest.

Re-Invention Scenario: The year is 2040. Sustainable Recreation Sciences is flourishing in universities. Programs related to recreation, sport, tourism, and other specialties have determined their common mission related to healthy individuals and sustainable communities. Recreation programs emphasize the importance of specialty areas, but more important, the contributions the field makes to society. Departments retain the word recreation in their titles and acknowledge how recreation is a link to other efforts such as community development, youth development, health promotion, and social justice. These units define themselves within the context of their university mission and the talents of faculty. They are mission driven and not resources driven. Interdisciplinary opportunities are designed related to curricula, and research is conducted mainly in interdisciplinary teams with recreation faculty leading these endeavors. The Academy of Leisure Sciences is flourishing as individuals from all disciplines became involved in promoting leisure as a social good and in supporting professionals involved in multiple sectors of recreation planning and promotion. Faculty and students are involved with other specialty organizations, but all come together under the umbrella of sustainable recreation sciences. Instead of making apologies for terms like recreation and leisure, educators lead in redefining these ideas and proudly look for opportunities to collaborate and contribute.

One concern for the future is the shifting meanings of leisure. Although the work ethic remains strong, leisure is not inconsequential. Unfortunately, sometimes researchers and educators become so focused on theory and practice that advocacy for leisure on a bigger scale does not occur. Aitchison (2006) described the importance of retaining leisure as an area of study since the whole is greater than the sum of the specialized parts. In addition to the legitimacy of leisure as an area of study (Fullagar, 2011), the legitimacy of leisure must be recognized regardless of how it occurs. For example, due to the obesity epidemic and concerns about inactivity, parks and recreation services are now recognized as major contributors to getting people active. Leisure scholars know the benefits of leisure but have not always connected the applications. This advocacy should be based on scholarship but also must be reflexive. If leisure has lost its signifier in uniting the specialties associated with the field, then new signifiers might be considered.

Leisure scholars in the future also must find a way to balance the need for advocacy and need for critical reflection (Parry, Johnson, & Stewart, 2013). Rowe (2011) offered that scholars must move beyond the missionary impulse to a more open, congruent, and acceptance of *messy* leisure. Rojek (2010) pleaded that viewing leisure as only good misses connections with the real world. Further, Samdahl (2000) also recommended discarding the use of only positivist and functional theories and replacing them with critical and postmodern perspectives will be helpful.

Traditional leisure services and their hegemonic reproduction should not be encouraged at the expense of critical intellectual pursuits.

Burdge's (1985) concern about the split between parks and recreation and leisure studies seems to have come to fruition to some extent. In the U.S., the NRPA continues to support research journals and the Leisure Research Symposium. Support of the efforts of educators has diminished with the dissolving of the Society for Park and Recreation Education (SPRE). Similar to colleagues in the United Kingdom and Australia/New Zealand, the Academy of Leisure Sciences, which was once strictly a honorary group has now opened its membership to anyone who subscribes to the mission: bringing together people from diverse backgrounds who share a mutual interest in better understanding the roles of leisure in life, including various contexts of recreation, park, tourism, outdoor adventure, health, therapy, and sport.

Curricula related to parks, recreation, and leisure have much to offer in a broader society. Students are receiving numerous skills when they major in the recreation field—leadership, programming, marketing, management, supervision, and evaluation. These curricula can prepare them to work in the broad field of human services whether in recreation specific organizations or other human service areas. Unlike a degree in liberal arts, students majoring in recreation specialties have abilities that may prepare them directly for the job market. Branding the degree is important, but it may not speak loudly enough to the skills students obtain. Further, what may be defined as a recreation job may be broader than traditional specialties. I believe many jobs are available for students who learn these skills, seek internship and part-time job experience, and know how to work with people.

Finally, partnerships are central to almost all endeavors today. Pritchard (2006) predicted the new leisure studies would be based on cooperation and collaboration, using multiple positions, practices, and insights. The challenge is to be clear about the contributions leisure scholars have to make through interdisciplinary learning or transdisciplinary scholarship. Scholars cannot give up their identity or the field will be swallowed by other areas. We must be clear, perhaps through recognizing the collective identities, about what can be offered. Perkins (2011) and Rojek (1995), for example, have argued leisure cannot be separated from the rest of life. However, the special contributions recreation and leisure offer must be articulated.

Godbey (2000) reiterated how both leisure studies and professional specialties could survive and prosper together with greater energy devoted to "Entrepreneurial effort, partnerships, interdisciplinary involvement... negotiating, promoting, explaining, and—above all—not apologizing for the subject material studied" (p. 41). Further, Fullagar (2011) stated the challenge is not to remove leisure from the discussion but to "carry forward a leisure studies ethos that values interdisciplinary engagement, industry relevance and 'public good' as we negotiate the vagaries of market forces in higher education to remain relevant . . . ." (p. 17). How change will be necessary to make leisure studies relevant as well as the facilitating the professional services that make life better for all individuals must be the focus of conversations to assure the re-invention of curricula and research.

REFERENCES

Aitchison, C. C. (2006). The critical and the cultural: Explaining the divergent paths of leisure studies and tourism studies. *Leisure Studies, 25*, 417–422.

Australian and New Zealand Association for Leisure Studies. (2009).The future of leisure studies. *ANZALS Newsletter, 44*. Retrieved from: http://www.staff.vu.edu.au/anzals/news44.pdf

Beard, E. (2011). A matter of degree. *Parks & Recreation, 46*(8), 46–51.

Burdge, R. J. (1985). The coming separation of leisure studies from parks and recreation education. *Journal of Leisure Research, 17*, 133–141.

Burton, T. L., & Jackson, E. L. (1989). Charting the future. In E. L. Jackson & T. L. Burton (Eds.), *Understanding leisure and recreation: Mapping the past, charting the future*, (pp. 629–642). State College, PA: Venture Publishing, Inc.

Burton, T. L., & Jackson, E. L. (1990). On the road to where we're going: Leisure studies in the future. *Loisir & Société, 13*, 207–227.

Chick, G. (1997). Crossroads and crises, or much ado about nothing? A comment on Mommaas and Coalter. *Leisure Sciences, 19*, 285–289.

Coalter, F. (1997). Leisure sciences and leisure studies: Different concept, same crisis? *Leisure Sciences, 19*, 255–268.

Cushman, G. (1995). The development of leisure studies in Aotearoa-New Zealand. *ANZALS Leisure Research Series, 2*, 44–60.

de Grazia, S. (1962). *Of time, work, and leisure*. New York: Twentieth Century Fund.

Driver, B. L. (1999). Recognizing and celebrating progress in leisure studies. In E. L. Jackson & T. L. Burton (Eds.), *Leisure studies: Prospects for the twenty-first century* (pp. 523–534). State College, PA: Venture Publishing, Inc.

Dustin, D. L., & Goodale, T. L. (1999). Reflections on recreation, park, and leisure studies. In E. L. Jackson & T. L. Burton (Eds.), *Leisure studies: Prospects for the twenty-first century* (pp. 477–486). State College, PA: Venture Publishing, Inc.

Fullagar, S. (2011). Where might the path less travelled lead us? A commentary on Stebbins (2011). *World Leisure Journal, 53*(1), 15–18.

Godbey, G. (1985). The coming cross-pollination of leisure studies and recreation and park education: A response. *Journal of Leisure Research, 17*, 142–148.

Godbey, G. (2000). The future of leisure studies. *Journal of Leisure Research, 32*, 37–41.

Hemingway, J. L., & Parr, M. G. (2000). Leisure research and leisure practice: Three perspectives on constructing the research-practice relation. *Leisure Sciences, 22*, 139–162.

Henderson, K. A. (2006). False dichotomies and leisure research. *Leisure Studies, 25*, 391–395.

Henderson, K. A. (2010). Leisure studies in the 21st century: The sky is falling? *Leisure Sciences, 32*, 391–400.

Henderson, K. A. (2011). A continuum of leisure studies and professional specialties: What if no connections exist? *World Leisure Journal, 53*(2), 76–90.

Jackson, E. L., & Burton, T. L. (1989). Mapping the past. In E. L. Jackson & T. L. Burton (Eds.), *Understanding leisure and recreation: Mapping the past, charting the future* (pp. 3–28). State College, PA: Venture Publishing, Inc.

Lynch, R. (1997). Whose crisis at the crossroads? *Leisure Sciences, 19*, 269–271.

Mommaas, H. (1997). European leisure studies at the crossroads? A history of leisure research in Europe. *Leisure Sciences, 19*, 241–254.

Parry, D. C., Johnson, C. W., & Stewart, W. (2013). Leisure research for social justice: A response to Henderson. *Leisure Sciences, 35*, 81–87.

Perkins, H. C. (2011). Sharing the road ahead: A commentary on Stebbins (2011). *World Leisure Journal*, 53(1), 19—22.

Pritchard, A. (2006). Listening to leisure voices: Getting engaged in dialogues, conversations, and entanglements. *Leisure Studies, 25*, 373–377.

Pronovost, G., & D'Amours, M. (1990). Leisure studies: A re-examination of society. *Loisir & Société, 13*, 39–62.

Roberts, K. (2010). Is leisure studies "ethnocentric"? If so, does this matter? *World Leisure Journal, 52*(3), 164–176.

Roberts, K. (2011). *Sociology of leisure. Sociopedia*. International Sociology Association. Retrieved from www.sagepub.net/isa/resources/pdf/Leisure.pdf

Rojek, C. (1995). *Decentering leisure*. London: Sage Publications.

Rojek, C. (2010). *The labour of leisure: The culture of free time*. London: Sage Publications.

Rojek, C., Shaw, S. M., & Veal, A. J. (Eds.). (2006). *A handbook of leisure studies*. New York: Palgrave Macmillan.

Rose, J., & Dustin, D. (2009). The neoliberal assault on the public university: The case of recreation, park and leisure research. *Leisure Sciences, 31*, 397–402.

Rowe, D. (2002). Producing the crisis: The state of leisure studies. *Annals of Leisure Research, 5*, 1–13.

Rowe, D. (2011). Serious leisure studies: The roads ahead less travelled. A commentary on Stebbins (2011). *World Leisure Journal, 53*(1), 23–26.

Samdahl, D. M. (2000). Reflections on the future of leisure studies. *Journal of Leisure Research, 32*, 125–128.

Schwab, K., & Dustin, D. (Eds.). (2013). *Just leisure: Things that we believe in*. Champaign, IL: Sagamore Publishing.

Sessoms, H. D. (1985, October). *Of time, work, and leisure revisited*. Presidential Address to the Academy of Leisure Sciences in Dallas, TX.

Sessoms, H. D. (1993). *Eight decades of leadership development*. Ashburn, VA: National Recreation and Park Association.

Sessoms, H. D., & Henderson, K. A. (2009). *The noble experiment: A history of NRPA*. Champaign, IL: Sagamore Publishing.

Shaw, S. M. (2006). Resistance. In C. Rojek, S. M. Shaw, & A. J. Veal (Eds.), *A handbook of leisure studies*. (pp. 533–545). New York: Palgrave Macmillan.

Smith, S. L. J. (1985). An alternative perspective on the nature of recreation and leisure studies: A personal response to Rabel Burdge. *Journal of Leisure Research, 17*, 155–160.

Stebbins, R. (2011). Leisure studies: The road ahead. *World Leisure Journal, 53*(1), 3–10.

Veblen, T. (1970[1899]). *The theory of the leisure class*. London: Allen and Unwin.

Williams, D. R. (2000). Anatomy of the Academy: Dissecting the past, resecting the future. *Journal of Leisure Research, 32*, 180–185.

40

CELEBRATING LEISURE STUDIES: ONWARD, OUTWARD, AND UPWARD

Daniel L. Dustin (University of Utah), Keri A. Schwab (California Polytechnic State University, San Luis Obispo), and Kelly S. Bricker (University of Utah)

In *The Rights of Nature: A History of Environmental Ethics*, Nash (1989) traces the idea of a liberal democratic tradition from its origins in the *Magna Carta* of 1215, which secured natural rights for a small group of English barons from a reluctant King John, all the way to present day debates over the appropriateness of extending natural rights to non-human living things and Earth in its entirety. At its core, this liberal democratic tradition reflects a general tendency toward an expansion of meaning to include wider and wider arcs of ethical consideration, thereby elevating the prospects for what it means to be fully human.

The purpose of this final chapter is to consider the place of leisure studies in this expanding liberal democratic tradition. More specifically, we believe leisure studies should be at the vortex of this ethical spiraling outward and upward, and we challenge leisure studies scholars to serve at the forefront. Drawing from the leisure studies literature, we highlight lines of thought that have contributed greatly to this spiraling outward and upward, and call for more and different kinds of contributions from the field's professionals, including collaboration with the fine arts to broadcast the significance of leisure in contemporary life, heightened political activism, and action-oriented research guided by a concern for social and environmental justice.

ONWARD

In *Leisure Studies: Prospects for the Twenty-first Century*, the predecessor to the current volume, Driver (1999) celebrated leisure studies' progress from the 1950s to the turn of the century. He assessed the state of the art, the state of management practice, and the state of academic education, concluding that the state of the art had become more science-based across a broad spectrum of topics, newly created scientific knowledge had begun to inform management practice, and the quality of academic education had improved on multiple fronts. While Driver encouraged the field to be proud of the progress made in a relatively short period of time (forty-plus years), he also challenged the field to better communicate the significance of leisure's contributions to social welfare. This is the challenge we take on later in this chapter. First, however, we want to follow Driver's lead by celebrating leisure studies' progress since his assessment 15 years ago. We underscore what we believe are important lines of inquiry that have spiraled the field outward and upward as part of the expanding liberal democratic tradition.

OUTWARD

In *The Sociological Imagination*, Mills (1959) coined the term "grand theory" to illustrate the possibility that social scientific advancements might someday be woven together into increasingly larger patterns of understanding until one explanation—one grand theory—could describe the entire working of things. While the field of leisure studies is a long way from any such comprehensive explanation of leisure's meaning, the prospect does fire the imagination. And while a grand theory of leisure is currently well beyond the field's grasp, a grand framework within which the purpose of leisure studies can be discussed is within reach (see also Walker, Kono, and Dieser, Chapter 36).

One of leisure studies' major advancements in the last 15 years is reflected in a movement away from a psychologized perspective of leisure that sees people as separate and autonomous beings with individual needs and wants, to a social psychological, or, one might even say, ecological perspective that sees people as interconnected and interdependent beings with needs and wants that are co-mingled with the needs and wants of the larger living world (Dustin, McAvoy, Schultz, Bricker, Rose, & Schwab, 2011). As Nash (1989) observes, ecology has brought with it a new appreciation for the meaning of community. No longer is community solely a human-centered construct. Propelled by more advanced ecologic understanding, and championed by Leopold's (1949) land ethic, the meaning of community is expanding outward.

Concomitant with ecologic thought is a growing realization that humankind, rather than being separate from and superior to nature, is interconnected with, interdependent on, and part of nature. Ushered in by Douglas's (1947) *The Everglades: River of Grass*, Krutch's (1956) *The Great Chain of Life*, and Carson's (1962) *Silent Spring*, a gradual environmental awakening has been under way since Earth Day in 1970, reflecting an emerging awareness that Earth is made up of intersecting and interlocking communities of life, of which humans are but one interdependent part. Echoes of American John Muir's late nineteenth century revelation that people can never do just one thing, that everything is connected to everything else, reverberate the world over.

Ecology has brought science and ethics closer together (Nash, 1989) to address the question of how human beings ought to live their lives as part of a much larger web of life. What interconnectedness and interdependence really mean, what respect for other living things really means, and what the concept of community really means, are now subject matters for scientists and ethicists alike. From Whitehead's (1920) writings on interdependence, to Leopold's (1949) "land ethic," to Schweitzer's (1965) "reverence for life," ethicists have joined the conversation about what ecologic understanding implies for human conduct.

Appreciating how ecology has informed ethical discourse and broadened ethical consideration, we now arrive at the first resting place on the journey outward and upward where we should pause to reflect on the implications for leisure studies. What is the relevance of ecology for leisure studies? Do leisure studies scholars think in ecologic terms? Is their research framed by ecologic considerations? Will the field ever engage in a leisure-centered dialectic to work through what it really means to be plain members and citizens of a larger community of life?

Hemingway's (1988) interpretation of the Aristotelian idea that leisure is much more than a private matter, that leisure is really about the virtuous employment of individual gifts to improve the quality of public life, suggests that leisure must also be about extending ethical consideration outward. This sentiment permeates Hemingway's writings (1988, 1999, 2006), Goodale's (2013, 1991), and Hunnicutt's (2000), to name but three of leisure studies' most introspective scholars. They each stress the public expression of individual virtue through leisure, if, in Goodale's (1991) words, leisure is to matter. Indeed, recent work in leisure studies suggests we may be turning a corner, or, as Hunnicutt (2000) puts it, "recalling those democratic vistas that once inspired us" (p. 61; see also Sylvester, Chapter 5).

Viewing leisure as a path for civic engagement and building social capital to enhance the quality of community life is increasingly common in leisure studies. Glover and Hemingway's foundational writings about the promise of leisure in a participatory democracy (Glover, 2006, Chapter 32; Glover & Hemingway, 2005; Hemingway, 1988, 1999, 2006), and subsequent writings about creating social capital via community centers (Glover, 2004a) and community gardens (Glover, 2004b), as well as Garcia and Strongin's (2013) on the ground activism in Los Angeles, are clear illustrations of leisure's potential to serve the public good. They also provide vivid examples of what it means to extend ethical consideration outward.

Equally promising is the work of leisure studies scholars who are bringing increasing attention to marginalized and underrepresented groups who have been largely invisible in leisure studies (e.g., Barnett & Johnson 2013; Johnson & Waldron, 2010; Rose, 2013; Samdahl, 2010, 2013). Building on Henderson and her colleagues' pioneering work in women's leisure (Henderson, Bialeschki, Shaw, & Freysinger, 1996, 1989), that work has been expanded to include other groups who have been disadvantaged and dispossessed by race, ethnicity, gender, and class. Operating within a social and environmental justice framework (Paisley & Dustin, 2011; Schwab & Dustin, 2013), their scholarship is bringing to light a host of leisure-related injustices, and their goal is to remedy those injustices through social action fueled by research and writing (Parry, Johnson, & Stewart, 2013). It is as if the field of leisure studies has finally responded to the clarion calls of pioneering leisure scholars (e.g., Gray & Pelegrino; 1973; Murphy, Williams, Niepoth, & Brown, 1973), who advocated tirelessly throughout the last half of the twentieth century for serving marginalized and oppressed people by going beyond the bounds of park and recreation areas and facilities to engage more directly with the community itself.

The sense of place literature provides even more evidence of the field's intellectual advancement outward. Focusing scholarly attention on the relationship between people and place marks another significant step forward in ethical consideration. The environment, rather than being viewed merely as a backdrop for the human drama, is beginning to receive equal billing. Connection to place matters and understanding why it matters is of increasing importance in leisure studies. Stewart and Williams's work in this area stands out (e.g., Stewart, 2006, 2007; Stewart, Williams, & Kruger, 2013; Williams, 2008; Williams & Patterson, 2008). Recognizing that people are in relationship with the environments enveloping them, and upon which human sustenance depends, is critical to an expanding liberal democratic tradition (see also Kyle, Chapter 31).

Ecotourism is also advancing outward as it demonstrates leisure's role in promoting the ecologic health of tourist destinations and the human health of their inhabitants

(Bricker, Black, & Cottrell, 2012; Schwab, Dustin, & Bricker, 2012; Stronza & Durham, 2008). Once again, the ecologic insight driving this expanding ethical consideration is the realization that human health and environmental health are inextricably intertwined, and that the future of human and environmental health, for better or worse, will unfold together (Chivian & Bernstein, 2008). While challenges remain in guaranteeing that touristic businesses are run in a socially and environmentally responsible manner (Higgins-Desboilles, Powys Whyte, & Tedmanson, 2013), examples of well-intended and well-thought-out tourism enterprises increasingly frequent the literature (e.g., Bricker, 2013; Stronza & Durham, 2008).

Leisure studies scholars have also made significant progress during the past 15 years in linking leisure, physical activity, and health (e.g., Bocarro & Edwards, Chapter 8; Godbey, Caldwell, Floyd, & Payne, 2005; Payne, Ainsworth, & Godbey, 2010). Scores of studies have demonstrated a strong positive relationship between physical activity and health promotion in leisure contexts (e.g., Broyles, Mowen, Theall, Gustat, & Rung, 2011; Floyd et al., 2011; Floyd, Spengler, Maddock, Gobster, & Suau, 2008; Mowen, Orsega-Smith, Payne, Ainsworth, & Godbey, 2007). As Godbey (2009) points out, the prospect of leisure pursuits serving as sustainable avenues to human health are especially promising because of their intrinsically rewarding nature. Enhanced health becomes a byproduct of what people find joy in doing during their free time.

The next step in the evolution of this health-related focus will be to guarantee that all citizens have access to parks and open spaces for health-promoting leisure activities and that they feel welcome and included in park programs and practices. This will require better understanding which members of the community are denied access or why they perceive barriers to access. Equal access does not necessarily mean equal opportunity, and leisure studies scholars must determine what inclusive policies, practices, and programs will best serve all groups (Devine & Piatt, 2013). Once access is ensured for all, the research focus can shift to ascertaining the relationship between healthy leisure activities and environmental health. If leisure studies scholars can make this connection, the field will have come a long way toward extending ethical consideration outward because it will have become apparent that human and environmental health are intertwined (Dustin, Bricker, & Schwab, 2010).

Linking environmental health to human health will also make it increasingly clear that humans cannot continue to act with disregard for the impacts of their actions on their fundamental ground of being, their earthly essence (Rolston, 1996). Expect intensified discussion and debate within leisure studies about the need for human restraint based on a growing awareness of the environmental costs associated with the benefits derived from leisure pursuits. A concern for nature's intrinsic value can be traced back to ethicists mentioned earlier, including Whitehead (1920), Leopold (1949), and Schweitzer (1965) as well as more recent ethical stances taken by Stone's (1974) *Should Trees Have Standing?*, Lovelock's (1979) *Gaia*, Wilson and Kellert's (1993) *The Biophilia Hypothesis*, and Shiva's (2006) *Earth Democracy*. While a few leisure scholars have pondered the ethical implications of these ecologically-based insights for leisure behavior (e.g., Dustin et al., 2011), the real work is still to come. Agreeing on the ethical rightness or wrongness of freely chosen recreation pursuits, and then educating the citizenry about those conclusions in a way that elevates their recreational tastes (Sax, 1980) is a challenge yet to be embraced by leisure scholars.

Finally, in addition to leisure studies' thematic expansion outward, there has been a corresponding expansion in research paradigms, methodologies, and practices representing increasing receptivity to multiple ways of learning and knowing what transpires in the name of leisure. Thoughtful considerations are sprinkled throughout the literature (e.g., Dustin, Schwab, & Rose, 2012; Fox, 2011; Stewart, Parry, & Glover, 2008), and paths to knowledge are now multi-branched. Though the field still has a long way to go, a wider range of voices are being heard, multiple ways of knowing are being explored, and new and innovative forms of reporting what is learned and known are making their way into the literature (Parry & Johnson, 2007). Leisure studies itself, then, is experiencing an expansion outward in what counts in knowledge creation, dissemination, and application (e.g., Ellis, Lee, & Satchabut, Chapter 38; Samdahl, Chapter 37).

What will the future of leisure studies look like? In our opinion, the grand framework within which to make sense of the work done in leisure studies should be built out of a concern for social and environmental justice. If the lessons of ecology apply to the human species, and if humans are part of nature, then the personal and professional responsibility of each and every human being is to do her or his best to cultivate a harmonious, sustainable lifestyle that honors people and nature in community. Promoting human and environmental health in tandem should be at the heart of this effort. Agreeing on, and operationalizing healthy, sustainable lifestyles is the task at hand. Fortunately, as countless philosopher/scientists have reiterated (Leopold, 1949; Oelschlaeger, 1991; Schumacher, 1977; Schweitzer, 1965), humankind's gift as a species is self-awareness. Paraphrasing Oelschlaeger (1991), human beings are nature's invention for keeping track of itself. So empowered, people have it within themselves to extend ethical consideration outward, advance the liberal democratic tradition, and elevate the prospect for what it means to be fully human.

UPWARD

Even as it is increasingly apparent that leisure studies are participating in the liberal democratic tradition of extending meaning outward and upward in wider and wider arcs of ethical consideration, there remains an insular interiority to leisure studies that troubled Driver and continues to trouble us. Communicating the field's relevance to the citizenry in a manner that inspires them and secures their support for leisure services is a daunting challenge. Several leisure studies scholars have lamented a "talking to ourselves" syndrome (Dahl, 1999; Pedlar, 1999; Samdahl & Kelly, 1999) while others have suggested the field has a wider reach than it is given credit for (Henderson, 2010). Nonetheless, there are several ways in which leisure professionals can do a much better job of communicating the significance of leisure in contemporary life to the larger culture. It is appropriate, then, to pause once more at this juncture to ponder those implications.

The most obvious way to reach more people is to write for the popular press. There are, however, two serious obstacles on this path. First, writing in a compelling way for the general reading public is very difficult. It is easier to write in jargon-laden language for fellow social scientists than to write in a manner that engages and holds the attention of lay people. Second, writing for the popular press is seldom encouraged or rewarded in academic circles. Blind peer-reviewed articles are favored in tenure and promotion processes and even applied writing for professional audiences is commonly frowned upon. Writing for the commercial market is a tough sell in more ways than one.

There are popular press success stories to be sure, but other than Czikszentmihalyi's (1990) they tend not to be the work of academicians. Blehm's (2007) *The Last Season*, for example, is a nonfiction account of the disappearance of a backcountry wilderness ranger in California's Sequoia-Kings Canyon National Park that earned Blehm, a former park and recreation undergraduate minor, the Barnes & Noble Discovery Author of the Year Award, and Barr's (2012) best-selling Anna Pigeon mysteries are set in national parks throughout the land. In both cases, these authors have reached thousands, if not hundreds of thousands, of members of the general reading public, who have learned a great deal about leisure services through their commercially successful works. In Blehm's case, *The Last Season* also resulted in the National Park Service (NPS) changing the way it outfits backcountry rangers, the way backcountry rangers check in on a daily basis, and the way benefits are processed for the families of NPS personnel lost in the line of duty. Of even greater note is Louv's (2006) *Last Child in the Woods: Saving children from nature-deficit disorder*. Louv's work is largely derived from what natural and social scientists have learned about human-nature relationships over the years, but his genius is in his ability to interpret natural and social scientific understanding to the general public in a way that has provoked them, and the agencies serving them at various governmental levels, to do something about reconnecting the citizenry, especially children, to nature.

Writing for the popular press is but one path to greater exposure for leisure services. Movie making is another. The impact of movies like *127 Hours* (2010), *Into the Wild* (2007), *A River Runs through It* (1992), and *Deliverance* (1972) on the general public's perception of outdoor recreation has been far-reaching. While some attention has been paid to the significance of movie making in addressing issues related to our field (O'Bannon & Goldenberg, 2007), the opportunity to be really creative is largely unexplored. A concerted effort is required to recruit undergraduate and graduate students who have a genuine interest in leisure but who aspire to make their living in the fine arts. The field needs poets, novelists, playwrights, filmmakers, and musicians, who have a passion for leisure to express that passion through the performing arts.

Leisure professionals also must become more active politically. When we described Hemingway's (1988, 1999, 2006) interpretation of leisure as the virtuous employment of individual gifts to improve the quality of public life, we could just as easily have been referring to political engagement as civic engagement. As More (2002) reported, "every decision at every level is political" (p. 107). Leisure services must be populated by a variety of individuals who are passionate about leisure and committed to advancing its ideals through active involvement in a participatory democracy (Wellman, Dustin, Henderson, & Moore, 2008a). Whether they volunteer or run for public office, their challenge is to advance leisure outward and upward into the citizenry's collective consciousness.

Finally, leisure studies scholars must commit themselves to a kind of emancipatory scholarship that uncovers social and environmental injustices and then does something about them (Parry et al., 2013). As many critics have noted, leisure studies scholars are effective at identifying social and environmental injustices, but they have not been effective in recommending tangible courses of action to rectify them. Their role has largely been limited to that of commentators. It is time to convert research findings into action items.

CONCLUSION

The prospects for leisure are bright, but for leisure to be of greatest service in the advancement of the liberal democratic tradition, and for leisure to be an energizing force in that vortex spiraling outward and upward toward greater ethical consideration, leisure must behave more like a verb than a noun (Wellman, Dustin, Henderson, & Moore, 2008b). It must be action-oriented. In *The Geography of*

Thought, Nisbett (2003) contrasts the emphasis placed on nouns by Westerners and on verbs by Asians. While Westerners favor nouns that sort phenomena into distinct and separate categories, Asians favor verbs that focus on the relationships between those same phenomena. What we have tried to demonstrate in this chapter is that the lessons of ecology teach that an expanding liberal democratic tradition characterized by the extension of ethical consideration outward is a function of recognizing humankind *in relationship* with nature.

As noted previously, nature's gift to humans is self-awareness. Humans have the capacity to step outside themselves, recognize the errors of their ways, and do something about them. For better or worse, humans are an empowered species. The attendant obligation is to exercise that power by taking an active socially and environmentally responsible role in public life. There is a strong parallel between democracy and leisure. They are both civic-mindedness in action. They are both concerned with people in community, not between the one and the many as Western thought teaches, but between the part and the whole as Eastern thought teaches (Wellman et al., 2008b); Eastern thought, that is, and ecology.

In *A Sand County Almanac*, Leopold (1949) contended that human progress as a species can be measured by the degree to which people extend ethical consideration outward from the self and others to the land and all of its creatures. We have shown throughout this chapter how leisure studies are moving in the right direction. The opportunity to join in this expanding liberal democratic tradition is open to each of us. Leisure professionals who populate the field, and who breathe much life into the "verb" leisure itself, are integral to this evolving generative process. There is much work to be done. While the leisure ideal might always remain just beyond our grasp, we toilers in the field can find comfort in the poet Browning's (1989) claim that our reach should exceed our grasp, or what's a heaven for?

REFERENCES

Barnett, J., & Johnson, C. (2013). Our town's a drag: Drag queens and queer space in Athens, Georgia. In K. Schwab & D. Dustin (Eds.), *Just leisure: Things that we believe in* (pp. 49–57). Urbana, IL: Sagamore Publishing LLC.

Barr, N. (2012). *The rope*. New York: St. Martin's.

Blehm, E. (2007). *The last season*. New York: Harper Perennial.

Bricker, K. (2013). Ecotourism as a venue for social and environmental justice: A case study of a Fijian vanua. In K. Schwab & D. Dustin (Eds.), *Just leisure: Things that we believe in* (pp. 160–166). Urbana, IL: Sagamore Publishing LLC.

Bricker, K., Black, R., & Cottrell, S. (2012). *Sustainable tourism & the millennium development goals*. Sudbury, MA: Jones & Bartlett Learning.

Browning, R. (1989). *A centenary collection of Robert Browning's poetry*. (Contributor: Michael Meredith). New York: Browning Institute.

Broyles, S., Mowen, A., Theall, K., Gustat, J., & Rung, A. (2011). Integrating social capital into a park use and active living framework. *American Journal of Preventive Medicine, 40*(5), 522–529.

Carson, R. (1962). *Silent spring*. Boston: Houghton Mifflin.

Chivian, E., & Bernstein, A. (Eds.). (2008). *Sustaining life: How human health depends on biodiversity*. New York: Oxford University Press.

Csikszentmihalyi, M. (1990). *Flow: The psychology of optimal experience*. New York: Harper & Row.

Dahl, R. (1999). A commentary on the perils of intellectual isolation. *Journal of Leisure Research, 31*(2), 199–201.

Devine, M., & Piatt, J. (2013). Beyond the right to inclusion: The intersection of social and environmental justice for inclusion of individuals with disabilities in leisure. In K. Schwab & D. Dustin (Eds.), *Just leisure: Things that we believe in* (pp. 17–26). Urbana, IL: Sagamore Publishing LLC.

Douglas, M. (1947). *The Everglades: River of grass*. New York: Rinehart.

Driver, B. (1999). Recognizing and celebrating progress in leisure studies. In E. L. Jackson & T. L. Burton (Eds.), *Leisure Studies: Prospects for the twenty-first century* (pp. 523–534). State College, PA: Venture Publishing, Inc.

Dustin, D., Bricker, K., & Schwab, K. (2010). People and nature: Toward an ecological model of health promotion, *Leisure Sciences, 32*(1), 3–14.

Dustin, D., McAvoy, L., Schultz, J., Bricker, K., Rose, J., & Schwab, K. (2011). *Stewards of access/custodians of choice: A philosophical foundation for parks, recreation, and tourism*. Urbana, IL: Sagamore Publishing LLC.

Dustin, D., Schwab, K., & Rose, J. (2012). Toward a more phronetic leisure science. *Leisure Sciences, 34*(2), 191–197.

Floyd, M., Bocarro, J., Smith, W., Baran, P., Moore, R., Cosco, N., Edwards, M., Suau, L., & Fang, K. (2011). Park-based physical activity among children and adolescents. *American Journal of Preventive Medicine,* 41(3), 258–265.

Floyd, M., Spengler, J., Maddock, J., Gobster, P., & Suau, L. (2008). Park-based physical activity in diverse communities of two U.S. cities: An observational study. *American Journal of Preventive Medicine, 34*, 299–305.

Fox, K. (2011). Can you hear the music? Toward a polyphonic leisure scholarship. In K. Paisley & D. Dustin (Eds.), *Speaking up and speaking out: Working for social and environmental justice in parks, recreation, and leisure* (pp. 181–192). Urbana, IL: Sagamore Publishing LLC.

Garcia, R., & Strongin, S. (2013). Healthy parks and communities: Green access and equity for Los Angeles. In K. Schwab & D. Dustin (Eds.), *Just leisure: Things that we believe in* (pp. 167–188). Urbana, IL: Sagamore Publishing LLC.

Glover, T. (2004a). The 'community' center and the social construction of citizenship. *Leisure Sciences, 26*(1), 63–83.

Glover, T. (2004b). Social capital in the lived experiences of community gardeners, *LeisureSciences, 26*(2), 1–20.

Glover, T. (2006). Toward a critical examination of social capital within leisure contexts: From production and maintenance to distribution. *Leisure/Loisir: Journal of the Canadian Association for Leisure Studies, 30*(2), 357–367.

Glover, T., & Hemingway, J. (2005). Locating leisure in the social capital literature. *Journal of Leisure Research, 37*, 387–401.

Godbey, G. (2009). *Outdoor recreation and health: Understanding and enhancing the relation*. Washington, DC: Resources for the Future.

Godbey, G., Caldwell, L., Floyd, M., & Payne, L. (2005). Contributions of leisure studies and recreation and park management research to the active living research agenda. *American Journal of Preventive Medicine, 28*(2), Supplement 2, 150–158.

Goodale, T. (1991). If leisure is to matter. In T. Goodale & P. Witt (Eds.), *Recreation and leisure: Issues in an era of change* (3rd ed.) (pp. 85–96). State College, PA: Venture Publishing, Inc.

Goodale, T. (2013). What will become of our 20 grandchildren? In K. Schwab & D. Dustin (Eds.), *Just leisure: Things that we believe in* (pp. 3–9). Urbana, IL: Sagamore Publishing LLC.

Gray, D., & Pelegrino, D. (1973). (Eds.). *Reflections on the recreation and park movement: A book of readings*. New York: Wm. C. Brown.

Hemingway, J. (1988). Leisure and civility: Reflections on a Greek ideal. *Leisure Sciences, 10*, 179–191.

Hemingway, J. (1999). Leisure, social capital, and democratic citizenship. *Journal of Leisure Research, 31*, 150–165.

Hemingway, J. (2006). Leisure, social capital, and civic competence. *Leisure/Loisir: Journal of the Canadian Association for Leisure Studies, 30*, 341–355.

Henderson, K. (2010). Leisure studies in the 21st century: The sky is falling? *Leisure Sciences, 32*, 391–400.

Henderson, K., Bialeschki, M., Shaw, S., & Freysinger, V. (1989). *A leisure of one's own: A feminist perspective on women's leisure*. State College, PA: Venture Publishing, Inc.

Henderson, K., Bialeschki, M., Shaw, S., & Freysinger, V. (1996). *Both gains and gaps: Feminist perspectives on women's leisure*. State College, PA: Venture Publishing, Inc.

Higgins-Desboilles, F., Powys Whyte, K., & Tedmanson, D. (2013). Tourism and environmental justice. In K. Schwab & D. Dustin (Eds.), *Just leisure: Things that we believe in* (pp. 91–100). Urbana, IL: Sagamore Publishing LLC.

Hunnicutt, B. (2000). Our reform heritage: Recovering the vision of community leisure services. *Journal of Leisure Research, 32*(1), 58–61.

Johnson, C., & Waldron, J. (2010). Are you culturally competent? In K. Paisley & D. Dustin (Eds.), *Speaking up and speaking out: Working for social and environmental justice in parks, recreation, and leisure* (pp. 171–179). Urbana, IL: Sagamore Publishing LLC.

Krutch, J. (1956). *The great chain of life*. Boston: Houghton Mifflin.

Leopold, A. (1949). *A sand county almanac*. New York: Oxford University Press.

Louv, R. (2007). *The last child in the woods: Saving our children from nature-deficit disorder*. Chapel Hill, NC: Algonquin Books of Chapel Hill.

Lovelock, J. (1979). *Gaia: A new look at life on earth*. New York: Oxford University Press.

Mills, C. (1959). *The sociological imagination*. New York: Oxford University Press.

More, T. (2002). The marginal user as the justification for public recreation: A rejoinder to Crompton, Driver and Dustin. *Journal of Leisure Research, 34*(1), 103–118.

Mowen, A., Orsega-Smith, E., Payne, L., Ainsworth, B., & Godbey, G. (2007). The role of park proximity and social support in shaping park visitation, physical activity, and perceived health among older adults. *Journal of Physical Activity and Health, 4*, 167–179.

Murphy, J., Williams, J., Niepoth, W., & Brown, P. (1973). *Leisure service delivery system: A modern perspective*. Philadelphia: Lea & Febiger.

Nash, R. (1989). *The rights of nature: A history of environmental ethics*. Madison, WI: The University of Wisconsin Press.

Nisbett, R. (2003). *The geography of thought: How Asians and Westerners think differently—and why*. New York: Free Press.

O'Bannon, T., & Goldenberg, M. (2007). *Teaching with movies: Recreation, sport, tourism, and physical education*. Champaign, IL: Human Kinetics.

Oelschlaeger, M. (1991). *The idea of wilderness: From pre-history to the age of ecology*. New Haven, CT: Yale University Press.

Paisley, K., & Dustin, D. (2011). (Eds.). *Speaking up and speaking out: Working for social and environmental justice through parks, recreation, and leisure.* (p. 233). Urbana, IL: Sagamore Publishing LLC.

Parry, D., Johnson, C., & Stewart, W. (2013). Leisure research for social justice: A response to Henderson. *Leisure Sciences, 35*(1), 81–87.

Parry, D., & Johnson, C. (2007). Contextualizing leisure research to encompass complexity in lived leisure experience: The need for creative analytic practice. *Leisure Sciences, 29*(2), 119–130.

Payne, L., Ainsworth, B., & Godbey, G. (2010). *Leisure, health, and wellness: Making the connections.* State College, PA: Venture Publishing, Inc.

Pedlar, A. (1999). Speaking each other's language: Should insularity concern us? *Journal of Leisure Research, 31*(2), 181–184.

Rolston, H. (1996). Nature, spirit, and landscape management. In B. Driver, D. Dustin, T. Baltic, G. Elsner, & G. Peterson (Eds.), *Nature and the human spirit: Toward an expanded land management ethic* (pp. 17–24). State College, PA: Venture Publishing, Inc.

Rose, J. (2013). Contesting homelessness: Public nature, political ecology, and socioenvironmental justice. In K. Schwab & D. Dustin (Eds.), *Just leisure: Things that we believe in* (pp. 58–66). Urbana, IL: Sagamore Publishing LLC.

Samdahl, D. (2010). What can American Beach teach us? In K. Paisley & D. Dustin (Eds.), *Speaking up and speaking out: Working for social and environmental justice in parks, recreation, and leisure* (pp. 83–93). Urbana, IL: Sagamore Publishing LLC.

Samdahl, D. (2013). At whose expense? How our commitment to conservation has propagated social injustice. In K. Schwab & D. Dustin (Eds.), *Just leisure: Things that we believe in* (pp. 10–16). Urbana, IL: Sagamore Publishing LLC.

Samdahl, D., & Kelly, J. (1999). Speaking only to ourselves? Citation analysis of the Journal of Leisure Research and Leisure Sciences. *Journal of Leisure Research, 31*(2), 171–180.

Sax, J. (1980). *Mountains without handrails: Reflections on the National Parks.* Ann Arbor, MI: The University of Michigan Press.

Schumacher, E. (1977). *A guide for the perplexed.* New York: Harper & Row.

Schwab, K., & Dustin, D. (2013). (Eds.). *Just leisure: Things that we believe in.* Urbana, IL: Sagamore Publishing LLC.

Schwab, K., Dustin, D., & Bricker, K. (2012). The role of sustainable tourism in mitigating HIV/AIDS, malaria, and other major diseases. In K. Bricker, R. Black, & S. Cottrell (Eds.), *Sustainable Tourism & the millennium development goals* (pp. 151–161). Sudbury, MA: Jones & Bartlett Learning.

Schweitzer, A. (1965). *The teaching of reverence for life.* New York: Holt, Rinehart, and Winston.

Shiva, V. (2006). *Earth democracy.* Cambridge, MA: South End Press.

Stewart, W. (2006). Community-based place meanings for park planning. *Leisure/Loisir, 30*(2), 405–416.

Stewart, W. (2007). Place meanings in stories of lived experience. In L. Kruger and T. Hall (Eds.), *Sense of place research for natural resource management.* Washington, DC: USDA.

Stewart, W., Williams, D., & Kruger, L. (2013). (Eds.). *Place-based conservation: Perspectives from the social sciences.* Dordrecht, Netherlands: Springer.

Stewart, W., Parry, D., & Glover, T. (2008). Writing leisure: Values and ideologies of research. *Journal of Leisure Research, 40*, 360–384.

Stone, C. (1974). *Should trees have standing?* Los Altos, CA: William Kaufman, Inc.

Stronza, A., & Durham, W. (Eds.). (2008). *Ecotourism and conservation in the Americas: Putting good intentions to work.* Wallingford, Oxfordshire: CABI.

Wellman, D., Dustin, D., Henderson, K., & Moore, R. (2008a). *Service living: Building community through public parks and recreation.* State College, PA: Venture Publishing, Inc.

Wellman, D., Dustin, D., Henderson, K., & Moore, R. (2008b). Democracy is a verb. *Service living: Building community through public parks and recreation.* (pp. 89–94). State College, PA: Venture Publishing, Inc.

Whitehead, A. (1920). *The concept of nature.* Ann Arbor: University of Michigan Press.

Williams, D. (2008). Pluralities of place: A user's guide to place concepts, theories, and philosophies in natural resource management. In L. Kruger, T. Hall, & M. Stiefel (tech. eds.), *Understanding concepts of place in recreation research and management* (pp. 7–30). Gen. Tech. Rep. PRW-GTR-744. Portland, OR: U.S. Department of Agriculture, Forest Service, Pacific Northwest Research Station.

Williams, D., & Patterson, M. (2008). Place, leisure, and well-being. In J. Eyles & A. Williams (Eds.), *Sense of place, health and quality of life* (pp. 105–119). Aldershot, UK: Ashgate Publishing Limited.

Wilson, E., & Kellert, S. (1993). *The biophilia hypothesis.* Washington, DC: Island Press/Shearwater Books.

Index

U

V

W

Y

Other Books by Venture Publishing, Inc.

21st Century Leisure: Current Issues, Second Edition
by Valeria J. Freysinger and John R. Kelly
Active Living in Older Adulthood: Principles and Practices of Activity Programs
by Barbara A. Hawkins
Adventure Programming
edited by John C. Miles and Simon Priest
Adventure Programming and Travel for the 21st Century
by Rosemary Black and Kelly Bricker
Boredom Busters: Themed Special Events to Dazzle and Delight Your Group
by Annette C. Moore
Brain Fitness
by Suzanne Fitzsimmons
Client Assessment in Therapeutic Recreation Services
by Norma J. Stumbo
Client Outcomes in Therapeutic Recreation Services
by Norma J. Stumbo
Conceptual Foundations for Therapeutic Recreation
edited by David R. Austin, John Dattilo, and Bryan P. McCormick
Dementia Care Programming: An Identity-Focused Approach
by Rosemary Dunne
Dimensions of Choice: Qualitative Approaches to Parks, Recreation, Tourism, Sport, and Leisure Research, Second Edition
by Karla A. Henderson
Diversity and the Recreation Profession: Organizational Perspectives (Revised Edition)
edited by Maria T. Allison and Ingrid E. Schneider
Effective Management in Therapeutic Recreation Service, Third Edition
by Marcia Jean Carter, Christen G. Smith, and Gerald S. O'Morrow
Evaluating Leisure Services: Making Enlightened Decisions, Third Edition
by Karla A. Henderson and M. Deborah Bialeschki
Facilitation of Therapeutic Recreation Services: An Evidence-Based and Best Practice Approach to Techniques and Processes
edited by Norma J. Stumbo and Brad Wardlaw
Facilitation Techniques in Therapeutic Recreation, Second Edition
by John Dattilo and Alexis McKenney
File o' Fun: A Recreation Planner for Games & Activities, Third Edition
by Jane Harris Ericson and Diane Ruth Albright
Finding Leisure in China
by Geoffrey Godbey and Song Rui
The Game Finder: A Leader's Guide to Great Activities
by Annette C. Moore
Health Promotion for Mind, Body, and Spirit
by Suzanne Fitzsimmons and Linda L. Buettner
Human Resource Management in Recreation, Sport, and Leisure Services
by Margaret Arnold, Regina Glover, and Cheryl Beeler
Inclusion: Including People With Disabilities in Parks and Recreation Opportunities
by Lynn Anderson and Carla Brown Kress
Inclusive Leisure Services, Third Edition
by John Dattilo

Internships in Recreation and Leisure Services: A Practical Guide for Students, Fifth Edition
by Edward E. Seagle, Jr., Tammy B. Smith, and Ralph W. Smith
Internships in Sport Management
by Robin Ammon, Jr., Matthew Walker, Edward E. Seagle, and Ralph W. Smith
Interpretation of Cultural and Natural Resources, Second Edition
by Douglas M. Knudson, Ted T. Cable, and Larry Beck
Intervention Activities for At-Risk Youth
by Norma J. Stumbo
Introduction to Outdoor Recreation: Providing and Managing Resource Based Opportunities
by Roger L. Moore and B. L. Driver
Introduction to Recreation Services: Sustainability for a Changing World
By Karla A. Henderson
Introduction to Therapeutic Recreation: U.S. and Canadian Perspectives
by Kenneth Mobily and Lisa Ostiguy
An Introduction to Tourism
by Robert W. Wyllie
Introduction to Writing Goals and Objectives: A Manual for Recreation Therapy Students and Entry-Level Professionals
by Suzanne Melcher
The Leader's Handbook: Learning Leadership Skills by Facilitating Fun, Games, Play, and Positive Interaction, Second Edition
by Bill Michaelis and John M. O'Connell
Leadership and Administration of Outdoor Pursuits, Third Edition
by James Blanchard, Michael Strong, and Phyllis Ford
Leadership in Leisure Services: Making a Difference, Third Edition
by Debra J. Jordan
Leisure and Leisure Services in the 21st Century: Toward Mid Century
by Geoffrey Godbey
Leisure Education I: A Manual of Activities and Resources, Second Edition
by Norma J. Stumbo
Leisure Education II: More Activities and Resources, Second Edition
by Norma J. Stumbo
Leisure Education III: More Goal-Oriented Activities
by Norma J. Stumbo
Leisure Education IV: Activities for Individuals with Substance Addictions
by Norma J. Stumbo
Leisure Education Program Planning, Fourth Edition
by John Dattilo
Leisure for Canadians, Second Edition
by Ron McCarville and Kelly MacKay
Leisure, Health, and Wellness: Making the Connections
by Laura Payne, Barbara Ainsworth, and Geoffrey Godbey
Leisure in Your Life: New Perspectives
by Geoffrey Godbey
Leisure Studies: Prospects for the Twenty-First Century
edited by Edgar L. Jackson and Thomas L. Burton
Leisure, Women, and Gender
edited by Valeria J. Freysinger, Susan M. Shaw, Karla A. Henderson, and M. Deborah Bialeschki
Making a Difference in Academic Life: A Handbook for Park, Recreation, and Tourism Educators and Graduate Students
edited by Dan Dustin and Tom Goodale
Managing to Optimize the Beneficial Outcomes of Leisure
edited by B. L. Driver
Marketing in Leisure and Tourism: Reaching New Heights
by Patricia Click Janes

More Than a Game: A New Focus on Senior Activity Services
by Brenda Corbett
N.E.S.T. Approach: Dementia Practice Guidelines for Disturbing Behaviors
by Linda L. Buettner and Suzanne Fitzsimmons
Parks for Life: Moving the Goal Posts, Changing the Rules, and Expanding the Field
by Will LaPage
Planning and Organizing Group Activities in Social Recreation
by John V. Valentine
Planning for Recreation and Parks Facilities: Predesign Process, Principles, and Strategies
by Jack Harper
Programming for Parks, Recreation, and Leisure Services: A Servant Leadership Approach, Third Edition
by Donald G. DeGraaf, Debra J. Jordan, and Kathy H. DeGraaf
Recreation and Youth Development
by Peter A. Witt and Linda L. Caldwell
Recreation for Older Adults: Individual and Group Activities
by Judith A. Elliott and Jerold E. Elliott
Recreation Program Planning Manual for Older Adults
by Karen Kindrachuk
Reference Manual for Writing Rehabilitation Therapy Treatment Plans
by Penny Hogberg and Mary Johnson
Service Living: Building Community through Public Parks and Recreation
by Doug Wellman, Dan Dustin, Karla Henderson, and Roger Moore
A Social Psychology of Leisure, Second Edition
by Douglas A. Kleiber, Gordon J. Walker, and Roger C. Mannell
Special Events and Festivals: How to Organize, Plan, and Implement
by Angie Prosser and Ashli Rutledge
The Sportsman's Voice: Hunting and Fishing in America
by Mark Damian Duda, Martin F. Jones, and Andrea Criscione
Survey Research and Analysis: Applications in Parks, Recreation, and Human Dimensions
by Jerry Vaske
Taking the Initiative: Activities to Enhance Effectiveness and Promote Fun
by J. P. Witman
Therapeutic Recreation and the Nature of Disabilities
by Kenneth E. Mobily and Richard D. MacNeil
Therapeutic Recreation: Cases and Exercises, Second Edition
by Barbara C. Wilhite and M. Jean Keller
Therapeutic Recreation in Health Promotion and Rehabilitation
by John Shank and Catherine Coyle
Therapeutic Recreation Practice: A Strengths Approach
by Lynn Anderson and Linda Heyne